PRESENT TENSE

PRESENT TENSE

THE UNITED STATES SINCE 1945

Second Edition

Michael Schaller
University of Arizona

Virginia Scharff
University of New Mexico

Robert D. Schulzinger
University of Colorado, Boulder

Houghton Mifflin Company   Boston   Toronto
Geneva, Illinois   Palo Alto   Princeton, New Jersey

We dedicate this book to our children:
Nicholas, Gabriel, and Daniel Schaller
Sam and Annie Swift
Elizabeth Anne Schulzinger

Senior Sponsoring Editor: Jean L. Woy
Senior Associate Editor: Jeffrey Greene
Associate Project Editor: Elena Di Cesare
Senior Production/Design Coordinator: Carol Merrigan
Senior Manufacturing Coordinator: Marie Barnes
Marketing Manager: Clint Crockett

Cover Designer: Harold Burch, Harold Burch Design, New York City

Cover Image: Wayne Thiebaud, "Holly Ridge Park" 1980 Courtesy Allan
Stone Gallery

Biographical Profile photo credits

*Credits continue on page I-23, which constitute an extension of the
copyright page.*

Printed in the U.S.A.
Library of Congress Catalog Card Number: 95-76985
ISBN: 0-395-74534-9

123456789-QM-99 98 97 96 95

CONTENTS

3

America at Home, 1945–1960 91

4

The General as President: Foreign Policy in the 1950s 138

5

The New Frontier at Home and Abroad, 1960–1963 *175*

6

The Dream of a Great Society *213*

7

The Vietnam Nightmare, 1961–1968 *250*

8

The Politics and Culture of Protest 295

9

The Illusion of Peace: Foreign Policy During the Nixon Administration 335

10

The Use and Abuse of Power: Domestic Affairs and the Watergate Scandal, 1969–1974   *366*

11

The Challenges of Change, 1974–1980   *403*

12

Right Turn: Conservatism Ascendant, 1980–1992   *443*

13

From the New Cold War to the New World Order *488*

14

Rumblings of the Future *529*

MAPS AND CHARTS

PREFACE

As we approach the year 2000, it is clear that the more than half a century elapsed since the end of the Second World War forms a coherent unit of United States history. As Americans born during the early Cold War, we experienced the many ways in which that struggle defined life at home and abroad. The end of that decades-long conflict during the 1990s makes it appropriate to take a fresh look at the events that have shaped our national and individual lives. Also, as teachers, we felt impelled to write a text that emphasized the topics, questions, and dilemmas raised by our students.

Present Tense provides a balanced account of domestic politics, social and cultural change, and foreign affairs. It highlights several interrelated themes, such as the legacy of the New Deal, the growth of an active federal government, the impact of the Cold War on American life, the ongoing struggle by women and people of color for equality, the contribution of immigration, and the role of the federal courts as engines of social and legal change.

We try to devote equal attention to all periods of the post-1945 era, while balancing coverage of domestic and foreign affairs. In the second edition we have reorganized coverage of domestic and foreign affairs, especially for the periods before 1960 and since 1980. For example, the onset of the Cold War is treated as more of a coherent unit, while domestic social, economic, and political change during the late 1940s and 1950s is discussed in one chapter. Similarly, coverage of the period from 1980 to 1995 highlights the social and political changes that occurred during these fifteen years, especially the emergence of a powerful conservative challenge to New Deal liberalism. A final chapter combines discussion both of recent politics and emerging social and cultural changes that are likely to shape future developments.

While reorganizing the text, we have included additional material on topics such as the domestic legacy of the arms race, the development of the West and Sunbelt, environmental issues, changing employment, population, and family patterns since the 1970s, and American cultural and political life. Throughout the book, we utilize a post-Cold War perspective to reexamine the decades before 1990 and developments since then.

To highlight some of the people who have had a significant impact on American life and culture, each chapter includes a "Biographical Profile" focusing on a representative figure from the period. Some of the people featured include Eleanor Roosevelt, J. Robert Oppenheimer, Jackie Robinson, Rachel Carson, Malcolm X, and Bill Gates.

Each chapter also includes an introduction, a conclusion, and suggestions for further reading as well as maps, charts, and photographs to enrich students' appreciation of the content. We also provide an Instructor's Resource Manual that includes learning objectives, chapter synopses, multiple-choice test items, and essay questions.

Our friends, colleagues, and students at the University of Arizona, University of New Mexico, and University of Colorado have assisted us in conceiving, writing, and improving this book. Since the appearance of the first edition, many readers have sent along useful suggestions on ways to improve the text. To all of them we extend our deep appreciation. We also thank the reviewers who commented on drafts of each of the chapters:

Gary Bailey, Indiana University of Pennsylvania
Bruce J. Dierenfield, Canisius College
John Gauger, Lehigh Carbon Community College
Larry D. Lankton, Michigan Technological University
Otis Pease, University of Washington
Charles Piehl, Mankato State University
Steven Ross, University of Southern California
Beryl Satter, Rutgers University-Newark
Jerold Simmons, University of Nebraska-Omaha

The challenge of reconciling their diverse viewpoints added rigor and richness to our interpretation of the last half-century.

We reserve a special thank you to Leonard Dinnerstein—friend, colleague, and mentor—who encouraged this project from its inception and has shared with us his deep knowledge of American society.

M.S., V.S., R.D.S.

1

New Deal and World War: Into the Modern Era

As the Second World War reached its fiery conclusion in 1945, Americans began to express their vision of the era that lay ahead. Henry Luce, the influential publisher of *Time* and *Life* magazines, celebrated the emergence of a new "international moral order" and the "first great American Century." Former vice president Henry Wallace believed the world stood on the threshold of a "Century of the Common Man," a time when the humane values of America's New Deal would transform the war-ravaged world.

These two men differed greatly in their political and social philosophies. But they shared a sense that the previous decade had fundamentally altered the nation and its role in the world. To understand the postwar era, we need to trace the basic changes that occurred during the war and the Great Depression that preceded it.

Politically, those years were dominated by a single figure: Franklin Delano Roosevelt, elected four times as president. As journalist Theodore White remarked in later years, "All contemporary national politics descend from Franklin Roosevelt." But the changes wrought during those years were far more than political. They were social, economic, military, and technological as well.

Our current vastly powerful federal government, which touches the life of every American in myriad ways, evolved during the years of Roosevelt's presidency. Direct government intervention in the economy, government provision of extensive social services, government involvement in science and industry—all these are by-products of the Great Depression and Second World War. For women and African-Americans, the Roosevelt years brought important expansions of opportunity, along with rising hopes and frustrations that had a great effect on postwar society. Most dramatically, the United States assumed a new, all-important position in international relations. By the end of the Roosevelt era, the United States had become a superpower—a difficult, uneasy role that has shaped the nation's history ever since.

THE ROOSEVELT REVOLUTION

Franklin D. Roosevelt's inauguration in March 1933 occurred in the midst of the Great Depression, with the American economy perched on the threshold of collapse. Following the dramatic stock market crash on October 24, 1929, over 13 million workers—one-fourth of the labor force—had lost their jobs, industrial production and national income had fallen by half, and foreign trade had fallen by two-thirds. The collapse of five thousand banks wiped out 9 million savings accounts. The ensuing panic created a run on solvent banks as well. Hundreds of thousands of homeowners and farmers faced foreclosure as financial institutions called in loans. On one day in 1932, one-fourth of the land in the state of Mississippi was sold at auction. Millions of homeless throughout the United States slept in makeshift camps derisively called "Hoovervilles," after the incumbent president, Herbert C. Hoover, who seemed paralyzed in the face of this national crisis. The title of a popular song asked plaintively, "Brother, Can You Spare a Dime?"

Accepting the Democratic presidential nomination in 1932, Roosevelt promised a "new deal" for the American people, and in his inaugural address the next March he sought to break the mood of despair that gripped the nation. "The only thing we have to fear," he proclaimed, "is fear itself." He made it clear that he intended to deliver what the nation demanded: "action and action now." Should Congress fail to respond to the challenge, he would seek "broad executive power to wage a war against the emergency, as great as the power that would be given to me if we were in fact invaded by a foreign foe."

As Roosevelt's words hinted, his New Deal required a federal government that would take a direct and prominent role in the economy and American society. This was a new phenomenon in American history—it was a virtual revolution. Within a few years, Roosevelt's administration enlarged the federal government's size and scope to an extent previously unimaginable. The new federal government touched more people in more ways than ever before. And the huge military-industrial complex needed to fight the Second World War further contributed to the expansion of government power after 1941.

Until 1933, the only routine interaction between the federal government and most citizens was the delivery of mail by the post office. Policies set in Washington rarely affected the everyday lives of ordinary people. There was no old age pension system, no federal unemployment compensation, no aid to dependent children programs, no federal housing support, no stock market or banking regulations, no farm subsidies, no withholding of taxes, and no minimum wage—to name only a few federal activities now taken for granted.

Traditionally, "good government" had meant "minimal government," with the greatest authority in the hands of state and local officials. The United States had no tradition of a federal government actively committed to solving social and economic problems. Yet minimal government had failed to stem the ravages of a massive depression with both national and international origins. In Roosevelt's view, the time had come when government had to save capitalism from its own folly by ensuring every American the "right to make a comfortable living." He predicted that a violent revolution of the Right or Left "could hardly be avoided if another president failed as Hoover has failed." His apprehensions may have been exaggerated. American citizens, in the words of one contemporary observer, appeared more in the grip of "fathomless pessimism" than of revolutionary fervor. Still, it seemed likely that disillusion with democracy and capitalism would spread rapidly if government failed to combat the depression. This had already happened in Germany and Italy.

Roosevelt's New Deal had roots in the turn-of-the-century Progressive movement, which criticized the concentration of private economic power and the loss of individual freedom brought on by industrialization. The Progressives looked toward state and especially federal government to regulate private business in the public interest. Drawing on this political philosophy, Roosevelt favored an *active* federal government that would safeguard the public welfare within a vibrant system of free enterprise. Throughout the 1930s he sought to rescue capitalism by curbing its excesses through reform and regulation.

The New Deal also reflected Roosevelt's complex personal background. Born an only child in a socially prominent Anglo-Dutch family in upstate New York, Roosevelt never had to struggle for money, status, security, or dignity. Like many young men of patrician roots, he viewed self-made millionaires and industrialists as unscrupulous. Roosevelt had an easy self-assurance that disarmed almost all those he met. Although not a deep thinker, he relished fiery intellects and recruited them as his advisers. His broad but undisciplined mind sought practical solutions rather than detailed theoretical analyses of vexing social problems. Supreme Court Justice Oliver Wendell Holmes succinctly described Roosevelt as a "second-class intellect, but a first-class temperament."

After serving Woodrow Wilson as assistant secretary of the navy during World War I and running unsuccessfully as the Democratic nominee for vice president in 1920, Roosevelt suffered a crippling attack of polio. Several years of therapy, beginning in 1921, failed to restore the use of his legs, but the ravages of the disease had two positive effects on his political career. Sidelined from active politicking during his prolonged recovery, Roosevelt avoided the bitter factionalism that divided the Democrats through most of the Republican-dominated 1920s. Also, his struggle with polio "humanized" Roosevelt. Previously considered something of an upper-class dandy who dabbled in politics as a hobby, Roosevelt had now suffered the kind of tragedy that afflicts ordinary people. When he re-entered politics to run for governor of New York in 1928, he related to people in an intimate way. His emotional vigor so overshadowed his physical handicap (he could stand only with the aid of braces, and generally sat in a wheelchair) that the handicap never emerged as a serious liability, even in an age when such disabilities often ended public careers. He charmed the press corps so effectively they refrained from writing about or taking pictures of his withered legs.

Unlike the cautious Hoover, Roosevelt was determined to take quick action to meet the national emergency. During the so-called First Hundred Days following his inauguration—a measure by which all subsequent administrations have been judged—Roosevelt mobilized the federal government. Working with an eclectic group of university professors, socially conscious lawyers, and social workers known as his "Brain Trust," the new administration drafted legislation and began staffing new agencies. Although not anticapitalist, most members of the Brain Trust believed that, in a complex economy dominated by large industrial corporations, government must force big business to share its power and, in Roosevelt's words, "distribute wealth more equitably." Congress gave the president most of what he sought, and even initiated some programs of its own.

Within a short time the New Deal produced a score of recovery programs, boosting prices and employment while shoring up banking and financial institutions. The National Industrial Recovery Act (NIRA) encouraged businesses to form associations to raise prices and profits in the hope that this would create new jobs. The Agricultural Adjustment Act sought to raise farm prices by limiting crop production in return for cash subsidies. The new Federal Deposit Insurance Corporation (FDIC) regulated and stabilized private banking through tighter supervision and federal insurance of individual deposits. The Securities Act of 1933 and the creation of the Securities and Exchange Commission (SEC) in 1934 put the nation's stock market under government supervision. The Home Owners Loan Corporation provided funds for refinancing mortgages to tens of thousands of homeowners, while the Federal Housing Administration insured private loans for new construction. To preserve basically sound industries that faced ruin, the Reconstruction Finance Corporation (started by Hoover) loaned some $10 billion to the private sector. This influx of capital saved millions of jobs and kept factories operating. The Tennessee Valley Authority (TVA)—an ambitious and unique new agency—undertook vast flood-control and electrical-power–generating projects in the Upper South. A variety of government bureaucracies launched massive dam-building ventures in the West, remaking the economy and ecology of the entire region.

With the passage of the National Labor Relations Act, also known as the Wagner Act, in 1935, the federal government recognized the

African-American schoolchildren in an art class sponsored by the WPA in Florida. *Franklin D. Roosevelt Library.*

right of workers to organize into unions and to bargain collectively with employers as a means of improving their wages and working conditions. Even so, a series of strikes and other militant actions occurred before the new Congress of Industrial Organizations (CIO) successfully organized such basic industries as steel, coal, and automobile manufacturing. Gradually, CIO unions abandoned their early anticapitalist stance (partly as a result of purging radicals from their membership) and became pillars of support for the Democratic party.

With state and local governments and private charities overwhelmed by the number of unemployed, the New Deal replaced reliance on private, local charity for the needy with a system of social rights, or entitlements. The Social Security Act of 1935 created a national system to administer old age pensions, unemployment insurance, and aid for the blind and handicapped, and it expanded aid to dependent children. Initially these programs, some financed by a payroll tax, paid meager amounts that varied widely from state to state. But for the first time, the federal government took primary responsibility to alleviate the impact of unemployment and poverty on individual Americans.

Eager to do good and to jump-start the economy, the Roosevelt administration also broke new ground by adopting programs to assist the unemployed. A host of agencies, such as the Federal Emergency Relief Administration (FERA), the Civil Works Administration (CWA), the Public Works Administration (PWA), the Works Progress Administration (WPA), the Civilian Conservation Corps (CCC), and the National Youth Administration (NYA), provided grants to states for welfare benefits or directly employed the poor in federal work projects. These programs, many inspired by Interior Secretary Harold Ickes and social worker and Roosevelt-intimate Harry Hopkins, provided work for the unemployed in a variety of fields. The unemployed were hired to build highways, municipal buildings, schools, seaports, airports, zoos, parks, and dams throughout the United States. The Federal Theater Project hired 12,500 actors to perform nationally. Artists were commissioned to paint murals in public buildings, writers to write travel guides. In New York City alone, the WPA employed more people than the entire American army. At its peak, the WPA had a national work force of 3 million.

Many in Roosevelt's inner circle justified this vigorous government action by citing the theories of an iconoclastic British economist, John Maynard Keynes. Keynes believed that active state intervention was fundamental to the success of mature capitalism. The depression of the 1930s had so shaken business confidence, he argued, that recovery without government intervention was unlikely. Corporations and entrepreneurs would not make new investments until consumer demand reappeared. To increase consumer demand, public money had to be pumped into the economy.

Government money might enter the economy in a number of ways. By hiring unemployed workers to build bridges or roads, for example, the government could generate a demand for raw materials and machinery. Workers receiving government paychecks would be able to pay for rent, food, and clothing, creating a market for consumer goods. This "pump priming" would create sufficient consumer purchasing power to restore the confidence of the private sector. As the system returned to normal, the government could withdraw its hand from the marketplace. Through "stimulative" deficit spending, the government could increase consumer demand by injecting money into the economy, recouping its losses through higher tax collections when economic conditions improved.

Orthodox economists and political conservatives bristled at the idea of government intervention in the economy, and they considered deficit spending a heresy. Even Roosevelt accepted Keynes's ideas only half-heartedly. He hesitated to support the massive federal spending and central planning that Keynes and his followers believed necessary to overcome the depression. Roosevelt also feared making citizens too dependent on the government as an

Eleanor Roosevelt

Between 1933 and 1945 Eleanor Roosevelt transformed the role of First Lady. Not content to be a mere hostess and model housewife, she crusaded for human rights and social justice, becoming a national symbol of reform and an inspiration to many women and minorities.

Little in Eleanor's early life foreshadowed her later rise to prominence. Born into an elite family, raised by a stern grandmother after her parents' death when she was only ten, she was a shy and emotionally insecure child. When she married her distant cousin, Franklin Roosevelt, his mother objected to the match and made life difficult for her daughter-in-law. The couple had six children, one of whom died in infancy. Although Eleanor and Franklin always admired each other, as early as 1918 his extramarital affairs created an emotional distance between them. For her own part, she formed close relations with other women, especially journalist Lorena Hickock.

employer of last resort. Nevertheless, his pragmatic approach to the crisis brought profound changes to the American economy and government.

Many of the New Deal programs and agencies had expired by the end of the Second World War. A number of them, however—including the SEC, the FDIC, the TVA, and the Social Security Administration—survive today. Most important, the New Deal established the principle that the federal government should intervene in the country's economic and social life on behalf of its citizens.

After polio crippled Franklin in 1920, Eleanor became politically active, often serving as his surrogate in Democratic party affairs. She played a role in Al Smith's 1928 presidential candidacy and in her husband's administration as New York governor from 1929 to 1933. During these years she worked closely with social workers, unions, and women's reform groups.

As First Lady, Eleanor Roosevelt vigorously promoted the New Deal agenda and, unfettered by the political restrictions that bound her husband, pushed a variety of progressive measures. Trade unionists, sharecroppers, and women's groups considered her their pipeline into the government. She also emerged as the administration's leading advocate for the rights of African-Americans. At a segregated meeting in Alabama, she insisted on sitting in the "coloreds only" section. When the Daughters of the American Revolution refused to rent a concert hall to African-American singer Marian Anderson, Eleanor Roosevelt of-fered the White House grounds for the performance. She always maintained that she acted first as a citizen and only afterward as a First Lady. Beginning in 1937, she wrote a popular newspaper column, "My Day," that appeared in hundreds of papers.

During the Second World War, when the federal government turned most of its attention toward boosting military production and directing the war effort, she played an especially influential role in advocating social causes, minority rights, and economic justice.

Even after 1945, Eleanor Roosevelt continued to speak and write on great issues of the day. Her achievements and her support for unpopular causes inspired hope in many of her contemporaries and established her as a model for younger generations of social activists. ■

Along with the revolution in the size and scope of government came a change in the profile of federal appointees. Previously most federal officials had been white, Anglo-Saxon men from the business community. The New Deal reached out to Catholics, Jews, African-Americans, and women with professional experience in social work, labor unions, and universities. These appointees brought diverse views to policy deliberations and acted as spokespersons in Washington for working, minority, and ethnic Americans. Some of Roosevelt's closest advisers, such as Thomas Corcoran, James Farley, Ben Cohen,

Sam Rosenman, Henry Morgenthau, Jr., and Felix Frankfurter, came from Irish or—even more controversial—Jewish backgrounds. Labor Secretary Frances Perkins, the first woman in a presidential cabinet, played a critical role in promoting new social legislation. Harry Hopkins, the first professional social worker to serve a president, became a frequent and influential adviser on both domestic and foreign affairs. First Lady Eleanor Roosevelt, a political activist who represented a national network of feminist, progressive women, also influenced Roosevelt's thought on social issues. This multiplicity of voices enriched Roosevelt's presidency and brought the concerns of diverse groups and classes to national attention.

To a large degree, Roosevelt relied on his appeal to the "forgotten man" to stimulate widespread interest in New Deal programs. Part of his effectiveness stemmed from his ability to speak to the American people en masse. Few national leaders have used the mass media—in his case radio—as effectively to bond with the public. Roosevelt initiated "fireside chats," live radio broadcasts through which he addressed millions of listeners in their living rooms. His audience considered the president a guest in their homes and planned their evening activities around his broadcast chats.

Roosevelt's appeal transcended traditional factions and was particularly strong for the disenfranchised. The New Deal coalition included not only the traditional Democratic Party machine, but also labor unions and voters from virtually every ethnic and minority group. The children of immigrants and minorities, helped by New Deal social programs, developed a greater sense of belonging and self-worth. These supporters contributed to Roosevelt's landslide presidential election of 1936 and his re-election in 1940 and 1944.

Millions of Americans experienced real, tangible benefits from New Deal programs. Some people were put to work, others received farm support payments or were able to refinance mortgages. Rural residents could recall the day on which electric power, funded by the federal government, first came to their homes and farms. Above all, Roosevelt's programs and personality restored hope to vast numbers of Americans and countered the lure of fascism and communism.

Yet there were signs, even in the heady early days of the New Deal, that it would not be an unqualified success. Although the unemployment rate fell dramatically from its high of 25 percent in 1933, it still hovered at 16.9 percent in 1936—as compared to just 3.2 percent before the stock market crash in 1929—and continued at an unacceptably high level throughout the 1930s. Moreover, many people fell through the gaps in the New Deal assistance programs. Some of the starkest images came from the "Dust Bowl" states of Oklahoma, Arkansas, and the Great Plains, where drought, wind, and plagues of grasshoppers forced the mass migration of small farmers. In the industrial cities of the North and Midwest, waves of strikes often led to violence and bloodshed as industrialists resisted organizing efforts. Because federal programs operated through and depended on the cooperation of local authorities, government administrators often bowed to local racial prejudices and distributed benefits in blatantly unequal proportions.

For millions of Americans, the New Deal either delivered too little or promised too much. Throughout the 1930s, radical alternatives to FDR's reforms were promoted by groups and individuals on both the Left and the Right. These included the American Communist Party as well as demagogues like Father Charles Coughlin, Gerald L. K. Smith, Francis Townsend, and Louisiana senator Huey Long. Each blamed "conspirators"—industrialists, bankers, Jews or other minorities—for America's problems. In the end, however, none offered a credible alternative to the New Deal.

Despite Roosevelt's landslide re-election in 1936 and the establishment of large Democratic majorities in Congress, the New Deal's struggles increased in the president's second term. Roosevelt caused one problem himself with a bungled attempt to pack the Supreme Court. Through 1937, a group of four conservative justices dominated the Supreme Court. These "Four Horsemen" together with Chief Justice Charles Evans Hughes and Justice Owen Roberts formed a majority that struck down such key New Deal legislation as the National Industrial Recovery Act and the Agricultural Adjustment Act. The conservatives insisted that not even a national economic emergency justified government interference in such private economic matters as the setting of wages and the sanctity of contracts. As a result, between 1934 and 1936, the high court voided so many pieces of federal legislation that it threatened the entire New Deal program.

Roosevelt insisted that the Constitution gave him the authority to meet "extraordinary needs by changes in emphasis." Fearing further judicial assaults on New Deal programs, he asked Congress in 1937 for the authority to appoint up to six additional Supreme Court justices. Most Republican and many Democratic members of Congress opposed this effort to pack the Court and rebuffed the president.

In mid-1937, however, one justice who usually voted with the conservatives switched sides, and another announced plans to retire. Although the effort to add additional justices failed, an emerging liberal majority on the court upheld the pro-labor Wagner Act, a minimum wage law, and key provisions of the Social Security Act. The court had turned a decisive corner. From 1937 on, the federal government exercised broad regulatory power over private contracts and commerce without fear of judicial intervention.

But just as the Supreme Court began affirming the right of the government to intervene deeply in the economy, a severe recession in 1937 and 1938 shook popular confidence in Roosevelt's leadership. Cuts in government spending and the initiation of the Social Security tax, which withdrew several billion dollars from circulation, probably brought on the downturn. The unemployment rate rose again, reaching 20 percent in 1938. Roosevelt committed himself to a higher level of public spending and even greater management of the economy. But his influence with Congress had waned, and he barely managed to shepherd the landmark Fair Labor Standards Act through Congress in mid-1938. The act banned child labor, established a federal minimum wage, and limited the regular work week to forty hours for many occupations. Yet the law did not cover agricultural and household domestic positions—jobs held largely by women, African-Americans, and Hispanics.

In the 1938 congressional elections, Republicans picked up eighty-one House and eight Senate seats. These Republicans joined with conservative Democrats in blocking further New Deal innovations. They demanded balanced budgets, curbs on labor unions, and, under the banner of states' rights, no federal help for racial minorities. The New Deal reform era reached a plateau in 1938 that it never surpassed. Many of the further goals of the Roosevelt administration would not be addressed until the 1960s.

The conservative bloc in Congress created the House Committee on Un-American Activities, which later achieved notoriety in the postwar years. The committee charged that Roosevelt's "left-wing-followers in the government are the fountainhead of subversive activities." Under attack from politicians whose support he needed in order to deal with growing threats from Germany and Japan, and hoping to repair his tattered relations with business leaders, Roosevelt backed away from reform. Soon the outbreak of war pushed social progress even further into the background.

AMERICA AND THE WORLD CRISIS

Until the late 1930s, the focus on the Great Depression limited public concern with foreign affairs. Roosevelt barely mentioned world events in his 1933 inaugural address. He did promise that America would act as a "good neighbor," especially in dealing with Latin America, and this policy resulted in the removal of occupation troops from Haiti, the lowering of tariffs, and the extension of trade credits to Latin American countries.

Early in his first term, Roosevelt extended diplomatic recognition to the Soviet Union. Ever since the Russian Revolution in 1917, the United States had refused to recognize the Soviet government. Public school teachers had often been urged not to mention the name "Soviet Union," and many maps showed the country as a blank spot. Recognition, the president hoped, might boost trade with the newly industrialized country and ally the Soviets with the Western democracies against Nazi Germany and Imperial Japan. However, lingering suspicion of communism, disputes over payment of Czarist debts, and revulsion toward Joseph Stalin's brutal collectivization of agriculture and his political purges prevented much cooperation before 1941.

By the mid-1930s, a spirit of isolationism was widespread. Many Americans, including a substantial number in Congress, believed that the nation should have little to do with conflicts between foreign countries. Congressional hearings of the mid-1930s focused on charges that British and French propagandists and American arms makers (the "merchants of death") had hoodwinked the United States into entering the First World War. These charges increased the public's distaste for foreign affairs and led Congress to pass neutrality acts between 1935 and 1937, which restricted the president and private Americans from giving economic assistance to foreign nations at war.

These laws, which did not distinguish between aggressor and victim, coincided with a burst of belligerence by Germany, Japan, and Italy. All three countries were ruled by Fascist or ultranationalist regimes that claimed special rights, frequently on the basis of race, to conquer their neighbors. The Italian invasion of Ethiopia in 1935, Italian and German support of the Fascist revolt in Spain in 1936, German remilitarization and the annexation of Austria from 1936 to 1938, and Japan's invasion of China in 1937 evoked little more than tongue-clicking from the American government.

In September 1938, when Adolf Hitler demanded the partition of Czechoslovakia, Roosevelt supported the decision by the British and French governments to "appease" Hitler's appetite, delay war, and, possibly, turn the German dictator's wrath toward the Soviet Union. After the fateful meeting in Munich, in which the British and French sealed the fate of the Czechs by agreeing to Hitler's demands, Roosevelt cabled British prime minister Neville Chamberlain two words: "Good man." Only later, when Hitler turned his fury on the West, did the Munich agreement and the term *appeasement* take on the aura of cowardly capitulation.

Like most Americans (and many Europeans), Roosevelt hoped to preserve the world balance of power while taking as few risks as possible. American leaders recognized the dangers of German domination of Europe and Japanese control of Asia, but they hoped other nations would take the responsibility for containing the aggressor nations' advances. Only after Hitler violated the Munich agreement by seizing all of Czechoslovakia, and then followed this onslaught with a demand for Polish territory, did the British and French abandon their policy of appeasement. By then it was nearly too late for them, or the United States, to act. In the months after the Munich debacle, Roosevelt got Congress to increase funding for a critical build-up of American air and naval forces.

In September 1939, after signing a nonaggression pact with the Soviet Union, Hitler invaded Poland. Britain and France responded by declaring war on Germany. With America's two major European friends facing the might of Nazi Germany, Roosevelt pressed Congress to permit England and France to purchase American arms, so long as they used their own money and ships to transport the weapons. This "cash-and-carry" policy helped the Allies, but at little cost or risk of involvement to the United States. Until mid-1940, Roosevelt hoped that indirect American assistance would suffice to resist Germany and Japan.

Just weeks after the outbreak of war in Europe, the president received a stark indication of the growing German threat. Nuclear physicist Albert Einstein, himself a Jewish refugee from the Nazis, sent Roosevelt a letter warning that German scientists had taken the first steps toward harnessing atomic power for military use. If German scientists developed an atomic bomb, Einstein predicted, Hitler would win the war.

Roosevelt authorized a group of high-level officials to begin an atomic weapons program, code-named the Manhattan Project. By 1945, some 150,000 people were working on some phase of the $2 billion project to construct the ultimate weapon. Many of the project's participants realized that the bomb would have a profound effect on the world, both during and after the war. The massive development project also marked a marriage of government, science, and industry that became a hallmark of post-1945 national security policy, as well as a force for social transformation of the nation.

By June 1940, Germany's mechanized *Blitzkrieg* ("lightning war") victories in Western Europe had left only Britain resisting Nazi power. (Russia remained neutral until attacked by Germany in June 1941.) Japan, which by then occupied large portions of China, joined Germany and Italy in the Axis Alliance and began threatening European and American colonies in Asia.

As Germany stepped up its air and submarine attacks against Britain, Roosevelt stretched his constitutional powers to the limit. He transferred war ships to the British and ordered the American navy to prevent German submarines from entering a large portion of the Atlantic. The American army, then comparable in budget ($500 million) and size (185,000 men) to the Bulgarian army, desperately needed to expand. When Roosevelt prodded Congress to pass the nation's first peacetime draft in 1940, his opponents labeled him a warmonger. One senator charged that Roosevelt's policies would "plow under every fourth American boy." Congress reluctantly extended the law in 1941, although many members opposed expanding the period of service from one to two years.

Polls in the summer of 1940 revealed that although 75 percent of Americans supported aid to England and China, the public opposed direct participation in the war. Roosevelt, who had decided to seek an unprecedented third term in 1940, felt obliged to pledge that the nation's youth would not be sent into any foreign wars. (If attacked, he later explained, the United States would of course respond.) Only after his re-election in November did Roosevelt publicly state his full commitment to the British and Chinese war efforts.

If England or China surrendered, Roosevelt declared, Americans would be "living at the point of a gun." To prevent this, he proposed a massive aid program called Lend-Lease, that would make America the "arsenal of democracy." In a vivid fireside chat, the president compared the aid to lending a fire hose to a neighbor whose house was in flames to keep the sparks from spreading. In March 1941, Congress, by a lopsided vote, passed legislation providing $7 billion in military aid for nations resisting Germany and Japan. This aid package was nearly as large as the entire federal budget! Secretary of War Henry Stimson referred to the Lend-Lease bill as a "declaration of economic war" against Berlin and Tokyo.

Roosevelt sent American troops to occupy Greenland and Iceland and ordered navy ships in the Atlantic to hunt down German U-boats. By the autumn of 1941, the German and American navies were engaged in an undeclared war that led to the sinking of an American destroyer. When Nazi armies invaded the Soviet Union in June, Roosevelt quickly approved Lend-Lease aid to the Soviets. He did so despite earlier American fury at Stalin for signing the 1939 non-aggression pact with Hitler, which freed the Soviets to seize the Baltic republics and eastern Poland.

With American attention turned toward the crisis in Europe, Japan took the opportunity to seize southern French Indochina, demand special access to oil from the Dutch East Indies, and insist that Washington stop military aid to China. In response, Roosevelt shifted naval units to the Pacific and imposed a trade embargo on Japan, leaving Tokyo with only a few months' reserve of petroleum.

Roosevelt insisted that Japan had to quit the Axis Alliance, withdraw its forces from China and Indochina, and make a nonaggression pledge before he would lift the oil embargo. Japan, under the de facto leadership of General Tojo Hideki, demanded the immediate resumption of oil sales and a cutoff of aid to China before considering any pullback.

When discussions broke off on November 26, 1941, American officials expected a Japanese attack on American bases in Southeast Asia or the Philippines and sent warnings to commanders there and in Hawaii. American intelligence had been intercepting Japanese communications, but they were unaware of Japan's plan to target the Pacific fleet at Pearl Harbor, in Hawaii.

On December 7, 1941—a date, Roosevelt said, that would "live in infamy"—Japan mounted a surprise air attack on the U.S. fleet and airfields at Pearl Harbor. The assault killed over 2,400 sailors and soldiers, damaged or sank eight American battleships, and destroyed a large number of planes. Suddenly, war had come to the United States. At Roosevelt's request, Congress promptly declared war on Japan. On December 10, Japan's allies, Germany and Italy, declared war on the United States. As Japanese forces rolled to a string of easy victories in Southeast Asia, shock and humiliation shook an American citizenry that had previously felt immune from the war in Europe and Asia. But Germany and Japan, although it was by no means clear at the time, had sown the seeds of their own doom by engaging America's vast military potential. Within a short time, American industry was producing more ships and planes each month than were lost to the Japanese during the "sneak attack on Pearl Harbor."

Pearl Harbor ended domestic dissent over participation in the war. On New Year's Day in 1942, the United States, Great Britain, the Soviet Union, and twenty-three other partners issued a "Declaration of the United Nations," a pledge to fight for victory against the Axis. Roosevelt and his military advisers resolved that the United States would provide additional Lend-Lease aid to Britain, Russia, and China, helping them to carry the bulk of the fighting against Germany and Japan. As soon as possible, British and American armies would open a second front invading Western Europe to relieve the pressure on the Soviets (who until 1944 had alone faced about two-thirds of all German forces). Roosevelt anticipated that once the Allies crushed Germany, the Soviets would then join in the final assault on Japan.

The proposed American military strategy encountered numerous obstacles. British prime minister Winston Churchill, who guided Britain throughout the war, feared high casualties in an early assault on Western Europe and preferred to wear down the Germans in North Africa and Italy. American commanders believed that failure to attack German forces in Western Europe would prolong the war, increase total casualties, and risk the collapse of the Soviet war effort. Roosevelt knew that Stalin would interpret any delay in opening a second front as encouraging Germany's devastation of the Soviet Union. Because the Russian army and Russian civilians were suffering enormous casualties in Europe, and out of fear that the Soviet Union might collapse and make a separate peace, Roosevelt promised Stalin a second front in 1942. At the same time, the air forces and navies of the United States and Great Britain played a critical role in destroying Germany's war-making capacity.

Supply problems, British stalling, the competing demands of the war against Japan, and other factors delayed the Allied entry into France until June 6, 1944. The massive invasion of Normandy on that date (see map) quickly broke the power of the Nazis in Western Europe. By then the Soviets had pushed German forces out of Russia and into Poland, at a cost of more than 20 million civilian and military dead. Stalin remained deeply suspicious of the Western Allies, even after they had opened the second front. He believed they would fight Germany to the last Russian and then move to control Europe themselves.

The behavior of Soviet leaders tended to arouse similar fears in London and Washington. For example, beginning in 1942 Stalin demanded that Roosevelt and Churchill approve the transfer of parts of prewar Poland and southeastern Europe to the Soviet Union. Although Western leaders believed such a concession would violate the rights of Poland and the other nations involved, they also recognized that the Soviets had a justified interest in creating a security zone in Eastern Europe, the route of two German invasions since 1914. Churchill and Roosevelt eventually accepted the Soviet demands in return for Stalin's promise to respect the political independence of the rest of Eastern Europe. Some American policymakers believed that at times Churchill seemed more interested in safeguarding British interests in the Mediterranean than in defeating Hitler. Like the Soviet Union, Britain also worried about America's power in the postwar world.

Roosevelt hoped that wartime trust and cooperation would create support for a new world political order. At a series of summits held between 1941 and 1945, the president sketched plans for a postwar international organization, the United Nations, that would be dominated by what he sometimes called the "Four Policemen"—the United States, the Soviet Union, Great Britain, and China. Each nation would police a particular security zone, or sphere of interest, that was most important to it. At the same time, each would work toward opening up world trade, decolonizing its own empire, and rehabilitating Germany and Japan to encourage their forming democratic societies. Roosevelt first pressed these points in August 1941, even before the United States formally entered the war, when he and a

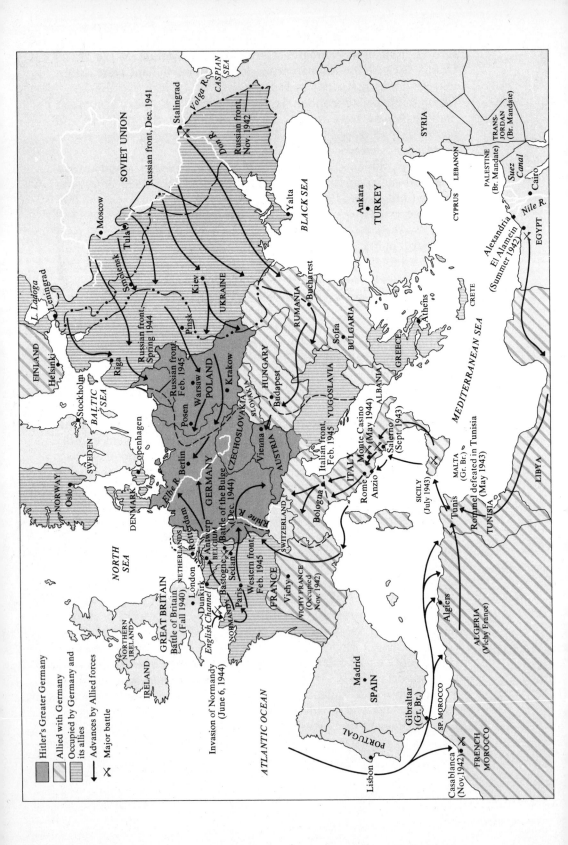

Hitler's Greater Germany

Allied with Germany

Occupied by Germany and
its allies

Advances by Allied forces

Major battle

SOVIET UNION

Russian front, Dec. 1941

Russian front, Nov. 1942

Russian front, Feb. 1945

Russian front, Spring 1944

Volga R.

Don R.

Stalingrad

Moscow

Tula

Smolensk

Kiev

UKRAINE

Pinsk

Krakow

Warsaw

POLAND

Posen

Yalta

BLACK SEA

Bucharest

RUMANIA

Sofia

BULGARIA

Ankara

TURKEY

SYRIA

LEBANON

PALESTINE
(Br. Mandate)

TRANS-
JORDAN
(Br. Mandate)

Suez
Canal

Cairo

Nile R.

EGYPT

Alexandria

El Alamein
(Summer 1942)

CYPRUS

CRETE

Athens

GREECE

ALBANIA

YUGOSLAVIA

Italian front,
Feb. 1945

Monte Cassino
(May 1944)

Salerno
(Sept. 1943)

Anzio

Rome

Bologna

ITALY

SICILY
(July 1943)

Tunis

Rommel defeated in Tunisia
(May 1943)

TUNISIA

MALTA
(Gr. Br.)

MEDITERRANEAN SEA

LIBYA

ALGERIA
(Vichy France)

Algiers

SP. MOROCCO

FRENCH
MOROCCO

Casablanca
(Nov. 1942)

Gibraltar
(Gr. Br.)

SPAIN

Madrid

PORTUGAL

Lisbon

ATLANTIC OCEAN

L. Ladoga

Leningrad

FINLAND

Helsinki

NORWAY

Oslo

SWEDEN

Stockholm

Copenhagen

DENMARK

BALTIC
SEA

Riga

NORTH
SEA

GREAT BRITAIN

Battle of Britain
(Fall 1940)

London

Dunkirk

English Channel

Invasion of Normandy
(June 6, 1944)

NORMANDY

Paris

FRANCE

Vichy

VICHY FRANCE
(Occupied
Nov. 1942)

SWITZERLAND

NETHERLANDS

Rotterdam

Antwerp

BELGIUM

Bastogne,
Battle of the Bulge
(Dec. 1944)

Sedan

Western front,
Feb. 1945

Rhine R.

Elbe R.

Berlin

GERMANY

CZECHOSLOVAKIA

SLOVAKIA

Vienna

AUSTRIA

HUNGARY

Budapest

NORTHERN
IRELAND

IRELAND

skeptical Churchill issued a proclamation called the Atlantic Charter. Plans for the United Nations went forward during the war, and it was chartered in 1945, shortly after Roosevelt's death. By then, however, growing mistrust between the United States and the Soviet Union frustrated efforts to have the UN serve as an international peace keeper.

Although the diplomatic and strategic logic of the war often seemed confused, by 1945 a pattern had emerged. As Stalin remarked, "whoever occupies a territory also imposes on it his own social system." Thus, between 1943 and 1945, the British and Americans, joined by Charles de Gaulle's Free French, gradually established pro-Western, anti-Communist regimes in North Africa, Italy, Greece, France, western Germany, Japan, and southern Korea. As American forces advanced across the Pacific (see map), Washington took possession of hundreds of islands formerly in the possession of Japan, declaring them "strategic trusteeships." The United States also became more involved in the Middle East, an area of immense petroleum reserves. Roosevelt met with the ruler of Saudi Arabia, King Ibn Saud, in 1943 and began a cooperative relationship that provided American access to Saudi oil for the next half century.

In truth, all the Allies looked after their own interests, even while pursuing common goals. For example, the British, French, and Dutch rushed to recolonize Southeast Asia as Japan retreated. As Russian forces pushed the Nazis toward Berlin, Stalin similarly imposed pro-Soviet regimes in most of Eastern Europe. Roosevelt, who was hardly naive, preferred delaying most bargaining until the war's end, when he thought the American position would be stronger. Nor did he favor any action jeopardizing wartime cooperation. Although several of his advisers urged confronting Moscow, perhaps even cutting off Lend-Lease aid once German troops had been pushed out of Soviet territory, Roosevelt refused to risk a break in the alliance and declared that everything would be negotiable after victory.

But by February 1945, as the imminent collapse of the Axis Alliance became apparent, the Allies could no longer defer discussing postwar issues. Roosevelt and Churchill joined Stalin for a crucial meeting at Yalta, a Soviet city on the Black Sea. There the "Big Three"—Great Britain, the United States, and the Soviet Union—agreed to participate in the new United Nations and to exact industrial reparations from Germany. They also agreed that the Soviets would enter into the war against Japan three months after Hitler's defeat. In exchange, Roosevelt granted Stalin certain concessions. Critics of the Yalta agreements later charged that Roosevelt acceded to Stalin's demands out of naïveté, deteriorating health, or perhaps even Communist

◀ **The Allies on the Offensive in Europe, 1942–1945**

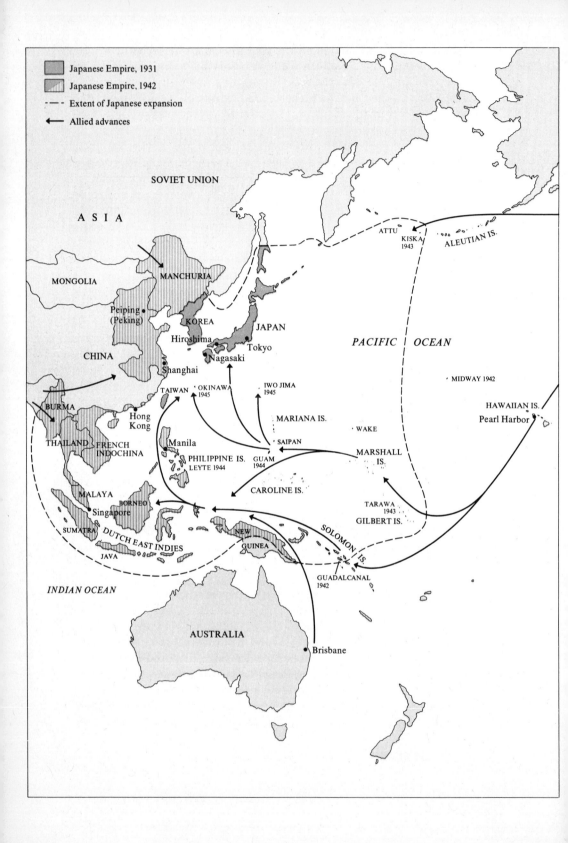

Japanese Empire, 1931
Japanese Empire, 1942
Extent of Japanese expansion
Allied advances

SOVIET UNION

A S I A

MONGOLIA

MANCHURIA

Peiping (Peking)

KOREA

CHINA

Hiroshima

Nagasaki

Shanghai

JAPAN

Tokyo

PACIFIC   OCEAN

ATTU

KISKA 1943

ALEUTIAN IS.

MIDWAY 1942

TAIWAN

OKINAWA 1945

IWO JIMA 1945

HAWAIIAN IS.

Pearl Harbor

Hong Kong

BURMA

THAILAND

FRENCH INDOCHINA

Manila

PHILIPPINE IS.

LEYTE 1944

MARIANA IS.

SAIPAN

GUAM 1944

WAKE

MARSHALL IS.

CAROLINE IS.

MALAYA

Singapore

BORNEO

SUMATRA   DUTCH EAST INDIES

JAVA

NEW GUINEA

SOLOMON IS.

TARAWA 1943

GILBERT IS.

GUADALCANAL 1942

INDIAN OCEAN

AUSTRALIA

Brisbane

sympathies. Why else would he sanction a dominant Soviet role in Poland or grant Stalin special economic privileges in Manchuria? "Yalta" became shorthand, especially among Republicans, for appeasement of Soviet territorial demands.

In fact, the Yalta agreement merely recognized what Stalin had already taken. Soviet forces occupied Poland, parts of Rumania and Bulgaria, and the Baltic states of Estonia, Latvia, and Lithuania. The Soviets were poised to invade Germany; and they would soon be able to attack Japan through Manchuria. Thus Roosevelt did not "give away," anything. Furthermore, American military leaders, who feared high casualties in the last stages of the war against Japan, pressed Roosevelt to make concessions to Stalin to get him into the Pacific war.

As part of the price for fighting Japan, Stalin demanded special economic privileges in Manchuria (northeastern China). In return he promised not to assist the Chinese Communists' struggle against the American-backed Chinese Nationalist government. Stalin also promised to reorganize the Soviet-installed regime in Poland along more democratic lines. A "Declaration of the Liberated Europe," signed by the three leaders, pledged cooperation in restoring democratic government in the liberated territories.

One Roosevelt aide complained that the agreement was "so elastic that the Russians can stretch it all the way from Yalta to Washington without technically breaking it." Roosevelt agreed, but added that it was the best he could do under the circumstances. Without continued Soviet cooperation, Roosevelt knew the Western allies would face a far bloodier road to Berlin and Tokyo. Soviet domination of Eastern Europe and northeast Asia—which Stalin could impose with or without western permission—seemed a reasonable price for saving American lives and shortening the war. Even American hard-liners did not seriously recommend fighting the Soviets to move them out of Poland. Most Americans rejoiced, in fact, when the Russians captured Berlin and when Germany surrendered on May 8, 1945. On the basis of earlier agreements, the Soviet Union turned over part of the German capital and other liberated territory to its allies.

It is important to recognize that when the war ended, the United States and its Western allies dominated most of the industrialized world, including North America, Great Britain, Western Europe, and Japan. The Soviets occupied much of Eastern Europe and a fourth of Germany, but their spoils did little to enhance their industrial or economic power. This fact, more than any other, ensured American supremacy after 1945 (in Chapter 2 we will examine the United States' postwar military power, including its early nuclear supremacy and its use of the atomic bomb to end the war in Asia). Among the warring

◀ The Pacific War

powers, the United States had made the smallest human sacrifice—about 400,000 dead, compared to a worldwide total approaching 50 million—and had gained the most. Russian civilian deaths during the three-year siege of Leningrad—just one city—exceeded the total number of military deaths sustained by the United States. America emerged from the war with the world's strongest economy and armed forces, as well as a monopoly on atomic power. When the killing stopped, the United States, with only 6 percent of the world's population, produced half the world's goods. This relative level of power and economic well-being was not surpassed in the subsequent half-century. As one contemporary noted, "while the rest of the world came out bruised and scarred and nearly destroyed, we came out with the most unbelievable machinery, trade, manpower and money."

WAR ON THE HOME FRONT

The war years brought most New Deal social programs to a halt. But even though the New Deal was gone, the war itself acted as a catalyst for far-reaching social and economic change. In 1941 the United States still had many characteristics of a rural and small-town society. Of 132 million Americans, only about 74 million, or 56 percent, lived in cities with more than ten thousand inhabitants. About one-third of dwelling units lacked indoor plumbing, and two-thirds lacked central heating. Moreover, only 40 percent of adults had an eighth-grade education. One-fourth had graduated from high school; one-tenth had attended college, and only half of these had completed a college degree. Almost 90 percent of white men (the most affluent group) made less than $2,500 per year. Over half of all wage-earning men and three-fourths of wage-earning women earned $1,000 per year or less. The economy was still depressed in January 1941. Around 9 million workers, or 15 percent of the labor force, had no job. Private investment stood 18 percent *below* the 1929 level. The gross national product (GNP) barely surpassed the 1929 figure.

All of this changed dramatically during the war years. As the war progressed, unemployment virtually disappeared, and ordinary Americans felt the shadow of the Great Depression finally lift from their lives. Private investment quickly surpassed the 1929 level and then continued to soar. The GNP swelled from a prewar level of $90 billion per year to over $212 billion in 1945. Universities and private industries vastly expanded their research facilities. Mass population shifts occurred as millions of Americans moved to cities. By the war's end, the United States had taken a giant leap from its lingering small-town past toward the urbanized, high-tech present.

The most obvious economic effect of the war was the surge in federal spending. Defense allocations rose sharply with the passage of

Lend-Lease in 1941. The initial Lend-Lease appropriation of $7 billion ballooned to a total of $50 billion for the war years—an enormous sum compared to the total federal budget of $9 billion in 1939. By the end of the war the annual federal budget increased tenfold between 1939 and 1945, to more than $95 billion (see figure, page 24). Correspondingly, the size of the federal bureaucracy more than tripled, reaching 3.4 million workers in 1945—a number still not surpassed as of 1995. The size and scope of the federal government expanded during earlier wars, especially during the Civil War and World War I. But after the earlier conflicts, it shrunk. This time the government grew and remained large.

Another portentous change was the rapid rise in the national debt. Although Treasury Secretary Henry Morgenthau, Jr., hoped to pay half of the war's costs by raising taxes, the other half had to be financed by the sale of bonds to individuals and banks. Until the war the United States had maintained a relatively small debt. But now, with the help of popular film and radio stars, the government promoted Treasury bonds so successfully it raised $135 billion. Small purchasers accounted for a third of the total sales, financial institutions for the rest. War-bond drives also served to involve American civilians in the common defense effort.

In addition to raising money, the government had to mobilize American industry for war. For this task Roosevelt turned to the business executives he had once denounced as selfish plutocrats. Thousands of corporate executives signed on to guide the national economy; they were called "dollar-a-year men" because they kept their business salaries and received only a token payment from the government. These "war lords of Washington," as one critic called them, exercised unprecedented control over the national economy by deciding what should be built, where, and by whom.

In May 1943, Roosevelt further centralized planning by asking his recent appointee to the Supreme Court, James F. Byrnes, to head the Office of War Mobilization (OWM). By relying more on incentives than on penalties, Byrnes and his business advisers proved remarkably successful in mobilizing the private sector to produce war goods.

Corporations were initially reluctant to invest the huge amounts of money needed to convert from civilian to military production. For example, it would cost General Motors a fortune to retool plants to produce tanks and jeeps in place of cars. Who would pay for conversion (and reconversion, when the war ended), and how could profits be guaranteed? Should private businesses invest in costly, experimental technology that might have no peacetime application? To encourage industrial production, the Justice Department relaxed antitrust enforcement. Washington offered manufacturers the innovative "cost plus a fixed fee" contract whereby the federal government paid

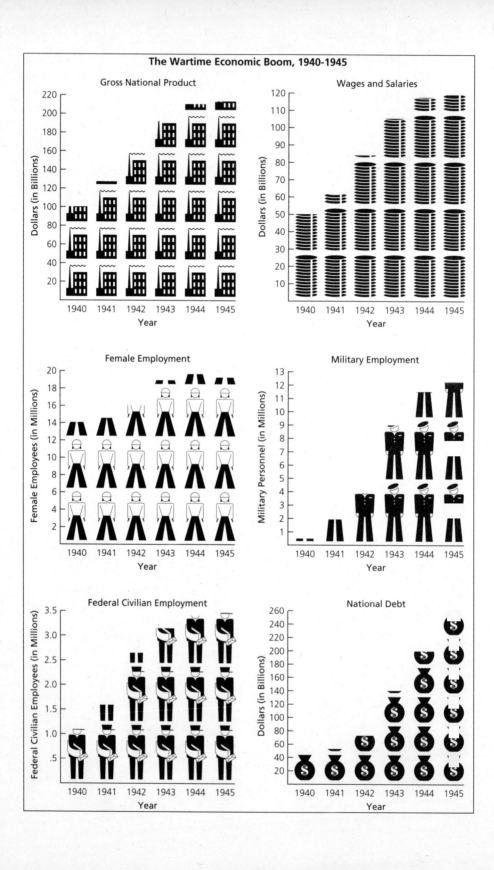

The Wartime Economic Boom, 1940-1945

Gross National Product

Dollars (in Billions)

220, 200, 180, 160, 140, 120, 100, 80, 60, 40, 20

Year: 1940 1941 1942 1943 1944 1945

Wages and Salaries

Dollars (in Billions)

120, 110, 100, 90, 80, 70, 60, 50, 40, 30, 20, 10

Year: 1940 1941 1942 1943 1944 1945

Female Employment

Female Employees (in Millions)

20, 18, 16, 14, 12, 10, 8, 6, 4, 2

Year: 1940 1941 1942 1943 1944 1945

Military Employment

Military Personnel (in Millions)

13, 12, 11, 10, 9, 8, 7, 6, 5, 4, 3, 2, 1

Year: 1940 1941 1942 1943 1944 1945

Federal Civilian Employment

Federal Civilian Employees (in Millions)

3.5, 3.0, 2.5, 2.0, 1.5, 1.0, .5

Year: 1940 1941 1942 1943 1944 1945

National Debt

Dollars (in Billions)

260, 240, 220, 200, 180, 160, 140, 120, 100, 80, 60, 40, 20

Year: 1940 1941 1942 1943 1944 1945

research and production costs and purchased items at a guaranteed markup. Largely as a result, corporate after-tax profits swelled from $6.4 billion in 1940 to $10.8 billion in 1944.

Defense mobilization led to other innovations. Before 1941, the federal government spent little money on scientific research. By 1945, not counting the $2 billion spent on atomic bomb research and the billions more used to construct plants to process steel and aluminum and to manufacture synthetic rubber and aircraft, Washington funneled $1.5 billion annually into research and development. Radar, electronic computers, jet engines, synthetic fibers, wonder drugs like sulfas and penicillin, nuclear weapons, and ballistic missiles all came out of wartime research. On the dark side, the war was used to justify government experiments on American citizens, including injecting unwitting people with radioactive substances as part of the research connected to the Manhattan Project.

The War Department's Office of Scientific Research and Development (OSRD), headed by Vannevar Bush of the Massachusetts Institute of Technology, poured $2 billion into the vast, highly secret, atomic bomb project. In three new "atomic cities"—Oak Ridge, Tennessee; Hanford, Washington; and Los Alamos, New Mexico—nearly 150,000 people conducted research, refined uranium, and produced weapons. The facilities rivaled the entire automobile industry in size. Additional government funds helped universities build modern scientific laboratories. Universities derived further support by enrolling several hundred thousand officers in army and navy programs for accelerated college degrees.

Research facilities mushroomed in private industry as well. By the end of the war, almost 2,500 private industrial research laboratories were employing 133,000 people, twice the prewar number. In an influential study called *Science: The Endless Frontier*, published in 1945, Vannevar Bush proposed the creation of a permanent government agency to fund basic research. Congress finally approved the idea in 1950, creating the National Science Foundation.

Overall, the administration's policies spurred military production that was little short of miraculous. Aircraft plants, which had produced barely 2,000 planes a year before the war, turned out nearly 50,000 in 1942 and 100,000 in 1944. By 1945, American industry had produced over 100,000 tanks, 87,000 ships of all types, 2.5 million trucks, 5 million tons of bombs, and 44 billion rounds of ammunition. As a result, Allied soldiers had a three-to-one advantage in arms over their Axis enemies. A story was told of a ship christening at which a woman at dockside was handed a bottle of champagne to do the honors. "But where is the ship?" she asked. "Just start swinging, lady," a worker remarked. "We'll have the ship there in time."

On the negative side, war production gave birth to what later critics, including President Eisenhower, would call the "military-industrial complex." In 1940 the hundred largest American companies produced only 30 percent of the goods manufactured in the United States. But wartime spending on high technology benefited large firms more than small ones. By 1945 the "Big 100" American companies produced a whopping 70 percent of the country's defense output, and the ten largest corporations accounted for nearly one-third of all war production. The close relationship between the military and large defense contractors would continue after the war, and the economic health of many American communities would come to depend on military appropriations.

As big business prospered during the war years, so did its traditional antagonists, the labor unions. For both patriotic and practical reasons, most labor leaders worked closely with government and business leaders. Buoyed by rising wages, most major unions took a no-strike pledge during the war, and this willingness to cooperate enhanced their emerging role as part of the economic and political establishment. (The one major exception was the United Mine Workers, led by John L. Lewis. Strikes in the coal mines caused major disruptions in 1943.) Among factory workers, union membership increased dramatically, from 10.5 million in 1941 to 15 million in 1945, a third of the non-farm work force. This represented the all-time peak of union membership.

To help pay for the war, the expanding government revised the tax structure and introduced tax withholding. Before 1941, most lower- and middle-income Americans paid little or no federal income tax. During the war the government sought to spread the costs equitably among wage-earning Americans. Taxes therefore rose, but not disproportionately. Before 1941, a married man without dependents earning $2,000 annually paid no federal taxes. In 1945, he paid just over $200. For individuals earning more, the tax bite increased at a progressive rate. As a result, tax revenues swelled from $5 billion to $49 billion by 1945.

At first, the combination of defense spending, full employment, and shortages of civilian goods fueled inflation. Agencies like the National War Labor Board and the Office of Price Administration imposed a variety of wage and price controls, along with rationing. Consumers needed ration coupons to buy items like gasoline, meat, and sugar. Children were encouraged to collect old cans, tires, and fat, which could be recycled into war goods. City dwellers cultivated millions of tiny "victory gardens" to supplement their diet.

But even while ordinary people conserved sugar and saved cans, a remarkable process was occurring. The war years brought about the most dramatic rise in income for working Americans in the twentieth century. With adjustment for inflation, real factory wages rose from $24 to nearly $37 per week during the war. The share of the national wealth held by the richest 5 percent of Americans declined from 23.7 percent to 16.8 percent. The number of families with an annual income below $2,000 fell by half, while the number with annual incomes over $5,000 increased fourfold.

Because of the high employment rate and the shortage of consumer goods, personal savings jumped from $2.9 billion annually in 1939 to over $29 billion annually in 1945. Purchases of "expendables" (jewelry, cosmetics, books, movie tickets) also grew, from $66 billion in 1939 to just over $100 billion in 1944. Record numbers of people frequented movies, nightclubs, and racetracks. Though wartime shortages continued, people found ways to enjoy their relative prosperity. Because of the war's stimulus to the economy, the Great Depression at last was history.

In addition to its economic impact, the war had a dramatic effect on *where* Americans lived and worked (see map, page 28). Most obviously, 16 million men and 250,000 women entered military service between 1941 and 1945. Almost all eligible men between the ages of eighteen and thirty-five years served in the armed forces. All told, over 12 percent of the total American population spent time in uniform. Many GIs were sent to parts of the country they had never seen before, and often they liked what they saw. In this way, the military helped break down regional barriers.

An upheaval among civilians also took place. Six million rural Americans headed for war work in the cities, while as many urban residents moved to jobs in new cities. Many of the migrants were African-Americans who left the states of the old Confederacy for jobs in the North and West. With shipbuilding, aircraft manufacturing, and other war industries concentrated on the East and West coasts and in the Upper Midwest, these areas grew rapidly. Not surprisingly, Washington, D.C., the seat of the expanding federal government, doubled in population.

The Sunbelt—the warm states of the South and Southwest—began its rise during the war years. Even as African-Americans left the old South, cities like Miami and Houston grew. The population also made a major shift westward. Along the West Coast the shipyards, aircraft plants, and staging areas for the Pacific front employed thousands of locals and hundreds of thousands of migrants. Not only war workers, but tens of thousands of military personnel migrated to San Diego, Portland, Seattle, Los Angeles, and San Francisco—or returned to these cities from overseas and decided to remain as permanent residents. California's population grew by over a third during the war, as 2 million people came from the South and from rural areas to work in the aircraft and shipbuilding industries. The population of Los

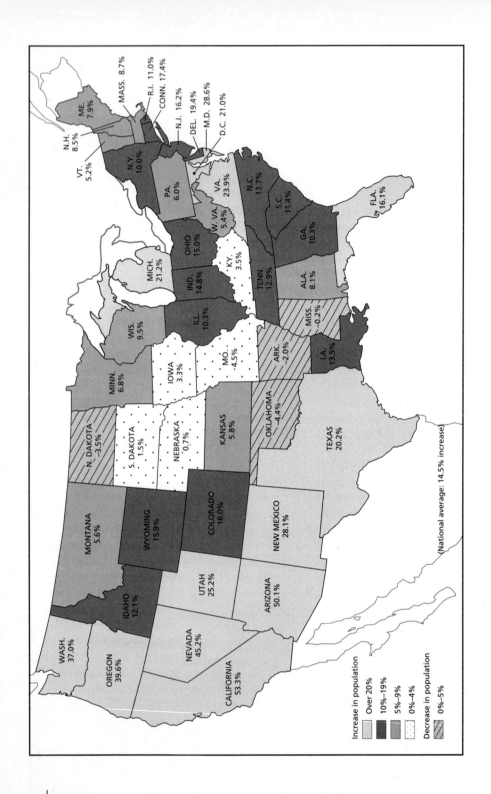

MASS. 8.7%
R.I. 11.0%
CONN. 17.4%
N.J. 16.2%
DEL. 19.4%
M.D. 28.6%
D.C. 21.0%
ME. 7.9%
N.H. 8.5%
VT. 5.2%
N.Y. 10.0%
PA. 6.0%
VA. 23.9%
W. VA. 5.4%
N.C. 13.7%
S.C. 11.4%
FLA. 16.1%
OHIO 15.0%
KY. 3.5%
GA. 10.3%
MICH. 21.2%
IND. 14.8%
TENN. 12.9%
ALA. 8.1%
ILL. 10.3%
WIS. 9.5%
MO. 4.5%
ARK. -2.0%
MISS. -0.2%
LA. 13.5%
MINN. 6.8%
IOWA 3.3%
N. DAKOTA -3.5%
S. DAKOTA 1.5%
NEBRASKA 0.7%
KANSAS 5.8%
OKLAHOMA -4.4%
TEXAS 20.2%
MONTANA 5.6%
WYOMING 15.9%
COLORADO 18.0%
NEW MEXICO 28.1%
IDAHO 12.1%
UTAH 25.2%
ARIZONA 50.1%
WASH. 37.0%
OREGON 39.6%
NEVADA 45.2%
CALIFORNIA 53.3%

(National average: 14.5% increase)

Increase in population
Over 20%
10%–19%
5%–9%
0%–4%
Decrease in population
0%–5%

Angeles alone increased by half a million. All told, the West's population grew by 40 percent between 1940 and 1950, with much of that explosive growth a direct result of the war.

Women's roles changed dramatically during the war, too, even though gender-based inequality remained deeply ingrained. In 1940, before the United States entered the war, about 27 percent of all women worked outside the home, but only 15 percent of married women did so. Moreover, most women in the labor force held low-paying jobs in light manufacturing, service, and clerical areas.

With the wartime labor shortage came a shift in public policy and private attitudes toward women in the labor force. Women were encouraged to work and to take jobs traditionally held by men—for the time being. A War Department pamphlet put it succinctly: "A woman is a substitute—like plastic instead of metal." The Office of War Information (OWI), an agency that produced radio plays, films, and posters in an attempt to mold public attitudes, chipped in with encouragements for women to join the work force. Such appeals swayed public opinion. Before the war, 80 percent of surveyed Americans opposed wives working outside the home; in 1942, 80 percent approved.

By 1945, over 6 million additional women, including 4 million who had been housewives before the war, had entered the industrial work force, accounting for a third of the total. They worked as riveters, welders, assembly line workers, aircraft fabricators, and in numerous other positions previously held only by men. Steelyards, shipyards, and aircraft plants employed virtually no women before 1942, but three years later women made up as much as 40 percent of the work force in key defense plants. African-American women contributed to the trend, entering manufacturing and clerical work in significant numbers for the first time.

In Los Angeles, at the peak of the war, 10 percent of all women residents worked in aviation factories. The fictional "Rosie the Riveter," a can-do, muscular woman in bulging overalls, was a familiar figure, celebrated in songs and on posters and magazine covers. Women also ran heavy equipment, drove trucks and trains, and took jobs as "cowgirls" and "lumberjills." They surged into the growing government bureaucracies as clerical workers, and even some professional opportunities improved, as newspapers, orchestras, radio stations, and financial institutions recruited women.

Despite the wartime labor shortage, however, women were often assigned to sex-segregated tasks, received lower wages than men for the same work, and found few support services such as day care for children. Social workers discovered babies sleeping in cars outside

Women welders at a Gary, Indiana steel plant prepare armor plating for tanks. *Margaret Bourge-White, Life Magazine ©1943 Time Inc.*

defense plants because their working mothers had nowhere else to leave them. Business and political leaders offered various rationalizations for denying women equal pay and access to day care. Women were encouraged to think of factory work as a temporary expedient, to keep their sights on the home, and to be prepared to resume the roles of housewife and mother when their husbands returned from the war. Black women faced additional obstacles stemming from racist treatment by management and co-workers.

As men entered military service, women's responsibilities increased in many ways beyond that of wage earner. Women became the center of family life as never before. They also assumed responsibility for critical unpaid work. They served as Red Cross nurses, canteen volunteers, and actresses on tours sponsored by the United Service Organizations (USO). These contributions were celebrated in films like *Stage Door Canteen*, the tale of three pretty USO hostesses who struck up romances with soldiers on leave. Max Lerner, a popular columnist, voiced a common male complaint that war work had created a "new Amazon" who could "outdrink, outswear, and outswagger the men." Surveys by the Labor Department found that although many women resented unequal pay and sexual harassment on the job, they found the new opportunities and responsibilities exciting. Women enjoyed spending and saving their higher earnings, valued the independence and self-confidence that came with earning an income, and liked acquiring new skills. Most employed women hoped to continue working when peace returned—but they did so, as we will see, under changed rules.

Just as war transformed women's roles, it also created new chances and challenges in race relations. Before the Second World War, over three-fourths of all African-Americans lived in the South, where they were employed mainly as tenant farmers or domestic workers. In the North, they occupied the lowest rung of industrial jobs. The Great Depression hurt these workers more severely than any other group. Reflecting political realities, New Deal programs never directly challenged segregation; after all, most African-Americans could not vote, and southern Democrats chaired key committees in Congress. Although Roosevelt sympathized with racial minorities, he declined to antagonize the southern Democrats whose votes he needed to move legislation through Congress.

Organizations like the National Association for the Advancement of Colored People (NAACP), the National Urban League, and the National Negro Congress protested the denial of work-relief benefits to African-Americans. They lobbied politicians and mobilized African-American voters in the North to demand changes. They found important supporters among left-wing political groups, the CIO, and white liberals.

Gradually the New Deal civil rights record improved. Top federal work-relief administrators like Harry Hopkins and Harold Ickes hired growing numbers of minorities. Although officials in the South resisted these moves, and segregation in federal programs remained common, African-Americans appreciated these efforts by Democratic New Dealers. As one leading black newspaper commented, "what administration within the memory of man . . . had done a better job . . . considering the imperfect human material with which it had to work? The answer, of course, is none."

The positive effect of New Deal policies on the racial climate in the United States, however incomplete, attracted millions of new voters into the Democratic coalition. In the 1932 presidential election, over two-thirds of African-American voters (nearly all in the North) supported the Republican candidate, Herbert Hoover. In 1940, over two-thirds of them voted for the Democratic ticket, and this number grew in later decades. Some critics have charged that Roosevelt deluded African-Americans with rhetoric, or that desperation made them appreciate any crumbs they could gather from New Deal programs. Yet, compared to what preceded it, the New Deal took important steps toward achieving racial justice.

African-American employment at all levels in the federal government tripled between 1933 and 1945, with most of the gains made during the war. Roosevelt's new federal agencies caused a sensation by abolishing segregated cafeterias and offices in their Washington headquarters. An informal "Black Cabinet" of prominent African-American citizens consulted regularly with agency heads and, on occasion, with the president. Eleanor Roosevelt, especially, championed the efforts of racial minorities. She met regularly with African-American leaders like Mary McLeod Bethune, an official of the National Youth Administration, invited them to the White House, and legitimized their concerns. She supported civil rights legislation and federal laws against lynching and the poll tax, sometimes even against the advice of her more cautious husband.

Roosevelt's judicial appointments also had a lasting impact on civil rights. With the exception of James F. Byrnes, Roosevelt's eight appointees to the Supreme Court—and especially Justices Felix Frankfurter, Wiley Rutledge, Frank Murphy, Hugo Black, and William O. Douglas—sympathized with efforts to dismantle legal discrimination. By the late 1940s they had struck down state laws excluding minorities from juries, established the right of workers to picket against discrimination in employment, outlawed racially restrictive covenants in housing, challenged segregation on interstate public transportation, forbade peonage of farm workers, overturned laws mandating lower pay for African-American teachers, and outlawed the system that barred nonwhites from voting in the all-important southern Democratic primaries. These Supreme Court rulings provided momentum for further legal challenges to segregation and for the civil rights movement of the late 1940s through the 1960s.

The war, however, brought new dissatisfaction with the pace of change. The United States was fighting enemies who proclaimed the right to enslave or exterminate "inferior" races. Presumably, American citizens were united in detesting such hateful ideologies. Yet American minorities at home and in the armed forces still faced discrimination and abuse. Law and tradition segregated African-Americans in school, at the workplace, and in numerous aspects of social life.

In 1941, as defense orders poured in to factories, African-American leaders expressed outrage that employment on military production lines remained largely segregated. A. Philip Randolph, head of the Brotherhood of Sleeping Car Porters, a union composed mostly of African-Americans, challenged racial economic discrimination directly. That spring he announced plans for a mass march on Washington in demand of equal employment rights.

To avert an embarrassing protest march, Roosevelt issued Executive Order No. 8802, which created a presidential Fair Employment Practices Committee (FEPC) to investigate complaints of discrimination in the defense industry. In exchange, the march on Washington was called off. Even though the FEPC lacked enforcement power, it pressed formerly segregated industries to hire about 600,000 additional African-American workers by 1945. The lure of these new jobs contributed to the migration of about 2 million African-Americans from the South to the North and West during the 1940s.

African-American leaders supported the war effort, seeking what they called a "double victory"—a victory over Nazi racism abroad and discrimination at home. The NAACP urged its members to "persuade, embarrass, compel, and shame" the federal government into acting against racism. Migration, employment in industry, and military service created a strengthened desire among African-Americans for the full rights of citizenship long denied them. Nevertheless, segregation and racism remained the norm, both in the military and in civilian life, during and after the war.

Ironically, the shared experience of war helped remove old ethnic barriers between whites. On the battlefields and in the canteens, white Americans from varied ethnic and religious backgrounds mingled and got to know one another. But the black-white barrier was much harder to crack. Although the military drafted a million African-Americans, it placed most of them in menial positions such as cook, driver, or construction worker. The Red Cross maintained segregated blood banks. African-American troops were often commanded by southern white officers, who treated them harshly. Still, African-American soldiers pressed ceaselessly for greater responsibilities and often challenged the status quo. For example, a young lieutenant named Jackie Robinson—who would later become the first black player in major-league baseball—refused to sit in the segregated section of a bus. He was court-martialed for his defiance, but he successfully defended himself and the charge was dismissed.

African-American anxieties were confirmed by several violent wartime race riots, most notably in Detroit in 1942 and in Harlem in 1943. In Detroit, a black-white fight at a park sparked the riot; in Harlem the violence started with the shooting of a black soldier by a policeman. White resentment of blacks seeking homes in segregated neighborhoods and applying for factory jobs previously reserved for whites contributed to the intensity of these conflicts.

In spite of such outbreaks of racial hatred, the war years generally had a positive effect on the struggle for equality and civil rights. Military service, even in a segregated system, brought black soldiers a certain sense of empowerment. New employment opportunities, exposure to the world outside the rural South, northward migration, and growing membership in civil rights organizations also gave a tremendous boost to African-Americans. The wartime generation of African-Americans was unwilling to suffer silently; their militancy and expectations were both on the rise. These people and their children would play a critical role in the postwar challenge to segregation.

Mexican migrants and Mexican-Americans also experienced hardship during the war. Since the early twentieth century, Mexicans had migrated in large numbers to the United States. During the depression, state and local authorities pressured 400,000 Mexicans residing in America to return to their native country. But after 1941, as large numbers of agricultural workers entered the armed services or sought more lucrative defense work, farm managers experienced severe labor shortages. Therefore, in 1942 the federal government negotiated a contract labor program with Mexican authorities which continued, in various forms, until 1964.

Under this so-called *bracero* ("laborer") program, the American government promised to supervise the recruitment, transportation, and working conditions of large groups of Mexican farm workers. During the war, this agreement brought in about 1.75 million farm and railroad laborers. However, the promised supervision of working conditions was incredibly lax, *braceros* were paid as little as 35 cents per day, and many lived under miserable conditions.

The nearly 2.7 million Mexican-Americans—or Chicanos, as many preferred to call themselves—faced additional problems. Living mostly in the Southwest, they were confronted with segregation in schools, housing, and employment. New social tensions flared in communities such as Los Angeles, where rapid growth inflamed latent racism. Mexican-American youth gangs, whose members dressed in flamboyant clothes called "zoot suits," were frequently harassed by the police and by white servicemen.

Ethnic relations in Los Angeles were worsened by the actions of sailors and Marines on shore leave, who frequently cruised the barrios in search of Mexican-Americans wearing zoot suits, whom they attacked and humiliated by stripping. Police often charged the zoot-suiters instead of the Marines with disturbing the peace. To many Chicanos, the flamboyant clothing was a way to assert their distinct identity and to flout white culture.

The tensions exploded in June 1943, when hundreds of sailors and Marines went on a several-day rampage, attacking Mexican-Americans, African-Americans, and Filipinos in East Los Angeles. Because local police participated in the attacks, military police were needed to quell the riot. The *Los Angeles Times* reported the incidents with headlines such as "Zoot-Suiters Learn Lesson in Fight with Servicemen."

When Eleanor Roosevelt suggested that long-standing discrimination against Mexican-Americans might have provoked the riots, the paper accused her of promoting racial discord.

But for Mexican-Americans, as for African-Americans, the war years brought some advances. Service in the military gave young Mexican-Americans a feeling of personal worth and power. After the war, Mexican-American veterans played a prominent part in organizing civil rights groups that campaigned against postwar discrimination in the Southwest.

The consequences of racism were, of course, nowhere more savage during the war than they were for European Jews. The Holocaust was a tragedy the United States did little to avert. In November 1938, after the German government had stripped German Jews of most civil and economic rights, Nazi mobs set upon Jewish businesses, synagogues, and homes, smashing and looting in an orgy that quickly became known as *Kristallnacht,* or "Night of the Broken Glass." Shortly after that incident, German police sent twenty thousand Jews to concentration camps, which later became the sites of mass extermination. Roosevelt remarked that he could "scarcely believe that such things could occur in a twentieth-century civilization." As the Nazis conquered eastern Europe, the murder escalated.

European Jews who attempted to flee confronted legal barriers everywhere. Since 1924, the United States' National Origins Act had restricted nearly all immigration from eastern and southern Europe. Even Jews who qualified under the unfilled German quota faced a maze of bureaucratic red tape that made it nearly impossible to obtain an entry visa.

Fear of competition for scarce jobs added to anti-Semitism in the United States, creating little sympathy for, and much agitation against, the immigration of even token numbers of Jewish refugees. Roosevelt, who worked closely with many Jewish advisers, was already the target of anti-Semitic remarks. Bowing to this pressure, he allowed the State Department to place impediments in the path of would-be immigrants seeking sanctuary.

Evidence surfaced in 1942 and 1943 that the Nazis planned to exterminate 10 million Jews with poison gas. Ultimately the Nazis would succeed in killing 6 million Jews. Yet even after the plans became known, British and American strategists rejected the idea of bombing the death camps and the rail lines leading into them. Such diversions from more important missions, Allied leaders argued, would delay victory. Congress rebuffed efforts to allow Jewish children into the United States. American officials even opposed granting temporary refuge to the few thousand European Jews who had slipped away from Nazi control.

The liberation of the Bergen-Belsen concentration camp—Americans confront the Holocaust. *Imperial War Museum*.

In 1944 Roosevelt finally created a War Refugee Board to establish camps in neutral countries and American-occupied territory overseas. Eventually these centers helped save the lives of a few hundred thousand refugees. Only one thousand refugees were admitted directly into the United States. As one scholar wrote, "Franklin Roosevelt's indifference to so momentous an historical event as the systematic annihilation of European Jewry emerges as the worst failure of his presidency."

Roosevelt's failure to champion the cause of Jewish refugees must be seen in light of the strong American sentiment favoring less, not more, support for Jews. Anti-Semitism flourished in the United States during the 1920s and 1930s. An opinion poll taken in 1942 found that many Americans believed Jews posed nearly as great a threat to national security as did Germany and Japan. Leaders of the American Jewish community anguished over the horrors of Nazi persecution, but they feared a backlash among Christian Americans if they spoke out forcefully. As a result, most Jewish organizations refrained from pressing politicians to rescue Holocaust victims. Instead, they called for creating a Jewish homeland in Palestine for those lucky enough to survive.

Meanwhile, in the U.S., the Japanese-American community was singled out for special persecution. Not only was Japan a wartime enemy, but the United States had a century-long tradition of anti-Asian agitation and hysteria. The surprise attack on Pearl Harbor, followed by Japan's initial victories in the Pacific, intensified the racial distrust and spurred exaggerated fears that Japanese-Americans would conspire to aid the enemy.

About 120,000 people of Japanese ancestry lived in the United States in 1941, nearly all in California or elsewhere on the West Coast. The 47,000 who had arrived in the United States before Asian immigration was banned in 1924 were barred from citizenship, but their 70,000 children, born in the United States, were full citizens. Although virtually no members of this community committed sabotage or illegal acts before or after 1941, their mere existence aroused public hysteria.

Journalists such as Westbrook Pegler demanded that every Japanese man, woman, and child be placed under armed guard. Congressman Leland Ford of California insisted that any "patriotic native-born Japanese, if he wants to make his contribution, will submit himself to a concentration camp." General John DeWitt, head of the Western Defense Command, declared that Japanese of any citizenship were enemies. A popular song chortled, "We're Gonna Find a Feller Who Is Yeller and Beat Him Red, White and Blue."

In February 1942 President Roosevelt issued Executive Order No. 9066—quickly backed by Congress—declaring parts of the country "military areas" from which any or all persons could be barred. Nearly every politician in the West applauded the move. Although the regulations also targeted German and Italian *aliens* (most Italians were later exempted), *all* persons of Japanese ancestry, regardless of their citizenship, were affected. In May, the War Relocation Authority ordered 112,000 Japanese to leave the West Coast in a matter of days. Ironically, in Hawaii—where, unlike California, the danger of a Japanese invasion was much more real—residents of Japanese descent made up such a large portion of the population and were so vital to the economy that only a few individuals were interned.

Nearly all those affected by the forced relocation orders complied without protest, abandoning their homes, farms, and personal property to speculators. Bleak internment camps were hastily established in several western states. While not equivalent to incarceration in the Nazi death camps, this mass imprisonment marked the greatest violation of civil liberties in wartime America. Families lived in rudimentary dwellings and were compelled to do menial work under armed guard.

Japanese-American families at the Manzanar War Relocation Center in California line up for "mess call." *AP/Wide World Photos.*

In 1944, the Supreme Court addressed the policy of forced relocation in a case against Fred Korematsu, a citizen who had refused to leave a designated war zone on the West Coast. The Court's decision in *Korematsu* v. *United States* affirmed the government's "right" to exclude individuals from any designated area on the basis of military necessity. The majority claimed that the defendant's race was irrelevant, because the government could, if it chose, exclude groups besides those of Japanese ancestry. In a powerful dissent, Justice Frank Murphy denounced the *Korematsu* verdict as a "legalization of racism" based on prejudice and unproven fears.

Despite the restrictive relocation orders and the degradation of life in the internment camps, Japanese-Americans contributed significantly to the American war effort. Many male internees volunteered for military duty and served in Europe, achieving recognition for their bravery in action. Others worked in the Pacific theater as translators, interpreters, or intelligence officers. As the war progressed, some internees were permitted to leave relocation camps if they agreed to settle in eastern states. By the summer of 1945 all could leave. A fortunate few found that friends had protected their homes or businesses; the rest lost the work of a lifetime.

Despite growing recognition that internment had been a grave error, Congress and the courts hesitated to make formal redress. Con-

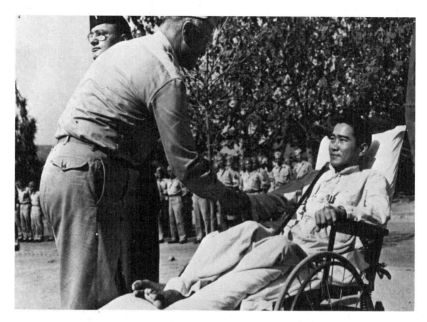

Howard Y. Miyake, a Japanese-American, receives a medal for his bravery during military service in the European theater. *National Archives.*

gress offered a token payment in 1948, but it was not until the 1980s that several Japanese-Americans convicted of wartime offenses successfully reopened their cases. Files from the Justice Department and the Federal Bureau of Investigation revealed that prosecutors had withheld evidence showing that no danger existed to justify relocation. Congress then made a formal apology and offered compensation of about $20,000 per surviving internee.

WARTIME POLITICS

As the wartime economic boom gradually erased memories of the Great Depression, many Americans felt that the reform programs of the New Deal no longer mattered. The 1942 congressional elections, in which 22 million fewer people voted than in 1940, proved disastrous for the Democrats. The Republicans gained 9 Senate seats (for a total of 43 out of 96) and 44 House seats (giving them 209 to the Democrats' 222). And nearly half the Democrats who were reelected came from the party's conservative southern wing. The new Congress proceeded to kill a number of New Deal agencies, including the Work Projects Administration (successor to the Works Progress Administration) and the Civilian Conservation Corps.

The president's chief of mobilization, James F. Byrnes, gloated that the war had helped elbow the "radical boys out of the way [and] more will go." His prediction proved accurate, as nervous Democratic party leaders blamed electoral losses on the left-leaning vice president, Henry A. Wallace. Unlike his more cautious boss, Wallace actively promoted civil rights and had called for postwar economic intervention by the government. Witnessing Roosevelt's obvious physical decline, the party barons feared that Wallace might assume the presidency upon Roosevelt's death or retirement.

Bowing to their complaints—and anxious to avoid having a conservative Democrat placed on the ticket—in mid-1944 Roosevelt agreed to replace Wallace with Senator Harry S. Truman, a moderate from Missouri. Truman had gained fame for conducting an investigation of profiteering by defense contractors. Committed New Dealers, like Librarian of Congress Archibald MacLeish, bemoaned the "collapse of liberal leadership."

In 1944 the Republicans nominated New York governor Thomas E. Dewey for president and Ohio governor John Bricker as his running mate. Despite Dewey's charge that the Democrats were "soft on communism" and prisoners of organized labor, he confounded conservatives by accepting many of Roosevelt's innovations and his plans for postwar America and international relations.

Roosevelt remained the people's choice, aided in part by Dewey's ineffective campaign style and by a big push from organized labor, which created the first political action committee, or PAC, to raise campaign funds. Roosevelt easily won a fourth term, though by his smallest majority yet (53.4 percent). The party lines in Congress remained largely unchanged.

Despite the political challenges and his own concentration on winning the war, Roosevelt made some effort in his last years to impart a vision for postwar reform. In his 1944 State of the Union address he called for drafting a "second Bill-of-Rights under which a new basis of security and prosperity can be established for all." He described a government committed to providing jobs, housing, education, and health and retirement insurance for all Americans. The original Bill of Rights had secured liberties by limiting the power of government. The new one, according to Roosevelt, would expand the government's power in pursuit of social and economic justice.

In a draft speech dictated on April 11, 1945, as victory in Europe loomed, Roosevelt appealed to the American people to "conquer the fears, the ignorance and the greed" that made the horror of world war possible. "The only limit to our realization of tomorrow," he declared, "will be our doubts of today. Let us move forward with strong and active faith." But the next day, April 12, the president died of a cerebral hemorrhage. Roosevelt's passing, as much as the imminent victory over the Axis forces, marked the threshold of the postwar era.

CONCLUSION

The Roosevelt years, stretching from the Great Depression to the last months of the Second World War, brought vast changes to the nation and to its role in the world arena. Those years molded the postwar world in fundamental ways that continue to affect us today.

Both the depression and the war prompted rapid growth in the federal government's size and scope of action. For the first time in the nation's history, the U.S. government had a direct and frequent effect on the daily lives of ordinary citizens. The government managed the economy to an unprecedented degree; it began to provide relief to the needy and the elderly; it funded scientific research that changed the face of American industry and made possible the high-tech society we now inhabit.

The Roosevelt years put Americans on the move, literally as well as figuratively. During the war, millions of rural or small-town Americans packed their bags and headed to the major industrial cities. African-Americans left the rural South in huge numbers, many making their new homes in the North and West. The *bracero* program contributed to a substantial influx of Mexican farm and railroad workers. The Sunbelt and the West Coast began their rise to prominence.

For women, the war meant a chance to take jobs traditionally reserved for men—a first step toward the revolution in women's lives that is still occurring today. For ethnic minorities, on the other hand, the depression and the war years were times of mingled hope, fear, and disappointment. The wartime internment of Japanese-Americans left a blot on the nation's record that no later compensation could remove. The government's failure to help European Jews escape the Holocaust seemed almost incomprehensible to later generations. Yet the Roosevelt era also brought a rising concern for the rights of minorities and new hopes that protest could lead to improvement— crucial ingredients for the civil rights movement of the postwar years.

Finally, as a direct consequence of the war, the United States emerged in 1945 as the world's leading military and economic power. Europe was devastated. The Soviet Union, though a mighty wartime ally and future competitor, had suffered terrible losses. In the postwar world, America's history would be shaped by its demanding new role as a superpower and by the conflicting ideas of Americans about how that role should be played. ■

FURTHER READING

On the depression and New Deal, see: Michael A. Bernstein, *The Great Depression: Delayed Recovery and Economic Change in America, 1929–39* (1988); Anthony J. Badger, *The New Deal: The Depression Years, 1933–40* (1980); William E. Leuchtenburg, *Franklin D. Roosevelt and the New Deal* (1963); Kenneth S. Davis, *FDR: The New Deal Years, 1933–37* (1986); Alan Brinkley, *Voices of Protest: Huey Long, Father Coughlin, and the Great Depression* (1982); Harvard Sitkoff, *A New Deal for Blacks* (1978); Lizabeth Cohen, *Making a New Deal: Industrial Workers in Chicago, 1919–39* (1991); Susan Ware, *Holding Their Own: American Women in the 1930s* (1982); Steven Fraser, *Labor Will Rule: Sidney Hillman and the Rise of American Labor* (1991); Steve Fraser and Gary Gestle, eds., *The Rise and Fall of the New Deal Order, 1930–1980* (1989). On American society during the Second World War, see: Doris Kearns Goodwin, *No Ordinary Time: Franklin and Eleanor Roosevelt: The Home Front During WWII* (1994); John Blum, *V Was for Victory: Politics and American Culture During World War II* (1976); Karen Anderson, *Wartime Women* (1981); Susan Hartman, *The Homefront and Beyond* (1980); Peter Irons, *Justice at War: The Story of the Japanese-American Internment Cases* (1982); Roger Daniel, *Prisoners Without Trial* (1993); Gerald D. Nash, *The American West Transformed: The Impact of the Second World War* (1985); Studs Terkel, *"The Good War": An Oral History of World War II* (1984). On military strategy and foreign policy, see: Robert Dallek, *Franklin D. Roosevelt and American Foreign Policy* (1979); Warren Kimball, *The Juggler: Franklin Roosevelt as Wartime Statesman* (1991); Russel D. Buhite, *Decision at Yalta* (1986); David Wyman, *The Abandonment of the Jews: America and the Holocaust, 1941–45* (1984); Michael Sherry, *The Rise of American Air Power* (1987); John Dower, *War Without Mercy: Race and Power in the Pacific War* (1986); Martin J. Sherwin, *A World Destroyed: The Atomic Bomb and the Grand Alliance* (1975); Michael C. C. Adams, *The Best War Ever: America and World War II* (1994); William O'Neill, *A Democracy at War: America's Fight at Home and Abroad in W.W. II* (1993).

2

Cold War and
Containment,
1945–1953

On April 12, 1945, Harry S. Truman sat with several congressional friends in the office of House Speaker Sam Rayburn. After chairing a tedious Senate debate on a water treaty, the vice president savored a stiff bourbon. A phone call from presidential press secretary Steve Early abruptly summoned him to the White House. There, Eleanor Roosevelt delivered the somber news: "Harry, the president is dead." Truman asked if there was anything he could do for her. "Is there anything we can do for you?" she replied. "You are the one in trouble now."

Regarded by many as a political nobody, the new president was suddenly in charge of concluding the world war and shaping a peace. "Trouble" was indeed an apt word—perhaps too mild a word—for what faced him. Although Germany was on the verge of surrender, Truman faced the thorny problem of how to handle relations with the Soviet Union, a wartime ally that was fast becoming a threatening competitor. Within a few months, Truman also had to decide whether to use the atomic bomb on Japan. Heading the most powerful nation in the postwar world, Truman found his every choice greatly magnified in importance.

During the five years following World War II an anti-Communist hysteria erupted onto the national scene. Fueled by legitimate worries about the Soviet Union as well as by political opportunism, the Red Scare distorted national politics from the end of the Second World War well into the 1950s. It frustrated attempts by progressives—including, to some degree, Truman himself—to expand the social reforms of the New Deal, and it led to widespread political intolerance and suppression of civil liberties.

Truman is often remembered as a feisty and irreverent folk hero, the president who posted the famous sign on his desk, "The Buck Stops Here." This image obscures the fact that for most of his time in office Truman was not a popular president. In the years of transition from world war to peace, the country's political and social divisions ran deep, and the public often doubted the abilities of those it chose to lead them.

TRUMAN TAKES CHARGE

Harry S. Truman came from a modest farming family near Independence, Missouri. As a young man he worked beside his father in the fields and as a bank clerk. When the United States entered the First World War in 1917, Truman, then thirty-three, enlisted in the National

Guard and commanded an artillery battery in Europe. At the end of his service he returned to Missouri, married Bess Wallace, and opened a clothing store in Kansas City. When the business failed, he turned to politics.

In the 1920s and early 1930s, Truman served as an elected judge in Jackson County, on the fringe of the area controlled by "Boss" Tom Pendergast's Kansas City political machine. Working in the shadow of corruption, Truman nevertheless earned a reputation as an honest and efficient administrator. In 1934, aided by Roosevelt's popularity as president, he won election to the U.S. Senate as a Democrat.

Truman's early social outlook reflected the racism prevalent in the midwestern border region. "I think one man is just as good as another," the twenty-seven-year-old wrote his future wife, "so long as he's honest and decent and not a nigger or a Chinaman." As he matured, Truman expressed greater toleration for ethnic minorities. After taking up his Senate seat in Washington, he worked to convince more liberal Democrats that he supported civil rights and civil liberties.

Although the freshman senator described himself as an enthusiastic supporter of Roosevelt, the president all but ignored Truman during the 1930s. During the Second World War, Truman won praise for chairing a Senate committee that exposed price gouging in defense programs. By the 1944 Democratic nominating convention he had emerged as a leading vice-presidential candidate. Roosevelt's deteriorating health worried the competing factions among the Democratic party leadership. Conservative party barons opposed renominating the very liberal incumbent vice president, Henry A. Wallace, as Roosevelt's running mate, favoring instead the more conservative James F. Byrnes. The third alternative, Truman, represented the centrist elements of the Democratic party. After much debate, the power brokers settled on Truman in a deal dubbed the "Missouri compromise."

During the three months in which they served together as president and vice president in 1945, Roosevelt and Truman had little contact. Truman knew nothing of what transpired in Roosevelt's meetings with Churchill and Stalin. He was, one scholar surmised, "too insignificant a subaltern to be trusted with secrets of state." When Truman became president, Secretary of War Henry Stimson took him aside after the first cabinet meeting to brief him on the Manhattan Project. The new president had known nothing about the development of the atomic bomb, now close to the testing stage.

Truman recognized that as vice president he had been kept in the dark on matters vital to national security and as president he was surrounded by better-informed men who were chary of their information. In consequence he grew distrustful of most of the Roosevelt cabinet he had inherited. There was not a "man on the list who would talk frankly," he later recalled. "The honest ones were afraid and the others wanted to fool me."

Within the first four months of his administration, Truman established his own chain of command, firing or easing out nearly all the cabinet members who had been close to Roosevelt. The profile of his appointees differed considerably from that of Roosevelt's advisers. In his first two years in office, Truman appointed forty-nine bankers, financiers, and industrialists, thirty-one career military men, and seventeen business lawyers to fill the top 125 federal job vacancies. Among those fired was Henry Wallace, dismissed as secretary of commerce in 1946 after a public dispute with Truman about how to deal with the Soviet Union.

Even though Truman proposed extending some New Deal reforms, progressives considered him a lukewarm liberal and never gave him the support Roosevelt had enjoyed. Nor was he accepted by the political Right, which wanted to eliminate all surviving New Deal programs. He wobbled on a political tightrope between the Right and the Left, and it often seemed both sides were shaking the rope, trying to make him tumble.

As British, American, and Soviet armies closed in on Berlin in April 1945, President Truman had to respond almost instantaneously to problems he knew little about. Determined to appear a forceful leader, he tended to make snap judgments. Hours after taking office, he boasted that, unlike his predecessor, he would "stand up to the Russians," implying that Roosevelt had been too easy on Joseph Stalin, the Soviet dictator.

The president's suspicion of Soviet goals was fueled by talks with the American ambassador to the Soviet Union, Averell Harriman, as well as by Secretary of the Navy James Forrestal, Chief of Staff Admiral William Leahy, and Undersecretary of State Joseph Grew. All had urged Roosevelt to demand a larger role for non-Communists in the government the Soviets had installed in Poland. Their advice appealed to Truman partly because the position they recommended would give him an opportunity to distinguish himself from his predecessor.

Ambassador Harriman flew to Washington from Moscow to express his fear that Stalin was breaking the agreements made at Yalta. He described Soviet actions—which included installing puppet governments and arresting real or imagined foes—as a "barbarian invasion of Europe." Communism, he told Truman, confronted America with "ideological warfare just as vigorous and dangerous as fascism or Nazism." Truman, who was not a party to the wartime deals, accepted Harriman's claim that Stalin considered compromise a sign of weakness. After all, had not appeasement encouraged Hitler? Truman, like many Americans, looked upon Soviet domination of the liberated countries of Eastern Europe as a replay of Nazi aggression and a possible prelude to global expansion.

On April 23, 1945, the president used "words of one syllable" to accuse visiting Soviet foreign minister Vyacheslav M. Molotov of violating promises made at Yalta regarding free elections in Poland. When Molotov disputed this interpretation and complained about Truman's harsh language, the president allegedly retorted, "Carry out your agreements and you won't get talked to like that." Truman spoke of giving Molotov the "straight one-two to the jaw," but in private wondered aloud if he had done right.

In fact, Truman's tough words had little effect on Soviet policy, in Poland or elsewhere. Responding to the president's charges of treaty violations, Stalin offered a blunt interpretation of the Yalta accords: "Poland borders with the Soviet Union [which] cannot be said of Great Britain or the United States." Moscow claimed no right to interfere in Belgium or Greece, where the Western allies had installed governments of their choosing. Stalin made it clear that he cared more about creating a security zone in Eastern Europe than about maintaining good relations with his wartime allies.

When Churchill confided to Stalin, in mid-1945, his fears about an "iron fence" dividing Europe, Stalin angrily dismissed the notion as a fairy tale. But Truman and Churchill were not fooled. Soviet forces had installed puppet regimes in Poland, Rumania, and Bulgaria. Later they used local Communists to take control of Hungary in 1947 and Czechoslovakia in 1948. Even if Stalin had no sinister master plan, the Soviets had behaved brutally in the areas that fell within their sphere of influence, and this aroused both anger and fear among Americans.

For his part, Stalin feared a revived Germany and capitalist encirclement of the Soviet Union, as occurred after the First World War. This encouraged his ironclad domination of Eastern Europe. In the tradition of the Russian Czars, Stalin measured Soviet security by the weakness of its neighboring states and by the intimidation and control he could exercise over them. Because of long-standing Eastern European distrust of Russia, nothing short of total Soviet control could keep the region under Moscow's thumb. The harsh imposition of Communist control and the large number of Soviet troops maintained in Eastern Europe appalled and frightened Western leaders. Ironically, Stalin's brutal exercise of power aroused the very hostility he feared from the capitalist West.

When Germany formally surrendered on May 8, 1945, Soviet troops occupied Berlin. The victorious Allies had agreed to partition Germany into occupation zones, but they had not addressed mechanisms for interzonal cooperation or how they would exact reparations from Germany. The Polish-German border problem sparked additional dissent. The Soviets annexed a swath of Polish territory along the Russian border and compensated Poland by grafting onto it part of eastern Germany. The swap displaced millions of ethnic Germans and moved Soviet power closer to central Europe, a chilling prospect to British and American leaders.

As the disputes over the postwar balance of power in Europe raged on, the war continued against Japan. After recapturing numerous Pacific islands, American air and naval forces operating from hastily constructed bases pounded Japan almost at will. In March 1945, for example, the fire-bombing of Tokyo killed nearly 100,000 civilians. American Marines, army troops, and naval personnel also suffered tens of thousands of casualties taking islands such as Iwo Jima and Okinawa. Still, the bulk of Japanese troops remained in China and Manchuria. American military planners dreaded the prospect of having to fight them. Yet there appeared few alternatives. The Chinese army remained a shambles, the Soviets had promised to fight Japan but Washington did not fully trust them, and no one could yet tell if the still-experimental atomic bomb would work. As a result, soon after he took office, Truman approved a tentative plan to invade Japan on November 1, 1945.

Truman, Churchill, and Stalin held a summit in mid-July in Potsdam, a once opulent suburb of bombed-out Berlin. Amid the rubble of the Thousand Year Reich, the Big Three spent most of their time arguing over German boundaries, the payment of reparations to Moscow, British and American demands that Stalin loosen his grip on Poland and Rumania, and the timing of Russia's entry into the Pacific war. The emergence of a new, postwar political outlook was evidenced by the defeat of Churchill's Conservative Party by the British Labour Party in elections held during the conference. Midway through the summit, Clement Attlee replaced Churchill as prime minister with a pledge to improve life for the British working class. On foreign policy matters, however, Attlee was as suspicious as his predecessor of Soviet behavior in Eastern Europe.

Although Churchill and Truman accepted the Polish-German boundary changes already made by Stalin, they refused to turn over to the Soviets industrial resources in the British and American occupation zones in western Germany. Stalin charged that this refusal to share resources violated earlier promises, and he wondered if American and British officials intended to rebuild western Germany as an anti-Soviet state.

Stalin tried to placate his allies by promising that Soviet forces would join the campaign against Japan by mid-August. Although American military planners still believed that Soviet assistance would help reduce American casualties, Truman now worried about the cost of Soviet involvement in the Pacific war. Specifically, he feared that

President Truman and Winston Churchill at the dawn of the Cold War. *Terry Savage/Courtesy Harry S. Truman Library.*

Soviet forces might assist the Chinese Communists and that the Soviets might set up an occupation zone in Japan.

On July 16, 1945, in the midst of the inconclusive discussions at Potsdam, Truman received a coded message that an atomic bomb had been tested successfully in New Mexico. The president's aides described him as excited and cheered by the prospect of having a weapon that might make Soviet help unnecessary in the war against Japan. Like Roosevelt before him, Truman maintained the policy of not telling Stalin about the atomic bomb. Instead, he casually mentioned the discovery of a new weapon of great power. Stalin, who knew of the Manhattan Project through espionage and had already ordered Soviet physicists to build a similar weapon, did not press for details, leaving Truman incorrectly thinking he had "fooled Mr. Russia." At the end of the conference, without inviting the Soviets to join in, the British and American governments issued the Potsdam Declaration, an ultimatum warning Japan to surrender at once or face utter destruction.

Truman ordered that the two available atomic bombs, code-named Fat Man and Little Boy, be used as soon as possible. On August 6 a

Time stops at Hiroshima, as the nuclear age begins.
© *1984 John Launois/Black Star.*

B-29 bomber named *Enola Gay*, for the pilot's mother, took off from the island of Tinian to drop the first bomb on Hiroshima, Japan. Two days later, as promised, the Soviets declared war on Japan and attacked their army in Manchuria. On August 9 a second bomb obliterated the city of Nagasaki. Nearly 200,000 Japanese civilians died in the two attacks, with radiation sickness later claiming additional lives. On August 10 Tokyo sued for unconditional peace, asking only that Hirohito be allowed to continue as emperor. On August 14 Truman accepted Japan's surrender, placing the nation and its emperor under the rule of occupation commander General Douglas MacArthur.

Publicly, Truman never admitted doubts about the decision to use the atomic bomb. He thanked God for giving him a weapon that saved "thousands and thousands of American lives" and "shortened the agony of war." Almost immediately, however, questions arose about Truman's decision. Some scientists had urged that the United States first demonstrate the bomb's power on unoccupied territory before using it in combat, to convince the Japanese to surrender. They questioned Truman's prediction that an invasion would have caused half a million American casualties, especially because intelligence estimates had predicted only fifty thousand. Truman later ridiculed the "crybaby" scientists who wanted to give Japan a demonstration of the bomb's potential before dropping it on Japanese cities.

American use of the bomb against Japan also raised the question of racism. Would American decision makers have used such a weapon against non-Asians? After all, the president had declared in private,

The devastation of Hiroshima after the use of the atomic bomb. © *1994 Dennis Brack/Black Star.*

"When you have to deal with a beast, you have to treat him like a beast." Some prominent Americans had called for "gutting the heart of Japan with fire" and "sterilizing every damn one of them so that in a generation there would be no more Japs." As racist as these remarks may sound, historians point out that European cities—Dresden, Germany, in particular—also suffered mass civilian casualties from Allied bombs.

Because Japan had already extended peace feelers, some critics thought the real motive for the atomic attack on Japan was to force a change in Soviet behavior in Europe and to speed victory in the Pacific to keep Russian forces out of China and Japan. Within days of Japan's surrender, Soviet leaders complained that Truman sought to intimidate Moscow through "atomic diplomacy." Remarks by Truman and his staff suggested that they did consider the effect on the Soviet Union in deciding to use the bomb. Secretary of State James F. Byrnes felt that a mistake had been made in allowing the Russians to become so powerful. He stressed the importance of using the bombs—not simply to defeat Japan, but to exclude Moscow from sharing in postwar decisions about Japan.

Clearly Truman felt ambivalent about the reasons for using the bomb. He probably hoped both to end the war with the fewest American casualties possible and to limit the Soviets' opportunity to gain a foothold in China and Japan.

But even without his growing suspicion of Stalin, Truman might have made the same decision to use the bomb. The United States had spent several billion dollars constructing the weapon. Military and civilian decision makers had always planned to use it as soon as possible. With the exception of a handful of scientists, few top leaders gave any serious thought to *not* utilizing the bomb. By 1945 the massive destruction of cities and civilians had become so commonplace that few moral objections were raised.

Victory over Japan confirmed the United States' place as the world's leading economic and military power. With only 6 percent of the world's population, it produced over half of the world's goods and controlled a majority of the world's wealth. This condition presented both opportunities and risks. Most Americans hoped to maintain this privileged status, but some realized that their continued prosperity depended on the revival of the devastated economies of Europe and, to a lesser extent, Asia. Moreover, wealth alone provided no easy way to halt the division of Europe by the "iron fence" or to stabilize Asia. When British, Soviet, and American foreign ministers met in London in September 1945, they argued bitterly over who threatened whom. The Western powers demanded relaxation of Soviet control in Eastern Europe, and Moscow responded by blasting "capitalist encirclement" and "atomic blackmail." The Cold War that grew from these mutual suspicions dominated world politics for two generations.

By the end of 1945, Washington and Moscow were already on a collision course in several major areas. Stalin's determination to forge an inviolable sphere of security around the Soviet Union led, inevitably, to his policy of dominating Eastern Europe. In doing so, he brutally suppressed all local forces he could not control. Stalin's talk of a coming world revolution understandably frightened the West, even if he did very little to assist Communists outside the Soviet Union and Eastern Europe. American leaders, for their part, insisted on breaking down international trade barriers and rebuilding the defeated Axis nations, policies that terrified the Kremlin. Washington often paid more attention to Soviet rhetoric about spreading communism—and to communism's harsh suppression of freedom in the areas it actually controlled—than to Stalin's actual posture, which was to hide behind the iron curtain he had created. In this atmosphere of distrust, Americans often blamed the Soviet Union for events over which it had only slight control, including much of the economic and political chaos that swept the world after the war ended.

EAST-WEST DISPUTES

Historians who have tried to fathom the causes of the Cold War often emphasize the differences in perception between United States and

Soviet leaders. Their hostility stretched backed to the Bolshevik Revolution of 1917, when Lenin's followers proclaimed their goal of world revolution and President Woodrow Wilson sent American soldiers to fight alongside troops from Western Europe and Japan to crush the Communists. In the subsequent decades, neither side understood or trusted the other much. In 1939, when Stalin and Hitler signed a nonaggression pact, American mistrust of Soviet intentions grew stronger. Only the common threat posed by the Nazis after 1941 drew them together.

The Soviet Union watched with deep suspicion as the United States extended its military power and influence. Well before the collapse of the Grand Alliance, American military planners had decided to establish a global network of naval and air bases in Europe, North Africa, and the Pacific. When the war ended, the United States quickly put this idea in motion. For example, numerous Pacific islands captured from Japan were annexed as "strategic trusteeships." The Joint Chiefs of Staff saw these bases as vital in order to protect American access to raw materials, to deter foreign aggression, and, if that failed, to intercept and counterattack aggressors. The advent of long-range bombers and atomic weapons, as well as popular pressure to demobilize American ground forces as quickly as possible after the war, made it seem imperative to U.S. planners to establish defensive positions as far from America as possible and as close to potential enemies as feasible. Not surprisingly, the Soviets reacted with concern as the United States developed military bases in a broad arc around the world—and around them.

Despite their mistrust of the Soviet Union, most American leaders did not expect the Soviets to unleash a sudden military attack against Western Europe or anywhere else. Rather, most officials guessed, the Soviets would try to take advantage of power vacuums created by economic chaos or anticolonial revolts in order to expand their influence. President Truman probably understood that the Soviet Union was more of a long-term rival than an immediate military threat. Yet early in 1946 he ruminated that he was tired of "babying" the Soviets. "Unless Russia is faced with an iron fist and strong language," he reasoned, "another war is in the making." With considerable insight, he told his wife and daughter that "a totalitarian state is no different whether you call it Nazi, Fascist, [or] Communist. [There] really is no difference between the government which [Soviet foreign minister] Molotov represents and the one the Czar represented—or the one Hitler spoke for."

Former British prime minister Winston Churchill encouraged anti-Soviet sentiment. At the time, Great Britain faced bankruptcy and required a multi-billion-dollar emergency loan from the United States. Like many of his compatriots, Churchill felt that he could garner U.S.

support by presenting Britain as a partner in a campaign against Soviet expansionism. Speaking in Fulton, Missouri, on March 5, 1946, to an audience that included President Truman, Churchill declared dramatically that "from Stettin [Poland] in the Baltic to Trieste [Italy] in the Adriatic, an iron curtain has descended" across Europe. He proposed an alliance of all English-speaking people, backed by the atomic bomb that "God has willed to the United States."

Joseph Stalin had his own doubts about the possibility of peaceful cooperation between East and West. Fearful of superior American economic and military power, he tried to isolate the Soviet heartland and the Eastern European satellite nations from contact with the outside world. Exposure, he feared, would alert the West to Communist weakness and make those living under Soviet control painfully aware of the better life enjoyed by their "enemies" on the other side of the iron curtain.

In a widely publicized speech to Soviet citizens delivered in February 1946, Stalin warned that it was in the nature of capitalism to prepare for war. He called on the hard-pressed Russian people to make greater sacrifices to develop heavy industry to safeguard their nation. Stalin invoked the threat of "capitalist encirclement" to justify his harsh rule and to suppress demands for greater liberty and more consumer goods.

There is little evidence that the Kremlin either anticipated an American attack or considered attacking the West. Nevertheless, Supreme Court Justice William O. Douglas, reflecting the view of many prominent Americans, called Stalin's speech a "declaration of World War III." For his part, the Soviet leader reacted angrily to Churchill's Iron Curtain speech that same month. He compared the British statesman's views to those of Hitler. The "racial theory" that those who spoke English should rule the world, Stalin complained, sounded like an incitement to war with the Soviet Union.

In the aftermath of these accusations, the Soviet government rejected membership in the American-sponsored World Bank and International Monetary Fund. These institutions were designed to promote trade and economic development by establishing orderly methods for making international loans, setting currency values, and reducing trade barriers among member states. As its most stable medium of exchange, the dollar—redeemable for gold at $35 per ounce—served as the world's reserve, or benchmark, currency. Washington's formula to boost world trade, Soviet foreign minister Molotov complained, might "look like a tasty mushroom," but it was really a "poisonous toadstool" designed to ensure American economic mastery and the exploitation of weaker peoples.

In 1946 Washington formally abandoned the plan of dismantling German heavy industry and making Germany pay reparations to

Russia—a plan, American officials complained, that had been drafted by economic idiots. American officials halted the shipment of reparations to the Soviet Union and instituted a merger of the British, American, and, later, French sectors into a single political unit, which eventually became West Germany. In September 1946, Secretary of State James Byrnes declared America's goal of reconstructing the German economy, and he suggested redrawing the German-Polish-Soviet borders to strip Moscow of its territorial gains. These actions were bound to antagonize the Soviets, who were extremely sensitive not only to territorial questions but also to any attempt to rebuild Germany, a nation that had invaded Russia in both world wars.

In another decision that moved the United States closer to its wartime enemy and further from its former ally, Washington dropped a prohibition against using the services of former Nazis. The War Department's secret Operation Paper Clip brought over seven hundred German scientists to the United States. Some were physicians who had performed horrible "medical" experiments on concentration camp inmates; others had overseen the death by exhaustion and starvation of slave laborers. Instead of prosecution, they were given new identities, if necessary, and hired as federal employees. In addition, both the United States and the Soviets eagerly recruited German rocket experts to build up their respective arsenals.

In 1946 Soviet-American tensions mounted when disputes arose in Iran and Turkey. During the Second World War the Allies deposed the pro-Nazi shah of Iran and jointly occupied that country. British and American forces had departed by early 1946, but the Soviets lingered, demanding an oil concession like the one the British had held for decades and supporting a separatist regime in northern Iran. Moscow also revived a long-standing demand that Turkey permit joint Soviet control over the Dardanelles, one of the strategic straits linking the Mediterranean with the Black Sea. Some American diplomats feared a Russian sweep across Turkey into the Mediterranean and across Iran to the Indian Ocean.

Declaring that the United States might as well find out now rather than later whether the Russians were bent on world conquest, Truman issued tough warnings to the Soviets and dispatched naval units to the Mediterranean. Stalin might be willing to probe, but he had no desire for a military showdown with the far more powerful United States. He backed down quickly in both Iran and Turkey. Although the Soviet Union may well have had expansionist goals, its motives— a quest for resources, security, and influence—were not much different from those of traditional empires.

Suspicion affected nearly all areas of Soviet-American relations, including efforts to control atomic weapons. Estimates varied as to when the Soviets would build an atomic bomb of their own. Some

American physicists thought it could be done within five years. Manhattan Project director General Leslie Groves, who had a low regard for Soviet science and mistakenly believed that Russia lacked high-grade uranium ore, thought the American nuclear monopoly would be secure for twenty years.

Hope that the atomic monopoly would compel Stalin to accept American demands faded quickly. Whenever the subject of the bomb entered Soviet-American discussions, Russian negotiators toughened their position. Determined not to allow the Americans to think he feared the weapon, Stalin told his colleagues that atomic bombs were meant to frighten those with weak nerves.

With the goals of preserving at least a modest edge in armaments and perhaps avoiding a dangerous arms race, the United States proposed in March 1946 that the Soviets accept a plan for international control of atomic energy. As originally drafted by Dean Acheson and David Lillienthal, the scheme called for placing nuclear research and materials under international supervision. The United States would retain its atomic monopoly for some time, surrendering it only when convinced that all nuclear potential abroad had been placed under firm control.

The next month, Truman named financier Bernard Baruch to present the plan formally to the United Nations. Baruch took a harsher line toward the Soviets, insisting on an American-dominated, veto-proof control commission with the right to manage all atomic facilities within the Soviet Union. Truman encouraged this approach, telling Baruch that "we should not under any circumstances throw away our gun until we are sure the rest of the world can't arm against us." The Soviets rejected the plan as a humiliating infringement on their sovereignty. They proposed an immediate ban on existing—that is, American—bombs, but suggested that a compromise might be possible. Baruch balked, insisting that Moscow accept his original formula, which was by that time known as the Baruch Plan.

In the middle of the United Nations debate, the United States conducted a dramatic series of atomic bomb tests at the Bikini atoll in the Pacific. Through these tests—some broadcast live over the radio—Truman hoped to sway the Soviets' position by demonstrating that the United States intended to keep its pre-eminent military power and continue with its development of nuclear weapons. When Stalin refused to blink, the Baruch Plan died, and the Soviets accelerated their own nuclear research.

The term "atomic age" had come into use in 1945, and the knowledge that nuclear weapons could destroy the world in a matter of minutes was affecting the national psyche. Some Americans made light of the danger by naming tavern drinks "atomic cocktails" or enjoying hit tunes like the "Atomic Polka" and "Atom Bomb Baby." In

1946 a French fashion designer christened a new type of bathing suit the "bikini," after America's Pacific test site. But the vision of a nuclear holocaust had begun to haunt people's imaginations.

The underlying anxieties were expressed in *Life* magazine's chilling fictional account of the "36-Hour War," published in November 1945. The article presented a lurid account of a mushroom cloud rising over Washington, D.C., and missiles hitting other cities. Although *Life* assured its readers that America "won" the fictional atomic war, the victory seemed dubious. Illustrations showed technicians in protective gear checking for radioactivity in front of the New York Public Library's marble lions—the only things left standing amid the city's rubble.

Despite the growing international tensions and hostile rhetoric, the Soviet and American governments actually reduced their military expenditures through 1946 and early 1947. For example, the United States cut its military budget and built few atomic bombs in this period. In fact, its tiny atomic arsenal consisted mostly of components requiring complex assembly, and relatively few planes were equipped to carry the weapons. Stalin, too, reduced military spending and troop strength, and he backed off in Turkey and Iran, withdrew troops from northern Norway, pulled Soviet forces out of Manchuria, and supported American mediation efforts in the Chinese civil war.

Nevertheless, by the end of 1947 the United States had begun major programs to resist Communist guerrillas in Greece, expand its nuclear arsenal, and forge a Western military alliance—and all of these steps were justified as responses to Soviet threats. How and why did this change occur? The answer involves a complex mix of factors, including instability in certain parts of the world, American strategic perceptions, Soviet actions, and domestic American politics.

By early 1947, chaos engulfed so much of the world that it appeared that vast new riches might simply fall into the lap of the Soviet Union. A nearly bankrupt Britain prepared to abandon India, Palestine, and Greece. Vietnamese and Indonesians had risen against their colonial masters. In China, civil war raged. Simply preventing starvation in occupied Germany and Japan cost the United States nearly $1 billion per year. Although the Soviets had not caused these problems, Americans feared that they stood to benefit from them.

George F. Kennan, second in command at the U.S. embassy in Moscow and the leading American expert on Soviet affairs, sent Washington a telegram in early 1946 detailing his conclusions about the deteriorating relations between the United States and the Soviet Union. In July 1947 the influential journal *Foreign Affairs* published an expanded version, written by Kennan under the pseudonym "Mr. X." In these documents Kennan argued that Stalin provoked tensions with the West as a means of justifying his harsh dictatorship to the

Soviet people. Kennan portrayed Soviet policy as a "fluid stream which moves constantly, wherever it is permitted to move," toward a goal of imperial domination. Although Soviet power was "impervious to the logic of reason," it remained "highly sensitive to the logic of force." Instead of accommodating the Kremlin, Kennan believed, Washington should respond with "long-term, patient but firm and vigilant containment." Before long, the term *containment*, or halting the extension of Soviet influence, wherever it might occur, became the operating principle of American foreign policy.

The timing of Kennan's "Long Telegram," immediately following Stalin's bellicose speech of February 1946 and just before the U.S.-Soviet confrontations over Iran, Turkey, Germany, and the Baruch Plan, prompted policymakers to view it as the definitive guide to Soviet behavior. American officials liked Kennan's assertion that Soviet leaders felt an ideological compulsion to treat the outside world as hostile. This explanation held the West blameless, dismissed the importance of the Soviet Union's huge wartime losses, minimized the Russian fear of a revived German threat, and obscured the reality of Soviet economic weakness which lay beneath its bluster.

A few months after Truman received Kennan's telegram he assigned his adviser Clark Clifford to use it as the basis for developing American policy toward the Soviets. Clifford's study, presented to Truman on September 24, 1946, further simplified Kennan's position by asserting that Stalin only understood the language of power. Four days before receiving Clifford's report, Truman had fired commerce secretary Henry A. Wallace for delivering a speech in New York City in which he condemned the arms race and the foreign policies of both Moscow and Washington, calling for a more conciliatory approach on both sides. Denouncing Wallace's speech, the president complained to Clifford that the "Reds, phonies and . . . parlor pinks are becoming a national danger."

Despite his condemnation of Wallace's remarks, Truman did not publicly release Clifford's inflammatory report. The gravest problem in Europe and Japan, as knowledgeable officials in Washington realized, was a huge "dollar gap" of more than $8 billion—the difference between the value of American exports and the amount of dollars foreign customers had available to pay for them. The dollar gap threatened to halt world trade. This imbalance could continue only as long as the United States government and private lenders provided credit. They would risk doing so only if Europe and Japan showed signs of industrial recovery. Once their credit disappeared, foreign nations would cease trading with the United States, perhaps causing the kind of global collapse that fed the Great Depression and Second World War. The Soviets might take advantage of such chaos by moving into vulnerable areas in Europe and Asia.

Policymakers agreed that successful containment of Soviet influence depended on reconstruction of the European and Japanese economies. As long as the "greatest workshops of Europe and Asia"—Germany and Japan—remained idle, Undersecretary of State Dean Acheson warned, peace and prosperity would never be achieved. Yet most members of Congress rejected this approach, because reconstruction of Europe and Japan would require a major increase in foreign aid, something never before done in peacetime. Only a simple, dramatic issue might mobilize Congress and the public.

Since 1944 a brutal civil war had raged between Greek monarchists, supported by Britain, and the leftist coalition known as EAM, from the Greek initials for National Liberation Front. The EAM had led the anti-Nazi resistance and now fought the corrupt and repressive regime in Athens. It included both Communists and non-Communists.

On February 21, 1947, the financially hard-pressed British government informed Washington it could no longer afford to support the Greek regime. Although the Truman administration had already provided $200 million in aid to Greece, to assume the full British burden would cost more. The United States ambassador to Athens warned that the Soviets regarded Greece as a ripe plum ready for picking.

The new secretary of state, George C. Marshall, who had served as army chief of staff in the Second World War, explained the Greek situation to congressional leaders. Never a dramatic orator, Marshall spoke of humanitarian reasons for assuming Britain's burden. As the politicians yawned, Undersecretary Dean Acheson took charge. He likened the battle to the classical struggle between Athens and Sparta. The United States and the Soviet Union, he said, were divided by an "unbridgeable ideological chasm." Acheson depicted the contest as one between democracy and liberty on one side and dictatorship and absolute conformity on the other. If the United States walked away, then, "like apples in a barrel infected by one rotten one," the "corruption of Greece would infect Iran and all to the east."

After a stunned silence, Senator Arthur Vandenberg, the Republican chairman of the Senate Foreign Relations Committee, reportedly said that if Truman told this to Congress, it would support an aid program. According to another version of the same meeting, Vandenberg declared that if the Democrats wanted to provide a WPA-style welfare program for Greece, Truman needed to "scare hell out of the American people." Whether or not the senator used this precise phrase, he made his point.

Acheson prepared a speech for the president that stressed the "global struggle between freedom and totalitarianism." When Truman addressed Congress on March 12, 1947, he declared that "it must be the policy of the United States to support free peoples who are resisting attempted subjugation by armed minorities or by outside pressures." Almost immediately, this statement was dubbed the Truman Doctrine. Specifically, Truman called for a $400 million program of aid to Greece and Turkey. Turkey was added to the program in part to defuse the Turks' anger over American aid to their traditional Greek rivals; moreover, by enlarging the area included in the aid program, the administration spurred Congress to take the danger more seriously.

Swayed by Truman's appeal, the Republican-dominated Congress passed the aid bill quickly. In practice, "supporting free peoples" meant defending *any* regime threatened by communism—or, often, non-Communist rebels—even if, as in Greece, the government in power was not democratic.

Years later, policymakers would use the successful Greek experience as a model for American intervention in Vietnam. Greece, however, was a unique case—and the civil war there did not involve direct Soviet influence. It was Yugoslavia, rather than the Soviet Union, that supplied aid to the Greek Communist rebels. Josip Tito, the Yugoslavian leader, had visions of annexing Greece to a Balkan federation dominated by Yugoslavia. But Stalin resented such empire building by his subalterns; in mid-1948 he denounced Tito as a renegade and tried to topple him. Searching for Western friends, Tito halted aid to the Greek rebels and forced them out of Yugoslavian sanctuaries. This change, along with American military aid to the Greek government, brought defeat to the insurgents by late 1949.

The greatest impact of the Truman Doctrine, however, was not in Greece but in Western Europe. On June 5, 1947, speaking at Harvard University, Secretary of State Marshall revealed the outlines of a European Recovery Plan (ERP) that soon became known as the Marshall Plan. To prevent the Soviets from taking advantage of European economic collapse, the plan offered a multiyear, comprehensive program to assist industrial recovery and trade in Europe. Although German industry was considered especially important, the program would include other nations as well. Truman asked Congress to back these ideas with a $27 billion appropriation. The Truman Doctrine and the Marshall Plan, he explained, were "two halves of the same walnut."

Technically the Marshall Plan did not bar participation by the Soviet Union or its satellites. However, in order to participate, Moscow would have had to open its financial books for American scrutiny and coordinate its economic policies with the West. Soviet foreign minister Molotov attended the first planning conference in Paris and proposed that each European nation present its own wish list to Washington, without establishing any common program. When this tactic failed, Molotov stormed out, to the great relief of American delegates.

Poland, Hungary, and Czechoslovakia also reluctantly withdrew to avoid offending the Soviet Union.

A Soviet-inspired coup in Czechoslovakia also helped convince a still reluctant Congress to act on the Marshall Plan. On February 25, 1948, Czech Communists—supported by a massing of Soviet troops on the Czech border—seized power in Prague and brought their nation into the Soviet bloc. The sense of crisis deepened on March 5, when General Lucius Clay, commander of the American forces in western Germany, warned of a "subtle change" in Soviet behavior. He felt that war might come with dramatic suddenness.

Neither the Czech coup nor Clay's warning really surprised American officials. State Department and military personnel had anticipated a Soviet move to stifle Czechoslovakian independence as a means of sealing off Eastern Europe from the Marshall Plan. Nevertheless, Truman played up these incidents in a speech to Congress on March 17, 1948. Pleading for passage of the Marshall Plan and measures to boost American military preparedness, he argued that recent events showed the intent of the Soviet Union to dominate the remaining free nations of Europe.

Congress finally passed a trimmed-down version of the Marshall Plan, which also included funds to rebuild the economy of Japan. Like Germany, Japan was envisioned as an anchor of containment. Also like Germany, the initial occupation policy for Japan, which stressed economic and political reform, was replaced by one that emphasized aid to big business and the return of the old political order. Over the next several years, the United States provided more than $15 billion in Marshall Plan assistance to Europe and Japan, the equivalent of about $90 billion in 1995 dollars.

The Truman administration also reformed the military and intelligence arms of the government. The National Security Act of 1947 addressed several problems. It consolidated the separate War and Navy departments into the Department of Defense, led by a civilian defense secretary. However, the three armed services (army, navy, air force) retained their separate identities. The act formally named the military head of each service to the Joint Chiefs of Staff and made all of these leaders military advisers to the president. Congress also revived the peacetime draft.

The new law created the National Security Council, to advise the president on foreign policy, as well as the Central Intelligence Agency (CIA), to gather and analyze intelligence. Soon the CIA expanded its role to include covert missions abroad.

In 1948 Washington began rebuilding American military power. The atomic arsenal grew from fifteen to more than two hundred bombs by 1950. The United States also encouraged Western European nations to form a mutual defense pact, the first step toward creation of the North Atlantic Treaty Organization (NATO) a year later.

In response to the Marshall Plan and the changes in the American military and intelligence services, Stalin imposed even tighter economic and political control on his Eastern European satellites and purged Communist Party members he feared might harbor liberal or independent tendencies. Most dramatically, in June 1948 the Soviets imposed a blockade on land routes into West Berlin, the non-Communist enclave deep inside eastern Germany.

The question of control over and access to the American, French, British, and Soviet occupation zones in Germany was a thorny issue and one that was ripe for exploitation. Before June 1948, the Western nations had already agreed in principle to unite their occupation zones into a single unit. Seeing that he had failed to prevent the restoration of a potentially powerful West German state, Stalin tried to drive the Western powers out of Berlin, lest that city become an anti-Soviet rallying point. When, as part of the unification process, Washington instituted currency reform in the Western-occupied zones, Moscow declared it a violation of earlier occupation agreements, and Russian troops were ordered to stop all road and rail transport into West Berlin.

Although air corridors over the Soviet zone had been guaranteed, the rules governing land access to Berlin were vague. Occupation commander General Lucius Clay urged Truman to allow him to shoot his way through the Soviet barriers. If Berlin fell, he warned, "western Germany will be next." Given Moscow's large advantage in ground forces, Truman opted instead for an airlift to bypass the blockade. He also bluffed by sending sixty atomic-capable B-29 bombers, without atomic weapons, to England.

As the president had guessed, Stalin did not want to start a war. Soviet planes never challenged the massive American air transport lifeline into the besieged city. In May 1949 the Soviets lifted the blockade. The Berlin airlift lasted nearly a year, becoming a symbol of American resolve and Soviet brutishness. It hastened the creation of what the Soviets greatly feared, an independent West German state, the Federal Republic of Germany, in May 1949. In rebuttal, the Soviet Union created the East German state, the German Democratic Republic, the following month.

The Berlin airlift had other, less tangible results as well. It modified the feelings many Europeans, the recent victims of Nazi aggression, harbored toward Germany. Instead of former enemies, the West Germans became fellow victims of the Cold War. The airlift also seemed a

Divided Europe ▶

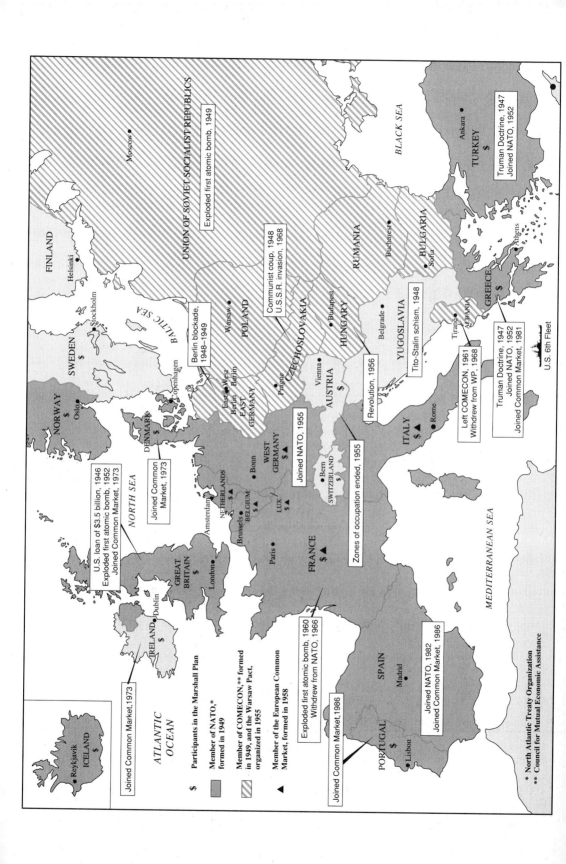

UNION OF SOVIET SOCIALIST REPUBLICS

Exploded first atomic bomb, 1949

Moscow

FINLAND

Helsinki

BLACK SEA

TURKEY

Ankara

Truman Doctrine, 1947
Joined NATO, 1952

BALTIC SEA

SWEDEN
$

Stockholm

Warsaw

POLAND

Communist coup, 1948
U.S.S.R. invasion, 1968

Berlin blockade,
1948–1949

RUMANIA

Bucharest

BULGARIA
Sofia

GREECE
$

Athens

NORWAY
$

Oslo

Copenhagen

East West
Berlin Berlin
EAST
GERMANY

CZECHOSLOVAKIA

Prague

Budapest

HUNGARY

Vienna

YUGOSLAVIA

Belgrade

Tito-Stalin schism, 1948

ALBANIA

Tiranë

Truman Doctrine, 1947
Joined NATO, 1952
Joined Common Market, 1981

DENMARK
$

Joined Common
Market, 1973

WEST
GERMANY
$ ▲

Joined NATO, 1955

AUSTRIA
$

Revolution, 1956

Left COMECON, 1961
Withdrew from WP, 1968

U.S. 6th Fleet

NORTH SEA

U.S. loan of $3.5 billion, 1946
Exploded first atomic bomb, 1952
Joined Common Market, 1973

NETHERLANDS
$

Amsterdam

Brussels
BELGIUM
$ ▲

Bonn

LUX.
$ ▲

Bern
SWITZERLAND
$

Zones of occupation ended, 1955

ITALY
$ ▲

Rome

MEDITERRANEAN SEA

GREAT
BRITAIN
$

London

Paris

FRANCE
$ ▲

Exploded first atomic bomb, 1960
Withdrew from NATO, 1966

ATLANTIC
OCEAN

Dublin

IRELAND
$

Reykjavik

ICELAND
$

Joined Common Market, 1973

SPAIN

Madrid

Joined NATO, 1982
Joined Common Market, 1986

Joined Common Market, 1986

PORTUGAL
$

Lisbon

Participants in the Marshall Plan

$

Member of NATO,*
formed in 1949

Member of COMECON,** formed
in 1949, and the Warsaw Pact,
organized in 1955

▲ Member of the European Common
Market, formed in 1958

* North Atlantic Treaty Organization
** Council for Mutual Economic Assistance

further illustration of the West's ability to make the Soviets back down through a show of strength.

When the frustrated Russians lifted their blockade of Berlin, the United States had, by most measures, won the Cold War in Western Europe and Japan. The Marshall Plan nations and Japan were on the road to economic recovery. Communism had lost its attraction for most Europeans. Stalin's efforts to keep Japan and Europe weak, divided, and isolated from the United States had failed miserably. George Kennan considered the American position so strong that he urged his superiors to approach Stalin with a deal to unify Germany as a militarily neutral nation. He thought this might stabilize Europe while reducing tension, but top American policymakers scoffed at the idea.

Following Truman's election in November 1948, he appointed Dean Acheson, the former undersecretary of state who had briefly left the State Department, as the new secretary of state, replacing the ailing George Marshall. Acheson favored a Western military alliance, including West Germany, to resist any potential Soviet threat. In April 1949 he oversaw creation of the North Atlantic Treaty Organization (NATO). The NATO pact pledged the United States, Britain, France, Belgium, the Netherlands, Italy, Portugal, Denmark, Iceland, Norway, and Canada to a common defense; Greece, Turkey, Spain, and West Germany joined later. NATO, Acheson told Congress, would go beyond maintaining a "balance of power," giving the West a "preponderance of power" over Moscow. Congress approved the NATO treaty in mid-1949.

The Soviets countered with the Council for Mutual Economic Assistance (known as the CMEA or COMECON) for Eastern Europe and later with the Warsaw Pact. By formal alliance as well as ideology, Europe was now divided in two (see map).

NATIONAL POLITICS, 1946–52

After the Republicans captured both houses of Congress in 1946, they looked forward confidently to winning the White House in 1948. In a way, the late President Roosevelt helped them, for whatever Truman's merits might have been, he inevitably suffered from comparison with his predecessor. Roosevelt had reshaped the nation's very concept of the presidency, making it difficult for Americans to think of someone else in the job.

Moreover, Roosevelt had been a master coalition builder, establishing an alliance of labor, urban ethnic groups, minorities, and farmers that is still known as the Roosevelt or New Deal coalition. Once the depression and world war were over, Truman found it difficult to maintain that consensus and build support for new initiatives. Like

Roosevelt, he favored moderate reform, believed in human progress, and supported an active role for the United States in world affairs. But his humble background, folksy style, and testy personality would never appeal to the public as the patrician Roosevelt had. By 1948, in fact, one survey found that only 3 percent of American voters listed Truman among the most admired leaders of recent decades.

Nevertheless, Clark Clifford, a young Missouri lawyer Truman appointed as his special counsel in 1947, developed a political strategy that proved remarkably successful. In November 1947, Clifford urged Truman to attack Republican efforts to unravel the economic and social reforms of the New Deal while pushing a liberal program of his own. Clifford argued that if former vice president Henry Wallace carried out his threat to run for the presidency as a third-party candidate, Truman should identify him in the public mind with communism.

Following this advice, in 1947 and 1948 Truman vetoed sixty-two Republican-sponsored bills attacking the New Deal legacy. Often the president's veto messages rang with angry language. Conversely, he proposed programs to increase aid to small farmers, raise the minimum wage, liberalize immigration policies, enhance civil rights, reduce taxes for working people, and increase Social Security benefits. As each measure went down to defeat at the hands of Republicans, Truman's standing rose among elements of the Roosevelt coalition. Truman also abandoned his antilabor stance and recaptured the support of unions through his stinging veto of the Taft-Hartley Bill, which he denounced as a slave-labor act (see Chapter 3). When Henry Wallace did challenge Truman, running as the Progressive party candidate, the White House and its liberal allies undermined his appeal. Truman announced, for example, that he was glad not to have the support of "Henry Wallace and his Communists."

Clifford's strategy also included an appeal to urban minorities, whom he predicted would form a crucial voting bloc in the 1948 election. By endorsing the recommendations of his Committee on Civil Rights, Truman solidified his support among African-Americans. At the same time, concerned about alienating moderate whites, he took only modest steps to put those recommendations into practice. The president also reached out to Jews and Eastern Europeans by supporting a liberalized immigration law and by extending diplomatic recognition to Israel.

At the same time that Truman was reaching out to labor and minorities, liberal Democrats moved closer to the center by taking a stand against communism. Labor leaders Walter Reuther and David Dubinsky; public figures such as Eleanor Roosevelt, Franklin Roosevelt, Jr., and Reinhold Niebur; and influential journalists created the Americans for Democratic Action (ADA) in 1947. The ADA rejected any "association with Communists or sympathizers with communism in the United States" and attacked Wallace's party as a totalitarian group. Endorsing Truman as the true successor to Roosevelt, the ADA prevented major defections to Wallace.

At the Democratic convention in July 1948, Truman tried to appease all factions by supporting an innocuous civil rights platform. However, a revolt by party liberals, including the young mayor of Minneapolis, Hubert H. Humphrey, forced the adoption of a stronger civil rights agenda. Angry southerners such as Senator James Eastland of Mississippi denounced attempts to "mongrelize the nation"; others complained that Truman was "kissing the feet of the minorities."

Some southern Democrats walked out of the convention and organized the States' Rights party. The presidential nominee of these "Dixiecrats," Governor Strom Thurmond of South Carolina, declared that his party represented the "deepest emotion of the human fabric— racial pride, respect for white womanhood and superiority of Caucasian blood." Civil rights, he insisted, was another term for the Communist ideology of the "radicals, subversives and Reds" surrounding Truman.

Now that the Democratic party had split three ways, many observers simply wrote off Truman's political prospects. In fact, the split may have actually helped Truman, as it allowed him to stress his anti-Communist credentials and to appeal to black urban votes. Nevertheless, as he began to campaign against Republican nominee Thomas E. Dewey, the governor of New York (who had run against Roosevelt four years earlier), Congresswoman Clare Boothe Luce described Truman as "a gone goose." The incumbent disagreed, ignoring polling data that gave Dewey a nearly fifteen-point lead during the summer of 1948. Truman crisscrossed the nation by train, delivering hundreds of combative speeches. Virtually ignoring the splinter candidates, Wallace and Thurmond, he concentrated his fire on the Republican-dominated Eightieth Congress, the "gluttons of privilege" who "stuck a pitchfork on the back of the farmers," tried to "enslave totally the working man," and wanted to do "a real hatchet job on the New Deal." A Republican president would bring back depression, he insisted. Enthusiastic crowds roared, "Give 'em hell, Harry."

In fact, Dewey was a moderate and a decent man who did not intend to roll back the New Deal. But his personality was stiff, and his campaign suffered from overconfidence. Dewey devoted more energy to planning his inauguration than to campaigning, failing even to rebut Truman's charges.

Gradually Truman's appeal to labor, farmers, urban ethnic voters, and blacks—the Roosevelt coalition—took hold. Also, Truman proved relatively immune to Republican redbaiting. He had proven his loyalty to the anti-Communist cause, and compared to the Progressive party he appeared conservative. The president's tough responses to Soviet pressure in Europe—notably with the Truman Doctrine and Marshall Plan—and his determination during the summer of 1948 to maintain the Berlin airlift were popular among voters. Many polling organizations, however, lost interest in the seemingly one-sided race and stopped taking surveys three weeks before the November election.

When the tally came in, Truman beat Dewey by over 2 million votes (24 million to 22 million)—one of the most dramatic upsets in the history of presidential politics. Henry Wallace and Strom Thurmond each received slightly more than 1 million votes, and their parties soon dissolved. Journalist Walter Lippmann, noting Truman's success in making the campaign a referendum on the New Deal, commented wryly, "of all Roosevelt's electoral triumphs, this one in 1948 is the most impressive."

Now president by election rather than simply by the death of his predecessor, Truman tried to emerge from Roosevelt's shadow. He proclaimed his own reform program, the Fair Deal. He introduced legislation for national health insurance, public housing, expanded Social Security benefits, a higher minimum wage, greater protection for civil rights, an agricultural support program that favored small farmers, and repeal of the Taft-Hartley Act.

Few of these measures came to a vote in Congress. The enduring coalition of Republicans and southern Democrats tied up most of the Fair Deal package in committee. Congress passed a very modest public housing bill and expanded Social Security, but Democrats could not muster the votes to repeal the Taft-Hartley Act. The outbreak of the Korean War in June 1950, Republican gains in that November's congressional election, and a series of scandals involving Truman cronies largely frustrated reformers.

Thus the Fair Deal remained more a promise than a reality. Nevertheless, Truman's proposals did set a social agenda for later administrations, and in this sense they were more influential than politicians of the time could guess. Ironically, Truman's own anti-Communist fervor had helped to block reform by inflaming public suspicion of liberal social policies.

EXPANDING DIMENSIONS OF THE COLD WAR

Even as the Marshall Plan and NATO were overcoming any serious threat of Soviet influence in Western Europe, the Cold War brought new concerns. Soviet development of an atomic bomb prompted

Washington to re-evaluate American security needs. Communist successes in China and Vietnam led to demands for deeper American involvement in those regions. Meanwhile, a number of sensational espionage cases raised fears that the Soviets could gain dominance simply by stealing American nuclear secrets.

In September 1949, American planes collected air samples indicating that an atomic explosion had occurred inside the Soviet Union. The Soviets had the bomb, years earlier than Americans had expected. Many feared that the Soviet Union's possession of nuclear weapons would place it on an equal military footing with the United States and encourage it to take direct military action.

The Soviet bomb triggered a debate in Washington over whether to build a new bomb a thousand times more powerful than the first atomic weapon. This superbomb, or hydrogen bomb, would derive its energy from the fusion of hydrogen atoms; current atomic bombs derived their energy from the splitting, or fission, of atoms. Some of those who opposed development of the superbomb, such as J. Robert Oppenheimer and George F. Kennan, doubted that Soviet atomic weapons would greatly alter the American military advantage, because the Russians lacked an effective delivery system. With some modification, American atomic bombs could be made far more powerful than the early prototypes. Thus the superbomb might not have any advantage in deterring an enemy. Others, who favored a slow approach to the exceedingly costly build-up of nuclear weapons, believed that Washington should first try to negotiate an arms control pact with Moscow. If Stalin stalled or raced ahead with his own hydrogen bomb project, the United States would still have the option of matching him.

Neither moral, political, or technical arguments swayed top policymakers against the new weapon. Acheson selected hard-liner Paul Nitze to replace Kennan as head of policy planning in the State Department, installing him as chair of a committee that urged rapid development of the hydrogen bomb. President Truman needed little convincing. America had to make the bomb, he said later, "if only for bargaining purposes with the Russians." After getting the nod to proceed in January 1950, American scientists exploded a prototype hydrogen device in November 1952. But a Soviet test of a hydrogen bomb occurred the next August.

When Truman asked Acheson to undertake a comprehensive study of American security policy, the secretary of state again tapped Nitze for the job. In the resulting top-secret document, issued by the National Security Council and numbered NSC-68, Nitze assumed that the risk of a Soviet attack was considerably greater than ever before. Without specifying why, he claimed that Soviet behavior showed a new boldness that "borders on the reckless." Nitze advocated a dramatic increase in American defense spending, from $13 billion to $50 billion annually. This increase would be used to fund both conventional forces and a new generation of nuclear weapons and delivery systems. Nitze confided to his staff that such huge sums were unlikely to be appropriated except as a result of a scare campaign designed to shock the public.

NSC-68, given to the president in April 1950, painted a lurid picture of a Kremlin motivated by "fanatical faith" to "impose its authority on the rest of the world." It greatly exaggerated Soviet military strength, claiming that by 1954 Moscow would possess the nuclear capacity to destroy the United States. The report called for an immediate, large-scale build-up of nuclear and conventional weapons to promptly meet each new Soviet challenge anywhere in the world.

Acheson, who privately admitted the study's verbal excesses, hoped it would "bludgeon the mass mind of government" into action. Other high officials supported the proposed increase in defense spending for a variety of reasons. For example, members of the president's Council of Economic Advisers argued that large defense expenditures would boost industrial output and employment, strengthening the economy. Yet Truman remained cautious. He endorsed NSC-68 in principle, but he worried about its high price tag. Although the document itself remained secret for decades, within months of its drafting the outbreak of the Korean War made vastly higher defense expenditures a reality.

In October 1949, a month after the U.S. confirmation of a Soviet atomic test, the administration received more bad news when Communist leader Mao Zedong (spelled Mao Tse-tung in the old transliteration) established the People's Republic of China. After four years of civil war, Nationalist party leader Jiang Jieshi (Chiang Kai-shek) had fled to the island province of Taiwan. The Communist victory outraged many of Jiang's Congressional supporters—the so-called China bloc—and disheartened Americans who considered China their favorite charity.

China's civil war between the Communists and Kuomintang (Nationalists, or KMT) had resumed as soon as Japan surrendered. Truman tried to help Jiang by giving him over $2 billion in military and economic aid between 1945 and 1949, but Nationalist incompetence and Communist strength nullified its effect.

During 1946, General George C. Marshall served a year as a mediator in China, trying to arrange a political compromise. Both Nationalists and Communists, however, believed they could win a military showdown and opposed real power sharing. Marshall gave up in January 1947, pronounced a plague on both Chinese factions, and returned to Washington to become secretary of state.

J. Robert Oppenheimer

In the immediate aftermath of the Second World War, J. Robert Oppenheimer acquired the glamour of a movie star. Celebrated as the father of the atomic bomb, he was featured on the cover of *Time*. Yet few people knew much about this shy, vain, and driven man.

"Oppie," as his colleagues called him, had grown up in New York City, attended Harvard, and studied physics in Europe before returning to teach at Berkeley and the California Institute of Technology. Before the war he helped educate a generation of physicists. He also supported many left-wing causes; and his wife, brother, and sister-in-law all supported the American Communist party at one time or another.

Despite these associations, Oppenheimer became head of the secret atomic weapons laboratory at Los Alamos, New Mexico, in 1942. In July 1945, while his

From then on the administration pretty much wrote off China, assuming it would either remain in chaos or come under Communist control. Military aid seemed pointless, as the Communists drove well-armed Nationalist troops from positions that American advisers regarded as easily defensible. In private, Truman called Jiang a crook, and many senators agreed that more aid to Jiang was "money down a rat hole." By 1949, Jiang and his army fled to Taiwan, then called Formosa.

Most professional diplomats recognized that Mao's relations with Stalin were strained, and in any case, China was so poor that any Chinese-Soviet alliance was likely to drain rather than enhance Soviet resources. State Department experts even predicted that the Chinese Communists might soon fall out with the bullying Soviets.

colleagues celebrated the successful test of the first atomic bomb, Oppenheimer recited to himself an apocalyptic passage from a classic Hindu text: "I am become death, the shatterer of worlds." Although he was the "father" of the weapon, "Oppie" remained profoundly uneasy with his offspring.

After the war he resumed his academic career and served as a high-level adviser to the Atomic Energy Commission. As an advocate of the international control of atomic energy, Oppenheimer helped draft the ill-fated Baruch Plan of 1946. But by the early 1950s his outspoken opposition to development of the hydrogen bomb, which he considered a militarily useless terror weapon, earned him the wrath of powerful enemies. In the politically intolerant climate of the Cold War, his criticism of the bomb was denounced as an effort to aid the Soviet Union; he was even accused of passing secrets to the Soviets. In 1954, during a review of his security clearance, the FBI played up his past friendships with Communists. Although no credible evidence linked him to espionage or any acts of disloyalty, in the tense atmosphere of the Red Scare the accusations proved damning. In May 1954 the AEC stripped him of his security clearance and dismissed him as an adviser on atomic policy.

This verdict ended Oppenheimer's public career, although he remained a forceful advocate of disarmament the rest of his life. He returned to academia, and in December 1963 President Lyndon Johnson belatedly awarded him a public service medal in recognition of his contributions to American science. Oppenheimer died in 1967. ■

In August 1949, the State Department issued a massive report known as the *China White Paper*. The report condemned the Communists for their subservience to Russia, but it insisted that Jiang, not the United States, had "lost China" and that he deserved no more help. Although Truman hesitated to establish formal relations with the Chinese Communist government in Beijing, he announced that American forces would not defend Taiwan against an anticipated Communist assault.

Truman and Secretary of State Dean Acheson tried to calm worried legislators by telling them that Washington would wait until the confusion of the Chinese civil war had settled before it would consider recognizing the Communist People's Republic of China. In January 1950 the president terminated military aid to Jiang's government-in-

Jiang Jieshi and Mao Zedong at an American-sponsored peace
conference in 1945. Civil war soon followed. *Jack Wilkes/Life
Magazine,* © *Time Inc.*

exile on Taiwan. Acheson, in a speech before the National Press Club
in Washington, urged turning away from China and concentrating instead on securing the "Great Crescent," the lands on the rim of China,
stretching from Japan through Southeast Asia to India. Southeast
Asian resources, he stressed, were more vital to both Europe and
Japan than was anything in China. In a remark little noticed at the
time, he also described South Korea as being outside the United
States' defensive perimeter in Asia. Republican critics labeled the
white paper a white wash and accused Truman and Acheson of coddling Chinese Communists.

By 1950 the United States had begun to assist French forces fighting
a Communist-led uprising in French Indochina (Vietnam, Cambodia,
and Laos). During the Second World War, Vietnamese guerrilla leader
Ho Chi Minh—a genuine Communist but also a figure highly re-
spected for his lifelong opposition to French rule—had cooperated in
the anti-Japanese struggle, and in 1945 he appealed for American support in securing Vietnamese independence. Roosevelt had urged the
French to loosen their hold on Vietnam, but Truman seemed less inclined to support anticolonial movements. Few American diplomats
knew much about Southeast Asia, and those who sympathized with
the independence movements were usually ignored.

In 1947 Dean Acheson, then undersecretary of state, spoke for the administration when he condemned Ho's Vietminh guerrillas as Soviet dupes. Acheson warned that their victory would expose all of Southeast Asia to Moscow's influence. He was also concerned that loss of the colony could weaken French resolve to resist Soviet expansion in Europe.

Still, Washington's uneasiness over supporting a colonial war led Acheson to insist that France go through the motions of naming a Vietnamese as the colony's nominal ruler, with the promise of eventual independence. To Washington's dismay, France selected Bao Dai, a disreputable playboy descended from Vietnamese royalty, as their puppet emperor. Nevertheless, in February 1950, after China and the Soviet Union recognized Ho's insurgent government, Washington felt obliged to recognize Bao Dai's puppet regime. That spring, the first American arms and advisers arrived in Saigon.

Drawing the line in Vietnam did not placate the loose coalition of legislators and citizens known as the China lobby, which blamed the administration for losing China and underrating the threat of communism in Asia. Republican senators such as Kenneth Wherry of Nebraska and William Knowland of California, together with Democrat Pat McCarran of Nevada, Republican representative Walter Judd of Minnesota, and publishers Henry Luce and Roy Howard, insisted that more American aid would have saved Jiang. They accused Dean Acheson and China specialists in the State Department of holding Communist sympathies. A young Democratic congressman from Massachusetts, John F. Kennedy, charged that the administration had deserted China, "whose freedom we once fought to preserve. What our young men had saved, our diplomats and president have frittered away."

THE RED SCARE

During the first decade following the Second World War, a mounting anti-Communist movement dominated American political debate. As mentioned earlier, American anticommunism stretched back to 1917 and the first "Red Scare," following the Bolshevik Revolution. Part of the tension after World War II came from disputes dating back to the 1930s, pitting left-wing factions in the Democratic party, the labor movement, and U.S. intellectual circles against centrists and conservatives who abhorred the Soviet Union and those Americans who defended it. Republican politicians who hated the New Deal aroused the public with charges that Roosevelt's programs had eroded liberty at home and contributed to the rise of communism abroad. This mixture of ideological fervor and political opportunism, combined with the legitimate reaction to Soviet domination of Eastern Europe, fed a Red Scare that began in 1946 to 1947 and soon grew to a fever pitch. Eventually the name of a Republican senator from Wisconsin, Joseph McCarthy, would become synonymous with the fear and persecution of the anti-Communist wave of the 1950s. But the Red Scare was well under way by the time McCarthy emerged as a national figure.

Domestic communism was, in fact, a tiny, nonviolent movement. The Communist Party of the United States—a legal organization— had some twenty thousand members at the end of the war, and it shrank quickly in the late 1940s. Although party leaders and members supported most Soviet policies and often served as apologists for Stalin's brutality, the party avoided violence, and ordinary members did not plot to overthrow the government. The Federal Bureau of Investigation (FBI) had infiltrated the party so thoroughly during the 1930s and 1940s that it could not organize so much as a picnic in secrecy. Nevertheless, anticommunism seized the popular imagination in the United States.

Numerous politicians exploited the rising fear and helped fan it into hysteria. Certain conservatives linked the New Deal, liberalism, and progressive politics to "the Reds," primarily as a way of discrediting them all. For example, racists labeled as Communist any who campaigned against segregation. Conservative union leaders found it was possible to oust left-wing opponents in the labor movement by calling them stooges of Moscow. Republican politicians, stymied by the continued popularity of New Deal reforms like Social Security, discovered that voters might desert the Democratic party if it could be tarred with charges of softness on communism. Pubic opinion proved volatile and easily swayed by such sensationalist charges.

The House Committee on Un-American Activities (HUAC) played a particularly influential role in stirring up the Red Scare. Between 1944 and 1946, Democrats John S. Wood of Georgia and John Rankin of Mississippi used the committee as a forum to attack liberal causes. Rankin, the most active member of the panel, took pride in extending to the nation's capital a law, modeled on laws in twenty-two states, banning interracial marriage. He accused the Red Cross of bowing to Communist pressure to "mongrelize the nation" by removing labels designating the race of donors from blood bank bottles. In 1945 he complained of a conspiracy among "alien-minded Communistic enemies of Christianity"—his code word for Jews—to take over the nation.

In November 1946, to counter charges of Democratic waffling on Communist subversion, President Truman established the Temporary Commission on Employee Loyalty. Stung by continued Republican attacks and Republican gains in the 1946 election, Truman issued Executive Order No. 9835 the following March, creating the Federal

Employee Loyalty Program to verify the loyalty of government employees.

Attorney General Tom Clark compiled a list of eighty-two supposedly subversive organizations. Applying even looser standards, congressional committees developed a list of over six hundred groups. Membership in any one of these "totalitarian, Fascist, Communist or subversive" organizations could, by itself, constitute reasonable doubt of a federal employee's loyalty and justify his or her dismissal. Clark warned that "[Communists] are everywhere—in factories, offices, butcher shops, on street corners, in private businesses—and each carries with him the germs of death for society."

The loyalty program required all current and prospective federal employees to undergo an investigation. Hearsay and anonymous accusations, as well as information from wiretaps and mail openings, could be used to discredit someone.

The FBI conducted most of the loyalty probes of government employees. Its director, J. Edgar Hoover, had been "chasing Reds," as he put it, since the first great Red Scare of 1919. Hoover, a consummate bureaucrat, used public relations and intimidation to build strong congressional support for his agency. Although relations between Truman and Hoover were frosty, the FBI director was on good terms with nearly every president he served under, from Harding through Nixon. During his long career, the FBI mirrored Hoover's contempt for Communists, African-Americans, and nearly every kind of political or social nonconformity.

At loyalty board hearings, the accused were typically asked whether they socialized with members of other races, whether they had any homosexual inclinations (itself grounds for removal), and what political or philosophical beliefs they held. Several diplomats stationed in China during the Second World War were fired for "consorting with known Communists"—a result of the fact that they had been assigned to Communist headquarters. By the early 1950s, over 5 million government employees had undergone some form of security check. Several thousand quit under protest. A few hundred were fired for associating with groups on the attorney general's list.

Neither the loyalty program nor later congressional witch hunts unearthed many real spies. Of course the Soviet Union, like the United States, routinely sought information on its opponent's nuclear capabilities, military plans, and high technology. Soviet agents typically recruited disgruntled employees who nursed grievances or needed cash, to gather and pass on information. Since few of the people the Soviets recruited had political motives, loyalty probes were virtually useless in uncovering their activities. The Kremlin generally avoided using American Communists as spies, because they were closely scrutinized by the FBI. Still, a few spectacular cases, such as the alleged treason of Alger Hiss (discussed on pages 78 and 79), created the impression that Communist sympathizers or even liberal Democrats might be spies.

A judicial attack on communism began in July 1948, when a federal grand jury indicted twelve top American Communist Party officials, including Eugene Dennis and Gus Hall, for violation of the Smith Act, a prewar law. The 1940 law, originally directed toward Fascists as well as Communists, made it a crime to advocate the overthrow of the government by force or to belong to a group advocating such action. In the postwar climate it was used almost exclusively against the Communist Party.

In October 1949 a jury found the party leaders guilty. And in 1951, in *Dennis* v. *United States,* the Supreme Court upheld the conviction. Writing for the majority, Chief Justice Fred Vinson ruled that citizens had no right to pursue violent rebellion where the opportunity for peaceful and orderly change existed. In vain, dissenting justices Hugo Black and William O. Douglas argued that American Communists did not in fact advocate violent opposition to the government.

By the time of that ruling, Democratic and Republican politicians had vied with one another to pass new and more stringent legislation to restrict subversive activities. Republicans Karl Mundt and Richard Nixon, as well as Democrats Pat McCarran and Hubert Humphrey, introduced anti-Communist legislation in 1949 and 1950. A compromise measure, the McCarran Act, or Internal Security Act of 1950, condemned communists as part of an international conspiracy that posed an immediate threat to the United States.

The law ordered all Communist-affiliated organizations and individuals to register with a Subversive Activities Control Board or face a $10,000 fine and five years in prison. If they did register, Communists faced social ostracism; if they did not, they risked being sent to jail. Mail sent by registered Communist groups had to be labeled "Disseminated by a Communist organization." Real or alleged Communists were denied passports and barred from jobs in government and the defense industry. The law permitted the deportation of naturalized citizens and the detention without trial of alleged subversives during periods of emergency.

With the cooperation of FBI director J. Edgar Hoover, the HUAC stepped up its activities in 1947. J. Parnell Thomas, a New Jersey Republican named to chair HUAC when his party won control of the House, announced the discovery of a Red plot to overthrow the government centered in Hollywood.

Even during the wartime alliance with the Soviet Union, Hollywood had never been much of a radical hotbed. The movie industry had released only a handful of films that were overtly sympathetic to Moscow. But other factors made Hollywood an enticing target for

HUAC. Jewish immigrants headed several of the eight major studios. Most had rejected their ethnic roots, Anglicized their names, and made movies celebrating an idealized America. Nevertheless, the anti-Semitic John Rankin found them an irresistible target, and Thomas was eager to generate publicity.

Communism had made inroads among only a small number of screenwriters. Poorly paid and frequently at odds with studio heads, the writers had formed a left-leaning union, the Screen Writers Guild. Studio bosses like Jack Warner and Sam Goldwyn hoped that by cooperating with congressional Red hunters, they could crush the guild and demonstrate their own patriotism. Warner, for example, complained to the committee about screenwriters who poked fun at the American political system or attempted to arouse sympathy for the "Indians and the colored folk."

The committee subpoenaed testimony from ten writers and directors it considered suspicious, including Dalton Trumbo, Ring Lardner, Jr., and John Howard Lawson. Several of the group were current or past Communist Party members. Expecting a sympathetic Supreme Court, dominated by Roosevelt appointees, to overturn any contempt citation from Congress, all of these writers and directors refused to testify, citing the First Amendment's protection of speech and political association. But the deaths of several members of the Roosevelt Court, and Truman's selection of more conservative replacements, changed the odds. The high court affirmed the convictions for contempt of Congress, and the writers and directors went to jail for terms of up to one year. As a small solace, HUAC's chairman, J. Parnell Thomas, was convicted of taking salary kickbacks from his staff and joined writer Ring Lardner, Jr., in prison.

Following the Hollywood hearings, studios pledged not to hire Communists. They created a blacklist of screen and television actors, writers, and directors who had either refused to cooperate with congressional investigators or had been named as suspect in someone else's testimony. Soon publications such as *Red Channels* listed the names of hundreds of artists, who found themselves locked out of jobs.

As the anti-Communist hysteria mounted, many public schools and universities required teachers to sign loyalty oaths or face summary dismissal. Labor unions purged their rolls of suspected Communists. The Catholic church, spurred by Francis Cardinal Spellman of New York, called on the faithful to combat the "aggression of enemies within." America would not be safe, the cardinal declared in 1949, "until every Communist cell is removed from within our own government, our own institutions, and not until every [Communist] country is returned to democratic leadership."

In 1948 the HUAC began its most famous campaign against a particular individual. For several years Whittaker Chambers, an editor at

Time, had been telling various government officials that he had been part of a Soviet espionage ring in the mid-1930s. Chambers claimed that members of the Roosevelt administration fed him material to pass on to Moscow. According to his account, he lost faith in communism after 1937 and became an avid Christian. Anxious to confess past sins, Chambers eventually told his story to Congressman Richard M. Nixon and other members of the HUAC. In August 1948 they presented him to the public.

In his initial testimony, Chambers described the espionage ring and mentioned that former State Department official Alger Hiss was a secret Communist, though not among those passing information. When Hiss fought back with a libel suit, Chambers counterattacked by naming Hiss as one of the informants.

In contrast to the disheveled and nervous Chambers, Hiss seemed a paragon of charm, eloquence, and professional accomplishments. He had worked for several New Deal agencies before rising in the State Department hierarchy, had attended the Yalta conference, and had helped organize the founding meeting of the United Nations. He had never been an influential policymaker, however, because his responsibilities lay in administrative and legal matters. After the war he had left the State Department to head the prestigious Carnegie Endowment for International Peace.

When Hiss first responded to the allegations, he denied even knowing Chambers. Following his persuasive rebuttal, some of the HUAC panel thought the committee had been embarrassed. Then California's Richard Nixon, who had won office in 1946 by linking his opponent to "subversive elements," took up the apparently lost cause. He arranged a face-to-face meeting between Chambers and Hiss, coaxing from the latter an admission that he had known Chambers under a different name—a real possibility, as Chambers had used many aliases. Subsequently it became clear that the two men had met several times during the 1930s.

The Republican party pushed the case with new vigor after November 1948, when, despite predictions, Harry Truman defeated Republican Thomas Dewey for the presidency. Nixon urged Chambers to escalate his charges. The HUAC and the FBI provided Chambers with derogatory information on Hiss; Chambers used the information to construct a new accusation, that Hiss had passed government secrets to him up until 1937 or 1938. To prove the point, he and Nixon accompanied reporters to Chambers's Maryland farm (later designated a National Historic Site by President Ronald Reagan), where Chambers reached into a hollow pumpkin and extracted several rolls of microfilm. The FBI determined that the film and associated papers (dubbed, collectively, the Pumpkin Papers) were secret documents, many of them retyped on a machine owned by the Hiss family. Al-

In 1950 Congressman Richard Nixon took grim satisfaction from learning that a federal jury had convicted Alger Hiss of perjury. *UPI/Bettmann Archive.*

though the statute of limitations on espionage had lapsed, a federal grand jury indicted Hiss for lying about his Communist affiliations and contacts with Chambers. Hiss's reticence about his relationship with Chambers, and the fact that some documents appeared to have been typed on Hiss's home typewriter, undermined the defense. Hiss never offered a convincing explanation of how the documents came to be typed on his machine.

The trial jury deadlocked in 1949. The government retried Hiss before a second jury, which convicted him on perjury charges in January 1950. Alger Hiss went to jail maintaining that the FBI had built a type-writer similar to his own and used it to forge the incriminating documents. Chambers went on to write *Witness,* a best-selling account of his troubled life, and to finger several other government officials as spies. Nixon parlayed his fame into a California Senate seat in 1950 and the vice-presidential slot two years later.

The Chambers-Hiss case became a political morality play for liberals and conservatives. Republicans felt they had proved a conspiracy. When Truman initially dismissed the HUAC's case against Hiss as a red herring, he drove Republicans wild. They believed that Secretary of State Dean Acheson, a friend of Alger's brother Donald, showed his true colors by vowing not to turn his back on Hiss after the conviction. This led Richard Nixon to complain that for years "traitors in the high councils of our own government have made sure that the deck is stacked on the Soviet side of the diplomatic tables." But Democrats who complained about Republican redbaiting had to account for Truman's own anti-Communist rhetoric and his promotion of the government loyalty program that legitimized the scare in the first place.

In February 1950, British police arrested Klaus Fuchs, an émigré German scientist, who confessed to being part of a spy ring that had passed secrets to the Soviets from the American nuclear laboratory at Los Alamos, New Mexico. By the summer of 1950 evidence from Fuchs led to the arrest of American Communists Julius and Ethel Rosenberg, who were charged with heading the conspiracy.

At a sensational and highly publicized trial, the Rosenbergs denied committing espionage, even though a relative who had worked at Los Alamos confessed to giving Julius information during the Second World War. After sifting the evidence for years, many historians concluded that Julius Rosenberg probably did pass a variety of industrial secrets to the Soviets, but the atomic data seem to have been relatively unimportant. Among those who spied for the Soviets, Fuchs probably passed on the most important information. Whatever the truth may have been, the two Rosenbergs were convicted, and in 1953 they died in the electric chair. Fuchs and several other confederates were sentenced to prison.

In retrospect, it seems clear that neither domestic subversion nor American Communists presented much of a threat to the republic. In the heightened atmosphere of the early 1950s, however, both government officials and ordinary Americans worried that traitors were giving the Kremlin vital data. After Fuchs's arrest, Indiana Senator Homer Capehart, a Republican, rose to ask, "How much more are we going to have to take? Fuchs and Acheson and Hiss and hydrogen bombs threatening outside and New Dealism eating away at the vitals of the nation. In the name of Heaven, is this the best America can do?"

In the charged anti-Communist climate of the early Cold War, immigration was often seen as a threat to America. The quota, or national origins, system established in the 1920s allowed a small number of people from western Europe to immigrate to the United States but restricted most others.

Shortly after the end of the Second World War, pressures mounted to amend these restrictions. The tragic condition of more than a million displaced persons (DPs) in postwar Europe proved especially problematic. These refugees included some 200,000 Jewish survivors of the Holocaust, ethnic Germans pushed out of Eastern Europe, and anti-Communist Latvians, Estonians, and Lithuanians who fled Soviet control. After intensive lobbying by citizens groups, in June 1948

Congress passed the Displaced Persons Act, which opened 200,000 slots for these people. An extension of the law let in an equal number in 1950.

Under continued pressure to revise the archaic quota system, in 1952 a reluctant Congress passed the Immigration and Nationality Act, also known as the McCarran-Walter Act. Senator Pat McCarran, co-author of the law, complained that the country already had too many "indigestible blocs" and did all he could to retain restrictions. Thus, while the law repealed the absolute ban on Asians, it set an absurdly low annual quota of one hundred persons for each Asian-Pacific nation. The law provided for the exclusion of suspected Communists and homosexuals and empowered the Justice Department to deport naturalized citizens accused of subversive activities. Passed over Truman's veto, this remained the basic U.S. immigration law until 1965.

Amid worries over international espionage and traitors at home, a hitherto obscure senator, Joseph R. McCarthy of Wisconsin, staked his claim to fame. A relative latecomer to the Red Scare, the senator so dominated the years from 1950 to 1954 with his antics that *McCarthyism* became the catchword for the era.

McCarthy came from a poor farm family and worked his way through high school, college, and law school. He won election to a county judgeship in the early 1940s by characterizing his opponent as senile. During the war he served as a Marine desk intelligence officer in the Pacific. He also flew several routine missions in the tail gunner's seat. He exaggerated this modest combat record in his 1946 Senate run, dubbing himself "tail-gunner Joe." A split within Republican ranks secured his nomination. He won the election over a weak Democrat, in a strong Republican year.

By 1950 journalists had given McCarthy the label "worst senator." His reputation sank even further when he spoke in favor of exonerating Nazi storm troopers convicted of massacring American prisoners of war. In need of a campaign issue, he borrowed reports of Communist sympathizers from his friend, California congressman Richard Nixon. On February 9, 1950, McCarthy told a gathering of Republican women in Wheeling, West Virginia, that America faced defeat because Dean Acheson, "this pompous diplomat in striped pants and a phony British accent," had turned over American foreign policy to subversives. "I have here in my hand," he declared, "a list of 205 [Communists] whose names are known to the secretary of state and who nevertheless are still working and shaping the policy of the State Department."

During the next week he repeated the speech several times, frequently changing the number of Communists. McCarthy soon labeled as Communists and traitors the "whole group of twisted-thinking

As lawyer Joseph Welch (hand on brow) listens, Senator Joseph McCarthy lectures a special Senate committee about the supposed Communist conspiracy in the United States. *UPI/Bettmann Newsphotos.*

New Dealers who have led America to near ruin at home and abroad."

McCarthy was a cynical opportunist who came to believe his own ravings. Taking advantage of Truman's own rhetoric and anti-Communist policies, which seemed to legitimize McCarthy's accusations of disloyalty, the Wisconsin senator and his supporters simply turned these charges against the Democrats. His conspiracy theory provided simple answers to complex questions. America did not need a Marshall Plan or NATO to win the Cold War, only a purge of Red sympathizers in its own government.

Democratic senators tried to expose McCarthy as a fraud during the spring of 1950. They established a committee, chaired by Democrat Millard Tydings of Maryland, that demanded that McCarthy document the charges of treason he had brought against diplomats. McCarthy's outrageous behavior turned the hearings into a circus. Each time he failed to provide details on one of his alleged "card-carrying Communists," the senator popped up with another name, just in time for reporters to insert it into the late editions of their newspapers. Ohio Republican senator Robert Taft and other supposedly responsible Republicans encouraged his guerrilla attacks. "If one case fails," Taft told him, "try another." The cascade of accusations and lies became difficult to refute, and the hearings ended in acrimony.

McCarthy's tactics and manipulation of the mass media presented journalists with an ethical problem. Journalist George Reedy recalled that covering McCarthy was a shattering experience for honest reporters, who felt obliged to take what McCarthy said at face value and give it coverage because he was a senator. Reedy knew that "Joe couldn't find a Communist in Red Square. He didn't know Karl Marx from Groucho." But for nearly four years McCarthy's charges paralyzed the State Department and terrified other government agencies. McCarthy's influence grew even stronger after the Republicans captured a Senate majority in November 1952.

Meanwhile, in the summer of 1950, the NSC-68 report, which advocated a massive increase in defense spending, languished on the president's desk while Truman pondered how to justify the cost of its proposals. Then, as one of Acheson's aides later remarked, "Korea came along and saved us."

THE KOREAN WAR AND ITS CONSEQUENCES

The North Korean invasion of South Korea on June 25, 1950, transformed the Cold War into a hot one. It also transformed American defense strategy and military spending. When the fighting stopped in 1953, American defense spending of about $50 billion per year approached the levels envisioned in NSC-68, and several hundred thousand American troops were stationed in Europe. Moreover, the war created a precedent of great significance: by committing the country to an extensive military effort without a congressional declaration of war, Truman set the pattern for Vietnam and other American military involvements in the following decades.

In August 1945, Soviet and American military planners divided the Korean peninsula, a Japanese colony since 1910, into temporary occupation zones north and south of the thirty-eighth parallel. When Moscow and Washington fell out, the division hardened. The Soviets sponsored a Communist regime, the Democratic People's Republic of Korea, led by veteran Korean Communist Kim Il Sung, north of the dividing line. In the South, the United States supported a right-wing government, the Republic of Korea, led by Syngman Rhee, a Korean exile who had lived in the United States for decades. Soviet and American occupation forces departed by 1949, leaving behind rival regimes, each claiming the right to rule an undivided Korea. Violence within and between both states was so common that between 1945 and 1949 an estimated 100,000 Koreans died in political strife.

"From the standpoint of military security," the Joint Chiefs of Staff wrote in 1947, the United States had "little strategic interest in maintaining the present troops and bases in Korea." For political reasons, however, State Department planners worried that abandoning the

South Korean government would be interpreted as a betrayal of U.S. friends and allies in the Far East. Whatever their misgivings about South Korea, American decision makers reacted to the North Korean invasion as if it were a direct Soviet challenge to Western security, rather than a civil war in a divided country. Although Stalin approved Kim Il Sung's invasion plan and provided him weapons, Moscow's involvement was limited. Evidence from Chinese and Soviet archives suggests that Kim Il Sung lobbied his patrons in Moscow and Beijing to support his attack on the South, and they agreed only after Kim assured them he would win quickly and not provoke American intervention. Stalin and Mao probably believed that a unified Korea would counterbalance their traditional enemy, Japan, which was then being rebuilt and rearmed by the United States. American policymakers focused on the Soviet threat in the region and largely dismissed the Korean origins of the war.

During the crucial days after the North Korean invasion, the Soviet delegate to the United Nations was boycotting UN meetings in order to protest America's refusal to seat the Chinese Communist delegation. Thus, with no Russian opposition, the United States was able to secure quick United Nations support for military aid to South Korea. On June 27 the Security Council called on United Nations members to furnish assistance to South Korea "to repel the armed attack and to restore international peace and security in the area." The same day, Truman ordered American air and naval forces into Korea, and three days later he sent ground forces as well. Congress was not asked to declare war; in fact, Truman referred to the military intervention as a "police action."

When the United Nations gave its imprimatur to sending in a joint force under an American commander, Truman assigned this critical role to General Douglas MacArthur, who headed the occupation forces in Japan. Although a number of countries eventually sent token forces, 90 percent of the United Nations troops were American, and MacArthur received instructions from Washington to keep the United Nations uninvolved in strategy and tactics.

The rapid collapse of the South Korean army drew the United States into a central combat role. In the early weeks, American troops could do little more than maintain a toehold at the southern port of Pusan. But American planes and ships controlled the air and sea lanes, and from his headquarters in Tokyo General MacArthur assembled a large force to counterattack. On September 15, 1950, MacArthur supervised a daring amphibious assault behind enemy lines on the coastal city of Inchon (see map). Within two weeks American troops had driven the North Koreans out of the South and achieved the original goal of the war.

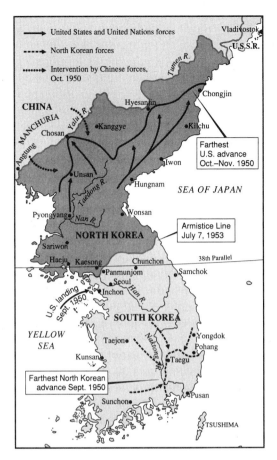

The Korean War, 1950–1953

The deceptively easy victory at Inchon, and the appearance of in-fallibility it gave MacArthur, persuaded President Truman to expand American goals. Instead of merely restoring the prewar border, Truman ordered MacArthur to cross north of the thirty-eighth parallel and unify the entire country under Rhee's regime. Truman and Secretary of State Acheson hoped this would deter future proxy aggression by Stalin and deflate Republicans who had accused the administration of "appeasement" in Asia.

From the opening round MacArthur chafed at talk of limited war, which brought only limited glory, and called for a crusade to crush the Communist regimes in Korea and China. The general confided to an aide his obsession with victory in a wider war and his hope that the Chinese Communists would provide a pretext for the United

States to expand the conflict. He would then "deliver such a crushing defeat it would be one of the decisive battles of the world, a disaster so great it would rock Asia and perhaps turn back communism."

Truman several times considered firing the general, whom he had earlier ridiculed as a "stuffed shirt, . . . play actor and bunco man." But as a potential Republican presidential candidate—he had sought the nomination in 1944 and 1948—MacArthur had to be treated with care. He could not be recalled without provoking a tremendous reaction among the many Americans who regarded him as a hero.

During the fall of 1950, administration officials actually worried more about the war ending too quickly, before Congress funded the NSC-68 proposals, than about its escalating out of control. Washington all but ignored warnings from the Chinese during October 1950 that American forces should not cross the thirty-eighth parallel into North Korea or approach the Yalu River, which separated North Korea from Manchuria, China's industrial heartland. MacArthur, like Truman, dismissed Chinese threats to defend North Korea as a bluff. During an October conference on Wake Island, the general assured the president that the war was practically won. If the Chinese dared enter the war, MacArthur predicted, there would be the "greatest slaughter."

In November 1950 Chinese troops stunned MacArthur—and Americans at home—by crossing into North Korea and driving American forces south to the thirty-eighth parallel in a humiliating retreat. MacArthur told the Joint Chiefs of Staff that he faced an entirely new war, one that could only be won if he received massive reinforcements, troops from Taiwan, and permission to attack China by air and by sea.

Most civilian and military officials in Washington disagreed. In their minds the real danger remained the Soviet threat to Europe and Japan. George Marshall, the former army chief of staff and secretary of state, recently appointed as secretary of defense, warned that Russia would be happy to see American and Chinese forces slaughter each other in a strategic backwater like Korea. Officials considered, but rejected, using the atomic bomb. Few appropriate military targets existed in North Korea, and ineffective battlefield use of the bomb might undermine its value as a deterrent threat. Using it against Chinese cities would be immensely destructive and, diplomats concluded, would almost certainly bring the Soviets into the war.

Once China entered the war and the front line bogged down, the public showed little sympathy for the limited aims of preserving South Korea and building up NATO and Japanese security. Soldiers complained they did not want to "die for a tie." Senator McCarthy insisted that Democratic sabotage had led to "American boys [lying]

American troops head toward the battle front in Korea as peasants flee the fighting. The war killed and wounded millions of Koreans. *UPI/Bettmann Newsphotos.*

dead in the mud [with] their faces shot away by Communist machine guns." Senator Taft accused Truman of violating United States law and the Constitution by sending troops to Korea without formal congressional approval. After less than a year of fighting, nearly two-thirds of the American public expressed dissatisfaction with the administration's handling of the war.

In the spring of 1951 the battle lines in Korea had stabilized; American forces had succeeded in stopping the Chinese army near the thirty-eighth parallel, without resort to atomic weapons or attacks on China. But when Truman prepared to send Mao a peace feeler in March 1951, MacArthur sabotaged it by demanding China's surrender. The general followed this with a letter to Republican congressman Joseph Martin in which he agreed with the politician's charge that Truman was guilty of the murder of American boys. Calling again for a wider war against China, MacArthur asserted, "There is no substitute for victory."

Outraged by MacArthur's grandstanding, Truman decided to recall him. On April 11 the president sacked MacArthur and replaced him with General Matthew Ridgway, the field commander who had blunted the Chinese drive south. Republican politicians were appalled by this rebuff. Senator Richard Nixon remarked that the "happiest group in the country are the Communists and their stooges."

On April 19, after arriving home to huge parades in his honor, MacArthur told both houses of Congress that Truman's policy of confining the war to Korea condemned all Asia to Communist rule. He brought the audience to tears by closing with the lyrics of an old army song, "Old Soldiers Never Die, They Just Fade Away." Although he obviously hoped *he* would not fade away, the general was stunned by how rapidly the public lost interest in him.

During inconclusive Senate hearings that summer into the general's recall, China agreed to peace talks. Nevertheless, the talking and fighting continued for two more years, until July 1953. In Chapter 4 we will see how the Eisenhower administration used force and compromise to secure an armistice restoring the boundary close to its prewar location. By then, over thirty thousand Americans and more than a million Korean and Chinese soldiers had died.

The Korean War set a precedent for American military intervention. It established the idea that the United States could and would engage in direct combat to preserve allied regimes against Communist-led aggression, even in far-flung corners of the world. Although some of Truman's critics charged that national defense should concentrate on regions closer to home, the administration's view prevailed. Further, by asserting his right to commit troops without explicit congressional authorization—and by overcoming the few opponents who challenged this notion—Truman defined a presidential prerogative that later inhabitants of the White House would use with increasing frequency.

TWILIGHT OF THE TRUMAN YEARS

Public resentment over the stalemate in Korea and the recall of MacArthur was not the only trouble Truman faced in 1951 and 1952. A series of petty scandals put his administration on the defensive. Truman appointees in several government agencies were condemned as bribe takers, "five-percenters" who awarded government contracts in exchange for 5 percent kickbacks. White House aide General Harry Vaughn confessed to accepting seven deep freezers as gifts from a contractor. And Senator McCarthy continued to accuse the administration of coddling Communists.

In mid-1950, Senator Estes Kefauver, a Tennessee Democrat, tried to deflect attention from the Red Scare by investigating organized crime. In dramatic televised hearings, he called witnesses who described an international criminal conspiracy nearly as frightening as communism—the Mafia. The public loved the parade of thugs Kefauver hauled before the television cameras. The attempt to divert attention from McCarthy failed, however, when the Korean War broke out. To make matters worse, Kefauver revealed links between mobsters and many Democratic city bosses.

The war issue, combined with charges of Democratic corruption and subversion, doomed the party of the retiring president. Republican Dwight D. Eisenhower beat Democrat Adlai Stevenson in a landslide, and Republican legislative candidates rode his coattails into slender control of both houses of Congress.

CONCLUSION

"I suppose," President Truman told the American people a few days before he left office in 1953, "that history will remember my term . . . as the years when the Cold War began to overshadow our lives. I have had hardly a day in office that has not been dominated by this all-embracing struggle—this conflict between those who love freedom and those who would lead the world back into slavery and darkness."

By the time Harry Truman left office, the basic outlines of American Cold War policy were firmly established. To contain the perceived Soviet threat and rebuild world trade, the United States had expanded its military budget, extended its bases worldwide, and committed itself to an ongoing nuclear arms race. It generously assisted Western Europe and Japan with the Marshall Plan and other aid programs. Through NATO, the CIA, and the National Security Council, it had institutionalized the Cold War. Most important, it had established the principle that America would intervene—with aid, with airplanes, or if necessary with American troops—whenever it appeared that the Soviet Union, China, or any of their clients were trying to extend Communist influence.

As the United States and the Soviet Union struggled to ensure their own security, each denounced the other's alleged aggressive intentions. Stalin and Truman both oversimplified complex problems; they blamed each other for many of the economic and political crises that afflicted postwar Europe and Asia. Historians have debated for years about the extent to which history might have been different if the two sides had understood one another better.

In Western Europe and Japan, at least, the United States largely succeeded in winning the Cold War by the early 1950s. But the frustrations of the Korean conflict, along with the fierce anti-Communism that Truman himself had helped to spawn, contributed to the Democrats' fall from power in 1952 and expanded competition between the United States and the Soviet Union in other parts of the world. ■

F U R T H E R   R E A D I N G

On the Truman presidency, see: Robert J. Donovan, *Conflict and Crisis: The Presidency of Harry S. Truman, 1945–48* (1977) and *Tumultuous Years: The Presidency of Harry S. Truman, 1949–53* (1982); Alonzo S. Hamby, *Beyond the New Deal: Harry S. Truman and American Liberalism* (1973); David McCullough, *Truman* (1992); Norman D. Markowitz, *The Rise and Fall of the People's Century: Henry A. Wallace and American Liberalism, 1941–48* (1973). On the Red Scare and McCarthyism, see: David Caute, *The Great Fear* (1977); Athan Theoharis, *Seeds of Repression: Harry S. Truman and the Origins of McCarthyism* (1971); Richard Gid Powers, *Secrecy and Power: The Life of J. Edgar Hoover* (1987); William L. O'Neill, *A Better World: Stalinism and American Intellectuals* (1983); Richard M. Freeland, *The Truman Doctrine and the Origins of McCarthyism* (1972); David M. Oshinsky, *A Conspiracy So Immense: The World of Joe McCarthy* (1983); Thomas C. Reeves, *The Life and Times of Joe McCarthy* (1982); Ellen W. Schrecker, *No Ivory Tower: McCarthyism in the Universities* (1986); Richard Fried, *Nightmare in Red: The McCarthy Era in Perspective* (1990). On the Cold War, see: Melvyn Leffler, *A Preponderance of Power: National Security, The Truman Administration, and the Cold War* (1991); Martin Sherwin, *A World Destroyed* (1975); Walter Isaacson and Evan Thomas, *The Wise Men: Six Friends and the World They Made* (1986); Paul Boyer, *By the Bomb's Early Light* (1990); Gregg Herken, *The Winning Weapon* (1981); David Holloway, *Stalin and the Bomb* (1994); Michael Hogan, *The Marshall Plan* (1987); Daniel Yergin, *A Shattered Peace* (1977); John Gaddis, *The United States and the Origins of the Cold War, 1941–47* (1972); Robert M. Blum, *Drawing the Line* (1982); Michael Schaller, *The American Occupation of Japan: The Origins of the Cold War in Asia* (1985). On the Korean War, see: Bruce Cumings, *The Origins of the Korean War* (2 Vols.: 1981, 1990); Michael Schaller, *Douglas MacArthur: The Far Eastern General* (1989); Callum A. MacDonald, *Korea* (1987); Burton I. Kauffman, *The Korean War* (1986). On immigration, see: David Reimers, *Still the Golden Door* (1992); Leonard Dinnerstein, *America and the Survivors of the Holocaust* (1982).

3

America at Home, 1945–1960

In the immediate aftermath of the war, Americans were glad to turn their attention to domestic matters. Young people were eager to return to peacetime jobs and raising families. The economy continued to grow. With money in their pockets, Americans rushed to new homes in suburbia, started having children in record numbers, and went on a spree of consumer buying, snapping up home appliances, automobiles, and the newfangled electronic gadgets called televisions.

By 1953, most Americans believed they had entered an era of well-deserved stability and prosperity. The "fifties" as a distinct era began with the election of General Dwight D. Eisenhower to the presidency and ended in 1961 when John F. Kennedy entered the White House. The Korean War and McCarthyism faded, Soviet dictator Joseph Stalin died, and the overwhelmingly popular Eisenhower brought a sense of security to American life.

Many of the era's symbols, such as hula hoops, Davy Crockett caps, rock 'n' roll, exaggerated automobile tail fins, and Disneyland, suggest the affluence and cultural complacency of the period. Especially for the white middle class, confidence in material progress and the perfectibility of American society coexisted alongside a fervent anti-Communist ideology and anxiety about nuclear destruction.

Following the turbulence of the last two decades, the home seemed a safe haven. Just as containment of communism characterized American foreign policy, a kind of domestic containment, stressing traditional gender roles and domesticity, dominated American social life. In the ideal suburban family, the American mother kept house and raised the children while her husband went off to a white-collar job. The kids grew up with a strong sense of American values.

But beneath the surface stability, the 1950s were years of change and upheaval. Not only did continued population movements, the automobile, television, and advanced technology change the face of American life, but critics began to complain that the apparent consensus of American society was hollow. American youth developed its own subculture, centered on rock-'n'-roll music, and it alarmed their elders. Meanwhile, the civil rights struggle erupted in the South, demanding that Americans confront issues that had too long been ignored.

THE AFFLUENT SOCIETY

Americans hoped that the end of World War II would mean a return to normal life, solidifying the economic gains brought on by wartime mobilization. Many New Deal economic programs continued, though not all Washington policymakers were willing to admit to perpetuating them. Whereas the Truman administration had unabashedly, and sometimes successfully, followed in FDR's footsteps, Eisenhower promoted massive government programs and public works while insisting that government ought to play a more passive role in the marketplace.

With the coming of peace, the first order of business was demobilization. Mustering out the 12 million GIs who had served in the war proved relatively easy. But the demobilized GIs returned to an economy in which the booming production of war goods had ceased. Even before the war ended, mass layoffs had begun at aircraft plants and in other key wartime industries. Within a few days of Japan's surrender, nearly 2 million more were out of work. With vivid memories of the Great Depression, many Americans feared a return of widespread unemployment.

However, returning servicemen had less difficulty finding jobs than many experts predicted. A significant number of ex-servicemen replaced women workers, for the industrial layoffs had included about 3 million women. Labor unions and factory owners followed the suggestion of a southern senator who called on Congress to force "wives and mothers back to the kitchen." Both private employers and the civil service gave veterans preference over other job applicants. Even though 75 percent of women who wished to continue to work eventually found postwar employment, they had to settle for clerical, sales, and light manufacturing work rather than more lucrative factory jobs. Typically, wages declined from about $50 to $37 per week for white women and to half that for black women. Men experienced a far smaller drop. Still, in 1950 nearly one-third of all women held paying jobs, up from 27 percent before the war.

The huge savings pool of nearly $140 billion that had accumulated since 1941 cushioned the transition to a peacetime economy. Consumers rushed to buy the cars, appliances, clothes, food, and housing that had been unavailable since 1942. The long postwar upswing in consumerism had begun—the transformation of America into what we now call the consumer society.

The American economy performed well during the Truman years. The steep inflation of 1946 to 1947 leveled off, reappearing only briefly early in the Korean War, and the gross national product rose an average of 4 percent annually. Meanwhile the immediate postwar surge in unemployment proved transitory, and the specter of massive unemployment never materialized. The number of Americans with jobs increased from a wartime high of 53 million in 1945 to 60 million in 1948 and 64 million by 1952.

With modest success, Truman's economic advisers tried to commit the federal government to a policy of full employment, so that

Breakfast with the family while clothes wash super clean

Set the dial at WASH—add a bit of soap—and your time's your own. The Bendix Automatic Washer does the work—all by itself. It fills itself with water—washes clothes—changes its water—rinses 3 times—damp drys clothes—cleans itself—drains itself—shuts itself off. No upset house. No putting hands in water. No need to hurry back.

Only the tumble-action principle of the BENDIX washes clothes so clean...so gently...with so little hot water and soap...*and no work at all!*

Postwar housewives welcomed appliances that made their work easier but no less time-consuming. *Cooper-Hewitt, National Design Museum, Smithsonian Inst./Art Resource, NY.*

everyone "able to work and seeking work" would find a job. A Full Employment Bill, introduced in Congress in 1945, would have empowered the president to take actions to stimulate the economy in times of recession. However, by the time Congress passed an amended version known as the Employment Act of 1946, the bill had been so watered down that it merely supported the principle of creating jobs.

Leon Keyserling, Truman's most influential economic adviser, believed that wealth could be distributed best by the private sector through consumer prosperity. Government should create demand—and thus jobs—by pumping more spending power into the economy through tax, welfare, and spending policies. As one leading economist put it, "consumption is the frontier of the future." By 1949 these economists were promoting new defense spending as a key to growth.

The line between defense spending and welfare, or what have more recently been termed "entitlement programs," is not always so clear. For example, veterans' benefits help the country staff its military establishment by providing incentives for enlistment; at the same time, such programs benefit a particular group of citizens. Prodded by President Roosevelt and the American Legion (which counted nearly half the House and Senate, Harry Truman, and twenty-six governors among its members), Congress had agreed in 1944 to establish benefits for returning soldiers.

The Servicemen's Readjustment Act of 1944, or the GI Bill, as nearly everyone called it, benefited millions of veterans and their families. The program provided veterans with temporary unemployment benefits, hiring preferences in civil service jobs, new hospitals and health benefits, low-interest loans to start businesses and purchase homes, and tuition and living stipends for college and vocational education.

Demobilized soldiers who could not find work received $20 per week—more than equivalent to the minimum wage of 40 cents per hour—for up to a year. This program alone paid out nearly $4 billion during the postwar years. Those pursuing a college education received $110 a month, plus an allowance for dependents and payment of tuition, fees, and books.

Before 1945 few people of moderate means could attend college. The flow of veterans into both public and private universities created a far more democratic system of higher education—a change with far-reaching social consequences. Over 2 million students, or half of the total male enrollment at institutions of higher learning, attended college on the GI Bill. Nearly half of the veterans were married, which forced colleges to drop their prohibitions against enrollment of married students. Couples were housed in Quonset huts, trailers, and converted fraternity houses. As the mass demand for higher education grew, state legislatures funded public universities more generously than before the war. Federal and state dollars built new libraries, classrooms, dormitories, and laboratories.

In addition to those attending college, nearly 6 million men went to technical and vocational schools on the GI Bill. By 1947, the total outlay for veterans' education had reached $2.25 billion, and that was just the beginning. When the program ended in 1956, the Veterans Administration (VA) had spent about $14 billion on schooling—compared to nothing before the war. The skills acquired by this generation boosted job mobility and incomes, allowing the government to recoup much of its outlay through higher income taxes.

Because a comparatively small number of women had served in uniform, women received few direct educational benefits. Although more women attended college after the war than before, they were steered away from careers that would place them in competition with men. Active sex discrimination and quotas continued to prevent women from enrolling in law, business, and medical schools. Harvard Business School, for example, did not admit women until 1963.

GEOGRAPHIC DISTRIBUTION OF UNITED STATES POPULATION, 1930–1970 (IN PERCENTAGES)

Year	Central Cities	Suburbs	Rural Areas and Small Towns
1930	31.8	18.0	50.2
1940	31.6	19.5	48.9
1950	32.3	23.8	43.9
1960	32.6	30.7	36.7
1970	31.4	37.6	31.0

Source: Adapted from U.S. Bureau of the Census, *Decennial Censuses, 1930–1970* (Washington, D.C.: U.S. Government Printing Office).

During the Truman years, white Americans flocked to suburbia (blacks and other people of color were often barred from buying homes in suburban enclaves.) Americans had begun leaving cities in the nineteenth century, but only after 1945 could the United States begin to be called a suburban nation. Between 1940 and 1970, the proportion of suburban dwellers increased from 19.5 to 37.6 percent (see table).

Up until 1945, the housing industry had focused on building custom homes or urban multifamily buildings. But housing prices in these units generally exceeded the $50 or so per month that most veterans could afford. After the war, the needs of veterans meshed with a new trend in the construction industry: the increasing dominance of large construction firms, those with over one hundred employees and building over one hundred houses per year. These companies discovered that they could operate profitably by building a great number of similar homes on large tracts of inexpensive, usually suburban, land.

Meanwhile, the National Association of Home Builders and the National Association of Realtors were lobbying to shape the federal housing policy that emerged during the late 1940s. By tradition, banks and other private lenders had followed restrictive mortgage procedures, often demanding 50 percent of the purchase price as a down payment and repayment of the balance within ten years. Following the war, however, the Federal Housing Administration (FHA) began insuring thirty-year bank mortgages with only a 5 to 10 percent down payment. The VA provided additional support under the GI Bill, so qualifying veterans could often take title for a token $1 down payment. By guaranteeing loan repayment, the FHA and VA persuaded private lenders to relax mortgage terms.

The result of these developments was a housing boom, particularly in suburbia. Housing starts jumped from 114,000 in 1944 to 1.7 million in 1950. By then, federal agencies insured more than a third of all mortgages—a figure that surpassed 40 percent by 1955. In addition to FHA and VA loan guarantees, the government's tax policy promoted housing growth by allowing a deduction for mortgage interest.

Levittown, named after builder William Levitt, became a synonym for suburban development. Levitt, a builder of luxury homes before 1941, pioneered prefabrication techniques for navy housing during the war. In 1947 he decided to mass-produce private homes that GIs would be able to afford. The first Levittown, a planned community of ten thousand homes, sprang from a 1,200-acre potato field on Long Island, New York. Larger projects followed in Pennsylvania and New Jersey.

In the words of one observer, Levitt made a "factory of the whole building site," doing for homes what Henry Ford had done for the automobile. Materials were precut and preassembled by teams of semi-skilled laborers and moved to lots when needed. Instead of hiring union painters and carpenters, Levitt trained workers to do specific tasks, such as spray painting or using power tools, on an assembly-line basis. The company bought its own forests, milled its own lumber, and bought standard-size kitchen and bathroom appliances in bulk to equip the new houses. At the height of Levittown construction, a house was completed every sixteen minutes. Construction costs were $10 a square foot, 30 percent below the industry standard. With a VA loan, a veteran could move into a new home for $56 per month, which was often less than the cost of renting an apartment. When one subdivision opened in 1949, fourteen hundred units sold in a single day.

The Levittown house, like Ford's Model T, set an affordable standard that made home ownership a reality for the postwar middle class. But Levittown was only the most conspicuous example of a widespread trend. Across the United States, surrounding its cities, new suburbs of similar-looking, middle-class houses began to appear. In a chaotic world, the freestanding, single-family, self-contained, all-electric suburban home was presented as a refuge. An associated phenomenon was the rise in suburban shopping centers, or malls; their number increased from eight to four thousand in the first postwar decade.

Suburbanization exacerbated racial segregation. Suburbia homogenized white society by mixing ethnic, social, and political groups that formerly had lived in separate urban neighborhoods. New institutions such as churches and civic clubs replaced extended families and kinship networks. Even though many architectural critics criticized suburbs, young families loved the new homes. Many looked

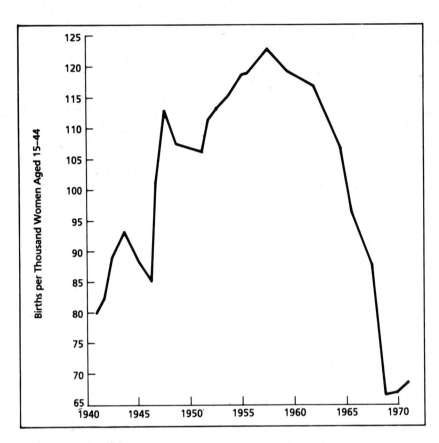

Birthrate, 1940–1970

forward to improving them and using their equity to trade up to fancier dwellings later.

By 1946, the nation was experiencing a baby boom that would last into the 1960s. The average number of children born to an American family increased from 2.4 to 3.2 between 1945 and 1957, when the boom peaked (see figure). The American population surged by 30 million in the 1950s, reaching 180 million by the end of the decade. When births peaked at 4.3 million in 1957, a third of all Americans were age 14 or younger. This created exceptional demands for new housing, appliances, toys, and schools. Between 1950 and 1960, total school enrollment in kindergarten through twelfth grade increased from 28 million to 42 million.

In previous decades, parenting manuals had described infants as nasty tyrants who, if indulged or overstimulated, would grow up with grave character disorders. Pediatrician Benjamin Spock challenged these assumptions in his 1946 *Book of Baby and Child Care*. Spock urged parents to have fun with their kids. He encouraged physical contact and emotional nurturing as keys to healthy development. The book sold over 20 million copies in ten years, and 40 million by 1990.

Even as young parents in suburbia read their Dr. Spock and enjoyed their electric kitchens, the same policies that promoted suburban growth were causing serious problems for cities, the poor, and minorities. The FHA gave preference to subsidizing single-family, detached homes in the $7,000 to $10,000 range. Until the 1960s, the FHA provided few loans to assist buyers in racially mixed neighborhoods or to improve existing multifamily housing . These redlining practices kept many African-Americans and other people of color out of the housing market and living in older, decaying urban neighborhoods. Meanwhile, minorities were barred from most suburban homes. In 1950, of 20 million suburban Americans, only 1 million were nonwhite. Levittown barred "members of other than the Caucasian race" from buying homes. A decade after the development opened, not one of the Long Island Levittown's 82,000 residents was black.

Public and private discrimination contributed to drawing a "white noose" around the increasingly nonwhite cities. As business firms and white families left the cities for the suburbs, they took with them the jobs and income that had contributed to urban tax revenues and employment. Generally speaking, the growth of suburbs around a city resulted in the decline of its economy. By 1960 the suburban population of 60 million equaled that of all urban areas. Except for the South and West, where rural-to-urban migration continued, most large cities either lost population or barely held steady during the 1950s.

Soon employment took the same route as the population. At first almost all suburbanites commuted to jobs in central cities, but by 1960 many worked closer to home. Suburban employment and manufacturing rose dramatically, while employment in the twenty-five largest U.S. cities declined about 7 percent during the decade. Downtown commercial districts lost business to suburban shopping centers surrounded by acres of parking lots.

The American population continued to shift west, with California, Florida, and Texas attracting many newcomers. The gains in urban population in the West and suburban population in the Northeast came partly at the expense of rural America. The number of agricultural workers fell to barely 6 percent of the population, down two-thirds since America entered the Second World War.

The rise of the suburbs had other lasting effects as well. One was the increased demand for cars and better roads. Between 1946 and 1950, domestic automobile production jumped from 2 million to

The thrill is pure Thunderbird . . .

By the 1950s, American culture was car culture. *Collection of Picture Research Consultants.*

6 million annually. By the 1950s, the highway lobby—an umbrella group of automobile makers, road builders, and trucking firms—began to pressure the federal government for a national highway system. Nine out of ten suburban families owned a car, compared to only six of ten urban households. Women driving station wagons full of children became emblems of suburban life.

On average, domestic auto manufacturers produced 7 to 8 million cars and trucks annually. By 1960 Americans had nearly 70 million vehicles on the road. Two-thirds of the nation's employees drove to work. In Los Angeles County alone, more cars plied the freeways than in all of Asia or South America.

These cars were not the staid models of the 1940s. Detroit built bigger, gaudier, more expensive machines than ever before. The public adored two- and three-tone models, tail fins, and wraparound windshields. Innovations like power steering, automatic transmissions, and air conditioning made cars more comfortable and convenient. Auto tourism became a major form of family leisure. Bobby Troupe's hit song "Get Your Kicks on Route 66" reflected Americans' love of the road. Families took cross-country trips to national parks and new amusement parks like Disneyland. Motel chains proliferated. So did other spin-off industries such as fast food restaurants and drive-in theaters.

Responding to demands from business, local governments, and auto-owning citizens, the federal government decided to upgrade the nation's inadequate highways. By 1956 a bipartisan movement in Congress, supported by organized labor, the construction industry, oil companies, car manufacturers, tire makers, and civil defense advocates (who argued that better roads would speed evacuation from cities in times of war), won passage of the National System of Defense Highways. This massive building program authorized the construction of forty thousand miles of new highways. Washington paid 90 percent of the initial $50 billion tab through excise taxes levied on tires and fuel, and the states paid the rest.

The interstate highway system dwarfed anything built by the New Deal. And although the title of the bill suggested the highways were needed primarily for defense purposes, the interstates' most important effects were social. By subsidizing the car culture with six thousand miles of city-to-suburb freeways while denying funds for inner-city mass transit, government promoted suburban development at the cities' expense.

The public's enthusiasm for the automobile allowed manufacturers to ignore their products' poor safety records and nonexistent fuel efficiency. The mounting highway death toll (forty thousand in 1959) elicited little concern, although a young Harvard law student, Ralph Nader, worried enough to begin probing auto safety as early as 1957. But the big Detroit automakers either ignored their few critics or dismissed them as deviants.

By the early 1960s, many urban planners and ordinary Americans began to question the wisdom of chopping up cities with smog-producing freeways while permitting mass transit to decay. But during the fifties nearly everyone celebrated public road subsidies for private automobiles. Gasoline was cheap, highways were "free," and America's future was on the road.

Leisure and entertainment in general were becoming big business. In 1947, radio still reigned as the nation's major source of information and entertainment. Out of some 38 million households, 34 million had at least one radio. Radio broadcasts brought news, music, comedy, melodrama, and soap operas to an immense audience.

Already, however, a newer electronic medium was poised to upstage radio. Considered an oddity when it was first invented in the 1920s, television had gestated for twenty years. In the late 1930s the National Broadcasting Company (NBC), an offshoot of David Sarnoff's Radio Corporation of America (RCA), began experimental commercial television broadcasts from New York. Only a few thousand people owned the 5-inch receivers, and there was little to watch on them anyway. Federal rules at the time limited the sale of

By the 1950s, television had joined the American family. *Courtesy of Motorola Museum of Electronics © 1995 Motorola, Inc.*

commercial advertising, which pays for the bulk of television programming today.

The war spurred technological progress in the mass production of high-quality electronics, which in turn made it possible to build better and cheaper television equipment. In 1946 the FCC licensed twenty-six new television stations to serve the public. Retooled factories hired many of the thousands of electronics workers trained during the war. Television sets remained both scarce and expensive for a time, and only a few programs were broadcast each night. Soon, however, enough television sets were produced that ordinary families could buy them. By 1949 about a million homes, mostly in large cities, received broadcasts from sixty-nine stations. Ten years later, six hundred stations reached 44 million households with televisions.

Television's influence on American life was soon manifest in ways both large and small. In 1948, both the Democrats and the Republicans held their presidential nominating conventions in Philadelphia because the city possessed a cable hookup that allowed viewing by an audience of 10 million. In cities with television stations, movie ticket sales plummeted, old-time vaudeville revues died, and attendance at live sporting events fell. "The Milton Berle Show," television's first great hit, attracted such large audiences that water pressure in cities dropped during the show's commercial breaks as viewers rushed to the toilet.

The television industry expanded quickly in the early 1950s, as the FCC sped up licensing procedures. As the size of TV sets increased, their quality improved and their price fell to an average of $200. By the time Eisenhower took office in 1953, half of all American homes had a set. For the rest of the decade sales ranged between 5 and 7 million units annually. By the early sixties, 90 percent of all homes had at least one receiver. As early as 1956, Americans spent more time watching television than working for wages.

At first the comedy shows, crime shows, Westerns, variety shows, quiz shows, and soap operas on television were like radio programs with scenery added. Some early comedy-variety offerings, like Sid Caesar's "Your Show of Shows" (1950–1954), provided quality writing and acting. A fair amount of sophisticated live drama aired through the mid-1950s on such shows as "Kraft Television Theater," "Playhouse 90," and "Studio One." But toward the end of the 1950s Hollywood began selling old movies to television and producing low-budget, made-for-TV movies. This effectively removed most original drama from television.

Among the most successful comedy shows of the 1950s was "I Love Lucy," which ran in several formats from 1951 through 1974 and became a model for many subsequent situation comedies, or sitcoms. Lucille Ball played Lucy Ricardo, the scatterbrained wife of Cuban-born band leader Ricky Ricardo, played by Desi Arnaz, her real-life husband. Each week Lucy and her friend Ethel Mertz schemed to get jobs, impress their husbands, and achieve respect. Their plans usually backfired, forcing Ricky and Fred Mertz to rescue their wives.

Because of technical limitations on live broadcasts and remote filming, news coverage was not a staple of television until the early 1960s. Still, Edward R. Murrow, a pioneer of radio and TV investigative journalism, produced some exceptionally good work for CBS, including an exposé of Senator Joseph McCarthy on "See It Now." But most television news came in a fifteen-minute format. As innovations such as the video camera made it possible to follow breaking stories, the television networks expanded nightly news coverage to half-hour broadcasts in 1963, promoting the programs heavily to win audience share.

Television generally provided entertainment, not intellectual enlightenment. "Howdy Doody," a lighthearted romp using marionettes and mock Indians, set the tone for children's programming. Westerns like "Hopalong Cassidy" and "The Lone Ranger" played to young viewers, before adult westerns such as "Gunsmoke" and "Maverick" came into vogue.

Soap operas and quiz shows dominated the daytime airwaves. Inexpensive to produce, they appealed to busy housewives, who could break up the household routine with TV viewing. "Queen for a Day," in which bedraggled women told hard-luck stories in return for prizes, merged the soap opera and quiz show formats.

In the evening, family-oriented sitcoms proliferated. The decade's big hits included "The Adventures of Ozzie and Harriet," "The Danny Thomas Show," "The Donna Reed Show," "Leave It to Beaver," "Father Knows Best," and "The Honeymooners." Except for the last, in which bus driver Ralph Kramden (Jackie Gleason) and his sewer-worker buddy Ed Norton (Art Carney) schemed to get rich— these were middle-class fables in which white suburban families with a homemaker mother and a breadwinning father lived pleasant lives. People of color appeared only as servants. Television's need to attract mass audiences to earn advertising revenue ensured that its content would appeal to the greatest possible number and that complex social or economic issues would not be discussed.

A quiz show scandal in 1959 tarnished television's reputation as the purveyor of clean values. In 1955 a few prime-time quiz shows with large cash prizes, such as "The $64,000 Question" and "Twenty-One," captured the public's fancy. In dramatic encounters, one or more contestants, isolated in glass booths, competed for cash prizes. To heighten the suspense, the questions were kept in bank vaults and brought to the studio by armed guards. Each week's winner proceeded to a new round, tougher questions, and bigger prizes. These shows attracted huge audiences and earned large profits for both the networks and sponsors. Producers often coached contestants on how to smile, grimace, fidget, and knit their brows while pondering the questions. Some contestants secretly received further help, including the answers to questions.

In 1956 Charles Van Doren, a young, articulate English professor at Columbia University, won $129,000 on "Twenty-One"—a great improvement on his $4,400 academic salary. NBC hired him as a consultant for $50,000 annually. Parents and teachers wrote to praise Van Doren as a role model for children. Two years later the bubble burst. In 1958 the man dethroned by Charles Van Doren complained to New York journalists that Van Doren had received answers in advance. Both a grand jury and a congressional subcommittee investigated the scandal. Van Doren first protested his innocence, but eventually he broke down and gave the investigating committee details of his cheating. The prospect of wealth and fame had corrupted him, Van Doren explained. In the wake of this scandal, networks canceled most of the quiz shows.

The scandal made many question the value of television. After all, TV had invaded the American home, taking center stage in the American living room. What happened when this new focus of family life lied to us? Should it be admired as a source of entertainment and information, despised as cultural pabulum, or feared for its demagogic potential? Just as social commentators disagree about television's worth in today's society, historians have mixed feelings about its contribution to the 1950s. Newton Minow, newly appointed chairman of the Federal Communications Commission (FCC), shocked a gathering of broadcast executives in 1961 by describing their industry as a vast wasteland.

Nowhere was the impact of television on popular culture clearer than in the area of sports. After the Second World War, professional and college sports assumed a growing significance in American life. By the late 1940s, professional leagues in basketball and ice hockey had joined those in baseball and football to provide increasing sports entertainment for an avid public. Sports took on the trappings of a secular religion as people gave vast significance to the fortunes of their favorite teams. In the suburbs, Little League baseball and football, modeled on the professional leagues, enrolled millions of children.

Television was part of this change, because it elevated players to unprecedented fame and gave fans a new and closer look at their idols. Initially TV cameras worked best in small arenas and other venues in which a single camera could pan the playing area. Boxing, wrestling, and roller derby fared well on TV, as did baseball. As the technology evolved, multiple and remote cameras improved the coverage of football and basketball, and sports occupied a growing portion of the TV schedule. By the 1960s sports had become a major part of broadcasting. Television also became the key to sports profits, for TV payments soon exceeded the revenue from ticket sales.

Desegregation proceeded slowly in professional and college athletics. After Jackie Robinson broke baseball's color line in 1947, professional teams began to hire black athletes, but the pace varied from one sport to another. Some southern college basketball teams refused to recruit African-Americans or play against teams that did. Because the segregated programs gradually became uncompetitive, they were eventually forced to recruit blacks as well as whites.

As the nation's population shifted toward the West and the Sunbelt, the owners of professional teams began to move franchises to these areas, often provoking outcries from loyal fans. When baseball owner Walter O'Malley took his Brooklyn Dodgers to Los Angeles in the late 1950s, New Yorkers decried his betrayal and demanded a congressional investigation. But during the next decade many teams relocated. While the old fans protested, fans in the new cities hastened to the stadiums and arenas or watched the games on television.

THE POLITICS OF MODERATION

By the fall of 1946, a wave of strikes in the automobile, electrical, coal, and transportation industries, along with inflation and shortages in consumer goods, had eroded support for the Democratic party. Truman was regarded by many as a man out of his depth; only 32 percent of survey respondents approved of the president's performance.

The Republican party picked up eleven Senate and fifty-six House seats in the November election, to hold a majority in both houses of Congress for the first time since 1930. Senator Robert Taft, nicknamed "Mr. Republican," emerged as the informal head of the party in Congress. Long critical of New Deal domestic and foreign programs, Taft denounced the "corrupting idea that we can legislate prosperity, legislate equality, legislate opportunity." In the past, he claimed, opportunity and equality had come from "free Americans freely working out their destiny."

Despite their new control of Congress, the Republicans had only modest success in unraveling the New Deal legacy. They did, however, effect significant changes in labor law. Moves to limit the right to strike and to abolish the closed shop—an arrangement that had compelled workers to join unions—began during the Second World War. Building on such antilabor sentiment, Senator Taft and New Jersey Republican congressman Fred A. Hartley introduced a law to curb union power. The Taft-Hartley Act of 1947, which passed over Truman's veto, outlawed the closed shop, barred secondary boycotts, made unions liable for a variety of monetary damages, established procedures for decertification elections, and permitted the president to impose an eighty-day cooling-off period in labor disputes, during which workers could not strike. Taft-Hartley also required union officials to sign affidavits proclaiming they were not communists. This requirement stirred up bitter internal feuding within labor ranks and encouraged public fears that left-wing labor activists were disloyal.

The law bolstered conservative labor leaders and discouraged new organizing drives, especially in the largely nonunion South, though it did not destroy existing unions that followed its provisions. The greatest impact of the Taft-Hartley Act was felt in the Sunbelt states of the South and West, where legislatures responded to business lobbying by passing right-to-work laws that barred making union membership a requirement for employment. To get out of union contracts, many labor-intensive industries, such as textiles, began to relocate to the Sunbelt.

Clearly, by the beginning of the 1950s national politics were swinging to the right. The question was, how far right? General Dwight D. Eisenhower, widely known by his nickname, "Ike," chose politics as a second career at age sixty-two. Despite this late beginning, he became one of the most popular and successful presidents in the postwar era. The public was reassured by his calming, grandfatherly style and seldom questioned his rather disengaged stewardship of domestic policy. Veteran journalist Walter Lippmann remarked, "Ike could be elected even if dead. All you would need [to do is] to prop him up in the rear seat of an open car and parade down Broadway."

Eisenhower was born in 1890 in Denison, Texas, into a large, pious, and poor family. He grew up in Abilene, Kansas, and attended West Point despite his parents' pacifism. He graduated in 1915, but because few promotions were available during the interwar period, he had risen only to the rank of major by 1939. With the start of the war in Europe, however, Eisenhower quickly ascended to prominence, helped by army chief of staff General George C. Marshall, who considered him among the most promising men in the army. By 1944 Eisenhower was a four-star general and commander of the Allied forces in the European theater. His ability to manage and conciliate the Allied armies sped victory and won him acclaim as a talented and humane leader.

After the war Eisenhower served successively as army chief of staff, president of Columbia University, and, during the Korean War, the first supreme commander of NATO. Ambitious but wary of politics, he rebuffed both Democratic and Republican invitations to seek the presidential nomination in 1948. Four years later he still coveted the White House but disdained the idea of campaigning for office, seeking instead a "draft" that would nominate him by acclamation.

Despite Eisenhower's wartime ties to Roosevelt, he held fairly conservative views on economics and social programs, favoring private enterprise over government intervention as a solution to most problems. He was, at the same time, a confirmed internationalist who supported containment of communism, the Marshall Plan, and the "Europe-first" orientation of the Truman administration. Eisenhower resented and feared the anti-NATO, "Asia-first" ideas of Republican presidential aspirants such as Senators Robert Taft and Joseph McCarthy and General Douglas MacArthur. Early in 1952 Eisenhower made his decision: he resigned his NATO command and entered the Republican primaries, securing enough delegates to defeat his chief rival, Taft, at the party's nominating convention. Eisenhower placated the Republican right by tapping California senator Richard M. Nixon as his vice-presidential running mate.

Eisenhower's campaign, an observer remarked, was "a masterpiece of evasion." He managed to calm fears that a Republican in the White House would roll back the achievements of the New Deal, and his war hero status seemed to provide assurance that he could handle foreign threats. When he promised that, if elected, he would "go to

Korea," voters interpreted it to mean that the general who had liberated Western Europe had a secret plan to end the Korean stalemate.

In contrast, the Democrats entered the campaign in disarray. Governor Adlai Stevenson of Illinois, a man of modest experience and reputation whose grandfather had served as vice president in the 1890s, received his party's nomination on the third ballot. Considered a liberal northerner, he tried to balance the ticket by choosing Senator John Sparkman of Alabama, a segregationist, as his running mate.

Stevenson, who wrote many of his own speeches, proved an extremely witty and articulate candidate. Neither in 1952 nor during his 1956 rematch, however, did he propose a feasible alternative to the Cold War or stirring solutions to unresolved domestic problems. Nor did Stevenson elicit much support from the large proportion of union members and minorities among the Democratic rank and file. Moreover, many Catholic Democrats objected to his earlier divorce.

Stevenson's eloquence and intellect, as well as his large, bald pate, led journalists to dub him an "egghead." Many voters disliked his uncanny ability to turn easy answers into difficult questions. He stressed that America faced tough choices and uncertain prospects. The Republicans, meanwhile, exploited public frustration with the Korean War and linked the Democrats to subversion and corruption. Vice-presidential candidate Nixon, who had won election to Congress by slandering his opponents as Communists, labeled Stevenson "Adlai the appeaser" and "a Ph.D. graduate of Dean Acheson's Cowardly College of Communist Containment."

The most exciting moment in the campaign occurred when allegations surfaced that Nixon had pocketed $18,000 in campaign contributions. Eisenhower considered dumping his young running mate until Nixon appeared on television with his family to deny any impropriety. In a maudlin but effective performance, Nixon admitted accepting one personal gift, a cocker spaniel named Checkers, on behalf of his daughters. He refused to give up the dog and suggested, in what became known as "the Checkers speech," that only Communists opposed him.

In the November election more Americans—over 61 million—voted than ever before. They opted for change, giving Eisenhower 34 million votes to Stevenson's 27 million (see map, page 109). White voters alarmed by the Democrats' connection to the civil rights movement gave the Republicans four states in the formerly solid Democratic South. Overall the Republicans won narrow majorities of nine seats in the House and one seat in the Senate.

Personally, Eisenhower seemed well suited to the conservative branch of his party. Whether on the golf course or at cabinet meetings, Eisenhower felt most comfortable in the presence of white, middle-aged corporate executives. He chose businessmen, financiers, and

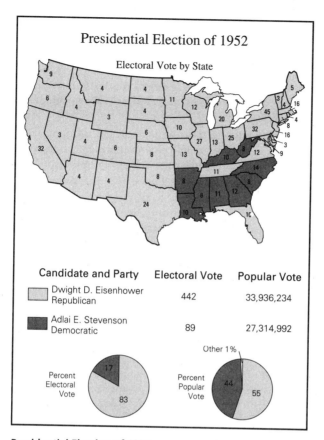

Presidential Election of 1952

Electoral Vote by State

Candidate and Party	Electoral Vote	Popular Vote
Dwight D. Eisenhower Republican	442	33,936,234
Adlai E. Stevenson Democratic	89	27,314,992

Percent Electoral Vote: 17, 83

Percent Popular Vote: Other 1%, 44, 55

Presidential Election of 1952

corporate lawyers for 76 percent of his high government appointments—nearly twice the figure of the Roosevelt and Truman administrations.

Nevertheless, Eisenhower had many disputes with conservative Republicans, including Senators Joseph McCarthy, Robert Taft, and William Knowland. He did not equate the GOP with patriotism or the Democrats with treason, and he expended little energy campaigning for other Republicans. This stance probably contributed to his public popularity, but it did not endear him to the hard-liners in his party.

Even more important, Eisenhower had no intention of trying to roll back the New Deal legacy—long a cherished plan of conservative Republicans. In his first term, in fact, he approved the extension of Social Security benefits to 10 million additional workers and signed a law raising the minimum wage from 75 cents to $1 per hour. He also reluctantly accepted farm subsidies and created the cabinet-level

Department of Health, Education, and Welfare. Despite his fiscal conservatism and his promise to balance the budget, Eisenhower met his budget goal in only three of his eight years in office. He would not slash services to serve an economic ideal.

On the issue of anticommunism, Eisenhower took a similarly moderate position. He maintained the loyalty program inherited from Truman and approved the firing of many innocent federal employees, but in his public utterances he downplayed the danger of internal subversion. The July 1953 armistice in Korea and the political demise of Senator McCarthy a year later (see Chapter 4) helped to quiet the Red Scare. Eisenhower also attempted to rein in the military budget, which had shot up rapidly during the Korean War.

Other items on his modest agenda were more pleasing to conservatives. He capped or reduced spending in many federal programs, lowered income taxes for the wealthy, eliminated price controls, eased business regulations, and returned some political authority to the states. In a huge boon to the embryonic nuclear industry, he backed the Atomic Energy Act of 1954, which licensed private firms to generate nuclear power while limiting their liability.

Overall, Eisenhower promoted a moderate conservative movement that recognized a strong domestic role for government and a permanent global role for America. Beginning in 1955, following the loss of the Republican majority in Congress, Eisenhower often cooperated with such powerful congressional Democrats as Sam Rayburn and Lyndon Johnson. At times he even considered forming a new, centrist political party that might bring Democrats and Republicans together.

CRACKS IN THE PICTURE WINDOW

While Eisenhower exuded his aura of political stability, American life was changing in significant ways. Technology continued the boom begun during the Second World War, and the economy reached new heights of prosperity in spite of three recessions. As the population swelled, Americans moved to the suburbs in ever greater numbers. Cars became much more than a means of transportation. Increasingly the home and family were the center of popular values, reinforced by a widespread religious revival. But critics surveying the social landscape began to insist that important flaws lay beneath the surface of prosperity and contentment.

Economic growth during the 1950s averaged more than 4 percent annually, despite recessions in 1954, 1958, and 1960. Inflation remained below 2 percent and unemployment below 5 percent. A record high employment of 66.5 million was reached in 1960. The

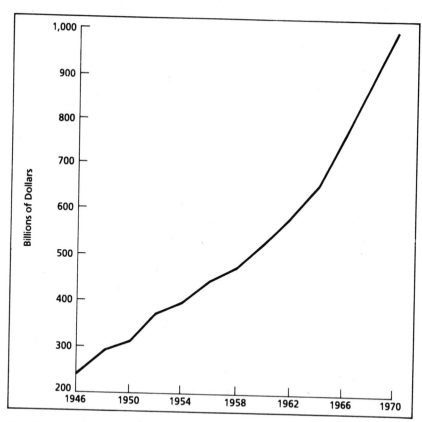

Gross National Product, 1946–1970

GNP nearly doubled between 1950 and 1960, to $500 billion (see figure). Measured in constant 1954 dollars, this represented a per capita increase of about 25 percent (from $2,096 to $2,536). Median family income grew from about $3,000 to $5,657. Real wages rose by 30 percent.

With high employment and higher incomes, Americans found more ways to spend their wages. Lenient bank lending policies and the advent of the credit card also stimulated consumer spending. The Diners Club and American Express credit cards were both introduced during the 1950s, followed by oil company, hotel chain, and department store credit cards. Sears promoted its cards so aggressively that by 1960 over 10 million Americans held them. As a record number of young families furnished homes and clothed children, private debt climbed from $73 billion to $200 billion between 1950 and 1960.

The profile of industry and business also changed. Mergers accelerated, with the result that the two hundred largest corporations controlled over half of all business assets by the end of the decade. Some corporations were beginning to expand across national borders. Traditional industries such as iron, steel, textiles, and mining shrank, while chemicals, aviation, drugs, plastics, fast food chains, discount retailers (such as Kresge's, later K-mart), and electronics expanded. Overall, heavy industry and manufacturing declined, and new job growth clustered in the service, clerical, and managerial sectors. By 1956, white-collar workers outnumbered blue-collar workers for the first time.

Meanwhile the labor movement struggled, with only partial success, to hold its own. The 1946 Full Employment Act, gutted in passage by Congress, promised only "maximum" employment, an ambiguous term that left plenty of room for shifting views of what represented an "acceptable" unemployment rate. In 1955 the American Federation of Labor and the Congress of Industrial Organizations overcame their long-time rivalry and merged to form the AFL-CIO. But congressional investigations into union ties to organized crime, along with the federal conviction of Teamsters Union president Dave Beck, tarnished labor's image and led to new legal restrictions on the labor movement. Although the number of union members remained fairly steady, the unionized proportion of the total work force declined with the loss of jobs in heavy industry. The unions that managed to penetrate the white-collar sector, such as the American Federation of State, County and Municipal Employees (AFSCME), accounted for a growing percentage of union membership.

Throughout the decade, business leaders and some economists boasted of creating a "people's capitalism" that ensured the equal distribution of abundance and erased class divisions. In fact, wealth remained highly concentrated, as it had throughout the century. In 1960, the richest 1 percent of the population possessed one-third of the nation's wealth, and the top 5 percent controlled over half its wealth. Yet half of all families had no savings account, and 40 million Americans, almost one-fourth of the population, lived near or below the poverty line (then figured as an income of $3,000 per year for a family of four). The poverty rate was especially high among the elderly, racial minorities, and rural Americans.

Superficially, Americans seemed a content lot, and they became increasingly devout. By the end of the decade, two-thirds of the population claimed formal church membership, up from 48 percent before the Second World War. Ninety-seven percent professed a belief in God. Religious popularizers like Billy Graham became media celebrities, appearing in newspapers, on radio and television, and on bestseller lists. A new translation of the Bible sold millions of copies. For those without time to read it, *Reader's Digest* issued an abridgment.

Congress added the words "under God" to the Pledge of Allegiance and put the motto "In God We Trust" on the nation's paper money.

Christianity, like parenthood and the suburban nuclear family, became a measure of Americanism and a rejection of atheistic communism. Surveys revealed that a large majority of Americans considered atheism a subversive threat. Like Eisenhower, few people stressed doctrinal differences or weighty theological issues; rather, religion served to unify society. As Will Herberg, a professor of Judaic studies, noted in his incisive 1955 study *Protestant-Catholic-Jew*, the nation's religions, especially in suburbia, tolerated almost any content in their observances—or lack thereof. Rather than reorienting life to God, religion served a social function in the new communities.

On one issue religious and secular opinion leaders agreed emphatically—the need for a "strong" American family founded on "traditional" values. "Of all the accomplishments of the American woman," *Life* magazine's editors boasted in a special Christmas 1956 issue on women, "the one she brings off with the most spectacular success is having babies." In Eisenhower's America, a "steelworker's wife and Junior Leaguer alike do their own housework." According to the magazine, when the new woman gracefully conceded to men the top jobs in the workplace, she fulfilled a timeless female destiny.

But the fifties family was nothing if not innovative. During the decade, American women reversed a hundred-year trend by marrying younger and having more babies. Reinforcing this trend, advice columns, television shows, and schools emphasized "traditional" gender roles placing the husband at work and the wife in the home. A fear of sexual chaos, brought on by the Cold War, emerged as a common theme. Popular literature discussed the dangers posed by "loose women" and "sex perverts" who might be in league with the Soviet Union. Senator Joseph McCarthy, whose close aide Roy Cohn was a closeted homosexual, joined Republican party chairman Guy Gabrielson in warning that "sexual perverts [had] infiltrated our government" and were "perhaps as dangerous as real Communists." Even the admirable Joseph Welch, counsel to the army in the hearings that finally exposed McCarthy's mania, was not above gay-baiting. When confronted with evidence obviously doctored by McCarthy's associates, he taunted Cohn, "Do you suppose fairies put it there?"

The dominant domestic ideology of the period, which Betty Friedan dubbed "the feminine mystique" in her 1963 book of that title, defined women as wives and mothers. But in fact, a third of all women worked for wages, and total female employment grew in the 1950s from 16.5 million to 23 million, representing a third of the work force. Nevertheless, in popular thinking women belonged at home, raising children and erecting a bulwark of social stability. Sex, though not discouraged, was to be limited to marriage.

Parenthood became an expression of responsible citizenship and motherhood the fulfillment of female sexuality. A book published in 1947 and popular for a decade thereafter, *Modern Women: The Lost Sex*, by Dr. Marynia Farnham and Ferdinand Lundberg, described unmarried, childless women as emotionally disturbed. The authors urged laws barring older single women from teaching, since they "cannot be an adequate model of a complete woman."

Despite warnings from self-declared experts that higher education inhibited fertility, a growing number of women attended college. Educated women, however, still faced discouragement. Adlai Stevenson exhorted women at Smith College not to feel frustrated by their distance from the "great issues and stirring debate" for which their education prepared them. A woman could be a good citizen, he claimed, by helping her husband find value in his work and by teaching her children the uniqueness of each individual.

Prodded by such assertions from civic leaders and the media, it is not surprising that the average mother of the 1950s had between three and four children, usually by age thirty. As noted earlier, the birth rate continued to rise until 1957. At the same time, contraception, accepted by all the major faiths except the Roman Catholic church, became common as a method for spacing pregnancies and limiting births.

In spite of the formal sexual orthodoxy of the era, there were portents of a more emancipated future. Notably, sex was more openly discussed and displayed during the 1950s than in most earlier periods. Popular science provided a vehicle for sexual openness in 1953 when Dr. Alfred C. Kinsey published his best-selling *Sexual Behavior in the Human Female*, which suggested that women, like men, engaged in a wide variety of sexual acts, both before and after marriage. In the climate of the times, many people considered this finding "dirty" and offensive.

But disapproval of the Kinsey report did not prevent artistic representations of sex from becoming more open in the 1950s. In the film industry, for example, the Hollywood Production Code had long barred use of words like "virgin" and "seduction" and restricted the sexual content of films. Even married couples were shown sleeping in separate beds. By the mid-1950s, the code was relaxed. The movies did not necessarily improve, but the sex in them became far more graphic than before.

During the same years, the Supreme Court overturned several state laws restricting publication of serious erotic literature, such as D. H. Lawrence's *Lady Chatterley's Lover*. Such books became more widely available, and writers of less renown also offered some steamy reading. The decade's most popular novel, *Peyton Place* (1956), sold almost 10 million copies. The book jacket promised that author Grace

Metalious, a young housewife, "lifted the lid off a small New England town," exposing lust, rape, incest, alcoholism, murder, and hypocrisy.

Playboy magazine was surely the most influential erotic publication of the decade. Its glossy centerfolds brought bare-breasted women into millions of homes, displaying them like one more new consumer product. When Hugh Hefner first published *Playboy* in December 1953, he featured the rising starlet Marilyn Monroe as "Playmate of the Month." Slick, upscale, and replete with the hedonistic "Playboy philosophy," selections from serious writers, and airbrushed photographs of busty beauties, *Playboy* represented a quantum leap from the grimy "girlie" magazines of the prewar years. By 1956 its circulation had reached one-half million per month.

Besides pressuring women into domestic roles, the massive pro-family propaganda of the fifties stifled many men, who, fleeing commitment, found *Playboy* a temporary escape. Hefner pitched his magazine to college students and young status-conscious men who wanted to date, not marry, the centerfold models. Willing to spend their salary on the expensive stereos and pricey liquor advertised in *Playboy*, they fantasized about worry-free sex with no house payments or children to complicate their lifestyle.

If *Playboy* spoke to the desires of young men, the emerging art form of rock 'n' roll touched a deep chord in American youth of both sexes. Before the advent of rock, mainstream fifties music featured fatuous songs like "How Much Is That Doggie in the Window." But as television gave radio increasingly stiff competition, radio stations became less profitable, and this prompted many of them to change their formats. In some large cities, radio stations began targeting a new audience, African-Americans. African-American popular music of the time, often called "race music," vibrated with religious and sexual energy. But white audiences had little exposure to it. To make the distinctive black style more acceptable, some disc jockeys called it rhythm and blues, or R&B. After 1945 R&B began to influence southern "hillbilly" and western "cowboy" music, creating the hybrid country-and-western style. And by the mid-1950s, increased exposure of R&B paved the way for its evolution into rock 'n' roll. This dynamic new musical form, along with improved recording technologies and the emergence of a large cohort of teenagers with money to spend, created a vast new commercial market in music.

In 1952 Cleveland disc jockey Alan Freed premiered an R&B radio show called "Moondog's Rock 'n' Roll Party." Like the term *jazz*, "rockin' and rollin'" originally referred to sexual intercourse. To appeal to his white audience, Freed downplayed this reference, connecting the words *rock 'n' roll* to the style of dancing associated with the music. From then on, the barriers between white and black music began to tumble. White audiences opened their ears to black music at the same time the civil rights movement was challenging the racism of white society.

In 1954, Bill Haley, a portly, nearly middle-aged white band leader, recorded "Rock Around the Clock," an exuberant tune that became the theme song of the popular film *Blackboard Jungle* (1955). The movie chronicled the struggle of a young teacher in a run-down inner-city high school who tried to motivate alienated, poor youth. It touched on problems of race, class, and delinquency—unusual themes in commercial art of the time. The film's message—crime does not pay, and middle-class values are a salvation—is scarcely remembered. But "Rock Around the Clock," critics and audiences agreed, gave *Blackboard Jungle* its "insurrectionary power." The music brought white middle-class youth to their feet. Theater owners reported spontaneous dancing in the aisles.

The record industry was especially eager to appeal to white youth, because they represented an enormous market. "Teen-agers," a relatively recent term for those who enjoyed a prolonged adolescence before entering the labor force, formed an expanding group during the 1950s. Their numbers and economic impact grew steadily, so that by 1959 the teenage market—including money spent by parents on teenagers and by teenagers on themselves—topped $10 billion per year. With so much at stake, record producers hustled to find more white recording artists who employed the black sound in a form acceptable to white teenagers.

The biggest find was a nineteen-year-old part-time truck driver from Tupelo, Mississippi—Elvis Presley. Born poor, he had taught himself the guitar and learned the R&B style. His first record in 1954 earned him appearances on regional radio shows, and within a year he was a star throughout the South. In live performances he aroused his fans, both female and male, by undulating his body and thrusting his hips in a style he attributed to revivalist preachers. Presley virtually created the image of the hypersexed male rock star, replete with long hair, leather jacket, a sneering expression, and a sultry demeanor.

By 1956 Presley had became a national sensation. He released a series of hits, including "Heartbreak Hotel," "Don't Be Cruel," "Love Me Tender," and "I'm All Shook Up," that sold over 14 million records that year. He appeared on Ed Sullivan's popular TV variety show, where the cameras focused above the waist to conceal the young man's suggestive thrusts. Over 80 percent of all American viewers watched this performance, a number unsurpassed until the Beatles made their television debut in 1964.

Between early 1956 and March 1958, when the army drafted him, Presley released fourteen consecutive million-seller records. By 1966

Elvis Presley in 1956. His exuberant singing style shocked adults and excited youths. *UPI/Bettmann Archive.*

he had sold 115 million records. Presley's success not only set a standard for other white rock singers, but also spurred white acceptance of African-American artists such as Ray Charles, Chuck Berry, Little Richard, and Fats Domino.

While the young went wild over rock 'n' roll, parents recoiled at its influence. Some rock lyrics made fun of middle-class values. Besides its generally sensual, even sexual emphasis, rock music ridiculed work ("Get a Job"), downplayed school ("Don't Know Much About History"), mixed religion with sex ("Teen Angel"), scoffed at authority ("Charlie Brown, He's a Clown"), and celebrated irresponsibility ("Rock Around the Clock"). Popular music had never before so blatantly defied social mores or so distinguished youth from older generations.

Adult fears, and the discontents that gave rise to concern, emerged plainly in films like *The Wild Ones* (1953), *Rebel Without a Cause* (1955), and *Blackboard Jungle* (1955). These three movies featured actors Marlon Brando, James Dean, and Sidney Poitier as young toughs who oozed anger, sexuality, and contempt for their elders. Their fictional characters presented an even stronger challenge to the social order than did Holden Caulfield, the alienated teenage hero of J. D. Salinger's popular novel *Catcher in the Rye* (1951). Despite the films' overt messages that violence and immorality were wrong, most teenagers who flocked to see Brando, Dean, and Poitier cheered the unrepentant rebels, not the characters who accepted their elders' advice.

Among parents who had just experienced World War II, peace and quiet seemed a good bargain. Young people, however, wanted something more. A youth subculture was beginning to emerge, and many parents worried about it. They blamed their music, movies, books, and comics, and even the television programs that to later generations would seem so innocent. Some people invoked the Communist specter. Early in the decade, Justice Department officials helped one Hollywood studio produce a film warning that "throughout the United States today, indeed throughout the free world, a deadly war is being waged." The "Communist enemy," the film declared, was trying to subvert American youth by spreading drugs and encouraging obscenity in the mass media.

Many political liberals and professional educators attributed juvenile delinquency and a host of other social ills to the lack of federal aid to public schools. Without more money for buildings, equipment, and libraries, they argued, teachers could not cope with surging enrollments and the constant accumulation of new information. Only higher salaries, paid for by taxes, would lure talented college graduates into teaching.

Conservatives, on the other hand, blamed the educational establishment itself, including teacher training colleges and unions, for poor student performance. The right wing believed that John Dewey's popular ideas of "progressive education," with their emphasis on social relevance, democratic ideals, and pragmatism, had undermined respect for the acquisition of basic skills, traditional values, and culture. They called for a return to basics, more classroom discipline, and the teaching of religious values.

Neither liberal nor conservative critics fully acknowledged that part of the problem lay in the changing nature of mass education. Before the Second World War, relatively few students finished high school, and even fewer went to college. Public primary schools sought merely to instill some basic discipline and rudimentary reading and arithmetic skills. The wealthy attended private schools, and talented students of modest means benefited from special college preparatory courses in public high schools.

Postwar prosperity resulted in many more working-class youths attending high school. As blacks and Hispanics migrated to urban areas, they became a major presence in public schools, increasing the cultural and social diversity in schools. Tension within this newly varied population, combined with the baby boom and the rapid expansion of the suburbs, put education at all levels under stress. Schools were expected to teach job skills, citizenship, and a sophisticated science, math, and literature curriculum to a broader cross section of students than ever before. To complicate the problem, by tradition American schools are locally funded and controlled, making it difficult to promote change at the national level.

The critique reached new heights after October 1957, when the Soviet Union launched the first artificial satellite, *Sputnik I*. (See Chapter 4 for a discussion of the space race.) Anxiety over the Cold War added fuel to the crisis in education. Journalists and politicians described the Soviet Union as the model of successful mass education. Communism, it seemed, had won the space race by winning the education race. What would Moscow win next?

In fact, Soviet success in education was greatly exaggerated. Nevertheless, *Sputnik* forged a national consensus in favor of federal aid to education. Before the crisis, southern Democrats opposed federal spending on education, fearing it would erode local control and spur integration. Northern liberal Democrats worried about opening public coffers to parochial schools. Parochial schools feared that higher school taxes would impact parents' ability to pay tuition and would thus erode their client base. Most Republicans simply opposed spending money on social programs. But the clamor to catch up with the Russians changed things.

Senator Lyndon B. Johnson of Texas, Democratic majority leader and presidential aspirant, chaired an investigating committee assessing the impact of Moscow's space coup. Long an advocate of federal support for education, he now warned of a widening science and technology gap. Congress and President Eisenhower cooperated in September 1958 to pass the National Defense Education Act (NDEA), a billion-dollar package, supplemented by state grants, to provide aid to schools and universities. It granted funds for construction, student loans and scholarships, and the teaching of science, mathematics, and foreign languages. In the following two decades, the NDEA and successor programs had a huge impact on American education at all levels, from primary grades through graduate and professional schools. As with the GI Bill of the decade before, loans and fellowships allowed many more students to pursue advanced degrees. By 1960 the United States granted ten thousand doctorates annually, three times the pre–Second World War number. Foreign students flocked to American universities, making the United States a world center of higher education.

With educational assistance provided by the NDEA, a record number of students enrolled in college during the 1960s. As never before, Americans assumed that a bright student, whatever his or her social background, should and would go to college. The large group of confident, intellectually curious students hitting college campuses coincided with growing American military involvement in Vietnam. Not surprisingly, this generation of college students would play a major role in challenging the Vietnam War in the 1960s.

The 1950s role models for college rebels were the Beats, a small, loosely defined group of iconoclastic writers who captured the public attention late in the decade. Their defiance of social and literary convention, as well as their dabbling in drugs, Eastern mysticism, and homosexuality, outraged the middle class and excited many teenagers and young adults. Beatniks, as they became known, shunned Christianity, work, materialism, family life, patriotism, and interest in winning the Cold War.

The Beat writers included poets Allen Ginsberg and Gregory Corso and novelists Jack Kerouac and William S. Burroughs. Most began writing in New York early in the decade and later drifted toward San Francisco. Ginsberg gained national attention in 1956 when San Francisco police charged him with obscenity for publishing his poem *Howl,* a highly personal cry against American materialism. The Beats achieved further fame in 1957 with Kerouac's best seller *On the Road,* a raucous, thinly fictionalized account of the author's cross-country travel with his unconventional friends.

The Beats' defiance of the "square" world struck a chord, but emulation of the Beats was confined mostly to the superficial element of style. Some people gathered in dark cafés to listen to poetry and jazz music and sip espresso. More important, college students, who were in general the epitome of conformity in the 1950s, began to read the Beats and ponder their challenges to social, sexual, and political conventions.

Despite such rumblings of rebellion, most social commentators agreed that the United States had solved the major problems afflicting society. Persistent pockets of poverty, such as among African-Americans, were seen as minor embarrassments rather than as major problems. An influential analysis published by Daniel Bell near the end of the decade, *The End of Ideology,* argued that the passionate ideological crusades of earlier years no longer had relevance. The United States had mastered the production of abundance and now had only to decide how to allocate the wealth.

Nevertheless, some critics began to question the social mores and culture that arose from this decade of calm prosperity. Such books as David Riesman's *The Lonely Crowd* (1950), Sloan Wilson's *The Man in the Gray Flannel Suit* (1955), William H. Whyte, Jr.'s *The Organization Man* (1955), John Keats's *The Crack in the Picture Window* (1957), and Richard Gordon's *The Split Level Trap* (1960) turned a critical eye on the fifties. Riesman and Whyte discussed the eclipse of the "inner-directed" personality. Instead of relying on internal drives and values, they charged, Americans had become "other-directed," little more than sheep who sought approval and rewards from their peers. According to Whyte, the bureaucratic structure of big business stifled a healthy competitive spirit. No longer spurred by drive and vision, the organization man looked to "the group as the source of creativity."

Critics also attacked the pervasive consumer culture. In a trilogy of best sellers criticizing the advertising industry—*The Hidden Persuaders* (1957), *The Status Seekers* (1959), and *The Waste Makers* (1959)— journalist Vance Packard blamed mass marketing and the concept of "planned obsolescence" for turning citizens into insatiable consumers.

Only a few social critics claimed to find basic structural flaws in American society. One of these was sociologist C. Wright Mills, whose book *The Power Elite* (1956) asserted that a small group of military, business, and political leaders controlled the country in such a way that the majority of Americans were left powerless. Herbert Marcuse, a German émigré philosopher, blended Freudian psychology and Marxism in his *Eros and Civilization* (1956), which argued that a tiny minority manipulated the lives of most people and developed unique forms of psychological repression. In *Growing Up Absurd* (1960), Paul Goodman criticized schools and other institutions for stifling creativity and individualism. These critics offered evidence that America's problems had not disappeared or been forgotten. Their dissent foreshadowed the radical challenges that emerged in the 1960s.

CONTINUING STRUGGLES: CIVIL RIGHTS AND CIVIL LIBERTIES

At a time when so many Americans enjoyed abundance, African-Americans were still denied basic human rights. Like much of the population, African-Americans were highly mobile after the Second World War, continuing their migration patterns of the war years. In the rural South, farm mechanization pushed black sharecroppers off the land. Some went to southern cities like Atlanta and Birmingham. More went north and west (see map, page 124). About one in five African-Americans left the South in the 1950s.

The migrants did not find residential integration in their new communities. Just as the newcomers arrived, white Americans were leaving the cities for the suburbs. During the 1950s the nation's twelve largest cities lost 3.6 million whites and gained 4.5 million nonwhites. By 1960 over half of all African-Americans lived in the largely poor

Before 1947, African-American baseball players could play only in the Negro Leagues, teams owned largely by the white major-league clubs. During the Second World War, activists demanded that baseball drop its color bar, but it was not until after the war that Branch Rickey, owner of the Brooklyn Dodgers, resolved to challenge the policy of racial exclusion.

Rickey searched for the perfect African-American to integrate major-league baseball—not only a superior athlete, but also a model citizen with an even temperament, a man who would not be fazed by white harassment. The ball player he found was Jack Roosevelt ("Jackie") Robinson.

Jack Roosevelt Robinson

Born in 1919 to a family of Georgia sharecroppers, Robinson was uprooted at an early age when his mother moved

and mostly black inner cities. The new suburban communities remained nearly all white.

In the South, segregation came under sharp attack. Court decisions, boycotts, and new laws undermined the legal and social pillars of racism. Led in many cases by war veterans, African-Americans organized voter-registration drives in the South, where they encountered white hostility and sometimes outright violence. After hearing reports of blacks killed for daring to assert their voting rights, President Truman acted. Even though he privately rejected social equality among the races, in late 1946 he established the President's Committee on Civil Rights to recommend steps for the federal government to take to ensure basic civil rights for all Americans. The panel urged government action to guarantee equal opportunity in education, housing, and employment. It called for federal laws against lynching and poll taxes, creation of a permanent Fair Employment Practices

the family to southern California. Jackie eventually attended UCLA, where he excelled in several varsity sports. As one of the small number of African-American officers during the Second World War, he successfully defended himself in a court-martial after challenging an order to move to the back of a military bus. In October 1945 Rickey gave him a contract to play with the Dodgers' top minor-league team in Montreal, where he led the league in batting in 1946.

His debut with the Brooklyn Dodgers—marking the integration of the major leagues—came in April 1947. Throughout his first season, Robinson had to endure racial epithets hurled by angry fans and white players alike. At least one team, the St. Louis Cardinals, threatened to walk off the field if Robinson appeared. Through it all, Robinson's extraordinary talent and personal resolve triumphed, and he won Rookie of the Year honors. He became so popular that the House Committee on Un-American Activities called on him to refute a claim by Paul Robeson, a famous black singer and actor, that African-Americans would not fight in a war against the Soviet Union. Within two years of Robinson's debut, several more black players received major-league contracts.

Robinson played for the Dodgers through 1956. After retirement, he served as vice president of a food company and became a close friend and political ally of Nelson Rockefeller, the Republican governor of New York. After suffering from diabetes for many years, Jackie Robinson died in 1972. ∎

Commission, and a strong Civil Rights Division within the Justice Department.

When Congress declined to act, Truman used executive authority to bolster civil rights enforcement by the Justice Department. He also appointed a black federal judge and made several other minority appointments. When labor leader A. Philip Randolph threatened in July 1948 to organize a boycott of the draft to protest the segregated armed forces, Truman issued an executive order calling for desegregation in the services. Still, the armed services moved so slowly that desegregation took another six years.

As the government inched forward, African-Americans pursued nonviolent direct action inspired by India's Mohandas Gandhi. Two women staged the first sit-in in Washington, D.C., during the war. (One of them, Patricia Harris, later became a cabinet secretary in the Carter administration.) After the war, the Congress of Racial Equality

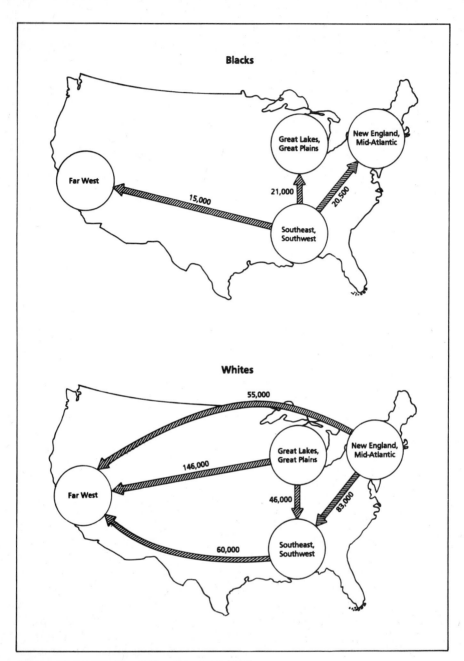

Blacks

Far West

Great Lakes,
Great Plains

New England,
Mid-Atlantic

Southeast,
Southwest

15,000

21,000

20,500

Whites

55,000

Far West

Great Lakes,
Great Plains

New England,
Mid-Atlantic

146,000

46,000

83,000

60,000

Southeast,
Southwest

Average Annual Regional Migration, 1947–1960

(CORE) carried out sit-ins at lunch counters in northern cities and organized a "swim-in" at Palisades Park in New Jersey. Although mobs beat the participants, the amusement park and many lunch counters were desegregated as a result of these demonstrations. These small and hard-won victories convinced activists of the importance of direct action for mobilizing their communities and maintaining political pressure on the white establishment.

In the legal realm, too, progress was being made. The Supreme Court gradually extended judicial protection for the civil rights of minorities. Even before the Second World War ended, in *Smith* v. *Allwright* (1944) the Court overturned the whites-only primary system that prevailed in some southern states. Two years later, in *Morgan* v. *Virginia* (1946), the Court held that racial segregation on interstate buses violated federal law. In 1947 CORE organized the first "freedom ride," to test the ruling. The group made it as far as Durham, North Carolina, before being arrested and sentenced to thirty days on a chain gang.

Other legal decisions helped combat segregation in housing and employment. The Supreme Court had ruled at the turn of the century that local laws enforcing residential segregation violated the Fourteenth Amendment. It undermined that decision, however, by permitting state courts to enforce private contractual agreements that barred minorities. But in *Shelly* v. *Kraemer* (1948), the justices ordered that state courts could not enforce restrictive clauses in private contracts. On hearing of the new ruling, a furious congressman declared that "there must have been a celebration in Moscow last night."

Nothing symbolized the unequal status of African-Americans more powerfully than school segregation. *Plessy* v. *Ferguson* (1896) permitted school systems that were "separate but equal." By 1938, Chief Justice Hughes suggested that southern states wishing to continue separate-but-equal education ought to make black-only schools truly equal. In 1948 the Court took up the case of Ada Sipuel, who had graduated with a strong record from the State College for Negroes in Langston, Oklahoma. She was refused admission to the University of Oklahoma Law School (the only one in the state) on racial grounds, but was told that a separate school for blacks with "substantially equal" facilities would soon open. Represented by Thurgood Marshall, chief counsel of the National Association for the Advancement of Colored People (NAACP), she sued for admission to the existing school.

Marshall argued the case before the U.S. Supreme Court in 1948. In *Sipuel* v. *Board of Regents of the University of Oklahoma*, the justices ruled unanimously that Oklahoma must provide Sipuel with a legal education "in conformity with the equal protection clause of the Fourteenth Amendment." The university regents then created a sham law school by roping off a tiny area within the state capitol building and assigning three teachers to Sipuel. Marshall challenged this ruse, but the Court declined further action.

Two years later, the University of Oklahoma admitted, under pressure, a sixty-eight-year-old African-American, George W. McLaurin, to its graduate program in education. The university ordered McLaurin to sit in a doorway outside the classroom, use a special desk in a segregated section of the library, and eat alone in a cafeteria annex. When the NAACP challenged these rules, McLaurin was permitted to sit inside the classroom so long as his seat was encircled by a railing with a sign that read "Reserved for Colored." A unanimous Supreme Court, in *McLaurin* v. *Oklahoma State Regents* (1950), struck down these rules on the grounds that the university had imposed inequality on McLaurin even while allowing him into a school with whites.

That same year, the Court decided in *Sweatt* v. *Painter* (1950) that Texas had not provided a black law student with equal facilities. The state had thrown together a makeshift classroom for Herman Marion Sweatt, without a law library or law school faculty, at segregated Prairie View University. The Court ordered Sweatt admitted to the University of Texas Law School at Austin.

In these various decisions, the U.S. Supreme Court did not outlaw segregation or overturn the separate-but-equal rule dating from 1896. But a majority of justices seemed willing to chip away at segregation by forcing states to honor the "equal" part of the "separate but equal" doctrine. Their rulings encouraged Marshall and the NAACP to escalate the attack on school segregation, placing the system under constant judicial siege. By 1952 the NAACP was pressing five suits before the Supreme Court against public school segregation.

These five suits were eventually combined under the heading of one key case, involving Linda Brown of Topeka, Kansas. Each morning she had to walk past a nearby "white only" school to catch the bus that would take her to a "colored only" school. NAACP chief counsel Thurgood Marshall decided to abandon his piecemeal strategy. He likened the "separate but equal" doctrine to the "black codes" established after the Civil War to restrict the rights of African-Americans. The doctrine could be sustained, Marshall argued, only if the Supreme Court agreed "that for some reason Negroes are inferior to all other human beings." Marshall insisted that segregation violated the Fourteenth Amendment, and he submitted research by psychologist Kenneth Clark suggesting that African-American children educated in single-race schools suffered lasting emotional and intellectual damage.

The Supreme Court heard arguments in *Brown* v. *Board of Education* late in 1952, but they delayed ruling. Chief Justice Fred Vinson, like several associate justices, had misgivings about segregation but thought states had a right to set their own school policies, however discriminatory they might be. In September 1953, in the midst of the Court's deliberations, Vinson died. Associate Justice Felix Frankfurter privately quipped that Vinson's timely demise was "the only proof I've ever seen of the existence of God." A year before, presidential candidate Eisenhower had secured support from Governor Earl Warren of California by promising him the first opening on the Supreme Court. Eisenhower had some qualms about appointing Warren to the most influential seat on the court, but he honored his promise.

Neither Eisenhower nor most other Americans imagined how fateful this appointment would become. Warren viewed the Supreme Court as a unique force for protecting the weak, the oppressed, and the disadvantaged. His vision and activism brought the Court into the center of national politics and made him the most influential chief justice in over a century.

Warren ordered a rehearing of *Brown* in December 1953. Then he persuaded all eight associate justices to join him in a unanimous opinion, issued in May 1954, that struck down segregation in public education. Warren rejected the *Plessy* decision of 1896 and put forth an essentially new interpretation of the Fourteenth Amendment.

For Warren, the issue was simple justice. To segregate schoolchildren solely on the basis of race, he wrote "generates a feeling of inferiority . . . that may affect their hearts and minds in a way unlikely ever to be undone. . . . Segregation with the sanction of law, therefore, has a tendency to retard educational and mental development of Negro children." In education, he declared, "separate but equal has no place. Separate educational facilities are inherently unequal."

Critics charged that the ruling misconstrued the Constitution and relied on dubious sociological data. Others accused the Supreme Court of usurping congressional and state power by making, rather than interpreting, the law. Warren's defenders retorted that the *Brown* decision yielded the morally correct verdict. In fact, the Supreme Court had taken action—reluctantly—to resolve a moral, legal, and political issue that neither Congress nor the president would confront. Civil rights had been stuck in a political gridlock that only the Supreme Court seemed capable of unraveling.

In practice, the *Brown* decision affected only public schools, not the comprehensive web of segregation laws that prevailed in twenty-four states and the District of Columbia. Moreover, the Supreme Court delayed implementing its ruling and called for consultation between local authorities and judges. During 1954 and 1955, while the high court heard the NAACP demand "integration now," southern states requested delays and demagogues called for "segregation forever." During this interim period, the Court's delay and President

Eisenhower's uneasiness over the desegregation ruling helped fuel a massive resistance movement.

Warren again spoke for a unanimous Court in May 1955, ruling in a case called *Brown II* that school segregation must be ended everywhere in the nation. Although desegregation should begin with "all deliberate speed," the court issued no timetable. Southern officials hoped that federal district judges would wink at delays and, as a Georgia official remarked, define a "reasonable time as one or two hundred years." When district judges insisted on early action, however, segregationists dug in their heels. In several southern states, "white citizens' councils" sprang up to intimidate parents and school boards attempting to integrate the schools. Over one hundred members of Congress signed a "Southern Manifesto" opposing the *Brown* decision. Senator Harry F. Byrd, a Democrat from Virginia, called for massive resistance, and several state legislatures in the South declared they would defy the "unconstitutional" Supreme Court rulings.

These states passed laws forbidding officials to carry out any action to mix races in public schools. Several states curtailed or abolished public schools, turning over the buildings to all-white private academies. At one point Mississippi and South Carolina actually amended their constitutions to abolish public education, and Virginia closed public schools for several months. Because of resistance and hostility, in 1960 most schools in the South and many in the North remained as segregated as before. Far from being resolved, the issue would become the focus of public debate again and again in later decades.

President Eisenhower did little to promote the Supreme Court rulings. As army chief of staff in 1948 he had defended military segregation, arguing that "if we attempt to force someone to like someone else, we are just going to get into trouble." Of course, equality under law, not the "liking" of minorities, was the real issue.

Pressed by the contending factions to endorse or denounce the *Brown* ruling, Eisenhower privately blamed Earl Warren for the crisis and called his appointment of the judge "the biggest damn fool mistake I ever made." Although the president accepted the desegregation decision, he declined to endorse it. He told Booker T. Washington's daughter, "We cannot do it by cold lawmaking, but must make these changes by appealing to reason, by prayer, and by constantly working at it through our own efforts."

Eisenhower's greatest effort on behalf of change came in response to a direct challenge to federal authority in Little Rock, Arkansas. In 1957, the Little Rock school board accepted a court order to allow nine African-American students to enroll in the city's Central High School. But Governor Orval Faubus, an ardent segregationist, called out the National Guard to block them. When a federal court ordered the

African-American students enter Central High School in Little Rock. *Ed Clarke, Life Magazine* © *Time Inc.*

troops to withdraw, a white mob surrounded the school, taunting and threatening the blacks attempting to enroll. Faced with massive local defiance of a federal court order—and embarrassed by Soviet propaganda publicizing American racism, which found a wide audience in the Third World—Eisenhower felt compelled to send a thousand army troops and ten thousand National Guardsmen to protect the students, maintain safety, and enforce the court order.

The troops stayed a year. In 1958 Governor Faubus closed the Little Rock schools in an effort to prevent integration (they reopened as white academies). A year later a federal court disallowed this move. The whole episode, including vivid pictures of the howling mob and the frightened but dignified African-American students, became an international embarrassment to the United States.

The administration tried to mollify critics by introducing a civil rights bill to Congress in 1957. Attorney General Herbert Brownell pushed the legislation while Eisenhower recuperated from an illness. Brownell had political motives for pressing a civil rights bill: he hoped that a debate on the question would divide the northern and southern wings of the Democratic party and curb the influence of presidential hopeful Lyndon Johnson. The ploy failed when Johnson used his talents of persuasion to convince a majority of Democrats to support the Civil Rights Act of 1957, an amended version of the administration's bill that declared support for black voting rights but offered no means of enforcement.

In passing the 1957 Civil Rights Act, Congress was responding to a rising tide of grassroots activism on the part of African-Americans. Shortly before Christmas in 1955, Rosa Parks, a tailor's assistant in Montgomery, Alabama, who was also secretary of the local NAACP branch, boarded a bus to ride home. When ordered to vacate a seat and move to the rear so that a white passenger might sit, she refused. Parks declared that she had decided to discover "once and for all what rights I had as a human being and a citizen." Besides, she added, "my feet hurt." For her trouble, she was arrested for violating the law requiring the separation of whites and blacks on public buses.

Rosa Parks was not the first black woman to be arrested for breaking this law; in three recent cases the city of Montgomery had dropped charges to avoid a legal challenge. The Women's Political Council, a group of African-American professional women, knew of Parks's good reputation in the community and her support for civil rights causes. They considered her case an ideal test case. The council conferred with other community leaders, including E. D. Nixon, a local NAACP official, and decided to mobilize grassroots support for a challenge to the law. They enlisted the help of Baptist ministers, including Ralph Abernathy and Martin Luther King, Jr., in organizing a black boycott of Montgomery buses.

King, then a twenty-seven-year-old preacher, was new to the community. He came from a prominent family in Atlanta. His father, Martin Luther King, Sr., ministered to a large congregation and encouraged his talented son to pursue a broad education, including a doctorate in theology from Boston University. Martin Luther King, Jr., did not initiate the challenge to racism in Montgomery, but he gradually emerged as its leader because of his talents and passionate oratory. He told local and national audiences that "there comes a time when people get tired . . . of being segregated and humiliated, tired of being kicked about by the brutal feet of oppression." The time had come for his people to cease tolerating "anything less than freedom and justice." Influenced by his reading of Thoreau and Gandhi, King applied the principles of nonviolent civil disobedience to the boycott. He would soon become the nation's most prominent African-American leader.

For a year, some fifty thousand African-Americans walked or rode in car-pools rather than ride the segregated buses of Montgomery. Organizer JoAnn Gibson Robinson compared the immense car-pool operation to a military campaign. Boycott leaders did not insist on full

Reverend Martin Luther King, shown here with his wife Coretta, became the nation's best-known civil rights leader as a result of the Montgomery, Alabama, Bus Boycott. *UPI Bettmann Archive.*

integration, asking only that passengers be seated on a first-come, first-served basis, with blacks seating themselves from the rear to the front and whites from the front to the rear. Despite the modest nature of this request, city officials responded by indicting protest leaders for violating state antiboycott laws and by banning car-pools as a public nuisance. Terrorists bombed churches and the homes of activists, including King's. But in November 1956, the Supreme Court overturned the Alabama bus segregation law under which Parks had been arrested. This left the city and the bus company no legal recourse and a financial disincentive to resist integration. Thus the combination of grassroots and judicial activism achieved victory.

African-American women sparked, organized, and staffed the Montgomery campaign. The boycott also illustrates the critical role that churches and ministers played in the early civil rights crusade. Because segregation excluded blacks from political activity, churches offered the one permissible setting for community organization. They provided a base of support, local leadership, some financial resources, a common language and culture, and a sense of empowerment that could be turned toward meeting political goals. Ministers such as King and Abernathy molded African-American religions into a political weapon by portraying heroes like Moses and Jesus as social revolutionaries. Just as the biblical Jews reached the Promised

Land after long tribulation, African-Americans could win freedom, these ministers told their congregations, through faith and a commitment to struggle.

Many other African-Americans had challenged segregation, independently and collectively, by the end of the decade. College students in the South took the boldest initiative. In February 1960, four students from the North Carolina Agricultural and Technical College, after shopping in a Greensboro, North Carolina, Woolworth's, sat down at the lunch counter to order coffee. When the manager refused to serve them, they stayed there until the store closed, when they were arrested.

This tactic spread quickly. Lunch counter sit-ins occurred in over thirty cities in seven states. Many protesters were arrested, and some were beaten. Most adopted a strategy of nonviolence in the face of assaults. The effort yielded notable successes, with many national chain stores integrating their lunch counters. Some of the student activists followed Ella Baker into the Student Non-Violent Coordinating Committee (SNCC), which she organized in 1960. Over the next few years, SNCC would play a major role in challenging segregation.

Despite these important achievements, at the close of the 1950s most African-Americans still attended predominantly segregated schools and lived in single-race neighborhoods. Few blacks in the South could vote. Many more personal sacrifices by civil rights activists, and the intervention of a sympathetic federal government, would be necessary to effect real change.

The Civil Rights movement brought together diverse Americans who had fought long and hard against discrimination. Mexican-Americans also organized on their own behalf in the postwar period. Such groups as the League of United Latin American Citizens (LULAC) and the GI Forum resisted discrimination and segregation in the West, mounting legal challenges that overturned school segregation in California and banned the exclusion of Mexican-Americans from Texas juries. Such organizations emphasized the rights of Mexican-Americans to be treated as full citizens, but they distanced themselves from Mexican immigrants coming into the country—both legally and illegally.

At the same time, many western Mexican-Americans, Indians, and other people of color resisted Anglo calls for cultural assimilation. They sought to maintain the languages and traditions that made their groups distinctive. The tension between the desire for equal rights and the demand for legal and cultural distinctiveness remains an issue for people of color in the West today.

Even as the federal government and the courts began to support African-Americans, the Eisenhower administration and Congress imposed several well-intentioned but ultimately calamitous policies on

Native Americans. Reversing New Deal efforts to expand assistance to Indian tribes, the federal government adopted the policy of "Termination," gradually eliminating many Indian reservations and social services. The administration and Congress justified these measures as ways to reduce costs, protect states' rights, and expand the rights of individual Native Americans.

Between 1954 and 1960 the federal government withdrew benefits from sixty-one tribes. Many reservations were absorbed by the states in which they were located, becoming new counties. The tribes now had to pay state taxes and conform to state regulations. To raise the cash required for taxes, many tribes and individuals had to sell land and mineral rights to outside interests. For example, the Klamaths of Oregon, enticed by offers from lumber companies, sold off most of their ponderosa pine forests. The Menominees of Wisconsin sold much of their reservation to wealthy Chicagoans, who built vacation cabins on former tribal land.

The financial gains from these deals proved fleeting. Within a few years the tribes were worse off than before. An increasing number of Indians abandoned the former reservation lands. By the end of the 1960s, half the Native American population had relocated to urban areas.

Starting in 1956 the Supreme Court began unraveling the restraints on free speech and political action that had been spun during the Red Scare. Although Eisenhower complained bitterly about Warren's liberal activism, he appointed as associate justice William J. Brennan, who became an even more forceful exponent of civil rights and civil liberties. Three other Eisenhower appointees, John Marshall Harlan, Charles E. Whittaker, and Potter Stewart, were moderates. Hugo Black and William O. Douglas, Roosevelt's appointees, joined Warren and Brennan in a solid four-vote liberal block. On occasion they won support from Justice Frankfurter or one of the three other Eisenhower appointees. In 1962, President Kennedy's appointment of Arthur Goldberg as associate justice solidified the liberal direction of the Warren Court.

The Court nullified antisubversion statutes in forty-two states with the 1956 *Pennsylvania* v. *Nelson* decision. Speaking for the majority, Chief Justice Warren ruled that only federal, not state, laws could make it a crime to advocate the overthrow of the federal government. In 1957, in *Jencks* v. *United States,* the Court dealt a blow to government witch hunts by insisting that accused persons had the right to examine the evidence gathered against them. That same year, in *Yates* v. *United States,* the Supreme Court overturned the conviction of fourteen mid-level Communist Party officials sentenced for violating the Smith Act. The justices ruled that verbal calls for toppling the government did not constitute a crime. To be illegal, an act must involve the attempt to "do something now or in the future."

EISENHOWER'S
SECOND-TERM BLUES

As Eisenhower entered the final year of his first term, the public seemed at ease with his casual style of leadership. The Korean War had ended, Senator McCarthy was a spent force, Stalin's successors called for peaceful coexistence, and the economy was robust. Only Eisenhower's health worried voters. He suffered a serious heart attack in September 1955 and a disabling attack of ileitis, followed by surgery, the next June. His speedy recovery, however, quieted most fears. Eisenhower decided to run again.

Eisenhower harbored doubts about keeping Vice President Richard Nixon on the ticket. He had never liked the brash young man, and now he pondered ways to ease Nixon out. When Nixon balked, Eisenhower relented rather than provoke the wrath of the Republican right. But his misgivings about Nixon undermined the vice president's stature and hurt his presidential candidacy in 1960.

The Democrats renominated Adlai Stevenson, following a challenge from Senator Estes Kefauver, who then beat out Senator John F. Kennedy for the vice-presidential slot. Stevenson raised serious questions about poverty, the lack of a national health program, and the administration's refusal to fund public schools. Stevenson also favored ending the draft and halting the open-air testing of atomic weapons; however, he condemned Eisenhower for losing half of Indochina to communism and for not building as many long-range bombers as the Soviets. Nevertheless, as one journalist commented, "The public loves Ike. . . . The less he does the more they love him."

On election day in November 1956, Eisenhower gathered 58 percent of the popular vote, over 35 million ballots to Stevenson's 26 million. The public liked Ike far more than it liked his party, however. The Democrats maintained a four-seat majority in the Senate and a twenty-nine seat majority in the House.

In November 1957, Eisenhower suffered a mild stroke. Although his mental powers were intact, his slurred speech made his public communication less effective than before. That autumn, several foreign and domestic events called his leadership into question. After his dispatch of troops to Little Rock to protect the black students at Central High School, critics called his actions either too great or too modest a response. The clamor over *Sputnik* prompted Democrats to ridicule Eisenhower for starving education and for spending too little money on space and defense projects. The new Soviet leader, Nikita Khrushchev, began making whirlwind tours of the Third World, offering aid and winning praise for his country's support of emerging nations. In 1958 Eisenhower's powerful chief of staff, Sherman Adams, resigned amid allegations that he had accepted expensive fur coats from a contractor. Democrats in Congress took the lead in funding the NDEA and space research. To many Americans, Eisenhower began to seem disengaged.

By 1960 political discontent was percolating just beneath the surface. The third recession since Eisenhower took office, along with new challenges from Moscow, a Communist revolution in Cuba, and a sense that America needed younger, more dynamic leadership, gave the Eisenhower administration a tired, somewhat shabby appearance. Yet Eisenhower remained a hero to most Americans. They credited him with ending the Korean War and delivering peace and prosperity. His bland, comfortable stewardship, like that of the typical father in the era's sitcoms, had reassured most middle-class Americans that they would be allowed to get on with their lives.

CONCLUSION

The early postwar years were a time of consolidation for the New Deal's social reforms. Neither President Truman nor more radical reformers succeeded in winning large-scale expansions of social services. Nor, in most cases, did conservatives succeed in turning back the clock. The Roosevelt legacy of a large, active federal government was preserved.

Among the most influential postwar domestic programs were those in education and housing. Because of the GI Bill of 1944, which eventually financed education for more than 2 million college students, higher education took on a more democratic character. At the same time, liberal FHA and VA loan-guarantee policies helped spark a postwar building boom, a key element in America's postwar prosperity.

Important characteristics of postwar America were emerging: higher education for greater numbers, a middle-class population shift from cities to suburbs, a growing concentration of minorities in the inner cities, surging interest in consumer products such as home appliances and televisions, and a baby boom that by the late 1950s and 1960s would lead to an increasingly youth-oriented culture.

For women, the heroic wartime days of Rosie the Riveter were gone. Women were turned out of wartime industrial jobs and encouraged to stay home with their families. Although many managed to return to work, they generally had to settle for lower-paying jobs. More attended college than before the war, but they were steered away from fields such as law and business.

For ethnic minorities these years brought similarly mixed results. Native Americans faced difficulties brought on by Termination.

Mexicans continued to migrate to the U.S., but like the Mexican-Americans already in the country, they faced persistent discrimination. Mexican-Americans and Indians grappled with the tension between seeking equality and maintaining their cultural distinctiveness. African-Americans made significant progress in establishing civil rights through voter-registration drives, legal challenges, nonviolent demonstrations, and symbolic acts like sit-ins and freedom rides. Sometimes the activists encountered bloody resistance, and the legislative and executive branches took only small and slow steps to help. Yet crucial court victories set the scene for the major civil rights victories of the 1960s.

In retrospect, the fifties seem a curiously contradictory period in American life. Eisenhower practiced the politics of moderation, churches increased their membership, and family values appeared dominant. Middle-class suburban families embraced the trappings of prosperity—the automobile, home appliances, television, sports, jet travel, and other new miracles of consumerism. But young people, inspired by their own emerging subculture, entered a period of ferment. Despite the emphasis on traditional family structures, sex was discussed more openly. Women were going to work in greater numbers, not quite fulfilling their idealized role as housewives and mothers. Intellectual critics challenged the era's conformity and consumerism, and the Beat writers dared to suggest that drugs, sex, and religious experiences might be more important than patriotism.

Perhaps the biggest contradiction of all was that despite the overall prosperity, one in four Americans lived near or below the poverty line at the end of the decade. And despite government inaction, some economists had begun to pay serious attention to this problem. By then, too, the civil rights revolution was under way; the African-American struggle to end segregation and claim equal rights was in the process of transforming the social landscape. With all of these developments interacting, the fifties were a period of considerable change beneath the guise of security and stability. ■

F U R T H E R   R E A D I N G

On Eisenhower and the politics of the 1950s, see: Charles Alexander, *Holding the Line* (1975); Stephen E. Ambrose, *Eisenhower: The President* (1984); Barbara B. Clowse, *Brainpower for the Cold War: The Sputnik Crisis and the National Defense Education Act of 1958* (1981); Fred I. Greenstein, *The Hidden Hand Presidency* (1982). On social change, see: Keith W. Olson, *The G.I. Bill, the Veterans, and the Colleges* (1974); Elaine T. May, *Homeward Bound: American Families in the Cold War Era* (1988); Kenneth Jackson, *Crabgrass Frontier: The Suburbanization of the United States* (1985); Herbert J. Gans, *The Levittowners* (1967); Erik Barnouw, *Tube of Plenty* (1982); Mark H. Rose, *Interstate: Express Highway Politics, 1941–56* (1979). On civil rights, see: Nicholas Lemann, *The Promised Land: The Great Black Migration and How It Changed America* (1991); Mark V. Tushnet, *The NAACP's Legal Strategy Against Segregated Education* (1987); Taylor Branch, *Parting the Waters: America in the King Years, 1954–63* (1988); David J. Garrow, *Bearing the Cross: Martin Luther King, Jr., and the Southern Christian Leadership Conference* (1986); Richard Kluger, *Simple Justice* (1975); Mario Garcia, *Mexican Americans: Leadership, Ideology, and Identity, 1930–1960.*

4

The General as
President: Foreign
Policy in the 1950s

Shortly after taking office in 1953, President Dwight D. Eisenhower gathered a group of military and diplomatic specialists in the White House sun parlor and asked them to reassess Cold War strategy. In a project dubbed Operation Solarium, the experts weighed the policy of containment against more radical proposals, including threatening Moscow with nuclear war should it cross a demarcation line, and attempting to push back existing areas of Soviet control through political, psychological, economic, and covert military pressure. Discussion even touched on launching a pre-emptive attack on the Soviet Union.

As a candidate, Eisenhower had pledged he would never rest until he had liberated the "enslaved nations of the world." John Foster Dulles, the newly appointed secretary of state, had denounced containment as a "treadmill, which at best might keep us in the same place until we drop exhausted." Both men had criticized Truman's foreign policy because it was not designed to win a conclusive victory, and Republican campaign rhetoric had castigated the Democrats for "abandoning people to Godless terrorism."

With this background, the new president might have been expected to support the more belligerent recommendations emerging from Operation Solarium. But instead Eisenhower quietly made George F. Kennan—the chief architect of Truman's containment policy—one of the study's coordinators, even though Dulles had already removed Kennan from the State Department. Ultimately, the president approved continuation of the containment policy, much as it had been received from the Truman administration.

With the campaign's rhetoric behind him, Eisenhower pursued a relatively moderate foreign policy during his two terms in office. His precise approach to foreign affairs was not easy to categorize. Although he had declared that America could never rest until the Communist yoke had been lifted from Eastern Europe and China, he resisted calls from the Pentagon and Congress to increase defense spending, fearing that large budget deficits would be as destructive as war in the long run. He was willing to threaten other countries with nuclear weapons, but he avoided full-scale conflict and never employed America's expanded nuclear arsenal against an enemy. Under Eisenhower's leadership, the United States and the Soviet Union gradually learned how to coexist. However, the two powers displaced much of their direct competition into an often unsavory contest for influence in the Third World.

EISENHOWER'S APPROACH TO FOREIGN POLICY

Eisenhower's choice for secretary of state, the formidable John Foster Dulles, seemed a marked contrast to the avuncular president. A powerful corporate lawyer active in the Presbyterian church, Dulles had long been touted as the Republicans' chief foreign policy expert. He often wore a sour expression, and he delivered frequent lectures on Christian virtue and Communist sin. He was so noted for his toughness against communism—in Asia and elsewhere—that Winston Churchill joked he was the only "bull" who carried around his own "China shop."

During the Eisenhower administration, Dulles and Vice President Richard Nixon frequently made bellicose and controversial statements, creating the widespread impression that they, not Eisenhower, were the real forces behind the administration's foreign policy. In fact, as historians have come to realize, Eisenhower kept both men on a short leash. He used them to float controversial ideas, warn adversaries, and appease Republican hard-liners. In some respects they served as lightning rods to draw criticism away from the president himself, whose own views were less extreme.

Operation Solarium, combined with a 1953 strategic plan called NSC 162/3, placed a greater emphasis than before on the use of atomic bombs, both as weapons and as bargaining chips in the Cold War. In contrast to the previous administration, which had seen atomic bombs as weapons of last resort, Eisenhower's advisers urged using the bombs as weapons of choice at least in theory.

For the president, this approach had economic as well as military benefits. By relying more on nuclear weapons and the air force, the United States could slash the size of its costly ground forces. Unlike military officials who wanted enough troops, ships, and conventional munitions to achieve a decisive *superiority* over the Soviet Union, Eisenhower favored *sufficiency*—enough striking power to deter or, if necessary, destroy the Soviet Union, but no more than was needed. Attempting to match the Soviets "man for man, gun for gun," he warned, would lead to national bankruptcy. He also pointed out that "every gun that is made, every warship launched, every rocket fired, signifies, in a final sense, a theft from those who hunger and are not fed, those who are cold and are not clothed." Following these principles, Eisenhower managed to reduce military expenditures from about $52 billion annually to about $36 billion at the end of his first term. During his second term, however, military spending increased again because of congressional pressure and renewed competition with the Soviet Union.

Eisenhower and Dulles christened their strategy the New Look. It depended on what Dulles called the threat of "massive retaliation" against Soviet or Chinese provocation. The administration had inherited a nuclear arsenal of about a thousand bombs. Over the next eight years this stockpile grew to eighteen thousand weapons. An important addition to the military's arsenal was the huge, eight-engine B-52 bomber. (First deployed by the air force in 1955, the B-52 is so effective it remains in service today.) Meanwhile, small, tactical nuclear weapons as well as intercontinental ballistic missiles (ICBMs) and submarine-launched missiles were under development. By the time Eisenhower left office in 1961, the United States had enough air-, sea-, and ground-launched nuclear weapons to destroy Soviet targets many times over—far surpassing Eisenhower's own goal of sufficiency.

Some critics, especially Democratic politicians and career army officers, argued that the New Look and the doctrine of massive retaliation locked the United States into an all-or-nothing response to foreign threats. Eisenhower and Dulles responded with three measures designed to soften the all-or-nothing posture. First, the administration entered into anti-Communist military alliances with numerous countries, promising American materiel support for local troops fighting in small wars. Second, for situations short of war, the president authorized the CIA to carry out covert military operations against unfriendly regimes or groups. Finally, the administration pushed the development of tactical atomic weapons for battlefield use. These explosives, small enough to be fired in artillery shells, were intended to counter a conventional attack by Soviet or Chinese forces without escalating to thermonuclear war. The army even developed a 58-pound atomic bomb commandos could carry in their packs and use to blow up bridges, factories, or military depots.

In support of this nuclear strategy, Eisenhower saw no reason why atomic artillery shells should not be used "exactly as you would use a bullet or anything else." Early in his presidency, he approved a policy stating that in the event of hostilities with the Soviet Union, the United States would "consider nuclear weapons to be as available for use as other munitions." Yet, in part because of his military background, Eisenhower was wise enough to fear a nuclear showdown. In 1954, when South Korean strongman Syngman Rhee wanted him to threaten Russia and China with war in order to unify Korea, Eisenhower replied that "if war comes, it will be horrible. Atomic war will destroy civilization." Clearly, the president hoped to avoid a nuclear conflict, and he saw the atomic arsenal as a deterrent. If deterrence failed, however, Eisenhower was prepared to "push the button."

The policy of relying more heavily on the nuclear threat received its first test in Korea, where fighting continued near the thirty-eighth

The B-52 Bomber

If any mechanical creation deserves a biography, the B-52 bomber is a strong candidate. In 1981, as a prod to Congress to fund the new B-1 and B-2 bombers, President Ronald Reagan complained that the aging B-52 was older than many of the pilots who flew it. Nevertheless, a decade later, B-52 bombers not only remained in the air force arsenal but proved especially effective in the American war against Iraq. Able to carry a larger bomb load than any other plane, the B-52, in the words of one air force general, "cannot be seen or heard until the bombs start falling, and then it's like rolling thunder."

Between 1955 and 1963, the air force purchased 744 of these immense eight-engine warplanes. The Boeing Company produced the B-52 at an average price per plane of only $8 million ($40 million in 1995 dollars, less than one-tenth the cost of its successors).

parallel despite two years of peace talks. A major unsettled point was China's demand that the United States observe international law by returning all Chinese and North Korean prisoners of war (POWs) held in South Korea, including several thousand who had sought asylum. Like Truman before him, Eisenhower feared a domestic backlash if he agreed to repatriate POWs to a Communist country against their will.

Determined to break the deadlock, Eisenhower ordered a study to consider the use of tactical atomic weapons in Korea. To his surprise, most military and diplomatic experts doubted that atomic weapons would do much good. As the Truman administration had realized, there were few suitable targets to bomb in North Korea. Inconclusive use of the bomb might "depreciate the value of our stockpile," strate-

The plane carries a crew of six and was three or four times larger than any other combat aircraft flown before 1955. With a 60-yard wingspan, its drooping wings appear to flap on take-off, giving it the appearance of a pre-historic creature bounding down the runway and struggling to fly.

The B-52 was conceived before the nation possessed long-range missiles. Defense planners assigned it the mission of carrying nuclear weapons seven thousand miles, from U.S. bases to the Soviet heartland. But even after the big ICBM build-up of the 1960s, the air force discovered new uses for the bomber. In fact, the plane has been used heavily for conventional warfare, especially in Vietnam and the Persian Gulf war of 1991.

Aircraft designers expected the plane to last only about five thousand flying hours before structural fatigue set in. But the use of new components has extended its useful life to about fifteen thousand hours. With upgraded engines, electronics, and weapons systems, designers now predict the B-52 can be used in combat until the year 2035, eighty years after it was first built. But with the end of the Cold War in the 1990s, the Air Force finally began to retire the aircraft.

During its nearly forty years in active service, the B-52 acquired a certain mystique. Because of its immense destructive power, one air force commander noted that "it has an ethos, a sense of awesomeness." A symbol of the nuclear age, the B-52 starred in two films about nuclear war, the satiric *Dr. Strangelove* and the somber *Fail-safe*. ■

gists warned. Attacking urban and industrial targets in China would cause huge civilian losses, something Eisenhower opposed.

Eisenhower decided to bluff about U.S. intentions concerning atomic weapons. American officials spread the rumor that Eisenhower planned to use the bomb. When an armistice was achieved in July 1953, Dulles claimed that he had made it known to the Chinese that they faced a nuclear threat, and that fear of it compelled them to accept the U.S. demand for voluntary prisoner returns.

In reality, several factors contributed to the breakthrough. Joseph Stalin's sudden death from a stroke in February 1953 brought to power Soviet leaders eager to improve relations with the United States. Moreover, China had grown weary of the costly war and sought better ties with the West. Even before Washington dropped hints about escalating the war, Chinese and American negotiators had made progress on a partial exchange of sick and wounded prisoners. They then compromised on the broader issue. POWs resisting repatriation would be remanded to a neutral commission to determine their ultimate fate. When South Korean president Syngman Rhee opposed this deal, an enraged Eisenhower threatened to depose him. Thus diplomacy and Stalin's death, as much as atomic threats, led to the Korean cease-fire.

Even before the Korean armistice, Stalin's death affected Soviet behavior. During the dictator's final years, he had expanded Soviet military power, behaved increasingly erratically, and initiated bloody new purges to stamp out imagined conspiracies within his inner circle.

Immediately after Stalin's death, a triumvirate, composed of Georgi Malenkov, Nikolai Bulganin, and Nikita Khrushchev assumed power. The three new leaders promised Soviet citizens a better life. There were some ideological differences among them, but they agreed to do away with Stalin's network of terror and to seek improved relations with the West. Malenkov announced that no dispute—even with the United States—was so bad it could not be settled peacefully through negotiations.

The Soviet Union resumed diplomatic ties with Yugoslavia and Israel, eased strains with China caused by Stalin's paltry aid during the Korean War, and began providing economic support to developing nations like Egypt. These and similar measures reversed Stalin's policy of intimidating other Communist nations while ignoring the nations emerging from the crumbling European empires.

Khrushchev initially seemed the least capable member of the triumvirate and the one most committed to the status quo. But by 1955 his skills at inner-party intrigue allowed him to oust his colleagues and emerge as the first among equals. In 1956, Khrushchev shocked his country and the world by denouncing Stalin's crimes. Downplaying his own role as one of Stalin's henchmen, the new party boss charged that Stalin's "personality cult" had distorted communism and led to the slaughter of several million loyal Bolsheviks and countless Soviet citizens.

Although both Russian and world opinion cheered this break with the past, the changes within the Soviet Union posed a challenge for the Eisenhower administration. Should Washington accept at face value Soviet talk of "peaceful coexistence," or should it increase pressure on Moscow now that a less oppressive regime held power? Did Malenkov and, later, Khrushchev really seek cooperation with the West, or were they merely deceiving us? Should the United States try to break up the Sino-Soviet alliance? If so, should the administration moderate its hostility toward China or continue its efforts to isolate

Mao's government? Some Western leaders, among them Winston Churchill, urged Eisenhower to meet with the new Kremlin bosses and to allow commercial ties with China; but, restrained by Dulles, Eisenhower reacted cautiously to changes in the Communist camp. For whatever reason—fear of a political backlash, a preference to wait passively for the demise of communism, or conflicting advice from his advisers—not until late in his presidency did he begin a serious dialogue with Soviet leaders.

THE EBBING OF McCARTHYISM

The ebb and flow of the domestic Red Scare also influenced Eisenhower's approach to foreign policy. During 1953 and 1954, Senator Joseph McCarthy continued to attack supposed Reds in American government. Although Eisenhower personally found McCarthy vile, he had done little during the presidential campaign to alert the public to McCarthy's excesses. Even when McCarthy labeled George C. Marshall a traitor who had perpetrated "a conspiracy so immense as to dwarf any previous such venture in the history of man," Eisenhower refused to condemn the senator in public or defend the accused. Not only was Marshall a former army chief of staff, secretary of state, and secretary of defense—and the architect of the Marshall Plan—he was the man who had raised Eisenhower from military obscurity during the Second World War. Yet Eisenhower merely told aides he would not "get into the gutter" with McCarthy.

Eisenhower made numerous other concessions to the Republican right wing. In 1953 he refused to block the execution of Ethel and Julius Rosenberg, convicted of atomic espionage for Moscow, even though he harbored doubts about Ethel's guilt. In another high-profile case, Eisenhower approved stripping physicist J. Robert Oppenheimer of his security clearance in retaliation for his opposing the development of the hydrogen bomb. Eisenhower allowed Dulles to appoint Scott McLeod, a McCarthy protégé, to purge China specialists in the State Department who had predicted the Communist victory. Foreign Service officers had to demonstrate "positive loyalty,"—an indefinable quality—to keep their jobs. Dulles ordered that books by "Communists, fellow travelers, et cetera" be removed from U.S. Information Agency libraries abroad. "Et cetera" included works by such "radicals" as Mark Twain. During Eisenhower's administration, about fifteen hundred federal employees in various agencies were fired as security risks, and another six thousand were pressured to resign.

But McCarthyism was on the wane after 1954, the year McCarthy began to self-destruct. Early in that year, piqued at the army's refusal to give his staff aide David Schine a draft deferment and other special treatment, McCarthy charged the army with coddling Communists. The bizarre allegation focused on a dentist, Irving Peress, who had been drafted, promoted, and honorably discharged despite his admitted Communist sympathies. When high army officials, acting on the president's orders, refused to apologize or give personnel records to the senator, McCarthy charged them with incompetence and treason. Ignoring White House warnings to back off, the Wisconsin Republican declared he "did not intend to treat traitors like gentlemen."

With Eisenhower's quiet encouragement, the army countercharged that McCarthy had tried to blackmail them into giving David Schine special treatment. In April 1954 the Senate launched an inquiry. At the same time, television journalist Edward R. Murrow aired a segment of his show "See It Now" that highlighted some of McCarthy's most unsavory actions. Soon several members of the Senate began to question their colleague's behavior.

During a dramatic, televised Senate inquiry, known as the Army-McCarthy hearings, 20 million viewers had their first close look at McCarthy's vicious attacks on the loyalty of all who resisted him. Army counsel Joseph Welch, the soul of telegenic respectability, parried McCarthy's shrill tirades and refused to be provoked by the slashing attacks of Roy Cohn, the senator's legal aide.

Although only a small number of observers realized it at the time, a sexual undercurrent was present in an exchange between Cohn, a closeted homosexual who ridiculed gay men as perverts and subversives, and Welch. When Cohn could not explain how certain evidence he had placed in the record had been tampered with, Welch taunted Cohn by suggesting that "fairies"—common slang for gay men—had been responsible. By hinting broadly that Cohn was homosexual, Welch implied that McCarthy's villainy even extended to hiring homosexuals. In the timbre of the times, homosexuality was considered so unsavory that even liberals and civil libertarians felt free to use allegations of it to attack the red-baiters.

After weeks of failing to prove any Red plot within the army, a frustrated McCarthy charged that Frederick Fisher, a young lawyer who worked for Welch's Boston firm but was not a member of the army's legal team, had Communist leanings. Welch, who had anticipated the accusation, responded to McCarthy's mudslinging with a sad shake of the head, saying, "I think I never really gauged your cruelty or your recklessness." Unable to stop himself, the senator resumed his attack on Fisher. Finally, Welch could tolerate McCarthy's slander no more. He declared that McCarthy's forgiveness would "have to come from someone other than me." The lawyer then issued a historic query: "Have you no sense of decency, sir, at long last? Have you left no sense of decency?"

Even though the Army-McCarthy hearings rendered no formal verdict, the senator had failed a critical media test. Opinion polls taken during and after the televised sessions revealed a dramatic slide in McCarthy's approval rating, from nearly 50 percent at the beginning of 1954 to only 30 percent in June. By December, the Senate voted to censure him for "unbecoming conduct."

Eisenhower, who took a bit more credit for the senator's humiliation than was warranted, hosted Welch at the White House and remarked that "McCarthyism had become McCarthywasim." McCarthy's loss of public and Senate approval gave Eisenhower more freedom to maneuver. The witch-hunter himself never recovered from these public defeats. Shunned by old friends, he increased his legendary drinking, lost political influence, and died of alcohol-related illness in 1957.

AMERICA AND THE CHALLENGES OF THE THIRD WORLD

In the fifteen years following the end of the Second World War, thirty-seven nations emerged from colonialism to independence, eighteen during 1960 alone. Most of these new states were nonwhite, poor, nonindustrialized, and located in Asia, Africa, or the Middle East. Many had gained independence through armed struggle; in some the violence continued after independence. They had much in common with poor noncolonial nations, especially those in Latin America, where political unrest often became armed rebellion. During the 1950s, at least twenty-eight prolonged guerrilla insurgencies were under way.

Most of these emerging and underdeveloped nations, loosely called the Third World, existed outside the bloc of the industrialized democracies (the First World) and the Communist nations (the Second World). Few had democratic governments. Most sought to remain neutral in the Cold War while pursuing economic development and soliciting aid from both sides. Poor nations both envied and resented American power. They often employed the rhetoric of socialism, even as they sought the material rewards of capitalism.

Under Stalin, the Soviet Union had ignored or criticized most non-Communist liberation movements. Khrushchev proved more adroit, offering economic and military assistance to emerging nations whether or not they adhered to Moscow's line. This probably represented a Soviet effort to avoid a direct challenge to the United States while still supporting revolutionary goals.

The United States increasingly shared Moscow's concern with the Third World. The emerging nations contained vast raw material

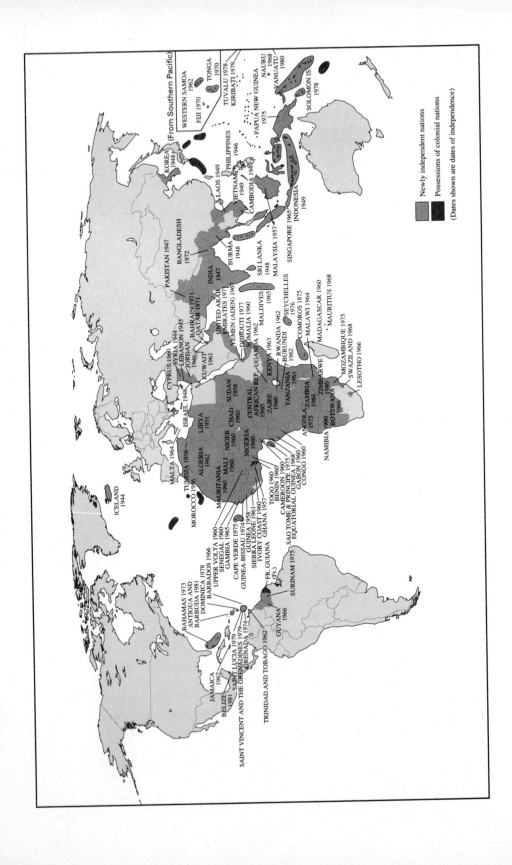

(From Southern Pacific)

WESTERN SAMOA 1962
FIJI 1970
TONGA 1970
TUVALU 1978
KIRIBATI 1979
NAURU 1968
VANUATU 1980

KOREA 1948
LAOS 1949
PHILIPPINES 1946
VIETNAM 1949
CAMBODIA 1949
SOLOMON IS. 1978
PAPUA NEW GUINEA 1975

PAKISTAN 1947
BANGLADESH 1972
INDIA 1947
BURMA 1948
SRI LANKA 1948
MALDIVES 1965
MALAYSIA 1957
SINGAPORE 1965
INDONESIA 1949
SEYCHELLES 1976
MAURITIUS 1968

CYPRUS 1960
SYRIA 1944
LEBANON 1943
JORDAN 1946
BAHRAIN 1971
QATAR 1971
UNITED ARAB EMIRATES 1971
YEMEN (ADEN) 1967
SOMALIA 1960
DJIBOUTI 1977
RWANDA 1962
BURUNDI 1962
COMOROS 1875
MADAGASCAR 1960

ISRAEL 1948
KUWAIT 1961
SUDAN 1956
UGANDA 1962
KENYA 1963
TANZANIA 1961
MALAWI 1964
MOZAMBIQUE 1975
SWAZILAND 1968
LESOTHO 1966

MALTA 1964
LIBYA 1951
CHAD 1960
CENTRAL AFRICAN REP. 1960
ZAIRE 1960
ZAMBIA 1964
ZIMBABWE 1980
BOTSWANA 1966

ICELAND 1944
TUNISIA 1956
MOROCCO 1956
ALGERIA 1962
MAURITANIA 1960
MALI 1960
NIGER 1960
NIGERIA 1960
ANGOLA 1975
NAMIBIA 1990

UPPER VOLTA 1960
SENEGAL 1960
GAMBIA 1965
CAPE VERDE 1975
GUINEA-BISSAU 1974
GUINEA 1958
SIERRA LEONE 1961
IVORY COAST 1960
GHANA 1957
TOGO 1960
BENIN 1960
CAMEROON 1960
SAO TOME & PRINCIPE 1975
EQUATORIAL GUINEA 1968
GABON 1960
CONGO 1960

BAHAMAS 1973
ANTIGUA AND BARBUDA 1981
DOMINICA 1978
BARBADOS 1966
SAINT LUCIA 1979
SAINT VINCENT AND THE GRENADINES 1979
GRENADA 1974
FR. GUIANA (Fr.)
SURINAM 1975

JAMAICA 1962
BELIZE 1981
TRINIDAD AND TOBAGO 1962
GUYANA 1966

Newly independent nations

Possessions of colonial nations

(Dates shown are dates of independence)

wealth and a huge population. Eisenhower and Dulles worried that the Third World's criticism of imperialism and capitalism would provide a wedge for Soviet influence. And many Americans mistrusted any model of national development that deviated from the United States experience.

To halt Communist inroads in the Third World, the Eisenhower administration forged numerous anti-Communist alliances based loosely on NATO. These included the Central Treaty Organization (CENTO) in the Middle East and the Southeast Asia Treaty Organization (SEATO), as well as bilateral defense agreements with Taiwan, South Korea, Spain, and the Philippines. Unlike NATO, most of the new pacts committed Washington only to provide aid and consultation in cases of aggression. The pacts had more psychological and political than military value, for when major American interests in Asia, the Middle East, or Latin America were at stake, the United States usually acted on its own.

Foreign aid also played a growing role in the administration's effort to influence the Third World. Under Truman, nearly all foreign economic assistance had been sent to Western Europe and Japan. Eisenhower first called for eliminating most aid, offering two-way trade as the best way to help poor countries. But because the poorest nations had little to export and no money to buy foreign goods, two-way trade would not substantially help them. Eventually the Eisenhower administration not only increased overall aid levels, but also sent most of its assistance—surplus food, credits to buy American products, military equipment, construction loans—to emerging nations.

Critics pointed to faults in the aid programs for developing nations. For example, providing surplus grain to poor nations under the "Food for Peace" program fed the hungry and helped American farmers dispose of surplus crops, but it often delayed sound agricultural development in needy countries. Construction loans were frequently squandered on glamorous, expensive projects like sports arenas while basic necessities like irrigation systems and wells went unfunded.

In 1958, writers William J. Lederer and Eugene Burdick highlighted these problems in their best-selling novel, *The Ugly American*. They described a fictional Southeast Asian country, resembling Vietnam, in which ignorant American diplomats knew nothing about their host nation and lived in an isolated "golden ghetto." The fictional diplomats contemplated grand development schemes but ignored the plight of the peasant farmers. The hero, a physically unattractive diplomat, defied the stereotype by learning the local language,

◀ **The Rise of the Third World: Newly Independent Nations Since 1943**

associating with ordinary people, discovering their real needs, and successfully defending the nation against communism.

Whatever the impact of its aid programs, the Eisenhower administration believed they were not enough to counter the threat of Communist influence in the Third World. By supplying military advisers and authorizing covert actions by the CIA, Eisenhower deepened American involvement in Vietnam, and soon the United States was intervening in Iran and Guatemala as well.

During his first term, Eisenhower appointed General James Doolittle to chair a secret study of the CIA's ability to counter Soviet activities. The resulting report warned that America faced "an implacable enemy whose avowed objective is world domination by whatever means and at whatever cost." There were "no rules in such a game," because "previously acceptable norms of human conduct" no longer applied. Americans "must learn to subvert, sabotage and destroy our enemies by more clever and sophisticated and more effective methods than those used against us."

Using the CIA to conduct secret operations had a strong appeal to American leaders. Covert actions provided the opportunity to achieve foreign policy goals without the direct costs of war or the scrutiny of public debate. The secrecy of CIA operations also permitted the government to act in ways the American public found too uncomfortable to discuss.

For example, during the 1950s many scientists thought mind-altering drugs might be used against U.S. troops or as a means to entrap and brainwash individuals. To assess this danger, the CIA undertook a secret project in which doses of LSD—lysergic acid diethylamide, a hallucinogen—were given to unsuspecting American citizens. After the people were drugged, CIA operatives studied their behavior. Hundreds of Americans—the exact number is unknown—became unwitting guinea pigs in these experiments. Several went insane, and at least one committed suicide or was murdered to keep the project secret. Information about the operation remained secret until the late 1970s.

The CIA began to play an important role in America's interventions in the Third World. As a covert arm of government policy, the CIA bolstered friendly governments and sponsored coups against unfriendly regimes the administration felt it could no longer tolerate. During the Eisenhower years the public heard few details of the CIA's operations; only in later decades were some of these actions brought under public scrutiny.

Eisenhower inherited the war in French Indochina and passed it on to his successors. In 1953 and 1954—as later—policymakers worried that if the Communist Vietminh guerrillas won in Vietnam, first all of Southeast Asia, then resource-starved Japan, would "fall like dominoes." After this, Eisenhower predicted, the Pacific Ocean would "become a Communist lake."

Since 1950, the United States had spent over $1 billion in Vietnam, providing about 70 percent of the cost of France's war against the Vietminh and its leader, Ho Chi Minh. Yet, as American analysts admitted, French rule was unpopular in Vietnam and unlikely ever to be accepted. Eisenhower and Dulles hoped that if the French granted real power to non-Communist Vietnamese rather than the puppet emperor Bao Dai, the war would change from a colonial struggle to a battle against communism. Defending the "freedom" of an independent Vietnam would prove more popular among Americans than saving a colony.

In the spring of 1954 the war in Indochina reached a climax. Vietminh guerrillas, assisted by Chinese military aid and advisers, trapped twelve thousand French troops at Dienbienphu, a valley in northern Vietnam. Washington again urged the French to grant Vietnam independence as a way of building support for expanded American and British military aid. Vice President Richard Nixon went further, recommending sending in American troops. Eisenhower compared the threat in Vietnam to the earlier dangers posed by Hirohito, Mussolini, and Hitler. The French, Eisenhower privately complained, were "a hopeless, helpless mass of protoplasm."

As the battle for Dienbienphu approached a climax late in April, Dulles, Nixon, and the heads of the armed services formulated plans for American air strikes against the Vietminh. General Nathan Twining proposed dropping three small atomic bombs around the battle zone to clean out the Communists. Eisenhower urged restraint, declaring, "You boys must be crazy. . . . We can't use those awful things against Asians for the second time in ten years." However, Eisenhower did consider a conventional air strike, and he allowed Dulles to threaten atomic retaliation if China sent combat troops to help the Vietminh. But when Britain declined to commit troops to aid the French, and congressional leaders proved unenthusiastic, Eisenhower refused to intervene.

Early in May 1954, the French base at Dienbienphu fell. The political uproar in Paris resulted in the election of a new prime minister, Pierre Mendes-France, who pledged to negotiate a quick end to the Indochina war. Talks took place at an international conference in Geneva. Nearly everyone present predicted the Vietminh would soon control all of Vietnam. Eisenhower sent an American observer to the Geneva talks, and Dulles also attended briefly. When asked if he planned to meet with Chinese representative Zhou Enlai, Dulles responded, "only if our cars collide." The United States feared that whatever arrangement emerged from Geneva would merely enhance Communist power and prestige.

Cartoonist Herblock depicted the anxiety many Americans felt about the Eisenhower-Dulles foreign policy. *From* Herblock's Special for Today *(Simon & Schuster, 1958).*

China and the Soviet Union actually played a moderating role at the Geneva talks. Eager to win points with the West, the major Communist states pressed Ho Chi Minh to accept a temporary division of Vietnam rather than immediate total control. The Geneva Accords, reached in July, drew an armistice line, intended as a temporary military division, along the seventeenth parallel, with French forces moving to the south and Vietminh troops to the north. The key provision called for the departure of all French forces from Vietnam by 1956, followed by free national elections. As the French withdrew from Indochina, they also granted complete independence to Laos and Cambodia, which bordered Vietnam.

American leaders feared that Ho Chi Minh would probably win the promised election. Dulles warned European leaders that the West must never surrender Southeast Asia. To bolster the wobbling dominoes, Dulles flew to Manila in September 1954. There he signed the SEATO alliance, essentially a Western pact to police Asia. Only two Southeast Asian nations, Thailand and the Philippines, were signatories. Dulles also negotiated a defense treaty with Taiwan.

Meanwhile, the United States began providing substantial economic and military assistance, as well as military advisers, directly to non-Communist groups in southern Vietnam. As the French departed, American personnel, many working for the CIA, backed Ngo Dinh Diem, a Vietnamese Catholic (in a largely Buddhist nation) who had lived for several years in Europe and the United States. Attracted by his pro-Western rhetoric, his Christianity, and his anti-Communism, army and CIA officers helped Diem organize a government and army in Saigon. To expand Diem's base of support, the CIA encouraged northern Catholics to move south.

In 1956 Diem staged carefully controlled elections south of the seventeenth parallel. He deposed Emperor Bao Dai, who went into exile on the Riviera, and proclaimed himself president of the Republic of Vietnam. Washington recognized this republic, better known as South Vietnam, as an independent nation, and dismissed the Democratic Republic of Vietnam (North Vietnam) as a Communist puppet state with no claim on the south. Between 1956 and 1960 the United States spent over $1 billion in an effort to create a viable South Vietnam.

During these years Diem achieved nominal success in establishing his regime. Prominent Americans, including Senator John F. Kennedy and Frances Cardinal Spellman, as well as influential media such as *Life* magazine, portrayed Diem as a democratic leader and a model for Asian development, ignoring the many things that made him unpopular in his own land. These included a haughty style, persecution of Buddhists, favoritism toward the Catholic minority, support for landlords against the peasantry, and toleration of widespread corruption. They described Diem's strong-arm tactics as "one-man democracy." Despite such wishful thinking, by 1960 a powerful guerrilla movement was challenging Diem and raising once again the specter of a Communist Vietnam. In effect, Eisenhower's policy of supporting Diem had merely passed the problem on to his successor.

Concern over Vietnam stemmed from the larger fear of the People's Republic of China (or Red China, as most Americans called it during the 1950s). In 1954 to 1955 and again in 1958, the United States and China came close to war over the fate of several small Nationalist Chinese-held islands in the Taiwan (Formosa) Strait. The most important of these, Quemoy and Matsu, lay only a few miles off the coast of mainland China. The pro-American Chinese government on Taiwan (Formosa) stationed troops on these islands in an effort to maintain its claim to the Chinese mainland, using them as a staging area for commando raids against the Communist regime. In retaliation, and in hope of destabilizing and eventually taking over Taiwan, the Chinese began shelling Quemoy in September 1954. The United States responded by signing a mutual security pact with Taiwan.

In private, both Eisenhower and Dulles had little respect for Jiang Jieshi (Chiang Kai-shek) and ridiculed his claim to the Chinese mainland. In negotiating the security pact with Jiang, Dulles insisted that no major Nationalist attack be launched against Communist China without American approval. He also made it clear that the United States would protect Taiwan but not necessarily the small, disputed islands close to mainland China. Eisenhower and Dulles felt compelled to assist Jiang, in part because they had criticized the Democrats for deserting him but also because they feared further Chinese expansion if Taiwan fell. The administration convinced Congress early in 1955 to approve the Formosa Strait Resolution, which empowered the president to use force to protect the security of Taiwan and "related positions and territories in that area." The president and secretary of state also issued a veiled warning of atomic retaliation if Chinese forces invaded Quemoy or Taiwan.

The 1955 crisis ended when China seized a few minor islands in the Taiwan Strait but abandoned efforts to capture Quemoy. Washington and Beijing then began diplomatic talks in Warsaw and Geneva that continued, with little success, for fifteen years. Tensions resumed in 1958 when China renewed its shelling of Quemoy and Eisenhower ordered the American navy to resupply Nationalist troops on the island. After some tense moments, the Chinese declined to shoot at the American ships. The Americans convinced Jiang to stop provoking China. The Chinese artillery gradually abated, first firing only on odd-numbered days and soon after substituting propaganda bombs for real shells.

The Chinese resented both U.S. support for Taiwan and what they saw as a lack of Soviet assistance to themselves. The 1958 confrontation in the Taiwan Strait contributed to the growing friction between China and the Soviet Union. When Khrushchev refused to provide Mao with a prototype atom bomb, the Chinese leader began a crash program to develop China's own bomb. Mao denounced the Soviet leadership for "yielding to evil" and "coddling wrong," and Khrushchev called Mao a warmonger. While these tensions between Moscow and Beijing pleased Americans, historians are unsure whether the policies promoted by Dulles and Eisenhower split the Communist powers apart. In any case, the United States and China continued to see each other as enemies after the Soviets and Chinese fell out.

Eisenhower used the CIA to deal with a variety of threats in both the Middle East and Central America. The agency played an especially important role in deposing regimes that challenged American or Western domination of raw materials and in situations where the Soviets were not directly involved. Examples occurred in Iran, Guatemala, and Cuba.

During the Second World War, American oil companies began to displace British, French, and Dutch control of Arab and Persian Gulf petroleum. Inexpensive oil played a major part in the postwar economic growth of the United States, Western Europe, and Japan. When Eisenhower took office he inherited a smoldering dispute over control of Iranian oil. In 1951 Iran's nationalistic (but non-Communist) prime minister, Mohammed Mossadeq, seized the holdings of the Anglo-Iranian Oil Company without compensating its (mostly British) owners. In retaliation, major European and American oil companies organized a boycott, refusing to purchase, transport, or refine Iranian petroleum.

In May 1953, as the boycott caused economic havoc in Iran, Mossadeq cabled Eisenhower that, unless the boycott ended, he might seek Soviet assistance. Eisenhower rejected Iran's request for support and urged Mossadeq to reach a "reasonable settlement" along the lines demanded by the British.

Shah Mohammed Reza Pahlavi, Iran's nominal monarch, had played only a minor role in the nation's politics since succeeding his father during the Second World War. The young shah resented Mossadeq's influence and saw the crisis as an opportunity to regain real power by playing up the Soviet threat. His interests coincided with those of American diplomats and oil companies, who hoped to preempt Britain's dominant role in the Iranian oil industry. To prevent any Soviet role in Iran and to preserve access to the region's petroleum, Eisenhower authorized a CIA coup to topple Mossadeq and put the shah in control.

Kermit Roosevelt, grandson of Theodore Roosevelt and a veteran spy, played a key role in the coup. Arriving in Teheran in August 1953, he made contact with the shah and with a general in the Iranian army, Fazollah Zahedi. Roosevelt financed violent demonstrations against Mossadeq, enlisting mobs led by circus performers along with army and police personnel. The shah fled briefly to Rome while the army moved to restore order. Zahedi's forces stormed the parliament and arrested Mossadeq, and the general became prime minister. The shah returned to power, and Washington promptly extended $45 million in aid to his government.

An American delegation sent by Eisenhower mediated a deal between Iran and the British oil companies. The settlement allowed Iran to retain control of its oil fields so long as it agreed to market its petroleum at a low price through a consortium, in which American companies were granted a 40 percent stake. The British discovered that the cost of calling in the United States included losing a large measure of its oil monopoly.

Aside from Iran, the Middle East remained in political turmoil throughout the 1950s. Arabs felt humiliated by Israel's military victory in 1948 and the continued ability of the tiny Jewish state to defeat its numerous Arab neighbors. Although at the time Britain and France, rather than the United States, provided most of Israel's weapons, American Jews, with Washington's blessing, made substantial private contributions to Israel. Many Arabs considered Israel a vestige of Western colonialism; they also found it a useful scapegoat for their own problems.

Such was the situation when Gamal Abdel Nasser, an Egyptian army officer, toppled the inept, pro-British King Farouk in 1952. Nasser emerged as a popular and ambitious leader who envisioned Egypt as the center of a revived Arab world. He bought arms from the Soviet bloc; but at the same time he sought economic assistance from the West to finance construction of the immense Aswan Dam across the Nile, designed to provide electricity and water for Egyptian farmlands. Dulles initially favored American financing for the project, but he canceled the aid in July 1956 when Nasser extended diplomatic recognition to Communist China. By this time, the Eisenhower administration feared that Nasser's appeal to pan-Arab nationalism would destabilize the oil-rich region—even though Egypt had little oil of its own—opening a path for Soviet influence or endangering the West's supply of cheap petroleum.

Nasser retaliated for the withdrawal of American support by nationalizing the British-owned Suez Canal, through which much of Europe's oil supply passed. Egypt's seizure of the canal enhanced Nasser's image among Arabs and provided tolls that would help pay for the Aswan Dam. The British and French governments decided to send forces to recover the canal (and, they hoped, topple Nasser). They coordinated their plans with Israel, which feared Nasser's influence on other Arabs.

In accordance with the joint plan, on October 29, 1956, the Israeli army attacked and defeated the Egyptian army on the Sinai Peninsula and camped just east of the canal. Britain and France then announced the dispatch of troops with the stated goal of protecting the Suez Canal from destruction. The European powers demanded that both Egyptian and Israeli armies withdraw from either side of the waterway and return it to European control.

These actions by America's allies infuriated Dulles and Eisenhower. They feared that European intervention in the Suez dispute would strengthen Arab radicals and distract world attention from the crisis in Hungary, where Soviet forces were crushing an uprising. The fact that America's two closest allies, England and France, had acted secretly both embarrassed and angered the American leaders. The United States therefore joined the Soviet Union in condemning the Suez attack, and the otherwise rival superpowers supported a United Nations-mandated cease-fire. With sunken vessels blocking oil shipments through the canal, Dulles pressed Latin American exporters to embargo petroleum sales to Britain and France until the European forces left Egypt. Washington also threatened to block private American aid to Israel. By December 1956, the invaders had left Egypt,

Nasser had claimed a victory over imperialism, and British prime minister Anthony Eden had resigned in disgrace.

Following this fiasco, Britain and France moved to accommodate Arab sentiment by distancing themselves from Israel, and the United States took a more active role in the Middle East. In January 1957, Eisenhower got Congress to approve a resolution giving him the power to use force, if necessary, to "block Communist aggression" in the region. Washington hoped to woo conservative Arab rulers in Saudi Arabia, Jordan, and Iraq by posing as their protector against both Soviet influence and Nasser's radical followers.

The so-called Eisenhower Doctrine held that the United States could intervene in the Middle East if any nation there requested help to resist a Communist takeover. During 1957 a series of plots, coups, and countercoups swept Syria, Jordan, and Iraq. In 1958 Nasser forged an alliance between Egypt, Syria, and Yemen, creating the United Arab Republic. In July a pro-Nasser officer, General Abdel Karim Kassim, toppled the pro-Western King Faisal of Iraq, and considered allying his new government with Egypt.

American officials feared that Nasser and his followers throughout the region would block the world's access to Middle Eastern oil, forcing the United States, Europe, and the Soviet Union to bargain with them for petroleum. Determined to block Nasser's influence, the Eisenhower administration made a show of strength in the tiny country of Lebanon, where for months a political crisis had shaken the government.

Before abandoning control of Lebanon during the 1940s, France imposed on the Lebanese a constitution that gave greater political power to the Maronite Catholic minority than to the Muslim majority. As the number of Muslims grew, so did their resentment at their second-class status; many were attracted to Nasser's vision of a unified, Arab Middle East. In July 1958, Lebanese president Camille Chamoun, a Maronite, outraged Muslims by suggesting he might stay in office when his term expired a few months later. Radio broadcasts from Egypt called on Muslims to depose the Christian-dominated government in Beirut, and rioting erupted. When Chamoun looked to the United States for assistance, Eisenhower saw an opportunity to intimidate Nasser.

Eisenhower believed that Nasser's true object was to gain control of vital Middle East petroleum supplies in order to destroy the Western world. Similarly, Dulles feared that unless American forces intervened in Lebanon, all governments in the Middle East not affiliated with Nasser would be overthrown. The impact would be felt worldwide, he worried, as people surmised that the United States was "afraid of the Soviet Union."

On July 14, 1958, Eisenhower ordered fourteen thousand Marines, with tactical nuclear capability and backed by a large fleet, to suppress what he called a "Communist-inspired" threat to Lebanon. Actually, by the time the Marines landed in Beirut, most of the rioting had ended. Sunbathers gaped in awe as landing craft disgorged troops prepared to fight their way ashore.

The operation achieved its basic aim of limiting Nasser's influence over Middle East oil supplies. The Lebanese factions patched together a compromise, and Chamoun surrendered his office to another Christian. Iraq dropped plans to ally with Egypt and promised to protect Western-owned oil facilities. Even Nasser backed off, after receiving word from Khrushchev that the Soviet Union would not assist him in any direct challenge to the United States. Although the Middle East remained chronically unstable and the Arabs and Israelis would fight several more wars, Eisenhower's show of force held the line through the end of the decade.

The Eisenhower administration also had great concern with blocking Communist influence in Latin America. In Senate testimony in 1953, Dulles described a growing Communist conspiracy in Central and South America. In the past, Dulles explained to his brother Allen, director of the CIA, Washington could afford to ignore turmoil in Latin America. Now, however, unrest and upheaval would lead to control by Communists.

Throughout the 1950s the United States provided very little aid, aside from military assistance, to Latin America. For example, the army established special training programs in Panama and elsewhere for Latin American military officers. By paying only lip service to democracy, ignoring the region's social problems, and aligning itself closely with repressive regimes, Washington showed that it opposed communism in Latin America but turned a blind eye to its dictatorships and poverty. In 1953 Eisenhower and Dulles identified the major crisis in Latin America as the "Communist infection" in Guatemala, one of the region's poorest nations.

In 1944 a group of reform-minded Guatemalan army officers had overthrown long-time dictator Jorge Ubico. After a relatively fair election in 1945, reformer Juan Jose Arevalo became president. He inherited a desperately poor country in which the European-descended elite held nearly feudal control over the large Indian population. Some 2 percent of the population controlled 70 percent of the land. In addition, the American-owned United Fruit Company, a banana grower, held vast tracts of farmland, much of which remained uncultivated. United Fruit also controlled the railroads, ports, and communications infrastructure. Although United Fruit was not the most exploitative employer in Guatemala, its American employees lived in luxury while its peasant workers eked out a living on a dollar a day.

Arevalo abolished forced Indian labor, extended voting rights, imposed a minimum wage, and began a modest land-reform program. In 1951 Arevalo's elected successor, President Jacobo Arbenz Guzman, ordered the redistribution to the poor of large uncultivated land holdings and sponsored new labor and wage reforms. In the Guatemalan context, these actions were revolutionary. Arbenz drafted plans to build new roads and ports that would break United Fruit's monopoly over the transportation system. He also expropriated 400,000 acres of uncultivated company land, offering $3 per acre compensation, a figure based on the declared tax value of the property.

United Fruit demanded $75 per acre and got the Eisenhower administration to intercede on its behalf. The State Department—several of whose top officials had past business associations with United Fruit—claimed the issue was neither social justice nor land reform but a Communist assault on private property. American officials then cooperated with United Fruit publicists in a propaganda campaign that labeled Arbenz a Communist dupe. By casting the dispute over compensation for banana plantations as a battle between communism and Western-style democracy, the administration and United Fruit created a pretext for intervention. By removing Arbenz, Dulles told the president, Eisenhower would achieve a "Czechoslovakia in reverse." He was referring, of course, to the Soviet military pressure that toppled the non-communist government in Prague in 1948. Washington boosted aid to several key Latin American nations, which then joined the United States in sponsoring a resolution before the Organization of American States, a regional organization the United States had helped to found in 1948. The resolution declared that no nation in the Western Hemisphere had a right to a Communist government.

In the summer of 1953, Eisenhower authorized a CIA plan to stage a coup in Guatemala. To undermine Arbenz's support within the military, Washington cut off aid to the Guatemalan army and increased assistance to neighboring states. From bases in Honduras and Nicaragua, the CIA organized a small Guatemalan exile force under Carlos Castillo Armas. It began a disinformation campaign, using pamphlets and radio broadcasts to confuse the Guatemalan people. The broadcasts declared that a large rebel army would soon attack. When Arbenz purchased a small arms shipment from Communist Czechoslovakia in May 1954, American officials immediately described it as part of a "master plan of world communism" that threatened the Panama Canal.

In June, a thousand or so CIA-directed exiles entered Guatemala and set up a base camp. CIA radio stations broadcast reports of a massive invasion. A few small planes dropped anti-Arbenz leaflets in the capital while the pilots threw sticks of dynamite out of their cockpits. In a panic, Arbenz tried to arm a peasant militia. The regular army was frightened of fighting the United States, and they also feared being supplanted by peasants. Fooled into thinking he faced a large invasion, and deserted by his army, Arbenz resigned on June 27. As the CIA had planned, Castillo Armas and his comrades took over.

Eisenhower considered the Guatemalan coup a model Cold War triumph. At a dinner in their honor, Eisenhower told a gathering of key CIA participants that, thanks to them, America had averted the establishment of a Soviet beachhead in the Western Hemisphere. The new Guatemalan rulers restored United Fruit's lands and rolled back most other reforms. Over the next three decades, a succession of military governments slaughtered an estimated 100,000 Indians, labor organizers, students, and intellectuals who challenged the ruling elite.

Eisenhower later approved CIA operations to overthrow President Sukarno of Indonesia, General Rafael Trujillo of the Dominican Republic, and Premier Patrice Lumumba of the Congo (now Zaire). Although Sukarno survived a botched coup attempt, Trujillo and Lumumba both fell to assassins' bullets. American complicity in the assassinations remains unclear.

Despite the success in Guatemala, chronic poverty in Latin America led to instability. When Eisenhower sent Vice President Nixon to Venezuela on a good-will tour, an angry mob stoned his car and nearly killed him. The crowd was reacting, in part, to Nixon's praise of Latin American military leaders as a "great stabilizing force" against communism.

The Cuban Revolution of 1959 proved even more frightening. Washington had tolerated Cuba's long-lived military dictator, Fulgencio Batista, because he protected foreign investments and supported the United States in the Cold War. As a reward, Cuban sugar producers enjoyed privileged access to the American market. This profited wealthy landowners, among them many Americans, but few benefits trickled down to plantation workers.

Batista's regime collapsed in January 1959 when Fidel Castro led a guerrilla army into Havana. The son of a well-to-do family, Castro had lived for a time in New York, when he dreamed of pitching for an American baseball team. Trained as a lawyer, he led a failed rebellion in the early 1950s, spent time in a Cuban prison, and launched a second revolt in 1956. Initially Castro called for socialist reform but had no specific Marxist program or links with the Soviet Union.

At first Washington took a wait-and-see attitude. Castro legalized Cuba's small Communist party, made anti-American speeches, ousted moderates from his movement, postponed promised elections, and publicly executed about five hundred of Batista's henchmen. During a visit to Washington in April 1959, Castro insisted he wanted good relations with America. But he later signed a trade deal with Russia and expropriated foreign-owned plantations, paying the owners—with bonds rather than cash—a price based on deflated tax valua-

Fidel Castro with Richard Nixon in April 1959 during his visit to the United States. *Wide World Photos.*

tions. Eisenhower decided the Cuban leader was a dangerous pro-Soviet puppet.

Although Castro lost his popularity among the Cuban elite, many ordinary Cubans admired his bold challenges to Uncle Sam. Castro's spunk in standing up to the United States also made him something of a hero elsewhere in Latin America. To counter his appeal, Eisenhower approved long-term economic aid to Latin America, a program President John F. Kennedy later dubbed the Alliance for Progress.

After cutting trade and diplomatic ties with Cuba, in mid-1960 Eisenhower decided to eliminate Castro. He authorized the CIA to covertly undermine Castro's image and regime and to train an army of exiled Cubans to invade the island. Mindful of the overthrow of Guatemala's Arbenz, Castro organized a popular militia armed with Soviet weapons. A year later, the CIA plan led to the disastrous Bay of Pigs invasion, for which the next president, John F. Kennedy, took the principal blame.

THE HUNGARIAN UPRISING AND REFUGEE POLITICS

Although the Eisenhower administration showed few qualms about intervening in Third World countries when there was any question of

Hungarian freedom fighters celebrate their brief victory before Soviet forces over-whelmed them. © *Stern/Black Star.*

Communist influence, little could be done about the regions under direct Soviet control. This fact was emphasized by the 1956 uprising in Hungary. In the autumn of that year, inspired by Khrushchev's own speech denouncing Stalin, ordinary Hungarian citizens as well as local Communist officials revolted against Soviet domination.

A reformist faction gained control of the Hungarian Communist party and began to dismantle the Stalinist police apparatus. Moscow held back at first, but intervened brutally when reformer Imre Nagy declared that Hungary intended to quit the Warsaw Pact, the military agreement that bound Eastern European states to Moscow. Early in November, in the middle of the Suez crisis, Khrushchev sent Russian tanks into Budapest to crush this heresy.

Although CIA-supported Radio Free Europe had urged Eastern Europeans to revolt, when the Hungarians did rise against the Soviets, Washington refused to help. To a degree, the simultaneous crisis in the Middle East limited Washington's ability to act in Europe. Eisenhower also feared that American intervention would destroy Hungary rather than free it. "[The] Russians are scared and furious," he noted, and "nothing is more dangerous than a dictatorship in that frame of mind." The president even barred sending to Hungary a group of CIA-trained exiles prepared for guerrilla operations.

The uprising in Hungary created a major refugee problem for the United States. Some 200,000 people, mostly noncombatants, fled the reimposition of Soviet control. Because the 1952 McCarran-Walter Act barred most immigration from Eastern Europe, few could enter the United States. As President Truman had predicted, the law became a slap in the face to those "fleeing barbarism."

In 1953 Eisenhower had persuaded Congress to enact the Refugee Relief Act. This allocated about 200,000 special visas outside the quota system, with half reserved for "escapees" from "Communist-dominated" areas of Europe. A few Chinese also came under its provisions. But in spite of this one-time relaxation, strict immigration quotas remained in place. Senators William Revercomb of West Virginia and Pat McCarran of Nevada warned that refugees might be Communist "sleeper agents" sent to subvert America, and many Americans complained that too many foreigners were entering the country. In 1954, Eisenhower responded to complaints about large numbers of illegal Mexicans by authorizing the deportation of 1 million undocumented migrants during "Operation Wetback."

The mass Hungarian exodus prompted the United States to bend its regular immigration policy as well. Eisenhower found a loophole in the existing law that permitted the attorney general to grant refugees "parole," a legal status that allowed them to enter the United States "for emergency reasons or for reasons deemed strongly in the public interest." This provision had been written to accommodate individual hardship cases, not large groups. Nevertheless, Congress approved use of the parole power to admit 38,000 Hungarians; it also voted special aid for them. Most of the rest settled in Europe.

Lawmakers and the public showed compassion for several reasons. The Hungarians were seen both as victims of Soviet oppression and as an easily assimilated group. The situation repeated itself in 1959 and 1960 when over 125,000 middle- and upper-class Cubans fled Castro's revolution. Furthermore, by utilizing the special parole provision, Congress avoided prolonged debate over immigration quotas, letting the existing law stand.

The response to the plight of the Hungarian, Cuban, and, later, Indochinese refugees must be understood in light of the Cold War. Policymakers viewed these refugees not merely as victims but as assets in an ideological struggle. Mexicans were deported while Hungarians and Cubans were welcomed as symbolic freedom fighters.

THE SPACE RACE AND THE ARMS RACE

In October 1957 the Soviet Union captured world attention by launching an earth-orbiting, basketball-sized satellite, *Sputnik I*. White House Chief of Staff Sherman Adams dismissed the achievement as an "outer space basketball game." A month later, however, the

Russians launched the thousand-pound *Sputnik II,* carrying a dog into orbit. Senator Lyndon Johnson of Texas, chair of the Armed Services Committee's Preparedness Subcommittee, expressed astonishment that another nation might achieve technological superiority over the United States. Like millions of Americans, he wondered what it would mean if *Sputnik* carried a nuclear bomb instead of a dog. Senator Henry Jackson of Washington called for a "National Week of Shame and Disgrace." *Life* magazine added to the panic when it described the Soviet satellite as a major defeat for the United States.

The space and missile race had begun during the Second World War with the German V-2 rocket. After 1945, both Moscow and Washington utilized German scientists to help develop rocket programs. Because the American air force preferred the glamour of piloted aircraft to impersonal missiles, and because American bombers could be based in Europe, near the Soviet Union, Wernher von Braun's rocket team in Huntsville, Alabama, received modest funding. In contrast, the Soviet Union, which lacked air bases near the United States, saw missiles as a cost-effective way to deliver bombs. Consequently, Moscow initially pushed harder to develop long-range missiles.

With the growth of the Pentagon's budget after 1950, and with increasing reliance on atomic weapons under Eisenhower's New Look, the pace of rocket research accelerated. Eisenhower was also keen to use rockets to launch reconnaissance satellites capable of providing reliable intelligence on Soviet capabilities. By observing what the Russians really had, the United States could avoid arming too lightly or heavily.

But because spy satellites would take years to develop, Eisenhower approved a stopgap—the U-2 spy plane. A brilliant team of aircraft engineers designed and built the U-2 prototype in eighty-two days at a secret site run by Lockheed Aviation. In 1956 the high-flying spy plane began crisscrossing the Soviet Union at 80,000 feet, photographing rocket test sites and allowing intelligence analysts to keep close tabs on their rivals' progress.

The U-2, Eisenhower later explained, produced intelligence "of critical importance to the United States." Besides revealing what the Soviets *did* have, it revealed what they *did not* have. The spy plane, Eisenhower said, "provided proof that the horrors of the alleged 'bomber gap' and the later 'missile gap' were nothing more than the imaginative creations," put forth by irresponsible Americans who wanted to build more weapons than U.S. security needs required.

Because of uncertainty over the legality of space-based reconnaissance, Eisenhower wanted America's first prototype satellite to be launched on a civilian, rather than military, rocket. This required building a separate booster, the Vanguard, rather than using the military's Redstone rocket, already near completion. Waiting for the Vanguard meant that the Russians would probably win the first lap in the space race. Eisenhower accepted the delay, reasoning that if the Soviets orbited a satellite first, they would establish a legal precedent by overflying America from space. Despite the impression of tardiness, during the late 1950s research and development was begun for nearly all of the rocket boosters and missile systems deployed by the United States through the 1980s.

When *Sputnik I* went aloft, Eisenhower assured his cabinet it posed no threat. He explained his reasons for relying on a nonmilitary rocket and hinted at a closely guarded secret: U-2 pictures revealed that, despite the success with *Sputnik*, the Soviets possessed only a small and unreliable rocket arsenal. The president urged his colleagues to play down *Sputnik,* lest public hysteria force an unnecessary boost to America's space budget.

Administration spokespersons therefore belittled the Russian achievement as a gimmick and attributed it to German scientists rather than Communist technological superiority. But this did little to quell public anxiety. Democrats, educators, journalists, and military contractors alike charged in the media that the Russians had humiliated the United States and threatened its national security. Each of these groups used *Sputnik* as leverage to achieve its own agenda: to embarrass the administration, to secure more funding for education, or to force an increase in defense spending. At the Senate committee hearings chaired by Lyndon Johnson, a parade of critics claimed that the Soviets had achieved the scientific equivalent of the Japanese attack on Pearl Harbor.

In response, Eisenhower advanced the date for launching an American satellite. In December 1957, in the middle of the Senate hearings, a hastily prepared Vanguard rocket exploded on takeoff. Critics promptly dubbed it "Flopnik." Reluctantly, Eisenhower approved the use of a military rocket, which launched a satellite a few months later.

As the Senate hearings wound down, Johnson warned of widening gaps between the United States and the Soviet Union in aircraft, missiles, submarines, and high technology. Because the United States stood on the verge of losing the "battle of brainpower," he called for increases in space and military appropriations as well as massive federal funding for education. Eisenhower responded by appointing a White House science adviser and increasing funding for the National Science Foundation. He worked with Congress to create the National Aeronautics and Space Administration (NASA), with an initial budget of $340 million. As noted earlier, he also supported passage of the National Defense Education Act (NDEA), a billion-dollar package of federal grants for schools and universities.

Shortly after *Sputnik*'s launch a high-level advisory panel, the Gaither Commission, reported to Eisenhower on the expanded Soviet threat. Hoping to force Eisenhower's hand, the authors leaked their conclusions to journalists. Headlines warned that the United States was about to become a second-class power exposed to immediate danger from a Soviet Union bristling with missiles. The Gaither report predicted that the Soviets would soon deploy hundreds of nuclear-tipped long-range missiles, threatening America's survival. The authors called for accelerating American missile production, increasing military spending by 25 percent, and building a massive system of fallout shelters, at a cost of $30 billion, to protect civilians. Democratic presidential hopefuls, among them Senators Stuart Symington, John F. Kennedy, and Lyndon Johnson, warned that the administration ignored a perilous "missile gap."

To Eisenhower's credit, he tried hard to resist unwarranted increases in defense spending. Unlike the Gaither panel, Eisenhower doubted that civilians could be protected against nuclear bombs. Moreover, U-2 reconnaissance revealed that the Russians had not put their rockets into full production. As with their bombers, they had deployed a few prototype rockets as a bluff—to impress the Third World, refute Chinese criticism, and cover up their comparative weakness. Because Khrushchev knew of the U-2 missions, it is difficult to guess why he thought boasts would intimidate Eisenhower. By reinforcing the widespread overestimate of Soviet rocket technology, Khrushchev's rhetoric actually helped the cause of Americans who wanted to accelerate the arms race. A military gap did exist—but it favored the United States. Because of American bombers in Europe and Asia, medium-range missiles in Turkey and Italy, and the deployment by 1960 of Polaris nuclear submarines in oceans around the world, the United States had a commanding lead in the arms race.

THE STIRRING OF DÉTENTE

Even as the space race joined the arms race in heightening public anxiety in America and creating new reasons for disagreement with the Soviets, a countervailing trend began to emerge. Eisenhower and Khrushchev took significant steps toward détente, talking with each other at summit meetings and establishing a temporary moratorium on nuclear tests. Although these efforts produced no lasting agreement, they did set a precedent for future negotiations.

The relaxation of tensions stemmed in part from the fact that by 1955 the Soviets possessed a substantial atomic arsenal. The Cold War rivals had struck a balance of power, or terror; either side could greatly damage or destroy the other. Eisenhower acknowledged that under these circumstances there was little possibility of victory in a full-scale war, only varying degrees of mutual devastation. In spite of

Dulles's boast that on several occasions his willingness to go "to the brink of war" had forced China and the Soviet Union to back down, Soviet leader Nikita Khrushchev probably hit the mark when he explained that Dulles "knew how far he could push us, and he never pushed us too far."

Moreover, by the mid-1950s growing prosperity in Europe and the changing of the Kremlin guard had taken some of the edge off the Cold War. The creation of an independent West German army and its inclusion in NATO in 1955 formalized the postwar division of Europe. The Soviets responded by creating their own military alliance, the Warsaw Pact, but otherwise they accepted Western moves. The Soviets surprised the United States in 1955 by agreeing, largely on American terms, to a treaty ending the joint occupation of Austria that had begun in 1945.

Prodded by the NATO allies and his own desire to lessen the nuclear threat, Eisenhower agreed, in July 1955, to meet the Soviet leadership at a summit conference in Geneva. At the gathering, Eisenhower stunned the Soviets by calling for a policy of "open skies," whereby each side would be free to conduct aerial reconnaissance of the other's military facilities. The United States had little to lose and much to gain from such an arrangement. The Russians dismissed the proposal as a "bald espionage plot," and it went nowhere. Despite the lack of any formal agreement, both sides left the summit praising the "spirit of Geneva"—a willingness between opposing blocs to talk.

During Eisenhower's final three years as president, he tried harder to reach some form of accommodation with the Soviet Union. For example, the perennial problem with Berlin re-emerged in 1958. Since the early 1950s, about 300,000 East Germans had fled Communist rule annually, most of them through Berlin. Faced with this population hemorrhage, Khrushchev demanded the withdrawal of Western forces and the creation of a "free," meaning East German-controlled, city. He announced a six-month deadline for the removal of Western troops, prompting members of Congress to demand a sharp increase in American military strength.

Eisenhower responded creatively to both Moscow and Congress. A war over Berlin, he observed, would be a nuclear, not conventional, conflict; therefore it made little sense to expand the size of the army, as some in Congress demanded. To the Soviets Eisenhower declared that American forces would stay in Berlin; at the same time, however, he informed Khrushchev that if the deadline for Western withdrawal were set aside, a superpower summit could be arranged. Khrushchev quickly allowed the threat to lapse and accepted an invitation to visit America in the fall of 1959.

In July, before the scheduled visit, Eisenhower sent Vice President Richard Nixon on a good-will trip to the Soviet Union. During an impromptu debate with Khrushchev, held in a model American kitchen at a Moscow trade fair, Nixon proposed shifting the terms of the superpowers' competition. During what journalists dubbed the "kitchen debate," the vice president boasted that most Americans owned houses stocked with appliances that made life easier for home-makers. A flustered Khrushchev dismissed these "useless gadgets," but insisted that Soviet housewives had even better washing ma-chines. Confident that America had the edge in the appliance race, Nixon asked, "Would it not be better to compete in the relative merits of washing machines than in the strength of rockets?"

Democratic critics of the Eisenhower administration lambasted this effort to encourage non-military competition. Senator John F. Ken-nedy, positioning himself as a presidential candidate, ridiculed what he labeled Nixon's female-like "experience in kitchen debates" as a prime example of the administration's weakness and the reason for its failure to build more missiles.

A few months later, the Soviet leader visited the United States and conferred with Eisenhower at Camp David, the presidential retreat in Maryland. The absence of the hard-liner Dulles, who was terminally ill with cancer, improved the atmosphere of conciliation. As in the earlier meeting between Eisenhower and Khrushchev, no formal agreements emerged from the summit. But the two leaders found it useful to measure each other up, and both spoke of a "spirit of Camp David," which observers took to mean an informal reduction in ten-sions. The Soviet leader traveled through the United States and agreed to meet Eisenhower in Paris the following spring.

To Eisenhower, the summits with Khrushchev offered a chance to reduce the danger of nuclear war and to slow the development in America of a garrison state obsessed with security. The president be-lieved that massive defense spending had contributed to America's emerging international trade deficit and to the economic recession of 1958. Khrushchev, for his part, hoped that a reduction in tension would improve his ability to hold off Soviet hawks, including mem-bers of the military establishment who demanded greater missile pro-duction. For both Khrushchev and Eisenhower, one of the central is-sues was an agreement to limit nuclear testing.

NUCLEAR DILEMMAS

In December 1953, Eisenhower proposed an "Atoms for Peace" pro-gram to secure international cooperation in expanding the peaceful use of atomic technology. Congress passed legislation assisting con-struction of domestic nuclear power plants, but the proposal had little effect on curbing the arms race. In fact, for the rest of the decade both the United States and Soviet Union produced tens of thousands of additional nuclear weapons. In the United States this required a crash effort to expand uranium mining, plutonium production, and weapons testing, mostly in western states and on Pacific islands.

In the red rock mesas and valleys of Arizona, for example, government engineers descended on Navajo villages and convinced sheep herders to take up uranium mining "in defense of the nation." Hundreds of small mines, employing over 1,500 Navajos, were opened during the 1950s and 1960s. The miners were offered good wages, but they were never warned about the dangers of breathing uranium dust. By the 1970s many of the miners were ill with a variety of fatal cancers. In some families, two or three generations of fathers and sons died from mining-related cancers.

Uranium ore was turned into weapons-grade material at processing facilities in Hanford, Washington and Rocky Flats, Colorado. Some small subcontractors, like the Albecroft Machine Shop, located in a residential neighborhood of Oxford, Ohio, also built bomb components. Under pressure to produce enriched uranium and plutonium at an accelerating pace, such facilities observed few environmental safeguards. Radioactive residue was dumped into streams, vented into the air, or buried in the ground. When Albecroft closed in the 1960s, it left behind polluted ponds that local children used as swimming holes. Five of six girls in one family living adjacent to the abandoned plant died of cancer. As one Defense Department official admitted in 1980, "the army considered what was inside the fences [of the nuclear facilities] our problem, and no one should know about that."

Between 1945 and 1963, atmospheric tests were conducted at sites in Nevada and the South Pacific. During these tests thousands of soldiers and sailors were stationed as close as three miles from ground zero. In Nevada, infantry units were often marched to the detonation point within an hour of the explosion; the intent was to "train military units to become familiar with new weapons and their characteristics." From a present-day perspective, the ignorance of the hazards of radiation is astounding.

Thousands of Americans living in small towns in Nevada, Utah, and Arizona—the so-called downwinders—were exposed to high levels of wind-blown fallout following each test. In 1955 the government distributed brochures to people living near the test sites. It informed them that "you are in a very real sense active participants in the nation's atomic test program." Many residents recall having family picnics outdoors to watch the giant plumes of colored clouds from the explosions. Little did they suspect that their "active" participation would eventually be measured by high rates of leukemia and other cancers from radioactive fallout.

Atomic dummier at Yucca Flat, November 1955. *Loomis Dean, Life Magazine, © 1955, 1983 Time Inc.*

Similar misfortune plagued the Bikini islanders, whose Pacific atoll was selected as the location for the first hydrogen bomb test in 1954. The Defense Department moved the population to another island, but this failed to protect them when the unexpected power of the bomb and shifting winds dusted them with radioactive debris. Forty years later, Bikini remains uninhabitable. A Japanese fishing boat, the *Lucky Dragon,* sailed too close to the test area, and was contaminated by what its crew called "the ashes of death", causing a brief but intense dispute with the Japanese government after one of the sailors died. The dramatic mushroom cloud from the Bikini explosion was featured in the 1956 Japanese horror film *Godzilla,* a parable about the dangers of radiation.

While most early cases of contamination were caused by ignorance, accident, or cutting corners to speed weapons production, cases of willful injury also occurred. Beginning in 1945 and continuing through the early 1970s, top medical scientists at government laboratories and in prominent research institutions subjected unsuspecting patients to injections of plutonium and other radioactive substances. Generally these patients were poor, prison inmates, minorities, or already suffering from grave illnesses. Most had no idea of the risks involved. Several hundred pregnant women, for example, were offered free pre-natal "care" that included injections of small amounts of plutonium to determine its effects on fetal development. The purpose of many of these experiments was to determine "safe" radiation dosages for workers in the nuclear industry.

Before the 1970s the Atomic Energy Commission, citing national security, downplayed the danger from all forms of radiation, even though by the late 1950s its own studies had confirmed the injury to the miners, soldiers, and downwinders. The AEC actually promoted routine use of X-rays in shoe stores to fit children. Soldiers at the Nevada test site were instructed merely to avoid breathing sand. The downwinders were told to dust off their clothes and brush off their shoes if debris fell on them. The best action, according to the AEC, was "not to be worried about fallout." Navajo miners and workers at Rocky Flats and other weapons plants were not even provided with paper face masks when digging ore or sweeping up plutonium dust. Cartoons with "Bert the Turtle" assured American schoolchildren they would be safe if they remembered to "duck and cover" beneath their desks during a nuclear attack.

In 1990, as medical evidence mounted about the devastating health effects of exposure to radiation, Congress passed the Radiation Exposure Compensation Act. Under its provisions, uranium miners, military personnel, workers in government nuclear arsenals, and downwinders who had suffered certain types of cancer were eligible for between $50,000 and $100,000 in compensation. In many cases, however, the eligibility criteria were so complex that victims had difficulty making a case. For example, by 1990 most of the Navajo uranium miners had died. Many of their widows could not produce marriage certificates or employment stubs from forty years before and were barred from collecting damages.

Opposition existed to atmospheric testing of nuclear weapons even in the 1950s. British author Nevil Shute's best-selling novel *On the Beach* (1957) depicted the end of human life, caused by fallout from a nuclear war. Nobel Prize-winning chemist Dr. Linus Pauling appeared on Edward R. Murrow's popular television show, "See It Now," to warn of the health effects of fallout. Ten thousand scientists from numerous nations signed a petition in favor of a test ban. At congressional hearings, scientists reported that even small amounts of radioactive strontium in milk consumed by pregnant women increased the danger of cancer and genetic injury to their fetuses. A citizens group, the Committee for a Sane Nuclear Policy (SANE), formed in 1957 and soon boasted twenty-five thousand members in 130 chapters. Its officers included such prominent Americans as writer John Hersey, magazine publisher Norman Cousins, labor leader Walter Reuther, and pediatrician Benjamin Spock. As part of a disarmament program, they called for halting weapons tests. Many of these nuclear critics were accused of disloyalty or pro-Communist leanings for challenging government policy.

Eisenhower sympathized with some of the concerns voiced by nuclear critics, but he would not agree to a test ban unless the Soviets dropped their opposition to on-site inspection. When Moscow hinted that it might relent, American hard-liners panicked. Dr. Edward Teller told Eisenhower that if he were allowed to conduct tests a while longer, he could build a fallout-free weapon. Because of Teller's claim, which had little validity, Eisenhower temporarily slowed negotiations on a ban. In 1958, however, the president changed tack when his newly appointed science adviser, James Killian, invited to the White House a number of scientists who refuted Teller's views. They also explained that atmospheric testing was unnecessary to maintain a nuclear arsenal, especially if underground testing continued.

During 1958 the two superpowers conducted several rounds of large atmospheric nuclear tests. To assuage fears that the Soviet Union might sign a test-ban treaty and then continue testing secretly, American scientists assured Eisenhower that a network of seismic stations could detect most nuclear explosions, even those underground. While their subordinates worked on the terms of a treaty, Khrushchev and Eisenhower agreed to an informal test moratorium, effective in October.

Eisenhower proposed banning fallout-producing atmospheric explosions but allowing continued small underground tests. The smaller tests were difficult to detect, and as American hard-liners noted, they were useful in designing new types of weapons. Khrushchev surprised American negotiators by proposing a comprehensive ban on all testing, coupled with limited on-site inspection within the Soviet Union to guard against cheating. Although uncertainties remained, agreement at the upcoming Paris summit seemed possible.

However, the May 1960 Paris summit proved a fiasco. On the eve of the conference, an American U-2 spy plane crashed inside the Soviet Union, brought down either by a Soviet missile or by engine failure. Eisenhower had approved this risky mission in the hope of gathering photographic evidence confirming that, despite Khrushchev's bluster, the Soviet Union had not deployed many long-range rockets. Such data would justify greater flexibility in arms control discussions. Sadly, the failed mission proved fatal for this cause.

After American officials released a cover story about a missing weather aircraft, Moscow announced that in fact it had captured a spy plane. When Eisenhower denied this, Khrushchev amazed the world by displaying pilot Francis Gary Powers, who confessed to espionage. The CIA had assured Eisenhower that Powers could not have survived a crash. Eisenhower was so depressed he considered resigning.

When the two world leaders met in Paris, Khrushchev demanded that Eisenhower apologize to the Soviet people for the U-2 mission.

Eisenhower refused, and the summit broke up. An important opportunity to limit nuclear testing and slow the arms race had slipped away. The informal moratorium on nuclear testing lasted until the fall of 1961, when both the Soviets and the Americans resumed their tests.

CONCLUSION

By the end of his presidency, Eisenhower sensed the limitations of his achievements in foreign policy. He also worried that American society would face increased regimentation as the nation remained shackled to its huge and growing defense budget.

His reflections on these matters were evident in his remarkable farewell address of January 1961, which has been quoted repeatedly ever since. Eisenhower warned against the temptation to solve domestic problems through "some spectacular and costly action" abroad. The old general deplored the view that a large increase in defense spending would create a miraculous solution to the nation's troubles. The greatest threat to democracy, he observed, came from a new phenomenon, the "conjunction of an immense military establishment and a large arms industry." Americans needed to guard against the unwarranted influence of this "military-industrial complex."

With this turn of phrase, the former military man had sounded a warning that would ring down the decades. It had little immediate effect, however, on the administrations that followed.

Eisenhower began his presidency proclaiming the New Look, which emphasized the use of nuclear weapons and the doctrine of massive retaliation. Accordingly, he presided over a dramatic build-up of the nuclear stockpile, including the development of ICBMs. He also intervened repeatedly in Third World conflicts, often employing the CIA to undermine governments that he considered dangerous. He deepened the American involvement in Vietnam, which would have tragic consequences in the 1960s and 1970s.

Nevertheless, most historians see Eisenhower as a president who basically kept the peace. After ending the Korean War, he avoided further direct conflicts with the Soviet Union or China. Although he and Dulles brandished nuclear weapons as the ultimate threat, he never authorized a nuclear attack. In the early years of his administration, he made significant efforts to restrain defense spending, and in his second term he took steps toward détente with the Soviet Union. The next chapter will examine how his immediate successor, John F. Kennedy, handled such issues as the space race, missiles, détente, and unrest in the Third World. ■

FURTHER READING

On foreign policy, the arms race, and the Cold War during the 1950s, see: Stephen E. Ambrose, *Eisenhower: the President* (1984); Stephen E. Ambrose, *Ike's Spies* (1981); H. W. Brands, Jr., *The Cold Warriors* (1988); Robert A. Divine, *Eisenhower and the Cold War* (1981); Richard Immerman, *John Foster Dulles and the Diplomacy of the Cold War* (1990); Richard Rhodes, *Dark Sun: The Making of the Hydrogen Bomb* (1995); Howard Ball, *Justice Downwind: America's Nuclear Testing Program in the 1950s* (1986); Robert A. Divine, *Blowing on the Wind: The Nuclear Test Ban Debate, 1954–60* (1978); Tad Bartimus, *Trinity's Children: Living Along America's Nuclear Highway* (1991); Jonathan Weisgall, *Operation Crossroads: The Atomic Tests at Bikini Atoll* (1994); Carole Gallagher, *American Ground Zero* (1993); Walter A. McDougall, . . . *The Heavens and the Earth: A Political History of the Space Age* (1985); Stephen G. Rabe, *Eisenhower and Latin America* (1988); George McT. Kahin, *Intervention: How America Became Involved in Vietnam* (1986); David L. Anderson, *Trapped by Success: The Eisenhower Administration and Vietnam* (1991); John Gaddis, *The Long Peace* (1987); Michael Beschloss, *Mayday* (1986); Thomas Paterson, *Contesting Castro: The United States and the Triumph of the Cuban Revolution* (1994); Gordon Chang, *Enemies and Friends: The United States, China, and the Soviet Union, 1948–1972* (1989).

5

The New Frontier at Home and Abroad, 1960–1963

By the end of the Eisenhower administration, many Americans were ready for a change. Not only had Eisenhower's grandfatherly style begun to seem unexciting, but social and political attitudes were evolving. Especially among young people, the ideal of a stable, secure, middle-class family in the suburbs was giving way to a desire for more adventure, a greater challenge. In politics, too, the nation's young adults admired high style rather than cautious consensus. Those who embraced this new perspective found a leader to suit their tastes in the glamorous, wealthy, and witty John F. Kennedy.

Often known informally as Jack Kennedy or JFK, he embodied urbane masculinity, combining a dazzling smile and youthful appearance with what his admirers called toughness—the ability to act decisively without expressing agonizing self-doubt. He exuded curiosity about public affairs and people, read voraciously, absorbed information like a sponge, asked probing questions of subordinates, and spoke beautifully. His press conferences were works of art, and journalists found him a welcome relief from the stolid Eisenhower. He came from a large, rambunctious, wealthy family that always seemed to be in motion—sailing, playing touch football, goading each other on with constant competition. His wife, Jacqueline, was slim, sophisticated, and cool. She spoke softly and wore her designer clothes effortlessly. The Kennedys kept company with celebrities from the worlds of art, literature, the mass media, and entertainment. Jack's friends winked at his parade of mistresses; those who knew him from afar adored his personal style and his mastery of American politics.

The Kennedy style captivated the mass media, and through them the public. Kennedy's presidency raised the expectation that problems could be solved by wit, intelligence, knowledge, energy, and skillful management. Many middle-class Americans felt more optimistic about their country's social, spiritual, and economic prospects during the thousand days of Kennedy's presidency than they did for years thereafter. His murder on November 22, 1963, permanently wounded the American outlook.

In retrospect, however, Kennedy's administration has lost much of its luster. His toughness, knowledge, and energy alone could not meet many of the challenges facing the country. His principal skills were those of technique and style. He was less adept at outlining a compelling vision of the future. Kennedy was a splendid politician, but he was not an advocate of any particular cause. He and his supporters considered it a source of strength and a sign of their maturity that they treated public affairs coolly and dispassionately.

In domestic affairs this detached, pragmatic attitude made Kennedy slow to respond to important emerging issues. Although he courted black voters, he hesitated to commit himself to significant support for civil rights. Only after violent attacks on black and white Freedom Riders and a bloody confrontation over university desegregation in Mississippi did Kennedy announce that he would ask Congress to pass a civil rights bill. On the issue of poverty he responded with some sensitivity, but he did not manage to develop a program before his death. Many of the initiatives that progressive Americans expected from him remained unrealized until Lyndon Johnson took office.

In foreign policy Kennedy also failed to develop a genuinely new approach, choosing instead to apply his own variant of the policy of containment that had been established more than a decade earlier. His belief in a need for toughness with the Soviet Union encouraged him to risk nuclear war more dramatically than Eisenhower and Dulles had done. Although the American public backed him at the time, historians have taken a more ambivalent view, balancing admiration for his energy and intelligence with disappointment over his obsessive waging of the Cold War.

THE ELECTION OF 1960

The election of 1960 demonstrated how much American politics had changed since the Second World War. Democrats expected that the New Deal coalition of liberals, working class people, Catholics, southerners, and racial minorities would continue to give them an advantage in presidential elections. They believed that the idea of an activist government, promoted by the New Deal, had been accepted by a majority of Americans. They explained away the popularity of Dwight D. Eisenhower as a reflection of his personal appeal rather than an endorsement of the Republican party. However, the 1960 election results revealed serious limits to the New Deal coalition and the public's acceptance of government activism. The Democrats barely won with John F. Kennedy, a moderate candidate from the party's center. Richard Nixon, the Republican candidate, did so well that he remained an important figure in American politics. White southerners continued their flight from the Democratic party, preparing the way for future Republican and conservative triumphs.

Only forty-two years old when he announced his candidacy for the presidency in January 1960, John F. Kennedy shook up Democratic party professionals, who dismissed him as a brash outsider. But these leaders were unaware of the advantages Kennedy's celebrity would bring to the 1960 election. He was already well known to the public: laudatory stories about him and his wife had appeared in many newspapers and magazines; he had won the Pulitzer Prize for his 1956 book *Profiles in Courage* (though most of it had been written by others); and he had made a memorable impression by nearly winning the Democratic nomination for vice president in 1956. His fresh, youthful vigor stood in sharp contrast to Eisenhower's age and apparent passivity—a difference Kennedy planned to emphasize in his campaign.

Kennedy also believed his moderate stance on the controversial issues of the 1950s would distinguish him favorably in voters' minds from the party's liberal wing. He astutely concluded that the public mood had become more conservative since the New Deal, that voters would respond best to a candidate who projected energy and managerial competence rather than passionate commitment to causes. The growing influence of television bolstered Kennedy's approach. Impassioned or flowery oratory—a necessary attribute for candidates before the age of television—often irritated TV viewers rather than inspiring them.

Although party professionals and most liberals had their doubts about the young candidate, they could not agree on an alternative. Kennedy dashed the hopes of the older men by winning victories in seven presidential primaries. By the time the Democratic convention met in July, only Senate Majority Leader Lyndon Johnson of Texas could mount a last-ditch campaign against Kennedy.

Johnson's bid came so late, and Johnson had opposed so many liberal initiatives, that his attempt to gain the nomination fizzled. Kennedy won on the first ballot. He then astonished his own staff—and disturbed party liberals—by offering the vice-presidential nomination to Johnson. Much to Kennedy's surprise, Johnson accepted.

Two days later, Kennedy addressed fifty thousand Democrats at the Los Angeles Coliseum. He announced that "we stand on the edge of a New Frontier—the frontier of the 1960s—a frontier of unknown opportunities and perils—a frontier of unfulfilled hopes and threats." The crowd cheered when he offered not "a set of promises [but] a set of challenges." Kennedy's New Frontier came with "the promise of more sacrifice instead of more security," and the public was intrigued.

Nevertheless, Richard Nixon, the Republican candidate, had the advantages of experience in national office and the inherited mantle of the popular president Eisenhower. Nixon's steadfast loyalty to the president helped him win the Republican nomination over a last-minute challenge from New York governor Nelson Rockefeller, who had spent the previous two years on an ambitious project of public works in the Empire State. Shortly before the Republican nominating convention, Nixon met Rockefeller and agreed to lead a much more activist government than Eisenhower had directed.

To win the presidency, Kennedy had to demonstrate that he was Nixon's equal. A key element in the campaign was a series of four face-to-face televised debates. Already television was changing the nature of American campaigns. To achieve an illusion of intimacy with their viewers, candidates had begun to hire media experts to make them appear warm, trustworthy, knowledgeable, energetic, and wise. The first Kennedy-Nixon debate proved crucial, because most voters had never seen Kennedy before, whereas Nixon had been a familiar figure for the last eight years.

Instead of seeing an inexperienced youth easily defeated by his opponent, viewers saw Kennedy as a knowledgeable, self-assured, handsome candidate. His crisp, fact-filled delivery made him appear Nixon's equal, erasing "experience" as an edge for the incumbent vice president. Nixon, on the other hand, looked tired and haggard. Sweat poured down his face, smearing his make-up. The candidates' appearance affected audience perceptions of who had won the debate. People who watched the debate on television considered Kennedy the clear winner, whereas those who listened to it on the radio thought Nixon did a better job.

During the campaign, each man tried to convince voters that he would confront the "Communist threat" with greater conviction than his opponent, and both indicated they would oppose the Soviet Union more vigorously than had the Eisenhower administration. Nixon vowed to defend Quemoy and Matsu, two small islands off the coast of the People's Republic of China that Eisenhower and Dulles had protected. Kennedy responded with an attack on Eisenhower and Nixon for tolerating a "Communist outpost" in Cuba, just ninety miles from Florida. Shortly before the final debate, Kennedy's office released a statement promising "to strengthen the non-Batista democratic anti-Castro forces." Nixon, aware that the CIA had already developed plans for an invasion of Cuba, feared that Kennedy had deliberately revealed a plot to overthrow Castro. Nixon characterized such a plan as a violation of international law that would rouse anti-American passions throughout the Western Hemisphere.

Kennedy deftly turned the issue of his Catholicism to his advantage, neutralizing anti-Catholic sentiments and winning the hearts of his fellow Catholics. He gave a brilliant televised performance before the Houston Ministerial Association—a highly skeptical audience of several hundred Southern Baptists—telling them, "I am not the Catholic candidate for President, I am the Democratic candidate, who happens to be Catholic." He promised to resign if he was ever forced to choose between violating his conscience and violating the Constitution.

John F. Kennedy and Richard M. Nixon exchange small talk after one of their four televised debates. In these debates, Kennedy's cool self-assurance gave him an edge over a defensive Vice President Nixon.
Ed Clarke, LIFE Magazine © Time Warner Inc.

Another brilliant gesture helped him secure the votes of blacks. African-Americans had been cool to Kennedy because of his noticeable lack of interest in civil rights legislation during his years in Congress. Kennedy and his brother Robert melted the animosity with two telephone calls in late October 1960. Civil rights leader Martin Luther King, Jr., had been sent to a rural Georgia jail to serve a four-month sentence on trumped-up charges involving a demonstration against a segregated lunch counter at an Atlanta department store. John Kennedy called the prisoner's wife, Coretta Scott King, to express his interest in her husband's welfare. His brother Robert, Kennedy's campaign manager, secured King's release by calling the judge and telling him the harsh sentence made the state of Georgia look bad. The judge relented and ordered King freed. In gratitude, King's father, Martin Luther King, Sr., a Protestant minister, announced that he was dropping his opposition to the Catholic Kennedy. The Kennedy campaign then distributed 2 million copies of a booklet describing the Kennedy brothers' efforts on King's behalf.

In the November election Kennedy won a razor-thin plurality, beating Nixon by only 118,574 votes out of a total of 68,334,888 votes cast. And even that narrow victory was tainted by charges of voter fraud in several key states Kennedy won by a small margin. Sixty-four percent of Americans voted, the largest proportion since 1920. The issue of Kennedy's religion reduced his popular-vote margin, but it actually helped him win electoral votes. Although he lost the backing of about 1 million Protestants who had supported Democrats in earlier elections, these people were concentrated in midwestern farm states that customarily voted Republican anyway. Among Catholics, Kennedy won 80 percent of the vote, up from the approximately 63 percent who had voted for Democratic candidates since Roosevelt, and this gain proved important in the electoral college. African-Americans, too, helped Kennedy win such key northern industrial states as New York, Pennsylvania, and Michigan. Although most blacks still could not vote in the South, those who did provided crucial victory margins in North and South Carolina and Texas.

PERSONALITY AND STYLE

Although historians later criticized his assertive rhetoric, at the time Kennedy captured his listeners with his stirring phrases and his calls to sacrifice. The speech included what were probably Kennedy's most famous words: "And so my fellow Americans, ask not what your country can do for you—ask what you can do for your country."

The brilliant inauguration set the tone for the remaining thousand days of the Kennedy administration. He and his family projected a sexy image of vigor and refinement that the nation responded to. The president's staff participated in bone-wearying fifty-mile hikes; the nation's public schools began requiring physical education. Although he personally disdained classical music and ballet, Kennedy invited cellist Pablo Casals to perform at the White House to show that the nation's political leadership admired high culture. Intellectuals felt valued, in sharp contrast to the harassment they had experienced during the McCarthy era. Jacqueline touched a similar nerve with her efforts to refurnish the White House with authentic antiques.

In choosing his advisers and key administrators, Kennedy appointed a group that writer David Halberstam would later call "the best and the brightest." Relatively young, often educated in the most distinguished colleges and universities, many of them boasting fine records in business or academia, these new stars in Washington added to the Kennedy aura. But they, too, were not passionately dedicated to specific social causes. Kennedy assembled a cabinet of men who shared his view that managerial competence, not commitment to any particular program, mattered most in the conduct of public affairs. Feeling the need for continued counsel from his closest adviser, he named his thirty-six-year-old brother Robert as attorney general. He included two Republicans in his cabinet: C. Douglas Dillon as treasury secretary, to reassure business leaders, and Robert S. McNamara, the young president of Ford Motor Company, as secretary of defense. McNamara—ferociously intelligent, impatient with ignorance, a numbers-and-facts kind of man—set the tone of the New Frontier. If information could not be summarized numerically, McNamara would not use it.

Kennedy also chose a Republican to fill another important post, outside the cabinet. McGeorge Bundy, forty-one-year-old dean of the faculty at Harvard and a long-time friend, became national security adviser. Kennedy believed that Eisenhower's disengaged style had hampered the nation's conduct of foreign affairs; he wanted to elevate the importance of the national security adviser to help make the president the central figure in foreign policy. Under Kennedy the influence of the secretary of state—a cabinet position—declined. After a long search for a secretary of state, Kennedy settled on Dean Rusk, formerly Truman's assistant secretary of state for Far Eastern affairs.

At the same time that he sought to strengthen his control of foreign policy, Kennedy limited his options in domestic affairs by retaining J. Edgar Hoover as director of the Federal Bureau of Investigation. From the beginning, Hoover and Robert Kennedy fought bitterly. Hoover refused to acknowledge the existence of the Mafia; Robert wanted the FBI to infiltrate it. The attorney general also pressed Hoover to obtain evidence against Jimmy Hoffa, president of the Teamsters Union, but Hoover resisted that idea as well. The FBI director, in turn, forced Robert into approving wiretaps on African-American civil rights leader Martin Luther King, Jr., whom Hoover detested and suspected of ties to the Communist Party of the United States. With these tapes, Hoover compiled lurid evidence of King's many sexual encounters with women other than his wife. Yet the Kennedys had to keep Hoover in office, because the FBI chief had in his files damaging tape recordings that proved a 1941 sexual liaison between twenty-three-year-old navy lieutenant John F. Kennedy and a woman who may have worked for Nazi intelligence. Although President Kennedy often seemed to flaunt his extramarital encounters, he feared that Hoover's files could destroy him.

The uneasy secret shared with Hoover was only one example that Kennedy was not the glittering knight he appeared to be. For close observers, a gap soon developed between his dashing media image and the more mundane reality. Even while he remained popular, the public hopes raised by his high style and thrilling oratory were often disappointed.

FBI director J. Edgar Hoover flanked by two men who distrusted and feared him, Attorney General Robert F. Kennedy (*left*) and President John F. Kennedy. *Photo No. ST-C147-2-63 in the John F. Kennedy Library.*

FOREIGN POLICY: THE QUEST FOR VICTORY

Like his predecessors, Kennedy pursued a policy of containing the Soviet Union and opposing revolutionary change in the Third World. Discarding Eisenhower's doctrine of massive retaliation, Kennedy substituted the principle of "flexible response," designed to increase the administration's options for dealing with both the Soviet Union and revolutionary movements elsewhere. In practice this strategy led to greater emphasis on counterinsurgency fighters in addition to more intercontinental ballistic missiles (ICBMs), and the overall military budget rose. Through 1961 and 1962 the United States confronted the Soviet Union and its Third World clients as assertively as ever before, hoping for a decisive victory in the Cold War. And in the Cuban missile crisis of October 1962, Kennedy's assertiveness brought the world to the verge of nuclear disaster.

In the aftermath of the missile crisis, however, ordinary citizens and policy planners paid more attention to the danger of nuclear war with the Soviets. Cold War tensions began to ease in 1963 as authorities in both countries looked for alternatives to their permanent

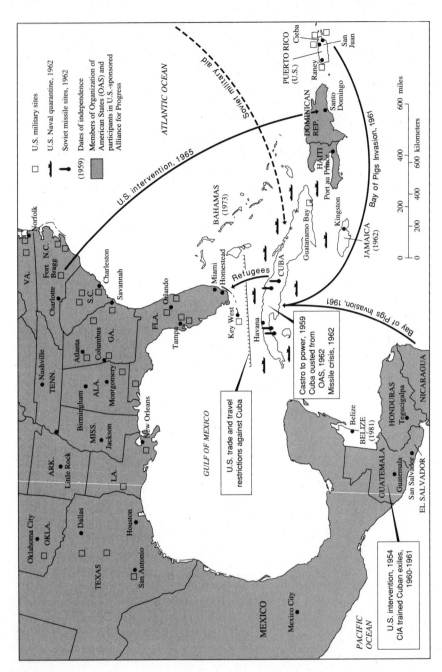

The United States in the Caribbean and Central America

Legend:
- □ U.S. military sites
- ⌐ U.S. Naval quarantine, 1962
- Soviet missile sites, 1962
- (1959) Dates of independence
- Members of Organization of American States (OAS) and participants in U.S.-sponsored Alliance for Progress

U.S. intervention, 1965

Soviet military aid

ATLANTIC OCEAN

PUERTO RICO (U.S.) — Cieba, San Juan, Raney

DOMINICAN REP. — Santo Domingo

HAITI — Port au Prince

BAHAMAS (1973)

Bay of Pigs Invasion, 1961

Guantanamo Bay

JAMAICA (1962) — Kingston

600 miles

600 kilometers

0 200 400

Norfolk
VA.
Fort Bragg N.C.
Charlotte
Charleston
S.C.
Savannah
GA.
Columbus
Atlanta
ALA.
Montgomery
Nashville
TENN.
Birmingham
MISS.
Jackson
ARK.
Little Rock
LA.
New Orleans
Orlando
FLA.
Tampa
Miami
Homestead
Refugees
Key West
Havana
CUBA

**Castro to power, 1959
Cuba ousted from OAS, 1962
Missile crisis, 1962**

U.S. trade and travel restrictions against Cuba

GULF OF MEXICO

Oklahoma City
OKLA.
Dallas
Houston
TEXAS
San Antonio

MEXICO
Mexico City

Belize
BELIZE (1981)
GUATEMALA
Guatemala
San Salvador
EL SALVADOR
HONDURAS
Tegucigalpa
NICARAGUA

PACIFIC OCEAN

**U.S. intervention, 1954
CIA trained Cuban exiles, 1960–1961**

competition. Unfortunately this early *détente,* or relaxation of tension, did not last.

Fidel Castro was like a toothache to the new president: the pain would not get better and Kennedy could not take his mind off the Cuban dictator. Castro's actions in 1960 and early 1961 made Kennedy even more frustrated. Knowing that the United States was arming exiled opponents of his government, Castro began supporting revolutionaries throughout Latin America in response. "That is the reason President Kennedy can't sleep at night," Castro said.

In 1960, under President Eisenhower, the CIA had begun planning an invasion of Cuba by these armed exiles. By the time Kennedy took office, the operation was nearly ready. When the CIA presented its plans for the invasion, most of Kennedy's inner circle of advisers approved. CIA chief Allen Dulles informed the president that the prospects for success in an invasion of Cuba were greater than they had been in 1954, when the agency had sponsored an invasion of Guatemala. Dulles predicted that once the invasion force landed, a general revolution would sweep over Cuba, expelling Castro from the island.

Kennedy's main concern was for the administration's ability to maintain "plausible deniability" of its involvement. In response, the CIA changed the proposed landing site to the remote swampy Bay of Pigs, and the president banned the American air force from providing cover to the invaders. Some analysts later claimed that these alterations doomed the operation. In fact, the plan was flawed from the beginning. Castro was broadly popular among poor Cubans throughout the island. Castro's large, well-supplied army of peasant supporters was ready for an attack. Indeed, some of Kennedy's own advisers doubted the workability of the plan.

Yet the invasion went forward anyway, because it seemed easier to continue than to cancel an advanced plan. The president feared looking weak should word leak out that he had scrapped a plan prepared by the Eisenhower administration. He worried that if the members of the brigade were forced to return to the United States from their bases in Guatemala, they would inform the media of the plan, making it appear that Kennedy's toughness was just a pose for the election.

The invasion began at first light on April 17, 1961 (see map, page 184). The brigade hit the beaches shortly after a CIA broadcast from Honduras entreated Cubans to rise against Castro. That plea had no effect, but Castro's own call to arms for his 200,000-man militia worked perfectly. The Cuban defenders sank many of the invaders' landing craft. Attackers who made it ashore became easy targets for Castro's tanks and fighter planes. By the evening of the first day, officials in Washington knew that the operation had failed. Within seventy-two hours the Cuban army had captured 1,189 invaders and killed 114; only about 150 escaped death or capture.

In the aftermath of the Bay of Pigs debacle, Kennedy set about restoring the image he had tried to craft of a decisive, successful, active leader. He embarked on a public relations offensive against Castro, implying that the United States would look for other ways to end Castro's regime. In a speech before the American Society of Newspaper Editors, Kennedy blamed the victim, explaining that American "restraint" toward Cuba was "not inexhaustible." He pledged never to "abandon . . . the country to communism." The public loved Kennedy's tough reaction. A Gallup poll taken the week after Kennedy's speech revealed that 71 percent approved of his overall handling of the presidency and over 80 percent backed his Cuban policy.

Kennedy's obsession with Cuba continued after the failure of the Bay of Pigs invasion. The American government ransomed the approximately twelve hundred captured Cuban exiles with $120 million worth of drugs, medical supplies, trucks, tractors, and agricultural implements. Veterans of the brigade were given a tumultuous reception in Miami's Orange Bowl. Kennedy accepted one of their battle banners and promised to return the flag "in a free Havana." All the while, his administration proceeded with efforts to discredit, overthrow, or kill Fidel Castro and drafted plans to invade the island once more.

In late 1961 the CIA initiated Operation Mongoose, the code name for various schemes to oust or assassinate the Cuban leader. The CIA developed a series of fantastical plans. Psychological warfare experts suggested that a full beard represented sexual potency in Cuban culture, so agents tried to drop depilatory powder in his boots. Another scenario involved agents slipping him cigars either laced with LSD to make him incoherent or injected with poison to kill him. At various times would-be assassins tried to poison him, spear him with harpoons as he snorkeled in the Caribbean, or induce him to don a wet suit rigged with explosives. None of these attempts worked.

In frustration the CIA turned to the Mafia, hoping to tap its assassination expertise. Mafia chiefs had helped the Eisenhower administration in its efforts to kill Castro, hoping to regain control of casinos closed by the revolutionaries. Eventually the connection between the U.S. government and the criminals became too hot for top Kennedy administration officials, and the partnership was severed. One of the president's several mistresses also shared a bed with the boss of the Chicago Mafia. FBI director Hoover knew of this bizarre triangle, and he ultimately persuaded Robert Kennedy that any exposure of this connection could severely embarrass the administration. Kennedy stopped the affair. Castro learned of the American-sponsored plots on his life and sought help from his patrons in Moscow. Nikita

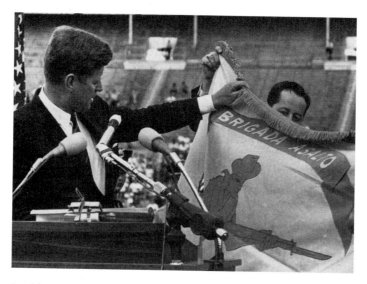

President Kennedy receives the combat flag of the Bay of Pigs invasion brigade at a ceremony in Miami's Orange Bowl. *Wide World Photos.*

Khrushchev responded with Soviet troops equipped to repel another U.S. invasion. In mid-1962, the Soviets also agreed to station in Cuba a few dozen intermediate-range ballistic missiles (IRBMs) armed with nuclear bombs.

Elsewhere in the developing world, the Kennedy administration used a variety of methods—some far gentler than Operation Mongoose, some equally violent—to encourage people and governments to support the United States in its global competition with the Soviet Union. During the election campaign of 1960, Kennedy accused the Eisenhower administration of indifference to poverty in Latin America and a lack of support for independence movements in Africa and Asia. Eisenhower, he said, had ignored the winds of change sweeping the Third World and had opened the way for the Soviet Union to gain advantages there. The new administration sought to restore America's prestige among the poor or newly independent states of Latin America, Africa, and Asia by helping to build modern societies there.

Fearing that many Latin American states, racked by poverty, social inequality, and political repression, stood on the verge of revolutions similar to Cuba's, the Kennedy administration developed a foreign assistance program called the Alliance for Progress. Kennedy obtained from Congress a down payment of $500 million to eradicate illiteracy, hunger, and disease in the Western Hemisphere. Over the next eight years, the United States provided about $10 billion in assistance to Latin American governments; an additional $8 billion came from private agencies. Kennedy also promised to advance political and social reform in Latin America by pressuring the region's political leaders to revise tax and land laws that favored the rich.

The hopes inflated by the Alliance for Progress made disappointment almost inevitable. Creating just and prosperous societies in the Western Hemisphere proved far harder than restoring modern, industrial European countries to the prosperity they had enjoyed before the Second World War. Throughout Latin America, economic growth stalled at an unimpressive average of 1.5 percent per year during the 1960s. Unemployment rose, and the average figures for life expectancy, infant mortality, adult illiteracy, and amount of time children spent in school remained the same.

The Kennedy administration found it harder to practice concern for democracy and social justice than to preach it. Kennedy produced a mixed record in his efforts to promote popular, elected governments. The administration did hasten the end of Rafael Trujillo's dictatorship in the Dominican Republic, and it supported constitutional regimes in Venezuela, Colombia, and Mexico. But it acquiesced in allowing military coups in Argentina, Guatemala, Honduras, and Haiti. The CIA also secretly funded moderate and conservative candidates in Chile to undermine the Socialist candidate, Salvador Allende Gossens, in the presidential race of 1964. In most cases a government's attitude toward Castro determined the American response to it. Those that opposed Castro received American aid. Those that expressed sympathy for him or questioned U.S. actions in the Bay of Pigs were suspected of leftist sympathies and denied Alliance for Progress funds.

Another program, not involving covert actions, had perhaps a more lasting benefit. The Peace Corps, a project arising from the Kennedy administration's desire to encourage active commitment among American young people, became one of the most popular government programs in recent history. Like the Alliance for Progress, the Peace Corps originated from Cold War preoccupations and a sense that Eisenhower had done too little to oppose communism abroad. The day after his inauguration, Kennedy asked his brother-in-law, Sargent Shriver, to organize the Peace Corps. Congress created the new organization in September 1961. In the remaining twenty-seven months of the Kennedy administration, about seven thousand Peace Corps volunteers, most under twenty-five, went to work in forty-four countries in Asia, Africa, and Latin America. More than half worked in education, fighting adult illiteracy and teaching children. The rest helped with community development, public works, health care, and agricultural programs. The personal impact of their service lasted for decades. Most recipients of the aid admired the

A Peace Corps volunteer in the West African nation of Mali helps with the planting. *Courtesy of the Peace Corps.*

earnest young Americans, but to the surprise of some Corps volunteers, they did not choose to transform their culture into one based on an American model. Some Americans learned from the exchange of ideas the Peace Corps promoted. More sophisticated volunteers returned home with a heightened appreciation for other cultures. Many came to question the simplistic anti-Communist assumptions that had created the Peace Corps in the first place. Instead of seeing the problems of poorer lands in terms of the competition between the United States and the Soviet Union, many returning volunteers believed that the United States should try to understand poorer countries in terms of their own culture and history.

Africa was only a slightly higher priority to Kennedy than it had been to Eisenhower. And when the administration did act decisively in Africa, it assisted conservative elements. In the former Belgian Congo (now called Zaire), for example, a nation that had been independent since mid-1960, the Kennedy administration spent two years trying to install an anti-Communist labor leader as head of the government. The CIA bribed the Congolese legislature into electing Washington's choice, a move Rusk hailed as a "major Soviet defeat."

The victory proved ephemeral, however, and the Congo sank into civil war. During this conflict the United Nations tried to arrange cease-fires and create stability, but Washington resented these efforts, fearful that they would interfere with American efforts to promote an anti-Communist faction.

Obsessive anticommunism and preoccupation with events elsewhere also hampered American efforts to advance independence in Portugal's African colonies of Angola and Mozambique. At first the Kennedy administration backed a United Nations resolution condemning Portuguese rule. Later, however, Portugal's dictator threatened to tear up the lease for American military bases on the Azores, a group of islands in the mid-Atlantic. Portugal's friends in the United States argued that the bases were vital outposts in the Cold War. Faced with stiff opposition, the Kennedy administration gradually dropped its support for self-determination and independence from European rule for the remaining colonies in Africa.

In addition to challenging Fidel Castro and attempting to fend off further leftist gains in the Third World, the Kennedy administration also intensified direct American opposition to the Soviet Union. The frigidity in United States–Soviet relations that began with the U-2 incident and the collapse of the Paris summit in May 1960 continued throughout the first year of the new administration. Hoping to demonstrate his mastery of foreign affairs, Kennedy met Soviet Communist Party General Secretary Nikita Khrushchev at a hastily arranged summit conference in Vienna in June 1961. The meeting took place less than two months after the catastrophe at the Bay of Pigs. Although the American public had rallied around their young president after the Cuban debacle, Kennedy's standing abroad had suffered. Earlier reservations among world leaders regarding his youth and lack of experience in foreign affairs seemed to have been borne out by the fiasco in Cuba. Thus Kennedy went to Europe in June to reassure French president Charles de Gaulle that he could recover from his blunder and also to impress Khrushchev with how tough he could be.

The stop in Paris buoyed the president. As the first lady charmed the aging President de Gaulle, Kennedy's knowledge and his ability to speak clearly and cogently relieved French suspicions. But in Vienna, instead of the get-acquainted session he had expected, the president found himself caught up in a dangerous conflict with Khrushchev over the future of Berlin.

The former capital of the Third Reich had been occupied by the four victorious allies (the United States, the Soviet Union, Great Britain, and France) since 1945. Emerging Cold War tensions had blocked progress on a formal peace settlement with Germany, leaving the future of Berlin unresolved. The city was divided into eastern and western sectors, and the entire municipality was completely surrounded by the German Democratic Republic (East Germany). Created by German Communists in 1949, East Germany maintained its capital in the part of Berlin controlled by the Soviet Union. The Western powers, however, refused to recognize the sovereignty of the German Democratic Republic or its control over East Berlin. The Federal Republic of Germany (West Germany), also established in 1949, had installed its capital in the quiet Rhine town of Bonn. Since its inception, West Germany had insisted that the two Germanies must eventually be reunited and that East Germany was a puppet of the Soviet Union. Meanwhile, the Western powers had retained their rights to supervise the affairs of Berlin.

At the Vienna summit, Khrushchev raised the issue of Berlin as a way of bolstering the sagging legitimacy of East Germany. He had complained about the West's refusal to acknowledge East German sovereignty at the Camp David summit with Eisenhower in September 1959, but the situation had persisted. In the interim, the East German government had pressed the Soviets to do something to boost its prestige. Now, at his meeting with Kennedy in Vienna, the Kremlin leader insisted that the allies finally resolve the German problem by signing a peace treaty recognizing the legitimacy of East Germany, with a capital at East Berlin. If no progress occurred soon, he threatened, the Soviet Union would sign a separate peace treaty with East Germany, ceding to that government control over land and air access to Berlin. Under such a treaty East Germany would be in a position to strangle West Berlin, because the city's economy depended on trade with the rest of West Germany, 120 miles away. The Western powers had been strongly committed to West Berlin's existence ever since they had airlifted supplies to the city in 1948. The loss of West Berlin, many feared, would erode faith in Washington's ability to defend other friendly areas challenged by the Soviet Union.

In addition to his tough stand on Berlin, Khrushchev surprised Kennedy by affirming Soviet support for what he called "wars of national liberation" in Southeast Asia and Latin America. Kennedy responded to Khrushchev's unexpected demands by expressing hopes for friendly relations with the Soviets, but he clearly had been caught off guard. Robert Kennedy felt that his brother's failure to crush Cuba had led Khrushchev to believe Kennedy was a weak president.

In the aftermath of the Vienna summit the United States came close to war with the Soviet Union over Berlin. Within hours after returning to the United States, Kennedy delivered a somber televised report on his encounter with Khrushchev. He told the public that meeting the Soviet leader had been a frightening experience. He explained that Khrushchev believed "the tide of history was moving his way" and "the so-called wars of national revolution supported by the Kremlin would replace the old method of direct aggression and invasion."

Behind the scenes, Kennedy prepared U.S. forces for a showdown with the Soviets over Berlin. He recognized that Khrushchev had manufactured the Berlin crisis in order to demonstrate his own toughness to the Soviet military and to assure the East German government of his support. Nevertheless, the United States behaved as if the crisis could turn into a war. To prevent the Soviets from making good on their threat to limit access to Berlin, Kennedy let them know that Washington no longer felt bound by its pledge not to unloose a preemptive nuclear strike. He decided that Khrushchev "won't pay attention to words. He has to see you move."

On July 25 Kennedy further defied the Soviets with a bellicose speech. "If we do not meet our commitments to Berlin, where will we later stand?" he asked the American public. He reactivated some reserve units, which were to go immediately to Germany, and increased the armed forces by over 200,000 troops by doubling draft calls and dropping the exemption for married men. The next day he asked Congress for an additional $3.5 billion for military outlays. Included in that figure was $207 million more for civil defense—an amount that prompted morbid speculations among ordinary citizens about the likelihood of nuclear war. Seventy-one percent of those questioned in a Gallup poll agreed that Americans should fight their way into Berlin if access were blocked.

While American anxieties grew, in early August events in Germany changed the course of the crisis. The constant stream of refugees from East to West Germany became a flood in July. That month more than thirty thousand of the best-educated and most skilled East Germans left their dreary police state for the robust economic opportunities of the West.

The East German government responded to the exodus on the night of August 13 by beginning construction of a concrete and barbed-wire fence between East and West Berlin. Within three days what became known as the Berlin Wall became an almost impenetrable barrier preventing East Germans from fleeing to West Berlin. The wall would remain in existence for almost three decades, and hundreds of East Germans would be shot trying to escape through it or over it. Yet in 1961, despite the moral outrage in the West, construction of the Berlin Wall actually defused the crisis. It allowed the Soviets and East Germans to stop the flow of refugees without a diplomatic confrontation with the West. Khrushchev spoke no more about a separate peace treaty.

The wall caught the Kennedy administration completely by surprise. Its construction demonstrated that the American military buildup had not intimidated the Communists. Nor had it left the United States the kind of flexible options the Kennedy administration wanted. On the other hand, many of Kennedy's advisers privately accepted the logic of the solution. Although Kennedy drew cheers from hundreds of thousands when he spoke at the wall in June 1963, declaring "Ich bin ein Berliner" ("I am a Berliner"), it is clear that his Berlin policy did not present the flexible, skeptical approach to world politics his intellectual supporters expected from him. Instead of greater nuance, less posturing, and a deeper appreciation for the subtleties of world politics, Kennedy fell back on simple anti-Communist rhetoric and threats. He confronted the Soviets and Communists everywhere with military force, and then was surprised to discover that the military approach did not yield victory.

The Kennedy administration adopted a more complex mixture of military threat and diplomatic bargaining during the Cuban missile crisis of October 1962, one of the most pivotal and dangerous episodes of the Cold War. In the end the United States forced the Soviet Union to remove missiles and manned bombers from Cuba, but for thirteen days, from October 15 to 28, 1962, the United States and the Soviet Union approached the brink of thermonuclear war.

In the summer of 1962 the Cubans believed that another American-sponsored invasion of their island might be launched at any time. Their fears were realistic: the Defense Department had already drafted plans for a second, larger attack on Cuba. In July Raul Castro, Fidel's brother and Cuba's minister of defense, visited Moscow and pleaded for Soviet help against the CIA's Operation Mongoose. It was in response to this plea that Khrushchev supplied Cuba with intermediate-range ballistic missiles (IRBMs) and technicians to operate them. The missiles were capable of delivering nuclear warheads to targets in the eastern third of the United States. By this time the Soviets had also stationed manned bombers and an estimated ten thousand to forty thousand troops in Cuba to repel another invasion.

Missiles offered little effective protection against the small-scale harassment of Operation Mongoose, but the weapons served Soviet interests in several ways. They retaliated against the United States, which had stationed its own IRBMs in Turkey, aimed at the Soviet Union. The weapons would probably make Castro feel safer and more grateful than ever for Moscow's help. Most of all, Khrushchev believed that sending the missiles to Cuba had little cost. They really had not increased the threat to the United States, a fact noted at the height of the crisis by Secretary of Defense McNamara. "A missile is a missile," he said at the time. "It makes no difference if you are killed by a missile fired from the Soviet Union or from Cuba." Applying the same reasoning, Khrushchev did not expect that the United States would risk world war to force the missiles out.

Khrushchev did not reckon on America's obsession with Cuba and the emphasis that would be placed on the Cuba issue as the fall congressional campaigns approached their climax. Even before Kennedy knew the exact extent of the missile build-up, some Republicans, led by Senator Kenneth Keating of New York, claimed that the Soviets had installed IRBMs capable of launching a nuclear attack at any moment. (Keating's information came from a group of anti-Castro Cubans.) On October 10, Keating declared that the Soviets in Cuba had the "power to hurl rockets into the American heartland." Fearful of a public outcry and of charges that the Democrats were "soft," Congress passed a resolution promising "by whatever means may be necessary, including the use of arms . . . to prevent in Cuba the creation or use of an externally supported military capability endangering the security of the United States."

On the night of October 15 the CIA developed photographs, taken by a U-2 spy plane, that showed the construction fifteen miles south of Havana of a launching site for missiles with a range of about two thousand miles. The president saw the pictures at nine o'clock the next morning and exploded, saying he had been "taken" by the Soviets, who had assured him in September that only defensive antiaircraft missiles would be situated in Cuba. The missiles had to be removed, he said. Otherwise, the United States would be vulnerable to attack, the public would be terrified, and "Ken Keating will probably be the next president of the United States."

An executive committee made up of the administration's principal foreign policy and defense officials met secretly over the next twelve days. Their task was to force the Soviets to back down, without igniting a world war. Robert Kennedy chaired most of the meetings. The president attended some of them but usually kept quiet to allow uninhibited deliberations. From the beginning the participants agreed that the missiles presented an unacceptable threat. Moreover, allowing them to stay in Cuba would represent a humiliating setback for an administration committed to waging the Cold War more aggressively than the apparently cautious Eisenhower had.

Although the advisers were united in their refusal to tolerate the missiles, they were divided on tactics. They weighed the risks and potential opportunities offered by a blockade of Cuba or air strikes against the missile installations. As the discussions proceeded, a majority of the executive committee began to endorse the idea of a quarantine of Cuba as a way of forcing the Soviets to remove the missiles. The committee eventually recommended a blockade.

By Sunday, October 21, the Washington press corps was abuzz with speculation that something was about to happen. On Monday, the blockade began; 108 U.S. Navy ships patrolled the Atlantic and Caribbean, intercepting and inspecting the cargo of any vessel bound for Cuba, to make certain it was not carrying offensive weapons. At 7 P.M. that evening Kennedy went on television, delivering one of the most somber speeches any president had ever given. He announced the existence of the CIA photographs, explaining that they showed "a series of offensive missile sites . . . now in preparation on that imprisoned island."

Americans anxiously waited out the next several days. When the president received news that Soviet ships were steaming toward the navy's blockade line, the tension seemed too much to bear. Robert Kennedy remembered that his brother's face was drawn, his eyes pained. A few hours later, however, navy officials radioed that the Soviet vessels had stopped without challenging the blockade. The U.S. navy allowed only tankers and passenger ships through. As a symbolic gesture, sailors from two United States destroyers boarded a cargo ship chartered by the Soviets. Finding no forbidden weapons, the navy allowed the ship to pass through to Cuba.

The blockade succeeded in preventing movement of further weapons to Cuba, because neither the Americans nor the Soviets wanted the situation to deteriorate into war. The quarantine did not, however, settle the matter of the missile sites already under construction. In a series of telegrams to Khrushchev and in several secret face-to-face meetings in Washington between United States and Soviet representatives, Kennedy pressured the Soviet leader to demolish the sites and remove the missiles already in Cuba. At one point a Soviet representative in Washington offered to remove the missiles and bombers. Khrushchev confirmed the offer in a telegram, but he added a condition: he would act only if the United States removed its IRBMs from Turkey. Kennedy ignored the offer of an exchange, and he also did not respond when Khrushchev seemed to reverse himself in a later telegram. Instead Kennedy repeated that the Soviet missiles had to be eliminated, and he focused on Moscow's initial offer to remove them. Faced with overwhelming American military might and astonished that the young American president would actually risk a nuclear war over a largely symbolic issue, Khrushchev capitulated. He wired Kennedy that he had instructed his officers to "discontinue construction of the . . . facilities, to dismantle them, and to return them to the Soviet Union."

It appeared to relieved Americans that Kennedy had won a great victory. In the aftermath of the crisis the United States quietly removed its missiles in Turkey. Washington also promised never to invade Cuba. In return, the Soviets took their manned bombers out of Cuba and pledged never to install offensive weapons on the island.

Fidel Castro felt betrayed by Khrushchev's surrender; the suspension of Operation Mongoose a few days after the crisis subsided did little to mollify him. He believed that the United States still wished him dead and that now he had no protector. His anxieties had a factual basis. The next spring the State Department created a secret Cuban Coordinating Committee to bring down Castro's government.

In October 1963 the committee approved sabotage operations against twenty-two targets on the island.

During the crisis and for years afterward, Kennedy won high praise for his grace under pressure and the way he sifted conflicting advice and made decisions. By skillful diplomatic initiatives that allowed Khrushchev room to maneuver, he forced the Soviet Union to retreat without a fight. The eventual removal of American missiles from Turkey offered the Soviets a small satisfaction. Yet Kennedy had risked nuclear war to show his toughness toward Khrushchev and Castro. The missiles in Cuba never threatened the security of the United States to the extent the president indicated at the time. As his trusted aide Theodore Sorensen later observed, "the United States was already living under the shadow of Soviet missiles, which could be launched from Soviet territory or submarines, and, therefore, there was no real change in our situation which required any kind of drastic action."

The Cuban missile crisis sobered both the Americans and the Soviets, encouraging officials and ordinary citizens in both countries to look for ways to avoid future confrontations. In the aftermath of the showdown, relations between the superpowers began to improve. In the next six months the two governments agreed to install a direct communications link—a Teletype hot line—connecting the Kremlin with the White House. Kennedy abandoned some of his harsh anti-Communist rhetoric and urged other Americans to do the same. Americans and Soviets had a mutual interest in ending the arms race, the president declared: "We all breathe the same air. We all cherish our children's future."

In 1963 the United States and the Soviet Union signed the first Limited Test Ban Treaty, ending the above-ground nuclear tests that had resumed in 1961. The treaty banned explosions of atomic devices in the atmosphere, in outer space, and under the ocean. The two sides promised to work on a more comprehensive treaty banning underground nuclear explosions as well.

NEW FRONTIERS AT HOME

On the domestic front, the Kennedy administration tried to shake the torpor of the Eisenhower years by promoting an expanding American economy. Kennedy's efforts to improve economic conditions began slowly, but they gained momentum over time. Administration officials initially resisted endorsing efforts to redistribute wealth, fearing that such programs would provoke antagonism from wealthy and middle-class Americans. Similarly, the Kennedy administration at the beginning paid more attention to the economic and social concerns of the white middle class than to the deprivation of the poor or the hardships endured by people of color. In 1963, the last year of his life, Kennedy adopted a more liberal position, calling for aggressive government action to eliminate poverty.

The president's curiosity and his wide reading eventually made him alert to the previously hidden crises of widespread poverty and degradation of the environment. Kennedy and his principal advisers had come of age politically in the late 1940s and 1950s—a time when leaders were expected to stress the positive aspects of American society as it confronted the Soviet Union in the Cold War. In the early 1960s, however, Americans looked more critically on their country's shortcomings. Kennedy had spoken eloquently during the 1960 presidential campaign about the need for vigorous action both at home and abroad, and although he did not develop many specific details for a domestic program, it was to his credit that he grew intellectually as president by recognizing the flaws and inequities in American society. By late 1962 the Kennedy administration had begun to lay the foundations of the major domestic reforms that would be undertaken by his successor.

When Kennedy promised in 1960 to get the country moving again, to a large extent he was promising to engineer an economic recovery. Economic growth had averaged about 3 percent per year from 1953 to 1960, but the averages masked wild yearly swings, from declines of 2 percent in some years to growth of 5 percent in others. And although prices had increased little during the Eisenhower years, the country had suffered sharp recessions in 1954, 1958, and 1960. Rising unemployment had helped Kennedy win some important industrial states in the Midwest in the presidential election of 1960.

Kennedy's efforts to bolster economic growth worked slowly, but eventually the economy expanded robustly. Rather than stimulating the economy directly, as liberal advisers urged, by creating government programs to aid depressed areas, the Kennedy administration decided that a safer course was to adjust taxes to encourage private investment. In April 1961 Kennedy urged Congress to eliminate the complicated system of tax deductions, or "loopholes," that had arisen since 1945. At the same time he stated that businesses would invest more if Congress enacted investment tax credits to encourage them to modernize their plants and equipment. At first the proposed legislation received little attention, because concern over the Bay of Pigs and heightened tensions with the Soviets preoccupied Congress. When Congress resumed work on the tax issue in the summer of 1963, it preserved most of the tax loopholes while giving more preferences to corporations than Kennedy had originally requested. The revised bill finally passed in the early months of the Johnson administration.

The economy improved overall in the Kennedy years, though its performance fell short of what had been promised. In contrast to the fluctuations of the 1950s, economic growth held to a steady 3 percent per year. Unemployment began to decline from 6 percent to under 5 percent. In 1961 and 1962, inflation, as measured by the consumer price index, fell to a nearly negligible rate of 1 percent per year. Business leaders were reassured by the administration's resistance to policies designed to redistribute wealth and income.

Public concern grew over the plight of the fifth of the American population—approximately 25 million people—living in poverty. Largely forgotten since the end of the Second World War, the poorest Americans lived in decaying cities and remote rural areas. Eighty percent of them were white, the remainder ethnic minorities. The poorest of the poor were people over the age of sixty-five living in rural areas. The Democrats of the 1950s and early 1960s, heirs of the New Deal but eager for acceptance from the business community, had mostly ignored their needs. In 1962 Michael Harrington, a former social worker, challenged this indifference in his book *The Other America*. Harrington decried a vicious cycle in which "there are people in the affluent society who are poor because they are poor; and who stay poor because they are poor." He spoke directly to the country's leaders, explaining to them that "the fate of the poor hangs on the decisions of the better off."

The Other America made a deep impression on intellectuals and opinion makers. Kennedy found in Harrington's book a troubling critique of his own timid efforts to revitalize the American economy and to make the New Frontier reach everyone in the country. He asked the chairman of the Council of Economic Advisers to develop plans for a more vigorous assault on poverty. Unfortunately, before a program was ready, Kennedy was murdered.

THE PUSH FOR CIVIL RIGHTS

The movement to end discrimination based on race reached its peak in the 1960s. By the end of the decade the degrading system of legal segregation had ended. America underwent a revolution in race relations. This so-called Second Reconstruction altered the American racial landscape even more than the first Reconstruction, which took place in the decade after the Civil War. African-Americans had mobilized against segregation for years; by the 1960s their efforts commanded the attention of most white Americans, provoking both support and resistance. As public officials gradually realized how important it was to end legally sanctioned segregation, the Kennedy administration began to take steps to aid the effort.

In 1961, fully six years after the Supreme Court ruled that segregation in the public schools had to end "with all deliberate speed," separation of the races remained a fact of life across the nation, especially in southern and border regions (including Washington, D.C.). Not only were many public schools and universities closed to blacks, so were many public transportation vehicles, bathroom facilities, and parks, as well as privately owned restaurants and hotels. The National Association for the Advancement of Colored People (NAACP), the most prominent of the black civil rights organizations, had sought to build on the victory in the landmark *Brown* v. *Board of Education* case by persuading the courts to order quicker desegregation and encouraging Congress to pass civil rights legislation protecting black voters. The NAACP desegregated some school districts and saw passage of a civil rights law in the late 1950s, but progress was painfully slow. As noted in Chapter 4, President Eisenhower did not speak out against racial discrimination, and he only belatedly ordered federal troops to Little Rock, Arkansas, in 1957 to ensure the safe admission of black students to that city's Central High School. The modest Civil Rights Act passed that year did not, as African-Americans had hoped, outlaw discrimination in public or privately owned accommodations. After the sit-in at a Greensboro, North Carolina, lunch counter in 1960, the sit-in movement spread, along with marches, demonstrations, and other protests against legally sanctioned discrimination. Many of these actions involved the newly formed Student Non-Violent Coordinating Committee (SNCC).

As a senator John Kennedy had taken few positions on racial discrimination. During the presidential campaign of 1960 he became somewhat bolder, but he continued to walk a narrow line on civil rights, hoping to retain the support of traditional white southern Democrats while also winning the votes of blacks. He refrained from endorsing new civil rights laws, but condemned Eisenhower for his timidity in not putting the moral authority of the presidency on the side of victims of racial prejudice. The president, Kennedy said, could end discrimination in public housing "with the stroke of a pen," by signing an executive order. He promised that his protection of minorities would be more vigorous, and blacks believed that the Kennedy brothers' telephone calls on behalf of the jailed Martin Luther King, Jr., signaled sympathy with their cause.

At first, however, Kennedy's administration did little to advance civil rights. Particularly galling to those blacks who had supported him was Kennedy's failure throughout 1961 to sign an executive order ending discrimination in public housing. By the end of the year the Congress on Racial Equality (CORE), a rival of the NAACP that favored more militant action, sought to shame Kennedy into making good on his promise. CORE organized the "Ink for Jack" campaign, in which supporters of civil rights mailed thousands of ball-point pens to the White House. Eventually, in 1962, Kennedy signed an executive order outlawing racial discrimination in public housing.

The "Ink for Jack" campaign represented only a small part of the civil rights effort. Many ordinary citizens believed that much more was required to achieve civil rights and that the government would not act unless pressured from below. In the spring of 1961, blacks and whites joined together in a campaign of civil disobedience to force the federal government to take a more aggressive stand. In early May, two busloads of blacks and whites left Washington, D.C., bound for New Orleans, with interim stops scheduled along the way throughout the South. Calling themselves Freedom Riders, the travelers challenged state laws prohibiting mixed seating on interstate buses and requiring public accommodations along the way to maintain "whites only" and "colored only" facilities. In practice such laws meant nonwhites could not enter most restaurants or relieve themselves in most public rest rooms.

At first the Freedom Riders encountered icy stares from white people and found bus stations mysteriously closed when they arrived. This silent resistance was difficult enough; but when the travelers reached Alabama, the opposition proved much more dangerous. In Anniston, Alabama, a white mob attacked one bus with pipes, slashed the tires, and demanded that the Freedom Riders leave the bus. Although the local police escorted the bus and its passengers out of town, the gang continued its pursuit in cars. After the bus's tires went completely flat, the mob surrounded it, and someone threw a bomb through the window. When the Freedom Riders ran out of the bus, the mob beat them. One white Freedom Rider was punched in the face while others stomped on his chest until he lost consciousness.

This inexcusable refusal by local authorities to protect United States citizens goaded Kennedy into action. The violence had been photographed and shown in newspapers and on television, shocking many Americans. Scenes of the howling mob attacking unarmed Freedom Riders also offered a propaganda boost to the Soviet Union on the eve of the Vienna summit. The president, sickened by the sight of this violence, ordered United States marshals to Alabama to protect the Freedom Riders, and the Justice Department enjoined racist organizations from further interference with the buses.

At the same time, the reluctance of the administration to take decisive action was evident. No matter how offensive the attacks on Freedom Riders became, Washington officials remained reluctant to antagonize southern whites who had been an essential element of the Democratic party's coalition. Robert Kennedy asked for a "cooling-off period" of a hundred days to let tempers subside. James Farmer, executive director of CORE, acidly replied, "We've been cooling off for one hundred years. If we got any cooler we'd be in the deep freeze." Accordingly, CORE ignored advice to stop the demonstrations and continued to arrange Freedom Rides for the rest of the summer of 1961. Federal marshals offered protection against physical assaults on the buses and riders. At the same time, Robert Kennedy sought unsuccessfully to persuade the Freedom Ride organizers that voter registration, rather than public demonstrations, would do more for the cause of civil rights.

Like many other white northerners, the Kennedy brothers gradually developed greater concern over racial discrimination as the demonstrations continued. They expressed their greatest commitment to civil rights in September 1962, during a confrontation with Mississippi Governor Ross Barnett over the enrollment of James Meredith, a black man, at the state's university in Oxford. Meredith, an air force veteran, had applied for admission to the University of Mississippi in January 1961. A high school graduate and resident of Mississippi, he was entitled to admission to the state university, but it refused to enroll him. He appealed the decision in federal court, and on September 13, 1962, Supreme Court Justice Hugo Black, a native of Alabama and former member of the Ku Klux Klan, ordered the university to admit him. Mississippi's state legislature responded by making Governor Barnett a temporary registrar of the university. Playing to strong racist sentiments throughout the state, Barnett vowed not to surrender to "the evil and illegal forces of tyranny." He promised that Meredith would never register.

The president and attorney general spoke several times on the telephone to Barnett. For a while it appeared that a compromise had been arranged: the governor would save face by resisting the federal marshals who had been sent to Oxford to escort Meredith into the university, but Meredith would be allowed to register later. That deal fell through, however, as hundreds of whites converged on the college town, intent on chasing Meredith away. When Meredith and his escort of federal marshals finally reached the campus, over a thousand white demonstrators blocked their path, screaming "Go to Cuba, nigger lovers, go to Cuba!" They threw rocks and bottles at the line of marshals. Then several members of the mob, now numbering over two thousand, opened fire with shotguns and rifles, killing an English reporter and wounding a marshal and a United States border patrolman.

In the midst of this violence, Kennedy addressed the nation. He spent more time calming the fears of white Mississippians than explaining the evils of racial discrimination. He appealed to that state's "great tradition of honor and courage, won on the field of battle." He urged the university's students, most of whom had not been involved in the demonstrations, to continue to stay on the sidelines, because "the eyes of the nation and the world are upon you and upon all of us." At the same time, Kennedy ordered 23,000 army troops to Oxford to quell the rioting and to ensure that Meredith could enroll for classes and study in relative peace. Five hundred troops remained stationed in Oxford until Meredith graduated in June 1963. Martin Luther King, Jr., thought the Kennedy brothers had helped the cause of civil rights but did not fully appreciate how much work remained to be done.

In 1963 Martin Luther King, Jr., sought to increase the civil rights movement's momentum. In May he helped organize demonstrations for the end of segregation in Birmingham, Alabama. The protesters found the perfect enemy in Birmingham's police commissioner, Eugene "Bull" Connor, whose beefy features and snarling demeanor made him seem a living caricature of a racist southern sheriff. Connor's police used clubs, dogs, and fire hoses to chase and harass the demonstrators. Kennedy watched the police dogs in action on television—along with the rest of the country—and confessed that the brutality made him sick. He later observed that "the civil rights movement should thank God for Bull Connor. He's helped it as much as Abraham Lincoln." The president dispatched the head of the Justice Department's civil rights division to Birmingham to try to work out an arrangement between King's demonstrators and local business leaders that would permit desegregation of lunch counters, drinking fountains, and bathrooms. The president made several calls to the business leaders himself, and they finally agreed to his terms.

On June 10, during a national address focusing on civil rights, Kennedy acknowledged that the nation faced a moral crisis. He rejected the notion that the United States could be the land of the free "except for the Negroes." Reversing his earlier reluctance to request civil rights legislation, he announced that he would send Congress a major civil rights bill. The law would guarantee service to all Americans, regardless of race, at all establishments open to the public—hotels, restaurants, theaters, retail stores, and the like. Moreover, it would grant the federal government greater authority to pursue lawsuits against segregation in public schools and universities and would increase the Justice Department's powers to protect the voting rights of racial minorities.

African-American leaders found Kennedy's commitment to legislation encouraging, but they wanted assurances that the president would follow through. To maintain pressure on Congress, several civil rights leaders revived the idea, first presented in 1941, of a March on Washington to promote civil rights. The Kennedy administration was not in favor of such a march. Already public opinion polls indicated that a plurality of voters thought the president was pushing integration too fast, and Kennedy worried about the political cost of endorsing the black push for equality.

Martin Luther King, Jr., delivering his "I Have a Dream" speech on August 28, 1963. *Francis Miller, LIFE Magazine © 1963 Time, Inc.*

The March on Washington went forward anyway, on August 28, 1963. A crowd of about 300,000 people, mostly black but including people of all races, filled the mall facing the Lincoln Memorial. Led by folk singer Joan Baez, they sang the spiritual "We Shall Overcome," which had become the unofficial anthem of the civil rights movement. They heard other songs and listened to speeches. John Lewis, a leading Freedom Rider, prepared a militant address that was toned down by march organizers before he delivered it. He spoke of "blacks" rather than "Negroes," a terminology that took hold over the next few years.

The climax came when Martin Luther King, Jr., offered to the watching world an inspiring vision of the future. Although he had invoked these images many times before, much of white America was listening to him for the first time: "I have a dream that one day *all* God's children, black men and white men, Jews and Gentiles, Protestants and Catholics, will be able to join hands and sing in the words of the old Negro spiritual, 'Free at last! Free at last! Thank God Almighty, we are free at last!'" President Kennedy watched on television and told an aide in admiration, "He's damn good." But within three months Kennedy was dead, and the civil rights legislation advocated by the March on Washington needed the support of a new president.

TECHNOLOGY: HOPE AND FEAR

Americans had developed a new appreciation for the benefits of technology by the early 1960s. Yet by the time Kennedy was murdered in November 1963, fears had grown about the potential negative impact on everyday life of modern science and engineering. In April 1961, days before the defeat at the Bay of Pigs, a Soviet cosmonaut, Yuri Gagarin, became the first man to orbit the earth. Americans felt ashamed and frightened. The shock of the 1957 *Sputnik* launch was still fresh in everyone's mind. Members of the joint congressional committee on space demanded that the Kennedy administration make good on its campaign pledge to restore the country's flagging prestige. One member told the director of the National Aeronautics and Space Administration (NASA), "tell me how much money you need, and this committee will authorize all you need." A newspaper concluded that Soviet successes in space had "cost the nation heavily in prestige" and that "neutral nations may come to believe that the wave of the future is Russian."

In this atmosphere, the Kennedy administration wanted to act quickly. NASA's own reports indicated that the United States led the Soviets in every area of space science; but in the tense aftermath of Gagarin's flight and the Bay of Pigs, Americans wanted a definitive victory in the space race. The president told a press conference that he was tired of the United States' being second best. He made Vice President Lyndon Johnson chairman of the Space Council and instructed him to look for ways of "beating the Russians." In late May the president went before Congress to announce a goal of "landing a man on the moon, and returning him safely to earth . . . before the decade is out."

To fulfill this lunar mission, Congress encouraged NASA to create the Apollo program. Johnson made certain that friends in Texas and nearby states received the lion's share of the scientific and construction contracts for Apollo. The Apollo complex followed the contours of the Gulf of Mexico, from Texas to Florida, providing jobs, income, and a stake in federal projects to traditionally poor but fast-growing southern states. Johnson called it a "second Reconstruction" for the area. In four years the number of workers employed directly by NASA had grown from 6,000 to 60,000. Another 411,000 scientists, engineers, technicians, and clerical staff flocked to the region to work for private firms under contract to NASA.

Even as the Apollo scientists worked feverishly preparing for the moon mission, NASA tried to top Gagarin's orbital flight. In the summer of 1961 two astronauts, Alan Shepard and Virgil Grissom, made space flights lasting about fifteen minutes in capsules launched by Atlas ICBMs. Then, in February 1962, ten months after Gagarin's orbit, Marine Lieutenant Colonel John Glenn was strapped into *Friendship 7* and blasted into orbit. In the next five hours Glenn made three trips around the globe. His success buoyed Americans, who had seen too many events that seemed to point to a decline in United States power, influence, and scientific pre-eminence. Glenn was a guest at the White House and enjoyed a ticker-tape parade down Manhattan's Broadway, the likes of which had not been seen since Charles Lindbergh returned in triumph after his solo flight from New York to Paris in 1927.

Americans also began to focus on another concern, which would become increasingly important in later years: the quality of the environment. In 1962 science writer Rachel Carson published *Silent Spring*, a lengthy indictment of the damage done to the environment by the pesticide industry. Use of synthetic pesticides, a product of technology developed during the Second World War, had increased 400 percent between 1947 and 1962. The United States now sprayed 650 million pounds of deadly chemicals per year over farms, gardens, and homes. As Carson wrote, these poisons did not distinguish among their victims and "should not be called insecticides but biocides." The chemicals remained in the environment, filtering through the soil, entering the ground water, and eventually finding their way into the food chain, where they contaminated animals and humans alike.

Carson's work alarmed the American public. Some 200,000 copies of her book were snatched up within a month, and members of Congress and newspapers were deluged with letters demanding federal action. Kennedy met Carson, and he instructed the President's Science Advisory Committee (PSAC) to study the pesticide problem. In May 1963, the PSAC reported that pesticides had done extensive damage to fish, birds, and other wildlife and that traces of toxic chemicals had been found in humans. The report urged elimination of the use of toxic pesticides. Pesticide manufacturers opposed the recommendations, but seven years later the newly formed Environmental Protection Agency (EPA) banned the use of DDT, the most harmful pesticide, in the United States.

A new environmental movement arose in the West in response to the explosive growth of cities. Western environmentalists tended to be city people who wanted to protect the wild places where they sought recreation and renewal. In the 1960s they often focused on issues involving water and wilderness. The Sierra Club, led by David Brower, successfully fought the construction of a dam at Echo Park on the Colorado River, which would have flooded part of Dinosaur National Monument in Utah, and managed to prevent the construction of dams that would have flooded parts of the Grand Canyon. Their

Rachel Carson

The Second World War stimulated research and development of new chemicals and synthetic materials generally hailed as miracle products. But miracles do not come free. While other scientists pursued the perfection of plastics, biologist Rachel Carson (1907–1964) spent the war years working for the U.S. Bureau of Fisheries, writing conservation bulletins. In the years following, she would turn her talents to exposing the hazards of new industries spawned by wartime economic mobilization.

Unlike most government writers, Carson combined the insights of a scientist with the grace of a poet. As a child growing up in Pennsylvania, she had aspired to a literary career, publishing her first story at the age of ten. But in college she was inspired to study biology,

victories, however, were sometimes Pyrrhic. Instead of building a dam at Echo Park, for example, the Bureau of Reclamation built one that flooded Glen Canyon, a place of such extraordinary grandeur that its loss would become the cardinal symbol of environmental degradation to a later, more militant generation of wilderness advocates. And when the Sierra Club argued against the Grand Canyon dams, they insisted that developers could instead garner electrical generating capacity by building coal-fired and nuclear power plants. As a consequence, the Black Mesa on the Arizona Navajo and Hopi reservations was strip-mined, and the coal-burning Navajo Power Plant was built at Page, Arizona. Such trade-offs convinced more and more advocates of environmental protection that they would have to take a more systemic, ecological view of their cause.

and she earned a master's in zoology at Johns Hopkins University. During summers in graduate school, she worked at the Marine Biology Laboratory at Woods Hole, Massachusetts, where she developed a lifelong passion for the sea and wetlands.

"I have always wanted to write," Carson once told a friend, "but I know I don't have much imagination. Biology has given me something to write about. I will try in my writing to make animals in the woods and the waters where they live as alive and as meaningful to others as they are to me." She lived up to her aspirations.

After writing award-winning nature books, including *The Sea Around Us* (1951) and *The Edge of the Sea* (1955), Carson wrote the book that would change the way Americans thought about their world. She had long been concerned about the indiscriminate use of one purported miracle product, the insecticide DDT, a substance both lethal and long-lasting. When a friend's private bird sanctuary was sprayed with DDT under a state-mandated mosquito-control program, Carson was horrified by the subsequent mass death of the sanctuary's birds and other insects. In 1962 she published *Silent Spring,* an indictment not only of DDT but of numerous other materials humans poisoned the earth, air, and water with. Despite vicious attempts by the chemical industry to discredit the book, *Silent Spring* spawned a worldwide outcry and gave birth to the modern environmental movement. ■

ASSASSINATION

Kennedy's endorsement of the civil rights movement during the fall of 1963 complicated his re-election chances in the South. As in 1960, a key state was Texas, where the Democrats feuded over policies and patronage. Governor John Connally, leader of the Texas Democrats conservative faction, opposed Kennedy's plans for a civil rights bill. The governor was not on speaking terms with the state's liberal senator, Ralph Yarborough, and both Connally and Yarborough distrusted Vice President Lyndon Johnson, whose shifting positions did not satisfy either liberals or conservatives. Seeking to bolster his own standing in his home state, Johnson persuaded several prominent national officeholders, including the president, to visit Texas in the fall.

When United Nations ambassador Adlai Stevenson spoke in Dallas in October, he encountered ugly demonstrations organized by vocal conservatives. Handbills appeared with pictures of Kennedy labeled "Wanted for Treason." The mob swarmed around Stevenson, someone hit him in the face with a sign, and only the protection of a police squad got him out of the hall safely. The attack on Stevenson was only the most recent in a series of violent protests against the administration. The Secret Service had compiled thirty-four credible threats on the president's life from the Dallas area since 1961. Many came from those who espoused extreme right-wing views, but the Secret Service also documented threats from leftists, anti-Castro Cubans, Puerto Rican nationalists, black militants, and several mentally disturbed individuals.

One month after Stevenson's encounter with the mob of Dallas demonstrators, on November 21, Kennedy flew to San Antonio with Jacqueline to begin a three-day swing through the Lone Star State. Johnson joined them later that day in Houston and the next day in Fort Worth, where the president addressed businessmen about the importance of Texas defense contractors to the nation's military strength. At 11:20 A.M. Air Force One took off from Fort Worth for the brief flight to Dallas. The presidential jet landed in Dallas at noon, and Governor Connally, his wife Nellie, and President and Mrs. Kennedy entered an open-air limousine for a trip downtown, where Kennedy was scheduled to speak before another business group. The motorcade route had been published days before to ensure the largest crowd possible. Thousands lined the route, and most were smiling, cheering, and waving. Mrs. Connally told the president, "You can't say Dallas doesn't love you." Kennedy replied, "That's obvious." Seconds later, at 12:33 P.M., three shots rang out. Two bullets hit the president; one passed through his throat and the other exploded through the back of his head. In shock, Mrs. Kennedy rose and climbed onto the rear hood of the car to retrieve part of the president's skull. The Secret Service agent who moved to shield her and guide her back into her seat heard her say, "I have brains in my hand." The motorcade raced to nearby Parkland Hospital, where Kennedy was pronounced dead at 1:00 P.M.

Later that afternoon, police arrested twenty-four-year-old Lee Harvey Oswald in a movie theater. A Marine Corps veteran and lonely drifter, Oswald had recently returned from a long stay in the Soviet Union. He worked in the Texas Book Depository, the building from which the shots were fired. Oswald had flitted among political causes of the left and right, making it difficult for later investigators to determine his motives. He had contacted the Cuban embassy in Mexico City earlier in 1963, but the Cubans had refused to speak with him, fearing he was a provocateur sent by the CIA. To complicate matters

President Kennedy's casket is borne away from the Capitol en route to burial at Arlington National Cemetery. *Photo No. Ar 8255-10 in the John F. Kennedy Library.*

further, Oswald had family ties to a Mafia member who had spoken of his desire to kill Kennedy in order to halt the Justice Department's investigations of organized crime.

The chances of ever discovering Oswald's true allegiances probably disappeared two days after the Kennedy assassination. That Sunday most Americans sat glued to television sets, watching hundreds of thousands of grief-stricken mourners file past a closed casket in the Capitol rotunda. When the networks cut away to the basement of the Dallas police station to show Oswald being escorted to another jail, millions of viewers saw nightclub owner Jack Ruby step out of a crowd and kill Oswald with a bullet to the abdomen.

In December President Johnson appointed a special commission, chaired by Chief Justice Earl Warren, to investigate the assassination. Less than a year later, the Warren Commission filed a report concluding that Oswald, acting alone, had killed Kennedy. The Warren Commission worked hastily, because it believed a speedy report would still rumors of a conspiracy. That did not happen. For years after the murder, many Americans, at times a majority, believed that a conspiracy was behind Kennedy's murder. The list of suspected conspirators was varied and shifted from year to year: extreme conservatives, the Mafia, the CIA, Fidel Castro, conservative Vietnamese, even Lyndon Johnson. In 1979 a House committee concluded that more than one person had fired shots at Kennedy's limousine, but FBI scientists rebutted the committee's findings. In the decades after the Warren Commission's report, little tangible evidence has come to light to demonstrate that its conclusions were flawed.

The persistence of the belief that Kennedy died at the hands of conspirators represented an effort to make sense out of a shocking act that deeply shook many Americans' faith in their institutions. In the years following Kennedy's death, other prominent figures fell to assassins, and shots were fired at other presidents in 1975 and 1981. Within five years of that fateful November afternoon, Americans had come to see their society as dangerous, violent, and led by people who lacked Kennedy's ability to inspire the nation. Many traced the beginning of their sense that America's public institutions did not work properly to the day Kennedy died.

CONCLUSION

After his death, Americans quickly elevated John Kennedy to martyrdom. His optimism, wit, intelligence, and charm—all of which encouraged the feeling that American society could accomplish anything its people wanted—were snuffed out in an instant. He was only forty-six years old. Within six months of his murder, journalist Theodore White bestowed on his administration the name "Camelot." Popularized by the 1962 Broadway musical of that title, the term referred to the mythical kingdom of Arthur and his Knights of the Round Table. In this view, Kennedy's 1,037-day administration represented a brief, shining moment during which the nation's political leaders spoke to Americans' finest aspirations.

The reality was more complicated. Kennedy and his advisers had been formed by the experiences of the postwar world. They represented a new generation, nurtured by the Cold War, an activist government, and the military-industrial complex. Skeptical of ideology and serenely self-confident, officials of the Kennedy administration and their circle of friends believed problems could be mastered and managed. That was their strength, because it encouraged their curiosity about people, trends, and ideas. They learned from their setbacks and mistakes, and by 1963 their skepticism even extended to the beliefs they expressed in 1960 that the United States could vanquish the

Soviet Union through sheer will power. Their self-confidence offered Americans hope.

Yet the style of cool self-reliance favored by Kennedy and his advisers also betrayed their primary weakness. Their resistance to emotion and passion stunted their ability to empathize with groups that had been excluded from the bounty of American society. The Kennedy administration did more for civil rights than its predecessor had, but its principal efforts in this area came as a result of intense pressure and dramatic events that could not be ignored. On the questions of poverty and the environment, Kennedy took important first steps; whether his administration would have accomplished significantly more if he had lived longer, historians can only speculate. Overall, his domestic program reflected the politics of consensus, much like his predecessor's.

In foreign affairs he also continued an earlier trend, the reflexive anticommunism of the Cold War, but with a particularly aggressive twist. His propensity for tough confrontation with the Soviets led the world to the brink of nuclear holocaust. Only after the near-disaster of the Cuban missile crisis did he begin to move toward détente.

Advocates of the New Frontier had promised the country a new youth and vigor in the White House, and the Kennedy administration provided these qualities in abundance. It was less successful in offering new substance and new solutions. The burden of acting on many unsolved problems fell on Lyndon Johnson, a very different man, who was suddenly elevated to the presidency. ■

F U R T H E R   R E A D I N G

On politics and policies in the Kennedy administration, see: James N. Giglio, *The Presidency of John F. Kennedy* (1991); Allan Matusow, *The Unraveling of America: A History of Liberalism in the 1960s* (1984); Herbert Parmet, *JFK: The Presidency of John F. Kennedy* (1983); Richard Reeves, *President Kennedy: Profile in Power* (1993); Thomas C. Reeves, *A Question of Character: A Life of John F. Kennedy* (1991); Theodore Sorensen, *Kennedy* (1965); Arthur M. Schlesinger, Jr., *A Thousand Days* (1966) and *Robert F. Kennedy and His Times* (1978); Theodore H. White, *The Making of the President, 1960* (1961); David Knapp and Kenneth Polk, *Scouting the War on Poverty: Social Reform Politics in the Kennedy Administration* (1971). On the assassination, see: Gerald Posner, *Case Closed: Lee Harvey Oswald and the Assassination of JFK* (1993). On space policy, see: Walter A. McDougall, . . . *The Heavens and the Earth: A Political History of the Space Age* (1985). On civil rights, see: Taylor Branch, *Parting the Waters: America in the King Years, 1954–1963* (1988); David Garrow, *Bearing the Cross: Martin Luther King, Jr. and the Southern Christian Leadership Conference* (1986). On environmentalism, see: Samuel P. Hays, *Beauty, Health, and Permanence: Environmental Politics in the United States, 1955–85* (1987); Marc Reisner, *Cadillac Desert: The American West and Its Disappearing Water* (1993). On foreign policy, see: Thomas Paterson, ed., *Kennedy's Quest for Victory: American Foreign Policy, 1961–1963* (1989); Thomas Paterson, *Contesting Castro: The United States and the Triumph of the Cuban Revolution* (1994); Michael Beschloss, *The Crisis Years: Kennedy and Khrushchev 1960–1963* (1991); Montague Kern, Patricia W. Levering, and Ralph B. Levering, *The Kennedy Crises: The Press, the Presidency and Foreign Policy* (1983); Richard Walton, *Cold War and Counter-revolution* (1972); John Lewis Gaddis, *Strategies of Containment* (1981); Thomas Schoenbaum, *Waging Peace and War: Dean Rusk in the Truman, Kennedy and Johnson Years* (1988); Trumbull Higgins, *The Perfect Failure: Kennedy, Eisenhower and the Bay of Pigs* (1987); Richard D. Mahoney, *JFK: Ordeal in Africa* (1983).

6

The Dream of a
Great Society

In 1962 Michael Harrington's best-selling book *The Other America*, a critique of economic inequality in contemporary America, helped spark renewed concern for the problems of the poor in the United States. By the early 1960s many middle-class Americans believed the apparent prosperity of the postwar years masked serious flaws in their society. They wanted something better and more uplifting, even if they were uncertain what that might be.

President Lyndon Johnson acknowledged the nation's desire to redistribute the benefits of affluence to those who had been left behind. He had witnessed deprivation firsthand during the Great Depression and was strongly moved to erase it. Addressing Congress in support of the 1965 Voting Rights Act, he recalled the poverty of the rural school where he had taught in 1928: "My students were poor and they often came to class without breakfast, hungry. They knew even in their youth the pain of injustice. . . . Somehow you never forget what poverty and hatred can do when you see its scars in the hopeful face of a young child." He had never expected to be in a position to do much about the problem. But now that he had the chance, he told Congress, he meant to use it: "I mean to be the president who educated young children . . . who helped to feed the hungry . . . who helped the poor to find their own way."

But Johnson was a man of many contradictions. He came to political maturity in the 1930s, as a New Dealer; but as a veteran of rough Texas politics, he learned to moderate his positions according to the currents of the times. He often had to shelve his commitment to the poor, sometimes serving the interests of the richest and most reactionary factions in the Lone Star State, in order to advance politically. In his thirty years of public life before assuming the presidency, Johnson—a huge man, six feet four inches tall, big-handed, with an enormous face and an overbearing presence—had charmed, flattered, and bullied his way to the top. Rivals and political foes feared, resented, and eventually hated his abusive manner and the twists and turns of his political position.

As president, Johnson articulated a vision of a "Great Society" that would bring an end to racial discrimination, afford equal opportunity to all people, eliminate poverty, and provide all Americans with adequate health care. The scale of this undertaking was so vast that disappointments were almost inevitable. Also, by 1966 the consensus Johnson had carefully cultivated in support of these goals began to erode under the weight of the war in Vietnam and a white backlash against government efforts on behalf of African-Americans. Unfortunately, Johnson's own shortcomings—his abrasiveness, untruthfulness and manipulation of others—made him an unsuitable leader for such times of political discord. When he lost congressional support for his initiatives, Johnson turned his back on the Great Society he had so eloquently described in 1964. He withdrew on occasion into passivity and paranoia. Finally he left Washington in 1969 a nearly broken man, his dream of a Great Society largely unfulfilled.

The successes and failures of the Great Society reflect the triumphs and disappointments of political liberalism in general. From the time of the New Deal until the mid-1960s, the liberal ideal—expanding government power in order to improve social and economic conditions—dominated American politics. By the end of the 1960s, however, many Americans no longer believed that government programs, agencies, or officials delivered tangible benefits. The early 1960s were years of enormous hope and promise for many; by the end of the decade, a more somber mood prevailed. America's faith in liberalism became a casualty, to some extent, of liberalism's most ambitious endeavor.

LYNDON JOHNSON: THE POLITICIAN AND THE PRESIDENT

Johnson told his biographer, Doris Kearns, about a recurring dream from his childhood: "He would see himself sitting absolutely still, in a big, straight chair. In the dream, the chair stood in the middle of the great, open plains. A stampede of cattle was coming toward him. He tried to move, but he could not. He cried out again and again for his mother, but no one came." According to Kearns, Johnson longed for the approval of his refined mother and the world of books, culture, and morality she brought to his frontier Texas home. However, he had also absorbed his brutal, alcoholic father's contempt for "dreamy thinkers whose idealism led inevitably to ruin and collapse." Thus throughout Johnson's life an urge for morality, justice, and culture warred with the bullying side of his nature that he had absorbed from his father. This inner conflict created a fear of paralysis, evidenced in the dream, along with a corresponding compulsion "to move, keep control, stay in charge."

Johnson went to Washington in 1931, in the depths of the depression, as an aide to a newly elected Texas congressman. The congressman let Johnson run his office and decide how he should vote; within months, the young aide was congressman in everything but name. In 1933 Johnson persuaded his boss to drop his entrenched conservatism and support the New Deal. Two years later, in 1935, Johnson used the contacts he had made within the Texas congressional delegation to win appointment as the Texas director of the newly created National Youth Administration.

In 1937 Johnson won a special election to Congress as a New Dealer. He took the courageous step for a Texas politician of courting black and Mexican-American voters, telling the black leaders of Austin that if they supported him he would someday back voting rights and perhaps a hot lunch program.

Back in Washington, he mastered the rules of the House and faithfully voted for Roosevelt's programs. By 1948 Johnson wanted to be a senator. In keeping with the Truman administration's ambivalent attitude toward New Deal reforms, he tempered his earlier populism, ran a viciously negative campaign as a moderate against a conservative former governor, stuffed ballot boxes in some key precincts, and won the election by 87 votes. From there he rose fast, becoming the majority leader in the Senate by 1954.

For the remaining six years of the Eisenhower administration, Johnson ran the Senate as no one had before him. He perfected the "treatment," a combination of flattery, cajolery, threats, empathy, blackmail, and horse trading, to get his way. His relations with the Eisenhower administration were excellent, but liberal Democrats came to distrust him as a Texas wheeler-dealer. He eliminated references in the 1957 civil rights bill to equal treatment in public accommodations, and he sided with business interests against labor unions in the debate over the Landrum-Griffin Labor Reform Act of 1958. Liberals were offended, seeing such actions as the work of a compromiser and perhaps even a reactionary.

Johnson toyed with the idea of a presidential run in 1960, but he hesitated. By the time he declared his candidacy—the week before the Democratic convention—it was too late even in the age before presidential primaries became the principal means of selecting a candidate. John Kennedy had virtually assured himself the nomination, and Johnson's attacks on his inexperience did nothing to endear him to Kennedy's political intimates. After Kennedy had won the nomination, Robert Kennedy, the candidate's brother and campaign manager, relayed word to Johnson that Kennedy wanted him as vice president. Johnson dithered, reluctant to abandon his powerful position as majority leader, and liberals expressed dismay. But eventually the senator from Texas, reviled by many of Kennedy's most ardent backers as a southwestern political fixer and manipulator, became the Democratic vice-presidential candidate. He accepted the nomination in order to win the election for the Democrats; his job during the campaign was to carry Texas and as much of the South as possible.

Johnson helped Kennedy carry Texas by forty-six thousand votes. His presence on the ticket also contributed to Kennedy victories in much of the lower South and New Mexico. His service during the campaign temporarily warmed the hearts of Kennedy's inner circle, but for Johnson it proved a curiously joyless victory. One of the supporters who gathered with him to watch the election returns in an Austin hotel thought he "didn't want to be vice president."

Johnson was worried that he would have little power as vice president. His concern was justified. When there were important decisions to make—on Berlin, Cuba, Vietnam, taxes, civil rights—Kennedy and his inner circle made them without consulting Johnson. Instead, the vice president chaired the newly created National Aeronautics and Space Council and the Presidential Committee on Equal Opportunity. In 1961 these seemed remote outposts of the New Frontier. They were, however, important proving grounds for Johnson's own presidency.

Johnson found solace in travel. When he left Washington for trips to Africa, Europe, and Southeast Asia, he was like a man released from jail. But by 1963, even the delights of travel had paled. Kennedy's staff could not stand Johnson, and he knew it. Once the master of the Senate, he withdrew from his old colleagues. The criminal conviction of Bobby Baker, onetime secretary to the majority leader and a man Johnson likened to the son he never had, revived charges that the vice president had illegally made millions while presiding over the Senate. In the summer of 1963 some of Kennedy's aides openly expressed the wish that Johnson—"Uncle Corn Pone," they called him—would voluntarily step down from the Democratic ticket in 1964. In early November 1963 a dispirited Johnson confided to an aide that his future as vice president seemed bleak, and he mused about a new career. It came in an unexpected way. On November 22 Kennedy was shot in Dallas, on a trip arranged to quell the endemic feuding among Texas Democrats.

Johnson took the oath of office aboard Air Force One with a stricken Mrs. Kennedy looking on, her clothes splattered with the blood of the slain president. Many of Kennedy's most ardent supporters viewed Johnson as unworthy of the office held by a fallen hero.

Unlike Harry Truman, who became president following the death of Roosevelt in 1945, Johnson asked his predecessor's staff to stay. But it was nearly impossible to cultivate harmony between Kennedy's circle and the assistants who had served Johnson in the vice presidency. The more inconsolable of the Kennedy people resented Johnson as a usurper. Johnson's aides believed Kennedy did not deserve his golden reputation. After all, Kennedy's domestic agenda had made little progress in Congress; but a legislative master like Johnson might turn the dreams of racial justice and expanded economic opportunity for the poor into law.

Initially Johnson rose above such pettiness. He was a whirlwind, putting in a 14- to 18-hour day. Immediately after Kennedy's funeral he addressed Congress, calling for unity, consensus, and the continuance of Kennedy's vision. A few weeks later he stood before Congress to deliver his first State of the Union address. In it he pledged to continue Kennedy's program, but with a distinctly activist and legislative stamp. Along with civil rights—the basic moral issue of the day—he emphasized the need to eliminate the blight of poverty. "This administration today, here and now, declares unconditional war on poverty in America. . . . It will not be a short or easy struggle, but we shall not rest until that war is won."

After his stirring words to Congress, Johnson plunged immediately into the effort to pass the landmark civil rights bill advocated by the demonstrators in Washington in August 1963. Despite Johnson's best efforts, the bill languished in the Senate in the fall. The provisions outlawing segregation in privately owned restaurants, overnight lodgings, and transportation were anathema to southern senators, who complained that they interfered with property rights. Nevertheless, in 1964 the House of Representatives, with the assistance of the Johnson administration, added two additional provisions to the bill. One empowered the Justice Department to intervene and file suit when a person's civil rights had been violated. The other created the Fair Employment Practices Commission, giving it the power to enforce equal opportunity in hiring and promotion in firms employing more than one hundred people. The House also added a provision forbidding discrimination based on sex as well as race; this later had a dramatic impact in reducing discrimination against women. The bill sailed through the House on February 10, by a vote of 290 to 130. Representatives explained their votes as a tribute to John Kennedy.

Things were more difficult in the Senate, however, where southerners and other opponents of the bill threatened to defeat it with a filibuster. Johnson went to work with his legendary "treatment" to force senators to vote for cloture (an end to debate), in order to bring the legislation to a vote on the floor. With the aid of Minnesota Democrat Hubert Humphrey, he wooed Everett Dirksen, the minority leader. They convinced Dirksen that the party of Abraham Lincoln could not afford to be responsible for the defeat of civil rights legislation. Finally, two and a half months after the filibuster began, the Senate passed the law on July 2, 1964, by a vote of 73 to 27. The act banned discrimination based on race in public accommodations—restaurants, theaters, hotels, motels, and rooming houses. State-supported institutions, such as schools, libraries, parks, playgrounds, and swimming pools, could no longer be segregated. The Justice Department now had the right to intervene to protect those whose civil rights had been violated. The Fair Employment Practices Commission could bring suit to end discrimination in private employment.

Johnson looked forward to signing more civil rights legislation after the election of 1964. He told the new attorney general, Nicholas deB. Katzenbach (who took over in the summer of 1964 after Robert

Making good on the promises of the Kennedy administration, President Johnson signs the Civil Rights Act on July 2, 1964. *Cecil Stoughton/LBJ Library Collection.*

Kennedy resigned), "I want you to write me the goddamndest, toughest voting rights act that you can devise."

Before submitting a voting rights bill, however, Johnson wanted to be elected president in his own right. He hoped not just to win, but to demolish the Republican nominee. As "president of all the people," he could emerge from the shadow of John Kennedy's legacy. He believed that winning a wide majority would enable him to successfully preside over a legislative program as rich as the New Deal.

Johnson's task appeared to be made easier by recent changes within the Republican party. Ever since the New Deal, Republicans had suppressed their most conservative inclinations during presidential campaigns, nominating nonideological, centrist candidates they hoped could win. Whatever else they believed in, Republican presidential candidates Dewey, Eisenhower, and Nixon all accepted the basic premise of the New Deal, that the federal government had a role to play in managing social and economic affairs. Party conservatives complained, but they were regularly outvoted at convention time.

But by 1964 the more conservative Republicans, including Senate Minority Leader Everett Dirksen, House Minority Leader Charles Halleck, old supporters of Senator Robert Taft, members of far-right groups like the John Birch Society, and various newcomers to the party (among them Ronald Reagan, a former president of the Screen

Actors Guild), had had enough. Enraged by what they considered the arrogance of "the Eastern Establishment," they railed against "Wall Street," "international finance," "Madison Avenue," "Harvard," *The New York Herald Tribune,* and "Ivy League prep schools." One advocate of this militant new conservatism, Phyllis Schlafly, complained that in the past "a small group of secret king-makers, using hidden persuaders and psychological warfare techniques, [had] manipulated the Republican national convention to nominate candidates who had side-stepped or suppressed the key issues." Never again, vowed the conservatives, promising to nominate one of their own for the presidency.

For their part, eastern Republicans such as Governors Nelson Rockefeller of New York and William Scranton of Pennsylvania were contemptuous of the backwardness and ignorance of the people they called "primitives"—midwestern, southern, and western politicians who had never valued the role of government in modern society. Fighting for the nomination were Rockefeller, a man whose pedigree and career proclaimed "Eastern Establishment," and Senator Barry Goldwater of Arizona, standard-bearer for the new conservatives.

Goldwater was a product of the Sunbelt, the fast-growing region that had gained wealth, power, and population since the Second World War. He grew up in Phoenix, a city that had swelled from thirty thousand inhabitants in his youth to over eight hundred thousand in the metropolitan area by the 1960s. Freed, they hoped, from the crowding, dirt, crime, and zoning regulations of older cities, the residents of the Sunbelt adopted new political habits. They distrusted government—especially the federal government, which controlled hundreds of thousands of acres of land in the western states—and they resented easterners. Few of them publicly acknowledged that federally funded roads, dams, and electric power grids had made the Sunbelt's growth possible.

Goldwater capitalized on the Sunbelt's animosity in his 1964 campaign. He sealed his nomination for the presidency with a narrow win over Governor Rockefeller in the California primary in early June. Goldwater quickly dashed moderate Republicans' hopes that he would soften his rhetoric and run as a centrist. His speech accepting the Republican nomination gave no quarter, saying that "those who do not care for our cause, we don't expect to enter our ranks." Finally, he dismissed party moderates with his famous pronouncement, "Extremism in the defense of liberty is no vice! . . . Moderation in the pursuit of justice is no virtue!"

In Goldwater, Lyndon Johnson found the perfect opponent. Choosing Senator Hubert Humphrey of Minnesota as his running mate, Johnson campaigned as a unifier and a builder of consensus. In contrast to Goldwater, who seemed sharp, divisive, and ultimately frightening to the public, Johnson looked conciliatory. The Arizona senator alarmed voters with talk of permitting battlefield commanders to have control over nuclear weapons. His proposals to make Social Security private and to sell the Tennessee Valley Authority confirmed suspicions that he was a radical "kook" who wanted to dismantle the most popular programs of the New Deal.

Democrats capitalized on these fears with a series of hard-hitting television advertisements designed to portray Goldwater as untrustworthy. The most famous of the TV spots showed a young girl counting the petals on a daisy. The image of the girl faded as a solemn announcer counted backward from 10. The sight of a mushroom cloud rising from an atomic explosion filled the screen, and Johnson was heard in a voice-over: "These are the stakes. We must learn to love one another, or surely we shall die." Johnson refused to debate Goldwater, letting TV ads carry his message instead, with devastating effect.

Johnson summarized his goals as "to move not only toward the rich society and the powerful society, but upward to the Great Society." He defined the Great Society as "abundance and liberty for all . . . an end to poverty and racial injustice . . . a place where every child can find knowledge to enrich his mind and to enlarge his talents." Johnson drew huge, responsive crowds throughout the country, and a wide coalition supported his campaign: whites and blacks, business and labor, liberals and moderates, Democrats and Republicans.

Johnson's victory on election day was the greatest presidential landslide since the previous century. He carried forty-four states and 60.7 percent of the popular vote (see map, page 222). Nevertheless, there were some ominous signs in how the popular vote was distributed. Throughout the South—the base of the Democrats' success in presidential elections since 1932—Johnson received only 51 percent of the white vote, a signal that his party's control of that region had slipped. In fact, this would be the last time a Democratic presidential candidate would win a majority of the southern white vote. In the Deep South, Goldwater's conservative appeal was especially effective. In addition to his native Arizona, Goldwater carried South Carolina, Georgia, Alabama, Mississippi, and Louisiana. White voters there were enraged by the Civil Rights Act, and grave fissures had appeared in the New Deal coalition.

But in the aftermath of Johnson's dramatic victory, it was hard to predict any difficulties for the Democrats. Alongside the Johnson landslide the Democratic party added 37 House seats and 2 more seats in the Senate. When the new Congress convened in January 1965, House Democrats outnumbered Republicans by 295 to 140. In the Senate there were 68 Democrats and only 32 Republicans. Not since Franklin Roosevelt's election of 1936 had either party

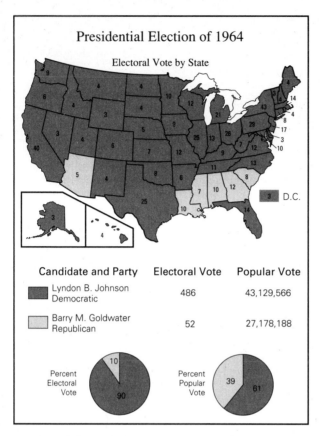

Presidential Election of 1964

Electoral Vote by State

Candidate and Party	Electoral Vote	Popular Vote
Lyndon B. Johnson Democratic	486	43,129,566
Barry M. Goldwater Republican	52	27,178,188

Percent Electoral Vote: 10, 90

Percent Popular Vote: 39, 61

Presidential Election of 1964

assembled such massive majorities in Congress. Johnson appeared to have the congressional backing he needed to use the government to revitalize American society.

THE GREAT SOCIETY: SUCCESS AND DISAPPOINTMENT

Spurred by Lyndon Johnson, in 1965 and 1966 Congress enacted the most sweeping social reforms since the New Deal. Designed to win the War on Poverty and create the Great Society Johnson had promised, these programs enhanced the role of the federal government in promoting health, economic welfare, education, urban renewal, and civil rights. The Great Society programs originated in the work of numerous social thinkers, reformers, and activists. In the late nineteenth and early twentieth centuries, progressive social reformers believed that the poor were mostly immigrants whose culture did not conform to that of the dominant white Protestant majority. The poor could be helped to achieve a stable position in American society by extending down to them the hands of the well-to-do and the intellectuals who studied their problems. In the 1960s the federal government revived this approach. Intellectuals studied the conditions of poor Americans and sought solutions to their problems. Consultants came to Washington to help draft laws reflecting the ideas social scientists had created over the past twenty years.

The Great Society was not limited to programs designed to eliminate poverty; Great Society legislation also served the needs of Americans who were not poor. The creators of the Great Society hoped to give everyone a stake in its success. They wanted to avoid policies that appeared to take resources from one group and give them to another. By steering clear of redistribution, the Great Society was able to gain the support of white, middle class Americans. But the effort to maintain a consensus carried substantial costs, and eventually support for the War on Poverty faded in the middle class. On the one hand, the effort to shy away from redistribution diluted the War on Poverty's effectiveness. On the other hand, *some* redistribution did take place, a development that undermined middle class support.

These ambitious new programs not only increased government spending but also required a greater number of bureaucrats to administer it. In contrast to the 1930s and 1940s, however, the greatest need for new government employees was at the state and local levels (see figure, page 224). Some of the new programs were very successful, but others left a legacy of disappointment and controversy.

Extending federally-funded health care benefits to the elderly was one of the first and most popular of the Great Society initiatives. In 1965, heeding the president's call to improve access to health care for elderly Americans, Congress enacted the ambitious program known as Medicare. Fulfilling a pledge first made by the Truman administration, the legislation created universal hospital insurance for Americans over 65 who were covered by Social Security. Congress also included voluntary insurance to cover doctors' fees. A complementary program, Medicaid, was enacted in 1966; it allowed participating states to receive matching federal grants to pay the medical bills of welfare recipients of all ages. After a slow start, all states but Arizona agreed to participate in Medicaid.

Medicare and Medicaid gained wide popularity because they covered nearly everyone at one time or another in their lives. The programs substantially reduced the gap in medical treatment between the poor and the rich. By 1970 the proportion of Americans who had never visited a physician fell from 19 percent to 8 percent. Prenatal

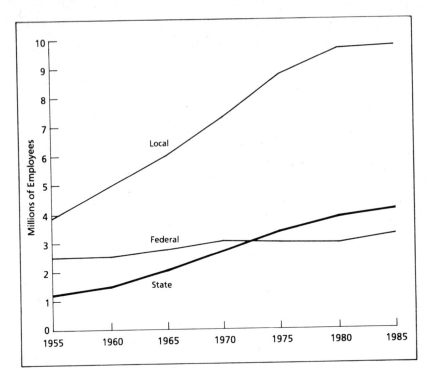

Growth of Government, 1955–1985

visits increased, helping lower the infant mortality rate by 33 percent. Among African-Americans the change in infant mortality was especially noticeable, declining from 4 percent of live births in 1965 to 3.1 percent in 1970 and 2.4 percent in 1975.

One problem, however, was the cost of these medical programs, which far outstripped original estimates. To overcome resistance from the American Medical Association, the administration had agreed that medical services would continue to be provided by private doctors chosen by the patients themselves. Moreover, hospitals and physicians would receive "reasonable and customary" payments for their services. When the inflation rate climbed during the late 1960s, medical charges rose even faster. Partly as a result, the annual cost of these government programs soared from $3.4 billion to $18 billion in ten years.

In 1965 Congress also passed a spectacular array of measures aimed directly at reducing poverty. Many of these programs were designed to alleviate the urban poverty that had led to race riots in numerous American cities in the summer of 1965. Congress created the Office of Economic Opportunity (OEO) to supervise the War on

Poverty. Johnson appointed Sargent Shriver, who had successfully headed the Peace Corps, as the first director of the OEO. Congress created the food stamp program, which provided assistance to people whose income fell below a level set by the government. The program worked well. Ten years after its enactment, research indicated that government efforts were "almost fully effective in reducing flagrant malnutrition."

Because experts considered education a key element in helping young people climb out of poverty, Congress created the Head Start program to reach the preschool children of impoverished families. This too was successful. Later studies revealed that Head Start children gained substantial advantages over poor children who did not enroll. They gained an average of 7 points on IQ tests and were half as likely as nonparticipants to repeat grades in school or to be assigned to special education classes. Long-term studies suggested that, as teenagers and young adults, "Head Starters" completed more years of school, worked more steadily, and engaged in less criminal behavior. Congress also provided grants to school districts with large numbers of poor children and scholarships and loans for underprivileged college students.

Another step was the creation of the Job Corps, patterned on the Civilian Conservation Corps of the New Deal. Reformers believed Job Corps members would develop effective work habits that they would continue to use once they gained employment outside the government. The corps employed one hundred thousand young men and women from poor families. Eight years later, in 1973, Congress expanded the Jobs Corps with the Comprehensive Employment and Training Act (CETA). CETA provided on-the-job training for the chronically unemployed. For those who could not find positions with private employers, the government created full-time public service jobs for them. Although costly, this program met its goals. A study conducted in Baltimore concluded that 94 percent of CETA graduates had jobs five years after they participated. Their wages were good, too—89 percent of the average wage in their city.

To aid urban renewal, Congress created the Model Cities program, but this was less successful. Originally planners had hoped to concentrate on a few targets, mobilize local leadership, and try a variety of methods to invigorate dying communities. If a few cities could be revitalized, their slums renewed and their residents provided with useful work, these demonstration projects would act as beacons for other places. As first conceived, the Model Cities program would target six communities. By the time it got under way in 1966, however, the number had grown to over a hundred, while the amount of money appropriated remained the same. Powerful members of Congress channeled the lion's share of the benefits to their own districts. As one urban affairs expert put it, "the law provided too little money for too many cities." The program could not even approach fulfilling the vision of its founders. Congressional leaders recognized the need to treat urban blight as a complex social as well as physical problem; but the decision to alter it from a demonstration project to a national effort—while at the same time starving its funding—doomed the program from the start.

To oversee the distribution of grants for Great Society programs, Congress established the cabinet-level Department of Housing and Urban Development (HUD) and Department of Transportation (DOT). These departments made a start in reducing the grinding poverty in urban centers, but Congress did not fund them fully in the period from 1965 to 1967. By the time the Johnson administration asked for a new housing act in 1968, much of the enthusiasm for the Great Society had ebbed. The costs of the Vietnam War made Congress reluctant to fund programs designed to replace dilapidated inner-city tenements. Consequently, the president's request to build 6 million low-income dwellings was slashed to less than one-quarter of the original proposal.

Funding problems also bedeviled the OEO, headed by Sargent Shriver. The OEO was supposed to coordinate several other programs, including the Job Corps; VISTA (Volunteers in Service to America), a domestic version of the Peace Corps; and the Community Action Program (CAP). Despite Shriver's best efforts, the OEO had to oversee a vast proliferation of programs, with little increase in funds. There were organizational troubles as well. One task of CAP was to encourage recipients of government assistance to participate in administering government programs; the goal was defined as "maximum feasible participation." But this goal provoked clashes between local authorities and the neighborhood activists assisted by the OEO. In Philadelphia, for example, poor, mostly black residents were elected as representatives to the local boards overseeing the allocation of OEO funds. The white mayor objected to the authority of these local boards, and he appointed a prominent black supporter to be the real power in Philadelphia's Antipoverty Action Committee. Similarly, in Atlanta, the business community ran the poverty program, refusing to let poor people sit on the board.

Such conflicts undermined congressional support for the OEO after 1966. The CAP's difficulties typified some of the Great Society's larger problems. The Johnson administration was trying to satisfy irreconcilable groups and factions. Johnson truly believed in building a consensus—a legacy of his congressional career—and he thought the way to foster consensus was to satisfy competing interest groups. But the antipoverty programs, as the historian Allen Matusow observed, "sought to appease vested interests that had resisted reform or occasioned the need for it in the first place." As time went on, administrators of Great Society programs came to believe that they had been underfunded and could not possibly meet the vast needs of the country's poor. Opponents of the programs, on the other hand, came to believe that they gave too much power to groups who previously had not had a voice. However modest this empowerment of the poor was, it threatened the political and social position of the people who had previously been dominant.

Despite the many flaws of the antipoverty programs and the resistance they sparked, they had some real successes. They helped reduce the number of people living in poverty by about 50 percent in a decade. Standards of medical care improved dramatically. Education reached impoverished rural and urban children in ways that had never before seemed possible. Job training provided a means of breaking out of the cycle of poverty. If the Johnson administration did not vanquish poverty in the United States, it at least gave many Americans an opportunity for a better life.

The issue of reform became inextricably bound up with race. Some of the most far-reaching changes created by the Great Society involved expanding the voting rights of people who had been persistently excluded from the polls because of their race. A series of demonstrations in Alabama helped set the stage for congressional action. For six weeks in early 1965, Martin Luther King, Jr., and the Student Non-Violent Coordinating Committee organized demonstrations in Selma for the right to vote. Marching demonstrators were clubbed and tear-gassed by Alabama state troopers, and the violence appeared on national television. The president sent an emissary to King to arrange a tactical deal that helped prevent further violence. For the culminating march to Montgomery, thousands of people flew in.

Johnson seized the opportunity to deliver a moving speech before Congress, calling for a voting rights act. If African-Americans did not gain equal voting rights, Johnson declared, "we will have failed as a people and a nation." He asked his fellow citizens to "overcome the crippling legacy of bigotry and injustice." Adopting the slogan of the civil rights movement, he insisted that "we *shall* overcome."

Congress obliged with the Voting Rights Act of 1965, which gave the Justice Department the power to register voters directly in localities where discrimination existed. If fewer than 50 percent of the citizens of a district voted or were registered to vote in 1964, the Justice Department assumed there had been discrimination at the polls. Literacy tests for voter registration were also outlawed. Over the next three years the law resulted in the registration of an additional 740,000 black voters (see map, page 228). The overall rate of registration among African-Americans rose from 31 percent to 57 percent. The law eventually produced an increase in black officeholders as well. The number of blacks in the House of Representatives rose from

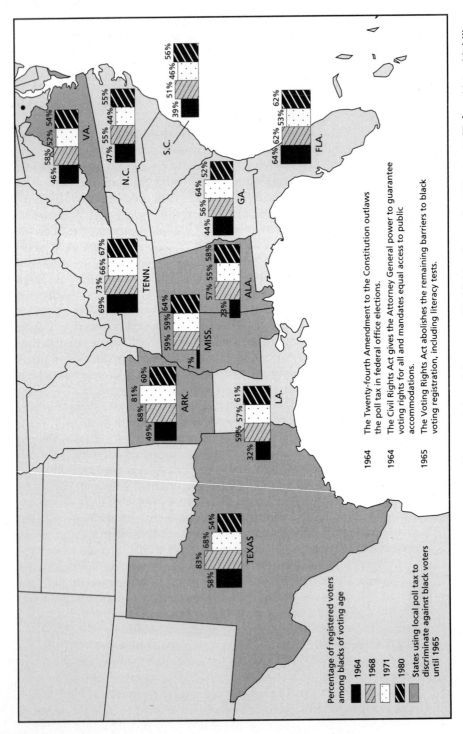

Black Voting Rights, 1964–1980. *Source: Reprinted by permission of Greenwood Publishing Group, Inc., Westport, CT, from Voter Mobilization and the Politics of Race: The South and Universal Suffrage, 1952–1984, by Harold W. Stanley. Copyright ©1987 by Harold W. Stanley and published in 1987 by Praeger Publishers.*

five to seventeen in the next twenty years, and the total number of black public officials in the entire nation increased from 103 to 3,503. In the 1970s and 1980s, African-Americans were elected to the mayor's office in cities ranging from Newark, New Jersey, and Gary, Indiana, to New York, Los Angeles, and Chicago. The change was even more startling in the Deep South: Atlanta, New Orleans, Birmingham, and even Selma selected black mayors.

Although the Great Society is remembered for its attempts to erase poverty and discrimination, it also sponsored programs that appealed directly to the American middle class. By funding the arts and humanities, promoting nonprofit television, and helping to clean up the nation's highways, the Johnson administration produced benefits even the wealthy could appreciate.

To fulfill his promise to "build a richer life of mind and spirit," Johnson sent Congress legislation to create the National Foundation for the Arts and Humanities, a smaller version of the National Science Foundation, which had been in existence since 1950. The new foundation consisted of two divisions: the National Endowment for the Arts (NEA) and the National Endowment for the Humanities (NEH). The Federal Council on the Arts and Humanities was created to supervise the two endowments. Both directly and through state councils, each endowment offered grants to individuals and to institutions such as universities, museums, ballet companies, and local arts centers.

The NEA and NEH sponsored conferences, produced films, offered fellowships for scholars and creative writers, and funded university courses and new curricula. In the beginning the endowments grew slowly, from a budget of $2.5 million apiece in 1966 to roughly $6 million each in 1970. But ten years later each endowment was spending $106 million per year. Together the NEA and NEH had a profound effect on the arts and humanities throughout the nation. The proliferation of local theater and dance companies, the development of many young artists and writers, the expansion of scholarly research—all of these were made possible by the NEA and NEH.

The Great Society influenced American television, too. To offer American people an alternative to commercial programming, Congress in 1967 reserved 242 channels on the nation's wavebands for local public, noncommercial TV stations. It also provided direct federal subsidies for public programming with the creation of the Corporation for Public Broadcasting (CPB). Governed by a presidentially appointed board, the CPB distributed grants to produce TV shows and helped with the operating budgets of local public TV stations. Programs such as "Sesame Street," an educational hour for preschoolers, and "Nova," a highly regarded series on science, received support from the CPB. Five years later, in 1972, Congress added National Public

Radio, a network of noncommercial radio stations. Those stations, and some of the programs they aired, received support from the CPB.

The Great Society also demonstrated a concern for the natural environment, to an extent. Congress enacted legislation mandating improvements in air and water quality. The president's wife, known to the nation as Lady Bird Johnson, took the lead in fostering a more pleasant environment along the nation's roads. Deathly afraid of air travel, she commuted between Texas and Washington on the nation's highway system. She was appalled by the junkyards and unsightly billboards lining the interstates. She pressed her husband to submit to Congress the Highway Beautification Act, which was passed in 1965. By increasing the federal contribution to interstate highway construction from 85 to 90 percent for states that joined the program, the law encouraged states to ban billboards and remove roadside junkyards. Because the law allowed billboard companies wide latitude in adhering to regulations, it resulted in only minor improvements. Nevertheless, this early gesture toward beautification, along with the measures designed to clean up the air and water, set the stage for stronger environmental laws in the 1970s.

Johnson's Great Society had a profound influence on immigration as well. When Johnson took office, an immigration quota system dating from the 1920s was still in effect. In setting limits on entry for many foreign nationals, the quotas reflected deep-rooted racial and ethnic biases. Hoping to erase the inequities of this system, President Kennedy had presented Congress with an immigration-reform package abolishing discrimination against immigrants on the basis of national origin.

The bill languished until Kennedy's death, but Johnson resubmitted it to the reform-minded eighty-ninth Congress in 1965. When it passed that year, it seemed only a moderate modification of America's immigration policy. It phased out the national quota system over the next three years. After 1968 there would be a total of 290,000 slots available each year, divided into 170,000 visas for immigrants from the Eastern Hemisphere and 120,000 for immigrants from the Western Hemisphere. In place of quotas based on national origin, Congress created seven categories to set priorities for granting entry. Two categories of immigrants received the highest priority: those holding desirable job skills and those with close relatives (parents and siblings) in the United States. Political refugees were given the lowest priority and accounted for the smallest number of visas. This situation was largely overlooked at the time but generated controversy later.

Because the law gave first preference to family members, Congress expected that the new mix of immigrants would closely resemble the old one. Although this reasoning made sense at the time, it failed to anticipate a profound change in immigration patterns in the next decade. For a few years the law worked as planned, admitting immigrants from southern and eastern Europe in large numbers.

By the middle of the 1970s, however, immigration patterns had changed, due to worldwide economic trends. Job prospects brightened in Europe, making America less attractive. European immigrants made up 45 percent of the total in 1965 but only 15 percent in the late 1970s. During this period immigration from Asia, the Caribbean, and South America shot up. Residents of these lands found the American economy extraordinarily attractive compared to the meager opportunities available in their own countries. This was especially true for educated people, whose skills qualified them for special preference under the terms of the 1965 law.

Congress did not envision that the family reunification provision would create an immigration chain. For example, a foreign student attending college in the United States could gain the skills needed to qualify for immigration preference. Within a short time he could use the family reunification provision to bring over his parents, spouse, and children. As these relatives attained citizenship, they too became eligible to sponsor relatives. Thus an ever-wider network evolved, bringing many additional immigrants to the United States.

This pattern, which held true for immigrants from nearly every Asian nation except Japan, actually reduced poverty in the United States. Many Asian immigrants came from upper-class, highly educated backgrounds. Within a decade of the new law's passage, tens of thousands of Asian physicians and nurses entered the United States. They became the backbone of many public hospitals' staffs. So many professionals emigrated from South Korea, Taiwan, the Philippines, India, Pakistan, and the British colony of Hong Kong that officials in these countries sometimes accused the United States of promoting a "brain drain" of talent that they needed for progress at home.

By 1979 the seven largest groups of immigrants were all of non-European origin:

Mexico	52,000
Philippines	41,300
China, Taiwan, and Hong Kong	30,180
Korea	29,348
Jamaica	19,714
India	19,708
Dominican Republic	17,519

Refugees and undocumented aliens swelled these figures even further. All in all, the 1965 immigration act resulted in an unprecedented boom in non-European immigrants to the United States during the 1970s.

CHANGES IN THE NATIONAL ECONOMY

In the early years of his administration, when his Great Society programs were springing into bloom, Johnson's efforts were bolstered by the greatest peacetime economic boom since the end of the Second World War. The administration's Keynesian strategy—adjusting government spending to encourage employment and growth and to dampen inflation—seemed to work. Unemployment fell to 3.7 percent of the labor force, its lowest level since the Korean War. Economic activity, as measured by changes in the gross product, grew by over 4 percent per year from 1964 to 1966. Government expenditures and receipts were roughly in balance for these years.

The boom hastened the rise of the Sunbelt. Spending for the military and the space program continued to flow to the South and the West. California consolidated its position as the premier defense contracting state, while Texas surpassed New York as the second. By the end of the 1960s, the federal payroll in the ten Sunbelt states amounted to $10 billion per year, double the amount in all other states combined.

Business prospered in the Sunbelt as well. For example, the oil industry, long headquartered in the Northeast, began to relocate to Texas, Oklahoma, and California. Getty, Union, Occidental, and Signal Oil, all based in Los Angeles, grew to prominence. Phillips Petroleum of Bartlesville, Oklahoma, and Tenneco, in Houston, challenged New York-based companies such as Mobil and Texaco.

The sixties also saw an explosion in banking in the Sunbelt. North Carolina National Bank grew the fastest, earning more money than any other bank in the country. San Francisco's Bank of America became the country's largest, with hundreds of branches serving retail customers. It heavily promoted its BankAmericard, the first bank credit card, sparking a new trend in consumer spending. In 1965 four big Chicago banks started MasterCard; two years later four California banks created Master Charge. Ads urged consumers to use their plastic to purchase everyday items—gasoline, clothing, meals, television sets, lawn mowers. The banks made money from these cards three ways: charging interest for purchases not paid off within a specified grace period, collecting fees from merchants accepting the cards, and licensing other banks to issue their own cards bearing the now famous BankAmericard, MasterCard, and Master Charge names. Eventually Bank of America sold its credit card business to a consortium of other banks, who changed the name of the card to VISA, and Master Charge merged with MasterCard, retaining the latter name.

Sunbelt banks also took the lead in developing bank holding companies, financial concerns that bought small local banks. The new entities, among them the United Bank of Los Angeles, Valley National Bank of Phoenix, and Columbia Savings and Loan of Los Angeles, had assets of over a billion dollars each, a large sum for the time. Thus they were able to provide loans for large real estate and industrial development programs, which had previously been forced to rely on major Wall Street firms for financing.

Wall Street also did well. The New York Stock Exchange enjoyed its greatest growth since the 1920s in the period 1963 to 1966, with prices more than doubling. One effect of this bull market was the development of industrial conglomerates. Audacious deal-makers, often from the Sunbelt, arranged for one firm to buy another in an unrelated industry. The parts of the resulting merged enterprise had little to do with one another economically, but the balance sheets showed increased profits. As if to emphasize the company rather than the product, the combined firms took names that had little intrinsic meaning. American Tobacco became American Brands. Ling Temco Vought became LTV. Some of these marriages joined highly unlikely partners. Litton Shipyards, renamed Litton Industries, acquired the Stouffer food company; the renamed LTV, a defense contractor, bought the Wilson meat-packing corporation.

But celebrations of the economic boom were premature. By 1966 the growing war in Vietnam (see Chapter 7) had unleashed unexpected and uncontrollable inflation. The inflation rate began to fluctuate between 2.5 percent and 4 percent per year. For people accustomed to the many years of price stability since the Korean War, this was a frightening development. Keynesians explained the rise as a result of too much business demand in the wake of the war in Vietnam. They urged the president to raise taxes in 1966 in order to pay for the war and stem inflation. Johnson refused, fearing that if he emphasized the need to pay war bills, conservatives would force him to squeeze his Great Society budget. Liberals criticized him too, when they saw how much the war hurt the reform effort. Wanting to satisfy everyone, Johnson believed the country could afford both guns and butter. The administration did monitor price and wage increases, and it established guideposts for business and labor to follow. But it had little success in rolling back those increases it considered excessive.

Interest rates soared in 1966. Banks began paying more than 5.5 percent interest on passbook accounts, more than savings and loan institutions were legally permitted to offer. Thereafter, owners of savings and loans lobbied Congress to relax the ceilings on what they could pay depositors. Rates on government securities, consistently below 3 percent in previous years, rose to 6 percent. The credit crunch, as it was called, also sent the stock market sprawling in 1966. All of this was supposed to slow the rise in prices, but it did not. In 1966 and 1967 prices rose by more than 4 percent per year; in 1968 inflation hit 6 percent.

Inflation hurt pensioners living on fixed incomes and small savers, whose return was kept low by regulation. But in the beginning it helped those poor people who had obtained jobs during the boom, because wages for marginal workers rose faster than those for skilled workers. Businesses lost to inflation, however, as higher wages reduced profits, from 10.6 percent of the nation's income in 1966 to 7.2 percent in 1970. Inflation also took its toll internationally. Since 1945 the dollar had been the standard currency of international trade. As prices rose in the United States, European holders of dollars began redeeming their currency for gold. The United States Treasury obliged, but by 1968 the $20 billion U.S. gold reserve represented less than one-third of all dollars held by foreigners.

What seemed the worst about inflation was its persistence and its tendency to rise over time. A 3 percent rate of inflation might be tolerable if it went no higher. In the last years of the Johnson administration, however, the annual rate of inflation rose steadily, discouraging savings, making long-term investment difficult, and souring the public on further costly programs to aid the poor.

THE SUPREME COURT AND CIVIL LIBERTIES

While Lyndon Johnson promoted his Great Society, the Supreme Court was engaged in another sort of liberal reform, the expansion of constitutionally guaranteed rights. Still led by Chief Justice Earl Warren, the Court expanded on its work of the 1950s, protecting the rights of individuals, altering criminal law, and regulating national and state voting systems.

Together, Presidents Johnson and Kennedy appointed four justices to the Supreme Court. Byron White (1962–1993), named by Kennedy, became one of the more conservative members. But Arthur Goldberg (1962–1965), Abe Fortas (1965–1969), and Thurgood Marshall (1967–1991) joined with Warren, Hugo Black, William O. Douglas, and William Brennan to consolidate the Court's liberal majority.

While acknowledging that the freedoms of speech, assembly, press, and religion guaranteed by the First Amendment sometimes had to be balanced against other interests, the Court's liberal majority required the government to show a compelling need to restrict liberty. If it could not, citizens' freedoms could not be abridged.

In *Bond* v. *Floyd* (1966), for example, the Court ruled that the Georgia House of Representatives could not refuse to seat an elected representative of the people, even though he expressed admiration for those who had opposed conscription for the war in Vietnam. A unanimous court held that neither public officials nor private citizens could be punished for opinions that did not violate the law. The Court also offered protection to "symbolic speech." In *Tinker* v. *Des Moines School District* (1969), the Court ruled that students could not be expelled for wearing black arm bands protesting the war in Vietnam. Writing for the majority, Justice Fortas argued that students did not lose their rights when they entered a schoolroom.

In *New York Times* v. *Sullivan* (1964), the Court loosened restraints on what the news media could write or broadcast about well-known figures. The Court ruled that public officials could not win a judgment of libel against a publication merely because a statement was untrue. Only "recklessly false statements" made with "actual malice" were covered by the libel laws. Justice Brennan held that "even a false statement may be deemed to make a valuable contribution to public debate." The decision emboldened the press, but it also resulted in a complete lack of privacy for public figures.

Nothing produced more public debate and more confusion on the Court than its efforts to define obscenity. From 1957 to 1968 the Court decided thirteen obscenity cases, issuing fifty-five separate opinions. It never did satisfactorily resolve the questions of what is obscene and how much latitude the government should have in restricting such material. Justice Brennan thought he had found an answer in *Roth* v. *United States* (1957), when he observed that expressions containing "the slightest redeeming social importance" could be protected by the First Amendment. The Court agreed that government could regulate as obscene materials that "the average person, applying contemporary community standards," would regard as appealing to "prurient interests." For the next decade the Court tried to write rules determining what materials fit that mold. It failed to do so, acknowledging that the process had to be subjective. Obscenity would remain a controversial issue for subsequent Courts. The Warren Burger Court (1969–1986) changed the definition of obscene materials from "utterly without redeeming social value" to "lacking serious literary, artistic, political or social value." This definition permitted more government regulation, but it was no more successful than the earlier definition in creating a universally accepted standard.

The Warren Court won praise from civil libertarians and stirred opposition from traditionalists with a series of decisions interpreting the First Amendment's ban on the establishment of a state religion. In *Engel* v. *Vitale* (1962), the Court banned states and localities from instituting prayers in public schools. Justice Black, writing for the majority, said "it is no part of the business of government to compose official prayers for any group of American people." Over the next several years, the Court ruled that schools could not require devotional reading of the Bible. The justices also revived memories of the famous 1925 "Monkey Trial" of John Scopes in Tennessee when they struck down an Arkansas law requiring the teaching of "creation science" as a valid alternative to the theory of evolution. Such a law, the Court decided, was an unconstitutional attempt to establish a state religion.

Conservatives denounced these cases as examples of judicial lawmaking. One member of Congress complained that "they put the Negroes in the schools, and now they have driven God out." To a substantial minority of Christians, the Court's rulings were highly offensive. From 1963 through the mid-1980s, opponents of the rulings tried to pass constitutional amendments permitting prayers or Bible-reading in public schools. Although these efforts failed, they were a key element in the conservative tide that rose in the late 1970s. Many religious men and women who had once voted Democratic became ardent supporters of Ronald Reagan and the Republicans in 1980.

The Court also expanded the rights of citizens accused of crimes and set new procedural standards for law enforcement officers. In *Mapp* v. *Ohio* (1961), the Court forced all states to conform to the exclusionary rule, which holds that evidence gathered outside the specific terms of a search warrant cannot be used against a defendant. In another landmark case, *Gideon* v. *Wainwright* (1963), the Court observed that Clarence Earl Gideon, a man who had spent over half of his adult life in jail or prison, had never had a lawyer to defend him. The decision affirmed that a "fair trial" meant a right to qualified legal counsel. If a defendant could not afford an attorney, a state had to provide one.

In a more controversial, 5-to-4 ruling in *Miranda* v. *Arizona* (1966), the Warren Court extended the Fifth Amendment's ban against self-incrimination. Ernesto Miranda, arrested for burglary in Phoenix, had been coerced into confessing by police, who told him that if he remained quiet judges would sentence him harshly. In its opinion on this case, the Warren Court set standards for police to follow when arresting suspects. Accused persons had to be informed in clear language (later called the Miranda warnings) that they had a right to remain silent and that anything they said could be used against them in a court of law. Police officers had to tell suspects that they had a right to a lawyer and that if they could not afford to hire one, legal counsel would be provided free by the state.

The Warren Court also enhanced the right to privacy, in a decision that had profound reverberations both for individual behavior and for legal reasoning and scholarship. In 1965 the Court struck down an 1879 Connecticut law prohibiting the use of any contraceptive device and penalizing anyone giving advice on birth control. The law had long been ignored, but Planned Parenthood managed to bring it before the Court as a test case. In *Griswold* v. *Connecticut,* Justice Douglas held that the state's ban on contraception violated a long-established right to privacy. Although such a right is not specified in the Constitution, Douglas inferred it from other rights that are specified there. Three other justices, Brennan, Goldberg, and Warren, concurred, but they were troubled by what they saw as Douglas's invention of a new right. Instead of following Douglas's reasoning, therefore, they relied on the rarely used Ninth Amendment, which reserves for the people any rights not enumerated in the Bill of Rights. They argued that the right of privacy was ancient, older than the Constitution, and that the framers intended to incorporate it through the Ninth Amendment. One of the Court's liberals, Hugo Black, dissented. Black considered himself a strict constructionist, and he could find no specific guarantee to a right of privacy contained in the Constitution. Black's reservations gave some legal scholars pause, but the popular reaction to the *Griswold* decision was highly favorable—few people wanted state intrusion into their bedroom.

The Court also established new rules for elections, making them more representative and democratic. In *Baker* v. *Carr* (1962), the Court overruled earlier precedents when it declared that it and lower courts could decide if the boundaries of state congressional districts were fair. In many states, legislatures had not reapportioned the districts for decades. As a result, rural districts often contained fewer than one-fifth the population of their urban or suburban counterparts. City dwellers complained, but they were reminded that the U.S. Senate also did not represent voters proportionally. But after *Baker* v. *Carr,* underrepresented voters had a wedge with which to sue. They based their appeals on the simple rule of "one person, one vote," and the Court agreed with them.

By 1968 Earl Warren had been chief justice for fifteen years. He was seventy-seven years old and had presided over some of the most far-reaching decisions in the Court's history. In March of that year Lyndon Johnson announced that he would not seek re-election. Because Warren wanted Johnson to have the opportunity to appoint a chief justice, he told the president that he intended to resign as soon as his successor could be confirmed. The president had a candidate in mind—Abe Fortas. An associate justice since 1965, Fortas was a longtime friend who had continued to give Johnson political advice after his appointment to the Court, often violating the tradition of judicial impartiality. During those three years, Fortas had become a stalwart member of Warren's liberal majority.

Fortas's nomination faced immediate difficulties in the Senate. Democrats still had a majority, but Republicans used a number of delaying tactics throughout the summer. They expected Richard Nixon to win the upcoming presidential election, and they wanted him to appoint the chief justice. Fortas's support for the Vietnam War, as well as his intimate ties to the now-unpopular Johnson, had made him unattractive to some Democrats as well. During the confirmation hearings, the Senate Judiciary Committee learned that Fortas had received $15,000 for teaching some summer law courses; the money had been paid by men who might have had cases before the Court. Faced with charges of cronyism, Fortas asked Johnson to withdraw his nomination in October. Warren remained chief justice until 1969, when President Nixon named Warren Burger, a conservative federal judge from Minneapolis, to replace him. Fortas remained an associate justice until the spring of 1969, when further allegations of financial impropriety forced him to resign. While sitting on the Court, Fortas had received $20,000 per year from a foundation underwritten by a man who had been convicted of securities violations. Rather than face impeachment, Fortas stepped down.

The end of the Warren Court marked the conclusion of a sixteen-year era of expanding individual rights and curtailing arbitrary government power. At the beginning of this period the Court outlawed segregation in public schools; by the end it had expanded First Amendment protection in ways that affected the daily lives of most Americans. It had validated the growing pluralism in American life. Yet its endorsement of social changes exacted a substantial price, in effect eroding the Court's own authority in the years that followed. Traditionalists who bemoaned the very pluralism the Court had affirmed attacked the justices' work. Over the next twenty years, conservatives gained advantage by deriding what they characterized as the social engineering and judicial activism of the Warren Court. While the subsequent Burger and Rehnquist Courts did not reverse most of the decisions of the Warren years, they curtailed many of their applications.

DECLINE OF THE GREAT SOCIETY

Despite the high hopes raised in 1964 and the amazing spate of Great Society legislation in 1965 and 1966, the good feelings lasted barely eighteen months. By late 1966 the impetus behind the Great Society had dwindled. Among the principal reasons for this decline were the war in Vietnam and a white backlash against the extension of civil rights.

Johnson's efforts to secure equality for all races peaked with the Voting Rights Act of 1965. That act, together with the Civil Rights Act of 1964, allowed the Johnson administration to put the weight of the federal government behind efforts to end formal, legal discrimination against racial minorities. Yet most observers realized that ending social and economic inequality between races would require more than removing the legal barriers.

In the summer of 1965, addressing the graduating class at predominantly black Howard University in Washington, D.C., Johnson spoke of the vicious circle of "despair and deprivation" among African-Americans. He explained that the Voting Rights Act was "the beginning of freedom . . . but freedom is not enough." He noted that the unemployment rate for blacks was now double that for whites, although thirty-five years earlier it had been the same. The unemployment rate for black teenage boys was 23 percent, compared to 13 percent for whites. The poverty rate for whites had fallen 27 percent while that of blacks had diminished by only 3 percent.

The reasons for the increasing economic gap between whites and blacks were complex, Johnson said, mostly deriving from "ancient brutality, past injustice, and present prejudice." But Johnson placed some of the responsibility for black poverty on the current cultural norms of African-Americans themselves. Drawing on a report called *The Negro Family: The Case for National Action,* by Assistant Secretary of Labor Daniel Patrick Moynihan, he emphasized the dreadful effects of "the breakdown of the Negro family structure." Assuming that this structure consisted of an adult male wage earner and a female homemaker, his argument implied a sentimental, idealized view of the family, hardly representative of the reality for either black or white Americans. Yet both Moynihan and Johnson ignored the complexity and variety of family life in their effort to demonstrate links between culture and poverty. "When the family collapses," Johnson said, "it is the children that are usually damaged," because of the absence of a strong father figure. "When it happens on a massive scale," the president explained, "the community itself is crippled."

Johnson's speech and Moynihan's report were supposed to set the agenda for further government action to reduce poverty. Moynihan had expected that by concentrating on cultural reasons for African-American poverty, the administration would be able to secure better antipoverty programs. But that was not to be. A White House conference met in November with the goal of expanding earlier civil rights legislation, but it broke up in acrimony over the Moynihan report. Some African-Americans, expressing new feelings of racial pride and

Malcolm X

The chief spokesmen for the new black militancy that arose in the sixties was Malcolm X, a man who could never be surprised by the depths of white resistance to the civil rights movement.

His original name was Malcolm Little. Born in Michigan in 1925, he was the son of a Baptist minister who worked as an organizer for Marcus Garvey's Universal Negro Improvement Organization. His father was killed when Malcolm was only six, probably by members of a white terrorist group. His mother suffered a mental breakdown soon afterward, and Malcolm and his siblings were sent to foster homes. After the eighth grade Malcolm dropped out of school and headed east, where he fell into criminal activities ranging from running numbers to procuring prostitutes and selling narcotics.

In 1946 he was arrested in Boston for burglary and larceny, and he spent the next six years in prison. There he was converted by the Nation of Islam,

resenting what they perceived to be condescending meddling by white liberals, denounced Moynihan's conclusions as racist. A number of critics concluded that the report blamed the victims of discrimination for their plight. Analysts found flaws in Moynihan's methods and described unique strengths in African-American families and culture.

Despite its apparently condescending tone, the Moynihan report represented a serious attempt to address a complex problem. But the early criticism undermined support for it. At the same time, Johnson was distracted by the growing problem in Vietnam. In July 1965 he

the religious group popularly known as the Black Muslims. According to the leader of that faith, Elijah Muhammad, white people were a satanic race sent by Allah to punish blacks, but the day of judgment was near at hand. Abandoning his "slave name" of Little, the young convert began to call himself Malcolm X.

After his release from prison, Malcolm X gradually became the best-known evangelist for the Nation of Islam. He became so popular that he made his rivals jealous. He took every occasion to denounce not only whites in general, but also blacks who joined the nonviolent civil rights movement, which he called a "mealy-mouthed, wait-in, beg-in, plead-in kind of action." A believer in racial separation, he advocated violence as a necessary tool for combating racist evils.

After he referred to John F. Kennedy's assassination as "the chickens coming home to roost," his Muslim opponents had him suspended from the Nation of Islam. Undeterred, he established his own movement, blending orthodox Islam with African socialism, anticolonialism, and black nationalism. In this period he moved away from the idea that whites must always be the enemies of blacks. But his political evolution came to an abrupt end when he was shot and killed in 1965, evidently by another Muslim in an act of vengeance. His autobiography, published after his death, established him as a prophet of the rising Black Power movement. ■

committed U.S. ground forces to the war, and over the next years, as the war consumed ever more of the government's resources and the administration's attention, the problems of poverty and racial inequality received less priority.

Another problem intervened as well. In the summer of 1964, race riots struck New York City and several other cities in New York and New Jersey. These proved only preludes to what was to come. In August 1965 a major riot erupted in Watts, a predominantly African-American section of Los Angeles. The insurrection sprang from economic frustration and black rage at the brutality of the all-white police force. Nevertheless, the events in Watts shocked moderate whites, who only five months before had been moved by the nonviolence and moral force of the demonstrators at Selma. White support for racial equality began to erode.

Over the next year, whites resented the efforts of Martin Luther King, Jr., and other civil rights leaders to desegregate housing in northern cities. Suspicion was also aroused by the Supreme Court's extension of the rights of people accused of crimes. Moreover, the race riots spread from one city to another after 1965; by 1968, Detroit, Newark, Washington, Cincinnati, and many other cities across the country had experienced major rioting. Whites were further alienated by the militancy of a newer generation of black leaders (see Chapter 8). By the time of the 1966 congressional elections, white anger at blacks was a key underlying issue.

That year a Gallup poll reported that 52 percent of whites believed the administration was pushing too hard on civil rights, 20-percent more than four years ago. Some Republican candidates denounced "crime in the streets," a euphemism for the African-American uprisings. They opposed the Great Society's plans to desegregate public housing. Democrats, too, fanned white fears of blacks. The unsuccessful Democratic candidate for governor of Maryland ran on the slogan "Your home is your castle—protect it." One Democratic congressman from Chicago ruefully reported that in "any home, any bar, any barber shop" you will find people "talking about Martin Luther King and how they are moving in on us and what's going to happen to our neighborhoods."

The white backlash, along with voter dissatisfaction over the administration's handling of the Vietnam war (see Chapter 7), propelled a Republican gain of forty-seven seats in the House and three in the Senate in 1966. The backlash had an effect at the state level as well. In California, conservative Republican Ronald Reagan, who condemned the Watts rioters, won the governorship with a margin of nearly 1 million votes. After the election results were in, the defeated Democratic governor, Edmund G. Brown, concluded that "whether we like it or not, people want separation of the races."

Over the next two years, white distrust of social reform grew. Working-class whites, many descended from eastern or southern European immigrants, came to despise the Johnson administration. As prices rose and the government seemed powerless to stop inflation, these white ethnics believed that their needs had been overlooked in the effort to end poverty and forge a Great Society. The urban riots and the Supreme Court's extension of protections to criminal defendants particularly infuriated white ethnic groups. Johnson seemed bereft of ideas to reconstruct his shattered consensus. After the U.S. Army had quelled the Detroit riots in July 1967, at a cost of forty-four lives, the president called for a day of prayer for "order and reconciliation among men." He created a presidential commission, headed by former judge Otto Kerner, to study the causes of urban violence. Yet when Kerner submitted his report in 1968, describing the emergence of "two nations, separate but unequal, white and black," Johnson refused to receive it.

Johnson's aides told him he needed more than prayer to restore his public standing. By the fall of 1967 his public approval rating had slipped below 33 percent, the lowest figure since Truman's dismal rating at the end of the Korean War. Assistants suggested that Johnson might revive his standing in the polls by showing support for police. In an address to the International Association of Chiefs of Police, Johnson drew prolonged applause with an attack on African-American rioters: "We cannot tolerate behavior that destroys what generations of men and women have built here in America—no matter what stimulates that behavior and no matter what is offered to try to justify it."

From that point on, the Great Society ground down. The flood of legislation begun in 1965 slowed to a trickle after the new Congress assembled in 1967. The only major law passed was a housing bill, submitted in 1968, designed to replace the dilapidated dwellings devastated by riots in northern cities. This law also banned racial and religious discrimination in the sale or rental of housing. Modified during the Nixon administration, the law ultimately led to the construction of 1.3 million low-income housing units, but the building program benefited rich developers and investors more than poor people.

Other Great Society programs withered at the end of the Johnson administration. Unwilling to fund both the war in Vietnam and the War on Poverty, Congress cut back on the latter. The president lost heart too at the end of his term, as he saw his support for the poor become a liability among whites. This reduction of support for the War on Poverty further fueled the backlash over the next decade. Conservative opponents of government assistance to the poor now pointed to the failure of the Great Society to eliminate poverty as proof that such programs could not work. In fact, these programs were underfunded, often mismanaged, and had little input from poor people themselves.

ASPECTS OF JOHNSON'S FOREIGN POLICY

The excitement and controversy created by the Great Society, and the dramatic escalation of the war in Vietnam, left the Johnson administration with neither the time nor the inclination to think deeply about relations with the rest of the world. Essentially, the administration continued the efforts begun earlier in the Cold War to project American power around the globe. Not comfortable with foreign affairs himself, the president relied on advice from the national-security experts he had inherited from Kennedy. Together with men like Secretary of State Dean Rusk, National Security Advisers McGeorge Bundy (1961–1965) and Walt Whitman Rostow (1965–1968), and Secretary of Defense Robert McNamara (1961–1968), Johnson involved the United States in a series of regional disputes in Latin America, the Middle East, and Europe. These controversies produced little success, and they strained relations with long-time friends. By 1968, experts inside and outside government were calling for a new direction in foreign affairs. At that point the administration attempted to dampen the passions of the Cold War and relax tensions with the Soviet Union. But its efforts at détente were cut short, and it remained for the succeeding Nixon White House to put them into effect.

The Johnson administration reversed its predecessor's halting efforts to foster social reform in the Western Hemisphere. In March 1964 the director of the Alliance for Progress announced that the alliance would change its emphasis; instead of focusing on land reform and reducing the gap between rich and poor, the Alliance would encourage economic growth. Henceforth, he said, the United States would be neutral on social reform and would protect its private investments. The United States would not force Latin American governments to adopt democracy if they faced Communist or other revolutionary movements. This policy served as an excuse for relying on Latin American military regimes to protect U.S. interests.

Besides its suspicion of social reform in Latin America, the Johnson administration also displayed an insensitivity to issues of national pride and identity in the region. Early in 1964, for example, the administration had to confront a host of angry Panamanians. For sixty years Panama had resented U.S. domination of the Canal Zone. The 1903 treaty granting the United States the rights to the Zone "as if it were sovereign" offended Panamanian pride. In 1964 the Panamanians became upset when American high school students in the Canal Zone tore down the Panamanian flag and U.S. authorities refused to raise it again, despite promising to do so. Four days of rioting in Panama left twenty-four Panamanians and four American soldiers dead. Thousands of Panamanians were forced to flee their homes. Johnson took matters into his own hands. Speaking to the Panamanian president personally, he promised to discuss Panamanian grievances in detail at an upcoming summit. But when talks opened between the two nations, Washington downplayed the issue of the offensive canal treaty. Most Panamanians believed Washington was merely stalling.

In 1965, faced with a potential leftist government in the Dominican Republic, the Johnson administration reverted to direct military intervention. Covering half of the Caribbean island of Hispaniola, the Dominican Republic had long been dominated, directly or indirectly, by the United States. A dictator, Rafael Trujillo, had ruled with American connivance from 1940 to 1961. Toward the end of his regime, however, Washington lost patience with his brutality. In May 1961 he was assassinated, and the Kennedy administration encouraged the democratic election of a successor. In December 1962 the Dominicans elected Juan Bosch as president. Bosch, a leftist but not a Communist, soon ran afoul of the Dominican military, which overthrew him in the fall of 1963.

In April 1965 young army officers sympathetic to Bosch ousted the military-backed government. Their more conservative seniors panicked and appealed to the American ambassador for help. Shooting broke out on the streets of Santo Domingo, and the United States envoy wired Washington that a Communist revolution was at hand. The embassy passed out a false press release stating that fifty-eight "identified and prominent Communist and Castroite leaders" were directing the pro-Bosch forces. President Johnson decided to send the Marines and the army to quell the uprising and install another conservative government. At first the president justified the intervention as necessary to preserve American lives and property. Two days later, on April 30, he explained instead that "people outside the Dominican Republic are seeking to gain control."

The United States forces trounced the leftists and eventually helped put a conservative, Joaquin Balaguer, in power. But the intervention produced a furious reaction. Bosch complained that "this was a democratic revolution, crushed by the leading democracy in the world." At home, liberal opinion was discouraged that the United States had reverted to force, intervening in a way repugnant to most Latin Americans.

While the intervention in the Dominican Republic helped to further dampen domestic consensus over foreign affairs, the war in Vietnam dealt it a fatal blow as it grew into a major controversy. At the same time, strains appeared in the NATO alliance, considered the cornerstone of American foreign policy since 1949. French President Charles de Gaulle attempted to restrain what he considered Washington's high-handed control of the alliance. Europeans were unhappy about the Cuban missile crisis of 1962, when the United States and the Soviet Union had approached the brink of war without consulting their allies. In the aftermath of the crisis, France went forward with its own atomic bomb project, and in 1966 the French president announced that his nation's forces would no longer participate in the military arm of NATO. He forced the alliance to move its headquarters

President Johnson whispers to Defense Secretary Robert S. McNamara during a news conference at Johnson's ranch in Texas. The president relied heavily on the foreign policy advice of McNamara, one of the holdovers from the Kennedy administration. *UPI/Bettmann Archive.*

from Paris to Brussels. The Johnson administration dismissed de Gaulle as a bitter old man making a futile attempt to restore France's faded glory.

Events outside Europe also challenged American leadership in international affairs. In June 1967 the Six-Day War between Israel and the Arab states of Egypt, Syria, and Jordan further strained America's foreign relations and created a bitter legacy. For ten years Egypt had smarted from the military embarrassment it suffered at the hands of Israel during the October 1956 Suez conflict. Egypt's President Gamal Abdel Nasser wanted to restore his standing at home by erasing the stain of the Suez loss. With his army resupplied by the Soviet Union, and goaded into action by other Arab states, Nasser looked for ways to threaten Israel in the spring of 1967.

He did so by demanding that the United Nations remove its emergency forces from the Sinai Peninsula, separating Israel and Egypt. Much to his surprise, the United Nations agreed. The Soviet Union urged caution, but Nasser was trapped by his own inflammatory rhetoric. He closed the Strait of Tiran to ships bound for Israel's important southern port of Eilat.

At this point the United States stepped in to head off a war. Johnson begged the Israelis not to respond to Nasser until the United States could organize an international flotilla to break the blockade. But the Europeans, fearful that the Arab states would cut off their oil, declined to join the effort.

Faced with what they believed to be a half-hearted American effort on their behalf, the Israelis took matters into their own hands on the morning of June 5. In a pre-emptive strike, the Israeli air force destroyed Egyptian planes on the ground while Israeli tanks knifed across the Sinai. Later that day, Jordan's King Hussein ordered his artillery forces to shell the Jewish sector of Jerusalem; in response, the Israelis turned on Jordan and two days later attacked Syria as well. Within six days Israel had taken the Sinai from Egypt, the West Bank (an area composed of the western bank of the Jordan River and the eastern part of Jerusalem) from Jordan, and the Golan Heights from Syria. After the war, the United Nations called for Israeli withdrawal from the captured territories in return for Arab recognition of Israel's right to exist. The United Nations also asked the combatants to settle the Palestinian problem, a constant source of conflict ever since Israel replaced the British colony in Palestine after the Second World War. Hundreds of thousands of Palestinians were now left homeless by Israel's conquest of the West Bank and Gaza. Neither Israel nor the Arabs implemented the UN resolutions, and the dispute between Israel, the Arab states, and the Palestinians, who wanted a state of their own, became more bitter than ever.

Two weeks after the Six-Day War ended in 1967, Soviet prime minister Alexei Kosygin visited New York for a special session of the United Nations General Assembly, called to discuss peace in the Middle East. While in New York, Kosygin accepted Johnson's invitation to meet him at Glassboro State College in southern New Jersey to discuss U.S.-Soviet relations. At this, the first superpower summit since the melancholy conversations between John Kennedy and Nikita Khrushchev in May 1961, the president sought the Soviet leader's help in arranging an end to the war in Vietnam. Kosygin refused, because he wanted to show the North Vietnamese that the Soviet Union could do more for them than the People's Republic of China, now the Soviets' rival.

The two men did agree to begin arms control negotiations. However, steps toward détente went no further in the remaining eighteen months of the Johnson administration. In August 1968, Secretary of State Rusk planned to announce that Johnson would repay Kosygin's visit with a trip to the Soviet Union to begin talks on limiting strategic arms. But on August 20, Soviet tanks rumbled into Prague, Czechoslovakia, to crush a Czech experiment in liberalized socialism. Moscow feared that Czech leader Alexander Dubcek secretly wanted to dismantle the one-party state. *Pravda*, the newspaper of the Soviet Communist Party, explained that Communist states could not stand idly by as one of their number fell "into the process of antisocialist degeneration." Western journalists quickly dubbed this position the Brezhnev Doctrine, after Soviet party chairman Leonid Brezhnev. In the climate of hostility evoked by the Soviets' crushing Czechoslovakian freedom, Johnson decided he could not afford the political risk of meeting Soviet leaders to discuss arms control. As in previous administrations, genuine détente with the Soviet Union remained only a tantalizing possibility.

CONCLUSION

By the end of 1968 it appeared that Lyndon Johnson's administration could be characterized largely by its failed aspirations. Johnson had done more than any other president since Franklin Roosevelt to spur Americans to reform their society. The Civil Rights Act of 1964 and the Voting Rights Act of 1965 had helped remove the legal barriers facing African-Americans. The War on Poverty reduced hunger and suffering, and Medicare improved access to health care. Meanwhile, Johnson's appointees to the Supreme Court helped the Court expand civil liberties and ensure that electoral districts were correctly apportioned. Yet by the end of Johnson's presidency, most of the public's early enthusiasm for his agenda had been lost. The Vietnam War was draining the government's funds and energy. Too many Great Society programs were underfunded or mired in administrative troubles. Race riots had erupted across the country, and a white backlash arose to block further attempts at social reform.

But it was foreign policy, not domestic affairs, that ultimately led to Lyndon Johnson's downfall. As demonstrated by his administration's intervention in the Dominican Republic, Johnson believed in the usefulness of military power for suppressing leftists and Communists in the Third World. In this he was fundamentally no different than his predecessors. Yet, as Chapter 7 explains, it was Johnson who dramatically raised the stakes in Vietnam and who received most of the blame for America's failure there. ■

FURTHER READING

On the personalities and policies of the Johnson administration, see: Robert Caro, *The Path to Power* (1983) and *Means of Ascent* (1989); Robert Dallek, *Lone Star Rising: Lyndon Johnson, 1908–1960* (1991); Doris Kearns, *Lyndon Johnson and the American Dream* (1977); Merle Miller, *Lyndon: An Oral Biography* (1980); Allan M. Matusow, *The Unraveling of America: A History of Liberalism in the 1960s* (1984); Richard Goodwin, *Remembering America: A Voice from the 1960s* (1988). On Great Society programs, see: James M. Sundquist, *Politics and Policy: The Eisenhower, Kennedy and Johnson Years* (1968); Daniel P. Moynihan, *Maximum Feasible Misunderstanding* (1970); David Reimers, *Still the Golden Door: The Third World Comes to America* (1992); John E. Schwarz, *America's Hidden Success: A Reassessment of Public Policy from Kennedy to Reagan* (1988); Charles Murray, *Losing Ground: American Social Policy, 1950–1980* (1986); Michael Katz, *The Undeserving Poor: From the War on Poverty to the War on Welfare* (1989); Nicholas Lemann, *The Promised Land: The Great Black Migration and How It Changed America* (1991); David M. Chalmers, *And the Crooked Places Made Straight: The Struggle for Social Change in the 1960s* (1991); William L. Van Deburg, *New Day in Babylon: The Black Power Movement and American Culture, 1965–1975* (1992). On the Supreme Court, see: Melvin Urofsky, *The Continuity of Change: The Supreme Court and Individual Liberties, 1953–1986* (1991); Bernard Schwartz, *Super Chief: Earl Warren and His Supreme Court* (1983); Fred Graham, *The Due Process Revolution: The Warren Court's Impact on Criminal Law* (1977). On foreign affairs, see: Philip Geyelin, *Lyndon B. Johnson and the World* (1968); Diane B. Kunz (ed.), *The Diplomacy of The Crucial Decade: American Foreign Relations During the 1960s* (1994); Thomas Schoenbaum, *Waging Peace and War: Dean Rusk in the Truman, Kennedy and Johnson Years* (1988); Steven J. Spiegel, *The Other Arab-Israeli Conflict: Making America's Middle East Policy from Truman to Reagan* (1985).

7

The Vietnam
Nightmare,
1961–1968

Amerincan involvement in the war in Vietnam grew from a minor issue of little interest to most people into a frightening nightmare, affecting nearly every aspect of American life. The seemingly endless war threw the country into agony, opening deep fissures in many American political, social, cultural, and religious institutions. The war became a major cause of the American people's disillusionment with government and of their abandonment of political liberalism. Chapter 8 explores the culture of protest the Vietnam War helped foster; this chapter focuses on the war itself and its impact on American politics and foreign policy.

From the beginning of America's involvement, during the late 1940s, until the fall of Saigon in 1975, U.S. politicians, diplomats, and military leaders consistently misunderstood the rapidly changing conditions in Vietnam. Their failure to grasp the intensity of revolutionary nationalism in Southeast Asia led to a futile attempt to sustain a non-Communist regime in the southern half of Vietnam. In the devastating war that developed during the 1960s, American bombs, guns, and money ruined Vietnam physically, economically, and socially. The grueling conflict also took a profound toll on many of the American soldiers who fought it.

As the war dragged on, Americans at home became sick of the brutal, inconclusive fighting. The general consensus on U.S. foreign policy that had developed in earlier decades eroded as the public became increasingly frustrated with the war. Many Americans continued to believe the United States should oppose communism, but they became disillusioned with this war because it made little progress. Other people believed the war should not have been fought at all. These misgivings about Vietnam spread into doubts about the overall principle of containment that had governed American foreign policy since the Second World War.

In the 1968 presidential election, Americans voted for change, hoping that a new administration could extricate them from the Vietnam morass. But more than four years—and another presidential election—would pass before a cease-fire agreement was signed.

THE GROWTH OF AMERICA'S COMMITMENT TO VIETNAM, 1945–1964

John Kenneth Galbraith, Harvard economist and U.S. ambassador to India, once asked President John F. Kennedy, "Who is the man in your

251

administration who decides what countries are strategic? I would like to . . . ask him what is so important about this [Vietnamese] real estate in the space age?" The president declined to identify the planner, because it was Kennedy himself who attached such importance to Indochina. Like most other high government officials in the years since 1945, Kennedy believed that the containment of communism should be the principal goal of American foreign policy. But because involvement in Vietnam represented only a small part of the larger U.S. strategy of confronting revolutionary nationalists in the postcolonial world, Americans never thought deeply about events in Vietnam until the United States was deeply involved in the war. From Truman through Kennedy, successive administrations gradually enlarged the U.S. commitment to Vietnam, setting the stage for a dramatic escalation under Lyndon Johnson.

Since 1945, the United States had backed alternatives to the Communist Democratic Republic of Vietnam (North Vietnam), established by Ho Chi Minh in Hanoi on September 2, 1945, the day the Second World War ended in Asia. The Truman administration, preoccupied with more pressing issues in Europe and other parts of Asia, paid little attention to Ho. The United States declined his pleas for diplomatic recognition. During 1946, war broke out between Ho's Vietminh guerrillas and French troops trying to re-establish French colonial power in Indochina. Despite some uneasiness about supporting colonial rule, the Truman administration backed France and its puppet Vietnamese regime. By the end of 1952, Washington was paying 40 percent of the cost of the war.

During the Eisenhower administration, the French required even more American aid. Despite the confident assertion of Secretary of State John Foster Dulles that an additional infusion of $400 million would help France "break the organized body of Communist aggression by the end of the 1955 fighting season," the Vietminh gained strength. By March 1954 the United States was paying 70 percent of the cost of the war, and the French military position at Dienbienphu had become desperate. Eisenhower toyed with the idea of ordering an air strike, but ultimately he decided against it. The Vietminh overran Dienbienphu on May 7, 1954.

Although Dienbienphu was a catastrophe for France, Washington almost welcomed the defeat as a chance to demonstrate American anti-Communist resolve. Unlike France, which was tainted as the colonial power, the United States could sponsor a so-called third force, composed of Vietnamese nationalists who opposed both the Communists and the French. This was the approach Eisenhower had in mind when the peace conference convened at Geneva, Switzerland. Although the United States sent representatives to the conference, it

Ho Chi Minh, a revolutionary strongly opposed to foreign domination of Vietnam, led the Vietminh against France and the Democratic Republic of Vietnam (North Vietnam) against the United States and the Republic of Vietnam (South Vietnam) from 1945 until his death in 1969. *Sovfoto.*

was not a signatory to the Geneva Accords. In fact, it soon helped undermine them.

After the Geneva Accords partitioned Vietnam along the seventeenth parallel, the United States became more deeply involved in Southeast Asia than ever. In late 1954 the Eisenhower administration sponsored the creation of the Southeast Asia Treaty Organization (SEATO), a military alliance patterned roughly on NATO. Although the southern part of Vietnam never formally joined SEATO, the United States based its involvement in Vietnamese politics partly on its having accepted protection from the alliance. Washington helped set up Ngo Dinh Diem as prime minister of the southern section. In 1955, Diem proclaimed a new nation, the Republic of Vietnam, with himself as president. Neither side (North or South) recognized each other. In 1956 the United States supported Diem when he refused to allow the nationwide unification elections, to include both North and

South, promised by the Geneva Accords. The United States further assisted Diem in creating the Army of the Republic of Vietnam (ARVN) and a police force.

Eisenhower espoused what came to be known as the domino theory, which said that if Indochina fell to communism, the rest of Southeast Asia would topple like a row of dominoes. General J. Lawton Collins, the special U.S. representative to Vietnam, recommended in 1955 that Washington withdraw support from the haughty, unpopular Diem, a Catholic in a predominantly Buddhist land; but Secretary of State Dulles declared that "the decision to back Diem has gone to the point of no return."

Vowing to exterminate all vestiges of the popular Vietminh in the South, Diem had his army and police arrest twenty thousand members of the movement, killing over a thousand in a span of three years. These bald actions won praise from American lawmakers looking for signs of a legitimate third force. Senator John F. Kennedy, for example, glorified the new South Vietnam as "the cornerstone of the Free World in Southeast Asia, the keystone to the arch, the finger in the dike."

Despite Diem's harassment, the remnants of the Vietminh in the South, assisted by North Vietnam, managed to mount a campaign of their own. On December 20, 1960, they proclaimed a new National Front for the Liberation of Vietnam (NLF) and began guerrilla attacks against the South. By mid-1961 the NLF forces, referred to as the Vietcong by the South Vietnamese, had succeeded in gaining control of 58 percent of the territory of South Vietnam.

When Kennedy became president, he decided that the Eisenhower administration had not done enough to help Diem. And after the catastrophic Bay of Pigs invasion and his chilly summit meeting with Nikita Khrushchev, Kennedy especially desired some measure of success against Communist movements in the Third World. "How do we get moving?" he asked his staff. They suggested using the army's Special Forces, commonly called the Green Berets, against the Vietcong insurrection.

Kennedy responded with an additional $42 million beyond the $220 million already being spent each year on aid to South Vietnam. He sent hundreds more troops to advise the ARVN on how to fight, and he ordered four hundred Green Berets to lead nine thousand mountain tribesmen in an effort to stop infiltration from North Vietnam. He also had the CIA conduct commando raids against North Vietnam. The United States provided heavy weapons to South Vietnamese provincial civil guardsmen (local militias) to use against the Vietcong in rural areas. By late 1961 there were 3,205 American advisers in South Vietnam; that number rose to 9,000 the next year. The American advisers—who did not limit their activities to advising—

helped the ARVN move hundreds of thousands of peasants from their homes to relocation centers, or "strategic hamlets."

The massing of peasants into strategic hamlets—separating them from land their families had tilled for generations—made it easier for the South Vietnamese government to hunt for NLF fighters. But it also gave the NLF a weapon in its propaganda war against the Saigon authorities. Once the rural South Vietnamese were relocated, the ARVN bombed and napalmed the countryside to rout out the NLF. Thousands of civilians, including women and children, lost their lives. The NLF told South Vietnamese peasants that the Saigon government was bombing and burning its own citizens. General Paul D. Harkins, in charge of the American advisory forces, dismissed warnings that this indiscriminate bombing only alienated the population from the government in Saigon, saying that napalm (highly flammable petroleum jelly) "really puts the fear of God into the Vietcong, and that is what counts."

While Harkins kept up a stream of optimistic reports flowing back to Washington, American field advisers grew disgusted with what they considered the cowardice and corruption of the ARVN and the South Vietnamese government. ARVN officers showed more interest in stealing their subordinates' pay than in engaging the NLF. On January 2, 1963, the NLF scored a huge triumph against the ARVN at the battle of Ap Bac, twenty miles from Saigon. Colonel John Paul Vann, an American adviser who witnessed the ambush and defeat of a powerful ARVN contingent by an NLF unit, lamented the "miserable damn performance" of the ARVN. Angry at the "failure" and "futility" of the ARVN commanders at Ap Bac, Vann told his superiors that the ARVN leaders were sadly "characteristic of virtually all of the senior officers of the Vietnamese armed forces."

By mid-1963 the Kennedy administration, once so supportive of Ngo Dinh Diem, viewed him and the rest of the Ngo family as obstacles to success against the NLF. The Vietnamese peasantry despised the strategic hamlets and hated Diem's connections to the old landlord class. Leaders of the Buddhist sects to which over two-thirds of the South's population belonged condemned Diem's pro-Catholic policies and demanded his resignation. Buddhists and students led street demonstrations against the government in June; the police responded with clubs and tear gas. On June 11 a seventy-three-year-old Buddhist monk, Thich Quang Duc, turned the Buddhist uprising from a local affair into an international crisis by immolating himself in the middle of a busy Saigon intersection. His ritual suicide was captured on film and broadcast around the world.

Americans reacted with horror. Senator Frank Church, an Idaho Democrat, told the Senate that "such grisly scenes have not been witnessed since the Christian martyrs marched hand-in-hand into the

Buddhist monks demonstrate popular opposition to the dictatorial ways of President Ngo Dinh Diem in 1963. © *1995 Burt Glinn/Magnum Photos Inc.*

Roman arenas." Church was in fact mistaken, as Buddhist monks had practiced self-immolation in the nineteenth century as a protest against French rule, but virtually no Americans knew such details of Vietnamese culture, and their shock ran deep. President Diem's sister-in-law, Madame Ngo Dinh Nhu, provoked further outrage against herself and her family when she scoffed that she would be "happy to provide the mustard for the monks' next barbecues."

The Kennedy administration decided that General Collins had been right eight years before: Diem's family must either change its ways and broaden its government to include non-family members and non-Catholics or be removed from office. That summer, to secure Republican support for his policies, the president appointed an old Republican rival, Henry Cabot Lodge, Eisenhower's ambassador to the United Nations and Nixon's vice-presidential candidate in 1960, as the new ambassador to South Vietnam. The day after his arrival in Saigon, Lodge encouraged a plot by some of the ARVN's top generals to oust the Ngos, but the generals aborted their plans, fearful that Diem had discovered the plot. Meanwhile, American officials in Washington kept up the pressure for change in Saigon.

Diem refused invitations to go quietly into exile. He dug in his heels and turned on the Americans. His brother Nhu hinted darkly at a deal with North Vietnam that would leave the Ngo family in charge of a neutral South Vietnam. At this point Ambassador Lodge, in Saigon, along with Secretary of Defense Robert McNamara and Assistant Secretary of State for Far Eastern Affairs Roger Hilsman, the officials in Washington most concerned with Vietnam policy, decided to encourage the dissident ARVN generals to reactivate their plans for a coup. On November 1, 1963, the plotters seized control of the presidential palace and captured Diem and Nhu. Informed in advance of the coup, Ambassador Lodge made no attempt to protect the Ngos or offer them safe conduct out of the country. They were murdered by the plotters early on the morning of November 2, and a new government took over, headed by General Duong Van Minh.

Word of Diem's death shook Kennedy, once one of the Vietnamese president's staunchest backers. When the murder was confirmed, Kennedy turned white and retreated from the room. Hilsman, who was intimately involved in planning the coup, seemed much happier. "Revolutions are rough. People get hurt," he nonchalantly told a reporter.

At first the existence of a new South Vietnamese government seemed to present an opportunity to wage war against the NLF with renewed vigor, but by January 1964 American officials in Saigon and Washington had grown impatient with General Minh's inability to subdue the Vietcong. Despite later claims by some Kennedy insiders that, had the president lived, he would have reduced the American commitment after the 1964 election, Kennedy remained dedicated to victory until the date of his assassination, three weeks after Diem's death. In remarks prepared for his ill-fated trip to Dallas, Kennedy wrote, "We in this country in this generation are—by destiny rather than choice—the watchmen on the walls of freedom. . . . Our assistance to . . . nations can be risky and costly, as is true in Southeast Asia today. But we dare not weary of the task."

Overall, the Kennedy administration left Lyndon Johnson a terrible burden in South Vietnam. By the time Johnson took office, sixteen thousand United States Army, Navy, and Marine Corps "advisers" were conducting daily operations against the NLF. And yet this effort produced diminishing returns, as the NLF continued to increase its control over the countryside. The more fighting the American soldiers did, the less the ARVN soldiers and officers seemed willing to do. The government of South Vietnam enjoyed little support except from a coterie of ARVN generals, who preferred the ease of life in Saigon to fighting in the field. In the countryside, where over 80 percent of the population resided, the national government had become at best a nuisance and at worst an enemy. While Kennedy pleaded with the American public not to weary of the war, many Vietnamese peasants had already lost patience and perhaps hope. The hated strategic hamlets and the government's widespread use of napalm and other defoliants proved powerful recruiting agents for the NLF. Johnson would have a difficult time pursuing Kennedy's vision of a victorious Republic of Vietnam.

Soon the new South Vietnamese government of Duong Van Minh proved no more receptive to American advice than had Ngo Dinh Diem and his family. The resistance of the Saigon government to American suggestions for waging the war presented the new Johnson administration with a painful dilemma, one it never resolved. The South Vietnamese authorities seemed incapable of winning the war without American assistance. Yet the more the Americans helped, the less the South Vietnamese did for themselves, thereby encouraging the Americans to get more deeply involved. The growing U.S. presence, in turn, seemed to validate NLF and North Vietnamese claims that the South Vietnamese authorities were American puppets.

On his one trip to the region in 1961, Lyndon Johnson, then vice president, had called Diem "the Winston Churchill of Southeast Asia." When skeptical reporters questioned him about this strange exaggeration, Johnson responded, "He's the only boy we've got out there." Now new to the presidency and trying to follow Kennedy's policies, Johnson relied on the advice of his predecessor's foreign policy experts. Almost to a man, they believed that the United States needed to increase its presence in South Vietnam, pursue the war more vigorously, and, if necessary, replace General Minh with someone more compliant to Washington's desires. Early in 1964, Walt Rostow, now head of the State Department's policy-planning staff, urged "a direct political-military showdown with Hanoi" before the end of the year. The president, facing the upcoming election, favored delay, hoping to keep Vietnam off the nation's front pages and the evening news. The president would not turn his subordinates away from their militant course, but neither did he want to disrupt the consensus he expected to carry him to victory in the fall.

As Johnson procrastinated, U.S. military planners and diplomatic officials moved to alter the military situation in South Vietnam. In late January 1964 the Pentagon helped engineer another coup in Saigon, replacing General Minh with General Nguyen Khanh, who the Americans thought would aggressively fight the war. Johnson ordered Lodge to do what he could to stiffen Khanh's resolve, cabling the ambassador that "nothing is more important than to stop neutralist talk whenever we can by whatever means we can."

In June 1964 some of the president's principal advisers floated the idea of seeking a congressional resolution supporting American air or ground action against North Vietnam. Six weeks later, after the raucous Republican convention had nominated Senator Barry Goldwater for president, two controversial incidents off the coast of North Vietnam justified introduction of such a congressional resolution and provided an excuse for air strikes by U.S. forces against North Vietnamese naval bases and oil storage facilities. Two U.S. destroyers, the *Maddox* and the *C. Turner Joy*, had been conducting so-called De Soto patrols in support of South Vietnamese naval operations along the North Vietnamese coast bordering the Gulf of Tonkin (see map, page 260). During these patrols, American ships sailing inside the twelve-mile territorial limit claimed by North Vietnam conducted surveillance against North Vietnamese coastal radar installations. The surveillance was designed to force the North Vietnamese to activate their radar devices, revealing their location. The *Maddox* and the *C. Turner Joy* would then notify accompanying South Vietnamese patrol boats of the positions of the North Vietnamese installations, and the southern boats would attack.

The De Soto patrols provoked the North Vietnamese navy to attack the *Maddox* on the night of August 2, 1964. Two nights later, in heavy seas, the commander of the *C. Turner Joy* thought his ship was under attack and ordered his crew to return fire. They did so, but hit nothing—probably because no North Vietnamese patrol boats were in the area and there had been no hostile fire. As Johnson later acknowledged, "For all I know, our navy may have been shooting at whales out there." The assault on the *Maddox* did actually occur, although Secretary of Defense McNamara was not telling the truth when he claimed that "the *Maddox* was operating in international waters and was carrying out a routine patrol of the type we carry out all over the world at all times."

Despite their falsehood, McNamara's claims carried the day in Congress, which passed the Tonkin Gulf Resolution on August 7. The House voted unanimously in favor of this resolution, and in the Senate only two members, Oregon Democrat Wayne Morse and Alaska Democrat Ernest Gruening, voted against it. The resolution authorized the president to "take all necessary measures to repel any armed attack against the forces of the United States and to prevent further aggression." The resolution also called for "all necessary steps, including the use of armed force, to assist" any member of SEATO that asked for American military aid. Although South Vietnam was not in fact a member of SEATO, the alliance had agreed to extend its protection to South Vietnam.

The resolution's extraordinarily broad grant of authority to the nation's chief executive included no time limit. Later Johnson would use it to justify a greatly enlarged American presence. Senator Morse predicted that the other lawmakers would eventually regret having approved such a blank check. One who did was J. William Fulbright, an Arkansas Democrat and the chairman of the Senate Foreign Relations Committee, who presented the resolution on the Senate floor. Within a year he opposed further U.S. participation in the war. He later

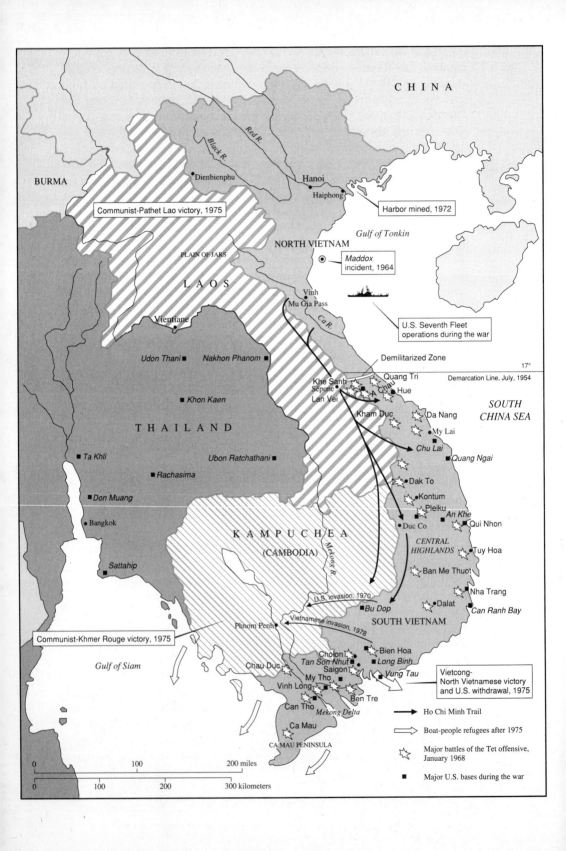

CHINA

Red R.

Black R.

BURMA

• Dienbienphu

Hanoi

• Haiphong

Harbor mined, 1972

Communist-Pathet Lao victory, 1975

Gulf of Tonkin

PLAIN OF JARS

NORTH VIETNAM

⊙ *Maddox* incident, 1964

L A O S

Vinh

Mu Gia Pass

Vientiane

Ca R.

U.S. Seventh Fleet operations during the war

Udon Thani ■ ■ Nakhon Phanom

Demilitarized Zone

17°

Demarcation Line, July, 1954

Khe Sanh   Quang Tri

Sépone   ☆ A ☆ Hue
Lan Vei

SOUTH
CHINA SEA

■ Khon Kaen

Kham Duc   ☆ Da Nang

THAILAND

☆ Chu Lai   • My Lai

■ Ta Khli

Ubon Ratchathani ■

☆ *Chu Lai*   ■ Quang Ngai

■ *Rachasima*

☆ Dak To

• Don Muang

• Kontum
☆ Pleiku   *An Khe*

• Bangkok

K A M P U C H E A

(CAMBODIA)

Mekong R.

• Duc Co ☆ Qui Nhon

CENTRAL
HIGHLANDS ☆ Tuy Hoa

Sattahip

☆ Ban Me Thuot

U.S. invasion, 1970

☆ Nha Trang

Vietnamese invasion, 1978

■ Bu Dop

☆ Dalat   *Can Ranh Bay*

Phnom Penh

SOUTH VIETNAM

Communist-Khmer Rouge victory, 1975

Gulf of Siam

Chau Duc

☆ Bien Hoa

Cholon   ■ Long Binh
Tan Son Nhut
Saigon   ☆ Vung Tau

Vietcong-
North Vietnamese victory
and U.S. withdrawal, 1975

My Tho ☆

Vinh Long

Ben Tre

Can Tho   *Mekong Delta*

➤ Ho Chi Minh Trail

Ca Mau

⇨ Boat-people refugees after 1975

CA MAU PENINSULA

☆ Major battles of the Tet offensive,
January 1968

0   100   200 miles

■ Major U.S. bases during the war

0   100   200   300 kilometers

lamented that he was "hoodwinked and taken in by the president of the United States, the secretary of state and the chief of staff and the secretary of defense," who had lied to him about what happened in the Gulf of Tonkin.

The Tonkin Gulf Resolution effectively removed Vietnam from the political debate during the 1964 election campaign. Goldwater, who had earlier berated Johnson for timidity in Vietnam and had even suggested the possible use of nuclear weapons against North Vietnam, fully supported the resolution and the limited air raid Johnson ordered against North Vietnam. For his part, Johnson stood serenely in the middle of the road on Vietnam. Most people believed he wanted to keep the United States out of a full-scale shooting war while preventing a Communist victory. His major campaign speech on Vietnam sounded moderate but left considerable room for greater American involvement at a later date. He said that "only as a last resort" would he "start dropping bombs around that are likely to involve American boys in a war in Asia with 700 million Chinese." He could not guarantee the future, he said, but "we are not going north and drop bombs at this stage of the game, and we are not going south and run out and leave it for the Communists to take over."

THE AMERICANIZATION
OF THE WAR, 1965

The year 1965 marked the point of no return for the United States in Vietnam. By July Johnson had made a series of fateful decisions that transformed the fighting in Vietnam into an American war. Nevertheless, throughout the period of gradually increasing American military involvement in Vietnam, the Johnson administration waged a limited war. Johnson wanted to break the will of the North Vietnamese without provoking a military response from the Soviet Union or China. Officials believed that limiting the extent of the war would lessen the impact on the American public, making it easier to sustain political support for the war. It proved nearly impossible, however, to wage a limited war effectively. Every step up the ladder of escalation alarmed potential adversaries abroad and created anxiety at home. At the same time, efforts to restrict the scope of the war relieved pressure on North Vietnam and generated opposition from a different group of Americans, those who wanted to defeat North Vietnam quickly with the use of massive military force.

◄ **Southeast Asia and the Vietnam War**

In the summer of 1965 Johnson took the final steps toward committing 100,000 U.S. ground troops to the war. No longer would the administration maintain the fiction that American soldiers were acting only as advisers; U.S. forces began conducting large-scale operations on their own, without accompanying ARVN units. Undersecretary of State George Ball, one of the few high officials skeptical of the importance of Vietnam and doubtful that the United States could prevail, described the United States as being mounted "on the tiger's back" in Vietnam. It would prove difficult, he warned, to decide "where to dismount."

As the South Vietnamese government grew continually weaker, the succession of military regimes nearly drove Johnson into apoplexy. News of yet another uprising provoked him to explode, "I don't want to hear any more." One of the president's assistants suggested that the coat of arms of the Saigon government display a turnstile.

In this atmosphere, Pentagon planners concluded that bombing the North would help save the South. General Maxwell Taylor, the ambassador to South Vietnam, told Johnson early in 1965 that air raids would "inject some life into the dejected spirits" of South Vietnam. The president, more prescient than some of his military advisers, worried that "this guerrilla war cannot be won from the air." Taylor reassured him, however, that although bombing would not destroy the enemy, it would "bring pressure on the will of the chiefs of the DRV [North Vietnam]. As practical men, they cannot wish to see the fruits of ten years of labor destroyed by slowly escalating air attacks."

Sustained bombing of North Vietnam began within a month of Johnson's 1965 inauguration. On February 7, 1965, a company of Vietcong soldiers attacked the American barracks at Pleiku, in the central highlands of South Vietnam, killing 8 Americans, wounding 126, and destroying ten planes. Although the assault hardly surprised high American officials, they believed that this attack on American forces would further undermine the shaky morale of the South Vietnamese government. Pleiku therefore provided the justification for sustained bombing of the North. Johnson first ordered a single retaliatory mission, similar to the one undertaken after the Gulf of Tonkin incident the previous August. But this did not stop calls for harsher action. Former vice president Richard Nixon urged night-and-day bombing of the North. On February 13 Johnson authorized Operation Rolling Thunder, an extensive campaign of sustained bombing against the North. In April, American and South Vietnamese pilots flew 3,600 sorties against targets in the North—fuel depots, railroad yards, bridges, power plants, and munitions factories.

The initial results of the campaign disappointed the air war advocates. Despite the expectations of Pentagon planners, the North Vietnamese quickly adapted to round-the-clock bombing. There were few industrial targets in the North, and the North Vietnamese quickly rebuilt destroyed bridges. The thick jungle provided cover for thousands of North Vietnamese men, women, and children (as young as ten years old) carrying supplies by hand and bicycle to the South along what became known as the Ho Chi Minh Trail. The North Vietnamese and NLF fighters did not capitulate, and the South Vietnamese government did not become stronger. American military officers urged even more air attacks. General Taylor complained that Rolling Thunder should be more than a "few isolated thunder claps." He urged a "mounting crescendo" of air raids against North Vietnam. In response, Johnson relaxed restrictions on targets over the next several months.

For the remainder of his term, Johnson worried about provoking Chinese intervention in the war. China's entry into the Korean conflict had proved disastrous for the United States. To minimize this risk, Johnson avoided bombing close to China's border with Vietnam. For the same reason, he denied repeated requests from the military to invade North Vietnam with ground troops. Such precautions worked, and China and the Soviet Union did not go beyond supplying North Vietnam with weapons. Yet air war advocates within the United States military believed that Johnson acted too cautiously. They doubted that the Chinese or Soviets intended to enter the war, and they believed the restrictions on bombing targets limited the effectiveness of the air campaign.

Since Rolling Thunder resulted in little more than temporary setbacks for the Vietcong, the American commander in South Vietnam, General William Westmoreland, called for direct American ground action throughout the South. There is no solution, he wrote the president, "other than to put our own finger in the dike." But Johnson still resisted a full Americanization of the war, and at a speech at Johns Hopkins University in April 1965, he offered "unconditional discussions" with North Vietnam to end the war.

In early May, McNamara, Taylor, and Westmoreland acknowledged that bombing alone would not win the war. At a meeting in Honolulu they agreed that the United States had to fight the war on the ground, in the South, if the Saigon government were to have a chance of surviving. They did not, however, adopt Westmoreland's preference for a comprehensive operation throughout the South; instead they called for an additional forty thousand U.S. troops to fight within fifty miles of American enclaves near the coast.

By June 1965 this approach had failed to stem the NLF's advance, and Westmoreland wanted another 150,000 troops deployed to fight the ground war throughout the South. Secretary of Defense McNamara cut Westmoreland's request to 100,000 troops and forwarded it to the president. Throughout July, Johnson consulted with his principal advisers on the future course to take in Vietnam. In these meetings Johnson appeared skeptical of the usefulness of committing additional American troops, but he was unwilling to accept an NLF victory. The only course he could tolerate, therefore, was a continued gradual increase in the American commitment—the very policy that had failed over the previous year. He hoped to keep the build-up as quiet as possible to avoid a raucous debate in the press or Congress and to prevent public disillusionment of the sort that had plagued the Truman administration during the Korean War. He also worried that a congressional debate on Vietnam would ruin his plans for the Great Society.

During the July 1965 meetings he asked General Earle Wheeler, chairman of the Joint Chiefs of Staff, "Tell me this. What will happen if we put in 100,000 more men and then two, three years later you tell me you need 500,000 more? How would you expect me to respond to that? And what makes you think Ho Chi Minh won't put in another 100,000 and match us every bit of the way?" To which Wheeler responded, "This means greater bodies of men from North Vietnam, which will allow us to cream them." Johnson's fear proved prophetic, and Wheeler's reply revealed the folly of the American commanders' war methods.

Undersecretary of State George Ball offered the most spirited dissent, explaining to Johnson that the United States could not win in Vietnam. He predicted that the struggle would be long and protracted, as in the Korean War, and that once again public opinion would turn against an inconclusive war. The United States would lose more prestige abroad when it became obvious that the world's greatest power could not defeat the guerrillas. Johnson seemed troubled by Ball's comments. He wondered if Westerners could successfully fight Asians in jungles and rice paddies. Still, the thought of a Communist victory appalled him. "But George," he asked, "wouldn't all these countries [the rest of Southeast Asia] say that Uncle Sam was a paper tiger, wouldn't we lose credibility breaking the word of three presidents?" Ball's assurances that the United States would gain more by removing itself from an imprudent situation failed to change Johnson's mind.

Eventually all the president's advisers, with the exception of Ball, concurred that adding 100,000 Americans to the 90,000 troops already in Vietnam would help stabilize the situation without causing a backlash in Congress or with the public. Most agreed to reject the request from the Joint Chiefs of Staff to call up the reserves. Such a move would dramatically raise the stakes, both at home and abroad, and would perhaps necessitate a presidential declaration of a state of emergency and a request to Congress for several billion dollars. In that event, Johnson worried, the Great Society would cease, and worse, "Hanoi would ask the Chinese and the Soviets for increased aid."

At the end of July, Johnson decided to inform congressional leaders that he intended to send another 100,000 men by the end of the year, without calling up reserve units. With few exceptions, both Republican and Democratic leaders in Congress supported the move. Speaker of the House John McCormack thought there was no alternative. "The lesson of Hitler and Mussolini is clear," he reflected. Senator Russell Long, a conservative Democrat from Louisiana, wondered, "If a nation with 14 million can make Uncle Sam run, what will China think?" Only Senator Mike Mansfield of Montana, Johnson's successor as majority leader, doubted the wisdom of Americanizing the war. "Whatever pledge we had was to *assist* [South Vietnam] in its own defense. Since then there has been no government of legitimacy. . . . We owe this government nothing." Mansfield also pointed out the limited American stakes in Vietnam. Even if the United States won the war, Mansfield said, "what have you achieved? It is by no means a 'vital' area of U.S. concern."

Johnson was unpersuaded. At a low-key, mid-day press conference on July 28, 1965, he announced the plan to send an additional 100,000 troops. That afternoon Mansfield wrote Johnson that most of the public approved of what he was doing because they trusted him as their president, but "not necessarily out of any understanding or sympathy with policies on Vietnam." He thought people backed Johnson for now because they sensed that "your objective [is] not to get in too deeply."

FIGHTING THE WAR, 1966–1967

During 1966 and 1967, the number of U.S. troops in South Vietnam rose from 190,000 to 535,000 (see figure, page 266). Yet even this size force could not prevail against the NLF and in fact contributed to the further deterioration of the government and armed forces of South Vietnam. The Americans were trying to apply tactics learned in the Second World War and Korea to a very different kind of struggle, against a guerrilla force. The "army concept" that had developed over the past twenty-five years held that wars could be won with advanced materiel and technology—aerial bombardment, tank attacks, artillery, electronic detection fences—rather than with soldiers armed with rifles. These principles seemed to make sense for a productive, industrial society that relied on conscripts. If machines could substitute for soldiers, the casualties would decline and public support would continue. But advocates of a high-tech war misunderstood the realities of the war in Vietnam. The army concept removed the American forces from direct contact with the people they were ostensibly helping and ultimately contributed to the loss of the war.

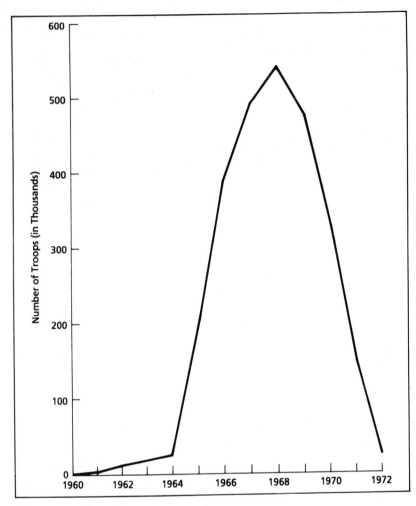

Levels of United States troops in Vietnam, at year's end

General Westmoreland tried to perfect a strategy of attrition—that is, a gradual wearing down of the enemy—against the Vietcong and North Vietnamese. Westmoreland never fully grasped that the NLF and the North Vietnamese fought a guerrilla war, in which they, not the Americans, determined their level of casualties. Persuaded that American technology could carry the day, Westmoreland used helicopters to send American units into the countryside on search-and-destroy missions to root out and kill enemy soldiers. Americans would fly out in the morning, pursue the Vietcong in firefights, count the dead, and return to their bases in the evening. The measure of success became "body counts" rather than territory captured, the standard in

Wounded American soldiers after a battle in Vietnam. *Larry Burrows, LIFE Magazine © 1966 Time Inc.*

earlier wars. The tactic encouraged abuses. Local commanders, hoping to please their superiors in Saigon, inflated the death figures. Moreover, reliance on body counts offered an incentive to shoot first and ask no questions. One Marine remembered that during his first night on patrol, "about fifty people shot this old guy. Everybody claimed they shot him. He got shot 'cause he started running. It was an old man running to tell his family. . . . Any Vietnamese out at night was the enemy." The army developed strict rules of engagement designed to prevent indiscriminate shooting of non-combatants. But the confusion of a war without clearly defined front lines, with enemy forces who looked like civilians, with the presence of civilians on the battlefield, and with the demands of the body count led to some atrocities.

Before U.S. troops descended from their helicopters, giant B-52 bombers and smaller fighter jets pounded the battlefields. The United States dropped more bombs on Vietnam, a country about the size of California, each month than fell on all of Europe during the entire Second World War. But the B-52 raids, code-named Arc Light, alerted the Vietcong and North Vietnamese forces that the Americans were on the way, giving them time to withdraw or to dive into hundreds of miles of tunnels to protect themselves from the massive firepower. Also, the Vietcong used unexploded American bombs and artillery shells as a weapon against the Americans. About 2 percent of the artillery shells and 5 percent of the bombs from the B-52s did not explode on impact. The enemy developed shrewd booby traps using these unexploded bombs, killing or wounding thousands of inexperienced American troops. In 1966 over one thousand American soldiers died of wounds caused by booby traps, and in the first six months of the following year, 17 percent of all American casualties resulted from mines or booby traps. The dollar cost of the bombing also mounted quickly, to about $2.5 billion per year.

The NLF kept gaining strength on the ground, using guerrilla tactics developed earlier by the Vietminh. They avoided firefights where they could, forcing the Americans to waste enormous energy and materiel for meager gains. They continued political organization in the countryside even as American bombers flew overhead. One American correspondent, alarmed at the apparent inability of U.S. commanders to acknowledge the strengths of the NLF, complained to a general, "How do you expect our forces to win the hearts and minds of the people when all they do is take off from one army base and fly overhead at 1,500 feet while Charlie [one of many nicknames for the NLF] is sitting down there and he's got 'em by the testicles jerking, and every time he jerks their hearts and mind follow?"

Despite such complaints, the United States Army continued to rely on search-and-destroy operations. The largest occurred in late 1966 and early 1967. In one such mission, which lasted from September to November 1966, twenty-two thousand U.S. and ARVN troops, supported by B-52 bombers and massive artillery fire, pursued the NLF northwest of Saigon. In another search-and-destroy operation, from February through May 1967, American B-52s reduced the South Vietnamese landscape to the eerie bleakness of the moon, making hundreds of square miles uninhabitable by the peasants the Americans were supposedly helping. Americans entering villages to root out the Vietcong sometimes carried out so-called Zippo raids, igniting the peasants' thatched huts with tracer bullets, flame throwers, and cigarette lighters to deny sanctuary to the enemy.

Such actions not only enraged the peasantry, but also shocked Americans watching the carnage on the evening news. Yet this enormous firepower failed to eradicate the Vietcong, who would simply melt away until an assault stopped. One reporter likened each blow to "a sledgehammer on a floating cork; somehow the cork refused to stay down." An American general later acknowledged that it was physically impossible to keep the enemy from slipping away.

All the while, North Vietnamese commander General Nguyen Vo Giap, the victor at Dienbienphu, had the Americans playing into his hands as he waged a protracted guerrilla war. The search-and-destroy operations took Americans away from the heavily populated coastal plain, where the NLF and the North gained strength among the popu-

American fire sometimes hurt friendly South Vietnamese. A father carries his child wounded by
American soldiers who mistook him for a Vietcong
fighter. *Philip Jones Griffiths/Magnum Photos Inc.*

lation. As the Americans engaged in inconclusive battles in the interior, they paid less attention to "pacification," the effort to bind the
peasantry to the government in Saigon.

If anything, the Saigon government lost even more support among
the South Vietnamese as the American war devastated the countryside. As part of their effort to deny sanctuary to the enemy, American
forces used giant transport planes to spray trees with defoliants. Between 1962 and 1972 the Americans dropped over 1 million pounds of
toxic chemicals such as Agent Orange over South Vietnam, destroying more than half its forests. Some American crews jokingly adopted
the motto"Only You Can Prevent Forests." But many crew members
later suffered serious health problems, probably from contact with the
toxins they dropped.

The effect of this tactic on the crops of South Vietnamese farmers—
the ostensible beneficiaries of the war effort—was immediate and

devastating. Deadly defoliants dropped from planes onto a suspected Vietcong area in the afternoon would soon drift over friendly villages; by the next morning, fruit fell from the trees and the leaves on rubber plants turned brown and broke off. Farmers blamed the Americans for their loss of crops, and they feared the defoliants would harm animal and human life as well. The birth of a physically or mentally impaired infant was often blamed on the defoliation campaigns. American forces also used poisons to destroy the rice crop grown in Vietcong areas, expecting the hungry enemy to emerge and fight. The theory overlooked the NLF's practice of buying or taking rice from the peasants; in effect the Americans ruined ten pounds of rice grown by friendly farmers for every pound of Vietcong rice they destroyed. South Vietnam, once an exporter of rice, began importing it from neighboring countries (and even the United States) as the war ground on.

The havoc in the countryside forced hundreds of thousands of peasants to flee their homes. Between 1964 and 1969 more than 4 million South Vietnamese—one-fourth of the population—were refugees at one time or another. Those who remained on their land often did so only because they feared the Vietcong would redistribute it if they were gone. Many of those who fled the terror from the skies, the defoliants, the artillery barrages, and the Zippo raids swarmed to cities that had neither room nor facilities for them; others languished in squalid refugee camps.

The population of Saigon, under 500,000 in the 1950s, swelled to 1.5 million by the mid-1960s. The capital and other cities near American installations—Danang, Cam Ranh Bay, Hue, to name a few—changed from Asian commercial centers, conducting business in traditional ways to army boom towns. Seedy bars and brothels sprang up near American bases, with women and girls as young as thirteen prostituting themselves for the GIs. Senator J. William Fulbright complained that the United States had transformed South Vietnam into "a gigantic whorehouse." Over 100,000 Amerasian children were born of liaisons between American soldiers and Vietnamese women. These children were scorned by the Vietnamese, and after the Americans departed they suffered terrible privation.

The presence of over 500,000 Americans transformed the Vietnamese economy. Production of food and rubber fell as the Vietnamese concentrated on servicing the newcomers. At first the GIs paid cash in U.S. dollars. Prices zoomed 170 percent in 1966 and 1967, and many Vietnamese could no longer afford the basic necessities of life. To halt the inflation, the army started paying its soldiers in scrip, which could only be used to purchase consumer goods on U.S. bases. Vietnamese entrepreneurs responded by importing watches, tape recorders, motorcycles, radios, and the like to sell to local people who worked for the Americans and were paid in South Vietnamese currency.

Corruption, already a problem before the Americans arrived en masse, vastly increased in 1966. The South Vietnamese government rented space to the Americans at exorbitant prices. South Vietnamese officials took bribes from contractors wishing to do business with U.S. agencies, including military bases and rural development organizations. Others demanded payment for licenses, permits, visas, and passports. Some Saigon officials traded in opium, and many engaged in the flourishing black market. Everything was for sale—U.S. government scrip, South Vietnamese piasters, Scotch whiskey, watches, hand grenades, rifles.

Americans were often aware of the corruption that eroded South Vietnamese society, but Westmoreland thought that curing it would alarm the very government the United States wanted to help. General Nguyen Cao Ky, who became prime minister in 1966, acknowledged that most of the generals were corrupt, but he thought it did not matter. "Corruption exists everywhere, and people can live with some of it," he explained, adding, "You live with it in Chicago and New York." Some midranking American officials wanted to threaten the government of Saigon with loss of aid if it did not remove corrupt officials. Westmoreland overruled such advice, fearing it would only annoy the government, without producing appropriate changes, or perhaps lead to the government's collapse.

By late 1967 the build-up had not won the war. McNamara's comment in late 1966 that he could "see the light at the end of the tunnel in Vietnam" inspired the rueful rejoinder that what he had glimpsed was the headlight of another train engineered by Ho Chi Minh. Thirteen thousand U.S. servicemen had been killed. Only the lowest American goal—denying a victory to the NLF—had been realized, and continued success was not assured. Other American war aims—creating a stable South Vietnamese government capable of waging the war on its own and winning the affection of its people, and forcing the North to quit—had become more elusive than ever. As American involvement intensified, South Vietnamese society dissolved. People either became dependents of the United States or went underground to join the NLF. The South Vietnamese government, once the bedrock of Washington's strategy to defeat communism in Southeast Asia, slipped into dependence and obstructionism.

MILITARY SERVICE AND THE DRAFT

Although the fighting took place far from the United States, the war deeply affected the way many Americans lived their lives. Military service became an important, life-changing experience for over

2 million American men. Combat soldiers often encountered racial tensions, boredom, drugs, and brutality against the Vietnamese. Most soldiers accepted these unpleasant realities as part of the hardships of military service, but many bore psychological and emotional scars for years after they returned from Vietnam. Nearly 80 percent of the U.S. troops in Vietnam served as support personnel, not combat troops, and their service was far less traumatic. But even those Americans who did not fight were changed by the war. Back home, millions of young men spent a substantial part of their late adolescence or young adulthood wondering whether they would be conscripted, seeking ways to avoid participating in the fighting. Far more men did not go to Vietnam than went, but the war created deep divisions among people of an entire generation. Those who fought in the war often resented those who did not, and people who did not go to Vietnam sometimes treated those who did with scorn, pity, or condescension.

Unlike the Second World War, for which the armed forces needed nearly every able-bodied American man, the military effort in Vietnam required less than half the eligible population. Of the 27 million available men between the ages of nineteen and twenty-six, 16 million never served in the armed forces. Of the approximately 11 million who did, 9 million enlisted more or less voluntarily and 2.2 million were drafted under the terms of the Selective Service Act of 1947. A total of about 2.8 million men, along with 6,400 women, actually saw service in Vietnam between 1961 and 1973.

Although the draft took only about 10 percent of the men subject to its call, the Selective Service affected the lives of nearly everybody. A major study conducted after the war concluded that the draft "cast the entire generation into a contest for survival." Working "as an instrument of Darwinian social policy," the draft, "through an elaborate structure of deferments, exemptions, legal technicalities, and noncombat military alternatives, . . . rewarded those who manipulated the system to their advantage." As the war became more dangerous and American casualties rose to three hundred dead per week, many young men wanted to reduce the risk to their personal safety. A number of options were available: deferments for marriage (dropped in 1965), fatherhood, or student status; enlistment in the National Guard or the reserves; enlistment in the armed forces, with a promise to serve in places other than Vietnam; and service in noncombat zones in Vietnam.

The wealthy and educated, those most aware of the intricacies of the system, knew best how to avoid the most dangerous duty. As a result, only 24 percent of eligible men from high-income families entered the military, 9 percent served in Vietnam, and 7 percent saw combat, mostly as officers. Of the eligible men from middle-income families, 30 percent served in the military, 12 percent in Vietnam, and 7 percent in combat. For low-income men, 40 percent entered military service, 19 percent went to Vietnam, and 15 percent saw combat. Such discrepancies produced a distressing inequity in the make-up of the forces bearing the brunt of the heaviest fighting.

The Selective Service system appeared corrupt and demeaning to many of those who faced conscription. Kingman Brewster, president of Yale University, perceived "a tarnishing of the national spirit and a cops-and-robbers view of national obligation," as young men looked for ways to avoid the draft. One young inductee who had the job of filing case histories at a local draft board had his eyes opened observing the ruses others used to avoid being called up. He telephoned his mother and reported, "The whole set-up is corrupt. I don't need to *be* here! I don't need to *be* here! I don't need to *be* here! I simply didn't *need* to be drafted!" Nonetheless, he went to Vietnam and became one of the fifty-eight thousand men who died. His feelings that the draft was arbitrary and unfair were common; a Harris poll concluded that most Americans believed the men who went to Vietnam were "suckers, having risked their lives in the wrong war, in the wrong place, in the wrong time." This pervasive unhappiness with the Selective Service system contributed to Americans' growing disillusionment with many public institutions.

Three-quarters of the 16 million men who did not serve in Vietnam admitted that they had changed their life plans to stay away from Vietnam, and a majority (55 percent) said they actively took steps to avoid the draft. Male college enrollments were about 6 to 7 percent higher than they otherwise would have been. In one survey of college students, 12 percent reported that fear of the draft prevented them from taking time out from their studies, and 5 percent claimed they had changed their course of study to prolong their deferment. Until 1968 graduate students earned deferments, so graduate school applications shot up in 1966 and 1967. The dean of one business college reported that 90 percent of the male applicants to his school sought admission out of fear of the draft.

Other options remained for those without deferments. Even if drafted, a man had to be physically fit before he could be inducted. Some young men had their family doctor prepare false documents to keep them out of the service. One physician commented that "the traditional doctor-patient relationship is one of preserving life. I save lives by keeping people out of the army." But some doctors resented such requests. One Bloomington, Indiana, physician agreed to write letters to the local draft board on behalf of some of his patients, ostensibly to keep them out of the service. But instead his letters noted that the men were fit and urged the army to induct them as punishment for manipulating the system.

A network of draft counselors, initially sponsored by churches and other pacifist organizations, arose to advise young men of their rights under the Selective Service Act and of legal ways to avoid induction. After the 1965 Supreme Court ruling in *United States* v. *Seegar*, conscientious objector status was available to anyone with a "sincerely founded reason" for opposing war. Before then only members of recognized pacifist sects—such as Mennonites, Quakers, Jehovah's Witnesses, Brethren—had been entitled to register as conscientious objectors. After *Seegar*, draft counselors advised young men on how to present their antiwar beliefs in a persuasive way: "Sit down and think about why you are against killing people in war. Write down short sentences or ideas (for instance: love . . . brotherhood . . . peace . . . equality . . . personal responsibility)." Counselors advised obtaining testimonials from teachers, scout leaders, or clergy who would vouch for the sincerity of the applicant's beliefs. Not surprisingly, the educated and articulate fared better than the poor and the less well connected at obtaining conscientious objector status. The 172,000 men who did gain such status during the war were expected by their draft boards to perform some sort of alternative service, but almost 50,000 of them were never found by their draft boards.

Some men simply refused induction or tried to evade their draft boards. About 209,000 men were accused of some sort of draft-related offense, but only 25,000 were indicted, and only 4,000 received prison sentences. Even those who entered the military sometimes refused to accept service in Vietnam. Some 12,000 men went absent without leave (AWOL) to escape an assignment to Vietnam. About 50,000 deserters or accused draft offenders took flight during the war, with 30,000 of them going to Canada. Many of these men quietly came home over the next decade, but 11,000 remained fugitives until 1977, when President Jimmy Carter proclaimed pardon.

For the men who went to Vietnam, life in the armed forces bore little resemblance to the experiences of their fathers or older brothers in the Second World War and the Korean War—and no likeness at all to the idealized versions of those wars presented in movies and television programs. For combat soldiers, Vietnam was sometimes a demoralizing, brutal experience. One day a young man would be in the relatively familiar surroundings of a stateside military base; the next day, after eighteen hours on an airplane, he would find himself in the alien landscape of Vietnam, in a situation that provoked both frustration and terror. The enemy, often indistinguishable from the local population, could materialize suddenly from the jungle and attack with horrible efficiency. On patrol, a soldier might be blown apart at any moment by a booby trap. Conventional precautions and tactics often seemed irrelevant. It was especially difficult to maintain the troops' morale when they saw more and more lives lost for little or no gain.

The difficulties were compounded by the military's personnel policy. Unlike earlier wars, in which soldiers served "for the duration," soldiers in Vietnam had a one-year tour of duty, spread over thirteen months, with thirty days' leave for "rest and recreation." A mixture of demographics, politics, and military management techniques prompted this arrangement. Because the pool of available soldiers far exceeded the number needed, keeping 500,000 men at the front while allowing *all* others to steer free of battle would cause resentment among those who fought and would erode public support for the war. Therefore, the military limited time in service and continually rotated the forces.

According to General Westmoreland, establishing end-of-tour dates helped boost morale and gave each soldier a goal. In fact, however, GIs' goal often became self-preservation: men approaching the end of their tours became reluctant to fight. No one ever wanted to be killed or wounded, but risking death or injury a few weeks before mustering out appeared especially pointless. One commander called the twelve-month tour "the worst personnel policy in history." To make matters worse, units did not stay together throughout their tours, increasing soldiers' and officers' feelings of isolation. Napoleon once observed that "soldiers have to eat soup together for a long time before they are ready to fight," but Americans discarded that lesson in Vietnam. Troops killed or wounded were replaced by newcomers, whose tour of duty expired later than that of the other men in their unit. Combat soldiers relied on friends who entered Vietnam with them, and they found it difficult to bond with others. Men mostly relied on themselves.

Officers, too, never remained with the same unit throughout their term, because the armed forces rotated commanders, down to the level of platoon lieutenants, every six months. Disgruntled commanders complained that the same war was fought over again every six months. The policy arose because it allowed officers to experience a variety of commands, a sure way of gaining promotion in the professional force developed after the Second World War. But such résumé enhancement—"ticket punching," as it came to be known—eliminated the possibility of strong bonds forming between officers and men. In many cases, the young lieutenants who served as platoon commanders had never even learned the basic combat skills that would inspire confidence in the soldiers under their command.

The lack of rapport between commanders and soldiers sometimes made personal hostilities difficult to control. The murder of officers by enlisted men—often with a fragmentation grenade or other anonymous weapon—became frequent enough, especially late in the war, to earn its own slang name, "fragging." Moreover, the armed forces were susceptible to the same racial tensions that plagued American society as a whole. As these animosities grew in the late sixties, racial divisions rose inside the armed forces. Many black soldiers had no white friends in the ostensibly integrated units. Inevitably, some of the violence between GIs took on a racial tone.

News of atrocities against the Vietnamese, whom some GIs referred to as "gooks," undermined support for the soldiers back home. In this long war against an enemy that struck without warning and then instantly melted away, soldiers sometimes disregarded the so-called Rules of Engagement regulating behavior toward the enemy. Once the body count became the principal means of measuring success in the war, some soldiers became excessive and brutal. A few men chopped off the ears of dead Vietnamese for trophies. They would "take [their] dog-tag chain and fill [it] up with ears," one infantryman recalled. "If we were movin' through the jungle, they'd just put the bloody ear on the chain and stick the ear in their pocket and keep on going. Wouldn't take time to dry it off. Then when we got back, they would nail 'em up on the walls of our hootch, you know, as a trophy." Some GIs gave up the nearly impossible task of distinguishing the Vietcong from uninvolved civilians; besides burning peasants' houses, they shot any Vietnamese they saw. "If it moves, it's VC [Vietcong]" became a common slogan for American soldiers. The most dramatic atrocity of the war occurred in March 1968, when American soldiers massacred more than two hundred unarmed Vietnamese villagers, mostly women and children, at the hamlet of My Lai. The military managed to keep the incident secret until the next year. Americans were uniformly horrified when it was revealed, although like so much else about Vietnam, public opinion about the incident was divided. Some expressed sympathy for the young American soldiers, feeling they had succumbed to the stress of combat. A smaller but significant group saw My Lai as a symbol of all the reasons why the United States should quit Vietnam.

To escape the fear and absurdity of a war without front lines, leadership, or clear goals, some soldiers turned to drugs. Marijuana, opium, and heroin were freely available and inexpensive in the cities, because officials of the South Vietnamese government engaged in the drug trade. So did the CIA, which used profits from drugs to finance a secret counterinsurgency program in the South Vietnamese highlands and along the Laotian border. Soldiers used drugs not only on the base, but in the field. One infantryman who served from mid-1967 to mid-1968 remembered that "in the field most of the guys stayed high. Lots of them couldn't face it. In a sense, if you was high it seemed like a game you was in. You didn't take it serious. It stopped a lot of nervous breakdowns."

Overall, soldiers who experienced combat in Vietnam developed greater psychological and emotional difficulties than did the 80 percent who served in support roles. The latter readjusted relatively readily into American society once they returned home. Surveys taken ten and twenty years after the Vietnam War indicated that the subsequent careers of non-combat soldiers developed similarly to those of men who had not gone to Vietnam. The picture was darker and much more complex for combat veterans. Many experienced post-traumatic stress disorder. Symptoms included drug and alcohol abuse, difficulty sustaining family relationships, trouble finding and maintaining employment, violence, and suicide.

RISING DISSENT AND THE COLLAPSE OF THE COLD WAR CONSENSUS

In addition to the soldiers in Vietnam, at least one man in Washington approached nervous exhaustion as the war expanded: President Johnson. The war had gone on longer than his military advisers predicted, and still there was no clear end in sight. Continued war threatened to wreck his cherished Great Society, and it cast doubt on his chances for reelection in 1968.

Johnson's personal crisis was deepened by mounting criticism of the war from former supporters. Arkansas senator J. William Fulbright, chairman of the Senate Foreign Relations Committee and an old friend from Johnson's days as majority leader, was among the first moderate public figures to dissent. In September 1965 Fulbright told the Senate that "U.S. policy in the Dominican crisis [the previous April] has been characterized by a lack of candor," adding that the same problem plagued the administration's positions on Vietnam.

Over the next few months Fulbright undertook a crash course in American policy toward Indochina, and the following February his committee opened televised hearings on the war. Numerous foreign policy experts told the committee that the administration had headed down the wrong road in Vietnam. George F. Kennan, one of the architects of containment, worried that the "unbalanced concentration of resources and attention" on Vietnam diverted Washington from what he considered to be the proper focus of U.S. foreign policy—Europe. General James Gavin, a Second World War hero, urged that the United States stop the bombing, send no more troops, retreat to enclaves, and look for a negotiated settlement. Fulbright expressed disbelief at Secretary of State Dean Rusk's repeated assertions that "this is a clear case of international Communist aggression." The chairman thought that most of the world viewed the conflict in Vietnam as "a civil war in which outside parties have become involved." Two

Vo Nguyen Giap (1911–)

Vo Nguyen Giap, the most prominent military leader of the Democratic Republic of Vietnam, oversaw the defeat of two of the world's premier military powers, France (in the war of 1946–1954) and the United States (in the war of 1961–1975). Giap came from an educated but impoverished family. His mandarin father gave him a deep love of learning and an abiding hatred of foreign domination of Vietnam. Already a nationalist by age 13, his intelligence and superior performance on entrance exams gained him coveted places in a French secondary school and at Hanoi University. He obtained a law degree in 1937, and the same year he joined the Indochinese Communist Party. In 1938 he married Nguyen Thi Minh Giang. The couple soon became two of the top ten leaders of the Indochinese Communist Party.

At the outbreak of the Second World War Giap left Vietnam for China, where he first met Ho Chi Minh. Giap's wife, who remained behind, was soon arrested by French authorities for Communist activities. She was incarcerated and later died in Hanoi's central prison—a dismal jail that later held captured U.S. air-men. Her death hardened Giap's commitment to rid his country of foreign rule.

Giap spent the Second World War traveling back and forth from China to Vietnam, organizing small guerrilla bands to harass first the French colonial authorities and later the Japanese army of occupation. In August 1945 he led an organized army of Vietminh fighters to capture the northern city of Hanoi from the retreating Japanese. He exulted when Ho Chi Minh proclaimed the birth of the Democratic Republic of Vietnam (DRV) from the balcony of the governor's mansion in Hanoi on September 2, 1945. But France refused to recognize Ho's government and attempted to reestablish colonial rule. War erupted between France and the DRV in December 1946.

Giap, one of the most militantly anti-French members of the new government, became chairman of its military council. Over the next eight years he created an army of 250,000. He developed a theory of protracted war, in which a nation could throw off outside domination by patiently wearing down the colonial power, first with guerrilla raids and later with conventional battles. Years of guerrilla assaults against the French culminated in the climactic siege of Dienbienphu in the spring of 1954. Giap's capture of Dienbienphu on May 7 tore the heart out of the French war effort. France lost its will to continue the fighting, and the first Indochina war ended with the Geneva Accords that July.

Giap's defeat of the modern, well-armed French army provided a model for North Vietnam's war with the United States and South Vietnam from 1961 to 1975. Giap perfected his strategy for waging a war of attrition. He developed a complex system of paths, roads, bridges, and tunnels (the Ho Chi Minh trail) to resupply his forces in the South. Thus reinforced, he staged a protracted series of guerrilla raids and eventually conventional battles with the Americans and the South Vietnamese, wearing them down. Giap turned the Americans' huge advantages in mobility and high-tech weaponry against them, by teasing them into wasting their resources on unimportant objectives. He derided the Americans' tactics in the air war: "There were far too many targets, and so they dispersed their effort. They used planes worth millions to attack a bamboo pontoon bridge."

In early 1968 Giap tried to repeat his success at Dienbienphu with the Tet offensive. Although Tet did not lead to the general uprising among the South Vietnamese that Giap had anticipated, it had a devastating impact on American public opinion and changed U.S. strategy from search-and-destroy operations to defending population centers. Giap reflected that, before Tet, the Americans "thought they could win the war, but now they knew they could not." Tet sent the United States down the road toward negotiations and de-escalation, culminating in the Paris Peace Accords of 1973. Two years later Giap's theories of protracted war were vindicated with the victory of the National Liberation Front.

Giap remained a member of the government of Vietnam well into his eighties. Fifteen years after his victory over the Americans, relations improved between Vietnam and the United States. Giap happily received visits from his former foes. The U.S. admiral who commanded American naval forces in Vietnam told him, "You are a legend in your own time, and I know that you share my views that the time has come to bind up our wounds." ■

months later, Fulbright observed that the war had damaged the Great Society and hurt the nation's relations with the Soviet Union and Europe. He lamented "the arrogance of power," which he defined as a "psychological need that nations seem to have to prove that they are bigger, stronger, better than other nations." Johnson dismissed his old friend's complaints as the bitter recriminations of "a frustrated old woman" who was angry at not having been appointed secretary of state.

While Fulbright and about a dozen other senators dissented from escalation in 1966, more potent opposition to the war arose outside the government in the form of a citizens' peace movement. Opposition to the war joined diverse groups—peace liberals, pacifists, and social revolutionaries. Beginning in 1965, these groups organized "teach-ins," in which they lectured college audiences on the evils of the war. The peace movement also sponsored the 1967 "Vietnam Summer" of protests against the war and the 1968 "dump Johnson" campaign, which sought to replace the president with someone who would extricate the United States from the endless war.

Some members of the peace movement agreed with Kennan that Vietnam was diverting American attention from more serious issues. Long-time Socialist leader Norman Thomas acknowledged that more pressing problems were clamoring for attention, "but it is a practical and emotional absurdity to think that the government or people can or will deal with these and other pressing questions until it stops the war in Vietnam." By 1967 even the least radical participants in the peace movement believed, as Seymour Melman of the Committee for a Sane Nuclear Policy (SANE) put it, "policy change now requires institutional change as well." When Students for a Democratic Society, a New Left group (see Chapter 8), organized the Vietnam Summer in 1967, one Detroit organizer reported, "I find that I am not really working here to 'end the war in Vietnam.'. . . I am working here to make people *feel* Vietnam, to make them realize that it is part of a pattern which oppresses them, as well as Vietnamese peasants." Along with opposition to the war, a general dissatisfaction with American government began to spread.

Public antiwar activism surged in the spring of 1967. Martin Luther King, Jr., who previously had expressed quiet misgivings about the war, openly broke with the Johnson administration. He called for de-escalation, helped organize a new antiwar group (Negotiation Now!), and endorsed the Vietnam Summer. On April 15, crowds of 100,000 in New York and 50,000 in San Francisco heard speakers from both the antiwar and the civil rights movements call for an end to the war and a recommitment to the goal of racial equality at home. Johnson grew alarmed at the possibility that King and pediatrician Benjamin Spock, now an antiwar activist, might run for president and vice president, respectively, in 1968. The White House worried so much that Press Secretary George Christian leaked to the press FBI files purporting to show King's connections to the Communist Party.

Federal agencies constantly observed, infiltrated, and harassed antiwar groups. The FBI compared Senator Fulbright's position during the 1966 Vietnam hearings to those taken by the Communist Party. The CIA infiltrated such antiwar groups as Women Strike for Peace, the Washington Peace Center, SANE, the Congress on Racial Equality (CORE), the War Resisters League, and the National Mobilization Committee Against the War. In August 1967 the CIA initiated Operation Chaos, designed to disrupt and confuse the antiwar movement. Agents sent phony letters to editors of publications, defaming antiwar leaders; other agents infiltrated antiwar groups that called for bombings or violent confrontation with police. Eventually the CIA opened files on over seven thousand Americans—in violation of its charter, which stipulated that it could not operate inside the United States.

The president became frantic as plans developed for a massive march on Washington in October 1967 to demand a halt to the bombing and immediate negotiations to end the war. In order to discredit the antiwar movement, Johnson asked his attorney general, Ramsey Clark, to leak information about the left-wing and Communist affiliations of some of its leaders. Nevertheless, on October 21, a crowd estimated at 100,000 assembled on the Mall in front of the Lincoln Memorial to hear speeches against the war. Later, a group of about 50,000 marched to the Pentagon, where scores crossed police lines and were arrested.

These large demonstrations helped change public attitudes toward the war. Equally important were the nightly televised newscasts showing the fighting and the devastation of Vietnamese society. Satellite technology made it possible to air footage of the war the day it was shot. Reporters and camera crews traveled with platoons into firefights in Vietnamese villages. They captured on film the flames of the Zippo raids, the moans of wounded soldiers, the terror in the eyes of children left homeless by the fighting. What they could not show, because it did not happen, was scenes of GIs liberating villages to the cheers of grateful residents. For a public brought up on the heroic newsreels of the Second World War, where such images had brought tears of pride to the home front, the sharp contrast between "the good war" of 1941 to 1945 and the quagmire of Vietnam proved especially distressing.

As this "living-room war" ground on without progress, Americans at home, like the soldiers in the field, had trouble distinguishing friendly Vietnamese from the enemy, and wanted no part of either. The fighting appeared pointless, and the public longed for relief from a war it had not anticipated or approved. Distrust of the government rose sharply in 1967, as observers noted a yawning "credibility gap" between the optimism of the president and his advisers and the continuing violence shown on TV every evening.

Antiwar activities, the failure to achieve victory, and press coverage of the horrors of the fighting altered the way the public viewed the war. Throughout the country there was a sharp division between "hawks," who supported the war, and "doves," who opposed it. In the beginning of 1967 most Americans were still hawks, willing to escalate the war if it could be decisively won. Fewer than a third of the public believed the war had been a mistake. By July that figure had risen to 41 percent, and by the time of the march on Washington in October, 46 percent thought the United States should never have entered the war. Yet the number calling for an immediate American withdrawal from Vietnam remained low. In February a mere 6 percent wanted withdrawal; by December that figure had risen only to 10 percent. Nevertheless, in the fall only 28 percent of the public approved of President Johnson's handling of the war. Most Americans saw themselves neither as hawks nor doves; they simply wanted relief. As the American war entered its third year in 1968, Senator Mansfield's 1965 warning about the shallowness of public support had proved prophetic.

Although no agreement existed about what to do next, the general consensus on American foreign policy had shattered. A significant number of people began to question its very basis. Did the principle of containment mean that the United States should take part in any Third World conflict in which one side identified with socialism or communism? Were the Communists in places like Vietnam any worse than the regimes the United States chose to support? Would a triumph by such Communists truly weaken the U.S. position with respect to its principal Cold War opponent, the Soviet Union? Did it make sense, in any event, for the United States to fight a war with little chance of victory? Although relatively few Americans had clear answers to such questions in 1967 and 1968, the war led many people to think about them.

By the end of 1967, doubts over further escalation of the war assailed even some of the war's sponsors. The president wondered about the usefulness of bombing North Vietnam. Secretary of Defense McNamara became morose at the lack of progress. The effort to secure the countryside had, "if anything, gone backward," he admitted. At one point he recommended an unconditional halt to the bombing to get serious negotiations started, but Johnson refused after learning that the Joint Chiefs of Staff had threatened to resign, all together, if the bombing was stopped. As he began to despair of winning the war through advanced technology, McNamara wanted out. In the fall of 1967 Johnson accepted McNamara's resignation from the Defense Department, replacing him with long-time Democratic party adviser Clark Clifford in February 1968.

Johnson tried to open negotiations with the North Vietnamese in the fall of 1967. Harvard professor Henry Kissinger secretly relayed to Hanoi, through French intermediaries, an administration promise to stop the bombing, with the understanding that the pause would lead to prompt discussions. The United States would not demand that the North remove its troops from the South, but it would trust that Hanoi would not take advantage of the hiatus to raise its troop levels. Kissinger also indicated that the United States remained firmly committed to the South Vietnamese government, now headed by President Nguyen Van Thieu. Although Washington would permit Vietcong participation in the Saigon administration, the NLF would have to drop its revolutionary program. Washington offered no guarantee that it would reduce its troop commitments or halt the ground war while talks went forward. As Kissinger secretly presented these conditions, the bombing continued, suggesting that the military did not know what the Johnson administration was attempting. Suffering from the bombing, the Hanoi government rejected these overtures and called once more for the United States to quit what it described as an "illegal" intervention in Vietnam's civil war.

With this rebuff Johnson sank further into gloom, wary of escalation but incapable of devising a satisfactory alternative. After McNamara announced his resignation, the president's advisers became more hawkish. William Bundy, Clark Clifford, Dean Rusk, Walt Rostow, and Maxwell Taylor told Johnson that he could not satisfy his domestic critics with a halt in the bombing. Doves had "insatiable appetites," Bundy explained, and they would only demand more concessions. North Vietnam, too, would view a pause in the bombing as a sign of weakness, and "to stop the bombing now would give the Communists something for nothing."

The president hoped that an optimistic assessment of the war from General Westmoreland, the supreme commander in the field, might buy time with the restless public. In November Westmoreland returned to Washington and told reporters he was "very, very encouraged" because "we are making real progress." He told Congress that the North Vietnamese and Vietcong could not hold out much longer. He thought U.S. forces had reached a point where the end of the war was in view.

While Westmoreland's rosy scenario made headlines, Johnson's civilian advisers worried about the effect of the war on domestic tranquillity and U.S. prestige abroad. Johnson assembled his so-called

Wise Men, foreign policy experts who had served various administrations since 1940, to chart a future path in Vietnam. They supported Johnson's course up until that time, but they warned that "endless inconclusive fighting" had become a "most serious cause of domestic disquiet." At the end of 1967 Johnson agreed to review the ground war to find a way to reduce American casualties and turn more of the fighting over to the ARVN.

January 1968 brought a military embarrassment elsewhere in Asia, when the U.S.S. *Pueblo*, a navy intelligence ship, was captured off the coast of North Korea. The *Pueblo* crew would remain the North Korean's captives for almost a year, until negotiations finally produced their release in December. But this incident was minor compared to what the North Vietnamese and the Vietcong had in store.

At 2:45 A.M. on January 30, 1968—on Tet, the Vietnamese New Year—a squad of nineteen Vietcong commandos blasted a hole in the wall protecting the United States embassy in Saigon, ran into the courtyard, and engaged the Marine guards there for the next six hours. All nineteen commandos were killed, but the damage they did to Washington's position in Vietnam could not be repaired. The assault on the embassy was only the most dramatic part of a coordinated offensive by North Vietnamese and NLF forces against South Vietnamese population centers over the Tet holiday. They attacked the Saigon airport, the presidential palace, and the headquarters of the ARVN's general staff. With the benefit of complete surprise, the North Vietnamese and NLF battled with the Americans and ARVN for control of thirty-six of forty-four provincial capitals, five of six major cities, and sixty-four district capitals.

In most areas the Americans and ARVN repulsed the Communists, killing perhaps 40,000 while losing 3,400 of their own. The cost to South Vietnamese civilians ran much higher, with 1 million refugees swelling the already teeming camps in two weeks. One of the most grisly scenes occurred in the old imperial capital of Hue, once noted for its serene beauty. The Vietcong succeeded in controlling the city for six weeks. By the time the battle was over and the Americans and ARVN had recaptured Hue, their bombs and artillery had left it, according to one soldier, a "shattered, stinking hulk, its street choked with rubble and rotting bodies." The ARVN uncovered a mass grave containing the bodies of 2,800 South Vietnamese officeholders who had been executed by the Vietcong.

The principal American casualty was the cheery fiction of progress in the war. After Tet, Westmoreland's recent assertion that an American victory could be achieved within two years sounded hopelessly unrealistic. His claims in the midst of the battle that the United States had defeated the enemy provoked derision. CBS News anchor Walter

Cronkite, until this point supportive of the Johnson administration, growled, "What the hell is going on? I thought we were winning the war." Cronkite publicly denounced "the optimists who have been wrong in the past." One of the most famous photographs of the war, showing the commander of the Saigon police shooting a Vietcong suspect in the head in the middle of a busy street, outraged the public at home. So did the comment of a United States Army officer who had helped wrest the village of Ben Tre from the Vietcong: "We had to destroy the town to save it."

Johnson, already discouraged by the lack of progress and by Robert McNamara's defection, grappled with Westmoreland's request for an additional 206,000 men. Failure to provide them, the general implied, meant losing the war. To Johnson, however, sending that many troops seemed a major escalation: it would risk Chinese or Soviet intervention and would shock the American public. After Tet, 78 percent of the public told a Harris poll that they thought the United States was not making progress in Vietnam, and only 26 percent approved of Johnson's handling of the war. Before he would grant Westmoreland's request, the president asked the new secretary of defense, Clark Clifford, to undertake a complete review of Vietnam policy.

Like McNamara before him, Clifford, once a hawk, now doubted whether sending more troops promised any progress. "I see more and more fighting with more and more casualties on the U.S. side and no end in sight to the action," he told the president. Civilian experts in the Defense Department revived a 1967 proposal by McNamara to change from a strategy of search and destroy to one of "population security." According to this strategy, American forces should protect the bulk of the South's civilian population while encouraging the ARVN to bear more of the burden of fighting the Communists. American casualties would probably decline, reducing public unhappiness at home, but the hope of obtaining a military victory would vanish. Clifford therefore pressed for a negotiated settlement. In early March, Johnson rejected Westmoreland's request for another 206,000 men.

Before deciding on future commitments, Johnson held another series of White House debates in mid-March. On one side stood Clifford, who now argued that the public demanded an end to the war, noting the "tremendous erosion of support" among the nation's business and legal elite. These people thought it foolish for the United States to go deeper into the "hopeless bog" of Vietnam. He pointed to European disappointment with the American preoccupation with Vietnam, evidenced by French demands for payment in gold for their dollar holdings. On the other side were Secretary of State Rusk and National Security Adviser Walt Rostow. Rusk advocated a public announcement of a partial halt to the bombing, expecting the North

William C. Westmoreland

William C. Westmoreland grew up wanting to be a soldier. Born in 1914 in a South Carolina cotton-mill town, he thrilled to stories of his ancestors' heroics during the Civil War. After attending West Point, he rose swiftly through the army ranks during the Second World War and Korea, and at age forty-two he became the army's youngest major general. In 1960 he returned to his beloved West Point as superintendent.

Greater responsibility was thrust on Westmoreland in June 1964, when President Johnson named him commander of the American forces in Vietnam. Like most successful officers who had fought in Europe during the Second World War, Westmoreland believed that American military technology could overwhelm any potential adversary; he therefore

Vietnamese to reject it. Rostow told the president to "hang in there," in the face of a restless and fickle public. He likened Johnson's position to that of Abraham Lincoln's during the darkest days of the Civil War, when the public had reviled him. As it became clear that North Vietnam and the NLF had not won the war during Tet, Rostow predicted, the public would renew its support.

Clifford persuaded the president to reconvene the Wise Men. During the last week of March they delivered some shocking opinions to the president. Dean Acheson, secretary of state under Truman, who had endured his own agony during the Korean War, asserted that the United States could "no longer do the job we set out to do in the time we have left, and we must begin to take steps to disengage." Cyrus Vance, former assistant secretary of defense, worried that "unless we do something quick, the mood in this country may lead us to withdraw."

followed a strategy of attrition, or wearing down the enemy by use of massive firepower. At first the new commander seemed a welcome relief from his ineffectual predecessor, General Paul D. Harkins. Handsome and friendly, Westmoreland got along well with the soldiers, and *Time* magazine named him Man of the Year in 1966.

But Vietnam was not Europe, and Westmoreland never grasped that the United States was engaged in a struggle that was more political than military. Over the years his faith in a military solution became less persuasive. After the Tet offensive of early 1968, his optimistic promises to Congress the previous November seemed almost foolish, and President Johnson denied his request for more troops. In June 1968 Westmoreland was recalled from Vietnam to serve as the army's chief of staff for the next four years.

After his retirement from the military he became bitter about the eventual Communist victory in Vietnam and his own falling reputation at home. Military experts derided his strategy of attrition as ill-informed and unimaginative. From 1982 to 1985 Westmoreland pressed a libel suit against CBS News for claiming that he had deliberately misled Johnson by underestimating the number of enemy soldiers. Finally he dropped the suit, and CBS stated that it had not intended to cast doubt on his truthfulness. This awkward legal battle only served to emphasize the blight Vietnam had cast on the general's career. ■

Johnson did not like what he heard, but he could no longer ignore the mounting pressure to reverse course. Working with a trusted speechwriter, he prepared an address to the nation to be broadcast the evening of March 31, 1968. In it he promised a partial bombing halt, limiting American attacks to the region immediately north of the demilitarized zone at the seventeenth parallel. He promised to halt all bombing "if our restraint is matched by restraint in Hanoi." He named Averell Harriman, one of the Wise Men, as head of an American delegation to try to open peace talks with North Vietnam. Then, in a passage he wrote himself and kept secret from everyone but his wife, he withdrew from the 1968 presidential race. In order to devote himself to the negotiations he had just promised, he pledged that "I shall not seek, and I will not accept, the nomination of my party for another term as your president."

The frustration of the apparently endless war in Vietnam nearly overwhelmed President Johnson in 1968. *Jack Kightlinger/LBJ Library Collection.*

THE ELECTION OF 1968

Lyndon Johnson had another reason for not seeking the Democratic nomination for president in 1968: he might not have received it. Anguish over the war had turned the Democrats against one another. For several years, many liberals and Kennedy insiders had stifled their misgivings about Johnson because they supported his domestic reform agenda; now, however, they revolted and looked for someone to challenge him for the nomination. Finding a candidate to run for nomination against a sitting president, even one as unpopular as Johnson, proved difficult. Robert Kennedy, now a senator from New York, refused entreaties to join the battle, fearing defeat and the perception of his campaign as a family vendetta. Senator George McGovern of South Dakota, another Senate dove, also declined. Finally, an obscure Midwestern senator, Eugene McCarthy of Minnesota, allowed himself to be drafted into running in the March 12 New Hampshire primary.

McCarthy's campaign seemed laughable at first. A retiring, self-deprecating figure torn with self-doubt, McCarthy shunned the glad-handing customary to politicians. In the early weeks of his campaign, McCarthy had few assistants, little money, and virtually no press coverage. Everything changed in February, however, as the public reeled from the shock of the Tet offensive. Thousands of college-age volunteers hurried to New Hampshire to help the campaign. McCarthy made Vietnam the issue, demanding a halt to the bombing and immediate negotiations. Johnson's supporters took the bait, running TV ads warning that "the Communists in Vietnam are watching the New Hampshire primary." Johnson denounced McCarthy as "a champion of appeasement and surrender" and predicted that he would receive less than a third of the vote. On election day McCarthy received 42.2 percent, coming within a few hundred votes of defeating Johnson; the Minnesota senator also took twenty of twenty-four delegates to the Democratic convention.

McCarthy's showing rattled the president and shook Robert Kennedy, who reconsidered his earlier refusal to run now that it appeared a challenge to Johnson might succeed. After consulting old supporters and trying unsuccessfully to persuade McCarthy to withdraw in his favor, Kennedy announced his candidacy for the Democratic nomination on March 16. Johnson's worst nightmare had come to life. As he explained to a biographer, "the thing I had feared from the first day of my presidency was actually coming true. Robert Kennedy had openly announced his intention to reclaim the throne in the memory of his brother. And the American people, swayed by the magic of the name, were dancing in the streets." Two weeks later, Johnson announced his own withdrawal from the race.

Aftershocks from Johnson's speech were still rumbling when, four days later, on April 4, James Earl Ray killed Martin Luther King, Jr., as King stood on the balcony of the Lorraine Motel in Memphis, Tennessee. The assassination ignited another spurt of black rage. Riots erupted in more than a hundred cities; within a week, police, the army, and the National Guard had killed thirty-seven people. Several blocks of downtown Washington were burned and looted. In Chicago, Mayor Richard J. Daley ordered his police to "shoot to kill arsonists, and shoot to maim looters." Spiro T. Agnew, Republican governor of Maryland (elected in 1966 as a moderate on racial matters) summoned the leaders of his state's NAACP and Urban League chapters to Annapolis and warned them that he held them personally responsible for the devastation of Baltimore.

Two months later, Robert Kennedy met an assassin's bullet. Early in the morning of Wednesday, June 6, hours after he had eked out a narrow victory over Eugene McCarthy in the California primary, Kennedy was shot by Sirhan Sirhan, a Palestinian immigrant angry at the New York senator's support for Israel. Once more the country suffered through a funeral for one of the Kennedy brothers: a Requiem mass in New York's St. Patrick's Cathedral, followed by a sad train ride south to Washington. Hundreds of thousands of mourners lined the tracks under a blazing sun. One senator on the train recalled that as he looked into their faces, "I saw sorrow, bewilderment. I saw fury and I saw fright." Robert Kennedy was buried next to his brother John in Arlington National Cemetery.

With Kennedy dead, McCarthy continued as the standard-bearer for the antiwar Democrats, who hoped to deny the nomination to Vice President Hubert Humphrey, who was supported by the prowar faction. Nevertheless, Humphrey gained the nomination at the tumultuous Chicago convention in August. Inside the hall the McCarthy forces, joined by Kennedy supporters, now backing George McGovern, lost a narrow vote on a "peace plank" in the platform, repudiating the Johnson administration's handling of the Vietnam War. Humphrey won the nomination by a two-to-one margin. On that same sultry night, the Chicago police force went mad, clubbing and tear-gassing a crowd of ten thousand demonstrators who had come to the city to protest the war. The police chased demonstrators into McCarthy's suite in a downtown hotel, beating several of them bloody and unconscious. Television cameras caught it all, including the protesters' chant, "The whole world is watching."

After this chaos, the Democratic nomination appeared worthless for Humphrey. Polls put him sixteen percentage points behind the Republican nominee, former vice president Richard Nixon. After losing a 1962 race for governor of California, Nixon had resurrected his political career by traveling the country, supporting local Republican candidates. A third candidate also ran, Alabama governor George Wallace, who had broken with the Democrats over civil rights. Some polls showed Wallace gaining 20 percent of the vote, much of it from formerly Democratic, working-class whites, largely but not exclusively in the South.

Both Nixon and Wallace fed public disgust with Vietnam. The Republican nominee, a hawk when escalation began in 1965, condemned the present stalemate. While presenting no specific way to end the war, Nixon promised an early "peace with honor" and hinted at a plan to reduce U.S. participation. Nixon also pursued a "southern strategy" of seeking the votes of southern white Democrats enraged at blacks. Promising to restore respect for law and order, he decried the race riots Johnson and Humphrey had not been able to stop. His running mate, Spiro Agnew, helped this cause by recalling the angry lecture he delivered to African-American leaders after the April riots in Baltimore and on Maryland's eastern shore. Wallace intimated that he could end the war faster than Humphrey. He named retired air force general Curtis LeMay, an undisguised hawk, as his running mate, hoping to capitalize on nationalistic feelings. But LeMay's inflammatory remark that he would "bomb North Vietnam into the Stone Age" alarmed voters, and Wallace's campaign began to fade in late September.

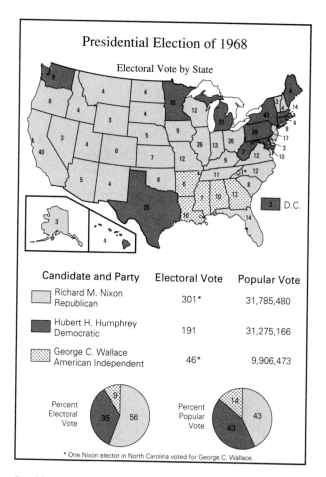

Presidential Election of 1968

Electoral Vote by State

Candidate and Party	Electoral Vote	Popular Vote
Richard M. Nixon Republican	301*	31,785,480
Hubert H. Humphrey Democratic	191	31,275,166
George C. Wallace American Independent	46*	9,906,473

Percent Electoral Vote: 9, 35, 56

Percent Popular Vote: 14, 43, 43

* One Nixon elector in North Carolina voted for George C. Wallace.

Presidential Election of 1968

Humphrey's campaign languished for six weeks after the Democratic convention. Liberals wanted nothing to do with him, even as he ran against Nixon, their old adversary. Johnson refused to release Humphrey from the political obligation to support the administration's Vietnam policy. Desperate for a way to distance himself from the stalemate in Vietnam, Humphrey announced on September 30 that he favored a total halt to the bombing "as an acceptable risk for peace, because I believe that it could lead to a success in negotiations and a shorter war." Suddenly Humphrey began to close the gap with Nixon, as many antiwar Democrats decided they preferred him to a man they despised.

Talks in Paris between the United States, North Vietnam, South Vietnam, and the NLF began in the summer, but stalled over the issue of who could participate. The delegations wrangled for months over this minor issue, and the seemingly endless talks about the talks came to symbolize in the public's mind their frustration with the interminable war. The North Vietnamese refused to grant the Saigon government a separate place at the table, and the United States denied recognition to the NLF. The conversations finally progressed in the days before the November election, since the Communist side preferred a Humphrey victory to a win by the more hawkish Nixon. The Nixon camp worried that a breakthrough in the Paris talks might give the election to Humphrey. Henry Kissinger informed the Nixon campaign that Johnson was preparing an "October surprise" to move the negotiations forward, thereby boosting Humphrey's chances. Anna Chennault, a conservative supporter of President Thieu who was in Nixon's employ, encouraged Thieu to resist reaching an agreement until after the American election, in the hope of aiding Nixon. Nonetheless, the weekend before the election Johnson announced a total bombing halt, along the lines Humphrey had promised. Serious discussions on ending the war were scheduled to begin immediately after election day, on November 5.

Nixon won by a scant 510,000 votes, taking only 43.6 percent of the vote (see map, page 291). Humphrey drew 42.9 percent, and Wallace got 13.5 percent. Humphrey's supporters believed that, given another four days, he would have won, because he had made up 7 percentage points in the polls in the five days before the election. That may have been wishful thinking: the drop in the Democratic portion of the vote from the 1964 election, when Johnson took nearly 61 percent, represented a striking decline. Nearly all of the 57 percent of the public who voted for Nixon or Wallace disagreed with Johnson's handling of the war in Vietnam, as did many of those who backed Humphrey.

The story of the events in Vietnam resumes in Chapter 9. Although Nixon took office with an apparent mandate for change, American troops continued to fight in Vietnam for another four years.

CONCLUSION

By the time of the 1968 election, most Americans wanted to end the Vietnam War, though they still disagreed about how. American involvement began quietly under President Truman and was gradually increased by Presidents Eisenhower and Kennedy. Lyndon Johnson took the fateful step of committing the United States to a massive air and ground war. Yet the more the United States contributed to the war effort, the more the corrupt government of South Vietnam grew dependent on American support. The result was a cycle of continual frustration.

The war devastated Vietnam—its land, its people, its society. It also proved tragic for many of the Americans who fought there. By the end of 1968, the war had already cost about thirty-seven thousand American lives, a number that would rise to over fifty-eight thousand by the time the United States withdrew its forces in 1973. And a significant number of American troops who returned physically unscathed suffered long-term psychological and emotional disabilities. Most believed their efforts in Vietnam had been futile and were unappreciated at home. The veterans' plight contributed to the overall feeling that the nation's public institutions had failed.

At home, disagreement over the war shattered the general consensus about the proper goals of American foreign policy. Opposition became widespread and bitter, ruining Johnson's chance for re-election in 1968 and throwing the Democratic party into turmoil. Because the war raised doubts about the power of American weapons and technology to mold events around the world, some Americans even began to question the basic doctrine of containment that had guided U.S. foreign policy since the late 1940s.

By dividing the American public, the Vietnam War also opened the deep chasms in American society that were the principal legacy of the 1960s. Chapter 8 describes how opposition to the war merged with other political and social movements to form a full-scale culture of protest. Many people became fundamentally disillusioned with American government and society. They distrusted not only the politicians in Washington, but all other forms of authority as well, and their rebellion stimulated an equally strong conservative backlash. ■

FURTHER READING

For overviews of the Vietnam War, see: William Duiker, *U.S. Containment Policy and the Conflict in Indochina* (1994); George C. Herring, *America's Longest War: The United States and Vietnam, 1950–1975* (1986); Stanley Karnow, *Vietnam: A History* (1983); Robert J. MacMahon, ed., *Major Problems in the History of the Vietnam War* (1994); Marilyn B. Young, *The Vietnam Wars* (1990). On the politics and diplomacy of the war, see: William C. Gibbons, *The U.S. Government and the Vietnam War,* (4 vol., 1986–1994); John M. Newman, *JFK and Vietnam* (1991); Robert S. McNamara with Brian VanDeMark, *In Retrospect: The Tragedy and Lessons of Vietnam* (1995); George M. Kahin, *Intervention: How America Became Involved in Vietnam* (1986); Larry Berman, *Planning a Tragedy* (1983) and *Lyndon Johnson's War* (1989); Clark Clifford, *Counsel to the President* (1991); George Herring, *LBJ and Vietnam* (1994); Brian VanDeMark, *Into the Quagmire: Lyndon Johnson and the Escalation of the Vietnam War* (1991). On fighting the war, see: Mark Clodfelter, *The Limits of Air Power* (1989); Neil Sheehan, *A Bright Shining Lie: John Paul Vann and America in Vietnam* (1988); Andrew

Krepenevich, *The Army and Vietnam* (1989); Peter G. McDonald, *Giap: The Victor in Vietnam* (1993); Wallace Berry, *Bloods: An Oral History of the War by Black Veterans* (1984); Mark Baker, *Nam* (1982); Don Oberdorfer, *Tet* (1979); Ronald Spector, *After Tet: The Bloodiest Year of the Vietnam War* (1993). On the home front during the war, see: Christian Appy, *Working Class War: American Combat Soldiers and Vietnam* (1993); Lawrence Baskir and William Strauss, *Chance and Circumstance: The War, the Draft and the Vietnam Generation* (1978); Myra MacPherson, *Long Time Passing: Vietnam and the Haunted Generation* (1984); Charles DeBenedetti, with Charles Chatfield, *An American Ordeal: The Antiwar Movement of the Vietnam Era* (1990); Melvin Small and William C. Hoover, eds, *Give Peace a Chance: Exploring the Vietnam Antiwar Movement* (1992); Tom Wells, *The War Within: America's Battle Over Vietnam* (1994); Nancy Zaroulis and Gerald Sullivan, *Who Spoke Up? American Protest Against the War in Vietnam, 1963–1975* (1984). On the political upheavals of 1968 (in addition to the discussion in Chapter 8) see: Lewis Chester, Godfrey Hodgson, and Bruce Paige, *An American Melodrama* (1970); James Miller, *"Democracy Is in the Streets"* (1987); Todd Gitlin, *The Sixties* (1987); David Farber, *Chicago '68* (1988); David Caute, *The Year of the Barricades* (1988).

8

The Politics and
Culture of Protest

Pandora's Box, a purple-painted music palace, was a Hollywood institution in 1965. The hip youth of Los Angeles flocked to the Sunset Strip nightclub to hear their favorite rock-'n'-roll bands, party madly, and see and be seen. When civic authorities decided the club had to be torn down to make way for a wider road and a three-way traffic light, Pandora's patrons held a sit-in in the middle of the Sunset Strip. "I felt like I *belonged*," wrote one teenage protester, "united with a thousand other kids, protesting what THEY were doing to US." Pop singers Sonny and Cher, clad in matching polka dot bell-bottom pants and fake-fur vests, wrapped their arms around each other. Some of the demonstrators held hands and beamed at one another in the moonlight. Others overturned a bus. The Los Angeles Police Department arrived, clubs swinging and sirens blaring. The next morning, the riot on Sunset Strip was front-page news. Songwriter-guitarist Stephen Stills, a member of the popular rock band Buffalo Springfield, found the whole scene deeply puzzling, and he recommended caution. "Something happenin' here," he wrote. "What it is ain't exactly clear. . . . We got to stop, children / What's that sound? / Everybody look, what's goin' down."

The Sunset Strip riot embodied the volatile political and cultural energies of the 1960s and early 1970s, a period that is often loosely referred to as "the sixties." By 1965 the spirit of protest had spread from young blacks unwilling to tolerate the slow pace of racial progress to young whites angry at government policies and sick of the bland pleasures middle-class life offered. Some in the baby-boom generation—those who made up the surge in the national birth rate that began in 1944—followed slightly older dissidents into the civil rights and peace crusades of the early 1960s. Some joined more radical movements, like Black Power and the Weathermen, a few concluding that only violent revolution could bring the necessary changes. Others sought to extend the boundaries of acceptable everyday behavior, sampling the psychological challenges, sensual pleasures, and physical risks of the emerging "counterculture." Many joined women's liberation groups, linking the personal and the political. Their political activism was sometimes enhanced, sometimes enfeebled by the cultural forms they created, as they gloried in sexual expressiveness, musical innovation, and pharmaceutical experimentation.

What people in the sixties would call the "generation gap"—the alienation of the young from the strategies and aspirations of their elders—had been brewing for some time. Among the "baby deficit" generation, born in the 1930s and 1940s, signs of discontent emerged in the 1950s. The pop culture antiheroes of that decade, from the brooding, doomed James Dean in *Rebel Without a Cause* to the lip-curling Marlon Brando in *The Wild Ones*, had shown adult America the face of restless youth. "I mean, how do you know what you're going to do till you *do* it?" asked Holden Caulfield, the touching adolescent protagonist of *The Catcher in the Rye*, J. D. Salinger's 1951 anthem for the newborn generation. "The answer is, you don't." Middle-class American parents in the fifties had planned ahead. They knew the price of affluence and were willing to sacrifice and save. Their children took material comfort for granted, but they wondered why so many Americans had to live in poverty. Relieved of the burden of financial worry by the growing American economy of the 1960s, the baby-boomers looked to expand the boundaries of peace, justice, and spirituality, as part of their quest for an ever-better good time.

By the mid-1960s, psychologists and sociologists had documented a growing alienation among America's young. Paul Goodman's *Growing Up Absurd*, Kenneth Keniston's *The Uncommitted*, and Philip Slater's *The Pursuit of Loneliness* depicted a generation at loose ends, disconnected from meaningful relations with other people, and lacking a sense of social purpose. Social critics and therapists alike wondered where this vast, free-floating constituency might end up. They wondered whether it would drag society down with its lethargy, lose itself in narcissism, or find something meaningful to do.

If even the children of privilege felt distant from the American dream, others had more reason to feel disaffected and to raise their voices in increasingly angry protest. African-American writer Richard Wright had sounded a note of black rage as early as 1940, with his novel *Native Son*. In the 1960s other black writers, from Black Panther leader Eldridge Cleaver to poet June Jordan, took up Wright's legacy. From rock singer Janis Joplin to the activists of the women's liberation movement, women too began to find words to defy the restrictions society placed on them. From these very diverse threads, the sixties wove a new politics and culture of protest.

FROM CIVIL RIGHTS TO BLACK POWER

For some fifty years, the National Association for the Advancement of Colored People (NAACP) and the Urban League, under the leadership of careful men like Roy Wilkins and Whitney Young, had led the African-American campaign for civil rights. They believed their cause was consistent with democratic and Christian principles, and they saw their movement as instrumental to realizing the promise of American life. They used a variety of methods. The NAACP and the Urban League concentrated on legal and judicial reforms. Others, particularly A. Philip Randolph of the Brotherhood of Sleeping Car Porters, encouraged public demonstrations against segregation. By the early 1960s, sit-ins, boycotts, and protest marches had become widespread. But the decade would soon see the emergence of more radical approaches.

By 1964, the civil rights movement had begun to focus on community organization and voter registration as primary tactics in the fight against racism. These methods were used primarily in the South, where racial segregation and hatred were particularly open and entrenched. Rank-and-file civil rights workers in organizations like the Congress of Racial Equality (CORE), founded in 1942, the Southern Christian Leadership Conference (SCLC), begun in 1957, and the Student Non-Violent Coordinating Committee (SNCC), founded at an SCLC conference in 1960, faced potential and actual white violence on a daily basis.

Black Mississippian Anne Moody joined first the NAACP, then the SNCC, knowing that doing so entailed grave risks both to herself and to her loved ones. One friend had been shot in the back because white townspeople suspected him of belonging to the NAACP; a local clergyman and his family had been run out of town because he had mentioned the NAACP in a sermon. While organizing blacks in the small towns of Mississippi, Moody learned to live with fear. Her uncle and three others were murdered in Woodville, Mississippi, in a campaign of what SNCC leader Robert Moses identified as "terror killings." Those who dared to speak out against the murders became targets themselves; when they asked federal authorities for protection, they were told, "We can't protect every individual Negro in Mississippi." Again and again, FBI and Justice Department officials stood by while demonstrators were beaten and illegally jailed. "I guess mostly the SNCC workers were just lucky," Moody wrote in her autobiography, *Coming of Age in Mississippi*. "Most of them had missed a bullet by an inch or so on many occasions. Threats didn't stop them. They just kept going all the time."

While Congress debated the Civil Rights Act of 1964, the SCLC's Martin Luther King, Jr., courted a national television audience, combining restraint and eloquence with the use of nonviolent boycotts, sit-ins, and demonstrations. A "conservative militant," King was a pivotal figure in the civil rights movement. He retained the support of white liberals, who provided much of the movement's financial backing, while trying to maintain ties with the increasingly frustrated younger African-Americans who staffed the front-line positions in the battle. King confronted white violence with dignity, leading peaceful protest marches against segregation and injustice. He dazzled the nation with his "I Have a Dream" speech at the massive 1963 March on Washington. Rank-and-file organizers, however, found King aloof and abstract, and referred to him sarcastically as "De Lawd."

During the summer of 1964, many black and white students spent their college vacations in Mississippi, where white resistance to integration was deep and militant. These student activists sought to break the white monopoly on political power in the South by using weapons dear to the American political system: voters. The Mississippi Freedom Summer Project, organized by the SNCC-affiliated Council of Federated Organizations, attracted more than a thousand students from the North, mostly white, to join veteran black and white southern workers in a campaign to register African-American voters for the newly-created, racially integrated Mississippi Freedom Democratic Party (MFDP). Volunteers also walked picket lines, attended innumerable meetings, and organized "freedom schools" at community centers to teach remedial reading, government, humanities, and other academic and vocational subjects.

The Mississippi state legislature reacted to the challenge by doubling the state police force, authorizing local authorities to pool their personnel and equipment for riot control purposes, and introducing an anti-invasion bill intended to keep civil rights workers out of the state. White vigilante groups mounted a campaign of intimidation ranging from harassment to bombings and killings. In June, civil rights workers Andrew Goodman, Michael Schwerner, and James Chaney—two northern whites and a southern black—were murdered. Yet the volunteers kept coming, sleeping in shifts on bare mattresses, living on peanut butter, cranking mimeograph machines, and tramping the hot streets. Sustained by idealism, SNCC workers wanted not only to end segregation and political repression, but also to oppose the fury of white hatred by living out their own vision of a racially integrated "beloved community" based on respect, affection, and a shared commitment to social justice. To one young white SNCC volunteer, African-American women like Fanny Lou Hamer, Ella Baker, and Ruby Doris Smith Robinson and men like the soft-spoken Bob Moses seemed "wise, caring, courageous, honest, and full of love." Blacks living under the burden of racism inspired younger white college students from the North with their bravery and their tirelessness.

The beloved community was, however, riddled with tension. Living in fear of "nightriders," who fired shots through their windows and telephoned bomb threats, civil rights workers also had to cope with racial friction within their own ranks. Long-time black workers worried that whites were trying to take over the movement without facing the risks blacks encountered daily. Interracial sexual relations caused conflict between black and white women and between women and men.

SNCC succeeded in mobilizing enough voters to enable the MFDP to mount a challenge to the all-white delegation the regular state party sent to the 1964 Democratic national convention in Atlantic City. MFDP delegation leader Fanny Lou Hamer electrified a national television audience as she testified before the party's Credentials Committee that she had been denied the right to vote and had been jailed and beaten in attempting to exercise that right. "We are askin' the American people," she said, "is *this* the land of the free and the home of the brave?" The MFDP demanded that its delegation be seated in place of the official state delegation. White liberals like Senator Hubert Humphrey of Minnesota and southern conservatives in the party leadership worked out what they termed a compromise: the white delegation was seated, after promising not to bolt the Democratic party later on, and two MFDP representatives received delegate-at-large status. To those who had put their bodies on the line all summer, this "compromise" seemed a betrayal, a triumph of expediency over morality. Two disillusioned African-American activists, Stokely Carmichael and Charles Hamilton, wrote that the lesson of Atlantic City was clear: "Black people . . . could not rely on their so-called allies."

By the time of the Atlantic City convention, African-Americans throughout the country were revealing their frustration at the limited success of nonviolent tactics. Martin Luther King, Jr., framed his endorsement of civil disobedience in the language and spirit of Christian forbearance: "One who breaks an unjust law must do so openly, lovingly, and with a willingness to accept the penalty." However, the black Christian churches King represented, which for a decade had emphasized the necessity of taking the moral high ground, were losing influence with their congregations. After a church bombing killed a group of Sunday school children, Anne Moody told her God,

You know, I used to go to Sunday school when I was a little girl. . . . We were taught how merciful and forgiving you are. I bet those girls in Sunday school were being taught the same as I was when I was their age. Is that teaching wrong? Are you going to forgive their killers? . . . Nonviolence is out. I have a good idea Martin Luther King is talking to you, too. If he is, tell him that nonviolence has served its purpose.

Black civil rights workers had learned through experience that white lawlessness seldom brought penalties. Even King was aware that activists' patience was wearing thin. If nonviolent civil disobedience failed to gain justice, King warned, "millions of Negroes will, out of frustration and despair, seek solace and security in black nationalist ideologies."

King's expectations were fulfilled. Many blacks began to reject Christian forbearance altogether. Some sought new meaning in a black separatist Islamic faith. Malcolm X, the nation's most prominent and eloquent Black Muslim (see pages 240–241), spoke out for black nationalism, explicitly rejected integration, and advocated meeting violence with violence. Rioting broke out in Harlem in the summer of 1964.

After the Democratic convention, the ranks of the SNCC split. One faction, which included black and white southerners and middle-class white college students, believed in participatory democracy and decision-making by consensus. The other group, dominated by long-time field organizers like James Forman and Ruby Doris Smith Robinson, wanted to move away from a focus on moral and procedural issues to questions of power. Bitterly disillusioned with the fickleness of their white allies, they argued that SNCC should be black-led and black-dominated.

By the early months of 1965, the concept of "black and white together" in the civil rights movement was becoming eclipsed. Malcolm X had begun to tone down his antiwhite message and to seek some new solutions to the problem of racism. But he was gunned down in February, allegedly murdered by less conciliatory followers of Black Muslim leader Elijah Muhammad. His death, ironically, convinced some African-American activists that power came only from the barrel of a gun. Other civil rights leaders persisted in trying to channel the movement's energies into coordinated, nonviolent action, but their protests seemed inadequate in the face of white brutality. In March a national television audience watched as Selma, Alabama, sheriff Jim Clark ordered his men to meet civil rights marchers with clubs and tear gas. Martin Luther King, Jr., and Ralph Bunche led a group of 3,200 people on a fifty-mile march from Selma to the heavily fortified state capitol at Montgomery, where they were joined by 25,000 supporters. In the course of the Selma campaign, three activists were killed. Many Americans were struck by the contrast between the violence of the Selma police and the peaceful nature of the march. The Voter Registration Act of 1965, signed in early August, passed partly as a result of the Selma march and of President Johnson's revulsion at the accompanying white violence. But the costs of pursuing peaceful tactics were becoming unbearable to movement veterans.

Around the nation, African-Americans responded to the slow pace of change with increasing fury. In August 1965, five days of looting and rioting broke out in Watts, a black ghetto in Los Angeles. Residents of Watts had reason to be frustrated: although Los Angeles as a whole was booming, blacks in the area were worse off than before. Median income in the area had dropped 8 percent between 1959 and 1965. Many complained that the white-controlled businesses in Watts jacked up their prices and paid low wages to black employees. Thirty percent of adult men in Watts were unemployed, and of those who did hold jobs, many lacked the cars necessary to navigate the nation's preeminent car-culture city. Los Angeles police, mostly white and sometimes openly racist, did little to win this community's trust. By the time the rioting subsided, thirty-four people had died, four thousand had been arrested, and much of the area had been leveled. The Los Angeles police chief blamed civil rights workers; the mayor blamed Communists. From the ashes arose a cry of despair that would fuel the revolutionary rhetoric of the Black Power movement and, in turn, the white backlash against African-American rights: "Burn, baby, burn." In Los Angeles, a race war seemed a real possibility.

On a march through Mississippi in the summer of 1966, the message crystallized. Those who still supported the goal of integration and the tactics of nonviolence, like Floyd McKissick of CORE and John Lewis, former chairman of SNCC, looked on as Stokely Carmichael, bringing news of the founding of the Black Panther party in Lowndes County, Alabama, announced a new goal—Black Power. To his African-American listeners he declared, "It's time we stand up and take over." To society at large he issued a warning: "Move on over or we'll move on over you."

Within a year, weary veterans of the civil rights movement had been displaced in the public eye by young militants. The SNCC became the organizing center of the Black Power movement. Carmichael and the new SNCC chairman, H. Rap Brown, viewed the increasingly common ghetto disturbances as a dress rehearsal for revolution. Meanwhile, the federal government offered only a weak response to urban rioting. President Johnson appointed Illinois governor Otto Kerner to head a commission to study the situation. When the Kerner Commission delivered a report concluding that the United States was shot through with racism and was rapidly becoming two nations—one black and poor, the other white and rich—Johnson did nothing. He was too preoccupied with the Vietnam War to pursue his promised Great Society.

Urging students at black colleges to "fight for liberation by any means necessary," Carmichael declared, "to hell with the laws of the United States." At a Black Power conference in Newark, held on the heels of a riot in which police killed twenty-five African-Americans, a thousand participants approved resolutions affirming black people's right to revolt and calling for a separate black nation and black militia. In 1968, Carmichael, Brown, and SNCC were replaced by the Black Panthers as the most visible militant group. Wearing leather jackets and carrying weapons, the Panthers often resembled an elite paramilitary unit. They aimed their radical rhetoric at the American capitalist system. During the next few years, as the Panthers provoked considerable uneasiness among the white middle class, they became the objects of heavy surveillance by the FBI. They had frequent confrontations with police, including shoot-outs that left some Panthers dead and others under arrest.

THE SDS AND THE RISE OF THE NEW LEFT

As African-American groups became more militant, so did other, predominantly white organizations that arose to challenge the structure of American politics and society. Collectively these groups came to be called the New Left, to distinguish them from the Old Left of the 1930s to 1950s.

The Old Left—liberal activists, socialists, and others who advocated fundamental changes—had run aground during the 1950s on the issue of communism. Partly to protect themselves against charges of communist sympathies, and partly from genuine abhorrence at Stalin's murderous tactics, liberals in groups like the Americans for Democratic Action had joined reactionaries like Senator Joseph McCarthy in trying to purge the nation of Communists. Most younger activists of the 1960s criticized this obsession with Soviet communism as irrelevant to the task of building progressive politics in the United States.

In contrast to the liberals and radicals of the fifties, who lived in the shadow of the Holocaust and Stalinism, those who came of age in the early sixties were the beneficiaries of the new American affluence and the huge postwar expansion of the nation's colleges and universities. Between 1945 and 1965, public spending on higher education rose from $742.1 million to $6.9 billion per year. University life provided the chance for a small but growing group of students to imagine things as they ought to be, rather than as they are. Many students became serious social critics. Among their mentors were radical sociologist C. Wright Mills and political theorist Herbert Marcuse. Uneasy in the presence of the world's growing atomic arsenal and ignited by the civil rights movement, they were less wedded to older allegiances than their Old Left predecessors and more optimistic about the prospects for sweeping social change.

Some of those who came of age in the early sixties founded the most influential and best-known New Left group, Students for a Democratic Society (SDS). At a 1962 SDS meeting in Port Huron, Michigan, Tom Hayden, one of the organization's early leaders, articulated its concerns and goals in his famous "Port Huron Statement." Beginning with his "Agenda for a Generation," Hayden declared that "We are the people of this generation, bred in at least modest comfort, housed now in universities, looking uncomfortably to the world we inherit." He went on to criticize college students' apathy toward politics and to deplore collegiate complacency. The country's widespread poverty and the unchallenged power of what Eisenhower had called the military-industrial complex threatened the nation's best traditions. Hayden called for a restoration of participatory democracy, to make political parties, corporations, and the government more responsive to ordinary people. "America," said Hayden, "should concentrate on its genuine social priorities: abolish squalor, terminate neglect, and establish an environment for people to live in with dignity and creativeness."

Embracing Hayden's hopeful message, white students flocked into civil rights work in the early 1960s. Some SDS members went south. Others, in 1964, set up the group's Economic Research and Action Project in northern ghettos, attempting to organize an interracial movement of the poor focused on issues such as jobs and community control of social programs.

Soon this involvement in the civil rights movement propelled student activists into taking up other issues in new places. Mario Savio and Jack Weinberg, two veterans of the Mississippi Freedom Summer, returned to the University of California at Berkeley in the fall of 1964 to continue recruitment for the movement. When campus authorities forbade their efforts, the Berkeley Free Speech Movement brought active radicalism on campus. Students took over the administration building, declared a strike, and enlisted faculty support for the removal of restrictions on free expression on campus. Free Speech Movement activists expressed both their joy and their anger in words once thought inadmissible in polite company, and conservative Americans began to see in Berkeley an outpost of lawlessness and libertinism. By 1966 California gubernatorial candidate Ronald Reagan was telling campaign audiences that campus activists indulged in "orgies so vile I cannot describe them to you."

Campus protests quickly spread. By 1965 there had been disturbances at Yale, Ohio State, the University of Kansas, Brooklyn College, Michigan State, and St. John's University. Campus disputes often arose over issues of personal conduct rather than national politics. College students of the fifties had accepted the time-honored doctrine of *in loco parentis*, according to which the institution had the right and the obligation to stand in for parents and regulate students' behavior. But by the mid-1960s, many campus regulations—particularly those attempting to preserve the conservative mating and dating rituals of the fifties—seemed quaint, artificial, and restrictive. Students began to oppose all kinds of limitations on their behavior, from dress codes and antismoking regulations to rules governing where they could live, what hours they could be out, and who could visit their rooms. Students at single-sex institutions agitated for coeducation. Returning from summers spent in loosely structured, sexually volatile communal households where they worked for the SNCC or the SDS, women and men students alike chafed at campus rules.

Even without these lifestyle issues, national politics provided more than enough cause for dissent, particularly as President Johnson escalated the war in Vietnam. As nightly news broadcasts brought television audiences graphic proof of the bloodiness and futility of the nation's foreign policy, official government pronouncements about the prospects for peace seemed patently false. Berkeley's Jack Weinberg admonished his fellow students not to trust anyone over thirty, and free-thinking American journalists began to believe there was no point in trusting *anyone* in power. On campuses, in cities, and on military bases, "underground" newspapers sprang up to offer a more radical alternative to conventional news sources. These papers penetrated the government's bureaucratic jargon and exposed its attempts to mislead the public. The language of the alternative press was itself sometimes so obscene or so riddled with Marxist jargon that it presented its own interpretation problems. Still, radical journalists' seeming paranoia about government surveillance was justified; the underground media were extensively infiltrated by government provocateurs, and undercover CIA agents joined the National Student Association in big numbers.

Even the mainstream press began to mistrust the information released by official sources. Investigative reporters like Seymour Hersh of the *New York Times* began to look beyond government press releases to get at the truth of national policy. Jeopardizing his sources in the military, Hersh broke the story of the My Lai massacre in Vietnam. Hersh and other journalists were willing to accept the professional risks inherent in upsetting the previously cozy relationship between reporters and their sources. As a result, they managed to uncover many important stories that government officials had attempted to suppress.

The Vietnam War soon became the main focus of student protest. Because students—male students, at least—were directly threatened by the draft, they represented a huge new constituency for the protest effort. When the SDS endorsed draft resistance, its membership swelled. Draft-counseling centers sprang up across the country. Women joined the protests in support of their male friends. Some movement members even tried to make resistance sexy; according to one slogan that appeared on protest signs, "Girls say yes to guys who say no." And by the late 1960s, many parents of draft-age men had changed their views on Vietnam as well.

In the spirit of participatory democracy, local SDS chapters and other draft-resistance groups tried a variety of tactics. Some initiated draft-card burnings. Others held sit-ins at Selective Service induction centers, opposed university Reserve Officers' Training Corps (ROTC) programs, protested military recruiters' visits to campus, or demonstrated against corporations involved in defense work. Dow Chemical, the manufacturer of napalm, became a particularly hated target. According to the National Student Association, between January 1 and June 15, 1968, there were 221 major antiwar demonstrations at 101 colleges and universities, involving some forty thousand students.

Across the country, college professors and even high school teachers initiated "teach-ins" to educate curious students about Vietnamese history and politics. There were notable efforts to join student groups with other organizations to orchestrate nationwide protests against the war. In the summer of 1967, twenty thousand people participated in the Vietnam Summer, an effort modeled on the Mississippi Freedom Summer and mounted by a coalition of pacifists, liberals, and radicals to mobilize the middle class against the war. Stop the Draft Week, from October 16 to 21, 1967, culminated in a march on the Pentagon. Fifty thousand people crossed the Arlington Memorial Bridge, some to picket, some to pray, others to attempt to storm the bastion of the military-industrial complex. The march was brilliantly (if egocentrically) recounted in Norman Mailer's *Armies of the Night,* a prime example of the "New Journalism," which used the narrative conventions of fiction to probe beneath the surface of real-world events. The march included not only students, but also representatives of many other groups ranged against the war. Among those present were Berkeley Free Speech activist Jerry Rubin, child-care expert Dr. Benjamin Spock, linguistics theorist Noam Chomsky, poet Robert Lowell, social philosopher Paul Goodman, and Dagmar Wilson of Women's Strike for Peace. The coalition even had its comic aspects: Ed Sanders, leader of a rock band called the Fugs, proposed a "grope for peace"; Sanders and radical leader Abbie Hoffman coordinated an attempt to levitate the Pentagon.

Sociologist Todd Gitlin, an early president of the SDS, noted that as the war became more militant, so too did the antiwar movement. Antiwar demonstrators had often tried to contrast their own peace-loving demeanor with the government's policy of violence, carrying signs reading "Make Love, Not War" and putting flowers in the barrels of the guns pointed at them by police and National Guardsmen at demonstrations. By 1967, however, antiwar activists were preaching a harder line, and demonstrators began adopting a tougher posture. In Oakland, California, protests during Stop the Draft Week turned into bloody confrontations with the police.

The SDS, its membership swelling, moved beyond the goals articulated at Port Huron, adopting the slogan "From Protest to Resistance." By 1967, SDS publications had begun referring to the authorities as "pigs." Insisting that the cause of justice in Vietnam—which they identified quite simply with the Vietcong and the North Viet-

Columbia University students occupy a professor's office in April 1968.
UPI/Bettmann Archive.

namese—could not get a fair hearing in the United States, some New Leftists declared free speech a sham and shouted down progovernment speakers. National Liberation Front flags began to appear at antiwar rallies, alienating many middle-of-the-road Americans. SDS leader Bernardine Dohrn wanted to bring the war home, to make the American people feel Vietnam's torment; such revolutionary tactics confused and angered many Americans, including many who opposed the war. Many sympathized with the radicals' demands, but found it hard to accept tactics that included violating property rights.

Nowhere was campus conflict more spectacular than at Columbia University in New York. Columbia embodied all that campus radicals condemned. A bastion of Ivy League privilege in the middle of the ghetto, the university was both a Harlem landlord and a holder of major defense research contracts. On April 23, 1968, the Columbia SDS chapter joined with black militants in taking over university buildings, including the president's office. Columbia students held the buildings for eight days, after which New York City police moved in with billy clubs. They arrested 692 people, three-quarters of them students. Though the siege was over, a student strike forced the university to close early for the year. The stage was set for violent confrontations between students and authorities on campuses across the nation in the next two years.

The American student protests were part of an international drive toward student militancy. The Columbia uprising had its counterpart in Paris, where angry protesters erected barricades in the streets and battled police. But not all students—and certainly not all young people—joined the protests. Some opposed only the war and the draft; some sympathized but stayed out of the streets. Many young people—political conservatives, white southerners, working-class youths who did not go to college, graduate students who had invested time and money in pursuit of professional careers—were either unaffected by the protests or opposed to them. Nevertheless, campus conflicts revealed a deep gulf between the "straight" social standards of the older generation and the beliefs of most of those who came of age in the sixties.

THE COUNTERCULTURE

At the same time that young people were becoming more radical in their political beliefs, they also began to experiment with new ways of living, inspired in many cases by the Beat writers of the 1950s. "The only ones for me," author Jack Kerouac wrote in his 1957 novel, *On the Road*, "are the mad ones, the ones who are mad to live, mad to talk, mad to be saved, desirous of everything at the same time, the ones who never yawn or say a commonplace thing, but burn, burn, burn like fabulous yellow roman candles." Along with other Beat writers, Kerouac came to symbolize the rejection of bourgeois comfort and the embrace of a life of sensation-seeking, adventure, and personal authenticity. The Beats also represented a male revolt against the middle-class family and the traditional masculine role of breadwinner. Going on drinking sprees, careening around the country, and embracing freewheeling sexuality, the Beats distanced themselves from the fifties family man in his gray flannel suits.

Some of the Beat literati, notably poet Allen Ginsberg, became political activists in the sixties. Others, like Kerouac, rejected politics as corrupt. All were involved in a protest against mainstream American culture. While "squares" pursued the American dream in suburban comfort—drinking martinis, listening to "Hit Parade" on TV, raising their kids, and fooling around only if they wouldn't get caught—the Beats, or "Hipsters," lived by another set of standards. They lived in bare apartments in urban enclaves like New York's Greenwich Village and San Francisco's North Beach, expanded the range of recreational drugs from sweet wine to marijuana and heroin, and listened to the incendiary, experimental jazz of Charlie "Yardbird" Parker, Dizzy Gillespie, and Miles Davis. Willing to die early and, they hoped, leave pretty corpses, young Beat poets celebrated their underground heroes' self-destruction. A Beat didn't need to worry about mundane matters. "If you believe you're a poet," said Gregory Corso, "then you're saved." These were the beginnings of a movement that widened by the later 1960s into the counterculture, a loosely defined phenomenon that involved new types of rock music, drugs, sexual freedom, and various other emblems of a liberated lifestyle.

Meanwhile, the popular culture the Beats despised was undergoing its own transformation. A revival of folk music—identified with the Old Left during the fifties—meant commercial success in the sixties for protest singers like Joan Baez and Bob Dylan. Their music sparked a yearning for social change and helped energize protesters. But it was rock 'n' roll that served as the primary musical catalyst for the counterculture.

For millions of American girls, the arrival of the Beatles in the United States in 1964 was a watershed. No musicians before or since ever achieved the mass popularity or cultural influence of these four young Englishmen: John Lennon, Paul McCartney, George Harrison, and Ringo Starr. While "Beatlemaniacs" fantasized about romance with their idols, they also found much to identify with in the "Fab Four." Playful, long-haired, wacky, and talented, the Beatles personified both personal independence and a new androgynous sexual ideal. One fan recalled, "I didn't want to grow up and be a wife, and it seemed to me that the Beatles had the kind of freedom I wanted: No rules, they could spend two days lying in bed; they ran around on motorbikes, ate from room service. . . . I wanted to be like them. Something larger than life." Another wrote, "I liked their independence and sexuality and wanted those things for myself."

As they had during the Elvis Presley phenomenon of the late 1950s (see Chapter 3), parents began to worry that their children were getting out of control. But the transformation of rock music and the youth culture it represented was only beginning. By the mid-1960s the sentimental love songs of the early Beatles gave way to the overt sexual come-ons of groups such as the Rolling Stones and the Doors. "I Wanna Hold Your Hand" gave way to the Stones' "Let's spend the night together," and the Door's "Touch me." Many girls accepted the idea. Hollywood clubs and the Sunset Strip attracted thousands of teenage girls. Parading in miniskirts, they sought fun and vicarious fame by having sex with rock stars. These "groupies" complied in their own sexual exploitation and subjected themselves to grave health risks, but they also represented a new, open, and defiant insistence on the right to sexual pleasure, for women as well as men. The birth control pill, first marketed in 1960, made pleasure without procreation more possible and galvanized the gradual repeal of state "blue laws" restricting the sale of contraceptives.

Janis Joplin

For a middle-class girl growing up in postwar Texas, looks mattered. Janis Joplin, born in 1943, was brainy, talented, and eager to be noticed, but conventional beauty was one thing she did not possess. Instead, she had "problems"—excess weight, severe acne—that made her wretched, rebellious, and outrageous. She began to dress sloppily, to hang out with wild boys, to venture across the Sabine River for nights of drinking and brawling in Louisiana roadhouses. She developed a "reputation." Classmates at Thomas Jefferson High in Port Arthur called her a pig.

Not surprisingly, she left Port Arthur after graduating in 1960, bound for the bohemian shores of Venice, California. But soon she returned to try Texas again. At the state university in Austin, she began to find a place in the spotlight, singing blues and folk and country music in local coffee houses. Listen-

Though groupies were only a small segment of the youth population, the ideal of sexual freedom was spreading rapidly, galvanized by the rock music that expressed the desires and demands of young people. As the counterculture developed, the music continued to evolve; performers invented new musical forms and hybrids, pushing folk and rock 'n' roll beyond all previous limits. Soon "psychedelic" music, often known as acid rock, was celebrating the use of mind-altering drugs. Groups like the Grateful Dead and Jefferson Airplane turned their sets into dizzying, deafening swirls of sound. A young white woman named Janis Joplin sang a steamy, screeching, tortured, blues-driven rock that gave her an almost legendary status as a prodigy of the counterculture.

Like Joplin, most of the avant-garde performers were white. Ironically, at a time when many black political leaders were turning from

ers began to realize she had remarkable talent and a unique, unforgettable style. But insecurity stalked her, and some students humiliated her with the title of "Ugliest Man on Campus." In 1963 she left Texas once again, heading for San Francisco.

This time, she found her niche in the hip life of California. Within a few years, Janis Joplin became the queen of the San Francisco psychedelic music scene, both a rock-'n'-roll star and a symbol of the counterculture. Bold, swaggering, cursing, she roared through town in beads and bangles, by turns clowning and sinking into despair. She fronted a band called Big Brother and the Holding Company, wringing ecstasy and torment from her amazing voice, reaching national acclaim with a stunning performance at the Monterey Pop Festival in 1967. Even after she had paused awhile to establish a new band and to redefine her music, she remained a celebrity, and a rock music phenomenon. Still, her personal troubles were never resolved.

"I just made love to twenty-five thousand people," she said after one concert, "and I'm going home alone." Sex was for her an obsession and a puzzle. She was attracted to both men and women, and she was deeply troubled by her bisexuality. Because none of her many partners could satisfy her for long, she was often lonely. Seeking reassurance and oblivion, she drank a sweet whiskey called Southern Comfort and shot heroin into her veins. Eventually, like all too many other stars of the counterculture, she became a victim of her own self-destructiveness. In 1970 she died of a drug overdose in a seedy Los Angeles motel. ■

civil rights to Black Power, African-American musicians succeeded in reaching a broad commercial audience by taking a fairly cautious approach. The best-known black recording artists were associated with Motown, the Detroit music company masterminded by black songwriter-entrepreneur Berry Gordy, Jr. Motown singers like Stevie Wonder and groups like the Temptations and the Supremes combined musical virtuosity with lush production, precise choreography, glittering costumes, and a bland message. One exception to this trend was James Brown, the godfather of soul music, who marked out the frontiers of raw sex appeal. Another black innovator was guitarist Jimi Hendrix, whose incendiary playing defined the psychedelic style.

Along with sex and rock 'n' roll, the counterculture featured the abundant use of drugs. The Beatles took lysergic acid diethylamide (LSD), a psychotropic chemical better known as "acid." Their path-breaking album, *Sergeant Pepper's Lonely Hearts Club Band*, declared "I'd love to turn you on." "More and more," former SDS president Todd Gitlin observed, "to get access to youth culture, you had to get high." Many people got "stoned" with milder drugs like marijuana, which was said to impair short-term memory but had limited long-term effects. Some, like rock idols Janis Joplin, Jim Morrison, and Jimi Hendrix, sought in drugs a release from deep-seated pain. They combined alcohol with barbiturates, amphetamines, cocaine, and heroin, until their dependencies killed them.

At first the term *psychedelic* referred to hallucinogenic drugs that altered perceptions. Counterculture adherents used these drugs as a means of expanding the mind to reach a higher level of experience and understanding. Drug use was also a way of expressing the anti-materialist, anti-authoritarian ethos of the era. For many, such perception-altering substances as marijuana and LSD became akin to religious sacraments. LSD was first introduced into the United States as part of a CIA program to develop drugs to use in questioning enemy agents. Harvard professors Timothy Leary and Richard Alpert conducted psychological experiments with LSD and, by 1960, were both enthusiastic advocates of hallucinogenic drugs. When Harvard fired them for using students as subjects in their research, they became outlaw heroes. Leary founded the League for Spiritual Discovery, established a commune at an estate at Millbrook, New York, and advised the nation's youth to "Turn on, tune in, and drop out." Alpert later embraced Eastern mysticism, reincarnating himself as the guru Baba Ram Dass.

Still others celebrated the recreational dimension of opening up what British writer Aldous Huxley had called "the doors of perception." Novelist Ken Kesey, who participated in CIA-sponsored drug experiments at Stanford, founded a mobile commune called the Merry Pranksters, which traveled in a wildly painted bus called "Furthur." In cities up and down the West Coast, the Pranksters held "acid tests"—parties with avant-garde rock 'n' roll, multimedia spectacles, and the mass distribution of free LSD. Journalist Tom Wolfe chronicled the Pranksters' activities in *The Electric Kool-Aid Acid Test*, a hyperbolic, typographically psychedelic piece of New Journalism. In San Francisco, the Pranksters joined forces with master businessman Bill Graham to produce the Tripps Festival, an event at the Fillmore Auditorium starring the city's premier acid-rock bands, the Grateful Dead and Big Brother and the Holding Company.

Soon new forms of popular behavior and expression grew up around the music and drug scenes. Adopting the Beats' notion that a posture of hipness constituted a form of social protest, counterculture devotees called themselves "hippies." The hippie style, with its flowing hair and bell-bottom jeans, transformed the appearance of American youth. As part of their rejection of Western civilization's "up-tight" materialism, devotees of the psychedelic culture adopted some of the trappings of Eastern mysticism, sporting bells, beads, flowing robes, and sandals. They perfumed their homes with incense and festooned them with Indian-print bedspreads. They wove flowers into their hair. They changed their diet, demanding more "natural" foods to enhance their spiritual health. They embraced the psychedelic art that appeared on rock posters and T-shirts, a style that used saturated colors, swirling calligraphy, and special photographic effects.

By the summer of 1967 there were hippie neighborhoods in most American cities and college towns. San Francisco's Haight-Ashbury district, in particular, had become a magnet for people preaching the virtues of love, dope, music, sex, and "flower power." While radical politicos proclaimed the summer of 1967 Vietnam Summer, hippies announced the "Summer of Love." This hedonistic interlude would transform society not by agitating for wide-scale social change or an end to the war, but by encouraging individuals to drop out of the rat race and sample the pleasures of the senses. The networks and news magazines predicted the migration of thousands of young people to the Haight that summer, to "crash" in communal "pads," "groove" at concerts in Golden Gate Park and at the Fillmore, and shower each other and the apprehensive local authorities with peace, love, and flowers. "If you're going to San Francisco," one song's lyrics advised, "be sure to wear some flowers in your hair."

There was plenty of good music, good vibes, and a profusion of flowers in the Haight that summer. Serious politics also made an appearance, in the street dramas and free feeds put on by the Diggers, a radical theater group that linked a savage critique of capitalism and militarism with a Thoreauvian plea for a simpler, more organic, ecologically responsible way of life. But despite the good feelings, there was also more than a measure of blight. Though at the time many observers believed the hippie influx into San Francisco represented a revolt against affluence, it was instead a sign that the idealized nuclear family of the 1950s was often a sham. Beneath the veneer of American family life, serious problems lurked. Class was no distinguishing factor among the migrants to San Francisco; the young people came from poor, working-class, middle-class, and wealthy backgrounds. Rather, those who ran off to the Haight were disproportionately children from severely troubled homes. They were as often throwaways as runaways; many were victims of parental abuse or neglect. "The surprising thing about this extraordinary moment in this extraordinary community," wrote journalist Nicholas Von Hoffman, who spent the summer of 1967 observing the scene in the Haight, "is not the number of anxious parents combing the place for their children, nor the number of sad little signs posted on bulletin boards asking dearly loved sons and daughters to return home, but how few there really are compared to the apparently large number of runaway minors."

Few migrants to the Haight had the skills to sustain themselves in a city suddenly flooded with multitudes of their kind. Thus the Haight hippies often turned to panhandling or to the perilous occupations of prostitution and drug-dealing to earn their keep. Drugs traded included marijuana and acid—destructive enough in large doses—and also such addictive substances as amphetamines, cocaine, and heroin, which led to overdoses and outbreaks of hepatitis from dirty needles. The cutthroat drug business kept Haight residents vulnerable to exploitation and physical violence.

Like dope, free love turned out to have a high price. Hippie girls, presumed to be sexually liberated, sometimes found they were expected to exchange sex for food and shelter, a practice that led some to conclude that prostitution for cash was a better bargain than sexual barter. The assumption that all "chicks" sought sexual liaisons left Haight women particularly exposed to sexual assault. Sexual promiscuity, whether chosen, forced, or economically necessary, led to epidemic venereal disease. Free medical clinics as well as soup kitchens were overwhelmed by demand.

At its root, the counterculture partook of the social problems and prejudices of American society in general. Crash pads, if hospitable, often re-created conventional household hierarchies. One young woman who went with a girlfriend to the Haight for a weekend reported with some disgust that her friend "moved into the first commune we entered and became a 'housemother,' which means she did all the cooking and cleaning," she added sarcastically. Racial tensions, like gender hierarchies, persisted among the hip as well as the square. Relations between the predominantly white hippies in the Haight and the nearby black community in the Fillmore were terrible.

Even as the Haight-Ashbury experience revealed contradictions in the counterculture, the music persisted, helping to keep the spirit of the cultural revolution alive. Promoters began staging large-scale, open-air rock festivals to attract the faithful. These reached a high point with the Woodstock music festival of August 1969, a rain- and mud-soaked gathering of 400,000 rock fans in upstate New York. The unexpectedly huge crowd presented many serious problems, particularly in providing sanitation, food, and water. The audience had difficulty actually hearing the music and seeing the stage. Traffic was so bad that state authorities closed down the New York State Thruway. In spite of these troubles, however, many members of the audience would look back on Woodstock as the grandest experience of the sixties, a demonstration that hundreds of thousands could come together for "three days of peace, love and music." The festival developed an almost mythological aura as the counterculture's finest hour.

At the opposite extreme was the festival at Altamont Speedway in California the following winter. In the spirit of drug fellowship, the headlining Rolling Stones made the common counterculture mistake of assuming that anyone who used illegal drugs must have humane values. The Stones invited the Hell's Angels motorcycle gang to provide the festival's security. The Angels, who resembled flower children only in their taste for dope, stabbed one person to death in front of the stage as Mick Jagger looked on aghast. Before the day was out, four people were dead, and many others had been severely injured. Whereas the promoters at Woodstock had worked hard to ensure that there would be enough medical facilities available to treat injuries and drug-induced freak-outs, medical care at Altamont was sadly inadequate to cope with even run-of-the-mill drug reactions.

Experiences like Haight-Ashbury and Altamont led many hippies to conclude that the only salvation for the counterculture lay in cultivating one's own garden. Across the country, disaffected hippies sought spiritual salvation and physical health by getting back to the land. College students moved out of dormitories and into rural farmhouses, bought sacks of brown rice, and planted organic gardens. Most communes were relatively short-lived, falling apart when faced with such issues as how to share expenses, whom to include or exclude, and how to divide up the work. Advocates of "doing your own thing" clashed with those who saw a need for organization, and those who took on the task of collecting money for food or rent were regularly turned away with a haughty admonition to not be so uptight and materialistic. The communes that lasted tended to be very hierarchical, like The Farm in Tennessee, or devoted to Eastern religious practices, especially various forms of Buddhism.

Authoritarianism, of course, did not guarantee stability or virtue. The most infamous of the communes, the murderous Manson Family, left the Haight-Ashbury to settle, finally, in the dry Santa Susana Mountains of southern California. Charles Manson held his mostly female followers so completely spellbound that by December of 1969 they were willing to commit murder at his orders. Even after they had been arrested for multiple homicides, including that of pregnant actress, Sharon Tate, Manson's disciples continued to express their loyalty to him from their prison cells.

Hippie communes reflected a fundamental tension in American society, the tension between a longing for connectedness and a desire for personal liberty. If most lasted only a short time and seemed more dedicated to escapism than to solving the problems of a postindustrial society, they nevertheless represented a desire for a way of life dedicated not to the pursuit of consumer goods but to a vision of a meaningful existence. Often as not, those who experimented with communal living pondered not only human relations, but also the

Hippies challenged social prescriptions by
forming communal families in the 1960s.
© 1979 Peter Simon/Black Star.

complicated connections between people and the natural world.
Some who began by raising organic vegetables became pioneers of
the environmental movement.

While communards sought a place apart from American consumerism and crass materialism, the counterculture spread to mainstream groups as well, becoming part of the everyday world of high
school students from the mid-1960s to the mid-1970s, and extending
beyond California and New York to other urban areas and even many
small towns. As it spread, there were many people ready to capitalize
on it. Bill Graham grew fabulously wealthy promoting rock concerts.
Psychedelic artist Peter Max eventually marketed his talents to some
fifty companies, including Sears and General Electric. The counterculture spawned new business opportunities for purveyors of dietary
and spiritual nostrums, record store owners, and proprietors of head
shops, T-shirt stores, health food stores, and hip clothing boutiques.

Jann Wenner, a particularly canny entrepreneur, spotted the marketing opportunity of the decade when he began publishing *Rolling
Stone* magazine, a tabloid that began by covering the rock scene and
soon expanded into long feature articles and investigative reporting.
Wenner made a fortune, meanwhile publishing some of the best of the
New Journalism. On the pages of *Rolling Stone*, politics and the counterculture came together in such extraordinary forms as Tom Wolfe's

perceptive history of the space program and Hunter S. Thompson's brilliant 1972 series on presidential politics, "Fear and Loathing on the Campaign Trail."

1968: A YEAR OF CATACLYSM

To some extent, the three movements this chapter has traced so far— Black Power, the New Left, and the counterculture—represented separate strands of antiestablishment sentiment during the sixties. Often they differed from one another in both goals and methods. For instance, the Black Panthers had no intention of wearing flowers in their hair; hippies were frequently indifferent to politics, believing that salvation lay in altering the mind and spirit; and some political radicals of the New Left could not fathom how anyone could lie around smoking marijuana when there was a rally to attend. But the membership of the three movements overlapped, and they generally shared a basic opposition to racism, social injustice, bourgeois consumerism, and the Vietnam War. As the climate of protest intensified in the late 1960s, there were more and more occasions when the various strands came together. This was particularly true in 1968, a cataclysmic year for American society and politics.

On December 31, 1967, some important members of the counterculture and the New Left joined forces. Radical leaders Abbie Hoffman and Jerry Rubin, black activist-comedian Dick Gregory, Beat poet Allen Ginsberg, counterculture writer Paul Krassner of *The Realist* (the nation's oldest underground newspaper), and several others founded the Youth International Party, better known as the Yippies. Hoffman, a great believer in employing humor to promote serious causes, was a master at manipulating the media. Applying a combination of militant tactics, freakish pranks, and humor, Yippies would try to make themselves the national media's front-page story. Their particular goals were sometimes hard to determine. They were for freedom, for spontaneity, against the Vietnam War, against racism, against politics as usual. They planned to turn the 1968 Democratic national convention in Chicago into a "Festival of Life" featuring rock music and elaborate practical jokes, a kind of revolutionary dance party.

The Yippies were not the only set of protesters on the political stage, nor were they by any means the group most representative of dissident youth. When Senator Eugene McCarthy decided to challenge Lyndon Johnson in the 1968 New Hampshire primary, thousands of students turned out for his campaign. Aware that their hippie style would alienate the middle-of-the-road and the middle-aged, they cut their hair, put aside their bell-bottoms, and donned coats and ties or skirts and sweaters, becoming "Clean for Gene." In a paroxysm of political idealism, they took the McCarthy campaign across the nation, converting flower power to grass-roots organizing, their Volkswagen Beetles sprouting the distinctive blue-and-white daisy-shaped McCarthy bumper stickers. When McCarthy nearly defeated Johnson in the New Hampshire presidential primary, they tasted victory and redoubled their envelope-stuffing and precinct-walking efforts. Johnson's announcement on March 31 that he would decline to run for re-election was their great moment of triumph.

This well-scrubbed foray into electoral politics fell victim to the national climate of violence and confrontation. The first great shock came on April 4, 1968, when Martin Luther King, Jr., was assassinated by a white supremacist in Memphis, Tennessee. King had gone to the city on behalf of striking sanitation workers; almost all of the workers were black, and they represented the abused, overworked, yet politically mobilized people he hoped to include in an interracial Poor People's Campaign. Seemingly prescient about his doom, King nevertheless maintained hope for the movement. The day before his assassination, he gave a speech in which he explained, "I've looked over and I've seen the Promised Land. I may not get there with you, but I want you to know tonight that we as a people will get to the Promised Land. . . . I'm not fearing any man. Mine eyes have seen the glory of the coming of the Lord."

Despite King's own optimism, many African-Americans could find no way to understand his murder except as proof of the futility of the nonviolent strategy he advocated. "When white America killed Dr. King," said Stokely Carmichael, "she declared war." The riots that broke out in more than a hundred cities lasted more than a week. More than sixty-five thousand federal troops were called out to try to restore order.

Yet, almost miraculously, thousands of activists clung to King's nonviolent vision. Two months after his murder, supporters of the Poor People's Campaign, led now by the SCLC's Reverend Ralph David Abernathy, built a makeshift settlement of tents and plywood shacks in the shadow of the Washington Monument. King's widow, Coretta Scott King, spoke often during the month-long existence of Resurrection City (as the protesters called their shantytown), stressing nonviolence but reminding her audience that "starving a child is violence, suppressing a culture is violence, contempt for poverty is violence."

Unfortunately, these words could not stem the tide of violence. After Robert Kennedy announced his candidacy for the Democratic presidential nomination, offering antiwar voters another choice, some of McCarthy's student supporters went over to the Kennedy camp. More significantly, Kennedy became the overwhelming choice of black and Mexican-American voters, who considered him the strong-

Violence erupted in Chicago during the 1968 Democratic convention. Though many Americans blamed demonstrators for the disorder, a presidential commission later termed the event a "police riot." *UPI/Bettmann Archive.*

est candidate on civil rights. Minority voters were impressed by Kennedy's support for Cesar Chávez and the United Farm Workers, a predominantly Mexican-American union trying to win basic, decent wages and working conditions from California grape growers. On the strength of minority support, Kennedy won the California primary on June 5, 1968, getting enough delegates to raise the possibility of a deadlocked Democratic convention. But his shooting by Sirhan Sirhan came only a few hours after the polls closed. When Kennedy died the next morning, many Americans believed that with him died the only chance for electoral politics to offer real change.

The city of Chicago became an armed camp in August 1968 as the authorities prepared for antiwar protests at the Democratic national convention. Barbed wire enclosed the convention center, twelve thousand Chicago police were deployed on twelve-hour shifts, and some six thousand troops of the Illinois National Guards were called out, along with about as many army troops. It is unknown how many FBI agents attended. The overwhelming majority of antiwar activists stayed away. On most days during the convention, there were perhaps four thousand demonstrators, with crowds peaking at possibly ten thousand on August 28. Thus, police generally outnumbered demonstrators by a factor of three or four to one, and federal records suggest that the ranks of the protesters were extensively infiltrated by government agents.

Those who did come to protest were hardly a representative cross section of the antiwar movement. For example, male demonstrators at Chicago outnumbered females by eight or ten to one, imparting a particularly macho flavor to the action. The Yippies came prepared to make a farce out of the convention by bringing along their own candidate, a live pig named Pigasus. "Our concept of revolution," said Abbie Hoffman, "is that it's fun." Paul Krassner terrified city residents by suggesting that demonstrators might attempt to alter people's consciousness by putting LSD into the city's water supply. An infuriated Mayor Daley refused to let demonstrators camp in city parks, a move that guaranteed there would be plenty of restless people looking for conflict. A small minority of demonstrators—perhaps as many as three hundred—representing the extreme Left came to Chicago hoping to provoke violence.

The police obliged them, acting without strategy or discipline in a week-long melee observers would come to call a "police riot." Over the course of the convention, they repeatedly cleared Lincoln Park with tear gas and clubs. Police and demonstrators clashed in Grant Park, across from Hubert Humphrey's headquarters in the Hilton, while television cameras recorded the head-bashing and some antiwar convention delegates went into the streets to support the demonstrators. Candidate Humphrey could smell tear gas from his hotel room. Reporters, bystanders, and demonstrators alike were beaten and gassed. A total of 668 people were arrested.

Meanwhile, inside the convention center, Mayor Daley refused to acknowledge the carnage, loading the galleries with supporters waving banners that read, "We Love Mayor Daley." Furthermore, most Americans seemed to believe the mayor and the police had responded appropriately. Less than 20 percent of those contacted in a national telephone poll thought the police had used too much force in putting down the demonstrations. Hubert Humphrey said the Chicago police had done "nothing wrong." To the strains of "Happy Days Are Here Again," he accepted the presidential nomination, his party in ruins around him.

No matter what Humphrey might do to placate voters who despised hippies and protesters, the Democrats were firmly linked in the public mind with those who had come to Chicago to demonstrate against the war. Ironically, the protests in Chicago aided the November victory of Republican candidate Richard Nixon, who was nominated at a carefully orchestrated meeting in Miami that looked like a love feast compared to the mayhem at Chicago. Nixon seemed a reassuring presence to those he would come to call "the silent majority" of Americans.

While the Right gained momentum after Chicago, spurred on by the inflammatory rhetoric of independent presidential candidate

George Wallace and Republican vice-presidential contender Spiro Agnew, the Left was transformed but not dead. SDS boomed. Some movement leaders, increasingly seduced by the romance of violent revolution, considered the convention a triumph, believing, with Tom Hayden, that "our victory lies in progressively demystifying a false democracy." Hayden and seven others, including Hoffman and Rubin, were indicted for conspiring to incite a riot at the convention. Their trial at the hands of reactionary judge Julius J. Hoffman became an emblem of the friction between radical dissidents and repressive authorities. When Judge Hoffman ordered one of the defendants, Black Panther leader Bobby Seale, bound and gagged, newspaper sketch artists had a field day depicting the fulfillment of the order. Seale was ultimately tried separately from the other defendants (all white), a judicial move that underlined the nation's persistent racial polarization.

Campus confrontation became the rule of the day. In May 1969, police and demonstrators at Berkeley clashed at the battle of People's Park. The park, which belonged to the University of California, had once been a weedy meeting place for dope dealers and their customers, but had since been turned into a community garden. The university, claiming it wanted to build a soccer field on the spot, asked police to seal off the area while bulldozers razed the gardens. When marchers moved in to take back the park, the police opened up with buckshot and tear gas. Governor Ronald Reagan sent in three thousand National Guardsmen, who occupied the park for seventeen days. People's Park became a symbol of radical struggle and the communal alternative to private property; it also underlined the emerging importance of ecological issues, pitting organic gardeners against bulldozers, tomatoes against tear gas.

Disturbances that spring at Harvard, Stanford, Cornell, and nearly three hundred other campuses included more than a hundred incidents involving arson and attempted or actual bombings. The voice of the counterculture grew more militant. Jefferson Airplane, a San Francisco rock group that had risen to fame by combining powerful vocal and instrumental performances with odes to the mind-expanding power of LSD, turned to celebrating insurrection, crowing "Look what's happenin' out in the streets / Got to Revolution!"

Meanwhile, some activists worked hard to repair the antiwar movement's damaged credibility. The New Mobilization, a coalition of moderate antiwar advocates, organized a nationwide peace demonstration in the fall of 1969, calling for a moratorium on the war. Millions of people responded, holding rallies, teach-ins, marches, and meetings. On the day of the demonstration, 100,000 people gathered on Boston Common; in New York City, a series of mass meetings were held, including one on Wall Street. Nationwide crowd estimates for the October 15 demonstrations ranged from 2 million to 15 million. The following month, more than half a million people gathered in Washington, D.C., for a second demonstration, the largest ever held in that city.

This huge, peaceful outcry against the war did have an impact; it demonstrated that millions of Americans supported neither the war nor the violent tactics of the extreme Left. Yet even moderate antiwar activists became angry and frustrated by their inability to stop the war. Moreover, the extremists made better copy, and their frequent clashes with police drew attention away from what the moderates regarded as their more serious attempts to affect the nation's policy in Vietnam.

On December 4, 1969, Chicago police raided the local Black Panther headquarters, killing Panther leaders Fred Hampton and Mark Clark in their beds. The SDS splintered, and it soon became dominated by a faction calling itself the Weathermen, after a line in a Bob Dylan song: "You don't need a weatherman to know which way the wind blows." Announcing their goal as "the destruction of U.S. imperialism and the achievement of a classless world: world communism," the Weathermen rejected coalition politics of any kind and embraced worldwide revolution. Their heroes included Chinese Communist Party chairman Mao Zedong and Central American revolutionary martyr Ché Guevara. Their enemies were "the pigs at home," their vanguard a revolutionary youth movement. "Kids used to try to beat the system from inside the army or from inside the schools," they said; "now they desert from the army and burn down the schools."

A week before the October demonstrations, two or three hundred Weathermen street fighters battled Chicago police in a showdown that came to be known as the Days of Rage. In the next year, the antiwar movement's conflicting philosophies were thrown into sharp relief. While thousands assembled to light candles and sing "Give Peace a Chance," a relatively few shock troops fantasized about violence, trained for street fighting, and built bombs. Between September 1969 and May 1970, there were at least 250 bombings at draft boards, ROTC buildings, federal offices, and corporate headquarters. In March 1970, three bombers from the Weather Underground, as the Weathermen now called themselves, died when they blew themselves up in a New York townhouse. The following August, a bomb exploded in the University of Wisconsin mathematics building, killing a graduate student working on a research project in a facility the bombers thought to be empty.

In 1970 there were 9,408 incidents of protest; 731 involved police and arrests, 410 involved damage to property, and 230 involved violence to persons. The confrontations peaked in May, when President

A student screams in horror over the body of an antiwar demonstrator slain by the National Guard at Kent State University on May 4, 1970. In the aftermath of the Kent State killings, college students across the country staged protests and strikes. *John Filo.*

Nixon announced that U.S. troops had invaded neutral Cambodia, a state neighboring Vietnam. The announcement set off a wave of student strikes; at least seventy-five campuses shut down for the rest of the academic year, and students at Northwestern University announced that their institution had seceded from the United States. Some thirty ROTC buildings were burned or bombed in the first week of May, including the one at Kent State University in Kent, Ohio. Governor James Rhodes called in National Guard troops to restore order on the Kent State campus; on May 4 nervous Guardsmen opened fire on student demonstrators and passers-by, killing four and wounding nine. Ten days later, police killed two more students and wounded nine at Jackson State, a predominantly black campus in Mississippi. Torn and bloody, the country seemed to be consuming its young—a cannibalism that some deplored, others embraced.

As radical Left and antiwar protests culminated in these violent confrontations, another protest movement was developing—more quietly at first, but perhaps possessing an even greater potential for long-term impact. This was the movement for women's liberation, a product of a new feminist consciousness.

THE RISE OF THE NEW FEMINISM

Even in the supposedly quiescent 1950s there had been some organized and articulate attempts to come to grips with women's issues. In the period immediately following World War II, some unions had sought to organize service and clerical workers, who were mostly women, as well as female factory employees like those in California's canneries. Sometimes uniting across ethnic lines, working-class women had pushed for such goals as equal pay for equal work and had begun to consider economic and social questions that would not be fully articulated until the 1980s. Even in its heyday, what writer Betty Friedan would in 1963 call "the feminine mystique"—the idea that women belonged at home because they were nurturing, timid creatures entirely different from competitive, capable men—did not go unquestioned. In the 1950s, magazines including *Ladies' Home Journal* and *Good Housekeeping* carried articles celebrating the benefits of paid work for women and featured profiles of successful career women.

By 1960, women's issues had begun to receive attention from the federal government. In 1961, President Kennedy established a Commission on the Status of Women (CSW), headed by Eleanor Roosevelt. Something of an anomaly in the masculine atmosphere of the New Frontier, the CSW took tentative positions, such as recommending new programs in adult education so that women might go back to work after raising their children. Such limited goals made it clear that women should not neglect their primary responsibility in the home.

In the early sixties, Congress began to discuss discrimination against working women. The Equal Pay Act of 1963 made it illegal to pay women less than men for doing the same job. However, the decade's most significant piece of legislation in the area of women's rights became law almost serendipitously. As Congress debated the 1964 Civil Rights Act, a reactionary Virginia congressman, Howard W. Smith, attempted to kill the bill by introducing an amendment that he believed would reduce the whole matter of civil rights to absurdity. Title VII prohibited discrimination on the basis of sex. Encouraged by business and professional women, liberal northerners led by Representative Martha Griffith of Michigan pushed the amendment through, and it became law along with the rest of the bill. The Equal Employment Opportunity Commission (EEOC), charged with enforcing the act's bans on workplace discrimination, did not at first take sex discrimination complaints seriously. But under increasing pressure from women's groups it ultimately began to enforce the law.

Meanwhile, as noted in Chapter 3, discontent had been brewing in the tranquil suburbs. Middle-class white women, supposedly fully absorbed in cleaning their houses and raising their children, found domestic life lacking. In 1960, when *Redbook* magazine ran an article titled "Why Young Mothers Feel Trapped" and invited readers to respond, the editors received an astonishing twenty-four thousand replies. In 1963 came the publication of Betty Friedan's *The Feminine Mystique,* which lamented the societal waste in isolating educated, talented women in the "comfortable concentration camp" of the American home. Middle-class American women, Friedan said, felt depressed, useless, and assailed by "the problem that has no name." Speaking for this constituency (and not, for example, for African-American mothers, whose families' survival had long depended on their ability to find paid work of any kind), Friedan believed that the solution lay in giving women meaningful jobs outside the home. In 1966 Friedan was among the founders of the National Organization for Women (NOW)—the first national lobby for women's rights since the suffrage era—dedicated to the goal of achieving for women political and economic opportunities equal to those enjoyed by men.

The women's movement gained momentum because it was rooted in widespread, elemental changes in American society. Among other factors, more and more women were becoming educated. Between 1950 and 1974, college enrollment for men increased by 234 percent; for women it increased 456 percent. Even more important, both married and single women were entering the paid work force. During the Second World War, female employment increased from 27 percent of adult women in 1940 to 36 percent five years later. Female employment dropped off temporarily immediately after the war, but by the beginning of the sixties, 37.7 percent of women aged sixteen and over were employed, constituting 33 percent of the total work force. A decade later, 43 percent of women aged sixteen and over, representing 38 percent of the civilian work force, were either working or looking for work. The numbers continued to rise steadily. More and more frequently, the working woman was a married woman: by 1962 married women accounted for 60 percent of the female work force. The working woman was also a mother: as early as 1970, one-third of women with children under six years of age held or sought jobs.

At the same time, women workers had fewer job options than their male counterparts. They generally crowded into female-dominated occupations—nursing, clerical work, teaching, domestic work—that paid less than men's jobs. In 1955, the median compensation for women in full-time, year-round employment was 64 percent of men's earnings. In 1960 the figure had dropped to 61 percent, and by 1975 full-time women workers were earning only 58.8 percent of what men earned. Even when they did the same work as men, they were paid less. The EEOC was understaffed and often reluctant to pursue complaints about violations of the Equal Pay Act. Moreover, employers could skirt the whole issue by writing slightly different job descriptions or giving different titles to men and women engaged in substantially the same activities.

Most women who worked reported that they did so out of financial necessity or to improve their family's standard of living, although some said they were seeking personal satisfaction. Still, most Americans assumed that even women who held full-time, paid jobs would continue to do most of the housework. According to figures that changed very little between 1955 and the early 1970s, full-time housewives spent between 52 and 56 hours per week doing housework. Wives who worked full-time outside the home still reported spending about 26 hours per week on housekeeping. And whether or not their wives worked, husbands spent about 1.6 hours per day, or 11.2 hours per week, doing household tasks, including yard work. Men helped at times with the shopping, cooking, and laundry, but in general did not do the cleaning or ironing.

Perhaps most important of all, the myth of the happy nuclear family was crumbling. Greater acknowledgment of the tensions within families (signaled by a rising divorce rate), concern about women who had been widowed or abandoned, and growing alarm over family violence and abuse, heralded an urgent need to re-evaluate women's place in American society. If women could no longer count on the family as a protected place, they would have to fashion new ways of making their way in the world.

The dramatic change in women's roles in society were bound to have political consequences, particularly as civil rights activists were uncovering racial injustice, liberal politicians were embracing social reform, and radical dissidents were questioning the distribution of power in American society. Although the civil rights movement and the New Left fell short of obtaining all their goals, both proved to be seedbeds for a feminist movement of lasting impact and immense scope.

In the fall of 1964, SNCC women, including Ruby Doris Smith Robinson, Casey Hayden, Mary King, and Maria Varela, drafted a paper on women's position in the SNCC. Robinson recognized that as a woman she shared some common ground with King and Hayden, both white, but as an African-American she also believed that the organization should be black-led and black-dominated. King and Hayden recognized that the turn toward Black Power would leave no place for them in a movement to which they had devoted years of their lives. But if Black Power as a political strategy left them out, as an ideology focusing on difference, it provided them with a model for how to distinguish the ways in which women's status diverged from men's. A year later, in the fall of 1965, King and Hayden anonymously composed "a kind of memo" to women in the peace and freedom movements, arguing that women and blacks both "seem to be caught up in a common-law caste system . . . which, at its worst, uses and exploits women." When they raised the problem of male dominance among their fellow activists, men generally responded by laughing at them. Several months earlier, at an SNCC meeting where the position of women in the movement had been raised, Stokely Carmichael had quipped, "The position of women in SNCC is prone!" Those who heard the remark, including Mary King, "collapsed with hilarity," but when the laughter faded, the serious question remained.

By June of 1967, women had found a language to express their grievances. They named the problem—sexism (sometimes called "male chauvinism")—and the solution—women's liberation. NOW activists focused on eliminating wage discrimination and fighting for legal guarantees of equality. They proposed the Equal Rights Amendment to the Constitution and pushed hard for its passage. The radical feminists, who sometimes began as NOW members but more often came out of the civil rights movement and the New Left, identified a new set of political issues, including child care, abortion, birth control, sexuality, family violence, and the sharing of housework. Soon, meeting in small groups to discuss not only war and racism but also problems that seemed intensely individual and private, they developed a new theoretical tool: consciousness-raising. By identifying their common grievances, they came to the fundamental insight of the new feminist movement—namely, that what appeared to be women's individual problems involved much larger questions of social power, or "sexual politics," in the words of feminist theorist Kate Millett. Feminist writer Robin Morgan turned this insight into the slogan, "The personal is political."

From the start, the new feminism, often called "the second wave" to distinguish it from the women's rights movement of the late nineteenth and early twentieth centuries, faced formidable obstacles. All kinds of people felt threatened by the prospect of women's liberation: conservative men, who stood to lose all manner of privileges; middle-class women, especially housewives, who worried that men would simply abandon their breadwinner roles and that women would lose whatever protections they had; fundamentalist Christians, who believed that women's traditional role was biblically ordained; and even leftist men, accustomed to treating women as assistant radicals and sex objects. In the late sixties and early seventies, the mainstream press used dismissive language to ridicule the movement. Reporters for *Time* and *Newsweek* who referred to Gloria Steinem and Shulamith Firestone as "women's libbers" never called Eldridge Cleaver or Rap Brown "black libbers."

Moreover, the task of building a movement based on women's common problems, interests, and objectives was deeply complicated by the very diversity of the women the movement hoped to mobilize.

The women's liberation movement brought young women into the streets to protest a variety of inequalities. *John Olson, LIfe Magazine* © *Time Warner Inc.*

Certainly race made a difference in how women approached feminism. Even in the early days of SNCC, racial differences among women had raised tensions: black women had articulated grievances and goals that diverged from those of their white sisters in the "beloved community." Class, age, sexual preference, and occupational status also divided women. Middle-class housewives who had invested their lives in the idea that their husbands would protect them were far less equipped to face the challenges of economic independence than were college-age women battling discrimination in law school admissions. Lesbian activists saw their interests as diverging in significant ways from those of heterosexual women. Mexican-American mothers working as migrant farm laborers or domestics had different needs from the affluent women who bought the produce they picked or hired them to clean their homes.

Some feminist activists, like Robin Morgan, took a page out of the Yippies' book and sought to create splashy media events to gain a national audience. A week after the 1968 Chicago convention, Morgan and almost two hundred other protesters at the Miss America Pageant in Atlantic City crowned a live sheep "Miss America." *New York Times* reporter Charlotte Curtis covered the protest in typically dismissive terms. Media critic Susan Douglas noted, that in Curtis's article, "charges about sexism in the United States were placed in quotation marks, suggesting that these were merely the deluded hallucinations of a few ugly, angry women rather than a fact of life." Print and broadcast media inevitably played up conflicts between women (Curtis saw fit to devote a full paragraph of her story to a "counterdemonstration" staged by three women). And they often went even further in demeaning feminist actions and goals. On August 26, 1970, feminists held the Women's Strike for Equality, featuring marches and rallies in major cities across the country. A march down Fifth Avenue in New York attracted between thirty thousand and fifty thousand supporters. ABC anchorman Howard K. Smith led the coverage of the event that night with a quotation from Vice President Spiro Agnew: "Three things have been difficult to tame. The ocean, fools, and women. We may soon be able to tame the ocean, but fools and women will take a little longer."

Because of the enormous diversity of issues affecting women, feminists had different views on both long- and short-term goals for the movement. Some argued that the first order of business was to dismantle a capitalist system that especially oppressed women. Others believed that the movement should concentrate first on eradicating male domination. Some believed men could be reformed and that women had an obligation to maintain relations with men. Shulamith Firestone declared that "a revolutionary in every bedroom cannot fail to shake up the status quo." Others rejected heterosexuality, some for political reasons, some because women's liberation allowed them to act on long-suppressed lesbian feelings. As visions of the women's movement proliferated, so did its tactics, its victories, its failures, and its institutions.

By the mid-1970s women had made inroads into male-dominated professions, mounted successful challenges to legal and economic discrimination, founded new enterprises, and claimed new rights. Yet much remained to be done. While the privileges of race and class enabled a few American women to "have it all," many more remained highly vulnerable. The wage gap between men and women persisted. If some women made strides in professional circles, many more fell deeper into poverty.

THE LEGACY OF THE SIXTIES

Although the women's movement has continued, with various shifts in emphasis, to the present day, the other protest movements of the sixties gradually faded or evolved into new, less sensational forms. The New Left never recovered from the cataclysmic spring of 1970, when the killings at Kent State capped a surge of bombings and confrontations. After that, some self-proclaimed revolutionaries went underground. Moderate dissidents seemed dazed by the escalating climate of hatred. Some, declaring themselves burned out, retreated from politics altogether. Many left the movement to pursue other political goals. Eventually, peace came to Vietnam, removing the principal issue that had united the many threads of the New Left. But the legacy of the 1960s political protest was not forgotten. Most obviously, future administrations knew that an unpopular war abroad might provoke widespread rebellion at home.

The counterculture saw many of its distinctive attributes absorbed into the mainstream culture. Hippie styles in hair and clothing and psychedelic music became popular enough to lose some of their revolutionary impact. Society at large became more sexually permissive; indeed, the "sexual revolution" was a primary legacy of the sixties. Recreational drug use spread far beyond hippie enclaves, winning converts in many segments of American society. As this happened, some of the erstwhile hippies drifted into more conventional lives— or at least their habits no longer seemed extraordinary. Others founded the "New Age" movement, reviving ancient religions and joining experimental therapy groups in search of spiritual fulfillment and expanded consciousness. Rooting out one's inner demons, whether through meditation, confrontation, long soaks in seaside hot springs, or hard labor in religious communes, occupied some inheritors of the countercultural tradition. Inevitably, business began to capitalize on nostalgia for the wild and crazy sixties. Nike launched a TV ad featuring the Beatles' song "Revolution." Tofu, yogurt, herbal tea, and organic rice began showing up on supermarket shelves.

Meanwhile, the civil rights movement, transformed by Black Power, fragmented. Some leaders went into exile; others were dead. Still others began to move into the political mainstream. SCLC workers Andrew Young and Jesse Jackson, who had stood with Martin Luther King, Jr., when he was shot in Memphis, led the next generation of activists. Both men became powers to be reckoned with in the Democratic party. Blacks and women held more and more local and national political offices. Beginning with Carl Stokes of Cleveland, elected in 1967 as the first African-American to become mayor of a major American city, blacks moved into positions of power in the nation's urban centers. By 1990 former SNCC president John Lewis would win election to the U.S. Congress, defeating a fellow movement veteran, Julian Bond.

The push for African-American rights also spawned a new, multicultural politics of difference. By the late 1960s, Native Americans organized to raise public awareness of the history of their oppression, adopting both militant and moderate tactics. Members of the American Indian Movement (AIM) occupied Alcatraz Island and staged a mass protest at Wounded Knee, South Dakota, the site of a notorious massacre of Lakota (Sioux) Indians in 1890. Other Indian advocates formed such organizations as the Native American Rights Fund to pursue legal change. By 1980 Native Americans had succeeded in forcing the federal government to return some important tribal lands and to provide compensation for other lands that had been confiscated by whites.

Mexican-Americans, galvanized by Cesar Chávez's charismatic leadership and his success in organizing the United Farm Workers, pressed for reform in the treatment of Latinos. Latinos shared a heritage based on their Spanish language and culture, but they had come from places as diverse as Mexico, Chile, Nicaragua, Cuba, and Puerto Rico, under enormously varied circumstances. As they struggled to articulate common goals—forming organizations like the League of United Latin American Citizens (LULAC)—and to come to grips with differences among themselves, they became an increasingly important part of the American political and economic picture, especially in the Sunbelt. Latino students, particularly Chicanos, organized campus groups that continue to play a prominent role at universities across the country.

Just as the protest movements of the sixties mobilized people to seek racial justice and gender equality, they also created the possibility of a civil rights movement for homosexuals. On June 29, 1969, police raided the Stonewall Inn, a gay bar in New York City's Greenwich Village. Instead of accepting arrest, the patrons fought back with rocks and bottles. This confrontation was heralded as the beginning of the gay liberation movement. Gay and lesbian activists moved quickly to redefine homosexuality not as a perversion but as a legitimate sexual identity. If they did not reach a consensus as to whether sexual preference was inborn or chosen, they enabled millions of homosexuals to come out of the closet, redrew the boundaries of sexuality, and organized to claim a share of political power in many American cities.

For others who carried on the political legacy of the sixties, the fate of the earth seemed the most pressing issue. Back-to-the-land hippies became environmental advocates. Others took a more political road to the ecology movement; peace advocates worried about the environmental threat of nuclear weapons, and activists focused on large corporations that sold shoddy and dangerous products in the United States and the Third World. In 1970, environmental activists held the first Earth Day—part teach-in, part demonstration—designed to promote awareness of human impact on the natural environment. Books like Rachel Carson's *Silent Spring*, an indictment of the use of pesticides; Paul Ehrlich's *The Population Bomb*, a vision of demographic doom; Barry Commoner's *Science and Society*, a critique of the nuclear power industry; and Ralph Nader's *Unsafe at Any Speed,* an exposé of the automobile business, inspired a new awareness of the connections between technology, politics, personal freedom, and environmental dangers.

A huge and diverse array of organizations would in ensuing years press and expand the environmentalist agenda. Middle-of-the-road, predominately white organizations like the Sierra Club, the Nature Conservancy, and the Audubon Society mobilized nature lovers on behalf of endangered animals and plants and against development in wilderness areas. More militant groups like Earth First! engaged in what they called "monkey-wrenching," after the title of a novel by environmentalist writer Edward Abbey. Their tactics included disabling construction equipment and driving metal spikes into trees to destroy loggers' chain saws. Other groups, like the Southwest Organizing Project, headquartered in New Mexico, made the connection between racism and environmental degradation. They noted developers' and policymakers' predilection for locating toxic waste dumps in minority communities, and they pointed out the seeming indifference of many white environmentalists to the ecological dangers minority communities disproportionately faced. In time, these environmental groups became a formidable national political force; Congress responded to their political clout by establishing the federal Environmental Protection Agency.

CONCLUSION

In the 1960s and early 1970s, the nation's youth launched a frontal assault on conventional behavior, smashing the barriers between public and private life, and legitimizing new ideas and new behaviors. They exposed the depth of racial oppression in the United States, catalyzed the American withdrawal from Vietnam, began a sexual revolution, helped found a lasting feminist movement, promoted recognition of the plural nature of American society, and pressed new concern for the environment.

But these innovations created controversy and carried troubling consequences. Young radicals contributed to the climate of violence that engulfed American society by the 1970s. Moreover, by justifying their sometimes outrageous behavior in the name of personal freedom, they paved the way for what historian Christopher Lasch called "the culture of narcissism"—the retreat of many Americans into the pursuit of personal pleasure. By 1980 pundits were referring to the 1970s as the "Me Decade," contrasting that era with the more socially involved sixties. But the cultivation of "me" was to some extent a legacy of those radical years, an outgrowth of the Yippies and the hippies, the rock festivals and the drugs and the summer of love. Values spawned by movements for social justice, it seemed, could just as easily be deployed on behalf of individualism.

Perhaps inevitably, there was a counterrevolution. President Nixon's attorney general, John Mitchell, looked at the turmoil of the late 1960s and predicted that "this country's going to go so far right, you won't believe it." That old enemy of the Left, Ronald Reagan, ultimately led the triumphal march as the Right seized power in the United States in 1980. Even some former hippies and leftists moved to the opposite end of the political spectrum. Jerry Rubin, who had helped lead the Yippie protest at the 1968 Democratic convention, put on a suit and became a Wall Street wizard; Black Panther Eldridge Cleaver so repudiated revolutionary politics that the 1980s found him running for public office in California as a Republican. The Religious Right of the 1980s and 1990s adopted, with immense success, the grassroots organizing techniques developed by the radicals of the 1960s and 1970s.

The politics and culture of protest demanded a great deal from those who took part in the movements, and there were casualties. Drugs ended too many careers too soon. Charismatic Panther leader Huey Newton died in a shoot-out over a drug deal. Some, like Anne Moody, simply wanted to retire from dangerous advocacy and live a quiet life.

However, not all sixties activists burned out or rejected the politics of their youth. SNCC's John Lewis took his commitment to racial justice to Congress. Another SNCC veteran, Maria Varela, moved to northern New Mexico to create institutions promoting economic self-sufficiency for Hispanic villagers. The SDS's Tom Hayden campaigned for economic democracy from the halls of the California state legislature. Feminist lawyer Ruth Bader Ginsburg was appointed to the United States Supreme Court. Grateful Dead member Bob Weir became a committed environmentalist, urging fans at Dead concerts to help save the Brazilian rain forest. The unruly, diverse, sometimes shimmeringly beautiful, sometimes corrosively ugly political and cultural energies unleashed in the sixties could not be entirely suppressed. A host of genies had been let out of a multitude of bottles. ■

F U R T H E R   R E A D I N G

For an overview of this period, see: David Farber, *The Age of Great Dreams: America in the 1960s* (1994). On civil rights and Black Power, see: Clayborn Carson, *In Struggle: SNCC and the Black Awakening of the 1960s* (1981); William H. Chafe, *Civilities and Civil Rights: Greensboro, North Carolina, and the Black*

Struggle for Freedom (1980); David J. Garrow, *Bearing the Cross: Martin Luther King, Jr., and the Southern Christian Leadership Conference* (1986); Harvard Sitkoff, *The Struggle for Black Equality, 1954–1981.* On the New Left and the antiwar movement, see: Wini Breines, *The Great Refusal: Community and Organization in the New Left* (1983); Todd Gitlin, *The Sixties: Years of Hope, Days of Rage* (1987); James Miller, *"Democracy Is in the Streets": From Port Huron to the Siege of Chicago* (1987); W. J. Rorabaugh, *Berkeley at War* (1989); Kirkpatrick Sale, *SDS* (1973). On the counterculture, see: Charles Perry, *The Haight-Ashbury* (1984); Theodore Roszak, *The Making of a Counterculture* (1969); Nicholas Von Hoffman, *We Are the People Our Parents Warned Us Against* (1968); Warren J. Belasco, *Appetite for Change: How the Counterculture Took on the Food Industry, 1966–1988* (1989). On women's changing lives and the women's movement, see: William H. Chafe, *The American Woman: Her Changing Social, Economic, and Political Role, 1920–1970* (1972); Flora Davis, *Moving the Mountain: The Women's Movement in America Since 1960* (1991); Susan J. Douglas, *Where the Girls Are: Growing Up Female with the Mass Media* (1994); Alice Echols, *Daring to Be Bad: Radical Feminism in America, 1967–1975* (1989); Barbara Ehrenreich, et al., *Re-making Love: The Feminization of Sex* (1987); Sara Evans, *Personal Politics* (1978).

9

The Illusion of Peace:
Foreign Policy During
the Nixon Administration

On July 20, 1969, astronaut Neil Armstrong climbed down the ladder of the *Apollo 11* lunar landing module and became the first person to walk on the Moon. When Armstrong radioed back to Earth, "That's one small step for man, one giant leap for mankind," the country rejoiced and temporarily set aside its bitter divisions over the war in Vietnam. When the astronauts returned to Earth, President Richard M. Nixon called their seven-day journey "the greatest week in the history of the world since the Creation." For a brief while it seemed that a new age had dawned and that Americans had regained their earlier faith in the future. Scientists predicted Americans would be taking cheap vacations on the Moon by 1990 and that astronauts would land on Mars and the outer planets by 2000.

The *Apollo 11* mission fulfilled President John F. Kennedy's pledge to "put a man on the Moon and return him safely to Earth in this decade." Kennedy had promoted space exploration as an important part of the political and scientific competition between the United States and the Soviet Union. His vice president, Lyndon Johnson, had explained that "failure to master space means being second best in every aspect in the crucial arena of our Cold War world." But by 1969 the catastrophic war in Vietnam had sapped Americans' optimism about dominating world politics. Richard Nixon won the presidency in 1968 in part by tapping the vast public dismay over the costs of global intervention. He assailed "the policies and mistakes of the past," complaining that "never has so much military, economic, and diplomatic power been used as ineffectively as in Vietnam." Yet his own plans for solving the Vietnam riddle remained murky: his campaign speeches promised only "an honorable end to the war."

Nixon, aware of the war's increasing unpopularity, agreed with many foreign affairs experts who considered Vietnam a drain on American resources and a diversion from what should be the principal focus of U.S. foreign policy—managing the dangerous competition with the Soviet Union. Reducing the attention paid to Vietnam and restoring the United States' freedom to act in the rest of the world became the new administration's first foreign policy goals.

Within a month of the election, Nixon began what *Time* magazine later called his "improbable partnership" with Henry Kissinger, the forty-five-year-old German-born Harvard professor Nixon selected as his national security adviser. Over the next five and a half years, Kissinger had more access to Nixon than anyone else in the government, briefing him daily on world events, discussing grand strategy in foreign affairs, hammering out negotiations with other countries, gossiping about politicians, and plotting retribution on rivals at home and abroad.

From 1969 to 1974, Nixon and Kissinger orchestrated some of the greatest reversals in U.S. foreign policy since the beginning of the Cold War. Contemptuous of the State Department bureaucracy, they worked secretly to arrange dramatic meetings with old adversaries. Together they altered the course of the war in Vietnam, reduced tensions with the Soviet Union, opened relations with China, and made the United States the dominant foreign power in the Middle East. The public cheered Nixon and Kissinger at the time, just as it had cheered the astronauts. It seemed that the United States was facing the rest of the world—not to mention outer space—with renewed imagination and purpose. A Gallup poll listed Kissinger as the most admired man in the world in both 1972 and 1973. Even long-time political foes came to believe that Nixon had a flair for foreign relations. But by the time the president resigned in disgrace over the Watergate scandal in August 1974, détente had soured and peace in Vietnam had proved illusory. What Nixon and Kissinger had heavily promoted in 1971 as their "structure of peace" appeared to have been little more than diplomatic sleight of hand. Nevertheless, Nixon and Kissinger did react positively to changes in the international environment, and some of their actions later led to the end of the Cold War.

Richard Nixon and Henry Kissinger complemented each other and helped fulfill each other's ambitions. The president sought respectability and acceptance from eastern politicians, journalists, and intellectuals, and Kissinger sought power and prestige.

Nixon and Kissinger quietly revived the Johnson administration's tentative first steps toward better relations with the Soviet Union. During the first six weeks of the new administration, Kissinger opened a secret, "back-channel" line of communication with Soviet ambassador Anatoly Dobrynin. The national security adviser circumvented Secretary of State William P. Rogers, fearing that the State Department could not be trusted to follow his blueprint for improving U.S.-Soviet relations. He tried to enlist Dobrynin's help in pressuring North Vietnam to negotiate a deal on the war. Kissinger also began exploring arms control and trade discussions with the Soviet representative.

THE RETREAT FROM VIETNAM

Supportive news stories about Kissinger's dazzling intellect helped relieve some of the pressure on the new administration to end the war in Vietnam immediately. Commentators trusted Kissinger to handle the situation. More important in buying the administration time was the confusion and disarray among the opponents of the war following the debacle at the 1968 Democratic convention. Nixon and Kissinger knew, however, that the public would not long stand for a continued stalemate. Nixon promised he wasn't going to end up like

Lyndon Johnson, "holed up in the White House, afraid to show my face on the street. I'm going to stop that war. Fast." Both Nixon and Kissinger wanted a negotiated settlement, one that would preserve what they called American honor. Ultimately, the Nixon administration pursued three somewhat conflicting goals at once: reducing public attention on Vietnam, negotiating a face-saving arrangement with Hanoi, and bolstering the military capacity of Saigon.

Nixon and Kissinger began what was called Vietnamization of the war in Southeast Asia. Vietnamization followed a pattern set in the last months of the Johnson administration. Because public opposition to the war rose and fell in response to reports of American casualties, the United States would reduce its military actions on the ground, turning more of them over to the ARVN, the South Vietnamese army. At the same time, the air force and navy would step up their bombing of North Vietnam, to speed the pace of the Paris negotiations.

In June 1969 Nixon conferred with South Vietnamese president Nguyen Van Thieu on Midway Island. He explained Vietnamization, the scheme of turning more of the fighting over to the ARVN. Nixon then publicly announced the withdrawal of twenty-five thousand American troops from the war zone. Fewer American troops meant lower monthly draft calls, which Nixon hoped would reduce young people's anger about the war. In 1969 he also replaced the aging, abrasive General Lewis Hershey as head of Selective Service with Curtis Tarr, who promised to make the draft fairer by introducing a lottery in which men were selected randomly on the basis of their birth date.

In June 1969 Nixon tried to further reduce public anxiety about the war by forswearing the future use of American troops in Asian wars. In a statement quickly labeled the "Nixon Doctrine" by the press, the president said that in the future the United States would provide military and economic assistance to foreign countries resisting communist revolution, but would expect "the nation directly threatened to assume the primary responsibility of providing the manpower for its own defense."

But at the same time, U.S. planes expanded the air war into neighboring Cambodia, with a series of secret air raids designed to stop the North Vietnamese from using Cambodian trails to bring soldiers and supplies into South Vietnam. Over the next fifteen months American B-52s flew more than 3,600 raids, dropping over 100,000 tons of bombs on Cambodia. Although the bombing pleased Joint Chiefs chairman Earle Wheeler, Secretary of Defense Melvin Laird remained skeptical. He ordered an assessment of "the risk of hitting Cambodian personnel." Wheeler responded that "the enemy is suffering human and material losses"; but he did not tell Laird whether the bombing had fulfilled its purpose of slowing the flow of supplies from North Vietnam to the Communist forces in the South.

Despite efforts to keep the attacks secret, the *New York Times* reported the bombings, asserting that they violated Cambodian neutrality. Nixon railed that he was "being sabotaged by bureaucrats," meaning civilian workers on the NSC staff whom he suspected of leaking word of the bombing to the *Times*. Kissinger, distraught over the leaks and worried that Nixon might suspect him of disloyalty, arranged for FBI director J. Edgar Hoover to conduct wiretaps on members of the NSC staff—that is, Kissinger's own staff—who were suspected of leaking information. The taps revealed little, but they set a dangerous precedent for the administration.

Meanwhile, Vietnamization went forward. ARVN troops rose from 850,000 to over 1 million men, and another 100,000 South Vietnamese were enrolled in military schools. The United States encouraged South Vietnam to modernize its armed forces' promotion and pay systems. The Americans turned over huge quantities of weaponry to the ARVN: 1 million rifles, 12,000 machine guns, 40,000 grenade launchers, and 2,000 heavy mortars. Washington also transferred hundreds of planes, ships, helicopters, and trucks to the South Vietnamese.

But it seemed unlikely that even a better-equipped and better-paid ARVN could prevail over the National Liberation Front (NLF) and the North Vietnamese in 1969. Despite reforms, many problems still plagued the ARVN. About 20 percent of the soldiers listed on ARVN rosters were "ghosts," men who had died or deserted but whose names were kept on the rolls so commanders could pocket their pay. Desertion rates remained high, and the officer corps remained corrupt and reluctant to fight.

Conditions in the American army in Vietnam deteriorated as Vietnamization proceeded. Formerly individual soldiers had been reluctant to fight as the end of their tour of duty approached; now whole platoons refused to proceed with the few remaining search-and-destroy operations that were ordered. No one wanted to be among the last Americans killed or wounded in a war that had become the responsibility of the Vietnamese. American commanders saw the army disintegrate before their eyes. Drug use rose. In 1970 the command estimated that sixty-five thousand soldiers used narcotics. More frightening were the more than two thousand reports in 1970 of "fragging," as soldiers attacked unpopular officers with fragmentation bombs or rifles. Furthermore, the unpopularity of the war made it difficult to recruit young men into the American military academies. Modernization efforts suffered as well, as the Pentagon continued to spend over $12 billion per year on Vietnam. By the fall of 1969, Secretary of Defense Laird wanted the war ended if only to prevent further deterioration in the armed forces' morale.

In the spring of 1970 Nixon decided to pursue a number of dramatic military gestures in Vietnam, even as he quickened the pace of

American withdrawal. In March he announced plans to remove an additional 150,000 troops by the end of the year. At the same time, Cambodia's chief of staff, General Lon Nol, overthrew the government of Prince Norodom Sihanouk. Unlike Sihanouk, Lon Nol sided solidly with the Americans and the South Vietnamese, and he wanted them to rid neutral Cambodia of the North Vietnamese, who used Cambodia's border region to support insurgents in South Vietnam. American generals, worried about the effect of withdrawing 150,000 American troops, also pressed Nixon to intervene in Cambodia and to show the South Vietnamese that the United States was still willing to help them fight. Furthermore, Nixon thought a flamboyant military move could help him seize the initiative from the Democratic Senate, which that spring had rejected two conservative Supreme Court nominees, Clement Haynsworth and G. Harrold Carswell (see Chapter 10).

In late April Nixon decided to invade Cambodia to bolster the sagging fortunes of its new government. On the evening of April 30 he went before the American public to plead for their support. "If when the chips are down the world's most powerful nation acts like a pitiful, helpless giant," he said, "the forces of totalitarianism and anarchy will threaten free nations and free institutions throughout the world." The invasion produced a modest military yield, killing two thousand enemy troops and destroying eight thousand bunkers, and it may have bought some time for additional Vietnamization. It failed completely, however, in its larger goal of reversing the trend toward a military victory for the North. The ARVN forces fought poorly, and their incompetence and unwillingness to fight were abundantly evident on evening news programs. U.S. and ARVN forces also failed to find the North Vietnamese "nerve center" reputedly located in Cambodia.

Worst of all, from Nixon's point of view, the Cambodian operation provoked some of the most furious antiwar demonstrations of the Vietnam era. As described in Chapter 8, protests against the war, the draft, military-sponsored research, and the Reserve Officers' Training Corps (ROTC) erupted on hundreds of college campuses across the country. After National Guard troops killed four protesters at Kent State University, news of the slaughter further inflamed antiwar passions. Over 100,000 young people spontaneously converged on Washington to petition Congress to end the war. Thousands gathered at the Lincoln Memorial, where early one morning they were astonished to receive a visit from none other than Richard Nixon, distraught over the outrage his actions had produced. Nixon did little to cool the protesters' anger with this ineffectual gesture. Uncomfortable with strangers and in situations he could not control, Nixon made small talk about college football with young people who wanted the war to end. The president further strained relations with his opponents by publicly describing some protesters as "bums" who were more concerned with burning and looting their campuses than with studying.

Some members of Congress were also infuriated by the Cambodian invasion. Arkansas senator J. William Fulbright, chairman of the Senate Foreign Relations Committee, thought Nixon's policies were "undermining the security of our country." Congress responded to public concern over the Cambodian invasion by repealing the 1964 Tonkin Gulf Resolution, used by Presidents Johnson and Nixon to justify continued American participation in the war. Two Senate doves, Democrat Frank Church of Idaho and Republican John Sherman Cooper of Kentucky, introduced legislation to block further funding of American operations in Cambodia after June 30. The amendment passed the Senate but failed in the House. In any event, Nixon had already said the troops would leave by that date. The president responded defiantly to lawmakers' efforts to restrict his actions in Vietnam, saying, "If Congress undertakes to restrict me, Congress will have to assume the consequences."

At the same time, Kissinger undertook a renewed public relations campaign to undermine support for the antiwar movement. When three members of his staff resigned in protest over the Cambodian invasion, he told journalists that their departure represented "the epitome of the cowardice of the Eastern Establishment." He also tried to calm his former colleagues in academia, asking for their patience and warning that further protest against the war would provoke a backlash among conservative Americans who favored greater military force in Vietnam.

Neither the counterattacks against the antiwar movement nor the invasion of Cambodia brought the war any closer to an end. The peace talks in Paris stalled. The North Vietnamese delegation dismissed as a farce American proposals to withdraw troops if the North Vietnamese left the South. Willing to wait for a better proposal, the North Vietnamese threatened to remain in Paris "until the chairs rot." In August 1969, hoping that North Vietnamese diplomat Xuan Thuy would be more forthcoming in private than in public, Kissinger opened secret conversations in Paris, but he returned home dispirited. The North insisted that the United States leave Vietnam and stop supporting the Thieu regime. Because North Vietnam had never acknowledged the division of Vietnam into separate countries, it would not withdraw its forces from what it considered part of its own territory.

By the middle of 1970, therefore, Nixon's honeymoon with the public over Vietnam had ended. The expansion of the war into Cambodia revived the domestic turmoil of 1968. Like Johnson before him, Nixon could not appear safely on college campuses across the country. Unlike his Democratic predecessor, however, Nixon appealed to the more hawkish section of the electorate. As long as that group was satisfied, the administration could make progress toward its other foreign policy goals. Antiwar outbursts after the Cambodian invasion polarized national opinion, making hawkish Americans even more committed to Nixon. A few days after the incident at Kent State, construction workers rampaged through New York's financial district. They beat up antiwar demonstrators, forced officials at City Hall to raise the American flag (which had been lowered in mourning after the Kent State killings), and smashed windows at nearby Pace College. Two weeks later, the head of the New York Labor Council led an estimated 60,000 to 100,000 flag-waving union members in a march supporting the invasion of Cambodia and opposing the antiwar demonstrations. Nixon received their support warmly.

The emotional exhaustion following the massive demonstrations of 1969 and the shock of the Kent State killings, combined with the American withdrawal from Cambodia in June 1970, took a toll on the antiwar movement. As another 150,000 American troops left Vietnam and casualty figures dropped below one hundred per week, public concern about Vietnam fell slowly until early 1971. Then anger revived as the ARVN, encouraged by the American command, invaded another neighboring country, Laos. Once again they were looking for a nonexistent North Vietnamese headquarters; instead they encountered thirty-six thousand battle-hardened North Vietnamese troops. Without the large contingent of Americans who had led them into Cambodia the year before, the ARVN forces stumbled badly. After six weeks of the bloodiest fighting of the war, in which the South Vietnamese suffered casualties of 50 percent of their forces, the ARVN retreated in disarray. Administration statements that the ARVN had exercised an "orderly retreat" from Laos made no sense to TV viewers, who saw film clips of terrified South Vietnamese soldiers clinging to the skids of helicopters, desperately trying to get back to South Vietnam.

On Sunday, June 13, 1971, the *New York Times* began a series of articles on the origins of U.S. involvement in the war in Vietnam. "My God, there it is!" said former Defense Department official Leslie Gelb when he opened his newspaper that morning. "It" was the forty-seven-volume *History of U.S. Decision-Making Process on Vietnam, 1945–1967*, popularly known as the *Pentagon Papers*, which Gelb had compiled at Secretary of Defense Robert McNamara's request in 1968. Daniel Ellsberg, a former Defense Department official who had grown disillusioned with the war, had leaked copies of the *Pentagon Papers* to *Times* reporter Neil Sheehan earlier that spring. The secret history contained therein cast a dark shadow over the foreign policy of every administration from Truman through Johnson. The documents revealed that American officials had ignored international agreements, manipulated the Saigon government, and deliberately misinformed

Congress and the public. The *Pentagon Papers* convinced some people who had previously remained undecided about the war that the U.S. government had long known that its original commitment to Vietnam was a mistake.

At first there was disagreement within the administration over whether publication of the *Pentagon Papers* would help or hurt its diplomatic position. But within forty-eight hours, the Nixon team had decided to try to block further publication. Fearful that the *New York Times* series might upset delicate negotiations with the Soviet Union over arms control and with China over normalizing relations, the administration obtained a temporary restraining order against the paper, barring further publication of the *Papers*. The Supreme Court issued a decision in favor of the *Times* with remarkable speed. On June 30, the Court ruled against the government's demand for "prior restraint" on publication, because the government had not met "the heavy burden of showing the justification for the importance of such restraint."

In the aftermath of the Court's rebuff, Nixon aide John Ehrlichman created the so-called Plumbers unit, a band of operatives charged with stopping leaks from government officials. The Plumbers' activities were more sinister than their playful name. One of them, a former CIA agent named E. Howard Hunt, proposed digging into Ellsberg's private life to find ways to "destroy his public image and credibility." Later that summer, Hunt and a squad of anti-Castro Cuban exiles with ties to the CIA broke into the office of Ellsberg's psychiatrist to look for discrediting information to leak to the press. John Ehrlichman later went to jail for his role in the break-in. The next year Hunt, the Cuban exiles, and G. Gordon Liddy, who had helped plan the burglary, organized the notorious break-in at the Democratic National Committee offices at the Watergate office complex (see Chapter 10).

Public concern over Vietnam diminished in the last half of 1971, after the uproar over the *Pentagon Papers* subsided. American casualty rates and troop levels had declined, and declining draft calls had removed some of the urgency from the protest movement. But the Paris peace talks stalled in 1971, as neither the United States nor North Vietnam would make any concessions. Washington would not jettison Thieu, and the Communists refused even to acknowledge that they had troops in the South. For the remainder of the year, the United States followed a combination strategy of negotiation, threats to the Saigon government, and ferocious bombing. American officials believed that détente with the Soviet Union and China would force Hanoi to offer concessions. But these hopes were in vain: North Vietnam remained firmly committed to a complete U.S. withdrawal from the South. By the beginning of 1972, Nixon was complaining to Kissinger that he felt terrible pressure to end the war before the

Few people supported the American war effort in Vietnam as ardently as Daniel Ellsberg did up until 1967. And after 1968, no one opposed the war more strenuously. Ellsberg, a brilliant former Marine officer employed as a civilian analyst for the Defense Department, was a man of contrasts and contradictions. He combined deep analytical power with a moral passion for whatever cause he embraced.

Like many other highly educated Americans, Ellsberg had devoted his career to the Cold War. Born in 1931, he graduated summa cum laude from Harvard University, then volunteered for three years as a Marine officer before returning to Harvard for his Ph.D. In 1965 he joined a Defense Department team that urged reforms on the South Vietnamese government and tried to build support among the peasantry. But

Daniel Ellsberg

November election. Kissinger advised delaying any settlement until just before the election. That way, Nixon would gain timely adulation as a peacemaker without having to risk disillusioning the voters should the South Vietnamese government later fall to the Communists.

North Vietnam launched a full-scale invasion of the South in March 1972, sending in 120,000 troops. Only 6,000 of the 95,000 American troops remaining in the South were combat soldiers. The North Vietnamese met little resistance, advancing to within sixty miles of Saigon. The ARVN threw all its reserves into meeting the assault from the North, which allowed Vietcong guerrillas in the South to overrun villages in the heavily populated Mekong Delta, near the capital. In response, on May 8 Nixon ordered the largest escalation of the war since 1968. U.S. forces mined Haiphong harbor, blockaded other North Vietnamese harbors, and engaged in the most sustained bombing of the North since the war began.

the devastation wrought by the United States in Vietnam gradually eroded Ellsberg's faith in the war. Deeply discouraged, he left Vietnam in 1967 and went to work for the Rand Corporation, a Defense Department think tank.

The slaughter during the Tet offensive of 1968 completed Ellsberg's conversion into an opponent of the war. The next year he concluded that the Nixon administration's policy of Vietnamization was a "bloody, hopeless, uncompelled, hence surely immoral prolongation of U.S. involvement in this war." Burdened with guilt, he decided to act. He wrote letters to newspaper editors, demanding American withdrawal from Vietnam. Privately he began to photocopy the seven-thousand-page *Pentagon Papers,* the secret Defense Department history of the war. In early 1971, with no resolution of the war in sight,

Ellsberg delivered copies of the *Papers* to a *New York Times* reporter, hoping that their revelation of high-level deceit would shock the public into demanding an end to the war.

The Nixon administration vowed to punish Ellsberg. The Justice Department indicted him for theft, espionage, and conspiracy, and the so-called Plumbers unit broke into his psychiatrist's office to search for damaging information. When the Watergate investigation revealed the extent of the White House's campaign to discredit him, the case against Ellsberg was thrown out of court. In later years he continued to speak out against the dangers of war and what he considered the immorality of American intervention in Third World countries. ■

Although some politicians and other public figures condemned the escalation, it provoked less public opposition than the Cambodian invasion, because it resulted in fewer American casualties. Then, in late summer, the Paris peace talks between Kissinger and Le Duc Tho, the North Vietnamese representative, finally moved forward. Kissinger pointed to public opinion polls that gave Nixon a 30-point lead over Senator George McGovern, who had been nominated by a divided Democratic party to oppose Nixon in the November election. Nixon would surely win a second term, Kissinger told the North Vietnamese, and therefore they would receive the best possible offer if they reached an agreement *before* the November election. His strategy seemed to work: in October the two sides agreed on an outline for a settlement. The United States would remove its troops within sixty days of a cease-fire, and the North would release its American POWs. The United States would limit military aid to the South to replacing lost weaponry and training replacement troops. The United States also held out a promise of reconstruction assistance for North Vietnam. The North could keep its forces in the South, but it could not increase their numbers after the agreement went into effect. The Thieu government would remain in power, but it would make a good-faith effort to include other factions, including the NLF. An international commission similar to the one created by the 1954 Geneva Accords would supervise the agreements.

On October 26, less than two weeks before the presidential election, Kissinger announced that "peace is at hand" as he made public the major provisions of his agreement with Le Duc Tho. Work remained, he acknowledged, but he expected the end of the war to come soon. Although Kissinger's announcement virtually ensured Nixon's re-election, it was not accurate in its prediction of an end to the war. The South Vietnamese president panicked: fearing abandonment by the United States and realizing that his regime had no more popular support than had earlier South Vietnamese governments, President Thieu balked at signing any agreement that permitted North Vietnamese forces to remain in the South. When no agreement had been signed by election day, McGovern charged that Kissinger had tricked the public. Few voters responded: Nixon carried every state but Massachusetts and the District of Columbia.

Safely re-elected, Nixon tried to persuade Saigon to drop its objections to the October agreement. Kissinger's deputy, General Alexander Haig, traveled to Saigon with bribes and threats. If Thieu would agree to the Paris accords, the United States would provide economic and military aid to South Vietnam; furthermore, hints were dropped that the United States would resume bombing if the North violated the agreement. On the other hand, if Thieu continued to reject the agreement, the United States would sign it anyway and leave South Vietnam to fend for itself. Kissinger authorized Haig to tell the South Vietnamese leader that the president was committed to ending the war and would forge ahead with the deal regardless of anything Saigon did to stop it. Still, Thieu would not sign the accords.

Neither would the North Vietnamese agree to consider significant modifications to the agreement in order to break the impasse. Faced with this recalcitrance, Nixon tried to bludgeon the North into reopening the talks. On December 22, 1972, the United States unleashed the heaviest bombing campaign of the war against the North. Over the next twelve days, B-52s dropped thirty-six thousand tons of explosives, more bombs than were dropped in the period from 1969 to 1971. Approximately sixteen hundred civilians were killed in Hanoi and Haiphong. Critics at home and abroad expressed outrage at Nixon's behavior. Several characterized him as a madman. The president's approval rating dropped to 39 percent. Yet Nixon and Kis-

Henry Kissinger and North Vietnamese representative Le Duc Tho (center) confer during the Paris peace talks to end the war in Vietnam. *National Archives/Nixon Presidential Materials.*

singer retained a solid core of support for their overall foreign policies among journalists and foreign affairs experts.

The bombing and Nixon's eagerness to end the war restarted the stalled negotiations. Talks resumed in Paris between Kissinger and Le Duc Tho in early January. They made a few changes to the October agreement, including strengthening the boundary at the Demilitarized Zone, but they kept the major provisions of the earlier draft. On January 27, 1973, the two men signed a cease-fire agreement. The United States promised to withdraw its remaining troops within sixty days in return for the release of its POWs. The North promised not to increase its troops in the South. The Thieu government would remain in power, but vague plans for "political reconciliation" would go forward in the South, supervised by an international commission. The Saigon government did not sign the agreement, but this time Thieu indicated his approval, provided the United States promised to protect South Vietnam from future North Vietnamese attacks.

Americans felt great relief at the apparent end of the war and the imminent return of the POWs. The White House press office reported gleefully that "there is great admiration for the president, which seems to grow as we move further from Washington." For example, an Alabama paper lauded the "patient, long-suffering efforts of the administration" in bringing about accords that "represent in fact a much better bargain than Sen. George McGovern or other 'dove' critics were willing to settle for."

On Veteran's Day, November 11, 1982, the Vietnam Veterans Memorial was dedicated in Washington, D.C. The names of more than 58,000 Americans who died in Vietnam were etched into the black granite. © *1995 Susan Meiselas/Magnum Photos.*

But the peace Nixon had promised in 1968 had been a long time in the making. Nixon's first term had seen some of the heaviest fighting and worst suffering of the war. Officials estimated that 107,000 South Vietnamese soldiers and approximately half a million North Vietnamese and NLF fighters lost their lives during that period. Another 20,553 American troops were killed during those four years, bringing the total number of American deaths to over 58,000. The number of civilians killed will never be known; most estimates place it at over 1 million.

There was considerable question about whether the cease-fire truly represented "peace with honor," the outcome Nixon had promised during the 1968 campaign. The agreement left the South Vietnamese government in place, but it did not resolve the fundamental issue of the war: would Vietnam be one country or two? The fact that the agreement gave official recognition to the NLF and allowed the North to keep troops in the South ensured that the struggle would continue. For the Communists, the Paris agreement merely represented another temporary delay in their thirty-year effort to unify the country under their leadership. Certain that history was on their side, they waited for the opportune moment to complete their revolution.

In the West, however, the Paris agreement appeared to be a major accomplishment. In October 1973 the Nobel Prize Committee announced it had awarded its 1973 Peace Prize to Kissinger and Le Duc

Tho for their work on the Paris agreement. Le refused his share, because the political future of the South had not been resolved and fighting could resume at a moment's notice. But Kissinger and Le Duc Tho won praise from many American editorialists.

Kissinger's winning the Nobel Peace Prize marked the high point of enthusiasm in the United States for the settlement arranged in Paris. Vietnam faded as an issue for the rest of Nixon's second term, as Watergate, a war in the Middle East, and relations with the Soviet Union took center stage. Yet the fighting in Vietnam had not come to an end. The cease-fire gradually eroded. Each side attacked the other, and the North Vietnamese reinforced their positions in the South. President Thieu refused to bargain in good faith with NLF leaders to bring them into the government. By the beginning of 1975, five months after Nixon had left the presidency in disgrace, Vietnam stood poised on the verge of a climactic struggle that would chase Thieu from power and give final victory to the Communists (see Chapter 11).

DÉTENTE WITH THE SOVIET UNION

Long before the cease-fire in Vietnam, the Nixon administration had taken major steps in other foreign policy arenas. One of the most significant was the administration's attempt to renew détente with the Soviet Union. Relations between Washington and Moscow had been strained since the August 1968 Soviet invasion of Czechoslovakia. But Nixon and Kissinger had several reasons for wanting to reduce U.S.-Soviet tensions.

First, they believed that improved relations with Moscow might produce a breakthrough in Vietnam. Second, Nixon and Kissinger saw that détente with the Eastern bloc would help them maintain control of the NATO alliance. In search of economic markets, Western European governments and businesses were beginning to work out their own pattern of détente. For example, after a new Social Democratic government came to power in West Germany, the Soviets arranged in 1969 to borrow over $1 billion from West German firms and invited scores of them to invest in joint ventures. Soon other Western European businesses joined the rush to sell electronic equipment, build truck factories, construct buildings, and drill for oil and natural gas in the Soviet Union. If the United States maintained its hostility toward the Soviets while Western Europe moved toward cooperation, NATO might disintegrate. Moreover, American businesses, wanting their share of the Eastern bloc markets, demanded that Washington lift restrictions on East-West trade.

Finally, Nixon faced the same basic worry as all other presidents since the Second World War: the danger of nuclear war with the

Soviet Union. An arms control agreement with the Soviets would reduce the likelihood of nuclear war and demonstrate that the two powers could find common ground. In political terms, progress on arms control could help the administration quiet the scientists, editorial writers, and members of Congress who complained that the world faced grave dangers from the development of highly accurate, long-range ballistic missiles.

The Nixon administration conducted three years of highly complicated negotiations, known as the Strategic Arms Limitation Talks (SALT), with the Soviet Union. At his inauguration Nixon promised "an era of negotiation" with the Soviets, and at his first press conference he advocated replacing U.S. superiority in nuclear arms with nuclear "sufficiency." While a SALT negotiating team opened public conversations with the Soviets in Helsinki and Vienna, Kissinger conducted his own conversations with Soviet ambassador Anatoly Dobrynin behind the scenes.

As the SALT talks went forward, Congress sought to delay development of an antiballistic missile (ABM) system, first proposed in the last years of the Johnson administration. In August 1969 the Senate came within a single vote of stopping further work on the ABM system. This close call encouraged the administration to work harder on reaching an agreement with the Soviets. In May 1971 Kissinger's conversations with Dobrynin bore fruit, and the two publicly announced that they had separated the ABM issue from that of intercontinental ballistic missiles (ICBMs). They promised to concentrate on limiting ABM development. Although they proposed only "vague measures" leading toward a SALT treaty restricting ICBMs, Nixon was ecstatic at the breakthrough.

Over the next year, conversations continued between U.S. and Soviet diplomats on other issues. In November 1971, Commerce Secretary Maurice Stans went to Moscow to sign a series of economic agreements between the two countries. The United States agreed to build a $500 million truck factory for the Soviets and to sell them $136 million worth of grain and $125 million worth of oil drilling and mining equipment. American farmers and businesspeople welcomed these agreements at first; but two years later, when drought raised grain prices at home, U.S. consumers complained that wheat sold to the Soviet Union should have remained in the United States to keep prices low.

In March 1972 Kissinger traveled to Moscow to lay the groundwork for a summit between Nixon and Soviet Communist Party secretary Leonid Brezhnev. Before Kissinger left, Nixon stressed to him the domestic political importance of the upcoming summit. He considered it "vitally important that no final agreements be entered into until we arrive in Moscow." Otherwise, there would be no "news value to them." Nixon explained that Democratic congressional critics "will try to make it appear that all of this could have been achieved without any summitry whatever."

Accordingly, when Nixon visited Moscow in May he conducted a dramatic series of late-night negotiations with Brezhnev, with only Kissinger and an interpreter in attendance. (Secretary of State Rogers was pushed into the background.) These high-level talks yielded three significant agreements. An ABM treaty limited each power to only two ABM sites. SALT-I, or Interim Agreement on Limitations of Strategic Armaments, included a five-year pledge to limit land-based missiles to the number then contemplated by the U.S. arms program—a number that reduced Soviet plans by approximately 33 percent. The agreement also called for continued talks toward a later, more complete arms control treaty. Finally, a document called the "Basic Principles of U.S.-Soviet Relations" contained a promise to base subsequent superpower relations on "the principle of equality." Together these three agreements formed the basis of détente between the two superpowers for the next two years.

Before returning to Washington, Nixon and Kissinger stopped in Iran to cement a strategic connection with Shah Mohammed Reza Pahlavi. "I need you," the president told the Iranian monarch. Nixon wanted Iran to act as a "surrogate" power in South Asia, as part of the regional security scheme envisaged by the Nixon Doctrine. As an inducement to protect Western strategic interests in the oil-rich region of the Persian Gulf, Kissinger offered to sell Iran any weapon in the American arsenal, except nuclear bombs. State Department arms experts objected that the United States might lose control of some of its most sophisticated hardware by giving the shah such free access, but Kissinger overrode the dissenters through his close relationship with the president. Over the next five years Iran bought $8 billion worth of American weapons. Ultimately, American support for the shah backfired. A revolution swept the country, and in January 1979 the Shah— hated for his repressive rule—was forced to flee the country. The new leaders blamed the United States for the Shah's reign of terror (see Chapter 11). But at the time of Kissinger's offer, this was all years in the future.

When Nixon returned to Washington from Moscow and Tehran, he appeared to have engineered a major turning point in U.S.-Soviet relations. Old adversaries like Democratic senators Fulbright, Church, and Claiborne Pell of Rhode Island rushed to support détente. Other lawmakers pointed to flaws in the SALT agreement, however. Democratic senator Henry Jackson of Washington objected that Nixon's concept of nuclear "sufficiency"—the guiding principle that determined the U.S. position during talks—allowed the Soviets three hundred more land-based ICBMs than the United States. Kissinger emphasized that the United States retained a technological edge. The Soviets' large numbers of nuclear weapons were now constrained by the SALT treaty. The United States, on the other hand, was making major scientific advances in weaponry, and the SALT agreement—on the advice of the Joint Chiefs of Staff—imposed no limitations on them.

That fall, Congress approved both the ABM treaty and the SALT-I agreement. Yet it also tied Kissinger's hands in negotiating the full SALT treaty promised in the interim accords. Jackson attached a proviso to the congressional ratification, requiring that in future talks the United States demand numerical equality between the two nations' nuclear arsenals, a condition he claimed, erroneously, had been promised in the "Basic Principles of U.S.-Soviet Relations." Jackson's restrictions became a straitjacket from which even the artful Kissinger could not escape. U.S. and Soviet forces were not "symmetrical." The United States relied on a triad of land-based ICBMs, submarine-based missiles, and manned bombers. Moscow's nuclear weaponry was concentrated in ICBMs, and therefore the Soviets wanted higher numbers of these to offset the American advantage in other weapons systems.

Over the next two years Jackson, other politicians, and various public figures suspicious of the Soviet Union chipped away at public support for détente. They berated Kissinger and Nixon for failing to make further détente dependent on the Soviet Union's improving its poor record on human rights. In 1973 Jackson joined with Ohio Democratic congressman Charles Vanik to introduce legislation forbidding the extension of equal trading rights—so-called most-favored-nation status—to the Soviets until they permitted all citizens who wished to emigrate, mostly Jews, to do so. In that year more than thirty thousand Soviet Jews left for the West, more than had ever before been permitted to leave; nevertheless, Jackson saw the emigration issue as one that would fuel his run for president in 1976. The passage of the Jackson-Vanik Amendment in 1974 prevented the Soviets from receiving most-favored-nation status, thereby irritating the Kremlin. The Soviets accused the United States of not treating them as an equal and legitimate power, and détente waned.

Arms control talks made little progress for the remainder of the Nixon administration. As the Watergate scandal grew in 1973 and engulfed the president in 1974 (see Chapter 10), Nixon attempted to regain his public standing with two more summit meetings with Brezhnev. The Soviet leader visited Nixon in Washington in June 1973, and Nixon returned the favor with a trip to Moscow and the Crimean Peninsula in late June and early July 1974, barely six weeks before his forced resignation. Neither meeting produced a major breakthrough in arms control, although subsidiary pacts were signed to help prevent nuclear war and to limit the power of nuclear test explosions.

THE OPENING TO CHINA

Nixon's most dramatic foreign policy achievement was his reversal of U.S. foreign policy toward Communist China. On July 15, 1971, President Nixon announced that National Security Adviser Kissinger had just returned from Beijing, where he had spent two days preparing the way for a presidential visit to China in 1972. Nixon and Kissinger had engineered one of the most dramatic diplomatic turnarounds of the twentieth century, in nearly complete secrecy. That Richard Nixon—one of the most vocal anti-Communists of the early Cold War—had engineered the reversal made it all the more stunning.

Both China and the United States had much to gain by resuming regular diplomatic relations, which had been nonexistent since the beginning of the Korean War. Since 1966 China's leader, Mao Zedong, had encouraged "the great proletarian Cultural Revolution," during which thousands of young "Red Guards" had roamed China's cities and countryside, terrorizing the population into ideological orthodoxy. Now other Chinese officials, led by Zhou Enlai, wanted to end the chaos of the Cultural Revolution and open better relations with the rest of the world. China's once close ties to the Soviet Union had deteriorated so badly that the two fought a bloody border war in 1969 and 1970. Fearful of greater conflict in the future, China wanted ties to the United States in order to deter Soviet aggression.

Washington, for its part, saw ties to China as a way of reclaiming prestige lost in the Vietnam War. Establishing a connection to China, the most populous country in the world and a huge potential market, would show the world that the war in Vietnam had not prevented the United States from pursuing a vigorous foreign policy agenda, as some critics contended. An added benefit might include Beijing's persuading Hanoi to accommodate American peace proposals. Even if China did not help end the war, restoration of relations after twenty years would show that the United States had interests in Asia beyond Vietnam. Closer relations with China could also help put pressure on the Soviet Union in arms control talks or regional disputes. Finally, the American policy of not recognizing the Communist regime in China was widely regarded as a failure. Most NATO allies had formal relations with the People's Republic of China, and the United Nations General Assembly was about to seat Beijing and evict Taiwan.

Kissinger discussed all these issues with Zhou Enlai during his whirlwind forty-nine-hour visit. He found the Chinese leader to be "one of the two or three most impressive men I have ever met. Urbane, infinitely patient, intelligent, subtle." They agreed that Soviet domination of much of Europe and Asia threatened world stability; they noted that the United States, the world's leading conservative power, could preserve that stability. Although the Chinese promised no help on

Vietnam, they indicated that differences over that war should not prevent the United States and China from making progress on other issues. Kissinger in turn observed that American ties to Taiwan should not prevent Washington and Beijing from working together. The two countries agreed to continue talking about their mutual interests over the next seven months as they prepared for Nixon's visit.

The highly favorable reaction to the Chinese breakthrough made the White House jubilant. Some American politicians set aside their traditional animosities toward the administration. Democratic senator Fulbright told Nixon, "I completely agree with what you are doing." Majority Leader Mike Mansfield promised understanding for the "delicacy and promise of the situation." Senator Edward M. Kennedy, whose own earlier efforts to travel to China had inspired the White House initiative, called the visit "historic." Praise also poured in from abroad.

Kissinger arranged the final details of Nixon's visit during the fall of 1971. The UN's decision to replace Taiwan with mainland China occurred as Kissinger prepared for another visit to Beijing. Kissinger's disregard for Taiwan caused a rift within the administration and provoked criticism from Democrats. Secretary of State Rogers advised Kissinger to postpone the visit to Beijing, but Nixon and Kissinger thought Taiwan's cause was lost anyway. Senator Kennedy criticized the administration for its haste to visit the Chinese capital before the 1972 presidential election.

In December 1971, war broke out between Pakistan and India over efforts by the residents of East Pakistan, known as Bengalis, to form a new state, Bangladesh. India supported the Bengalis with troops who fought Pakistani soldiers in both the eastern and western parts of the Indian subcontinent. Public opinion in Europe and America backed the Bengalis' desire for independence from western Pakistan, because the more populous but poorer easterners had suffered economically, socially, and politically at the hands of the westerners since the founding of Pakistan in 1947. Washington ignored the abuses committed by the Pakistani government against the Bengalis, however, and tilted toward Pakistan to cement its ties to China. Beijing supported Pakistan, whose leader, Ayub Khan, had helped arrange Kissinger's July trip. The Soviet Union supported India and Bangladesh, and the Bengali rebellion eventually succeeded.

Complaints that the United States had backed the wrong side in the conflict were drowned out by spectacular live television coverage of Nixon's five-day visit to China, which began on February 21, 1972. The president's handshake with Zhou Enlai at the Beijing airport erased the ancient snub made by Secretary of State John Foster Dulles in 1954, when he had refused Zhou's hand at the Geneva conference on Indochina. Nixon and Kissinger received a well-photographed audience with Chairman Mao Zedong. The president toasted the Chi-

President Nixon and his wife Pat visit the Great Wall during their visit to China in February 1972. *UPI/Bettmann Archive.*

nese in the Great Hall of the People in the heart of Beijing's Forbidden City. He and his wife Pat walked along the Great Wall, and she visited the Beijing Zoo to acknowledge its gift to the United States of two cuddly giant pandas.

While television crews produced miles of film that would later be used in Nixon's campaign ads, Kissinger worked on the terms of the new relations between the two powers. The final communiqué, issued at Shanghai at the end of the trip, announced that each country would open an "interest section"—an embassy, by another name—in the other's capital. The United States relaxed restrictions on trade with and travel to China. The two powers agreed to disagree over Taiwan, with the United States maintaining its formal embassy there. The communiqué observed that both the Communist and the Nationalist Chinese believed China to be a single country. While warning the Soviet Union that the United States and China mutually opposed Soviet domination, the communiqué promised that their new relationship threatened no one. They did not agree to work together to end the Vietnam War, and each country expressed support for its own favorite in that conflict. Nevertheless, by its very existence, the Shanghai communiqué demonstrated that the United States had moved beyond its preoccupation with Vietnam. At Shanghai, Nixon, Kissinger, and Zhou Enlai certified that friendship between Washington and Beijing could go forward regardless of what happened in Indochina.

In the wake of the tremendous popular response to the break-through in China, political opponents could only grumble that Nixon should have done more. Senator George McGovern, seeking the Democratic nomination in the 1972 presidential race, complained that if Nixon could go to China, he should be able to end the war in Vietnam. Another Democratic candidate, Hubert Humphrey, charged that the administration had sold out to Beijing. "Concessions were made by the president and by Dr. Kissinger," Humphrey said, "but not . . . by the Chinese." Representative John Ashbrook, a conservative Republican from Ohio, ran in the New Hampshire primary on the Taiwan issue, accusing Nixon of abandoning the island. He received only 7 percent of the vote. According to *Time* magazine, which named Nixon and Kissinger Men of the Year for 1972, détente with the Soviets and the opening of relations with China represented "the most profound rearrangement of the earth's political powers since the beginning of the cold war."

The breakthroughs in relations with Beijing and Moscow, combined with the Vietnam peace agreement of January 1973, established Henry Kissinger's reputation as a masterful negotiator and a brilliant innovator in foreign policy. During the summer of 1973, as Senate hearings on the Watergate scandal put Nixon in deep trouble, the president sought to recoup his flagging political standing by calling attention to his foreign affairs successes. Accordingly, in August he nominated Kissinger to replace the ineffectual and self-effacing William Rogers as secretary of state.

As evidence of what critics labeled his hammerlock on foreign policy, Kissinger retained his position as national security adviser as well. Yet the naysayers were few. Public and congressional reaction was overwhelmingly positive, and Kissinger sailed through his confirmation hearings. *Newsweek* magazine called him "the White House genius-in-residence," and *Time* labeled him a "Super Secretary." State Department officials were excited that their department would no longer be bypassed in major foreign policy decisions. As secretary of state, however, Kissinger continued his penchant for acting alone, using professional advice only when it suited his purposes. This characteristic, along with his domineering manner, eventually alienated many of the foreign affairs specialists.

OTHER CRISES, 1973

Vietnam was not the only Third World country to draw significant attention from the Nixon administration. Like earlier American presidents, Nixon wanted to hold the line against radical reform movements in Latin America. By 1970 his administration had become deeply involved in an effort to prevent socialists from controlling Chile.

In August of that year it appeared that Salvador Allende Gossens, a socialist, would receive the highest number of votes in the upcoming Chilean presidential election. If no candidate received a majority, Chile's congress would select the winner. Customarily, however, the congress had bestowed the presidency on the candidate with the highest number of votes. Allende's prospects alarmed the Nixon administration, which feared that a socialist president in Chile might serve as a model for other Latin American countries that were resentful of the United States but were unwilling to install a Castro-like dictator. Kissinger told the Forty Committee, an interagency intelligence group supervising covert operations, "I don't see why we have to let a country go Marxist just because its people are irresponsible." The Forty Committee tried bribing the Chilean congress into electing a Christian Democrat as president, but the congress chose Allende. The CIA chief in Santiago then helped arrange the assassination of the chief of staff of Chile's armed forces, General Rene Schneider, and tried to pin the blame on Allende and the socialists. The plot backfired. In Chile, Schneider's murder was widely regarded as the work of the CIA, and Allende took office as president.

Over the next few years, the United States tried, in Nixon's words, "to make the Chilean economy scream." Washington immediately stopped foreign aid to Chile and blocked loans from such government-sponsored agencies as the Export-Import Bank and the Inter-American Bank for Reconstruction and Development. It used its influence with its NATO allies and with international agencies like the International Monetary Fund and the World Bank to prevent them from helping Allende's government economically. In these respects Kissinger and Nixon acted against the advice of the American ambassador to Chile. Ambassador Edward Korry acknowledged that Allende's efforts to nationalize American-owned copper mines and telephone companies posed a "conscious challenge to the traditions of the United States' defense of its business interests in Latin America." Nevertheless, Korry urged that the United States "cultivate pragmatic relationships with Chile and avoid confrontation."

Despite divisions within the administration over how important Chile was to the United States, opponents of Allende eventually prevailed. From 1971 to 1973 the CIA supplied over $20 million to opposition newspapers and political parties in Chile, particularly the Christian Democratic party, which it had funded since 1964. It also paid striking truck drivers refusing to transport food from the countryside to the cities. By June 1973, the Chilean middle class had been squeezed into poverty, and no food was reaching Chile's major cities. The military became angry at the loss of American hardware.

Commanders feared the wrath of middle- and upper-class Chileans, whose ranks included the military's own officers. In August, with the encouragement of the CIA, conservative general Augusto Pinochet began plotting a coup.

On September 11, 1973, a right-wing junta of army officers, led by Pinochet, overthrew the Allende's government. The president was murdered or committed suicide during the coup, and in the next two weeks the new government arrested over twenty thousand socialists and their supporters, killed hundreds of them, and forced thousands more into exile. Pinochet ruled with an iron fist for the next sixteen years, brutally suppressing political parties, political speech, and union activities. Once he had established his power, the United States lifted the restrictions on military and economic aid. The economy eventually revived. In 1990 the Christian Democrats won a presidential election. Pinochet relinquished the presidency but remained the head of the armed forces.

American intervention in Chile revived charges throughout Latin America that the United States opposed movements for economic and social justice, even when they came to power peacefully through legitimate elections. In 1975 the U.S. Congress revealed the CIA's role in destabilizing Allende's regime. Many Americans expressed dismay that their government had so crudely violated the sovereignty of another state in the Western Hemisphere.

Less than a month after the Chilean coup, war broke out in the Middle East when Egypt and Syria attacked Israel on October 6, 1973. A scholar of American Middle East policy believed that the October war, commonly called the Yom Kippur War, "completed the transformation of the Arab-Israeli dispute from a nuisance into a conflict central to American diplomatic and strategic concerns."

Ever since the 1967 Six-Day War, little progress had occurred in bringing Israel and its neighbors to the peace table. The United States had become the principal arms supplier to Israel and Jordan, while the Soviet Union replenished the losses incurred by Egypt and Syria in the Six-Day War. The Arab states refused to meet Israel face to face, and the Jewish state vowed not to consider relinquishing the territories it had taken—East Jerusalem, the West Bank of the Jordan River, the Golan Heights, and the Sinai Peninsula—unless its neighbors agreed to make peace. Egypt's President Gamal Abdel Nasser then launched a so-called war of attrition against Israel's forces along the Suez Canal and in the eastern Sinai in 1969 and 1970. These events formed the background to the Middle East crisis of 1973.

Of all the agencies concerned with foreign policy in the Nixon administration, it was the State Department that paid the most attention to the Middle East from 1969 to 1972. Nixon and Kissinger concentrated on Vietnam, détente with the Soviet Union, and opening relations with China, leaving the daunting task of resolving the Arab-Israeli dispute to Secretary of State Rogers. Pleased to be out from under the thumb of the imperious national security adviser, Rogers floated an ambitious plan to resolve the conflict in a single stroke. He called on Israel to withdraw from most of the territory captured in 1967 in return for full diplomatic relations with its neighbors and their pledge to maintain peace. But Israel balked at Rogers's plan as a threat to its security. Realizing that Rogers carried less weight with Nixon than did Kissinger, Israel's diplomats accurately believed that they could ignore his unsolicited proposals without offending the United States. Nevertheless, in the summer of 1970 Rogers was able to arrange a cease-fire.

Two months later Nasser died suddenly, leaving Egypt's government in the hands of his little-known vice president, Anwar Sadat. Just as Sadat took power, King Hussein of Jordan evicted Palestine Liberation Organization (PLO) guerrillas from his country in a bloody three-day war. Nixon ordered the U.S. Mediterranean fleet to send planes and equipment to help Jordan. Thereafter, the Middle East receded from public view in Europe and the United States. Sadat consolidated his power, an uneasy calm persisted along the Suez Canal, and the PLO guerrilla raids from Jordan into Israel stopped.

But by 1973 Sadat found the "no war, no peace" situation intolerable. He resented the presence of the ten thousand Soviet soldiers Nasser had invited into Egypt, and he feared that Syria's radical government threatened Cairo's pre-eminence in the Arab world. Despairing that the United States or the United Nations would ever persuade Israel to withdraw from the captured territories, he agreed with Syria to coordinate an attack on Israeli positions in the Sinai Peninsula and the Golan Heights. On October 6, Yom Kippur, the holiest day of the Jewish religious calendar, Egyptian and Syrian forces struck. The attackers achieved more in the first three days of the conflict than Arab armies had gained in three previous wars with Israel. Egyptian troops crossed the Suez Canal and captured hundreds of stunned Israelis. In the north, Syria reclaimed a large portion of the Golan Heights and threatened to slice Israel in two. Within a week, Israel's military position appeared desperate, and Prime Minister Golda Meir begged Washington for a resupply of planes, tanks, and ammunition.

Nixon and Kissinger agreed to the largest airlift of equipment and armaments since the Second World War. Assured of new arms, Israel counterattacked, driving the Syrians off the Golan Heights and threatening Syria's capital, Damascus. In the south, Israel's tanks turned back the advancing Egyptians. A worried President Sadat asked Moscow for aid, a move that Kissinger and Nixon considered a threat to détente. Kissinger traveled to Moscow to cool the crisis. While there, he publicly rejected a Soviet call for a joint U.S.-Soviet military expedition to impose a cease-fire. It was "inconceivable," he said, for the United States and the Soviet Union to introduce enough troops to stop the fighting. He also warned the Soviets not to move their own military forces into the Middle East in any guise. Before leaving Moscow, he arranged for joint U.S.-Soviet sponsorship of a United Nations cease-fire resolution.

Now well supplied by the United States, Israel resisted an immediate end to the fighting. Its tanks crossed the Suez Canal and threatened to destroy Egypt's army and enter Cairo. The Soviets issued a warning to Jerusalem, and Nixon and Kissinger responded by ordering a full military alert of American forces in the Mediterranean and Europe. The alert occurred only days after Nixon had provoked nationwide outrage over his abrupt firing of the special prosecutor investigating White House involvement in the Watergate break-in and cover-up (see Chapter 10). One newspaper editorial speculated that "this White House may well have felt that it was necessary to display toughness on a worldwide scale to show that President Nixon was fully in command of foreign policy and in no way weakened by domestic events."

The alert passed after nine hours, and a cease-fire was finally cemented. Israeli forces occupied the east bank of the canal, Egyptian troops stood on the west bank, and Israel was in control of more Syrian territory than it had held at the beginning of the fighting. In Washington, Nixon's behavior during the war and his ordering of the military alert worried politicians of both parties. Massachusetts Democratic representative Thomas P. O'Neill, invited to a White House briefing during the height of the crisis, thought the president was unhinged. He recalled that Nixon "kept interrupting Kissinger" and acted inappropriately: " 'We had trouble finding Henry,' [Nixon] said. 'He was in bed with a broad.' Nobody laughed." Peter Lakeland, an aide to New York's Republican senator Jacob Javits, informed his boss that "if, as now seems inevitable, Nixon will soon go under in what is likely to be a nasty, squalid, destructive spasm of criminal defiance, Kissinger's own . . . capacity to operate . . . will be called into doubt."

Although Lakeland's prophecy about Nixon proved accurate, Kissinger's reputation climbed in the aftermath of the Yom Kippur War. In November 1973 he commenced several rounds of negotiations— quickly labeled "shuttle diplomacy," by the press—between the capitals of Israel, Egypt, and Syria. Over the next eighteen months he arranged the disengagement of the three countries' military forces in the Sinai and the Golan Heights. Israel's armies withdrew from the banks of the Suez Canal, permitting the reopening of that waterway. Kissinger also renegotiated the cease-fire between Israel and Syria, with the former removing its forces from the old Syrian provincial capital but retaining its control over the most strategic parts of the Golan Heights. Yet no permanent borders were drawn on either front.

The laudatory notices Kissinger had received throughout the Nixon years became even more glowing in the wake of this shuttle diplomacy. The Egyptians called him "the American magician." A Japanese paper referred to him as the "Middle East cyclone." *Time* magazine gushed that "as he whirled through the capitals of the Middle East last week, Henry Kissinger more than ever warranted comparison to Metternich, Talleyrand or other great foreign ministers of the past. . . . No other Secretary of State in U.S. history has ever carried so much power, so much responsibility or so heavy a burden."

The hero worship accorded Kissinger was intensified by the public's desire for relief from the grim news of the winter of 1973 and 1974. Nixon, re-elected by a landslide in November 1972, now faced impeachment for abuse of power and obstruction of justice. An oil embargo of Europe, Japan, and the United States by the oil-producing Arab countries, in protest of Western support for Israel during the October war, doubled the price of gasoline. Nixon encouraged Americans to turn off their lights and set their thermostats at 65 degrees. Dramatizing the need to conserve fuel, he traveled on an ordinary United Airlines flight to Florida during his Christmas holiday. Although in 1973 America produced 75 percent of the oil it needed, Western Europe and Japan depended on the Middle East for over 80 percent of their oil. To prevent their economies from falling into the worst depression since the 1930s, Washington agreed to make up most of their petroleum losses. As a result, the United States had to make do with approximately 80 percent of its average fuel consumption. Unemployment rose by over two percentage points, to 7 percent, in the six months after the embargo, the stock market fell to its lowest level since 1962, and the economy was thrown into a sharp, eleven-month-long recession.

Nixon tried to use Kissinger's soaring reputation as a Middle East miracle worker to arrest his own slide in Congress, where the House Judiciary Committee had scheduled public hearings on impeachment in July 1974. The president traveled to Egypt and Israel in June, apparently to divert attention from troubles at home. Tumultuous crowds of over 1 million people cheered him on a train ride from Cairo to Alexandria. He encountered a more somber reception in Israel, which had not yet fully recovered from the setbacks of the early days of the Yom Kippur War.

As public distrust of the Nixon administration mounted during the Watergate scandal, Congress tried to take back from the president some of its traditional powers in foreign affairs. On November 7, 1973, Congress overrode Nixon's veto of the War Powers Act. This law capped efforts, begun with the 1970 repeal of the Tonkin Gulf Resolution, to reassert congressional influence over foreign affairs and war making.

Although no president had asked for a declaration of war since 1941, the United States had used military force often in the postwar era. Presidents from Truman to Nixon had asserted that events moved so quickly in the nuclear age that no time remained to consult with Congress before deploying American forces abroad. But growing public and congressional unhappiness with Presidents Johnson's and Nixon's handling of the war in Vietnam rendered lawmakers less amenable to appeals from the executive branch for complete freedom of action. Earlier versions of the War Powers Act had passed either the House or Senate; now, as the Watergate scandal undercut Nixon's political standing, the two houses agreed on a single version. Many critics of American foreign policy, both inside and outside the government, had concluded that it was vital to restrict the power of "the imperial presidency"—a phrase coined to describe the chief executive's tendency to act without regard for constitutional checks and balances.

The law that was finally adopted was the work of New York Republican senator Jacob Javits and Wisconsin Democratic representative Clement Zablocki, chairman of the House Committee on Foreign Affairs. Both lawmakers were willing to grant the president wide latitude in setting foreign policy, but they also wanted Congress to play a clearly defined role. The act required that the president consult with Congress "when possible" before sending U.S. troops into combat or into a zone where hostilities were likely. If the president determined that he had to act before telling Congress, the act required him to inform lawmakers within forty-eight hours of dispatching U.S. troops. Congress would then have sixty days to formally approve the use of troops and to state a time limit for their continued use. If Congress failed to authorize the president's action, the president would have another thirty days in which to withdraw American forces.

Some critics of the War Powers Act charged that it did not go far enough. One disgruntled legislative aide predicted, "What you'll have now is a Pentagon file full of contingency plans for ninety-day wars." Yet every president since Nixon has resisted the act, considering it to be an unwarranted restriction on the chief executive's foreign policy prerogatives. Despite subsequent complaints from lawmakers who wanted the law strengthened, and from presidents and cabinet secretaries who wanted it abolished, the War Powers Act has helped set the boundaries of presidential use of force for two decades.

CONCLUSION

Immediately after Richard Nixon resigned the presidency in disgrace in 1974, analysts looking for something praiseworthy in his administration began focusing on his foreign policy record. The *Christian Science Monitor* believed that Nixon had turned the country away from the damaging stereotypes of the Cold War, in which Americans saw a Soviet plot behind every world problem. The result was a more flexible and intelligent foreign policy than was ever expected from a visceral anti-Communist like Nixon. The newspaper wrote that he had "risked alienating many of his longtime cold war supporters, by opening America's door to the Communist world." The authors believed his collaboration with Kissinger had re-established White House control over the fractured apparatus of foreign policy. Kissinger's travels to China, the Soviet Union, and the Middle East represented a triumph for U.S. foreign policy, the paper said, and his shuttle diplomacy between the capitals of the Arab states and Israel appeared to lay "the groundwork for the difficult and continuing negotiations for peace" that loomed ahead. In the years following Nixon's departure, other analysts recapitulated the view that Nixon conducted foreign policy well, whatever his failings in connection with the Watergate scandal. Indeed, Nixon made skillful use of his foreign policy reputation in his effort to rehabilitate his reputation in the twenty years between his resignation in 1974 and his death in 1994. He frequently wrote and spoke on foreign affairs, traveled widely, and advised his successors on what to do about contemporary issues.

Nevertheless, Nixon and Kissinger failed in their central goal of re-ordering American foreign policy to create what they proclaimed would be "a generation of peace." They concentrated solely on such issues as the Vietnam War and relations with the Soviet Union, China, the Middle East, and Chile—all problems left over from earlier periods. They made some progress on each issue, but ten years after Nixon resigned, it seemed that his initiatives had delivered far less than was promised. It was clear that Nixon and Kissinger had understood how both the United States and the Soviet Union needed to end their wasteful competition.

Nixon and Kissinger failed to appreciate certain dramatic economic and political changes in the international arena, such as the relative decline of the U.S. position in international trade and the rise of Third World nationalism. For example, Kissinger and Nixon ignored increasing friction with Japan over trade. They tried briefly to address economic tensions with the NATO allies in 1973, but then neglected the question as crises in the Middle East intervened. Economic issues bored Kissinger. His economic aide joked that "being economic adviser to Henry Kissinger was like being military adviser to the Pope." Nixon and Kissinger also paid little attention to Central America and Africa, where festering poverty and political repression only worsened. The costs of ignoring the Third World and the fate of individuals oppressed by foreign governments would become more apparent later in the 1970s.

Nixon and Kissinger fell short even in what they considered their greatest achievements—peace in Vietnam, détente with the Soviets, and a new relationship with China. Many of these apparent successes proved short-lived, breaking down by the election of 1976. The peace agreement in Indochina—for which more than twenty thousand additional American lives had been sacrificed after Nixon took office—collapsed in 1975. The much-heralded détente with the Soviet Union, already weakened by 1974, did not survive the Ford administration. The opening to China widened in the late 1970s, but it was the Carter administration (ironically, as Carter was often criticized for being inept at international relations) that actually made the greatest progress, by resuming formal diplomatic relations with China. The high hopes for peace in the Middle East had also diminished by 1974. The Carter administration exceeded Kissinger's efforts by brokering a peace treaty between Israel and Egypt in 1978 and 1979.

Nixon's and Kissinger's methods contributed to both the dazzling promise and the disappointing results of their supposedly innovative foreign policy. By concentrating power in their own hands, they could move quickly, with theatrical flair. Yet their exclusion of foreign affairs professionals and their disregard for congressional opinion came back to haunt them when support and follow-through on various initiatives became necessary. Instead of working with the permanent foreign policy bureaucracy or Congress, Kissinger mocked them. Not surprisingly, they came to resent his high-handedness. As progress toward achieving his most prized foreign policy objectives slowed toward the end of the Nixon years and during the Ford presidency, Kissinger blamed the difficulties on lawmakers, the bureaucracy, the press, an impatient public, the Democrats—virtually anyone who opposed or questioned him.

When public esteem for Kissinger was at its height, in 1973 and 1974, the press likened him to Metternich, Talleyrand, and Bismarck—all conservative figures from the nineteenth century. Seldom did Kissinger's admirers recognize the irony in comparing a modern American secretary of state to these figures from Europe's past. For all of its drama and excitement, the diplomacy of the Nixon years represented more the end of the era that began in 1945 than a new beginning for American foreign relations. ∎

FURTHER READING

For general accounts of foreign policy in the Nixon administration, see: Tad Szulc, *The Illusion of Peace* (1979); Raymond L. Garthoff, *Détente and Confrontation: American-Soviet Relations from Nixon to Reagan* (1994); William G. Hyland,

Mortal Rivals: Superpower Relations from Nixon to Reagan (1987); Richard Nixon, *RN: The Memoirs of Richard Nixon* (1978) and *In the Arena* (1990); Stephen E. Ambrose, *Nixon* (vols. 2 and 3; 1989, 1991); Herbert Parmet, *Richard Nixon and His America* (1990); Henry Kissinger, *White House Years* (1979), *Years of Upheaval* (1982), and *Diplomacy* (1994); Seymour Hersh, *The Price of Power: Kissinger in the Nixon White House* (1983); Walter Isaacson, *Kissinger: A Biography* (1992); Robert D. Schulzinger, *Henry Kissinger: Doctor of Diplomacy* (1989). On the later years of the Vietnam War, see: George C. Herring, *America's Longest War* (1986); Arnold Isaacs, *Without Honor: Defeat in Vietnam and Cambodia* (1983); Melvin Small, *Johnson, Nixon and the Doves* (1988); Nguyen Tien Hung and Jerrold Schechter, *The Palace File* (1986); Marilyn B. Young, *The Vietnam Wars* (1990). On the Middle East, see: Daniel Yergin, *The Prize* (1991); Steven J. Spiegel, *The Other Arab-Israeli Conflict: Making America's Middle East Policy from Policy from Truman to Reagan* (1985); William Quandt, *Decade of Decision* (1977) and *Peace Process* (1994); Alan Dowty, *Middle East Crisis* (1984). On the War Powers Act, see: John Hart Ely, *War and Responsibility: Constitutional Lessons of Vietnam and Its Aftermath* (1994); Harold Hyman, *Quiet Past and Stormy Present? War Powers in American History* (1986); Thomas Franck and Edward Wiesband, *Foreign Policy by Congress* (1979).

10

The Use and Abuse of Power: Domestic Affairs and the Watergate Scandal, 1969–1974

Soon after Richard Nixon's 1968 campaign manager, John N. Mitchell, became attorney general in 1969, he tried to calm fears that the new administration intended to demolish the Great Society. "Watch what we do, not what we say," he told reporters, implying that the harsh conservative rhetoric voiced by candidate Nixon had been misleading. Nixon and his subordinates might have stressed such favorite conservative issues as halting street crime, cracking down on campus protests, and ending the busing of schoolchildren to achieve racial balance; but in practice, Mitchell seemed to suggest, they would continue an activist government committed to intervening in most areas of American life. On one level Mitchell proved prophetic: the new administration preserved and even expanded many of the government programs of the 1960s. Nixon and most of his principal advisers accepted the major tenets of the New Deal—that the government had a positive role to play in the economic and social life of the country. Yet Nixon owed his election to public disillusionment with government and to the race-based resentment that intensified. The Nixon administration's domestic policy both fed these resentments and consolidated the legislation of the Great Society.

Mitchell's comment contained more irony than he realized at the time. Behind the scenes, Nixon administration officials abused their power and threatened the very foundations of American democracy. As Nixon and his subordinates expanded the role of the executive branch, they intimidated critics in the press, on college campuses, and in private research organizations. The administration treated opposition politicians, writers, commentators, and even some actors, athletes, and comedians as personal enemies rather than political opponents. Nixon's obsession with secrecy, his contempt for other officeholders, and his disregard of civil liberties culminated in many violations of the law. During the episode known as "Watergate," representatives of Nixon's re-election committee used illegal campaign contributions to finance burglaries and wiretaps against the Democrats. The White House then obstructed investigations of these activities; but dogged reporters, congressional committees, independent prosecutors, and federal judges brought the facts to light. Eventually Watergate became the gravest constitutional scandal of the twentieth century, and it resulted in Nixon's resignation from the presidency in August 1974.

RECASTING THE WELFARE STATE

Initially the Nixon administration seemed to adopt the Eisenhower strategy of consolidating rather than repealing the reforms of its predecessors. During the campaign of 1968, Nixon endorsed the aims of reducing economic inequality, conquering poverty, and ending racial discrimination, but he complained that the Great Society programs of President Johnson had failed to meet these goals. Nixon claimed that the War on Poverty had been lost because of mismanagement by incompetent bureaucrats. He spoke of the principles of better management and of helping the poor and underprivileged help themselves. But in spite of these goals, the overall tendency of the Nixon administration was to de-emphasize social programs and to oppose further efforts at racial equality. The primary social initiatives in the Nixon years came from the other branches of the federal government—Congress and the courts.

Following the philosophy of many conservative thinkers, Nixon wanted to transfer much of the responsibility for social programs from the swollen federal bureaucracy to states and municipalities. The stated aim was to increase efficiency, make programs more responsive to local interests, and reduce federal interference. Conservatives also hoped that programs already administered at the local level would be eliminated or be given a more conservative slant.

To accomplish this shift of responsibility, Nixon successfully sponsored a system of revenue sharing and block grants, a method of government funding that lasted for ten years. Under this system, funds were sliced from federally administered programs in order to make money available to states and municipalities for use in education, urban development, transportation, job training, rural development, and law enforcement. Few federal guidelines were attached to block grants; the specific spending decisions were to be made at the state and local levels. The program did help states and cities pay for new buildings, parks, police cars, and jails. However, when times were hard and resources scarce, cities used the revenue-sharing and block-grant funds to meet their daily expenses. Rarely did local governments use federal grants to directly aid the poor. To make certain that some funds were applied to job training, in 1973 Congress passed the Comprehensive Employment and Training Act (CETA), designed to educate poor people for jobs. Over the next ten years some six hundred thousand CETA graduates found work through its training programs.

At the same time that revenue sharing was used to transfer some responsibilities away from the federal government, Nixon created the Urban Affairs Council, a sort of National Security Council of domestic affairs. The Urban Affairs Council would create new programs to be managed directly by the White House rather than by federal agencies, over which Nixon had less control. To head this new council, Nixon chose Daniel Patrick Moynihan, giving him the task of directing domestic policy and bending the bureaucracy to his will. Like Henry

Kissinger, his counterpart on the National Security Council, Moynihan had been on the Harvard faculty, off and on, for nearly twenty years; he had also held several subcabinet positions since the Kennedy administration. Author of the controversial 1965 study *The Negro Family: The Case for National Action* (see Chapter 6), Moynihan was convinced that a bleak cycle of poverty kept millions of people in permanent economic bondage. He believed that the only chance to improve conditions for the poorest Americans lay in ending their dependence on welfare payments. This view appealed to Nixon, who believed that a plan that trimmed welfare would both reduce poverty and please a middle class that was increasingly resentful of the poor.

Reforming the welfare system presented Nixon with an opportunity to surpass the Great Society while pursuing harsh attacks on "welfare cheats," a theme he had sounded during the 1968 presidential campaign. By the end of the Johnson administration, even the advocates of the Great Society had become increasingly doubtful that the War on Poverty could be won. More and more children were growing up in poverty in the late 1960s. Inadequate funding of Great Society programs, racism, changes in the nature of work, and the cultural legacy of slavery combined to make the end of poverty an elusive goal.

The largest welfare program, known as Aid to Families with Dependent Children (AFDC), had provided welfare assistance since 1935. Many poor people seemed unable to break out of an apparently endless cycle of poverty. Under AFDC the states established the payment amounts. Eighteen of the poorest states offered less than $31 per month per welfare recipient. In all cases, every dollar earned by a working welfare recipient was deducted from his or her welfare check.

In 1969, Moynihan and the Urban Affairs Council proposed scrapping AFDC and replacing it with a Family Assistance Plan (FAP) designed to end the cycle of dependence on government assistance. Through a "negative income tax," in which poor people would receive money instead of paying taxes, the plan would end welfare by offering each poor head of household approximately $1,600 per year.

A crucial distinction between the FAP and AFDC was that aid recipients would have to hold paying jobs. This provision helped deflect conservative criticism that the Nixon administration had turned into a supporter of lavish government assistance to the poor. Privately, Nixon explained to Moynihan, "I don't care a damn about the work requirement. This is the price of getting the $1,600."

The issue of revising the welfare system languished until 1972. Every time the Democrats favored welfare reform, Nixon opposed their efforts for doing too much. Every time Nixon put forward a proposal, Democrats blocked it for doing too little. As a result, nothing

On Earth Day, April 21, 1970, hundreds of thousands of Americans rallied in support of laws requiring less pollution and a cleanup of the natural environment. © 1995 Leonard Freed/Magnum Photos Inc.

directly supplementing the low incomes of the poor became law. Welfare then became a focal point in the 1972 presidential campaign.

A few weeks before the presidential election, Congress finally passed a new welfare reform bill, without providing a guaranteed income for poor families with children. It did, however, include a new program, Supplemental Security Income, that provided a guaranteed income for the elderly—many of whom were not poor—and for the blind and disabled of all ages. At the same time, Congress authorized automatic cost-of-living increases, tied to the consumer price index, for all Social Security recipients. Such payments went to rich and poor alike. Over the next twenty years the annual cost-of-living adjustments to Social Security proved to be an enormously popular entitlement, but one that contributed substantially to large budget deficits. The attempt to find a better system for helping the poor went no further during the Nixon administration.

The government made more substantial progress in creating standards for environmental protection. In the early 1970s Washington began to respond to public demands that the government regulate businesses whose activities were deemed destructive to the environment, harmful to consumers, or dangerous to workers. In April 1970 hundreds of thousands of people rallied across the country on the first "Earth Day," showing their support for environmental causes. Soon after, Congress created the Environmental Protection Agency (EPA), empowering it to investigate and curtail practices destructive to the environment.

During the 1970s the EPA brought hundreds of suits against industrial polluters of the nation's water and air. For new construction involving federal funds, the agency required environmental impact studies that clearly delineated the project's effects on traffic congestion, pollution, housing, wildlife, and a host of other concerns. The EPA set fuel efficiency standards for cars and required manufacturers to reduce carbon monoxide emissions from automobile engines. In studies on the effects of electrical power-generating plants on the atmosphere, the EPA determined that the burning of high-sulfur coal had created "acid rain" in the Northeast and neighboring Canada, harming that region's forests and fisheries. Although such reports alerted the public to environmental dangers, they also contributed to a growing sense that some problems exceeded the government's capacity to provide solutions.

Although Nixon signed the act creating EPA, he tried to limit the amount of money the federal government spent on environmental regulation. In 1970, in order to appropriate about $7 billion to clean up the nation's air and water, Congress had to override the president's veto. Nixon then "impounded"—refused to spend—about $1 billion of the money. By 1973, concerned about excessive federal spending, Nixon had impounded about $15 billion, affecting over a hundred government programs for cleaning up the environment.

Even the usually compliant Justice Department thought the president had gone too far. Assistant Attorney General William Rehnquist wrote that there was no constitutional provision justifying "a refusal by the president to comply with a congressional directive to spend." Democratic senator Sam Ervin of North Carolina, chairman of the Senate Judiciary Committee's Subcommittee on Separation of Powers, held hearings on impoundment in 1971. At one point Ervin declared that the president "has no authority under the Constitution to decide which laws will be executed or to what extent they will be enforced." Legal experts agreed, but various White House officials claimed that such congressional interference would prevent the president from doing his job. White House officials argued that the bad economic effects of a budget deficit outweighed the benefits of a cleaner environment, and Nixon continued the process of impoundment. Disagreements between the president and Congress over impoundment helped set the stage for their far larger confrontation—over the use and abuse of presidential power—that grew out of the Watergate scandal.

During the Nixon years, Congress also created the Consumer Products Safety Commission (CPSC) and the Occupational Safety and Health Administration (OSHA). Both agencies were supposed to make daily life safer and healthier. The CPSC investigated the safety of a wide variety of common household items, from television sets to kitchen appliances. It imposed rules for baby products that were highly popular with parents, but industry leaders objected to the added costs of meeting the new standards. At one point the CPSC ruled that children's pajamas treated with Tris, a highly flammable substance, should be removed from the market. Relieved parents applauded the decision, but the manufacturer, stuck with unsalable merchandise worth millions of dollars, complained that unsympathetic Washington bureaucrats had ruined the company's ability to compete. The pajamas were eventually sold in South America.

OSHA required that work sites be safe for employees and that businesses submit to unannounced inspections to ensure safety codes were being followed. Unions and most working people believed OSHA reduced job-related accidents and even saved lives. Businesses, however, found OSHA's inspectors meddlesome and imperious. Many economists and conservative commentators shared this view. Advocates of deregulation, who argued that the economy would function better if government regulations were removed, turned some of their strongest scorn on OSHA.

The environmental and consumer protection agencies created in the early 1970s reflected the public concerns of the time. The Nixon administration enforced these laws, although with less enthusiasm than the laws' sponsors in the Democratic-controlled Congress. Overall, the government did more to address environmental and safety concerns in the early 1970s than at any time in the next twenty years. Nevertheless, Nixon's reluctance to administer congressionally mandated environmental regulations contributed to a growing atmosphere of suspicion in Washington. Already under fire for prolonging the Vietnam War, Nixon drew little sympathy from the liberal and moderate Democrats who dominated Congress. The fight between the president and Congress over impoundment heightened the sense, on both sides, that the other branch of government could not be trusted.

Even as the Nixon administration tried but failed significantly to help the poorest Americans, it energetically opposed further progress on civil rights for African-Americans. At first, administration officials were divided in their attitude toward civil rights. Some officials favored further advances for African-Americans, but the Justice Department tried to limit the effects of the very law it was charged to enforce, the Civil Rights Act of 1964. Leon Panetta, head of the Justice Department's Office of Civil Rights, did try to enforce the law, but he was fired. Before he changed parties and won election to Congress as a Democrat, Panetta complained of "a massive retreat on civil rights" by Nixon.

In fact, the Nixon approach to civil rights came to be governed more and more by the so-called southern strategy—an attempt to woo traditionally Democratic white southern voters by appealing to their racial prejudice toward African-Americans. The strategy was formulated by Kevin Phillips in *The Emerging Republican Majority* (1969). Phillips observed that the substantial number of people who had voted for George Wallace in the 1968 presidential election were "in motion between a Democratic past and a Republican future." Attorney General John Mitchell, one of Nixon's key political advisers, favored the southern strategy. To appeal to southern white voters, the administration would emphasize conservative themes such as law and order, and it would resist further advances in civil rights.

While the Nixon administration resisted further progress on civil rights for people of color, the government responded to the activism of a revitalized women's movement (see pages 324–329). Congress passed the Equal Rights Amendment (ERA) to the Constitution and submitted it to the states in early 1972. The ERA was soon ratified by thirty-five of the thirty-eight states necessary for it to take effect. Though the ERA eventually fell short of adoption, the widespread activism of its supporters helped to focus attention on women's issues.

Along with abortion and busing, crime and drug use became major issues in the Nixon years. The Nixon administration inflamed public fears that the widespread use of drugs, especially heroin, had created a major crime wave. But the administration had no solutions to match its rhetoric.

During the 1968 campaign, Nixon had blamed the "permissiveness" of Johnson's attorney general, Ramsey Clark, for the rise in street crime. Nixon soon realized, however, that the federal government had little direct law enforcement power to combat crime in the streets. Faced with a local problem the federal government could do little to remedy, the Nixon administration tried several tactics: it tried to shift blame for drug use and crime onto its opponents; it manipulated statistics to magnify both the original problem and the effect of its own remedies; and, finally, it engaged in drug raids that disregarded the civil liberties of the accused and possibly violated the Constitution as well.

In 1969 and 1970 the administration proposed several highly repressive anticrime statutes, which it expected would fail in Congress. "The administration's position in the crime field depends on our ability to shift blame for crime bill inaction to Congress," read one White House memorandum. Much to the administration's surprise, however, the Democratic majority in Congress, not wishing to appear "soft" on crime, passed Nixon's crime package in 1970. The new laws increased sentences for federal crimes, allowed federal marshals to hold suspects for longer periods without pressing charges or setting bond, and enhanced federal officers' ability to tap telephones.

Although the federal government did not have the power to control ordinary street crime, it did have jurisdiction over the illegal sale of narcotics. By concentrating on drug crimes, the Nixon administration expected to generate popular support without having to address the sorts of crimes that had engendered public fear to begin with. Officials played with numbers to make it appear that drug use and crime had recently grown tenfold. In 1971 Nixon announced that the number of heroin addicts in the United States had soared from 69,000 in 1969 to 315,000 in 1970 and 559,000 in 1971. In fact, the number of addicts had not changed much in those years; the Bureau of Narcotics and Dangerous Drugs had simply reworked old statistics. The administration also inflated by about twenty-five times statistics on the value of property stolen by heroin addicts.

Armed with these inflated statistics about a heroin-induced crime wave, the Nixon administration declared a war on drugs. In early 1972 Nixon created the Office for Drug Abuse and Law Enforcement (ODALE), a secret police force outside the control of the FBI or CIA. ODALE recruited G. Gordon Liddy, a former FBI agent and the planner of the break-in at Daniel Ellsberg's psychiatrist's office, to organize raids on suspected drug dealers. Over the next year ODALE agents conducted midnight raids without search warrants. They kicked in doors, grabbed people from their beds, pointed guns at their heads, and threatened them with death unless they revealed the whereabouts of drugs. If they determined they had gone to the wrong address, the agents simply said they had made a mistake and left.

Although the administration produced additional misleading statistics to indicate that progress had been made, the war on crime and drugs actually had a negligible impact on heroin use and street crime. The crusade did enhance Nixon's political position among middle-class Americans concerned about crime, and it put his Democratic opponents on the defensive. But most significantly, the actions of Liddy and ODALE set the stage for the Watergate scandal by establishing a precedent for how far the administration would bend or break the law to serve its own purposes.

THE BURGER COURT

A major element of Nixon's appeal to southerners, whites, and conservatives during the 1968 campaign was his promise to reverse the direction taken by the Supreme Court under Chief Justice Earl Warren. He promised to appoint conservative justices that would revise the Warren Court's decisions expanding civil rights for racial minorities, civil liberties for individuals, and legal rights for criminal defendants. Nixon appointed a new chief justice, Warren Burger, and three new associate justices, Harry Blackmun, Lewis Powell, and William Rehnquist. But the new members, together with the holdovers from the Warren era, surprised both their supporters and their detractors. Instead of reversing the Warren Court's emphasis on enlarging the rights of individuals and curtailing the powers of government officials, the Court in the early seventies consolidated the Warren Court's decisions.

The Burger Court's decisions usually consolidated and sometimes expanded the civil rights gains of the Warren years. For example, the Court concluded that discriminatory effects as well as intention had been outlawed by the Civil Rights Act of 1964. In *Griggs* v. *Duke Power and Light Co.* (1971), Burger spoke for a unanimous court in ruling that the 1964 Civil Rights Act prohibited an employer from requiring high school diplomas or intelligence tests for job applicants if the results would be racially discriminatory. The Court reasoned that the tests and the diploma requirements had no bearing on the job to be performed. Later, in *Washington* v. *Davis* (1976), the Court upheld the legality of a verbal test given to applicants to the District of Columbia's police force because the questions did relate directly to the work performed. A relevant test was permissible, even if it kept most black applicants off the capital's police force.

By far the most controversial civil rights issue to reach the Court during the Nixon years was the use of busing to achieve racial desegregation. In two important cases, *Swann* v. *Charlotte-Mecklenburg Board of Education* (1971) and *Keyes* v. *Denver School District No. 1* (1973), the Supreme Court elaborated on lower courts' rulings regarding busing. In the former case the Court turned its attention from rural southern school districts, where students of both races lived close together, to urban schools, where only busing could achieve integration. The Court upheld a desegregation plan mandating substantial cross-town busing in a southern city. In the *Keyes* case the justices extended busing to a northern district where legal segregation had never existed but the school board had divided the district along racial lines.

Both the Court and the local officials who implemented busing plans were subjected to heavy abuse from white parents. In many locations the protests turned violent. In Lamar, South Carolina, an angry white mob attacked school buses carrying black students. Other mobs fire-bombed buses in Denver, Colorado, and Pontiac, Michigan. Irate whites in South Boston cursed and beat blacks who attended classes with whites under court order. Congress responded to the public anger with legislation proclaiming a moratorium on court orders attempting to achieve "a balance among students with respect to race, sex, religion, or socioeconomic status."

The Supreme Court, however, thought Congress was sidestepping the issue. If Congress had wanted to end busing, Justice Lewis Powell ruled in *Drummond* v. *Acree* (1972), "it could have used clear and explicit language appropriate to that end." In 1974 Congress did pass legislation (submitted by the Nixon administration) stipulating that busing could be used only as a last resort. But it left it up to the courts to make this determination, as part of their duty to guarantee equal protection to all citizens. In the late 1970s, Congress took a further half-step by forbidding the use of federal funds to buy or maintain buses used for school desegregation.

The Nixon administration appealed to white conservatives by denouncing the 1968 Supreme Court decision in *Green* v. *Board of Education*. In this case, the Court ruled that the southern use of "freedom of choice" plans that allowed parents to select any public school within their district failed to guarantee racial balance and therefore violated the Court's earlier decision, in *Brown* v. *Board of Education* (1954), prohibiting segregated schools. Nixon declared that "the Court was right on *Brown* and wrong on *Green*," and administration officials tried to block implementation of the *Green* decision.

In August 1969, under heavy pressure from the White House, the Department of Health, Education and Welfare (HEW) petitioned the Fifth District Court for a three-month delay in the desegregation of twenty-three Mississippi school districts. This was the first time since 1954 that the federal government had intervened to *slow* the pace of desegregation. HEW's action shocked lawyers in Panetta's Office of Civil Rights. They refused to defend the administration's position and secretly supplied information to the NAACP's Legal Defense Fund.

The fund appealed to the Supreme Court to reverse the delay. In a unanimous decision in *Alexander* v. *Holmes County Board of Education* (1969), the Court ordered that "the obligation of every school district is to terminate the dual school systems at once." The Fifth District Court responded with 166 desegregation orders over the next ten months. Legally mandated segregation ended in the South in the subsequent two years. By 1971, 44 percent of black children in the South attended schools where white students constituted a majority. In the North and West, by comparison, only 28 percent of black school children studied in schools with a majority of white students.

The Supreme Court's support for busing helped the cause of school desegregation overall, but it also contributed to a decline in middle-class white trust in public schools. Many white parents in urban districts facing court-ordered desegregation either placed their children in private schools or fled to the suburbs. Over the next decade, as this so-called white flight undermined support for public education, proposed tax increases for schools brought before voters were defeated. By stimulating the white exodus, the busing conflict also hastened the transformation of northern and midwestern urban centers into predominantly poor, black, and Hispanic areas. The less stake the white middle class had in the fate of the cities, the less support it gave to government programs to revitalize urban life. By reinforcing this trend with its decisions on busing, the Supreme Court unintentionally spurred an ongoing crisis in the nation's cities.

The seventies produced an atmosphere of increased awareness of discrimination against women. The Burger Court rendered a number of decisions prohibiting discrimination on the basis of sex, an issue that was largely ignored by the generally more liberal Warren Court. Although they were pleased by these decisions, advocates of women's rights were worried by the Court's reasoning. Instead of finding a constitutional right to equality, the justices relied on portions of the 1964 Civil Rights Act and the 1973 Equal Pay Act to whittle away at sex-based discrimination. In *Reed* v. *Reed* (1971), for example, the Court invalidated an Idaho law that gave preference to men over similarly situated women as administrators of estates. The Court held that legislation differentiating between the sexes "must be reasonable, not arbitrary." The same year, the Court ruled in *Phillips* v. *Martin Marietta* that Title VII of the Civil Rights Act forbade corporate hiring practices that discriminate against mothers with small children. In *Frontiero* v. *Richardson* (1973) the Court applied Title VII to the military, requiring the armed services to provide the same fringe benefits and pensions to women that they provide to men.

The Court went beyond issues of equal pay and job rights when it overturned all state laws restricting abortion in *Roe* v. *Wade* (1973). Feminists and civil liberties lawyers had challenged a Texas law that made any abortion a felony. The test case involved a poor, single woman who believed she could not afford to raise a child. Justice Harry Blackmun, writing for a seven-member majority, opened a new era in reproductive law by ruling that the right of privacy established by *Griswold* v. *Connecticut* (1965) was "broad enough to encompass a woman's decision whether or not to terminate her pregnancy." Blackmun sought to balance the state's interest in the fetus with the mother's right to privacy. Therefore the decision declared an absolute right to abortion during the first trimester of a pregnancy, when experts agreed that the fetus was not "viable"—that is, when it cannot live outside the mother's body. During the second trimester, when a fetus might possibly survive outside the womb, states could regulate, but not outlaw, abortions. Only for the last thirteen weeks of pregnancy, according to the *Roe* decision, could state laws prohibit abortion.

Roe, along with the earlier *Griswold* decision, reversed a century of government opposition to contraception. The decision responded to a widespread public desire to make safe abortions available. Until then, many pregnant women had been forced to resort to unsafe, "back-alley" abortions. Others had turned to the so-called abortion underground, found in most cities and on many college campuses, through which they could receive information about abortion and access to safe practitioners. *Roe* changed all this by making abortion readily available; many women soon took for granted their right to a safe, legal abortion.

However, the *Roe* decision produced more public dissent than any other Court ruling since *Brown* v. *Board of Education* struck down school segregation in 1954. The justices who wrote the *Roe* opinion, and the women's rights advocates who supported it, probably underestimated the anger it would cause. Since 1869 Catholic doctrine has held that life begins at the moment of conception; thus many Catholics and other traditionalists assailed *Roe* as judicial sanction of murder. Over the next two decades following *Roe*, opposition to the decision became an even greater rallying point for conservatives than did the Warren Court's protection of the rights of criminal suspects.

MANAGING THE ECONOMY

The behavior of the U.S. economy in the early 1970s defied the expectations of nearly all conventional economists. The perplexing economic conditions led the Nixon administration to pursue unexpected policies. Prior to that time, prices had remained steady or fallen in slow times and risen only in boom periods. But in the Nixon years, the United States experienced both inflation *and* slow or stagnant growth. When Nixon confronted this "stagflation," he abandoned long-standing conservative economic philosophy. He adopted some policies, advocated by political rivals, that he had once derided. His change on economic policy was nearly as dramatic as the new foreign policy he crafted with Henry Kissinger. The sudden shifts in economic policy dismayed supporters who had taken Nixon for a conventional conservative, but they paid political dividends.

During the 1968 campaign Nixon had disparaged the Johnson administration's efforts to create "guideposts" for businesses to follow in setting prices. These standards were supposed to keep price increases in line with gains in worker productivity, thereby holding inflation down, but they had not worked. Citing his own experience with the Office of Price Administration during the Second World War, Nixon said that governmental price controls "can never be administered equitably and are not compatible with a free economy."

Yet the economy did not behave the way the rules predicted. Inflation, the scourge of the Great Society, stubbornly hovered at around 6 percent. Still worse, unemployment rose steadily, from 3.8 percent in 1968 to over 6 percent in 1971. According to orthodox economic theories, prices should *decline*, or at least not rise, when workers lose their jobs. Experts in the early seventies could describe stagflation, but they could not explain it. In later years economists identified some of the reasons for it: the baby-boomers, representing a large population bulge, had begun to reach maturity and were thus spending more money on consumer goods; there was an increased proportion of entry-level workers in the work force; the United States faced increased competition from the revived economies of Japan and Germany; and the Vietnam War had an inflationary effect on the economy. But even if economists and government officials had seen these problems clearly at the time, they could have done little about them. The causes of stagflation ran so deep, both inside and outside the United States, that government officials were limited in their ability to fine-tune the economy.

Because the experts could not explain why the economy had not followed the conventional patterns, the president decided it was time to pay less attention to the experts. In December 1970, Nixon shook up the management of economic policy by appointing John Connally, former Democratic governor of Texas, as secretary of the treasury. Connally had valuable political connections among conservative Democrats, southerners, and southwesterners, but he had no background in economic theory. The new treasury secretary spent the first six months in office avoiding deep analysis of stagflation; instead he urged a partnership between government, big business, and organized labor. Nixon was so impressed with his political skills that the president wanted Connally to be his successor, perhaps as the head of a new party made up of conservative Democrats and most Republicans.

Nixon faced more immediate problems, though, as he looked for ways out of the doldrums of stagflation before the 1972 election. He acknowledged that government wage and price controls might be necessary. Early in 1971 he had told an interviewer, "I am now a Keynesian in economics." Because Keynesianism had been a dirty word during the 1968 presidential election, this was a remarkable turnaround. One reporter likened it to "a Christian crusader saying 'All things considered, I think Mohammed was right.'"

Having acknowledged that it was appropriate to impose wage and price controls, Nixon had to decide when to act. Economic news worsened throughout 1971. Although the United States continued to export more than it imported, exports were beginning to slide. Also, foreign expenditures by the government (mostly for the maintenance of hundreds of overseas military bases) and those of private citizens meant that the number of dollars going overseas exceeded the value of foreign currency coming into the United States. Such an economic situation is known as a balance of payments deficit. The problem had worsened during the Vietnam War years, as the central banks of France and West Germany began converting some of their dollars into gold. Experts had been warning since the Kennedy administration that the United States could not forever afford to keep its promise to redeem its currency in gold and that a sudden rejection of dollars by overseas holders could upset the world's trading system. After a further slide in U.S. exports in mid-1971, international investors began worrying about the dollar's strength. Many bought West German marks instead of dollars. In August 1971 the Bank of England, previously supportive of U.S. economic policy, demanded that its holdings in American dollars be redeemed in gold.

Undersecretary of the Treasury Paul Volcker decided that "the jig was definitely up" when he heard the news from London. He telephoned Connally on Friday afternoon, August 13, with the grim warning that "a major crisis [was] developing in the world's monetary exchange system." Over the weekend, economic advisers huddled with the president at Camp David to devise a series of steps to save the dollar and halt inflation. Nixon, the recently converted Keynesian, was also a lifelong political animal, and he believed that wage and price controls would stop inflation before the 1972 election. His advisers agreed that wage and price controls, in conjunction with a plan to stop the international flight from the dollar, could work.

On Sunday evening, August 15, exactly one month after Nixon's startling announcement that Henry Kissinger had just returned from China, the president presented a program he called the New Economic Policy. He proclaimed a ninety-day freeze on wages and prices. Thereafter, a government wage and price commission would monitor price increases and employee contracts, rescinding excessive increases. This was precisely the policy, suggested by Johnson, that Nixon had derided in 1968. Nixon also announced that the United States would no longer convert its currency into gold. However, he added that American citizens, who had not been able to own the yellow metal since an earlier currency reform during the New Deal, were now free to buy and sell it at the market price. Over the next year the United States and the major trading nations ended the system, created in 1944, of fixed exchange rates among the world's currencies. By 1972 the value of currencies "floated," determined daily in currency exchange markets around the world.

The New Economic Policy tried to slow the escalating payments deficit with a temporary 10 percent surtax on imports. Nixon also cut social spending by $4.7 billion and reduced business taxes. Coming on the heels of Kissinger's trip to China, the New Economic Policy seemed another example of pragmatic action by an administration willing to break with orthodoxy. In a Gallup poll taken a week after the speech, 73 percent of respondents approved of the new policy.

Although Nixon's policy resulted in some limited economic improvement, nothing could halt inflation after the 1973 Arab-Israeli war and the subsequent oil embargo by Arab oil producers. The price of oil rose 400 percent, and the effects of that increase caused other prices to shoot up throughout the industrialized world. American prices rose by more than 7 percent in 1974 and 1975.

The most far-reaching consequence of the actions taken in August 1971 involved the disruption of the link between U.S. currency and gold. The United States gained in the short term, as overseas banks and businesses used their unbacked dollars to invest in U.S. government securities. Over the long term, however, floating the dollar hastened a serious decline in American manufacturing. Investment in new plants and research in new products slowed in the 1970s and 1980s. Such investments do not pay dividends quickly, and the flexible exchange rate made it more difficult for businesses to predict the return on merchandise they planned to sell overseas. Hence companies increasingly shifted their assets to predictable, often nonproductive investments that would turn a quick profit. By the end of the decade the return on nonproductive investments like land, commodities, gold, silver, jewels, and art soared. The value of some farmland in the United States increased 500 percent, without a similar rise in the value of crops. Banks preferred to lend money for the purchase of tangibles and land rather than for investing in rebuilding factories or developing new products. Investors shied away from the stock market in the late 1970s, fearing it would not offer a profitable return in the future. This sapped companies' ability to raise the capital necessary to modernize American manufacturing in the late 1970s. Managers of American manufacturing corporations contributed further to the decline of the country's industrial strength by concentrating on maximizing quarterly profits rather than considering their longer-term economic prospects.

The New Economic Policy demonstrated the potential and the limits of Nixon's nonideological, flexible approach to economic management at a time of rapid change. By endorsing Keynesian techniques to reduce inflation and foster growth, Nixon followed the practices of his predecessors since the Second World War. Yet fine-tuning the economy proved far more difficult than sponsors had hoped. The long-term ineffectiveness of wage and price controls contributed to a growing sense that government did not work.

THE ELECTION OF 1972

With the American economy in the doldrums, Democrats originally had high hopes for the 1972 election. Nixon's southern strategy had failed during the 1970 congressional election, with only one southern Democratic seat falling to a Republican candidate. On the eve of election day, Edmund Muskie, the Democratic vice-presidential candidate in 1968, had persuasively attacked Nixon's "politics of fear" in a televised address. In 1971 Muskie emerged as the favorite for the Democratic presidential nomination. With his rugged good looks and moderate views, Muskie appeared able to unite the Democrats. Early opinion polls showed him tied with Nixon at 42 percent.

Alarmed by Muskie's popularity rating, functionaries of Nixon's Committee to Re-elect the President (CREEP) made plans to discredit him, hoping to force the Democrats to nominate the weakest possible candidate. During the crucial New Hampshire primary campaign in early 1972, Donald Segretti, a CREEP specialist, forged a letter and sent it to William Loeb, the vitriolic editor of the *Manchester Union-Leader.* The letter accused Muskie of laughing at an ethnic slur against French Canadians, a major voting bloc among New Hampshire Democrats. Loeb printed the letter and also blasted Muskie and his wife on the front page. Outraged, the senator stood on a truck in front of the newspaper office and assailed Loeb as a "gutless coward." Muskie appeared to choke back tears as he defended his wife, and immediately the contrast between him, tearful and wounded, and Nixon, the strong world leader seen on TV that very week at the Great Wall of China, diminished his appeal. Muskie won the primary, but his margin over the runner-up, Senator George McGovern of South Dakota, was smaller than expected. Muskie's moderate, centrist opinions, which would have given him wide appeal in the general election, did not excite primary voters, and he dropped out of the race within weeks.

The McGovern campaign now took off. Unlike Muskie, McGovern had clearly articulated views demonstrating a belief in political liberalism. He expressed support for Great Society social programs, opposition to the war in Vietnam, and sympathy for the aspirations of young people, women, protesters, and other previously excluded groups. Opposition to the war in Vietnam united an army of fervent McGovern volunteers. Activists supporting McGovern opposed the Nixon administration's hostility to civil rights and its resistance to expanding the domestic welfare legislation of the Great Society. Over the next four months, McGovern won a string of primaries in a crowded Democratic race, giving him close to a majority of delegates.

McGovern's most prominent rivals during this time were George Wallace and Hubert Humphrey. Wallace won the Florida primary with white-hot rhetoric. He attacked Nixon as "a double-dealer, a two-timer, and a man who tells folks one thing and does another." Crowds roared when he complained about busing imposed by "anthropologists, zoologists, and sociologists." He did not know which was worse: the "judges who had just about ruined this country," hypocritical politicians who sent their children to private schools, or the "briefcase-totin' bureaucrats. . . . Yale Ph.D.'s who can't tie their shoelaces. . . . Hypocrites [who] if you opened all their briefcases, you'll find nothing in them but a peanut butter sandwich." But Wallace's political momentum ended abruptly in May when a gunman's bullet wounded him, leaving him paralyzed from the waist down.

By June Hubert Humphrey was the sole champion of the "Anybody but McGovern" coalition, an alignment of Democratic officeholders and labor union officials who feared that the South Dakota senator was too liberal and too much the representative of outsiders to win the general election. Assailing McGovern's liberal positions, Humphrey closed a wide gap to trail by only five percentage points in the June California primary.

By July, when the Democrats assembled in Miami for their national convention, McGovern's nomination depended on the interpretation of rules drafted in the aftermath of the chaotic 1968 convention. The new rules had resulted from complaints that Humphrey won the 1968 nomination because political bosses had controlled delegate selection in states that had not held primaries.

At the 1972 convention, Democrats decided on a strict interpretation of the new rules. On the first night of the convention, Chicago mayor Richard J. Daley and fifty-eight of his hand-picked delegates from Cook County were booted off the convention floor for violating the guidelines for selecting representatives in keeping with the racial, sexual, and ethnic make-up of a district. A new group of delegates, which included more women and blacks but fewer old-time politicians, took the Daley delegation's place.

The Democrats' endorsement of pluralism brought thousands of representatives of previously excluded groups into the party's decision-making process. The delegates at the 1972 convention were 38 percent female (in comparison to 13 percent in 1968), 23 percent under thirty (2.3 percent in 1968), and 15 percent black (5.5 percent in 1968). If the groups they represented voted in November, McGovern could win through the strength of an electorate that was younger, poorer, and more racially diverse than usual. But if traditionally excluded groups stayed away from the polls, as they had in 1968, he would lose, because he had alienated the old base of the Democratic party—the South, labor, Catholics, the white working class, and white ethnics.

The electoral reforms hurt the men who had run the Democratic party for decades. For instance, only 18 of the 255 Democratic members of the House of Representatives came to Miami as delegates, whereas customarily more than half attended the convention in that capacity. Those who were excluded grumbled and threatened. Wayne Hays of Ohio complained that commissions were "trying to reform us [elected officials] out of the party." A Pennsylvania member objected that "you've got quotas for everything—blacks, Chicanos, eighteen-year-olds. Pretty soon they'll want quotas for draft dodgers." No group seemed more old-fashioned and out of place than the leaders of organized labor. AFL-CIO president George Meany had led the "Anybody but McGovern" campaign. An old Cold Warrior, Meany found McGovern's opposition to the war in Vietnam absurd. Like most of the working class of his generation, Meany also decried the lifestyle of many McGovern supporters, blaming the senator for seeming to tolerate the open sexuality and drug experimentation of the young. Meany denied McGovern the AFL-CIO's endorsement; it was the first time organized labor had ever not supported the Democratic presidential nominee.

McGovern's chances declined further when he chose his vice-presidential running mate. Having given little thought to the vice presidency before the convention, McGovern selected Missouri senator Thomas Eagleton, hoping Eagleton's Catholicism and moderate views would appeal to traditional Democrats uncomfortable with the antiwar youth backing McGovern. The day after the nomination, news surfaced that Eagleton had been hospitalized three times in the 1960s for depression and exhaustion. Although perhaps 10 to 25 percent of all Americans suffer some form of depression at one time or another, psychological or emotional dysfunction carried a much more substantial stigma then than they do now. Initially McGovern decided not to cater to what he considered prejudice. He said he was "1,000 percent for Tom Eagleton" and that he did not intend to drop him from the ticket. But Eagleton then admitted he had received electroshock therapy while hospitalized and that he still took tranquilizers. Pressure from editorialists and his campaign staff convinced McGovern to drop Eagleton. Coming so soon after his "1,000 percent" endorsement of Eagleton, McGovern's abrupt reversal made him look unpredictable, weak, and possibly foolish. The process of finding a replacement became a fiasco. After seven prominent Democratic politicians refused to run, McGovern finally selected Sargent Shriver, the Kennedy relative who had formerly directed the Peace Corps and the Office of Economic Opportunity.

In November, Nixon won a massive landslide in which he gained 61 percent of the popular vote and carried 49 states (see map, page 385). Only Massachusetts and the District of Columbia went for McGovern. A number of social and political issues contributed to the size of Nixon's victory. McGovern's support from antiwar activists and political newcomers had alarmed traditional voters. Voter turnout declined in 1972, and the election was decided by the same segments of the electorate that typically went to the polls. Eighteen- to twenty-year-olds, allowed to vote for the first time under the terms of the Twenty-sixth Amendment (adopted in 1971), turned out in fewer numbers than any other group, and half of them voted for Nixon after he promised he would end the draft in 1973. White working-class

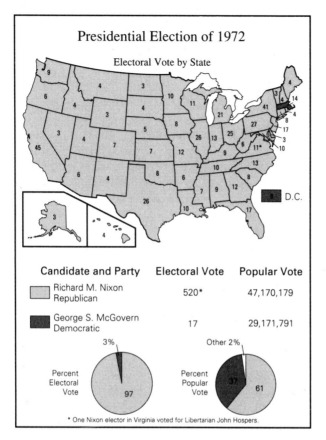

Presidential Election of 1972

Electoral Vote by State

Candidate and Party	Electoral Vote	Popular Vote
Richard M. Nixon Republican	520*	47,170,179
George S. McGovern Democratic	17	29,171,791

Percent Electoral Vote: 3% / 97

Percent Popular Vote: Other 2% / 37 / 61

* One Nixon elector in Virginia voted for Libertarian John Hospers.

Presidential Election of 1972

Democrats deserted McGovern in droves; 55 percent of blue-collar voters went for Nixon, as opposed to 34 percent in 1968. Fifty-three percent of Catholics voted for Nixon in 1972; 34 percent had voted for him in 1968. The southern strategy finally worked: three-quarters of those who voted for Wallace in 1968 supported Nixon in 1972.

Meanwhile, the New Economic Policy had tamed inflation, and unemployment had leveled off. Nixon's celebrated visits to Beijing and Moscow gave him and Kissinger the aura of successful statesmen. McGovern's opposition to the war in Vietnam faded as an issue with the public in the last two weeks of the campaign, when Kissinger announced (without much basis in fact) that "peace is at hand." Voters ignored McGovern's prescient warning that this was just one more trick from an administration that had quietly but steadily escalated the violence in Vietnam for three-and-a-half years while claiming it was preparing to end the war.

WATERGATE AND THE ABUSE OF POWER

Unknown to nearly everyone but a handful of trusted CREEP operatives and White House officials, an astonishing abuse of governmental power had begun as early as 1969. Ever since he had gone to Washington as a new congressman, in 1947, Nixon had considered himself a victim, never given proper respect by his political adversaries. Even the praise heaped on his foreign policy initiatives did not eliminate his feeling that he and his administration were embattled. He believed that Democrats wishing him ill occupied most permanent positions in the federal government. He complained bitterly about "sons-of-bitches that kick us in the ass." Feeling isolated and victimized, and taking little satisfaction in good news, Nixon lashed out at those he considered his domestic enemies. During his first term in office, he set in motion a series of events that represented serious illegal and unconstitutional abuses of presidential power. The scope of the illegalities was unprecedented, ranging from unfair campaign practices—sometimes trivialized by Republicans as "dirty tricks"—to using the Internal Revenue Service (IRS) to harass opponents, engaging in domestic espionage, and obstructing investigations into these actions by law enforcement agencies.

During the 1972 presidential campaign, George McGovern tried but failed to arouse public interest in a curious incident: a break-in at the Democratic National Committee headquarters, located in the Watergate office complex in Washington, D.C., on the night of June 17, 1972. As the public would later find out, the break-in had been perpetrated by five men employed by CREEP. Throughout the fall, McGovern expressed astonishment at White House press secretary Ron Ziegler's assertion that this had been a "third-rate burglary attempt" conducted by overzealous supporters, without direction from higher authorities. McGovern asked voters to consider the possibility that Nixon's men had engaged in "political espionage, political sabotage, and ... dirty tricks ... played to disrupt the democratic process." Few listened.

In fact, when the Washington police apprehended the five CREEP employees on June 17, they stumbled into a complicated web of lies and paranoia. The pattern had been set early on. For many years Nixon had considered himself undermined by various opponents: Democrats, journalists, intellectuals, academics, and even certain entertainment and sports celebrities. Early in his administration, Nixon concocted plans to derail opposition: he tapped the telephones of rivals and suspected leakers; he ordered a break-in at Daniel Ellsberg's psychiatrist's office; he endorsed a variety of schemes to make life

In the Oval Office of the White House, President Nixon confers with his top aides: *(from left)* National Security Adviser Henry Kissinger, Domestic Policy Adviser John Ehrlichman, and Chief of Staff H. R. "Bob" Haldemán. *National Archives/Nixon Presidential Materials.*

miserable for his perceived enemies. Nixon saw such enemies everywhere. They included Senator Edward Kennedy; actors Jane Fonda, Gregory Peck, Tony Randall, Julie Andrews, Connie Stevens, and Steve McQueen; the Brookings Institution; columnists James Reston and Rowland Evans; New York Jets quarterback Joe Namath; and comedian Richard M. Dixon, who did silly impersonations of Nixon. The president's lawyer, John Dean, compiled an "enemies list," at Nixon's request. The president told Dean to find ways "we can best screw" the more than one hundred people it named.

The White House commanded the IRS to harass political rivals, some of whom were on the enemies list. In two years the IRS investigated 4,300 such individuals and 1,025 groups, taking legal action against 43 people and 26 organizations. In addition, White House counsel Dean helped Nixon supporters who got in trouble with the IRS. Nixon insisted that "tax troubles be turned off" for friends of his. When career officials resisted turning the IRS into the president's private hit squad, Nixon complained.

G. Gordon Liddy, a former FBI agent who had helped plan the Ellsberg burglary and had run the administration's drug war, joined the

CREEP staff in late 1971. In early 1972 he presented to Attorney General John Mitchell—who was scheduled to leave the Justice Department soon to assume chairmanship of CREEP—a $1 million plan to disrupt the upcoming Democratic convention by kidnapping Democratic party leaders, putting them in bed with prostitutes, photographing them, and distributing the embarrassing pictures. Intrigued, but unhappy with the price tag, Mitchell told Liddy to come up with a more "realistic" plan. Liddy returned with a $250,000 scheme for eavesdropping on Democratic candidates during the 1972 campaign. Mitchell approved, and Liddy received $83,000 in hundred-dollar bills as a first installment for hiring surveillance operatives.

The money delivered to Liddy represented just a small part of a cornucopia of secret cash payments. Prominent individuals, corporations, trade groups, and lobbyists had curried favor with the Nixon administration by making substantial donations. Since 1969 Herbert Kalmbach, Nixon's personal attorney, had controlled $1 million in cash left over from the 1968 presidential campaign. Kalmbach kept the money in various safe-deposit boxes, adding to it as new money came in. During the 1970 congressional campaign, for example, Kalmbach collected another $2.8 million in cash. Donald Kendall, president of Pepsi-Cola, and H. Ross Perot, a Texas billionaire, each chipped in $250,000. Unreported by campaign treasurers, these contributions were illegal, and Kalmbach later served six months in jail for this surreptitious fund-raising.

After the 1970 congressional election Nixon told Kalmbach to concentrate on raising money for 1972. Remembering the 1960 election, when John Kennedy's wealthy father had come up with a fortune to help his son, Nixon wanted never to be outspent again. The indefatigable Kalmbach quickly collected millions. The desire to buy favors from the government stimulated the flow of a cash bonanza from various businesses. Dairy farmers dependent on government price supports had their lobbying arm, the American Milk Producers, pledge $2 million for CREEP. With this money in hand, Nixon overruled his own economic advisers, raising dairy price supports as the milk lobbyists wanted. In violation of the law, corporations subject to federal regulation also paid Kalmbach.

To hide the illegal source of this cash, Kalmbach took pains to see that it was properly "laundered," a process by which money is passed through intermediaries to obscure its origin. The problems intensified after April 1972, when a new campaign finance law went into effect requiring that the source of all contributions be reported. A typical scheme involved a $100,000 "donation" from Gulf Resources and Chemical Corporation of Houston. The Houston parent company transferred $100,000 to a Mexican subsidiary, which then paid a $100,000 "legal fee" to a Mexico City attorney. The attorney converted the $100,000 into cash and checks payable to himself, then delivered the cash and the endorsed checks to a Texas businessman. The businessman converted everything to cash and negotiable securities, mixed the $100,000 with $600,000 collected from Houston businesspeople, put it all in a suitcase, and flew it by courier to Washington for delivery to the treasurer of CREEP. Most such payments remained secret until 1973, when two investigative reporters for the *Washington Post*, Bob Woodward and Carl Bernstein, began to break the story of Watergate.

In April 1972, flush with cash from Kalmbach's fund-raising endeavors, G. Gordon Liddy hired James McCord and E. Howard Hunt, two ex-CIA operatives who had burglarized offices of Nixon's political opponents, to spy on various offices of the Democratic party in Washington. McCord and Hunt in turn recruited several Cuban exiles from Miami, veterans of the CIA's 1961 Bay of Pigs invasion and the burglary at Daniel Ellsberg's psychiatrist's office, to plant listening devices. In May they botched an effort to bug McGovern headquarters. Eventually they succeeded in planting bugs in Democratic Committee Chairman Lawrence O'Brien's office at the Watergate complex. Two weeks later, one of the bugs malfunctioned; the burglars returned to repair it on the night of June 16. At 1:50 A.M. on June 17, a night watchman noticed tape on the door of the Democrats' office and called the District of Columbia police. They arrived and apprehended McCord and four Cubans—Bernard Barker, Frank Sturgis, Virgilio Gonzalez, and Eugenio Martinez. Police were surprised to find the burglars carrying wads of hundred dollar bills. Howard Hunt's White House telephone number also turned up in an address book belonging to one of the suspects.

The arrests terrified Liddy, who scurried to destroy evidence linking him, CREEP, and the White House to the burglary. He asked Attorney General Richard Kleindienst to secure the release of the five men, but the request was refused. On the morning of June 17, Liddy went to his office at CREEP to shred files linking him and John Mitchell to plans to bug the opposition.

Immediately after the arrests, the White House began a cover-up. Presidential aide John Ehrlichman called H. R. Haldeman, who was with Nixon in Key Biscayne, Florida, to discuss Hunt's and McCord's involvement. Because both men had recently been employed by the White House, Ehrlichman and Haldeman feared that further investigation would implicate Nixon. Ehrlichman put John Dean in charge of keeping investigators at bay. White House press secretary Ron Ziegler dismissed reporters' concerns, asserting that "certain elements may try to stretch this beyond what it is."

Over the next three months, Dean, Haldeman, Ehrlichman, Mitchell, and Nixon successfully obstructed the Watergate investigation.

On June 20 Nixon told Haldeman to undertake a public relations offensive to squelch public interest in the Watergate break-in. Three days later, Nixon outlined to Haldeman a plan to have the CIA warn the FBI to "stay the hell out of this." Given Hunt's CIA connections, Nixon said, "we think it would be very unfortunate, both for the CIA, and for the country, and for American foreign policy" for the FBI to pursue the origins of the money found on the burglars. (Nixon's conversations with Haldeman on June 23 were caught on tape by listening devices the president had installed in the Oval Office. These conversations came to light in August 1974, providing proof of the president's efforts to obstruct justice.) Later that afternoon, acting FBI director L. Patrick Gray told Dean that the Bureau would not interview the Mexican lawyer whose checks had been the source of Liddy's cash.

Like the crime, the cover-up cost money. At the end of June, Dean met Kalmbach in Lafayette Park, across from the White House, and arranged for the master fund-raiser to collect money to purchase the burglars' silence. Kalmbach quickly gathered about $220,000, which was delivered to lawyers representing the Watergate defendants.

Reporters' efforts to turn public attention to Watergate by following the money trail received little attention at first. Bob Woodward and Carl Bernstein of the *Washington Post* covered the story because they routinely handled relatively insignificant metropolitan news, as the Watergate burglary initially seemed to be. More prominent national affairs reporters, intimidated by earlier administration campaigns against the press and dependent on access to powerful officials, shied away from covering Watergate. Woodward and Bernstein wrote several stories linking money laundered in Mexico to the Watergate burglars, but Nixon denied their significance. He told a news conference that "both sides" had made "technical violations" of the new campaign finance law, although he refused to say what the Democrats had done.

In mid-September it appeared that the cover-up had succeeded. A federal grand jury indicted Liddy, Hunt, and the five men arrested at Democratic headquarters. A Justice Department spokesman claimed that "we have absolutely no evidence that anyone else should be charged." Relieved, Nixon called Dean into his office late that afternoon and congratulated him: "The way you handled it, it seems to me has been very skillful—putting your fingers in the dikes every time that leaks have sprung here and sprung there." Nixon went on to ruminate about his plans for a second administration. He was pleased that Dean had been keeping notes on "a lot of people who are less than our friends." Those people "are asking for it," Nixon said, "and they are going to get it."

Investigative reporters Bob Woodward (*left*) and Carl Bernstein at work on the Watergate story at the *Washington Post. UPI/Bettmann Archive.*

Journalists Woodward and Bernstein kept reporting details of Watergate in the months before the November election, but their stories did not have a wide impact. They followed the money trail, assisted by an anonymous source who seemed familiar with all the personalities in the White House. They called this informant "Deep Throat," after a currently popular pornographic movie. Deep Throat would meet Woodward late at night in underground parking garages throughout the capital. He confirmed the journalists' suspicions that secret cash funds had been used for dirty tricks against the Democrats since 1970. By late October, Woodward and Bernstein believed they had traced the secret funds all the way up to Haldeman. Deep Throat informed them that "from top to bottom, this whole business is a Haldeman operation." On October 25, 1972, the day before Kissinger announced that "peace is at hand," Press Secretary Ziegler attacked the *Post* for "shoddy and shabby" use of confidential sources. He issued an unequivocal denial of Haldeman's connection to the secret funds. Two weeks later, Nixon won his landslide re-election.

Watergate faded but did not die in the winter following the election, while public attention was riveted on the savage bombing of North Vietnam and the subsequent Paris peace agreement. Democratic members of Congress kept an eye on news about Watergate, because they worried that CREEP's strong-armed fund-raising tactics threatened to put them out of business. Representative Thomas P. "Tip" O'Neill of Massachusetts, chairman of the Democratic Congressional Campaign Committee, noted that many long-time, reliable donors had not contributed to the Democrats' efforts in the 1972 campaign. The donors explained that they had been told by CREEP operatives to give only to the president and other Republicans—or suffer reprisals from federal agencies.

Early in 1973 the Senate decided to create a select seven-member committee (four Democrats and three Republicans), chaired by the conservative constitutional expert Sam Ervin of North Carolina, to investigate the break-in and sabotage against the Democrats in the 1972 campaign. As this, the Senate Select Committee on Campaign Practices—soon known informally as the Senate Watergate Committee—prepared to hold its first hearings, Nixon's staff formulated its strategy to disrupt the investigation. They would invoke "executive privilege," the idea that presidential agents could not be compelled to reveal information to Congress, an equal, not superior, branch of the government. Nixon advised subordinates involved in Watergate and the subsequent cover-up to "stonewall" the committee by forbidding White House assistants to testify.

The trial of the Watergate burglars revealed little at first, because they all pleaded guilty and denied White House involvement. The burglars continued to receive payments, and McCord heard from an agent that his wife and family would be taken care of if McCord had to go to jail for a year. Presiding over the trial, however, was U.S. District Court judge John J. Sirica, known as "Maximum John" for the tough sentences he handed down. Sirica expressed disbelief at prosecutors' claims that the men charged were the only ones involved in the break-in. He threatened the burglars with long prison terms. On March 19, McCord broke and wrote Sirica that he and other defendants had been under political pressure to plead guilty and remain silent, that others had lied under oath, and that higher-ups were involved in the break-in. On March 23, Sirica revealed the contents of McCord's letter and sentenced Liddy to six years in prison. He delayed sentencing the other defendants in the hope that they would reveal who else had participated.

As Sirica squeezed the burglars for information, Dean found it harder to maintain the cover-up. Hunt wanted another $130,000 in hush money from the White House, threatening that otherwise he would reveal the "seamy things" he had done. Dean told Nixon there was "a cancer growing on the presidency," because many of the people involved in the Watergate break-in and the burglary of Ellsberg's psychiatrist's office could be indicted. Those vulnerable to exposure included Mitchell, Haldeman, Ehrlichman, and Dean himself. Demands for hush money might go as high as $1 million, Dean said. Nixon replied, "We could get that. . . . And you could get it in cash. I know where it could be gotten." Nixon instructed Dean and other aides called to testify before the Ervin committee or the grand jury investigating the break-in to avoid perjury by saying "I don't remember; I can't recall."

Containment grew harder in April as prosecutors closed in on Dean, offering him immunity from prosecution if he divulged what he knew. Dean's possible defection frightened Nixon, who tried unsuccessfully to keep his wavering counsel in line. Fearing that Nixon might make him the fall guy, Dean decided to cooperate with the prosecutors. He began telling everything he knew about the cover-up to the Ervin committee's staff. Nixon then tried to discredit Dean, claiming he had directed a cover-up without the president's knowledge. He fired Dean on April 30. In a televised speech, he conceded that "there had been an effort to conceal the facts" about Watergate. He accepted no personal responsibility, implying instead that Dean had acted on his own. As he dismissed Dean, Nixon also decided to jettison Haldeman and Ehrlichman. He accepted their resignations, praising them as "two of the finest public servants I have ever known."

Nearly in a panic that the extent of the cover-up would be revealed, Nixon adopted a new tactic of appearing to cooperate with investigators. He bowed to public pressure and appointed Harvard law professor Archibald Cox as an independent counsel, or special prosecutor, to continue the Justice Department's investigation of Watergate. Cox, a long-time supporter of the Kennedys, apparently would be allowed to pursue the matter without political interference.

Nixon's strategy of pretending to accept responsibility for Watergate bought him a little time with the majority of the public, which did not know the extent of Nixon's involvement. However, on May 17 the Senate Watergate Committee began televised hearings, which continued throughout the summer of 1973. The committee began with the "foot soldiers" of Watergate—lower-level CREEP officials who explained how they handled the hush money. In the first month of the hearings, Sam Ervin, whose folksy appearance and manner could not hide a devastating wit and sharp intellect, became a celebrity. His vice chairman, Tennessee Republican Howard Baker, tried to focus attention on Nixon, repeatedly asking witnesses, "What did the president know, and when did he know it?" At hairdressing salons, muffler shops, bars, and business offices across the country, Americans interrupted their daily routines to stare at TV sets tuned to the Watergate hearings.

In late June, having been granted immunity from prosecution, Dean took the stand. For two days he read in a monotone a 245-page

Sam J. Ervin, Jr.

One of the most dramatic moments during the Senate Watergate Committee hearings occurred in July 1974, during the testimony of former domestic policy director John D. Ehrlichman. When asked if he believed that ordinary citizens could expect government break-ins and wiretaps in their own homes and offices, Ehrlichman replied that the ancient right to remain free from unlawful searches had been "considerably eroded over the years." That justification for the White House's lawbreaking was too much for Sam Ervin, the North Carolina senator who chaired the committee. His heavy jaws shook as he quoted an eighteenth-century English prime minister: "The poorest man may in his cottage bid defiance to all the forces of the Crown. It may be frail, its roof may shake, the wind may blow through it, the storm may enter, but the king of

statement describing the details of the cover-up. He characterized Watergate as emerging from "a climate of excessive concern over the political impact of demonstrators, excessive concern over leaks, an insatiable appetite for political intelligence." Trying to discredit Dean, Nixon leaked word to the committee that Dean had helped himself to some of the cash he had controlled. A columnist friendly to Nixon labeled Dean a "bottom-dwelling slug" for betraying his superiors. But he knew so much and had so many details at his fingertips that such slurs had little impact.

The testimony of Nixon loyalists made matters worse for the president. They stumbled, mumbled, forgot, or fought with the senators. Writer Mary McCarthy described John Mitchell's "small lifeless eyes, like those of a wintering potato," and his "voice, spouting insinuation." John Ehrlichman sounded supercilious as he explained the president's right, in the name of "national security," to order burglar-

England cannot enter." And yet, Ervin lectured, "we are told here that what the king of England can't do, the president of the United States can."

The exchange with Ehrlichman confirmed Ervin's status as a folk hero. Born in 1896, the senator seemed to represent the common decency of an earlier period. The sordid details of Watergate outraged him. His eye darted, his cheeks quivered. Though this former rural judge claimed that he was "just a country lawyer," he was no simple backwoodsman. His law degree was from Harvard, he read widely—as evidenced by his inexhaustible store of quotations—and he was as shrewd a politician as North Carolina had ever elected to the Senate.

For the liberals in his party he was an unlikely hero, for he had resisted legislation protecting the rights of racial minorities, women, and consumers. Yet, with his colorful personality and moral rectitude, he helped to bring people together at a time when the nation's political fabric was being torn apart. He convinced many conservatives—who might otherwise have seen the Watergate investigation as a liberal vendetta against President Nixon—of the gravity of the charges. He also helped northern liberals understand the common ground they shared with southerners.

The Watergate hearings represented the high point of Sam Ervin's public career. He retired from the Senate in 1975 and spent the next several years practicing law, lecturing on college campuses, and accepting accolades for his role in preserving the Constitution. He died in 1985. ■

ies and surveillance. Haldeman twisted and squirmed in his seat and refused to provide direct answers to the senators' questions.

The hearings climaxed in mid-July when Alexander Butterfield, the White House office manager, revealed that Nixon had tape-recorded his own conversations since 1970. Tapes existed that could show whether Dean was telling the truth. The Ervin committee, Judge Sirica, and Special Prosecutor Cox tried immediately to acquire the tapes. Nixon refused access to them, citing executive privilege. Returning from the hospital after a bout with severe viral pneumonia, the president denied rumors that he was going to resign. Such talk was "just plain poppycock," he said, adding, "Let others wallow in Watergate, we are going to do our job."

Another scandal hit the White House in late August, when the *Wall Street Journal* revealed that federal prosecutors in Baltimore were investigating Vice President Spiro Agnew for bribery, extortion, and tax fraud. Prosecutors had determined that Agnew, the former governor of Maryland, had received bribes from builders and engineers in his home state for the past ten years, in return for lucrative public works contracts. The payoffs had continued even after Agnew left the governor's office; the vice president had even accepted brown paper bags full of cash in his suite at the Executive Office Building.

Agnew fought against formal indictment with a strategy that made Nixon's position more precarious, because the vice president raised the specter of impeachment. The vice president's talk of impeachment angered Nixon, who did not want the notion implanted in the minds of members of Congress. The president hinted that Agnew should step down to avoid prosecution. Agnew refused the hint, telling a cheering throng of Republican women in Los Angeles that he would never resign. But only two weeks later he did. Prosecutors had hard evidence of bribery, and he realized he could go to jail if he did not strike a deal. He pleaded no contest to one count of income tax evasion, for not reporting or paying taxes on the bribes. Although he subsequently publicly affirmed his innocence, a no contest plea is considered an admission of guilt.

Agnew's resignation left a vacancy in the vice presidency. Under the terms of the Twenty-fifth Amendment, adopted in the aftermath of John Kennedy's assassination, the president could name a successor, to be confirmed by a majority vote in Congress. Nixon selected Minority Leader Gerald R. Ford of Michigan, a Republican stalwart who was well liked by his peers. He had little knowledge of or experience with foreign affairs. He was best known for his unswerving loyalty to Nixon through many dizzying turns of policy, and for his suggestion that Supreme Court justice William O. Douglas be impeached for expressing sympathy for the constitutional rights of antiwar protesters. If Nixon's own hold on the presidency were threatened, critics might think twice about forcing him out in favor of the untested Ford.

By October 1973, even the prospect of a Ford presidency could not save Nixon from the public's wrath as the full dimensions of the cover-up began to emerge. Archibald Cox and the Watergate Committee asked Sirica for subpoenas to force Nixon to produce the tapes of key conversations he had had with aides on Watergate. Cox declined as unworkable a compromise under which Mississippi's Democratic Senator John Stennis would listen to the tapes and certify the accuracy of a printed transcript. Realizing that such evidence would not stand in court, Cox persisted with his efforts to subpoena the tapes.

Nixon, mindful of his conversations with Haldeman and Dean plotting the cover-up, realized that releasing complete tapes to Cox would doom him. On Saturday night, October 20, Nixon asked Attorney General Elliot Richardson to fire Cox. Richardson, who had promised Cox independence, resigned rather than dismiss him. Richardson's deputy, William Ruckelshaus, also quit rather than execute the order. Only Solicitor General Robert Bork, third-in-command at the Justice Department, was willing to fire Cox. Nixon also abolished the special prosecutor's office and sent FBI agents to prevent Cox's subordinates from gaining access to their files.

A fire storm of protest engulfed Capitol Hill over the next forty-eight hours. Over 1 million telephone calls and telegrams flooded senators' and representatives' offices protesting the "Saturday Night Massacre." People who earlier had given Nixon the benefit of the doubt, believing he would cooperate with investigators, changed their minds and thought he wanted to hide his involvement in law-breaking. The next week, eight impeachment resolutions were referred to the House Judiciary Committee, chaired by New Jersey's Peter Rodino. The eruption of public anger over Nixon's stonewalling on the tapes forced another White House surrender. The president's lawyer announced the White House's willingness to release subpoenaed tapes to Judge Sirica. A new independent prosecutor, Houston lawyer Leon Jaworski, resumed the investigations.

As Jaworski gathered information about the state of the Watergate inquiry, more astonishing revelations fed the public's anger about Nixon's apparent duplicity. White House attorneys cataloguing the tapes discovered that some were missing and that an eighteen-and-a-half-minute gap existed on the tape of a June 20, 1972, conversation with Haldeman. Haldeman's notes revealed that he and Nixon had discussed Watergate at that meeting and the president had called for a "counterattack," presumably against any investigation of the break-in, during these crucial missing minutes. Soon after Judge Sirica revealed the existence of the gap, Nixon told Associated Press editors that "people have got a right to know whether or not their president is a crook. Well, I'm not a crook."

While the public struggled to assimilate this outburst, the IRS announced that it would re-examine the president's tax returns for 1970, 1971, and 1972. Nixon had claimed deductions of $576,000 for the gift of his vice-presidential papers to the National Archives. On incomes of over $200,000 he had paid only $700 in taxes one year and a few thousand dollars the other years. Moreover, his donation to the National Archives had been falsely dated to make it appear to comply with a new law prohibiting excessive valuation of such materials. Eventually, in April 1974, Nixon paid the IRS $264,706 in back taxes and penalties. News of the gap in the tape and of Nixon's tax troubles deeply rattled public opinion, turning many of his erstwhile supporters against him.

As public distrust of Nixon increased in 1974, the staff of the House Judiciary Committee carefully prepared a case for impeachment. Continual requests for tapes and documents produced White House delays or attempts to get away with half-compliance. In late April, Nixon appeared on television to explain that he would make edited transcripts of the tapes available to the committee. These documents, he claimed, would show no prior knowledge of the break-in and no participation in or knowledge of obstruction of justice.

That justification crumbled within days. The House Judiciary Committee voted not to accept edited transcripts and told Nixon that he had failed to comply with the committee's subpoenas. Nixon released transcripts anyway, and excerpts were widely published in newspapers. People were appalled by the conversations that had taken place in the Oval Office. The transcripts produced angry denunciations of Nixon, even from friends. Senate Minority Leader Hugh Scott said they revealed a "deplorable, shabby, disgusting and immoral performance" by everyone involved in the conversations. House Minority Leader John Rhodes told Nixon to consider resigning, and the *Chicago Tribune,* a long-time supporter of Nixon, called for quick action on a bill of impeachment.

By late July 1974 the committee had impeachment articles ready. On July 27, in a nationally televised session, six Republicans joined all twenty-one Democrats—forming a majority of 27 to 11—in voting to adopt the first article, charging Nixon with obstruction of justice for his involvement in the Watergate cover-up. On July 29 the committee voted 28 to 10 on a second, general article, charging abuse of power in connection to Nixon's harassment of domestic opponents. The next day, a narrower majority of 21 to 17 indicted the president for unconstitutionally defying its subpoenas. Two other articles of impeachment, involving tax evasion and the secret bombing of Cambodia, failed to pass; but the three that had passed were more than enough. If the full House of Representatives adopted these articles, Nixon would become only the second president in U.S. history to be impeached—the first having been Andrew Johnson in 1868. He would then be brought to trial before the Senate, which would decide whether to remove the president from office.

The Supreme Court quickly delivered another blow to Nixon. In *United States* v. *Nixon,* by an 8-to-0 ruling, the Court demanded that the president turn over to Sirica tapes of sixty-four conversations deemed to be essential evidence in the cover-up trials of six former aides. Chief Justice Burger acknowledged that the Constitution protected executive privilege, but he ruled that "when a claim of privilege is based only on the generalized interest in confidentiality, it cannot prevail over the fundamental demands of due process of law in the administration of justice." Nixon's lawyer agreed to turn over the tapes by an August 7 deadline set by Sirica.

On August 5 Nixon released transcripts of his June 23, 1972, conversations with Haldeman. On that date the two men had planned

The tape recording of Richard Nixon's June 23, 1972 conversation with H. R. Haldeman provided the crucial "smoking gun"—evidence of direct presidential involvement in the Watergate cover-up. *Reprinted courtesy of Susan Corn Conway Gallery, Washington, D.C.*

how to use the CIA to throw the FBI off the scent of the Watergate investigation. Here was the "smoking gun" his defenders had insisted did not exist, for the conversations showed Nixon's early knowledge of and participation in the cover-up. Nixon conceded in a written statement that the tapes were "at variance with certain of my previous statements," and he acknowledged that impeachment by the full House was "virtually a foregone conclusion." Two days later, all congressional support for Nixon collapsed with release of these tapes. All the Republican members of the Judiciary Committee who had voted against impeachment said they would now vote for it on the floor. Long-time Republican friends in the Senate told him he would have fewer than ten votes in that body when it came time to decide whether to convict him on the House's bill of impeachment.

Nixon's foreign policy advisers worried about his mental stability during these final days. Secretary of Defense James Schlesinger and Chief of Staff Alexander Haig informed military commanders around the world to check directly with them before executing any unusual orders from Nixon. Kissinger and Haig joined with congressional Republicans in attempts to convince Nixon to leave office before the crisis damaged foreign relations.

On the night of August 7, 1974, Nixon called Kissinger to the White House to tell him he planned to resign. Nixon wept openly and clearly felt his fall from grace keenly. He hoped for some later vindication, asking Kissinger, "Will history treat me more kindly than my contemporaries?" Kissinger tried to assure him that it would.

Nixon's impending resignation became public the evening of August 8. In a televised address he told the nation that he intended to leave office at noon the next day. The next morning he said farewell to his staff in a tearful, rambling, self-pitying speech; he recalled his father, his mother, his brothers' dying in their mother's arms, Theodore Roosevelt's dead young wife, and an early failure to pass the bar examination. At last Nixon recovered some composure and bade his staff and the nation good-by. He climbed into a helicopter on the White House lawn, flew to Andrews Air Force Base, and boarded Air Force One for a flight to California, becoming the first American president ever to resign. While Nixon was en route to the West Coast, Gerald Ford took the oath of office as the new president. Ford proclaimed that the "long national nightmare" of Watergate was over.

CONCLUSION

Richard Nixon's defenders, at the time of his resignation and in subsequent years, have tended to focus on his achievements in foreign policy, particularly the steps he took toward fostering cooperation with the Soviet Union and China. In some ways, however, his domestic record showed a similar vigor: for example, his early plan on welfare reform and his willingness to scrap his earlier economic approach in favor of wage and price controls exhibited a certain creativity and pragmatism for which he is not often remembered. But, unfortunately, he was most creative in devising ways to undercut his political opponents. His presidency became dominated by his obsession with supposed enemies and his determination to get them before they could get him. President Nixon did more to divide the nation than to unite it. In the end, more of the substantive changes in domestic affairs that came about during his term in office came from Congress and the Supreme Court, rather than from the executive branch. While the Court extended its civil rights rulings into the controversial areas of busing and abortion rights, Congress passed key legislation to protect the environment and promote public health and safety.

Ironically, it was Nixon's resignation that unified the country. No other event since John Kennedy's assassination had done more to bring Americans together. A president who had tried to exploit his power in illegal and unethical ways had failed to dominate the government and intimidate his opposition into silence. As his cynical manipulations of people and events became known during the Watergate investigations, Americans asserted their sense of justice and fair play. One of the flood of books that was eventually published on Watergate was entitled simply *How the Good Guys Finally Won*. Besides agreeing that justice had been done, Americans breathed a collective sigh of relief that the country's government had withstood the strain of the Watergate crisis. There was even a certain amount of national pride involved. It seemed that the American federal government, with its system of checks and balances allowing one branch to curb the excesses of another, was fully capable of overcoming the abuse of power.

Much of this national self-congratulation was deserved, and the revulsion people felt at Nixon's duplicity was real. Nevertheless, Nixon's downfall rested more on strokes of good fortune than on the smooth workings of a system of checks and balances. Many of the White House horrors—the buggings, the dirty tricks, the break-ins— were known before the election of 1972 and shrugged off as politics as usual. Had *Washington Post* reporters Bob Woodward and Carl Bernstein not kept the story alive in the fall of 1972, the Watergate scandal would have disappeared. Judge Sirica's prickly, skeptical personality also played a major role; a more complacent jurist might well have accepted the prosecution's claim that only seven low-level CREEP officials were responsible for the break-in. The investigations by the Senate Watergate Committee and the House Judiciary Committee helped focus public attention on the affair, but the Senate committee owed its existence as much to Democrats' outrage over CREEP's turning off their money supply as it did to concern for justice. Finally, the impeachment process began because of the fight over the tapes. If Nixon had not taped himself, if he had destroyed the tapes, or if Alexander Butterfield had not revealed their existence, the Watergate story probably would have turned out differently.

Overall, then, the implications of Watergate are difficult to assess. Nixon's abuse of power was finally checked, but perhaps only as a result of fortunate circumstances. Will the system work again if another president tries to subvert the country's laws and institutions?

A 1982 poll of over eight hundred historians identified Nixon as one of only four outright failures in the presidency. But some of the public anger at Nixon's actions had dissipated by the late 1980s, when he achieved a sort of rehabilitation, especially with respect to his handling of foreign affairs. At the time of his death in 1994 even old political enemies praised his skill at foreign policy and his astonishing tenacity in climbing back into the public arena in the two decades following his disgrace. More lasting than the public's anger at Nixon personally was a deepening public distrust of politicians, of government in general, and of many other figures of authority in American society. This perhaps was the most fundamental legacy of Richard Nixon and Watergate. ■

FURTHER READING

On politics and domestic policy in the Nixon administration, see: Richard Nixon, *RN: The Memoirs of Richard Nixon* (1978) and *In the Arena* (1990); Stephen E. Ambrose, *Nixon* (3 vols.: 1986, 1989, 1991); Joan Hoff, *Nixon Reconsidered* (1994); Herbert Parmet, *Richard Nixon and His America* (1990); William Safire, *Before the Fall: An Inside Look at the Pre-Watergate White House* (1975); Raymond Price, *With Nixon* (1977); A. James Reichley, *Conservatives in an Age of Change* (1981); Timothy Crouse, *The Boys on the Bus* (1976); Kevin B. Phillips, *The Emerging Republican Majority* (1969); Nicholas Lemann, *The Promised Land: The Great Black Migration and How It Changed America* (1991); Daniel Patrick Moynihan, *The Politics of a Guaranteed Income* (1973); Melvin Urofsky, *The Continuity of Change: The Supreme Court and Individual Liberties, 1953–1986* (1991). On Watergate, see: Stanley I. Kutler, *The Wars of Watergate* (1990); Kim McQuaid, *The Anxious Years: America in the Vietnam and Watergate Era* (1989); J. Anthony Lukas, *Nightmare: The Underside of the Nixon Years* (1976); Theodore H. White, *Breach of Faith: The Fall of Richard Nixon* (1975); Bob Woodward and Carl Bernstein, *All The President's Men* (1974) and *The Final Days* (1976); H. R. Haldeman, with Joseph Dimona, *The Ends of Power* (1978); H. R. Haldeman, *The Haldeman Diaries* (1994); John Ehrlichman, *Witness to Power* (1982); John Dean, *Blind Ambition* (1976).

11

The Challenges of
Change, 1974–1980

From the start of his presidency, Gerald Ford tried to put the memory of Watergate to rest and put the nation at ease. His homey style contrasted with Nixon's awkward defensiveness. The new president, an adored and adoring father of four happy young adults, seemed at peace with himself, his family, and his country. In contrast to Nixon, who had cheated on his income taxes, Ford paid his fair share. He was often photographed playing golf like a Midwestern small business-man. At first Ford relished his role as a regular guy: "I don't want a honeymoon," he told Congress three days after taking office, "I want a good marriage." He could take a joke, too. He laughed when photographers snapped pictures of his awkward moments—for instance, when his errant golf balls hit surprised spectators or when he stumbled on the Air Force One gangway, banging his head on the door.

But the good-natured Midwestern congressman-turned-vice-president found himself overwhelmed, when he assumed the presidency on August 9, 1974, by the public's feeling that government officials were incompetents or lawbreakers and the programs they administered inefficient or harmful. Ford tried to heal the wounds of Watergate by asserting, on taking office, that "our long national nightmare is over." But a few weeks later his popularity fell sharply when he gave Richard Nixon a blanket pardon for all crimes he might have committed while president. Ford's standing never recovered, and his plunging fortunes mirrored the public's frustration. In January 1975 he told Congress that "the state of the union is not good." Twenty months later the voters turned him out of office, electing a Washington outsider, former Georgia governor James Earl "Jimmy" Carter.

This rapid political turnover was a symptom of the nation's social volatility. Watergate had left Americans thinking they would have to solve their problems on their own, since politicians could hardly be trusted. Jimmy Carter promised the public "I will never lie to you"—but Americans would come to wonder what Carter really stood for. While they waited to find out, many women and men worked—sometimes against a flood tide of cynicism and apathy—to craft solutions themselves to the problems the country faced. Some got involved in local politics or in social issues, creating a new and more diverse generation of leaders. Others turned to religion. Many simply tried to make a living in the stagnant economy, keep their families from falling apart, and make sense of the sometimes bewildering world around them. Across the country it seemed that transformation began with the personal, and only later could it reach the level of national politics.

CHANGING ROLES FOR
WOMEN AND MEN

By 1974, profound changes in gender roles, family patterns, and personal desires had become apparent in American society. Fewer and fewer households conformed to the once-idealized nuclear family, with the father working outside the home and the mother caring for the children. The proportion of women who worked outside the home continued to grow. By 1970 one-third of mothers with children under six years of age held or sought jobs; 52 percent had joined the work force by 1984. In 1975 the Labor Department reported that only 7 percent of American families fit the category of a "typical" four-person household—a married couple living together with their two minor children.

The growing numbers of divorced men and women, people who had never married, unmarried couples living together, working women, single mothers, and openly gay men and women made for a visibly more diverse society, and Americans began speaking more openly about issues of sexuality and gender. Yet in many cases those whose way of life differed from earlier norms encountered hostility and economic hardship. Some traditionalists feared for their cherished values, and they joined a growing conservative movement to reverse threatening social trends.

Divorce became more commonplace in the 1970s, continuing a trend that began early in the twentieth century. By 1980, experts were predicting that one-half of all new marriages would end in divorce. For those marrying for the first time, 44 percent would divorce; for second or subsequent marriages the figure was 60 percent. Changing attitudes toward divorce coincided with the enactment of "no-fault" divorce laws in every state but South Dakota and Illinois between 1970 and 1980. California led the way with a liberal law permitting either party to sue for divorce if he or she believed "irreconcilable differences" had caused a breakdown of the marriage. Advocates of the new laws believed they would eliminate the phony accusations of abuse or adultery, the courtroom recriminations, and the spying by private investigators that had previously made divorce a nearly unbearable experience. It was also hoped that reduced acrimony would make it easier for divorced parents to cooperate in raising their children. Moreover, no-fault divorce changed the legal focus from assessing blame to dividing assets. The new laws tried to treat men and women equally, to recognize the wife's contribution to the partnership, and to end old assumptions that women's roles were subordinate to those of men.

No-fault divorce laws achieved many of these goals, but they also had unintended negative consequences for women and children. The divorce revolution particularly hurt at least two classes of women: older women who did not work outside the home and mothers of young children. The laws supposedly treated men and women equally, but they defined equality strictly in dollar terms. Older women who had been homemakers for years found they had few assets and limited job opportunities after divorce. The new laws ignored the immense, nonmonetary contributions these women had made to their families, and they expected women to be as able to support themselves after divorce as their husbands. Alimony, once a staple of divorce settlements, was rarely awarded under the new system.

The economic burden of divorce fell most heavily on women with young children. In 90 percent of divorces, children continued to live with their mother, but mothers fared poorly after divorce compared to fathers. In the first year after a marital breakup, the standard of living of divorced women and their minor children declined by an average of 73 percent; that of divorced men rose 42 percent. Judges divided marital property equally. In most cases the largest single asset was the family's house, which the court ordered sold. Thus a mother with minor children would find herself looking for new shelter—with only half the proceeds from the sale of her old home—at a time of rising housing costs. Judges ordered child support, but less than half of fathers paid the full amount of child support assessed by the courts: 30 percent of divorced mothers received only partial payments, and 25 percent received nothing at all. Feminist groups, whom conservatives accused of being "anti-family" and blamed for the rising divorce rate, set up support and training programs for former housewives transformed into "displaced homemakers" and lobbied state governments for tougher enforcement of child support.

In taking on these issues, women's groups confronted a social problem that would become more and more critical as the century neared an end. Women had become the fastest-growing segment of poor people in America, a trend sociologist Diana Pearce described as the "feminization of poverty." Of course this problem affected children as well as mothers. From 1970 to 1982, the proportion of children living in poverty grew from 15 to 21 percent. Most poor children lived in female-headed households.

At the same time, birthrates among unmarried women and teenagers began to rise (while declining among married women), placing further burdens on both mothers and children. Unskilled, uneducated, and poor young single mothers faced serious hardships. Good-paying jobs were scarce, especially in the depressed cities of the North. Even when they found work, these mothers often discovered that their paychecks barely covered the cost of child care, when they could find it.

Higher divorce rates were only one indication of profound changes in the American family. Throughout the 1970s, Americans adopted a variety of alternatives to the traditional nuclear family. The number of adults living alone increased 60 percent in the seventies; by 1980 this group constituted 23 percent of all households. At the same time, the number of unmarried couples living together tripled to 1.6 million, and one-third of them had children. No longer an anomaly, these unmarried households achieved some acceptance when the Department of Housing and Urban Development agreed to admit them into public housing as long as they exhibited a "stable family relationship." However, since welfare policies mandated that mothers receiving payments under the Aid to Families with Dependent Children (AFDC) program demonstrate that they were their children's sole source of support, the government offered women a Catch-22: if they lived with their partner they would lose their payments; therefore many mothers concealed or avoided stable partnerships, making it harder for them to climb out of poverty.

While rates of divorce and living together rose, so did the marriage rate. However their practices changed, Americans still pursued an ideal of eternal romantic attachment. Eighty percent of separated or divorced people remarried within three years. Sociologists described "blended families," in which children lived with stepparents, stepsiblings, and half siblings. Experts predicted that more than half of all children born in the seventies would spend part of their childhood living in a household other than the traditional model, headed by their own biological mother and father and with only their biological brothers or sisters. Forty percent would spend time in a single-parent household, almost always headed by a woman. One disadvantage of such situations was their unpredictability. On the positive side, the best of these blended families offered extended webs of nurturing and affection.

Child-rearing practices and expectations changed as more women entered the work force. Traditionally, mothers had borne the brunt of child care; now non–family members did more of the work. A substantial part of a family's income went to baby sitters or day-care facilities. Middle-class families improvised a variety of child-care arrangements. One survey of working mothers reported that their children "may experience three, four or even more kinds of care in a single week, as they spend part of the day in nursery school, another portion with a family day care mother, and are brought to and from these services by a parent, neighbor, or some other person." Single mothers, often poor, frequently left children with grandparents or other relatives. Older children let themselves into their homes after school. These so-called latchkey children had only the companionship of other youngsters or the TV set until their parents got home from work. Experts said the average child watched twelve to sixteen thousand hours of TV between the ages of two and sixteen.

Child-care advocates, including feminist leaders, worked hard to meet the growing need for day care. Marian Wright Edelman and others formed the Children's Defense Fund, soon to become the nation's most visible advocacy group on behalf of children. Leaders like Edelman and her friend Hillary Rodham Clinton pointed out that the United States was the only nation in the developed world without a national child-care policy. Beginning in 1971, Congress considered a number of bills that would have provided significant federal funding for child care, but conservatives fought the bills, which they feared would pave the way for "communal child rearing."

These changes in family life met resistance in some quarters, including women who felt that the new expectations seemed to dismiss their lives and achievements. American women did not move easily, or as a unified group, from family-centered domestic containment to feminist self-fulfillment. Opposition to the growing assertiveness of women crystallized in a movement to prevent ratification of the Equal Rights Amendment (ERA). Masterminded by conservative Illinois lawyer Phyllis Schlafly, the anti-ERA movement sought to recruit older women, women who did not work outside the home, conservative men, and religious organizations by arguing that the ERA would diminish women's standing and leave most women unprotected. Passed by Congress and sent to the states in 1972, the ERA had to be ratified by thirty-eight state legislatures before March 1979, or it would die. After quickly gaining passage in thirty-five states, the amendment was stymied in the three more it needed for acceptance. In July 1978, sixty-five thousand women marched on Washington to pressure Congress to extend the deadline for three more years. It did so, but opponents continued to block passage in state legislatures, and the proposed amendment was never ratified.

Another sign of trouble in the American family came from horrifying new reports of physical, sexual, and emotional abuse of children and spouses. Modern families may not have become more violent than earlier ones, but once feminists and child advocates insisted that the issues of wife battering and child abuse be taken seriously, behavior that was once considered acceptable was no longer tolerated. Most abuse went unreported, so documented cases represented only the tip of the iceberg. Although hard figures were difficult to obtain, experts estimated that between 1.5 and 2.3 million of the 46 million children between the ages of three and seventeen who lived with both parents had been battered by one or both of them sometime during their life.

Between 275,000 and 750,000 youngsters were beaten each year. Similar figures were reported for domestic partners, almost always women. Figures for children in single-parent households may have been higher, as these parents were often exhausted by the dual burdens of holding a job and raising their children. Sexual abuse of children also seemed to climb; an estimated 25 percent of girls and 20 percent of boys suffered molestation from parents, stepparents, other relatives, or acquaintances. Greater attention to women's rights also brought to light the growing problem of rape within marriage or living-together relationships. Reportings of rapes and wife beatings soared, and women successfully lobbied to allow prosecution of husbands for raping their wives.

The sexual revolution of the 1960s had left a complicated legacy. Much to the surprise of both its advocates and its critics, the idea of sexual freedom had been easily absorbed into the mainstream culture. Openness about sex and the erosion of old restrictions freed women. But at the same time, the decline of sexual taboos and the acknowledgment of female eroticism convinced some men that women were theirs for the taking. Sales of pornographic magazines, books, and movie tickets, mostly to men, surged, reaching $4 billion per year.

The growth of the pornography industry divided old allies and created unlikely alignments. Advocates of the new freedoms had once resisted all restraints on the dissemination of sexually explicit material. In the 1970s, however, feminists became divided over the issue of pornography. Some feminists, believing that pornography incited violence against women and degraded them, joined with religious traditionalists and social conservatives to call for the regulation or banning of pornography. Other feminists joined male advocates of sexual liberation, like *Penthouse* editor Bob Guccione, to argue that restricting pornography, however repugnant the material, violated the freedom of expression guaranteed by the First Amendment and would eventually foster a backlash against sexual freedom.

Greater openness about sexuality encouraged homosexual Americans to seek acceptance from "straight" society and an end to ingrained prejudice and stereotypes. The campaign for gay rights achieved notable gains in the seventies. For instance, the American Psychiatric Association dropped its classification of homosexuality as a mental disorder and joined a growing call for the extension of civil rights protections to homosexuals. A major women's conference in Houston affirmed solidarity with lesbians.

In their daily lives, gays and lesbians found new self-confidence and visibility during the 1970s. Gay men established well-defined, separate neighborhoods in many American cities. Lesbians, though less geographically concentrated, nonetheless created communities for themselves in various ways, claiming a culture of their own

Harvey Milk

Among the thousands of gay men who flocked to the Castro district of San Francisco in the 1970s was a middle-aged financial-analyst-turned-hippie by the name of Harvey Milk. During the five years he lived there, he agitated, politicked, and organized for gay rights, becoming a symbol of gay liberation and a martyr to the cause.

Harvey Milk was born into a middle-class family in Woodmere, New York, in 1930. In high school he was an athlete and class clown; he differed from his teenage friends only in his passion for opera. He knew, but did not divulge to his friends, that he was gay. After graduating from New York State College for Teachers in 1951, he served in the navy, held a series of jobs, and finally found that he had a flair for business. A conservative, Goldwater Republican, he became a successful analyst for a New York investment firm and kept his sexuality secret at work. But he lived the gay life openly in those handful of big American cities were it was acceptable, and soon his bohemian social life led him to change his politics and his way of living.

Like so many Americans of this era, Milk and his lover, Scott Smith, dropped out of the rat race and hit the road. The two landed in San Francisco in 1972, looking for a cheap place to live among people like themselves. In March 1973 they opened a camera shop on Castro Street, with a sign in the window that said, "Yes, We Are Very Open." But Harvey Milk wanted to be much more than a small businessman. As his theater-producer friend Tom O'Horgan put it, "Harvey spent most of his life looking for a stage. On Castro Street, he found it."

San Francisco had a long-standing gay community, and gays had exercised political clout there since the mid-1960s. The first openly gay candidate for public office had run for the city's board of supervisors in 1961. Building on the large gay constituency, but often at odds with political insiders (symbolized by the city's Alice B. Toklas Democratic Club), Milk determined that he would become the embodiment of gay politics, first in San Francisco, perhaps later in the nation. He would do so by combining populist appeals to outsiders and hippies with careful cultivation of gay-bar owners, corporate-minded bankers, and straight union bosses. From the time he first ran for city supervisor in 1973 until his victorious run for the same office in 1977, he built a coalition of neighborhood activists, labor unions, and rank-and-file gay voters. At his Castro Camera headquarters, drag queens and leather fanciers mingled with teamsters and firefighters.

Milk was not the only freshman on the board of supervisors in 1977. A former policeman named Dan White had also been elected, to represent a conservative district of the city. Milk, who was always independent (to the point of being considered a maverick by his admirers and a loose cannon by his detractors), thought at first that there might be some issues on which he and White could find common ground. But soon they began to differ, as Milk more and more often voted in support of the city's liberal mayor, George Moscone, and White grew more and more frustrated and alienated. What Milk did not know was that White was having personal problems that made him depressed and unstable. White resigned from office, then tried to have himself reinstated. Moscone opposed him; Milk offered no support.

On the morning of November 27, 1978, Dan White walked into city hall with a Smith and Wesson revolver and shot Moscone four times. He reloaded the gun with hollow-headed dum-dum bullets and moved on to Harvey Milk's office. White took Milk to the office he had lately vacated and shot Milk five times, twice in the head.

Harvey Milk's death brought thousands of gays, lesbians, and their supporters into the streets of San Francisco, first for a candlelight vigil and later for a massive, violent protest, dubbed "The White Night Riot," when Dan White was found not guilty by reason of insanity. In October 1979 over 100,000 people participated in a gay rights march in Washington, many carrying placards bearing Harvey Milk's picture. Journalist Randy Shilts later wrote that "For years afterward, when dull moments fell over a gay demonstration and the old slogans felt thin, someone could shout, 'Harvey Milk lives,' and it would not be hollow rhetoric. Harvey Milk did live, as a metaphor for the homosexual experience in America." ∎

through music, art, and literature, and founding successful businesses. Although some heterosexuals continued to oppose tolerance toward homosexuals, gays and lesbians spoke of the love and caring they experienced together. They openly acknowledged their sexual orientation, formed organizations to advance their interests, and published newspapers and magazines addressing their concerns. Gays and lesbians lobbied municipalities, states, and the federal government to guarantee equal access for homosexuals in employment, housing, and various government programs. Some laws changed, but Congress did not consider such legislation on the national level.

Opponents of gay rights mounted attacks against gays and lesbians. After Miami's city council banned discrimination against homosexuals, singer Anita Bryant began a campaign to repeal the new law. She complained that the "ordinance condones immorality and discriminates against my children's rights to grow up in a healthy, decent community." In June 1977, Bryant's Save Our Children movement organized a referendum that repealed the law by a two-to-one majority. The size of the vote shook gays and advocates of civil liberties across the country. The National Gay Task Force believed that the vote represented an effort to herd homosexuals back into the closet, where many had shuddered in fear of exposure before the openness of the sixties. San Francisco mayor George Moscone, elected with the support of the city's sizable gay community, condemned the repeal as "terribly wrong." Moscone backed a march by five thousand demonstrators against Bryant and other opponents of gay rights. But in November 1978, Moscone and Harvey Milk, the first openly gay member of the San Francisco Board of Supervisors, were gunned down by a former supervisor, Dan White, who had voted against San Francisco's gay rights law. Although the police arrested White with the smoking gun in his hand, he won acquittal on murder charges. The jury accepted White's strange claim that excessive consumption of Twinkies had left him temporarily insane. After the jury announced its verdict, about ten thousand supporters of Milk and Moscone rioted, chanting "He got away with murder."

ECONOMIC PROBLEMS AND SOCIAL DIVISIONS

Had the nation's economy boomed, as it had during the early 1960s, prosperity might have assuaged the social tensions and uncertainties of the 1970s. However, the economy began a serious decline in the mid-1970s. Inflation took a heavy toll on Americans, making many worry about the future. Stagflation—persistent slow growth coupled with rising prices—remained a serious problem. Prices rose because

American productivity had slowed and because a fourfold increase in petroleum prices produced an "oil shock" that rippled through the economy.

After September 1978, when a revolution in Iran sent oil prices soaring, inflation became rampant. The annual rate of increase in the consumer price index (CPI) climbed steadily from an already high 7 percent in May 1978 to 11.3 percent in July 1979. And this represented only a cumulative average: the cost of goods people bought and used every day rose even faster. Gasoline went up 52 percent from September 1978 to September 1979. Americans panicked, fearing they would not be able to get gas no matter what they paid. Oil producers, refiners, and service stations took advantage of the fear to gouge consumers. By the summer of 1979, cars were lining up five hundred deep at some service stations. Motorists shouted, shook their fists, and even stabbed one another to get gas. The apparent greed and callousness of the oil companies made people even madder. "It's sort of like sex," said a spokesman for Gulf Oil. "Everybody's going to get all the gasoline they need, but they're damn sure not going to get all they want." States imposed a crude form of rationing by demanding that drivers go to the pump only on alternate days.

Fear of shortages and high prices extended beyond gasoline. As prices on home heating oil, used mostly in the Northeast and Midwest, shot up during 1979, people in these regions glumly contemplated a cold, expensive winter. Food prices also took off. Consumers felt the pinch every time they went to the supermarket, and TV news broadcasts did not let them forget it when they returned home. In 1979 the "CBS Evening News" ran a popular weekly feature surveying the cost of a standard market basket of groceries in several cities across the country. Prices climbed everywhere; those soaring fastest included the basic staples of the American home—beer, eggs, plastic containers, even toilet paper.

American industry had, for some time, enjoyed a global edge that it believed would last indefinitely. As a consequence, many corporations, especially automakers and steel manufacturers, failed to undertake long-term planning, delayed modernizing, and underestimated their competition (especially from Japan and Germany). Inflation made it harder for businesses to modernize. As Secretary of the Treasury Michael Blumenthal explained, "you can't figure your rate of return, so you postpone investments." Competitors in Japan and Germany, where inflation remained below 3 percent, spent two to three times more than American firms on upgrading their manufacturing facilities. As a result, American manufacturing experienced a devastating decline. Observers began calling the industrial East and Midwest the "Rustbelt."

American workers also suffered as U.S. corporations grew more and more multinational, shifting their production facilities to Asia and Latin America, where labor was cheaper. Manufacturing jobs declined throughout the United States, especially in the large cities. New York City alone lost 234,000 industrial production jobs in the 1970s. The shrinking job market for unskilled workers had a severe effect on the urban poor. In earlier decades, American cities had been a magnet for unskilled European immigrants and southern rural blacks. With the loss of industrial employment, however, poverty worsened in many American cities. Especially in the northern cities, deindustrialization, a declining tax base, and increased poverty nearly overwhelmed municipal services. New York City came within days of defaulting on its debt before Congress approved loan guarantees—over Gerald Ford's resistance—in November 1975. In the first municipal bankruptcy since the Great Depression, the city of Cleveland actually defaulted on its bonds in 1978.

As its manufacturing industries declined, the American economy shifted toward services. The greatest job growth in the 1970s came in services such as information management, entertainment, transportation, and retail sales. While unemployed steel and auto workers contemplated the prospect of flipping burgers for $4 an hour instead of earning $16 plus benefits, local authorities struggled to arrest the decline in manufacturing by offering direct subsidies or tax abatements for service industries to relocate to their areas. New airports were constructed in Dallas and Atlanta, increasing the growth of these Sunbelt cities. Municipalities in both the Sunbelt and the Rustbelt wooed professional sports franchises by constructing new stadiums.

Confronted with social uncertainty and economic stagnation, some Americans developed a renewed interest in religion. In contrast to the earlier revival of the 1950s, when churches and synagogues had studiously avoided dogma and ritual, the most popular sects of the 1970s promised structure, authority, orthodoxy, and a return to lost moral values. The mainstream Protestant churches—Episcopalian, Presbyterian, Methodist, Congregationalist, and some Baptist groups—lost members and influence in the 1970s; so did the Catholic Church and Conservative and Reform synagogues. On the other hand, interest surged in fundamentalist, evangelical, and Pentecostal churches; Mormonism; Orthodox Judaism; and a rich variety of Eastern religions and spiritual disciplines such as Zen, Hinduism, yoga, and Tibetan Buddhism. Much of the gain in religious observance came from young people, including members of the sixties counterculture looking for meaning and connections in their lives.

Yet the positive contributions of religion were sometimes overshadowed by the unconventional and occasionally self-destructive behavior of some members of new groups. A few dramatic instances

An unemployed steelworker walks across the bridge near the Johnstown plant of Bethlehem Steel Corporation, where he has been laid off after sixteen years of service. Such layoffs signalled the decline of heavy industry in the United States; many workers were forced to trade well-paying skilled jobs for low-wage service work. *AP/Wide World Photos.*

suggested that some Americans had become so alienated from ordinary institutions that they had lost their grip on reality. The most chilling cult-related episode came in November 1978, when Jim Jones and his People's Temple became household words. Jones's temple attracted thousands of members, mostly poor blacks, in California in the 1970s. Jones promised a racially integrated community in which people of all colors would share everything. He became prominent in the San Francisco Bay Area, but growing public opposition persuaded him to lead about a thousand of his followers to the jungles of the South American country of Guyana, where they established the community of Jonestown. When a congressman visited in November 1978 to investigate claims that People's Temple members were being held against their will, Jones's followers murdered him. Soon thereafter, Jones and 915 of his followers drank cyanide-laced Kool-Aid and died. A tape recorder captured Jones's crazed voice encouraging believers to force poison down their children's throats and commit "revolutionary suicide protesting against the conditions of an inhumane world."

Americans reacted with horror to the news from Jonestown. Some anguished parents whose adult children had joined cults hired strongmen to seize the young people and "deprogram" them. Cultural observers decried the proliferation of nonrational and antirational approaches to spirituality. Historian Christopher Lasch assailed the "hedonism, narcissism and cult of the self" characteristic of several new religious movements. Writer Tom Wolfe went further, putting a label on the entire culture of the 1970s: the "Me Decade," he called it.

But despite such charges, many Americans continued to exhibit a deep dedication to social justice. Post-Watergate disdain for politicians, and a lingering repulsion to the Vietnam War, led people to take politics into their own hands. On the Left they joined feminist, environmental, gay rights, and civil rights organizations. A significant number continued to participate in political protests—which were generally smaller and more polite, but no less earnest, than those of the 1960s—as groups like the United Farm Workers; the American Federation of State, County, and Municipal Employees; and Friends of the Earth raised new issues and made steady gains. Reform-minded people trained to be teachers, inspired by an idealistic view of education as the path to a better society. Others worked in a wide variety of socially responsible businesses, from child-care centers, health collectives, and food co-ops to muckraking magazines and "ethical investment firms."

The Right also felt that the "culture of narcissism" was sapping America's vitality. Many Bible-oriented Christian leaders were particularly distraught at the direction the country was taking. They expressed their frustration by joining the political conservatives of the New Right, which had been growing ever since Barry Goldwater's unsuccessful presidential campaign of 1964.

Committed to overturning liberalism and restoring traditional values, these religious leaders gave a strong impetus to the movement. Many of them took to the airwaves with "electronic churches," which quickly developed a weekly audience of millions of viewers. The popularity of their TV programs further eroded attendance at mainline Protestant churches, which could not offer the same flashy showmanship. The TV preachers of the New Right damned liberalism, feminism, sex education, divorce, the practice of living together without marriage, homosexuality, and the teaching of evolution in the nation's schools. The most successful televangelists, as they were called—including Jerry Falwell, Pat Robertson, Jim and Tammy Bakker, and Oral Roberts—raised millions of dollars in contributions from their viewers. More and more, they connected religion with politics. "We have enough votes to run the country," Robertson declared. In 1979 Falwell formed the Moral Majority, an organization dedicated to "pro-God, pro-family policies in government." He urged other fundamentalist ministers to abandon Jimmy Carter and help raise converts for the Moral Majority and the Republican party.

Another member of the new political spectrum was a group of formerly liberal intellectuals, writers, and editors known as neoconservatives. Writing for small but influential magazines like *Commentary* and *The Public Interest*, neoconservatives assailed liberals for distorting the original purpose of the welfare state by changing the emphasis from promoting equal opportunity to guaranteeing equal results. They criticized affirmative action programs, which aimed to provide greater opportunity for groups that had historically been excluded from positions of economic, professional, and political power, as "affirmative discrimination." They maintained their earlier support of U.S. participation in the war in Vietnam, a stance that further alienated them from most liberals, who regretted the war and urged a less assertive American foreign policy. In 1975, neoconservatives formed the Committee on the Present Danger, which spent the next five years lobbying for additional American nuclear weapons to intimidate the Soviet Union. The emerging neoconservative movement added to the strength of former California governor Ronald Reagan's campaign for the Republican presidential nomination in 1980.

PRESIDENTIAL POLITICS

"Gerald Ford is an awfully nice man who isn't up to the presidency," wrote John Osborne in *The New Republic*. Osborne shared the feeling of millions of Americans who at first had welcomed Ford as a relief and a breath of fresh air. But Ford alienated potential supporters—on the right and the left—with two decisions taken within a month of his inauguration: the appointment of Nelson Rockefeller as vice president and the pardon of Richard Nixon. In some ways Rockefeller seemed a logical choice. An experienced Republican officeholder, he had served fourteen years as governor of New York before resigning in December 1973. He had run for the Republican presidential nomination in 1960 and 1964 and was widely regarded as the leader of the eastern, moderate wing of the Republican party. But therein lay a problem: the Republican party had grown increasingly western, southern, and conservative since 1968. The mainstream of the Republican party now consisted of people like those who had booed Rockefeller at the 1964 convention, and these conservatives never forgave Ford for elevating Rockefeller to the vice presidency. Nevertheless, Congress acknowledged that the new president had wide latitude in choosing a vice president, and Rockefeller was confirmed in December. For the first time in history, neither the president nor the vice president of the United States had been elected to their position by the voters.

President Gerald R. Ford and his daughter Susan visit Independence Hall, Philadelphia, during the Bicentennial celebration, July 4, 1976. *Wide World Photos.*

If choosing Rockefeller angered the Republican Right, pardoning Nixon did huge damage to Ford's public standing with the whole country. Ford believed that a protracted trial of the former president would only stir fresh anger about Watergate, diverting attention from what Ford wanted to accomplish and hurting Republican chances in the upcoming congressional elections. On September 8, 1974, Ford announced that he had provided a "full, free, and absolute pardon" to the former president. Nixon formally accepted the pardon, an act equivalent to acknowledging guilt, but he claimed only to have made "mistakes" in the Watergate affair. The public felt betrayed by Ford and was dissatisfied that Nixon would not admit he had broken the law. The new president's approval rating dropped from 72 percent to 49 percent.

Not surprisingly, in the 1974 congressional elections the Democrats overwhelmed the Republicans. Despite the low turnout (38 percent of eligible voters), the Democrats gained forty-six House seats, giving them a majority of 290 to the Republicans' 145 seats—enough to override a presidential veto without any Republican votes. They picked up an additional four seats in the Senate. They also won almost all the governorships in major states. After the election of 1974 there were more Democratic officeholders than ever—more even than after the Democratic landslides of 1958 and 1964.

Anger over Watergate and Nixon's pardon combined with frustration about the sour economy to produce the swing to the Democrats. Ford's response to the country's worsening economic state seemed tepid and inept. Committed to voluntary action rather than government intervention, he wore a button reading WIN, for "Whip Inflation Now." The president's button seemed silly, and it reminded voters of the childlike smiling "happy face" buttons that were popular at the time.

Troubles abroad contributed to the gnawing fear that events had slipped out of control, and the country's leaders had lost their sense of direction. The National Liberation Front, which was committed to reunifying Vietnam under Hanoi's Communist government, won the war in April 1975, less than nine months after Ford became president. Almost immediately after signing the cease-fire in January 1973, both the Saigon government and the NLF had broken it. The government of President Nguyen Van Thieu had hoped that its offensive against the Communists would encourage Washington to resume direct military support. But Thieu misjudged Americans' disgust with the war and their preoccupation with Watergate and their economic difficulties. In the fall of 1974 Congress cut in half Secretary of State Kissinger's request for $1.5 billion in additional military aid to South Vietnam.

In early 1975 Hanoi decided that the moment had arrived for a decisive victory. North Vietnamese forces captured an important outpost in the central highlands in March. When Thieu ordered his troops to withdraw, they fled in terror, leaving their weapons behind; the troops fought hundreds of thousands of panicked refugees for space in the clogged roads and on planes leaving for the South. Ford asked Congress for additional military aid, but his heart was not in it, and the aid was refused.

On April 29 the last American helicopters lifted off from the roof of the U.S. embassy in Saigon. The next day the remnants of the government of the Republic of Vietnam surrendered, and North Vietnamese and Vietcong troops renamed its capital Ho Chi Minh City. The Americans evacuated about 150,000 Vietnamese employees and supporters, but they left hundreds of thousands more behind. TV viewers at home were disgusted by images of United States Marines clubbing screaming, terrified Vietnamese to keep them away from the American embassy and of terrified people clinging to the runners of departing helicopters. Scenes of ARVN soldiers shoving and shooting the weak, the elderly, and women with small children in order to secure a place on the few evacuation planes represented to many the horror, chaos, and futility of the war in Vietnam.

Détente with the Soviet Union, already strained by the October 1973 Middle East war, declined further during the Ford administration. Kissinger and his Soviet counterparts never fulfilled their promise, contained in the 1972 SALT-I agreement, to conclude a full-fledged treaty by 1977. In November 1974 Ford met Soviet president Leonid Brezhnev in the Siberian port of Vladivostok, where the two signed the framework for an arms control treaty to be known as SALT-II; but this document never matured into a full-scale treaty. American opponents of détente complained that Kissinger had weakened the U.S. military position and ignored Soviet violations of human rights. The Kremlin considered complaints about its human rights record an unjustified interference in its internal affairs, and it believed such criticism was merely a smoke screen for American unwillingness to expand détente. Thus while Kissinger and Ford encountered domestic pressure to demand more of the Soviets, the Soviets began to stiffen their negotiating position.

In the fall of 1975 Ford continued to appear politically vulnerable, and he barely escaped two attempts on his life. Lynnette "Squeaky" Fromme, a member of the Manson Family—the group of cult murderers that went on a homicidal rampage in 1970—shot a pistol at the president in September. A few weeks later, a woman named Sara Jane Moore also fired at the president. Usually Americans pull together when the chief executive is in danger, but these assaults barely registered with the public. Because Gerald Ford lacked presidential stature, citizens largely ignored the danger to him.

His widely popular wife Betty made more of an impact when she called the Supreme Court's decision in *Roe* v. *Wade* "a great, great decision." She told an interviewer that she would not be surprised if her twenty-year-old daughter were to have an affair; she also expressed her belief that premarital sex probably reduced the divorce rate. Most Americans thought the first lady's views indicated a refreshing openness. But the reaction from conservative Republicans could not have been worse for Ford. The highly conservative *Manchester Union-Leader* headlined Mrs. Ford's remarks "A Disgrace to the Nation."

Another champion of the conservatives, former California governor Ronald Reagan, announced his candidacy for the Republican presidential nomination in November. He complained that "our nation's capital has become the seat of a buddy system that functions for its own benefit." He charged that Ford had become part of the cozy deal making of official Washington and was out of touch with the concerns of ordinary Republicans. Reagan stressed his opposition to a wide variety of institutions and trends: the federal government, Social Security, busing for integration, student radicalism, sexual promiscuity, abortion, the Equal Rights Amendment, détente, and accommodating the Third World. He advocated lower taxes, prayer in public schools, and an assertive foreign policy designed to erase the stain of Vietnam. Reagan defeated Ford in a series of southern and western primaries by criticizing the Nixon-Ford-Kissinger policy of détente with the Soviet Union. He complained that "this nation has become Number Two in military power in a world where it is dangerous—if not fatal—to be second best." Reagan won his greatest support with his ardent appeals to retain U.S. control over the Panama Canal, declaring, "We bought it, we paid for it, and we ought to keep it."

Ford eked out a narrow victory over Reagan at the Republican convention in Kansas City, pleading with party regulars not to humiliate a sitting Republican president. He capitulated to the conservatives by dropping Nelson Rockefeller as his nominee for vice president, replacing him with the sharp-tongued Kansas senator Robert Dole. The president toughened his stand on arms control, thereby blocking completion of a SALT-II treaty before the election, and suspended work on the Panama Canal treaty. Ford also accepted a conservative platform that adopted many of Reagan's positions—"less government, less spending, less inflation." The platform called for constitutional amendments prohibiting abortion and permitting prayer in public schools. The party did retain its support for the ERA, a fixture of Republican platforms since 1940.

Democratic voters chose Jimmy Carter, former governor of Georgia, to oppose Ford in the fall election. A graduate of the Naval Academy at Annapolis, Carter had served in a nuclear submarine before leaving the navy in 1953 to take over his family's peanut farm in the southern Georgia town of Plains. He won election to the Georgia state legislature and ran for governor in 1966, but lost to segregationist Lester Maddox. Like many other moderate southern politicians defeated by ardent segregationists in the twenty years after *Brown* v. *Board of Education*, he vowed never to be "out-segged" again; he won the governorship in 1970 in part by accusing his moderate opponent of excessive friendliness to blacks.

Once elected governor, Carter became a model advocate of the New South, which was too busy attracting modern industry to dwell on the racial divisions of its past. He declared in his inaugural address that "the time for racial segregation is over," and he ordered a portrait of Martin Luther King, Jr., hung in the state capitol. His governorship drew business to Georgia and healed many racial wounds of the previous decade. He forged an alliance between bankers, real estate agents, developers, and the black community. Two of his staunchest supporters were Martin Luther King, Sr., and Andrew Young, the first African-American congressman from Georgia since Reconstruction. After the catastrophic Democratic defeat in the 1972 presidential election, Carter decided to run for president. As he looked at Massachusetts senator Edward Kennedy and Alabama governor George Wallace, the two candidates believed most likely to run, he realized that each generated strong animosity among large segments of Democratic voters. A gap existed that could be filled by a moderate southerner unbloodied by recent controversies.

A deeply religious man, Carter stressed old Protestant virtues in his campaign for the presidency. Virtually unknown at the beginning of 1976, he followed the advice of political professionals who grasped what the public wanted in the wake of Watergate and Vietnam. Specific programs mattered less than confidence in the rectitude and competence of their leaders. At a time when nearly all Washington politicians were under suspicion, Carter effectively used his status as an outsider, untouched by the failures and scandals of the federal government. "I'm not a lawyer, I'm not a member of Congress, and I've never served in Washington," Carter told responsive audiences as he traveled the country in the winter of 1975–1976 looking for support in caucuses and primaries. He achieved his first breakthrough in the Iowa caucuses in January 1976 and won the New Hampshire primary in February.

If voters did not know where he stood on specific issues, they admired his honesty. He guaranteed "a government as good as the American people." When forced to take a stand on specifics—abortion, busing, amnesty for draft evaders—Carter tried to occupy the middle ground. He was "personally opposed to abortion" and did not want the government to fund abortions for poor women. Yet he also did not want to overturn the Supreme Court's judgment that abortion was a right. He opposed mandatory busing to achieve racial balance, but he also opposed a constitutional amendment outlawing the practice. He favored a pardon for draft evaders, but not amnesty, because accepting a pardon meant acknowledging having done wrong.

By April Carter had emerged as the clear front-runner, surpassing George Wallace, Senator Henry Jackson of Washington, and two liberals, Senator Birch Bayh of Indiana and Representative Morris Udall of Arizona. Carter's pre-eminence distressed some Democratic leaders. Part of the uneasiness about Carter derived from regional or religious snobbery: big-city liberals had little in common with southerners and evangelical Christians. But Carter also raised doubts among African-Americans when he explained his opposition to low-income housing in mostly white suburbs. He said, "I see nothing wrong with ethnic purity being maintained. I would not force racial integration of a neighborhood by government action." Carter's long-time support for the Vietnam War, his skepticism about many Great Society programs, and his disdain for Washington also seemed a slap in the face to Democratic party liberals.

Liberals looked for an alternative to Carter. In May two western Democrats, Idaho senator Frank Church and California governor Jerry Brown, defeated Carter in most of the remaining primaries. Brown's campaign drew the most enthusiastic response of the primary season. Like Carter, Brown doubted the capacity of government officials to solve many social problems. In an era of limits, Brown said, government programs could not afford to expand, and they should probably shrink.

Although Carter won no primaries outside the South after April, he continued to accumulate delegates. He wrapped up the nomination in June. A month later the Democrats met in optimism and harmony, a sharp contrast to their last two gatherings. To appease traditional liberals, Carter chose one of them, Minnesota senator Walter Mondale, as his vice-presidential nominee. Martin Luther King, Sr., who delivered a benediction, declared that "surely the Lord sent Jimmy Carter to come on out and bring America back where she belongs." When the convention adjourned, Carter enjoyed an enormous margin over Ford in public opinion polls, 62 percent to 29 percent.

During the fall campaign, each candidate reinforced persistent doubts about himself. Arthur Schlesinger, Jr., friend of the Kennedy family and advocate of traditional Democratic liberalism, complained on the eve of the election that voters had to choose between the "weirdness" of Carter and the "dumbness" of Ford. Carter's relatives, who presented a stark contrast to the bland, cheerful Ford family, contributed to the feeling that he was somewhat odd. Carter's mother, affectionately called "Miz Lillian," had left her quiet Georgia home when she was in her late sixties for a two-year stint with the Peace Corps in India. The candidate's sister, Ruth Carter Stapleton, was a traveling evangelist and faith healer. His brother, Billy, became a major embarrassment, guzzling beer in front of his gas station and letting reporters know that he resented his big brother's success.

Trying to modernize his priggish image, Carter told *Playboy* magazine that he had "looked on a lot of women with lust" and had "committed adultery in my heart many times." The *Playboy* interview had exactly the opposite effect from what Carter intended, and it suggested that he was losing his grip on how to appeal to the public. Conservatives and Evangelicals wondered why someone they considered one of their own was speaking to *Playboy* in the first place. Northerners, city dwellers, suburbanites, and well-educated professionals shook their heads at Carter's apparent naiveté.

Ford gave Carter a boost in the second of three televised debates when the president mishandled a question on détente and U.S. relations with Poland. He claimed that "there is no Soviet domination of Eastern Europe, and there never will be under a Ford administration." The camera then focused on Carter, whose face broke into a broad grin. "I would like to see Mr. Ford convince the Polish-Americans and the Czech-Americans and the Hungarian-Americans in this country," Carter replied. *Time* magazine labeled Ford's remark "The Blooper Heard Round the World" and questioned his "grasp of foreign policy and even his mere competence." On a more substantial level, Carter continued his denunciations of Republican foreign policy, claiming it had ignored the human rights abuses of other nations and turned the United States into "the arms merchant of the world."

On election day, Carter defeated Ford with 50.1 percent of the popular vote to Ford's 48 percent. Carter won 297 electoral votes; Ford won 241. Anger at the Nixon pardon, unhappiness with the sluggish economy, and doubts about Ford's ability to lead persuaded the majority to cast their lot with Carter. His backers admired his sincerity and morality and believed him to be more intelligent than Ford. That was enough to make them suspend their doubts about the ambiguity of his policies and their concern that he had gone too far in stressing his lack of ties to official Washington. Could such an outsider follow through on a program, even if he had one? Only time would tell.

The narrow victory revealed a divided and troubled electorate. Ford carried twenty-seven states; Carter won in twenty-three and the District of Columbia. Democrats maintained most of the congressional gains they had made in the landslide of 1974. Ford carried a majority of the white vote. Carter won all the states of the old Confederacy except Virginia. In each of those southern states, black voters turned out in substantial numbers, joining rural whites proud to vote for one of their own. But many Americans did not bother to vote in this largely issueless fight between two candidates about whom they had substantial doubts. Turnout was only 54.4 percent, which at that point was the lowest of any presidential election since the Second World War.

As president, Jimmy Carter relied on the advice of the pollsters and media specialists who had helped him win the White House. They told him to continue emphasizing his outsider status, to keep the Democrats who dominated Congress at arm's length, and to do things that symbolized his closeness to ordinary people. Following this advice made Carter popular temporarily, but it severely strained his relationship with the professional politicians of the party he ostensibly led.

Deeply divided, the Democratic party could not help the president, and it often hurt him when the country encountered hard times. "If this were France," complained Thomas P. "Tip" O'Neill, the new Speaker of the House, "the Democratic party would be five parties." Competing factions—southerners, blacks, urban ethnics, supporters of organized labor, feminists, former antiwar protesters, consumer advocates, environmentalists, educated professionals, traditional liberals and conservatives—coexisted in an uneasy coalition, broader but less secure than the one assembled by Franklin Roosevelt. The New Deal alignment had made the Democrats a majority party for thirty years, but the war in Vietnam and racial tensions had broken old political ties. The Democratic party of 1977 remained dominant, but it presented a variety of conflicting programs and approaches to government and society.

Perhaps no politician could have overcome this contentiousness in an era in which leaders commanded little respect. But in some ways Jimmy Carter was at a particular disadvantage. His rural, southern background and his moderate-to-conservative predilections distanced him from many of the leaders of his party. Moreover, as president he emphasized skillful management rather than a clearly stated set of principles; and when he did state his principles clearly, he tended to be inconsistent in acting on them. By the end of his term in office he had little authority over the nation he had tried to lead.

Carter's efforts to follow through on his campaign promises showed how difficult it was for the president to occupy a middle position. On his first day in office he offered a "full, complete and unconditional pardon" for all draft resisters. With this generous offer he established a pattern of trying to bridge the chasms separating Americans on divisive issues—and of winning little gratitude for his efforts. The pardon announcement helped retire lingering controversies over Vietnam, but it diminished the president's sparse political capital. The director of the Veterans of Foreign Wars called it the saddest day in American history. The Senate came close to passing a resolution of disapproval. At the same time, peace groups claimed that Carter did not go far enough. His pardon excluded military deserters and those with dishonorable discharges, people the American Civil Liberties Union noted were "more likely to be poor, from minority groups and less educated."

Many of Carter's early policy initiatives and nominations sparked congressional hostility. He offended important Democrats in February 1977 by abruptly canceling nineteen water projects in the South and West. These dams, river diversions, and irrigation systems were of dubious economic value in relation to their cost. They also represented tangible evidence of the wastefulness of the despised "Washington buddy system," in which legislators spent years building alliances by agreeing to support one another's pet construction projects. To Carter, who was committed to reducing waste and to judging each government program solely on its economic and social merits, the cancellations seemed logical. Politically, however, the decision angered many Democrats whose local support hinged on their ability to deliver public works projects to their districts.

Also, some of Carter's nominees ran into trouble with various factions of Democrats. He withdrew the name of Theodore Sorensen, formerly a close adviser to John F. Kennedy, as his choice for CIA director because conservatives objected to Sorensen's pacifism during the Second World War and his support for Daniel Ellsberg in the *Pentagon Papers* case. Liberals objected to Carter's nomination of an old Georgia friend, Griffin Bell, for attorney general. Bell belonged to clubs that excluded Jews and blacks; he had upheld the Georgia legislature's refusal to seat Julian Bond because of Bond's opposition to the war in Vietnam; and he had enthusiastically supported Nixon's controversial nomination of G. Harrold Carswell to the Supreme Court.

Carter's effort to compromise on divisive social issues dissatisfied important groups within his party and left an impression of a confused president who did not know where he wanted to lead the country. For example, he sought a middle ground on abortion where none existed, attempting to bridge the gap between Joseph Califano, head of the Department of Health, Education and Welfare (HEW), who opposed all abortions, and Midge Costanza, the White House liaison to women's groups, who favored a woman's unrestricted right to terminate a pregnancy. When the Supreme Court upheld a congressional action forbidding the use of Medicaid funds for abortion except in cases where the mother's life was threatened, supporters of reproductive choice complained that the decision unfairly penalized poor women.

The Carter administration also failed to resolve the nation's deep divisions on the question of affirmative action programs. These programs represented an effort by businesses, universities, and other organizations to compensate the victims of generations of prejudice by giving them preference for jobs or educational opportunities. To guarantee fair representation of minorities, many such programs established minimum quotas for minority groups and women, but this arrangement began to provoke strong resentment among those who did not benefit.

Carter supported the Supreme Court's effort to solve the dilemma in *University of California Board of Regents* v. *Bakke* (1978). Allan Bakke, a white man who had been denied admission to the university's medical school, argued that the university's affirmative action policy had produced a reverse form of discrimination, admitting less qualified black applicants in his place. Although the Supreme Court decided in Bakke's favor, the ruling was highly ambiguous. A majority of the justices allowed affirmative action programs based on race but invalidated rigid quota systems. Because many Democrats disagreed about affirmative action, the issue threatened to split the president's fragile coalition. The Court's sharply divided ruling failed to still the controversy about what steps, if any, institutions should take to redress previous discrimination.

The Carter administration tried to apply the *Bakke* ruling by insisting that agencies awarding federal grants and contracts adopt affirmative action programs but not require set quotas for specific classes of people. Neither supporters nor opponents of affirmative action considered Carter's position satisfactory. Disagreements about affirmative action and about "set-aside" programs for certain groups persisted long after *Bakke*. Many women and members of racial minority groups considered affirmative action meaningless without specific goals for hiring employees, admitting students, or awarding contracts. On the other hand, members of traditionally white labor unions feared that affirmative action threatened their jobs. And some European ethnics whose forbears had suffered discrimination felt affirmative action unfairly gave other groups an advantage they had never enjoyed.

As politicians squabbled in Washington and the president's popularity fell, a public backlash grew against government at all levels. In June 1978, Californians ignored the objections of Governor Brown and nearly every other prominent political figure, education professional, and businessperson in the state and voted by a two-to-one margin to roll back property taxes to the levels of the mid-1960s. The popularity of Proposition 13, as the tax limitation measure was called, was due to several factors. Because of the rapid inflation in the value of real estate, taxes on California homes had tripled in the preceding decade. Moreover, voters believed that government did not provide adequate services for the money it collected. Despite warnings that Proposition 13's restrictions on future tax increases would damage the state's schools, universities, parks, libraries, and highways, voters responded to the plan's sponsor, seventy-five-year-old gadfly Howard Jarvis, when he urged them to "take control of the government again or it will control you."

The passage of Proposition 13 alarmed officials across the country. Governor Brown quickly reversed himself and supported the tax rollback, because it was "the strongest expression of the democratic process in a decade." Elections in other states confirmed the extent of public anger but also demonstrated its limits. Measures similar to Proposition 13 passed in four states that had experienced sharp rises in housing prices in the previous decade, but tax limits or spending caps were defeated in four others.

Officeholders in both parties lost primaries to conservative insurgents who accused incumbents of supporting taxes. In Massachusetts, liberal Democratic governor Michael Dukakis, elected in the post-Watergate Democratic landslide of 1974, lost to a conservative who promised to reduce state taxes. Veteran liberal Republican senator Clifford Case lost to an advocate of the little-known theory of "supply-side economics." The idea of a substantial cut in income taxes grew from an eccentric theory into the centerpiece of the Republicans' 1980 campaign. Ronald Reagan, preparing for another run at the White House, told supporters that opposition to taxes was "a little bit like dumping those cases of tea off the boat in Boston Harbor."

Democrats felt the sting in Washington. Patrick Caddell, Carter's pollster, reflected that "this isn't just a tax revolt, it's a revolution against government." Opposition to new federal spending scuttled plans for national health insurance. Despairing of Carter's timidity and his increasing conservatism, Democrats took heart from Senator Edward Kennedy, who at a Democratic "miniconvention" in December 1978 encouraged support for traditional social welfare programs. "Sometimes," he said, "a party must sail against the wind." Kennedy's powerful speech thrilled Democrats embarrassed by Carter. By the spring of 1979 many Democrats wanted Kennedy to challenge Carter for the 1980 nomination, and the senator seemed ready to run. Public opinion polls taken among Democrats showed Kennedy defeating Carter by a two-to-one margin.

By July 1979 President Carter's approval rating had fallen to a dismal 29 percent, about where Nixon had stood on the eve of his resignation. The president knew he had to do something, but what? He rejected the counsel of Vice President Mondale, who argued that the country's problems did not stem from a psychological crisis of confidence; rather, Mondale believed, people were fed up with real economic problems and demanded concrete solutions. Disregarding Mondale's insight, Carter listened to pollster Caddell, who saw a "national malaise" in the public's alienation from traditional institutions. Carter decided to apologize for his administration's shortcomings in a nationally televised address. He acknowledged that the complaint that he had been "managing, not leading" the country had merit, and he begged citizens to "have faith in our country—not only in the government, but in our own ability to solve great problems." The next day he fired or accepted the resignation of five cabinet members.

As Vice President Mondale had predicted, blaming a "malaise" for the country's problems failed to restore faith in the national leadership. During the cabinet shakeup, the president appointed Paul Volcker, a twenty-year veteran of the Treasury Department and the New York Federal Reserve Bank, to chair the Federal Reserve Board. Volcker was confronted with an economic crisis consisting of high prices, slowed production, and mounting unemployment. As inflation continued throughout the summer of 1979, the stock market fell and economists predicted an economic slump for the following winter. Volcker responded by driving interest rates above 15 percent to stop inflation; but by the beginning of 1980 prices were still rising and 8 million Americans were out of work. In April 1980 the economy entered the sharpest recession since 1974. Americans wondered if people could buy a house with mortgage rates at 18 percent. Could they fill up their cars to drive to work? Would there be a job to drive to?

President Carter could do little about either the economy or the "malaise" Patrick Caddell had identified. In the aftermath of the Watergate scandal and the Vietnam War, Congress was less inclined than before to listen to the president. And by deliberately cultivating his outsider status in Washington, Carter had aggravated the problem. Even his own party granted him little authority. The public at large thought him ineffectual. After one of his attempts to reassure his fellow citizens that the nation's problems could be solved with time and careful planning, a Boston newspaper mocked his speech with the headline, "More Mush from the Wimp."

ENERGY AND THE ENVIRONMENT

Despite rising public skepticism, the Carter administration made serious attempts to confront long-term challenges. In April 1977 Carter unveiled a major legislative initiative promising a national energy policy. Like Carter's other programs, his energy policy sought to satisfy a variety of competing and antagonistic regional and economic interests. In the process, it offended more people than it pleased. He asked for the creation of a Department of Energy. He called for tax incentives and penalties to encourage consumers to conserve energy and producers to drill more oil and gas wells. As a last resort, he said, he favored further development of nuclear power.

Carter delivered his first energy speech at the height of his popularity. He warned that "the energy shortage is permanent." He encouraged his fellow citizens to turn their thermostats down to 65 degrees, and he called his energy program "the moral equivalent of war." Critics quickly pounced on the contradictory nature of the program. Speaking for conservatives, Ronald Reagan complained that "our problem isn't a shortage of oil, it's a surplus of government." Liberals objected that too much had been offered to oil companies and too little to the poor.

Congress finally passed a greatly modified version of his energy program in November 1978, about the time oil prices began another sharp rise after the revolution in Iran. The final law gave more benefits to both oil companies and their opponents. Appealing to advocates of alternative fuels, many of whom despised the huge multinational oil companies, the law created the Solar Energy Research Institute. At the federal, state, and local levels, governments sponsored research on a multiplicity of alternative energy sources and conservation programs, from wind power and geothermal energy to

The Organization of Petroleum Exporting Countries (OPEC) increased oil prices several times in the 1970s, fueling the rise of inflation and signalling the end of an era of easy abundance. *Don Wright in the Miami News, 1976, Tribune Media Services.*

new plans for mass transit and efficient building design. The federal government offered programs to make it easier for individuals to be environmentally responsible; for example, it gave home owners tax breaks for insulating. But there was also more than a little something for corporate America, such as government investment in the giant Synthetic Fuels Corporation—controlled by Exxon, Occidental Petroleum, and Union Oil of California—to extract petroleum from rocks in Colorado, Utah, and Wyoming.

As Congress struggled to craft an energy policy that would be acceptable to diverse regions and economic interests, Americans became increasingly skeptical about the ability of technology and engineering to improve their lives. Indeed, they feared that modern technology might not be safe. In the early 1970s, residents of the Love Canal neighborhood in Niagara Falls, New York, began to notice foul air, blackened trees, and increased numbers of cancer cases, miscarriages, and babies born with birth defects in their locality. For several years terrified residents demanded explanations, but they received no satisfaction. Experts eventually traced the problems to hazardous materials buried thirty years earlier by the Hooker Chemical Company. The federal government declared an emergency in the area and ordered the people in the neighborhood to move. None could sell their homes, and few thought the compensation the government offered was adequate. The Environmental Protection Agency (EPA) warned that the hazardous materials that poisoned the land, polluted the water, and fouled the air of Love Canal might be found in hundreds of locations across the country. "There are time bombs ticking all over," one EPA officer proclaimed. "We just don't know how many potential Love Canals there are."

Fears about the safety of nuclear power, which was heavily promoted in the 1950s as the cleanest, cheapest form of electricity available, expanded in March 1979 when a reactor at Three Mile Island near Harrisburg, Pennsylvania, badly malfunctioned. A stuck cooling valve overheated the reactor core, and a meltdown of the deadly nuclear fuel was barely avoided. One hundred thousand residents fled their homes, and many did not believe officials who told them two weeks later that it was safe to return. The power plant remained permanently disabled, its interior deadly to any who might enter it. In the wake of the incident, electric companies canceled over thirty proposed nuclear power plants.

The near catastrophe at Three Mile Island also fed more general fears about degradation of the environment. Washington created a $1.6 billion "Superfund," paid for by extra taxes on industries that pollute the environment, to clean up toxic waste sites. The Carter administration also placed over 100 million acres of Alaskan land under federal protection, barring mining or petroleum development. But such actions could not reverse the public's concern over the deterioration of the nation's land, air, and water. The environmental movement grew, and many environmentalists expressed increasing skepticism about the benefits of unrestrained economic growth.

At the same time, conservatives in the West gained new support for the "Sagebrush Rebellion" against federal control of vast amounts of land. As much as 60 percent of the land in Nevada, Utah, Arizona, Idaho, Montana, and Colorado belonged to the federal government. Several Rocky Mountain state legislatures passed laws demanding that the state take charge of its federal lands to allow more grazing, logging, mining, petroleum drilling, or recreational development than the federal Bureau of Land Management or the U.S. Forest Service would permit. Earlier generations of westerners had often approved of the federal government as a good steward whose efforts protected local resources for future generations. But advocates of the Sagebrush Rebellion saw Washington as the enemy, the home of haughty bureaucrats indifferent to the economic well-being of the West. Liberal westerners also sought local control over the region's resources (particularly its nonrenewable resources), to protect them not against the federal government but against multinational corporations. In 1974 the state of Montana, following the example of Texas's tax on oil, passed a severance tax on coal, assessed at the time of its removal from the state. By 1982, North Dakota, Texas, and Wyoming had followed suit, deriving between 25 and 35 percent of their revenues from the tax.

FOREIGN AFFAIRS IN THE CARTER YEARS

Despite Jimmy Carter's troubles on the domestic front, his administration initially succeeded in redirecting American foreign policy, turning it away from Cold War confrontation and toward advocacy of human rights abroad and sensitivity to the needs of poor nations. Early in his term, the president explained that "we are now free of the inordinate fear of communism which once led us to embrace any dictator in that fear." But Carter's foreign policy momentum stopped in 1979, and the last eighteen months of his administration saw a series of foreign policy setbacks and catastrophes.

The Cold War returned with a vengeance as the Soviets became more assertive on their southern borders, in the Middle East, and in Africa. Americans who had opposed détente felt vindicated. Distrustful of the Soviets and fearful of U.S. conservatives, Carter and his advisers dropped détente, and America became more hostile toward Moscow than at any other time since the early 1960s. Meanwhile, a revolution in Iran culminated in the seizure of the American embassy on November 4, 1979. Iranian revolutionaries held fifty-two U.S. citizens captive for 444 days. The Iranian hostage crisis virtually paralyzed Carter, undermined public confidence in his foreign policy, and eventually cost him reelection.

Carter achieved his greatest triumph in foreign affairs by arranging the first peace treaty between Israel and one of its Arab neighbors, Egypt. Carter believed that Egyptian president Anwar Sadat became a "man who would change history" when he courageously flew to Jerusalem in November 1977 to address Israel's parliament and offer an end to the thirty-year war. Israelis were euphoric in the wake of Sadat's trip, but the Palestinians and most other Arab states damned him as a traitor. The excitement faded in 1978 as Egypt and Israel made little progress in their talks. It was then that President Carter became personally involved as a mediator.

Carter invited Sadat and Israeli prime minister Menachem Begin to a series of conversations in Washington, and in September 1978 he arranged a joint meeting with them at Camp David, the presidential retreat in the Maryland mountains. An expected three-day conference extended to thirteen days. Carter dropped all other work to concentrate on bridging the gap between Egypt and Israel. The difficult details of the negotiations included Israel's withdrawal from the Sinai Peninsula and the future of the 1.5 million Palestinians living under Israeli control in the West Bank and Gaza Strip. Although these issues were not resolved, Carter's determination paid off with the signing of a framework for peace that promised a future treaty between Egypt and Israel, establishment of a five-year transitional authority in the West Bank and Gaza, and further negotiations on the status of the occupied territories.

However, the initial congratulations gave way to suspicion and recriminations. The Israeli-Egyptian treaty, which was supposed to be completed in three months, took six months and another round of personal diplomacy from Carter before it was signed in Washington in March 1979. The other Arab states and the Palestine Liberation Organization (PLO) ostracized Egypt and refused to join the Camp David peace process. Israel did not offer real autonomy to the Palestinians and continued its policy of not dealing with the PLO.

Like many other critics of Nixon's and Ford's foreign policy, Carter believed that the United States had ignored the fate of ordinary people in foreign countries who suffered mistreatment at the hands of their own government. Carter promised to pay far greater attention to promoting human rights abroad, hoping to thereby restore the United States' moral standing in the world, which had been badly tarnished by the war in Vietnam. The new administration made significant progress in promoting human rights during its first two years. Congress created a new State Department office, assistant secretary of state for human rights, and required the State Department to report on the status of individual rights around the globe. Governments that violated basic standards of decency might be shamed into altering their behavior by appearing on a list of abusive authorities. Congress might also reduce foreign aid to nations appearing on the list.

But the administration soon found it was difficult to apply standards of human rights strictly and impartially. The State Department did criticize some old friends in Latin America, but political expediency caused the administration to temper its criticism of other long-term partners in important areas of the world. For example, Carter went out of his way to praise the shah of Iran, and the United States continued its strong support for the corrupt regime of Ferdinand Marcos in the Philippines.

Similar inconsistencies arose as the government grappled with the escalating pace of immigration and refugee flight to the United States. War and its aftermath in Southeast Asia, combined with poverty and repression in Latin America, propelled millions of people toward the United States. Modifications of the 1965 immigration law led to the planned entry of almost half a million Asian and Latino immigrants annually. But this number accounted for only a small part of the total immigration.

The influx of South Vietnamese—some 130,000 in 1975—was hardly noticed at first, because most were educated, skilled, and easily assimilated into American life. From 1976 to 1980, however, a million more Vietnamese, Cambodians, Laotians, and others fled the harsh life and oppression of postrevolutionary Southeast Asia. About half of them eventually found a haven in the United States. The Carter administration funded resettlement programs for the immigrants, but their new neighbors greeted them coolly.

As Southeast Asians struggled for acceptance, a new wave of Cubans clamored to enter the United States. Unhappy with Fidel Castro's tough rule, many Cubans yearned for the freedom and prosperity they believed existed just a hundred miles north of their deprived island. In March 1980, thousands of Cubans took refuge in foreign embassies in Havana. President Carter believed he could embarrass Castro by offering these people asylum in the United States, but the Cuban strongman trumped his hand by announcing that any Cuban could leave from the port of Mariel. The United States organized a flotilla to transport the *Marielitos,* but a public relations disaster ensued when Castro emptied Cuba's jails and mental hospitals and ordered the inmates to board the boats for America. The criminals and mentally ill composed only a small number of the 130,000 fleeing Cubans, but opponents of immigration pointed to them to fan resentment against all refugees.

A refugee act passed in 1980 offered asylum in the United States for anyone facing a "well-founded fear" of persecution for religious, political, or ethnic reasons. In practice, people fleeing left-wing or Communist countries were usually granted asylum, but those escaping right-wing regimes found their entry to the United States barred. Some fifty thousand Haitians were excluded during the Carter years, and this inconsistency prompted criticism of the administration's refugee policy. Moreover, each year during the 1970s several million Mexicans crossed the border without official permission. Some left after a time, but enough stayed to create a permanent pool of between 5 and 15 million undocumented aliens—a further indication of a serious gap between administration policy and reality.

The influx of millions of non-European immigrants in the 1970s had a significant impact on the American population, hastening the development of a more multicultural society (see figure). Overall, the economy benefited from the new arrivals. Like earlier immigrants, they believed the United States provided greater economic and social opportunities than they could hope for in their homelands. They worked hard, settling in cities and towns across the country. Korean fruit and

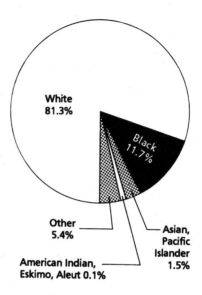

Racial Composition

White
81.3%

Black
11.7%

Other
5.4%

American Indian,
Eskimo, Aleut 0.1%

Asian,
Pacific
Islander
1.5%

Census Bureau figures. People of Hispanic origin can be of any race; the Census Bureau estimates Hispanics made up 6.4 percent of the population in 1980.

Population Profile, 1970–1980

vegetable stands became familiar sights in coastal cities. Southeast Asians changed the face of Los Angeles. Cubans asserted an increasingly powerful political and economic presence in Miami. The growth of the newer urban areas of the Sunbelt accelerated partly because of the new immigrants from Latin America and Asia. Yet since they arrived at a time of economic stagnation, the new immigrants confronted the prejudice that people of color have often encountered in the United States. In many cities, immigrants were beaten up and their businesses and property vandalized. A movement grew to enact more restrictive immigration laws that would reduce the overall number of immigrants and stem the flow of undocumented aliens.

Although it was becoming an increasingly multicultural nation at home, the United States continued to operate abroad within a Cold War context. Détente continued to decline. Carter tried to weave a coherent policy toward Moscow from the conflicting advice of his two principal foreign policy advisers, Secretary of State Cyrus Vance and National Security Adviser Zbigniew Brzezinski. Vance, a former Defense Department official in the Johnson administration, had come to doubt the effectiveness of military force as the Vietnam War wore on. He preferred conciliation and believed that competition with the Soviet Union was less important than proper management of new international economic and social trends. Brzezinski, a Columbia University professor and long-time academic rival of Henry Kissinger, regarded power politics as the key to international relations. He distrusted the Soviets and believed that competition between the Communists and the West remained as important as ever.

Carter first followed Vance's advice and tried to reduce tensions with the Soviet Union. The new administration tried to demonstrate that it could conclude a better arms control agreement than the SALT-II treaty, which the Ford administration had abandoned in 1976. In March 1977 Vance took to Moscow proposals to reduce each side's strategic nuclear weapons by 33 percent. Much to his surprise, the Soviets scornfully turned him down, suspecting a trick because the proposals went so far beyond what Kissinger had offered. Deeply embarrassed, the Americans resumed bargaining with the Soviets on the basis of the foundation laid previously. Two years later, in June 1979, Carter and Soviet leader Leonid Brezhnev signed the SALT-II treaty, limiting each side to 2,400 nuclear launchers. Had the SALT-II treaty been ready earlier in Carter's term, the Senate might have ratified it. By 1979, however, Carter was a weak president, with little political pull on Capitol Hill. That fall, the Senate Armed Services Committee voted against ratification.

In December 1979 the Soviets invaded Afghanistan to quell an uprising by Islamic fundamentalists against the Soviet-sponsored Afghan government. Carter used the invasion to justify shelving the SALT-II treaty, calling the invasion the "gravest threat to peace" since the end of the Second World War. In January 1980 Carter withdrew the treaty from Senate consideration, where it faced certain defeat anyway. To punish Moscow for the invasion, he refused to send athletes to the upcoming Moscow Olympics, a decision that upset hundreds of would-be American participants. He also embargoed grain shipments to the Soviet Union, infuriating thousands of American farmers, and he revived registration for the draft, alarming millions of young men. Carter now ignored Vance almost completely and relied on Brzezinski's advice in confronting the Soviets. His moderate supporters felt abandoned, whereas neoconservatives and other Cold Warriors did not trust his newfound toughness.

Still, Americans would likely have tolerated Carter's reversals had it not been for the rage and frustration generated by the capture of the U.S. embassy and its staff in Teheran, Iran, on November 4, 1979. The revolution in Iran had simmered beneath the surface for decades. In 1953 the United States had restored Shah Mohammed Reza Pahlavi to power in a CIA-sponsored coup against a government that had forced the shah into exile. The monarch then embarked on an expensive effort to modernize his country. Flush with oil revenue, the shah built the largest military force in the region with billions of dollars in weapons purchased from the United States. Along with the weapons and the development of the oil fields came fifty thousand American technicians and military advisers. The shah's revolution from above elevated a new class of merchants and technicians, who adopted Western mores and lifestyles. But many Iranians resented the monarch's iron-fisted rule. The shah's secret police jailed and tortured thousands of dissenters. Among those most hostile to the rapid social changes were Islamic fundamentalists. One of the men most eager to sweep out Western influences, depose the shah, and create a society based on the Koran was an elderly ayatollah, or religious leader, Ruholla Khomeini. A long-time opponent of the shah, the exiled Khomeini fervently encouraged revolution. By February 1979 Khomeini's followers had triumphed, evicting the shah and greeting the returning ayatollah as a savior.

The Iranian revolution affected American lives directly in the spring of 1979, when the new Islamic government raised its oil prices, causing gasoline lines in the United States. Throughout the summer of 1979 the United States tried to maintain a stable relationship with the new Islamic leadership in Teheran. But when President Carter admitted the deposed shah to New York for medical treatment in October, he infuriated the Iranian revolutionaries. Khomeini told his followers that the admission of the shah represented a plot by "the Great Satan"—the United States—in collaboration with "American-loving rotten brains" in Teheran to restore the shah to power. Khomeini demanded that the United States deliver the shah to Iran for trial and restore his "stolen wealth" to the Islamic regime. A week later, revolutionary students seized the American embassy.

The initial reaction in the United States to the capture of about seventy Americans—a group that included diplomats, Marines, CIA agents, and a few private citizens doing business at the embassy—temporarily revived Carter's flagging reputation. Showing his dogged energy, he froze Iran's assets in the United States, growled that American "honor" had been besmirched by the militants, and vowed not to travel out of Washington until the hostages came home. After some of the hostages were released, the number in captivity declined to fifty-two, but news broadcasts kept nerves raw by ticking off the number of days they had languished in Teheran since November 4.

Angry mobs in Tehran, November 1979, ridiculed and demonized President Carter. *AP/Wide World Photos.*

Relatives and friends of hostages tied yellow ribbons around trees, mailboxes, and telephone poles to keep the plight of the captives firmly in the public mind. Senator Kennedy assailed Carter for "lurching from crisis to crisis," and Ronald Reagan, running for the Republican nomination, implied that "our friend" the shah would not have lost his throne if the Carter administration had not betrayed him by criticizing his secret police for torturing political opponents. Reagan also suggested that Carter's inability to free the prisoners reflected his general lack of competence.

In April Carter accepted Brzezinski's advice to mount a military mission to rescue the hostages. Secretary of State Vance objected; he had promised European allies that the United States would not use force, and he believed the complicated plan would not work. He told Carter that he would resign after the operation, whether it succeeded or failed. On April 24, eight helicopters took off from an aircraft carrier in the Persian Gulf and headed for a desert rendezvous with transport planes. One chopper malfunctioned, and the remaining seven flew into a dust storm. Two of these were abandoned, and the site commander decided that the five remaining helicopters were not enough to mount a successful rescue operation. He telephoned the White House that he was withdrawing the rest of the force. After receiving orders to leave the desert landing site, another helicopter collided with a refueling plane, killing eight servicemen. The White House announced the mission's failure, Vance resigned, and some Americans believed the aborted mission was yet another demonstration of the limits of American military superiority.

Carter finally left the White House to campaign actively for reelection. Diplomacy proceeded behind the scenes, and the administration tried to arrange a deal with Iran for the captives' release before election day, November 4, 1980. Unfortunately for Carter, the efforts did not bear fruit until early 1981. The Iranians may have received promises of future favors from the Reagan camp if they kept the hostages until Carter left office. Gary Sick, a staff member on Carter's National Security Council, charged in 1991 that the Reagan campaign promised Teheran arms if it retained the American prisoners beyond the election. The hostages finally flew to freedom on January 20, half an hour after Ronald Reagan took the oath of office.

The failure to gain the release of the hostages sealed Carter's fate with the electorate. He defeated Kennedy for the Democratic nomination, but the fact that 35 percent of the convention delegates favored the challenger sent an ominous sign for the fall. Carter's advisers believed he could overcome Ronald Reagan by portraying him as a dangerous reactionary. They feared that an independent candidate, former Republican congressman John Anderson, presented the greater danger, because he could appeal to middle-of-the-road voters. By Labor Day, polls were showing Carter and Reagan running even, with Anderson receiving 15 percent of the vote. Carter refused to participate in a debate with Reagan and Anderson in late September, not wanting to add credibility to the third contender in the race. Anderson's support then dribbled away in October as voters concentrated on the only viable choices—Carter and Reagan.

Finally, Carter and Reagan debated head to head. Carter believed that his greater intelligence and command of the facts would make his conservative challenger appear unworthy, but the president badly miscalculated. In the debate, Carter stressed the severity of the last few years: "We have demanded that the American people sacrifice, and they have done that very well." Reagan, on the other hand, reminded voters how much austerity hurt: "We do not have to go on sharing in sacrifice," he said. In his summary remarks, Reagan looked directly into the camera with his cheerful blue eyes and urged Americans to "ask yourself, are you better off than you were four years ago?"

A week later, voters answered with a sharp No! Opinion surveys showed Carter's support collapsing in the weekend before election day, as it became clear that the hostages would not be coming home.

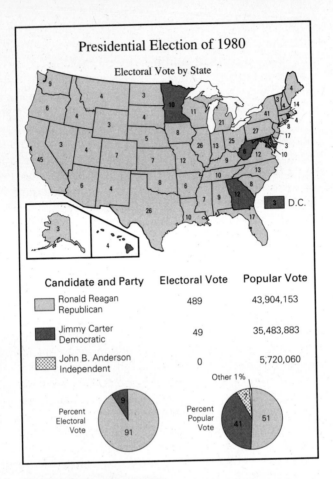

Presidential Election of 1980

Voters believed that whatever Reagan did would be an improvement over Carter's hand wringing, sermons, and demands for sacrifice. Reagan won 51 percent of the popular vote, Carter 41 percent, and Anderson 7 percent (see map). For the first time since 1954, the Republicans carried the Senate, and they gained 33 seats in the House. "It's a fed-up vote," observed Pat Caddell, Carter's pollster.

CONCLUSION

In the aftermath of Watergate, the Vietnam War, and the upheavals of the 1960s and early 1970s, Americans confronted changes in the late 1970s that demanded creativity and perseverance on an everyday basis. Disillusionment and disorientation from the recent past ran so deep that politicians found it virtually impossible to restore public faith in government. Gerald Ford, an unelected leader, lacked both a base of popular support and a clearly articulated vision of how to restore public confidence. Jimmy Carter had some advantages over his predecessor because he could credibly claim to be an outsider, who like most ordinary Americans, was not responsible for the disappointments of the Johnson and Nixon years. By 1980 it became apparent, however, that Carter's good intentions, intelligence, and firmly rooted moral values had not been enough.

Although many ordinary Americans continued to work hard to consolidate and extend the gains of the social justice movements of the 1960s, the economic and social developments of the times frustrated both the nation's leaders and the public at large. Increasing competition from foreign business, particularly from Japan, soaring inflation, and a decline in manufacturing put the country's economic future in doubt. The oil shock stimulated worries about scarce resources, and at the same time Americans became more aware of the environmental costs of industrial and nuclear development. The cultural changes of the 1960s had brought a new sense of freedom to personal relationships, but the growing diversity of American households presented new and sometimes bewildering challenges. Women demanded new respect, but pornography boomed. Gay men and lesbians achieved greater legitimacy, but the New Right singled out homosexuals with virulent attacks. Many alienated people took refuge from these bewildering trends in new religious sects, some of them authoritarian or violent. Others turned to a reaffirmation of traditional churches, and some were galvanized by televangelists who denounced liberalism, divorce, and all the new social and sexual freedoms.

Crystallizing many of the public's frustrations, the television preachers and other conservatives formed political organizations that helped mobilize support for conservative candidates. When President Carter failed to resolve the Iranian hostage crisis before the 1980 election, the public found a final reason to reject him. They turned instead to Ronald Reagan, a conservative champion who promised Americans that the future could still be bright. ∎

F U R T H E R   R E A D I N G

For general accounts of society and politics in the 1970s, see: Peter N. Carroll, *It Seemed Like Nothing Happened* (1982); Steve Fraser and Gary Gerstle (eds.), *The Rise and Fall of the New Deal Order, 1930–1980* (1989); Michael Barone, *Our*

Country (1990); Theodore H. White, *America in Search of Itself, 1956–1980* (1982). On public policy, see: Gerald Ford, *A Time to Heal* (1977); Robert T. Hartmann, *Palace Politics: An Inside Account of the Ford Years* (1980); A. James Reichley, *Conservatives in an Age of Change* (1980); Jimmy Carter, *Keeping Faith: Memoirs of a President* (1981); Mary Berry, *Why the ERA Failed* (1986); Nathan Glazer, *Affirmative Discrimination* (1975); J. Harvey Wilkerson, *From Brown to Bakke* (1979); William Julius Wilson, *The Truly Disadvantaged: The Inner City, the Underclass, and Public Policy* (1987). On women and the family, see: Flora Davis, *Moving the Mountain: The Women's Movement in America since 1960* (1991); Winnifrid D. Wandersee, *On the Move: American Women in the 1970s* (1988); Judith Stacey, *Brave New Families: Stories of Domestic Upheaval in Late Twentieth-Century America* (1990). On the emerging gay community, see: John D'Emilio, *Sexual Politics, Sexual Communities: The Making of a Homosexual Minority in the United States, 1940–1970* (1983). On economic changes, see: Barry Bluestone and Bennett Harrison, *The Deindustrialization of America* (1982); John P. Hoerr, *And the Wolf Finally Came: The Decline of the American Steel Industry* (1988); David Halberstam, *The Reckoning* (1986); Lester C. Thurow, *The Zero Sum Society* (1980); Daniel Yergin, *The Prize* (1991). On foreign affairs, see: Raymond L. Garthoff, *Détente and Confrontation: American-Soviet Relations from Nixon to Reagan* (1985); William Hyland, *Mortal Rivals: Superpower Relations from Nixon to Reagan* (1987); Gaddis Smith, *Morality, Reason and Power: American Diplomacy in the Carter Years* (1986); Zbigniew Brzezinski, *Power and Principle: Memoirs of the National Security Adviser* (1983); Cyrus Vance, *Hard Choices: Critical Years in American Foreign Policy* (1983); James Bill, *The Eagle and the Lion: The Tragedy of American-Iranian Relations* (1987); Gary Sick, *All Fall Down: America's Tragic Encounter with Iran* (1986); William Quandt, *Camp David* (1987).

12

Right Turn: Conservatism Ascendant, 1980–1992

In 1986, financier Ivan F. Boesky addressed graduating business students at the University of California at Berkeley. Boesky, celebrated for his success at buying underpriced shares of stock in companies about to be acquired in lucrative mergers, told his audience that "greed is healthy." Earning and flaunting great wealth, he implied, was the driving force of capitalism, the key to its growth and prosperity. The students sat rapt as Boesky affirmed the canon of the free market. That fall, however, the Justice Department charged Boesky with massive violations of security law. He pleaded guilty to buying inside information from corporate officials, which he then used to manipulate stock prices and acquire companies, making billions in profit. Film director Oliver Stone chronicled the rise and fall of a Boesky-like tycoon in the popular movie *Wall Street*, a cautionary tale about the glitter and deceit of the 1980s.

The chief emblem of the times was not Wall Street or Ivan Boesky, however; it was the reassuring, cheerful president, Ronald Reagan, who presided over the era. Reagan's favorite speech writer, Peggy Noonan, "had the feeling he came from a sad house and he thought it was his job to cheer everyone up." Catching the spirit of the man and the age, Noonan drafted the president's best-received lines for his 1984 re-election campaign. "America is back," she wrote; "it's morning again." College students especially liked this talk of renewal from America's oldest serving president. On campuses where a few years before undergraduates had hurled insults at Lyndon Johnson, twenty-year-olds screamed "U.S.A.! U.S.A.!" in response to Reagan's oratory. He tapped a popular yearning to restore a sense of community, real or imagined, that had been lost over the previous two decades. Reagan reflected the same mood as the television comedy series "Happy Days," which ran on ABC from 1974 through 1984. Expressing a nostalgia for the 1950s of the imagination, the show offered funny stories full of the innocence and hope that Americans wanted to believe they still possessed.

As he exhorted all Americans to believe in their country's greatness, Reagan pursued policies that benefited tycoons like Boesky while often neglecting those at the bottom of the economic ladder. During his two terms in office, Reagan challenged most and reversed many of the liberal programs and values that had dominated national politics since the New Deal. His administration worked to roll back the social welfare network, limit the role of federal courts in promoting civil rights and liberties, reduce government regulation of business and protection of the environment, slash income taxes, and foster a conservative social ethic in such areas as abortion rights and the role of religion in public life. Reagan's team insisted that by removing the dead weight of government from the private economy, they could unleash market forces that would create new wealth and foster greater equality. Some commentators said that the economic expansion of the 1980s proved that the Reagan approach was right. Others pointed to rising homelessness and the decreased mobility of the middle class as a sign that Reagan's happy days were not for everyone. Nevertheless, for most of his presidency, Reagan enjoyed a high level of public approval. Many Americans ignored the substance of his policies and the fact that the results of his administration's actions often contradicted the very beliefs and promises the president stressed.

THE EMERGENCE OF RONALD REAGAN

Born in Tampico, Illinois, in 1911, Ronald Reagan grew up in a series of small towns along the Mississippi River. He recalled his youth as "one of those rare Huck Finn-Tom Sawyer idylls." Although Mark Twain's novels actually chronicle hate, superstition, racism, and violence in nineteenth-century America, Reagan was referring to a sanitized vision of preindustrial America. His concept of America was subtly distorted, as one biographer noted, "toward small perfections, like the buildings in Disneyland." In truth, as the younger son of an alcoholic father and a fervently religious mother, Reagan had a childhood that resembled Twain's novels in ways he preferred not to recall. The family had little money and relocated frequently, often just ahead of the bill collector.

In spite of these problems, Reagan attended the religiously affiliated Eureka College, and after graduation he found work as a sports announcer at a small Iowa radio station. He narrated re-creations of baseball games based on reports that came into the station via telegraph, describing the games as if they were live. Reagan supplied colorful details and anecdotes so well that many listeners preferred his version to the real thing.

During the harshest years of the depression, Reagan's father sustained the family by working for a New Deal relief agency. Reagan became an avid Roosevelt supporter; he often memorized segments of Roosevelt's speeches and recited them for his friends. Long after Reagan had rejected the New Deal programs, he continued to sprinkle his public statements with lines from Roosevelt. But it was Roosevelt the political optimist and inspirational father figure, not the social reformer, who gripped Reagan's imagination.

While covering the Chicago Cubs' spring training in California in 1937, Reagan took a screen test and won a contract with the Warner

Brothers film studio. In 1940 he married actress Jane Wyman. The couple adopted one child and Jane gave birth to a second. Reagan spent the Second World War in Hollywood, working for an Army Air Corps unit that made morale-boosting films. He probably felt self-conscious about this comfortable assignment, because in later years he concocted elaborate stories about acts of heroism he claimed to have witnessed at the battle front. He even implied that he had helped to liberate a Nazi concentration camp. In fact, during the war Reagan never left the United States and rarely left Hollywood.

After 1945 Reagan's film career declined, but he became increasingly active in the Screen Actors Guild, serving as union president from 1947 to 1952. His marriage to Jane Wyman ended in divorce in 1949, and in 1952 he married another actress, Nancy Davis, who soon gave him two more children. During this period, fear of communism transformed his political outlook, as it did for many other Americans. He committed himself to the fight against what he called "the Communist plan . . . to take over the motion picture business" by cooperating with studio heads and the FBI in their efforts to blacklist suspect actors, directors, and writers.

Reagan's career took a new turn in 1954 when General Electric hired him to host its weekly television series and deliver corporate speeches. Over an eight-year period, Reagan visited GE plants throughout the country, speaking to executives, assembly-line workers, and local chambers of commerce. His after-dinner presentations invariably included an ode to "traditional values," a warning about threats to them, and entertaining anecdotes. Reagan warned of communism abroad and creeping socialism at home. Recanting his support for the New Deal—though not relinquishing Roosevelt's best lines—he praised business leaders for restraining the socialist tide, despite the burdens of high taxes and government regulations imposed by liberals. Even after he left GE's employment in 1962, Reagan devoted the bulk of his time to delivering the same speech, which he had been perfecting since 1954. It played particularly well among conservative groups in southern California.

In 1964 Barry Goldwater emerged as the champion of the conservative movement. As the Republican nominee for president, he promised to dismantle the New Deal legacy. Yet Goldwater proved a divisive and unpopular candidate, easily caricatured as an extremist itching to unleash a nuclear war and send the elderly and infirm into the poorhouse. Late in the faltering campaign, Reagan, by then a Republican, offered to make a televised fund-raising speech on Goldwater's behalf.

On paper the text seemed such a lifeless collection of antigovernment, anti-Communist clichés, with scant mention of the Republican nominee, that Goldwater's staff almost canceled the speech. But they underestimated Reagan's emotional appeal. Lifting some of the best-known phrases of Franklin Roosevelt, Winston Churchill, and Abraham Lincoln, Reagan declared,

"You and I have a rendezvous with destiny. We can preserve for our children this, the last best hope of man on earth, or we can sentence them to take the first step into a thousand years of darkness. If we fail, at least let our children, and our children's children, say of us we justified our brief moment here. We did all that could be done."

After Goldwater's defeat in 1964, wealthy friends urged Reagan to run for governor of California. During the 1966 gubernatorial primary campaign, Reagan spoke for short periods of time, before selected audiences, and avoided questions from the press. After winning the Republican primary he took aim at the Democratic incumbent, Governor Edmund G. "Pat" Brown.

"I am not a politician," Reagan declared. He characterized himself as an ordinary citizen opposed to high taxes, government regulation, big spending, waste, and fraud. He promised to reduce the size and scope of state government and to throw out the rascals who had mismanaged the state. In fact, Governor Brown had presided over a period of immense economic growth in California. Higher education, social services, highways, and water projects had expanded tremendously. But many middle-class citizens resented rising taxes, and the violent Watts riots of 1965, the Berkeley Free Speech Movement and the student antiwar movement had left them increasingly hesitant to support their Democratic governor.

Reagan proved to be an extremely adept campaigner, especially on television. He focused voter attention on abstract issues like freedom, personal autonomy, and "traditional values." He linked the moderate Brown to big government, high taxes, welfare cheats, ghetto riots, judges who "coddled criminals," and the "mess" at Berkeley. California voters viewed the challenger as a warm, pleasant man aroused by grievances they shared. In the November election Reagan trounced Brown by a margin of nearly 1 million votes.

Overall, during his two terms as governor, Reagan combined conservative rhetoric with fairly flexible policies. Several times he sent state police to quell disturbances on the Berkeley campus, and he forced out several liberal administrators. But he never followed through on threats to slash education spending and to investigate "communism and blatant sexual misbehavior" at Berkeley. In 1967 he blamed his predecessor for leaving him a budget deficit, then approved the largest tax increase in state history. Although he boasted of cutting state spending, during his two terms spending doubled, from less than $5 billion per year to $10 billion. When the legislature passed one of the nation's most liberal abortion bills, Reagan signed it. Later, when he campaigned against abortion, he said he had never read the law.

In 1974, after Nixon resigned and Ford became president, Reagan objected bitterly to Ford's selection of liberal Republican Nelson Rockefeller as vice president. Reagan resolved to challenge Ford for the presidential nomination in 1976.

Entering the Republican presidential primaries in 1976, Reagan proposed slashing federal social programs and returning others to state control. When this issue fell flat, he attacked President Ford and Secretary of State Kissinger for pursuing arms control and détente with the Soviet Union and for negotiating a "give-away" of the Panama canal. Reagan's challenge seriously undermined Ford's election prospects.

Reagan set the stage for his 1980 campaign by resuming his criticism of the pending Panama Canal treaty and demanding massive rearmament to counter the power of the Soviet Union. He also endorsed the Proposition 13 tax rebellion and proposed drastic cuts in federal income tax rates.

Economic stagnation, the collapse of détente, and particularly the Iranian hostage crisis made the public receptive to Reagan's call for a dramatic change in leadership in 1980. Although his chief rival for the Republican nomination, George Bush, referred to his tax cutting scheme as "voodoo economics," Reagan secured the nomination handily and then chose Bush as his running mate. In the general election campaign he downplayed his more extreme beliefs, such as his long-time dislike of the Social Security program; instead he focused on themes of renewal, strength, and national pride. "This is the greatest country in the world," he declared. "We have the talent, we have the drive, we have the imagination. Now all we need is the leadership." Most Americans, he believed, hungered for "a little good news" and for a leader who promised renewed American strength and success. Reagan projected common sense, spoke of heroes and grand traditions, and offered simple, reassuring answers to complex questions.

The generalities of his campaign paid off in his victory over President Carter in the November election. Only a tenth of those who voted for Reagan told pollsters that they had selected him because he was "a real conservative"; rather, they were disgusted with Carter and attracted to Reagan's vision of a happier, more powerful, less divided America. The election results also showed a notable "gender gap" and "age gap": Reagan drew far less support from women and from the elderly—who opposed his economic ideas—than from young men who liked his tough rhetoric. Significantly, barely half of those eligible to vote cast ballots.

Ronald Reagan made strategic use of TV in pledging to cut taxes, inflation, and wasteful social programs. *Ronald Reagan Presidential Library, TV courtesy of Zenith Electronics Corporation.*

Whether Reagan's victory represented a conservative mandate or not, the conservatives had in fact won considerably more power. Republicans took control of the Senate for the first time in nearly three decades, and they picked up some three dozen additional House seats as well. Several key liberals, such as Senators Frank Church and Birch Bayh, were unseated. The successful targeting of liberals by conservative political action groups left Democratic leaders like House Speaker Thomas P. "Tip" O'Neill shell-shocked and in awe of the new conservative champion, Ronald Reagan.

THE REAGAN STYLE

In his inaugural address, Reagan stressed a few general economic grievances, such as inflation and a burdensome tax system. Playing to the widely shared disillusionment with government programs, he declared, "In this present crisis, government is not the solution to our problem, government *is* the problem." He pledged to cut inflation, taxes, and wasteful social programs.

In an astute move, Reagan reached outside his conservative circle to appoint James A. Baker III, a close friend of Vice President George Bush, as White House chief of staff. A veteran of Washington politics,

Baker recalled Lyndon Johnson's insight after his landslide victory in 1964: "You've got just one year when Congress treats you right, then they start worrying about themselves." Baker argued that key legislation must be passed during the first few months of the Reagan administration, while the Democrats were in disarray and Congress offered its traditional deference to a new president. He persuaded Reagan to push for the two things the president wanted most: tax cuts and a defense build-up. "If we can do that," Baker predicted, "the rest will take care of itself." Many conservatives would have liked to see Reagan lead a crusade on key social issues during these months—for example, mounting a strong campaign for constitutional amendments outlawing abortion and legalizing prayer in public schools. But although the president often voiced his concern about these issues, he accepted Baker's advice not to press them very hard with Congress.

Ever since the 1950s, Reagan had criticized high taxes. A wealthy man, he believed that people should be rewarded for achieving wealth, not taxed at higher rates for doing so. He also gave much credence to anecdotes about "welfare queens" who drove Cadillacs and had their noses in the public trough.

Reagan was impressed by the tax theory of economist Arthur Laffer. In the mid-1970s, Laffer drew a graph on a restaurant napkin demonstrating, to his satisfaction, that if income tax rates declined, people would work harder. The government could then obtain sufficient revenue, even with lower tax rates. Unfortunately, Laffer could not say what the "right" tax rate should be—except that it should be less than the existing rate.

However, it was not just an issue of working harder for personal gain. Like many other conservatives, Reagan believed that a tax cut would promote industrial growth as well as personal wealth. Freed from the burden of excess taxes and given extra capital to work with, the nation's entrepreneurs would unleash the market forces that would spur an economic revival.

Reagan also emphasized the dangers of deficit spending by the government. The Democrats, he said, had "mortgaged our future and our children's future for the temporary convenience of the present." With the national debt approaching a trillion dollars, disaster loomed. The nation would have to stop living beyond its means; in particular, it would have to lower its social expenditures. Reagan also believed that lower social spending would encourage people to help themselves rather than depend on the government.

These beliefs prompted the new president to take up the call of Republican congressman Jack Kemp of New York and William Roth of Delaware to lower federal income tax rates. In the late 1970s they had propounded a plan to cut personal and business taxes by 30 percent in order to stimulate the economy. Dubbing their approach "supply-side economics," Kemp and Roth predicted that lower tax rates would encourage business activity and investments. But the Kemp-Roth tax cut languished in Congress—until a supporter occupied the White House.

In January 1981, President Reagan unveiled his economic plan before a joint session of Congress. He endorsed a proposal that cut most personal and business federal income tax rates by 25 percent over three years, lowered the top personal rate from 70 percent to 50 percent, eliminated "bracket creep" (the tendency for taxpayers to be pushed into higher brackets by inflation), reduced taxes on capital gains, lowered estate and gift taxes, and allowed faster depreciation on business investments. To reduce federal spending, Reagan also proposed to shift many social programs from the federal government to the states, to eliminate numerous welfare programs, to trim Social Security benefits, and to cut back federal regulation of business, the environment, and public health.

Congress enacted much of what the president asked for. Although the Democratic majority in the House managed to limit some of the proposed cuts in social welfare spending, public enthusiasm for the tax cuts proved so overwhelming that the Democrats could not stand in their way. Moreover, Reagan convinced many Democrats that a combination of tax reductions and spending cuts would jump-start the economy, leading to a surge in growth that would easily make up for the revenues lost by lowering tax rates. Congress therefore approved the tax cuts as well as many domestic spending reductions during the summer of 1981.

An economic recession, the worst since the 1930s, began late in 1981 and lasted almost two years. It was partly caused by the decision of Paul Volcker, the Carter-appointed chairman of the Federal Reserve Board to raise interest rates to stifle inflation. Unemployment rose to over 10 percent, and business failures, farm foreclosures, and homelessness increased dramatically. Critics began to charge that the reduction in taxes and benefits helped the rich and hurt the poor. Reagan's approval rating declined, and the Democrats made substantial gains in the 1982 congressional elections. Nevertheless, Reagan refused to alter his priorities. He blamed the recession and the growing budget deficit on problems inherited from President Carter, and he predicted that the worst would be over by 1984.

Reagan's prediction proved partially correct. The high interest rates gradually squeezed inflation out of the economy. The rate of inflation fell from about 14 percent in 1980 to below 2 percent in 1983. Interest rates gradually declined from 21 percent to a still-high 11 percent. Changes in world markets drove down oil prices and reduced the cost of imported fuel. Massive defense spending created a boom in high technology and in the aerospace industries of New England, the Southwest, and the West Coast.

By the end of 1983, the worst of the recession had passed. The subsequent economic expansion lasted beyond Reagan's departure in 1989. Supply-siders took credit for creating over 18 million new jobs, spurring economic growth, lowering federal tax rates, and tripling the average price of stocks. Many Americans agreed that the final six years of Reagan's term marked a period of broad prosperity.

But increased government spending on weapons, as well as easy bank credit, played an important part in this supposed free-market recovery. "Defense is not a budget item," Reagan told his staff; "you spend what you need." And spend they did. As the new administration took office, Defense Secretary Caspar Weinberger proposed an annual increase amounting to almost 10 percent of the last Carter budget. Over the next five years, defense expenditures totaled almost $1.5 trillion.

At a White House conference with Reagan, Weinberger displayed impressive charts that showed Soviet nuclear and conventional forces dwarfing those of the free world. Unlike Budget Director David Stockman, a true believer in small government, the defense secretary warned that even token reductions in military spending endangered national security. As Stockman later described it, Weinberger held up a poster showing three cartoon soldiers:

"One was a pygmy who carried no rifle. He represented the Carter budget. The second was a four-eyed wimp who looked like Woody Allen, carrying a tiny rifle. That was [Stockman's] budget. Finally there was G.I. Joe himself, 190 pounds of fighting man, all decked out in helmet and flak jacket and pointing an M-60 machine gun."

Stockman wondered whether Weinberger "thought the White House was on Sesame Street." But Reagan, who was committed to keeping the United States pre-eminent in military strength and was determined to challenge the Soviets, did not want to deny the armed forces anything they might conceivably need. He accepted Weinberger's proposal for a large increase in defense spending, and Chief of Staff Baker shepherded it through Congress. Reagan's two terms saw the largest peacetime defense budgets in history.

Unlike Jimmy Carter, President Reagan had a great deal of success in getting Congress to approve his agenda. Although the Democrats still controlled the House, they approved most of the defense increases, tax cuts, and social spending reductions he called for. Part of this success stemmed from the abilities of aides such as Baker, but much of it came from Reagan's own personality. He melted the resistance of hard-bitten senators and representatives with anecdotes and grins.

When charm failed, Reagan used television to urge the public to call or write their representatives in support of his programs. With his experience as a film star and television host, he proved a master of the electronic media, earning the nickname "The Great Communicator." Moreover, his three closest first-term advisers—James Baker, Michael Deaver, and Edwin Meese—understood the role the media played in ensuring success. As one observer commented, each presidential action was designed "as a one-minute or two-minute spot on the evening network news"; every presidential appearance was conceived "in terms of camera angle." With his uncanny ability to turn clichés into winning phrases, he fostered in his audience a sense of community even as he rallied them against government. In times of uncertainty, Reagan projected a reassuring decisiveness.

Even in personal suffering, Reagan appeared to advantage. When a crazed gunman, John Hinckley, gravely wounded the president in March 1981, Reagan told his wife in the emergency room, "Honey, I forgot to duck." About to go under the surgeon's knife, he jokingly asked if the doctor were a Republican. "We're all Republicans today" came the reply. Reagan's humor and spunk evoked immense affection among Americans who had questioned the warmth of some of his predecessors.

In other settings, however, Reagan's limitations became apparent. News conferences, where questions often confused him, were painful to watch—and were therefore kept to a minimum. He preferred to have every word and action scripted in advance; when a script was lacking, he seemed uninformed about many of his own programs. Once, when a bold reporter asked him to describe his arms control efforts, he drew a blank. Nancy Reagan whispered in her husband's ear: "Tell them we're doing all we can." He dutifully repeated the phrase. He tended to nod off during staff meetings. In fact, while Reagan supplied the vision and good looks, an inner coterie of advisers ran the country.

RE-ELECTION AND THE SECOND ADMINISTRATION

By 1984, as the economy climbed out of recession and into its long expansion, Ronald Reagan loomed as a formidable opponent for any Democratic challenger. Most voters enjoyed a few more dollars in their pockets from the tax cut, inflation had practically disappeared, and abstract difficulties such as the growing budget deficit had little immediate impact on individuals. Reagan's 1983 decision to invade the tiny island of Grenada was a whopping success with the public. In 1984 he even managed to share the glory of the American athletes at the Los Angeles summer Olympics, where they won a large number of gold medals.

By 1984 the Democratic party was struggling to mobilize an electorate no longer attuned to the New Deal legacy. Civil rights activist Jesse Jackson urged the Democrats to reach out to the poor and disenfranchised of all races in order to win elections. He felt the party had a better chance of electing a president by increasing the voting pool than by trying to wring more votes out of the mere 50 percent of Americans who normally cast ballots. Jackson claimed to represent a racially diverse "Rainbow Coalition," but his strength lay mostly among African-Americans. His association with Black Muslims and his anti-Semitic remarks (such as calling New York City "Hymie Town") frightened many whites, Jews, and European ethnics, who were core constituents of the Democratic coalition. The Democratic party, riven by competing interests, took on the appearance of Humpty Dumpty, after the fall.

Senator Gary Hart of Colorado, another outsider, also urged Democrats to reach beyond their New Deal past. Hart spoke about the need for "new ideas," though he revealed few. He was young, handsome, and telegenic, and he said the future mattered more than ideology. In his pursuit of the nomination, he reached out to socially liberal, economically conservative younger voters.

In contrast, former vice president Walter Mondale won endorsements from organized labor, ethnic organizations, women's groups, teachers, environmentalists, and other organized elements in the party. Critics, however, described Mondale's celebration of the glory days of the Democrats and his search for endorsements as pandering to "special interests." In the end, Mondale accumulated enough support to win the nomination, but Hart and Jackson gave him only grudging endorsements after the convention.

After a slow and highly visible search for an "appropriate" running mate, Mondale finally selected New York congresswoman Geraldine Ferraro as his vice-presidential candidate. As the first woman nominated for the national ticket by a major party, Ferraro excited millions of Americans. She proved a smart, articulate candidate who easily held her own in a debate with Vice President George Bush. Questions about her husband's financial dealings, however, obscured her critique of the Reagan presidency. Many voters concluded that having served only three terms in Congress, Ferraro was untested. Ultimately, Ferraro's presence on the ticket probably did not affect the election outcome.

Mondale tried valiantly to run a campaign based on the issues. He bombarded the public with warnings about runaway spending, an out-of-control arms race, environmental disasters, and the unfairness of Reagan's economic policies. His most famous campaign line was

"He'll raise taxes, so will I. He won't tell you, I just did." Commentators briefly praised Mondale's political courage, but within a week decided he had committed political suicide. United Nations ambassador Jeane Kirkpatrick, a conservative Democrat, dubbed him "bad-news Fritz Mondale," leader of the "blame-America-first crowd."

The president's speeches and commercials emphasized the themes of redemption, patriotism, and family. Reagan, Mondale rued, "patted dogs." In 1980 Reagan had run against government; in 1984 he *was* the government, but it made no difference. His campaign theme, summarized by a newspaper as "don't worry, be happy," carried him to a landslide sweep of forty-nine states. Democratic candidates nonetheless did much better at the congressional and state levels. The Democrats retained their majority in the House and pecked away at the slim Republican majority in the Senate.

During his second administration, several internal staff changes as well as external policy reverses diminished Reagan's luster. The problems began when the highly capable White House chief of staff, James Baker, wanted a change of pace. He and Treasury Secretary Donald Regan, a man not well known to the president, decided to switch jobs, soliciting Reagan's blessing for the move after they had made up their minds. Reagan would probably have had fewer difficulties in his second term if Baker had continued as chief of staff.

Assistant Chief of Staff Michael Deaver and presidential counselor Edwin Meese left the White House in 1985. Meanwhile, Reagan nominated Meese for attorney general. Soon reports began to circulate that Meese, through a close friend and financial adviser, E. Robert Wallach, had promoted the fortunes of a shady defense contracting firm, Wedtech. A lengthy investigation by the Senate Ethics Committee and a special prosecutor concluded that Meese had exercised terrible judgment but had not done enough to warrant indictment. These and other problems of numerous administration officials, which became known as the "sleaze factor," began to dog the administration.

Reagan recovered his poise by the summer of 1986. As the stock market surged to record highs, Congress passed a major tax reform bill, the economic centerpiece of Reagan's second-term legislative agenda. The new tax law, a modification of the flat-rate income tax system proposed by Democrats Bill Bradley and Richard Gephardt, was presented as a way to restore simplicity and equality to the complex tax code. It closed many tax loopholes and reduced the code's multiple tax brackets to just three, at rates of 15, 28, and 33 percent. The reform eliminated taxes for the poorest Americans, but a quirk in the law allowed the wealthiest Americans to pay a tax rate slightly below that of the upper middle class. Even though most taxpayers ended up paying about the same total as before, Reagan convinced middle class voters that the law had reduced their taxes.

In 1986 the president hosted a Fourth of July celebration at the Statue of Liberty that showed him at his best. The extravaganza featured a renovated Statue of Liberty, the biggest fireworks display ever assembled, and Ronald Reagan. Leslie Stahl, a White House reporter for CBS, commented that, "Like his leading lady, the Statue of Liberty, the president, after six years in office, has himself become a symbol of pride in America." However, despite Reagan's immense popularity, he failed to achieve any realignment in national politics. In the 1986 congressional elections, even as Reagan rode high in the polls, the Democrats regained control of the Senate and increased their majority in the House. The Democratic majority blocked administration proposals to make further cuts in social programs, expand defense spending, and intervene more directly in Central America.

By late 1986 the Iran-contra scandal—which involved a series of weapons-for-hostage deals with Iran and illegal arms transfers to a group of Central American "freedom fighters"—was becoming public, and during the next year it proved a profound embarrassment to the administration. Then, in October 1987, a collapse in stock prices jolted the confident economic mood that had prevailed since 1983. After the Dow Jones Industrial Average hit a record high of 2,700 points in August, it slumped. In mid-October it fell 600 points in a few days, losing almost a fourth of its value and reviving memories of the 1929 stock market crash that had ushered in the Great Depression. Although Wall Street recovered most of its losses within a year, the minicrash created anxiety about the economy that proved impossible to shake.

The combined impact of the Iran-contra scandal and Wall Street jitters in 1987 might have been Reagan's undoing. But the president's ability to adjust to circumstances once again surprised Americans. During 1988, relations between the United States and the Soviet Union improved dramatically, creating the possibility for an end to the Cold War. The public proved quite willing to forget the Iran-contra affair. Reagan left office with an overall 68 percent approval rating, higher than that of any president since Franklin D. Roosevelt.

REALITIES OF THE REAGAN ERA

Reagan's high public approval rating, along with his remarkable success at communicating his ideas and faith in America, often gave the impression that the nation's problems were vanishing before an onslaught of new pride and optimism. In many cases, however, the reality did not match the administration's glowing rhetoric. Some old

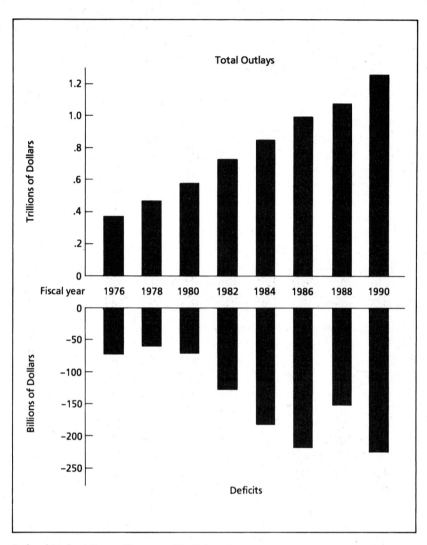

Federal Budget Expenditures and Deficits, 1976–1990

problems deepened, and some disturbing new economic and social trends arose.

When Reagan took office, he was bitterly critical of Carter's "runaway deficit of nearly $80 billion" and the cumulative national debt of almost $1 trillion. Yet over the next eight years his administration ran up annual deficits that ranged from $128 billion to well over $200 billion (see figure). The national debt tripled, to almost $3 trillion. The $200 billion annual interest tab became the third-largest item in the budget.

The president denied responsibility for any of this. He blamed runaway spending on what he called an" iron triangle" of Congress, lobbyists, and liberal journalists who conducted raids on the treasury. In fact, despite his assertions, in eight years as president Reagan never submitted a balanced budget proposal to Congress. New social programs were not to blame for ballooning deficits, for they were few and far between during the 1980s. Most of the red ink resulted from Reagan's insistence on increasing defense spending at the same time that tax rates were reduced. And even when the president endorsed a constitutional amendment mandating a balanced budget, he stipulated that it should apply only to his successors.

Reagan had been able to push large tax cuts and massive defense spending through Congress, but lawmakers were unwilling to make draconian cuts in the social programs their constituents demanded. Thus the public's eagerness to pay less while still receiving government benefits compounded the deficit problem.

Because the treasury had to borrow so much at home and abroad to fund the deficit, fewer dollars were available for investment in research, new plants, and machinery. Although the country began the 1980s with a positive trade balance in manufactured goods, the balance soon turned negative. The foreign trade deficit grew dramatically, surpassing $150 billion per year by the second half of the decade. Every week during the Reagan years, American consumers spent on average about $2 billion more on foreign goods than foreigners spent on American products. The cumulative imbalance for the decade approached $1 trillion.

The economic expansion of the 1980s was highly selective. Prosperity and wealth tended to flow to both coasts, partly because of defense spending. The Northeast and California boomed. After severe doldrums in the 1970s, Boston and Manhattan blossomed again during the 1980s. In these boom areas, real estate prices skyrocketed for both residential and commercial property.

At the same time, much of the upper Midwest experienced a loss of high-paying industrial jobs, continuing the decline that began in the 1970s. In addition, farm states and energy-producing states staggered. Small farmers abandoned the land in accelerating numbers, while cities like Houston, buffeted by falling energy prices, faced economic disaster. As Reagan spoke of "morning in America," the sun set on many traditional industries and small farms, and the Southwest experienced a prolonged recession.

Even in nationwide terms, the long economic expansion of the later Reagan years was less impressive than it looked. It was a marked improvement compared to the late 1970s, but compared to the entire period from 1945 to 1980, the recovery appears more modest. During most of the 1980s the inflation rate was twice as high as the average for the years from 1947 to 1967. Unemployment also remained higher than in most years between 1947 and 1973. Overall, the economy grew no faster in the 1980s than it had during the 1960s and 1970s.

Continuing a trend that began in the 1970s, real wages—that is, wages adjusted for inflation—remained stagnant; in fact, salaries declined slightly on average during the 1980s, although the impact was hidden by an increase in the number of working wives and mothers, whose earnings boosted total family income.

Meanwhile, incomes were not stagnant for the richest Americans. In 1980 a typical corporate chief executive officer (CEO) made about forty times the income of an average factory worker; nine years later the CEO made ninety-three times as much. Reagan-era policies nearly doubled the share of the national income going to the wealthiest 1 percent of Americans, from 8.1 to about 15 percent. Over 60 percent of income growth during the 1980s belonged to the top 1 percent of Americans. By the end of the 1980s, the top 1 percent, some 834,000 households, was worth more than the bottom 90 percent, or 84 million American households. The gap between rich, middle class, and poor in the United States was bigger than ever before.

Correspondingly, the 1980s witnessed a celebration of wealth—critics called it greed—unparalleled in America since the Roaring Twenties. For many people, it seemed that income had become the accepted measure of human value. Professional athletes earned immense sums, and college basketball, football, and baseball players looked forward to becoming fabulously rich. Conservatives such as Congressman Kemp and writers Jude Wanniski and George Gilder celebrated financiers and deal makers as secular saints who enriched society. Their heroes—colorful Wall Street operators like Carl Icahn, T. Boone Pickens, Ivan Boesky, and Michael Milken, and real estate speculator Donald Trump—earned billions of dollars buying and merging companies and constructing new office towers, apartment complexes, and resorts. Not since the days of the so-called Robber Barons in the nineteenth century had business leaders publicly voiced sentiments like Boesky's ode to greed or Trump's boast that "I like beating my enemies to the ground."

A "merger mania," fueled by the 1981 tax law and the Reagan Justice Department's relaxed attitude toward enforcing antitrust laws, gripped Wall Street through 1987. Many of the nation's biggest companies bought out competitors or were themselves swallowed up in leveraged buyouts financed by huge loans bearing high interest rates. Corporate raiders argued that these deals rewarded stockholders and eliminated incompetent management, thus increasing industrial competitiveness.

Because many multi-billion-dollar deals were too risky for banks, insurance companies, or pension funds to finance, Milken and others pioneered the use of so-called junk bonds, high-interest bonds with little security. Financiers attempting to take over large corporations would issue these corporate IOUs to raise money for the acquisition. But the purchaser was often compelled to sell off profitable portions of the newly acquired business in order to repay its heavy debt.

In some cases, like that of the new long-distance telephone company MCI, junk bonds did contribute to innovation and real growth. But more often than not these highly speculative financial deals did little to help the economy.

In addition to the Wall Street wizards, the decade celebrated "yuppies"—an extended acronym for "young urban professionals"—a group that exulted in its upward mobility during the 1980s. Journalists used the term lavishly in 1983 and 1984, partly to describe Gary Hart's unexpected following among young Americans as he campaigned for the Democratic presidential nomination. *Newsweek* dubbed 1984 "The Year of the Yuppie" and applauded the group's eagerness to "go for it" as a sign of the "yuppie virtues of imagination, daring and entrepreneurship." Yuppies existed "on a new plane of consciousness, a state of Transcendental Acquisition."

Bona fide yuppies—people born between 1945 and 1959, earning over $40,000 as professionals or managers, and living in a city—totaled about 1.5 million. As candidate Hart learned, they were not a big constituency for Democratic liberals. Even though they rejected restrictive ideas on abortion and enjoyed recreational drugs, most supported Reagan's economic policies. Yuppies aspired to become investment bankers, not social workers.

Yuppies spent and overspent on "leisure products" like Porsches and BMWs, designer sneakers, state-of-the-art electronic equipment, and gourmet foods. They also embraced the fitness craze, wore natural fibers, took up jogging, patronized health spas, and ate high-fiber diets.

By 1988 the overused term *yuppie* had evolved into a slur. Even people who fit the type perfectly did not want to be identified with it. Few of those who had acquired new wealth in the eighties gave up their stocks, bonds, or BMWs; but it seemed that the outright celebration of greed during the Reagan era was losing its appeal.

As the gap between the richest and poorest Americans widened to the largest it had been since 1945, poverty increasingly became the lot of women and children. The so-called feminization of poverty grew more severe during the 1980s, partly because of the rising rate of children born to single mothers. The rate of children living with a never-married mother soared by 70 percent between 1983 and 1993. In the early 1980s, 3.7 million children under age 18 lived with a single parent who had never married. A decade later, 6.3 million children, or 27 percent of all American children, lived with a never-married parent.

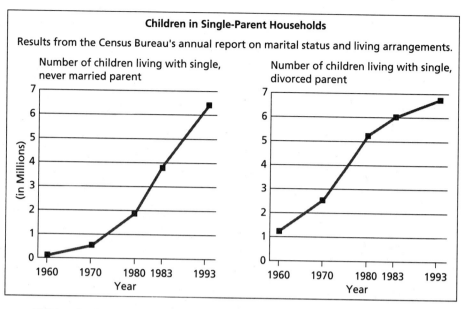

Children in Single-Parent Households

Results from the Census Bureau's annual report on marital status and living arrangements.

Number of children living with single, never married parent

Number of children living with single, divorced parent

Children in Single-Parent Households

An additional 5 to 7 million children lived with single divorced parents. By the early 1990s, one of every four births in the United States was to an unwed mother; the rate for African-American and Hispanic women was about 50 and 33 percent, respectively. Compared to married women, unwed mothers were less likely to receive prenatal care, finish high school, or hold a paying job. The Reagan administration made the situation worse by slashing funds for the Women, Infants, and Children (WIC) program, which provided prenatal and postnatal care to poor women.

President Reagan justified cutting many social programs with the quip that after twenty years of a war on poverty, poverty had won. Superficially, statistics seemed to confirm this view. In the early 1980s, the poverty rate for all Americans stood at about 13 percent, about where it was when Lyndon Johnson left office. However, the nature of poverty had changed over time. Before the passage of Great Society programs, the elderly and disabled had made up a larger share of the poor. But after 1965, increased spending on Social Security and Medicare had improved their lot dramatically; in other words, contrary to Reagan's implication, government programs *had* helped a large number of chronically poor. For the groups that made up the bulk of the poor in the 1980s—single mothers, young children, and younger men with few job skills—total federal welfare spending had not grown significantly, and with inflation, the value of welfare payments had actually decreased.

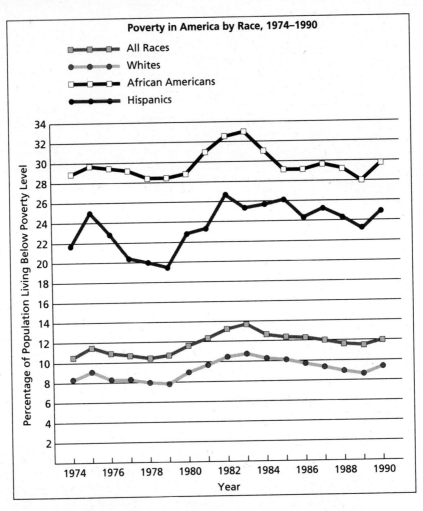

Poverty in America by Race, 1974–1990

▦	All Races
●	Whites
▢	African Americans
●	Hispanics

Poverty in America by Race, 1974–1990

One of the most troubling economic trends of the 1980s was the sharp increase in the number of people who worked full-time but could not by themselves lift themselves and their family out of poverty. The percentage of all Americans working full-time but earning less than a poverty-level income—about $13,000 a year for a family of four in 1991—rose by 50 percent between 1979 and 1992, from 12 percent of the work force to 18 percent. The trend toward lower wages was particularly sharp for young workers and those without college degrees.

The growing phenomenon of homelessness and the worsening plight of a seemingly unreachable "underclass" alarmed both conservatives and liberals during the 1980s. The homeless included a vari-

A mother begs for work and food—an increasingly common sight during the 1980s and 1990s.
© 1990 David Butow/Black Star.

ety of people, from women fleeing abusive spouses to the chronically mentally ill. Many lived on urban streets or in subway stations, begging for money and food. In another grim development, the decade saw more young African-American men in jail or on parole than attending college. The plight of the homeless and urban underclass shocked American sensibilities, but it did not affect public policy. Conservatives who saw poverty as the mark of personal failure believed that government efforts to help only deepened that failure. Liberals believed that government should help, but they had few new ideas to offer.

GOVERNMENT AND THE PRIVATE SECTOR

Government regulation of business, the environment, and banking had been one of the most important innovations of the New Deal. Conservatives had always criticized this intervention. Now, as the public expressed its own doubts about the competence of government, the Reagan administration initiated a major assault on the regulatory powers of the federal government.

As noted earlier, in the late 1970s the Carter administration began eliminating some federal regulations that interfered with competition. Prices declined in the airline and trucking industries after controls were removed. Reagan carried this policy even further, for the president and his advisers saw virtually all government regulation as anticompetitive.

Under Reagan, federal agencies abolished many of their earlier rules, ranging from requirements for stronger car bumpers to environmental restraints on offshore oil drilling. The budgets for agencies such as the Environmental Protection Agency (EPA), the Occupational Safety and Health Administration (OSHA), and the Securities and Exchange Commission (SEC) were slashed, ostensibly to save tax dollars. Because of the consequent staff shortages, these agencies were often unable to enforce regulations even if they wanted to. In a number of cases, Reagan appointed agency heads—such as Anne Burford Gorsuch of the EPA and James Watt of the Department of the Interior—who were openly hostile to the very regulations they purportedly enforced and who devoted their energies to weakening environmental protections.

One example of how the Reagan administration twisted the original purpose of a government program took place in the Department of Housing and Urban Development (HUD). The president appointed an African-American lawyer, Samuel Pierce, to head the agency. Pierce earned his nickname, "Silent Sam," by seldom speaking at cabinet meetings. Over a period of several years, the administration cut the HUD budget by nearly 75 percent. Pierce and his deputies used part of what remained in HUD coffers as a fund to award contracts to friends and political cronies. After Interior Secretary James Watt left the cabinet, he earned close to half a million dollars by making a few telephone calls to get favored developers access to HUD officials. In 1989 investigators discovered that billions of public dollars intended for low-income housing had been invested instead in luxury apartments, golf courses, swimming pools, and outright scams.

Pierce's misbehavior paled in comparison with the debacle in the savings and loan industry. During the 1970s, banks and savings and loan institutions (also called S&Ls or "thrifts") had lost large amounts of money and large numbers of depositors because unregulated money market funds paid a higher rate of interest. To make banks and S&Ls more competitive, Congress agreed at the end of the Carter years to raise the federal deposit insurance level to $100,000 on individual accounts and to allow the institutions to pay any interest rates they wanted. In 1982 the Reagan administration prodded Congress to go further and completely deregulate most S&Ls. Previously, their major lending activity was limited to low-risk, low-profit mortgages on single-family homes. But after 1982 they were permitted to invest their depositors' funds in undeveloped land, commercial real estate, shopping malls, fine art, junk bonds, and virtually anything else. Profits from such risky ventures primarily benefited S&L owners. And the existence of federal deposit insurance meant that neither the owners nor the depositors risked losing money; if bad loans led to an S&L collapse, the cost of repaying its depositors would be borne by the taxpayers.

Upon signing the Garn-St. Germain Act of 1982, which permitted these new S&L operations, Reagan called it the economic equivalent of a home run. Deregulation would liberate the creative energies of S&L managers and produce greater profits, which would make more money available for home loans. Instead, in many parts of the country, incompetent or corrupt lenders went wild. They invested insured funds in commercial real estate and other high-risk ventures, knowing they would reap any profits that accrued but would have no personal responsibility for losses.

In California, Charles Keating's Lincoln Savings and Loan became a multi-billion-dollar institution virtually overnight by paying high interest rates to attract $100,000 accounts. Most of these funds went into extremely speculative projects, whose high costs called into question their ultimate profitability. Colorado's Silverado Savings and Loan, whose board of directors included Neil Bush, son of the vice president, acted similarly. By providing easy commercial mortgage money, the freewheeling S&Ls created a construction boom in certain parts of the country, pumping billions of dollars into the economy. (In some ways, the S&L loans—which were eventually made good by the government—mirrored defense spending as a form of government-backed boost to the private sector.)

In addition to speculation, corruption soon entered the picture. Lenders found it easy and profitable to collude with builders to drive up the cost of projects, producing bigger fees all around. Some S&L officers made dubious loans to business partners or paid themselves exorbitant salaries, with little fear of exposure. Properties were often "flipped" (sold back and forth) several times in a day for ever-higher prices, with S&L managers authorizing the escalating loans in return for kickbacks.

Timely intervention by federal regulators might have limited the cost of the debacle, but Reagan's budget cuts had reduced the number of bank examiners. And even when auditors did find evidence of malfeasance, S&L managers' political influence could often stave off the day of reckoning. Charles Keating of Lincoln Savings and Loan made large contributions to influential senators, who pressed bank examiners to allow Lincoln to stay in business. By the time regulators closed it down, Lincoln had accumulated losses of about $3 billion—all chargeable to the federal agency that insured the institution's deposits. To put this loss in perspective, the cost of the Lincoln failure alone surpassed the cumulative value of all bank robberies in the United States over the previous twenty-five years.

By 1989, hundreds of S&Ls had failed, and few of those still in operation remained profitable. The federal government created the Resolution Trust Corporation to take over a huge inventory of vacant buildings and obligations from the failed institutions. Estimates for the final cost of the bailout ran to about $150 billion. By any measure, this was the biggest bank heist in the nation's history.

CIVIL RIGHTS AND CONSERVATIVE JUSTICE

"Conservatives have waited over thirty years for this day," commented Richard Viguerie, a leading New Right fund-raiser, when President Reagan nominated Judge Robert H. Bork in July 1987 to a vacant seat on the Supreme Court. Viguerie's feelings stemmed from anger about the Court's 1954 desegregation decision and many subsequent rulings by the Warren Court. President Reagan, like many other conservatives, shared these feelings. To him, liberal judges on the Supreme Court and throughout the judicial system were responsible for a decline in morals, a rise in premarital sex, and the banishing of God from public school classrooms.

Ronald Reagan had long opposed most civil rights laws and supported a constitutional amendment to outlaw school busing. Early in his presidency, trying unsuccessfully to stop Congress from establishing a federal holiday honoring Martin Luther King, Jr., he alluded to rumors about the civil rights martyr's left-wing leanings and steamy sex life. He also outraged civil rights groups by instructing the Justice Department to ask the Supreme Court to restore tax-free status to segregated private schools and colleges. (The Court turned him down, ruling in 1983 that the IRS had acted properly in denying tax benefits to such institutions.) When the 1965 Voting Rights Act came up for renewal, Reagan urged Congress to kill it. Congress renewed the law anyway, but the Reagan Justice Department then declined to investigate many allegations of infringements on minority voting rights.

In the field of civil liberties, Reagan believed that the court system overemphasized the rights of accused criminals, to the detriment of government power and victims' rights. A large portion of the American public, fearful of violent crime and increasingly suspicious of the courts, shared the president's views. During the 1980s, legislators on

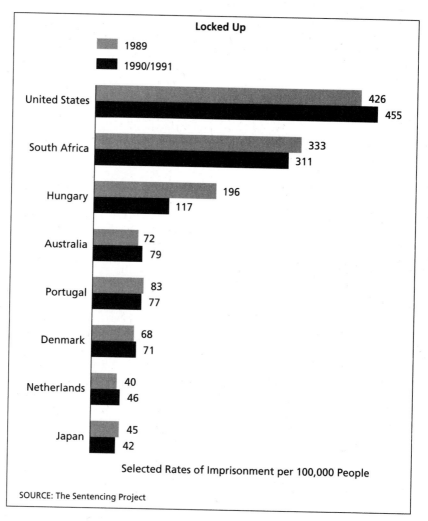

Locked Up

- 1989
- 1990/1991

United States	426	455
South Africa	333	311
Hungary	196	117
Australia	72	79
Portugal	83	77
Denmark	68	71
Netherlands	40	46
Japan	45	42

Selected Rates of Imprisonment per 100,000 People

SOURCE: The Sentencing Project

Selected Rates of Imprisonment per 100,000 people

both the state and national levels responded to public fears with laws that mandated longer, compulsory prison sentences for many crimes. As a result, prison populations doubled and prison construction costs became the fastest-growing category in many state budgets. By 1991, over 1 million Americans—nearly one out of every 250 citizens—were imprisoned. This gave the United States the dubious honor of having achieved the world's highest rate of incarceration, ten times that of many other industrial democracies. (And with the new federal and state sentencing laws from the Reagan era, the number of prisoners is expected to approach 2 million by the year 2000.)

President Reagan's principal contribution to the campaign for conservative justice lay in his judicial appointments. During his two terms he was able to appoint about four hundred federal judges—a majority of all those sitting in 1988—as well as the chief justice on the Supreme Court and three associate justices. He had the Justice Department screen candidates carefully to ferret out liberal views on civil rights, civil liberties, school prayer, and abortion. Nearly all of Reagan's appointees were white males of a markedly conservative bent, and nearly all were fairly young, ensuring that they would remain on the Court for many years to come.

The president's first three Supreme Court nominees were confirmed rather easily by the Senate. Sandra Day O'Connor—the first female Supreme Court nominee—and Antonin Scalia joined the Court as associate justices, and William Rehnquist was promoted to chief justice. But the Senate, which had a Democratic majority after 1986, rejected the 1987 nomination of Robert Bork, the outspoken conservative championed by Richard Viguerie and other members of the New Right. Many senators were offended by Bork's abrasive personality and disturbed by memories of his role in President Nixon's firing of Special Prosecutor Archibald Cox during the Watergate investigation. Moreover, Bork's contention that the Constitution offered little protection for privacy, free speech, women, and minorities aroused anger in the Senate. Undeterred by Bork's rejection, Reagan then nominated Anthony Kennedy, who also held conservative legal views but did not antagonize people as Bork did. Kennedy was easily confirmed in 1988.

Gradually the Reagan appointees changed the tenor of the Court's rulings. After 1984 the Court whittled away at previous decisions requiring police to alert suspects to their rights. The Court also approved limitations on bail, affirmed most state death-penalty laws, and allowed the introduction in court of some illegally seized evidence. At first, despite the Justice Department's attacks on affirmative action as a "racial spoils system," the Court tended to uphold affirmative action programs; but following Kennedy's confirmation, the conservative majority on the Court began to chip away at it. In a series of cases in 1989—the most important was *City of Richmond* v. *J. A. Croson Company*—the Court disallowed government set-aside programs, which had reserved a certain proportion of contracts for minority groups, and made it much harder for women, minorities, the elderly, and the disabled to sue private employers for job discrimination.

These decisions reflected a conservative view of justice that prevailed among the general public. Many Americans agreed with the president that "constitutional loopholes and technicalities" should not limit police and prosecutors. On civil rights issues, the use of school busing and affirmative action plans had created a lingering

In 1981, Sandra Day O'Connor became the first woman appointed to the Supreme Court. *UPI/Bettmann Archive.*

white backlash that drove large numbers of voters out of the Democratic Party.

SOCIETY AND CULTURE IN THE 1980s

In the social and cultural sphere, as in the judicial system, the 1980s were a decade when conservative values re-emerged. President Reagan and many of those who supported him stressed family values, clean living, religion, attention to the basics in education, and cultural unity. At the same time, however, the nation experienced a renewed drug crisis, a decline in the reputation of public education, a series of scandals among right-wing television evangelists, an AIDS epidemic, and a large influx of immigrants, which made the United States even more culturally diverse.

During the 1980s, as the scourge of AIDS and increased drug use aroused public concern, a health and fitness craze swept the nation. Americans began to pay heed to warnings that their health suffered from their often sedentary life, high-fat diet, and use of alcohol, tobacco, and caffeine. Exercise became popular, even fashionable. Low-salt, low-fat, all-natural foods were suddenly in great demand.

Groups such as Mothers Against Drunk Driving (MADD) campaigned to stiffen state laws against drunk drivers. Antitobacco advocates pressed local governments to mandate smoke-free work places and restaurants.

Meanwhile, illegal drug use continued to be commonplace. During the 1980s and early 1990s, an estimated 40 million Americans consumed an illegal substance each year. A 1987 survey revealed that half of all citizens under age forty-five had smoked marijuana at least once. In the first part of the decade, public concern about illegal drug use seemed minimal. In 1985 barely 1 percent of Americans surveyed listed drugs as a major national problem. But four years later, more than half of those surveyed described drug use as the gravest threat to national security.

What had happened to change the public attitude? To a large extent, the change stemmed from the appearance of "crack," an inexpensive cocaine derivative that became widely available by mid-decade. Newspapers, magazines, and television news reports carried frightening stories: robberies inspired by addicts' need for money to buy crack; crack-using parents who ignored or abused their children; preteen dealers; turf wars in which rival dealers shot not only each other but innocent bystanders as well.

Although accurate numbers are hard to come by, many experts believe that drug use among white Americans and the middle class peaked in the late 1970s or early 1980s. When cocaine and its derivatives became popular, the greatest concentration of users was among poor, inner-city, minority youth. For some of these young people, staying high relieved the miseries of daily life. For others, selling drugs provided one of the few avenues of economic and social mobility available to them.

The drugs themselves killed surprisingly few people, about 4,000 to 5,000 in a typical year during this period. About 8,000 others died in turf wars and drug-related crimes. In comparison, alcohol-related deaths approached 200,000 annually, and tobacco was responsible for some 400,000 American deaths each year during the 1980s.

Charging that the nation faced an unprecedented epidemic of drug use, President and Mrs. Reagan urged the public to fight back. "Just say no" was the widely circulated slogan of Nancy Reagan's antidrug campaign. Like most other citizens, however, the Reagans seemed more concerned about the escalation of drug-related violence than about why youth used drugs or how to rehabilitate them. The administration focused its antidrug efforts on a dramatic but largely futile campaign to intercept supplies, arrest dealers, and throw users in jail. By 1989 the federal and state wars on drugs cost almost $15 billion annually, with most of the money spent on police and prisons. Much less money and attention went into education and rehabilitation.

Meanwhile, among the young and all other sectors of the population, alcohol abuse remained the overwhelming drug problem.

In his enthusiasm to suppress drugs, Reagan urged compulsory urine tests for millions of workers in the transportation sector who showed no evidence of drug abuse. Although advocates of civil liberties objected, courts permitted the tests in many instances. By the early 1990s, federal and state prisons were bursting with drug felons, but cocaine remained as widely available as before.

In 1989, shortly after taking office, President George Bush declared a new offensive in the war on drugs. He kicked off the campaign with a television address during which he showed a dramatic (staged) "drug buy" in Lafayette Park, across the street from the White House. With the Defense Department freed from many of its Cold War duties, the president assigned the military to work with Latin American governments to suppress cocaine production and exports. Bush appointed a new "drug czar," William Bennett, to coordinate the campaign, and he got Congress to enact laws mandating long sentences for small-time users and the death penalty for drug "king pins."

As before, the bulk of the money allocated for the campaign was directed toward law enforcement rather than education and prevention. Drug czar Bennett promised a quick victory, but he spent most of his energy exchanging insults with other government officials and members of Congress. Unable to show any results beyond a slight decline in middle-class drug use that probably had nothing to do with government efforts, Bennett resigned after less than two years on the job. The war on drugs quickly lost the attention of both Bush and the American public.

A related, if less dramatic, concern arose over public education. Since the *Sputnik* scare of 1957, Americans had worried about how the nation's schools compared to those of its rivals. Concern mounted during the 1980s, when stories appeared about American high schools turning out illiterates and about Japanese students (the new challengers, replacing the Soviets) routinely outperforming Americans on standardized tests. The Department of Education's 1983 study, *A Nation at Risk*, reported that "if an unfriendly foreign power had attempted to impose on America the mediocre educational performance that exists today, we might well have viewed it as an act of war." Ironically, Reagan's own secretary of education, Terrel Bell, issued the report in the hope of generating public opposition to the president's deep cuts in school aid. Most Americans sympathized with the tone of the report, but few agreed on a remedy. Conservatives blamed the problem on permissive teachers, sex education, wasteful spending, and a lack of attention to Western cultural traditions and the "three R's." They especially criticized "multicultural" education, which stressed the contributions of non-Europeans and women to American society. Liberals complained that public schools were underfunded and hard put to teach both traditional subjects and the high-tech skills needed in a competitive world.

Sensing the public's mood, President Reagan applauded Bell's report and asked the education secretary to play a role in his reelection campaign. But soon after Reagan began his second term, he summarily fired Bell and appointed a successor who announced that schools needed more discipline, not more money.

To complicate matters, the urban middle class abandoned public schools in growing numbers. Continuing the trend of the 1970s, middle-class parents enrolled their children in private and parochial schools with selective admission policies. With many of their more motivated students gone, the public schools struggled to educate a larger proportion of poor, minority, and non-English-speaking children. Moreover, the flight of middle-class students reduced school districts' ability to raise needed revenues. Parents paying tuition for private education were reluctant to support new taxes. The gradual aging of the American population also contributed to the school crisis, because the elderly—with no young children of their own to educate—tended to oppose additional expenditures on schools. These problems in turn accelerated the decline of faith in public education, making it still harder to fund schools adequately.

Jimmy Carter was the first to link Bible-Belt Christianity with presidential politics, but Ronald Reagan captured the movement masterfully for the Republican party. Evangelical Christianity experienced a dramatic growth during the 1970s. When Johnson ran for president, only 24 percent of Americans described themselves as "born again" (having personally experienced salvation). By 1978 this figure had approached 40 percent. Although the experience had different meanings for different people, as a group these Americans tended to be angered by social permissiveness and Supreme Court rulings on school prayer and abortion. Many had simply stopped voting.

Reagan and his advisers recognized the immense impact these disaffected Christians could have if they were energized behind national and local candidates. Republican officials capitalized on the ability of television ministers to mobilize an audience of millions on behalf of the Republican cause. Preachers like Jim Bakker, Jimmy Swaggart, Oral Roberts, and Pat Robertson, who represented a variety of Protestant sects and traditions, saw themselves as potential kingmakers. Jerry Falwell, founder of the Moral Majority, boasted that he hoped to "bring about a moral and conservative revolution" by electing sympathetic politicians.

Reagan seldom attended church, but he spoke with verve and certainty on religious matters. In 1980 he told a meeting of self-described fundamentalist Christian leaders that he considered himself "born again" and that "it was a fact that all the [world's] complex and horrendous [problems] have their answer in that single book—the Bible." He criticized federal courts for not permitting "creation science" to be taught as a scientific alternative to the theory of evolution, and he urged amending the Constitution to permit the return of prayer to public schools. "You can't endorse me," he told cheering preachers, "but I endorse you."

By 1985, the electronic ministries were raising well over $1 billion annually. Viewer donations supported a variety of religious, charitable, political, and business causes. In organizations such as the Moral Majority, the 700 Club, and the PTL ("Praise the Lord") club, donations were often funneled into unaudited accounts. Indeed part of the surge in televised fund-raising could be traced to a change in federal regulations. Before the late 1970s, TV stations had donated air time to religious organizations in order to fulfill government requirements for public-service broadcasting. By the 1980s, however, the regulations permitted stations to count religious broadcasts as fulfilling these requirements even if the air time was paid for at regular prices. Therefore the stations charged high rates, which only those ministries adept at fund-raising could afford to pay.

The most successful televangelists preached two basic sermons. One fulminated against the threat posed to America by immorality, communism, abortion, and "secular humanism" (the belief that humans, not God, were the basis of moral law). The other celebrated a gospel of wealth, a belief that money and nice possessions represented a form of divine grace. The Reverend Jimmy Swaggart epitomized the former style and the Reverend Jim Bakker the latter. Both implied that grace was readily available to those who showed their faith by making generous donations.

The televangelists tapped into major trends in 1980s America. Jimmy Swaggart's talk of sin and Satan resembled President Reagan's campaign against godless communism and the Soviet Union's "evil empire." Jim and Tammy Faye Bakker's PTL show celebrated wealth and conspicuous consumption in much the same way that yuppies admired BMW's and cappucino machines. The Bakkers seemed to say that people could not do good unto others until they felt good about themselves, and feeling good about oneself required a lot of expensive possessions.

Many televangelists were honest and sincere, less inclined to flamboyant exaggeration and flagrant fund-raising than Swaggart and the Bakkers. The Reverend Billy Graham, for example, had used television to preach the gospel since the 1950s. While clearly a "conservative," Graham generally avoided partisan politics, and he showed no hint of financial impropriety. Moreover, not all viewers accepted the political dogma put forth by the media preachers. Many who watched the shows simply found the mix of "old-time religion," songs, and entertainment a comfort in an impersonal society. Other donors, pollsters found, contributed money out of a sense of obligation to pay for enjoying the spectacle, much like viewers who voluntarily sent money to public radio and TV stations during their annual pledge week.

Whatever the basis of their appeal, televised ministries suffered a major setback in 1987, when several of the most outrageous televangelists were tainted by scandal. Federal prosecutors indicted Jim Bakker on numerous counts of fraud and conspiracy for bilking followers out of $158 million they invested in a scheme involving his ministry's religious theme park, Heritage USA. In addition, a rival TV preacher revealed that Bakker had forced a female church member to have sex with him and had used donation funds to pay her hush money. A jury convicted Bakker of cheating investors, and he received a stiff jail term.

Other televangelists also fell from grace. Oral Roberts became an object of derision when he locked himself in a prayer tower, claiming God would "take" him in thirty days unless his flock mailed him $8 million—which they promptly did. Jimmy Swaggart admitted that he had bought sex from prostitutes, who in court depositions described him as "really weird." Pat Robertson's crusade for the Republican presidential nomination collapsed amid public ridicule after he announced he would use prayer to divert a hurricane from Virginia to New York.

The personal and financial lapses of certain televangelists had long been rumored. Evidence suggests that the Reagan administration pressured government agencies to overlook charges of lawbreaking in the early 1980s because the electronic churches supported the president. By the 1990s, many politically active televangelists and New Right religious activists had refocused their attention on local, rather than national, campaigns, throwing their support behind candidates for school boards, city councils, county governments, and Congress.

Ronald Reagan and the religious Right celebrated the "traditional" family, consisting of a breadwinning husband and a wife who served as mother and homemaker. (Fundamentalists either ignored or did not care that Reagan was the first divorced president, had married two career women, and had little contact with two of his four children.) Many Americans still found this image of an old-fashioned, stable family appealing. Yet the so-called traditional household continued to decline in the 1980s. In 1970, forty percent of the nation's households still conformed to that ideal; by 1980 that proportion had dropped to 31 percent, and by 1990 to 26 percent. In 1983 the proportion of adult women with jobs outside the home surpassed 50 percent for the first time in the country's history, and it continued to rise over the next decade.

With women holding a large share of the nation's paying jobs, feminists continued to press harder for affordable child care, approval of the Equal Rights Amendment, and an end to gender discrimination by employers. But Reagan opposed efforts to develop a national child-care policy, and Republicans in Congress blocked any reconsideration of the Equal Rights Amendment when the deadline for ratification expired in 1982. After Reagan left office, his appointees to the Supreme Court struck down civil rights legislation that would have facilitated women's ability to sue employers for gender discrimination. Despite Reagan's opposition to most feminist goals, he did win a measure of support from women for appointing a few women to high-profile posts. During his first term he made Jeane Kirkpatrick ambassador to the United Nations, Margaret Heckler the head of the Health and Human Services Department, and Sandra Day O'Connor the first female Supreme Court justice.

The issue of abortion remained controversial throughout the 1980s. Reagan persuaded Congress to bar Medicaid-funded abortions for poor women and to limit funding for other forms of birth control. In their place he advocated "chastity clinics," in which counselors advised teenage girls and unmarried women to avoid pregnancy by avoiding sex. (The role played by young males was largely ignored.) The president also encouraged "right-to-life" (antiabortion) groups to support politicians opposed to abortion and to work against candidates who favored a woman's right to choose.

Many commentators proclaimed that the 1980s were witnessing the end of the sexual revolution that began during the 1960s. This pronouncement was probably premature, but the outbreak of the AIDS epidemic in the early 1980s brought a health crisis that would indeed make Americans more cautious about sexual relations. The result of a virus apparently originating in Africa, AIDS (for acquired immune deficiency syndrome) destroyed the immune system and left victims vulnerable to opportunistic infections. The deadly human immunodeficiency virus (HIV) that caused AIDS was transmitted from one person to another through the exchange of body fluids, particularly blood and semen. In the early years of the epidemic, sexual transmission was especially prevalent among gay men. Intravenous drug users who shared needles were also at grave risk, as were their sex partners. Before tests were developed to check the nation's blood banks, many hemophiliacs caught the virus through blood transfusions. By the end of 1993, some 200,000 Americans had died from the disease, and an estimated 1 million others carried the deadly HIV infection. AIDS struck hard in other countries as well, especially in Africa, Brazil, and parts of Southeast Asia.

The fight against AIDS included a public education campaign to alert people to the danger. *Saatchi & Saatchi.*

Because many of the first people with AIDS were gay men or drug abusers, President Reagan was uncomfortable even discussing the disease. Along with his conservative backers, he opposed spending much federal money on AIDS research or preventive education during his first term. The president remained silent on the subject while televangelists spoke of God's sending a "gay plague" to punish sinners. Scientists urged public officials to endorse a "safe sex" program promoting the use of condoms in order to reduce transmission of the virus. But many religious authorities and cultural conservatives fought against the idea, believing that promoting safe sex merely encouraged promiscuity.

In October 1985 the death from AIDS of Rock Hudson, a popular film star and a personal friend of the Reagans, helped to humanize the disease, both for the president and for the public at large. The president appointed a commission that recommended much higher levels of funding for government and private research, education programs, and treatment. The virus had been identified by 1984, and now a search for ways to prevent or cure the disease began in earnest. Reagan urged compassion for people with AIDS, but he seldom spoke on the subject and he refused to endorse his own surgeon general's call for widespread publicity encouraging the use of condoms.

Immigration continued to arouse strong feelings among Americans. The changes in immigration law after 1965 led to increasing

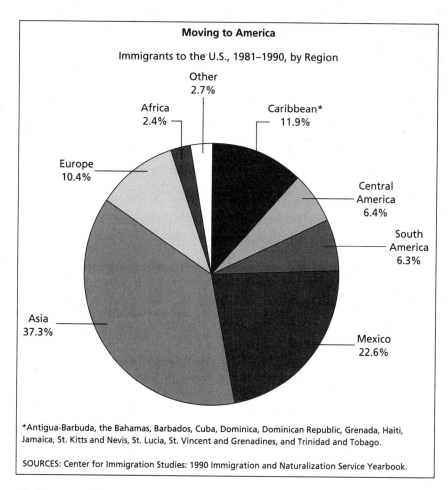

Moving to America

Immigrants to the U.S., 1981–1990, by Region

- Other 2.7%
- Africa 2.4%
- Caribbean* 11.9%
- Europe 10.4%
- Central America 6.4%
- South America 6.3%
- Asia 37.3%
- Mexico 22.6%

*Antigua-Barbuda, the Bahamas, Barbados, Cuba, Dominica, Dominican Republic, Grenada, Haiti, Jamaica, St. Kitts and Nevis, St. Lucia, St. Vincent and Grenadines, and Trinidad and Tobago.

SOURCES: Center for Immigration Studies: 1990 Immigration and Naturalization Service Yearbook.

Moving to America

numbers of Asians and Hispanics coming to the United States. By the 1980s, almost 45 percent of documented immigrants came from Asia and the Middle East, and about as many came from Latin America and the Caribbean; just over 10 percent came from Europe. Increased Asian immigration was especially dramatic during the 1980s, as 3.5 million Filipino, Chinese, Korean, and Vietnamese immigrants boosted the number of Asian-Americans in the United States by 100 percent. Although some Asians came as refugee "boat people," most were well educated, and many had family members already living in the United States.

The increase in immigration aroused mixed feelings among the general public. Some Americans responded by forming a sanctuary movement modeled on the Underground Railroad of the pre-Civil

War years, offering shelter to political refugees. Many African-Americans resented what they saw as favored treatment of the new arrivals. The large number of undocumented Mexicans living in the United States—a number estimated at anywhere between 3 million and 15 million during the 1980s—aroused special concern. Some whites feared the erosion of English as the national language with the proliferation of new cultures and tongues. Voters in California, Arizona, and Florida passed laws declaring English the official state language.

After years of debate about how to control immigration, Congress passed the 1986 Simpson-Rodino Act. It offered legal status to several million undocumented aliens living in the United States, but it imposed fines on employers who hired new undocumented workers. Despite hopes that the new law would ensure orderly immigration procedures, it had little effect on undocumented immigrants or on those who employed them. By the mid-1990s, about 1 million people immigrated legally to this country each year, historically a very high number.

THE 1988 ELECTION

As Ronald Reagan approached the end of his second term, Democrats once again hoped to win back control of the White House by restoring the New Deal coalition that had splintered in the late 1960s. But the Democratic party's divisions had not healed. Seven of the eight men seeking the Democratic nomination tried to steer discussion away from the contentious issues of race, social policy, and foreign affairs. They argued instead that Democrats were more competent managers and could adjust more rapidly to a changing world. Only Jesse Jackson—the first African-American to win a substantial political following at the presidential level—championed traditional liberal causes; he criticized his fellow Democrats for "moving their policies to the right like Ronald Reagan."

Early on, the 1988 presidential race took on the trapping of farce. Gary Hart, the front-runner in the Democratic race, destroyed his candidacy when newspapers published stories and photographs about his liaisons with Donna Rice, a fashion model. Hart, a married man, had denied rumors about his womanizing and challenged journalists to prove him a liar; he quickly withdrew from the campaign when they did.

The controversy over Hart's personal life set the tone for much of what followed. The media vigorously pursued stories that revealed politicians' failings and the hypocrisy behind their public image. A few months after Hart quit the race, the press reported that another Democratic candidate, Delaware senator Joseph Biden, had cribbed portions of his speeches from other politicians and had exaggerated his academic achievements. Biden, too, left the presidential race.

By the spring of 1988, only two major Democratic candidates remained: Jesse Jackson and Massachusetts governor Michael Dukakis. Although Dukakis was a relative unknown, he easily outpolled his opponent in the primaries, where Jackson's image as a radical dogged him. In securing the Democratic nomination, Dukakis shunned the unpopular label of "liberal," promised not to raise taxes, and claimed that he could achieve for the entire nation the rapid economic growth his state had experienced during his term as governor. But the so-called "Massachusetts' Miracle" had resulted more from high levels of defense spending than from anything Dukakis had done.

Vice President George Bush, pursuing the Republican nomination, had to fend off challenges from Reagan aide Patrick Buchanan and Kansas senator Robert Dole. Both accused him of being an inauthentic conservative, merely posing as a Reaganite to hide his "Eastern Establishment, liberal Republicanism." Although Bush secured his party's nomination, these accusations later came back to haunt him in office.

The Democrats considered Bush a soft target. "If we can't beat Bush," one Democratic strategist remarked, "we'd better find another country." Media attacks on the vice president appeared to help the Democrats at first. Columnists and cartoonists presented Bush as an inarticulate, unimaginative weakling. They ridiculed his upper-class background and prep-school education. Texan John Connolly deflated Bush's claim to be a true son of the Southwest, describing him as "all hat and no boots." Conservative writer George Will depicted Bush as a "lap dog," and "Doonesbury" author Garry Trudeau dismissed him as a cheerleader for Reagan who had "put his manhood in a blind trust."

But the Democrats failed to take Bush's competitiveness and accomplishments into account. The son of a wealthy Republican senator from Connecticut, Bush left college during World War II to become the youngest fighter pilot in the U.S. Navy. He was shot down in combat late in the war. A clip of his rescue, showing a smiling, boyish Bush waving his thanks to the men who had pulled him out of the sea, became one of the most effective TV spots of the 1988 campaign. After graduating from Yale, Bush moved from Connecticut to Texas, made a fortune in the oil business, and served two terms in the U.S. House of Representatives, from 1967 to 1971. Defeated in 1970 for a Senate seat, Bush became chairman of the Republican National Committee. He later became the U.S. ambassador to China and head of the Central Intelligence Agency.

In one of the most famous statements of the campaign, Bush paraphrased a line from movie hero Clint Eastwood: "Read my lips," he declared, "no new taxes." Although some critics thought a Washington "insider" like Bush could not possibly assume Reagan's "outsider" mantle—nor ignore the need to raise taxes to meet the mounting deficit—Bush convinced the public otherwise.

Bush and his advisers prepared carefully for the campaign against Dukakis. By interviewing small "focus groups" of voters, they identified vulnerabilities in the Dukakis record and capitalized on them. For example, while he was governor, Dukakis had vetoed a law requiring school teachers to lead their students in the Pledge of Allegiance. Dukakis had also supported (like governors in twenty-four other states) a furlough program for convicts, under which prisoners nearing the end of their sentences could spend time out of prison. Unfortunately, a convicted murderer named Willie Horton fled during a furlough from a Massachusetts prison and raped a Maryland woman. The fact that Horton was black and the woman white added to the emotional nature of the incident, allowing Bush to arouse white fears that Dukakis was "soft on crime."

Throughout the fall campaign, Bush hammered away on the issue of the flag salute—at one point visiting a flag factory and almost literally wrapping himself in the national banner—and crime. He attacked Dukakis as a "card-carrying member of the American Civil Liberties Union (ACLU)," in a tone reminiscent of Senator Joe McCarthy's condemnation of "card-carrying Communists." Dukakis, at best a wooden public figure, became so bogged down defending himself against these charges that he failed to articulate a program. Bush briefly appeared to jeopardize his own chances by selecting Dan Quayle, a forty-one-year-old senator from Indiana, as his running mate. Quayle had an undistinguished record in the Senate, and years earlier he had used his family connections to enter the National Guard as a way of avoiding service in Vietnam. But widespread misgivings about Quayle had little effect on election day. At the conclusion of a campaign that was utterly devoid of substance (one book on the campaign was called *The Trivial Pursuit of the Presidency*), Bush easily won with 53 percent of the popular vote and majorities in forty states. He ran especially strong among white men and in the South. Once again, however, voters returned a majority of Democrats to the House and Senate, resulting in a divided government.

Widespread lamentations after the election that the candidates should have provided a more serious debate overstated the quality of earlier campaigns. They also underestimated the dominant role played by television in shaping the way leaders communicated with the public. Because voters increasingly gained their information from television news rather than from printed media, candidates tailored their messages to the TV format. Media consultants—who largely held both the politicians they worked for and the voters in contempt—helped arrange the candidates' public appearances so as to produce thirty-second "sound bites" that played well on the evening news. Reasoned discussions of the issues did not fit into this format. Even the television reporters who analyzed the campaigns preferred to concentrate on the dramatic features of "the race"—as if the candidates were horses in a steeplechase—rather than on substantive differences between the candidates.

THE BUSH PRESIDENCY AT HOME

In accepting the Republican nomination for president, George Bush pledged to preside over a "kinder, gentler America." This prompted an understandably miffed Nancy Reagan to blurt out to a friend attending the convention with her, "kinder and gentler than whom?" Without directly saying so, Bush promised to create an administration that was more concerned with meeting people's needs than his predecessor had been. While Reagan had seen "government as the problem," the moderately conservative Bush saw responsible government as a solution to problems and public service as an honorable occupation. This outlook helped him win the election, but it also put him on a collision course with the extreme conservatives who now dominated the Republican party.

A number of trends helped make Bush popular and sustain good feelings about his administration through mid-1991. The economic expansion that began in 1982 continued well into 1990. The changes sweeping the Communist world, as well as U.S. military successes in Panama and the Persian Gulf (see Chapter 13), made it appear that Bush had both an active and successful foreign policy. The low esteem people had for Congress also boosted Bush's popularity.

The Republican president and the Democratic majority in Congress cooperated in pushing through some important pieces of legislation in 1990 and 1991. The Americans with Disabilities Act required government, business, and educational buildings to provide equal access for the physically handicapped. Buildings, walkways, elevators, classrooms, work stations, and rest rooms were to be reconfigured so that disabled persons could use them easily. The Clean Water Act expanded a law first enacted in the 1970s that set federal and state standards for water purity and provided funds for sewage systems and for cleaning up polluted waters. An overhauled version of the Clean Air Act set stricter standards for automobile and industrial emissions. The Radiation Exposure Compensation Act provided payments for victims of atomic mining and testing during the Cold War. The Native American Graves Repatriation Act forced museums to return bones and cultural artifacts to Indian tribes.

Claiming the title "the education president," Bush at first showed interest in improving the performance of the nation's public schools. During 1989 and 1990 he met with governors to outline a series of goals for public education. These included improved literacy and graduation rates and higher test scores in subjects like science and mathematics. The so-called "Goals 2000" project that grew out of this meeting was coordinated by the little-known governor of Arkansas, Bill Clinton. The president endorsed the Goals 2000 report, since it committed little new federal funding but provided an appearance of activism.

Economic realities forced Bush to retreat from the pillar of the Reagan revolution, a commitment to lower taxes. Faced with a growing deficit and complaints from foreign creditors worried about the value of the U.S. dollar, the president and congressional Democrats agreed on a budget in the fall of 1990 that required both modest tax hikes and modest spending cuts in social programs. Despite Bush's futile effort to make a distinction between "revenue increases" and "tax increases," conservative Republicans were enraged at him for breaking his "no new taxes" pledge. When a recession began at the end of 1990, conservatives attributed it to the president's reversal of Reagan's policy.

Despite a general belief that public policy in the 1990s would prove less contentious than in the previous fifteen years, controversy over individual rights struck a discordant note. Two Supreme Court decisions reminded people of issues that had recently divided them. In 1989 the Court revived an earlier controversy when it affirmed that the First Amendment's guarantee of free speech permitted citizens to burn the American flag as an act of political protest. President Bush quickly proposed amending the Constitution to forbid flag burning. Pollsters found the public strongly in favor of such a ban, and it seemed that Democrats might again find themselves on the defensive. But the issue faded almost as quickly as it arose, and by the end of the year Congress decided not to endorse an amendment. Instead, a new federal law banning flag burning was passed, which was then struck down by the Supreme Court.

A 1989 decision regarding abortion produced a longer-lasting controversy. In *Webster* v. *Reproductive Services of Missouri*, the court ruled by a five-to-four margin that abortion rights could be limited by state law. States could bar abortions in public hospitals, for example, or forbid public employees to assist in abortion procedures. Writing for the majority, Chief Justice Rehnquist asserted that "nothing in the Constitution requires states to enter or remain in the business of performing abortions." Although the ruling stopped short of reversing *Roe* v. *Wade*, Justice Harry Blackmun, the principal author of *Roe*, declared in a dissenting opinion that while the right to an abortion remained the law of the land "for today, at least . . . the signs are very ominous and a chill wind blows."

In the wake of *Webster,* several states, including Louisiana, Pennsylvania, and Utah, passed laws stopping just short of outright bans on abortion. Physicians, women's groups, and organizations such as Planned Parenthood filed suits to overturn these laws. Ruling on a 1992 Pennsylvania case, *Planned Parenthood* v. *Casey,* the Supreme Court again narrowly upheld the right to have an abortion while allowing states to impose a broad range of restrictions.

The politics of the issue became complicated when Republican pollsters discovered that many women who supported their party also favored abortion rights. Republican National Committee chairman Lee Atwater, known for his slashing attacks against liberals, now insisted that the Republican party was a "big tent" that tolerated diverse views on abortion. President Bush, who as a young politician supported the right to choose but in 1988 asserted that "abortion is murder," kept a low profile on the issue, again angering both abortion rights supporters and foes.

Abortion and rights issues came to the fore in 1990 and 1991 when justices William Brennan and Thurgood Marshall retired from the Supreme Court. The departure of two of the Court's most liberal justices gave Bush the opportunity to alter its ideological complexion decisively. To replace Brennan, he nominated the virtually unknown David Souter, a former judge of the New Hampshire Supreme Court who had served for a few months on the federal bench. Souter had never expressed himself publicly on such controversial issues as abortion, the right to privacy, and the death penalty. During his confirmation hearings he remained silent on nearly every controversial question. Despite doubts voiced by senators and citizens on all sides of these issues, Souter easily won confirmation. He emerged as a moderate during his first four years on the high court, willing to let *Roe* v. *Wade* stand.

To fill the seat left vacant by Thurgood Marshall—the Court's first African-American justice—Bush took a different tack. Already in trouble with the Republican right wing for breaking his no new taxes pledge and for other signs of "moderation," the president hoped to mend fences by appointing a high-profile conservative. Bush nominated Clarence Thomas, a forty-three-year-old African-American federal court of appeals judge who had publicly questioned many of the Supreme Court's past rulings on abortion, school prayer, privacy rights, and the death penalty.

As discussed in Chapter 13, the president's success in toppling General Manuel Noriega in Panama and in mobilizing a twenty-eight-nation coalition to liberate Kuwait from Iraq made Bush an extremely popular president through mid-1991. But once the excitement

Clarence Thomas and Anita Hill

When President Bush described Clarence Thomas as the American "most qualified" to sit on the Supreme Court, opponents ridiculed him and even supporters described this level of praise as an "overstatement." But few denied that Thomas had achieved many impressive goals in a life that began in poverty. Raised as a Catholic, he attended Holy Cross College in Worcester, Massachusetts. At Yale Law School in the early 1970s he flirted with radical black nationalism. After graduation, his politics became increasingly conservative. Thomas joined the staff of Republican senator John Danforth of Missouri, and following the election of Ronald Reagan, he went to work for the Department of Education's Office of Civil Rights. In 1982 he became head of the Equal Employment Opportunity Commission (EEOC). Later, President Reagan appointed him to the federal court of appeals. Although he opposed many of the positions advocated by civil rights organizations, groups such as the NAACP were reluctant to oppose the nomination of an African-American to the Supreme Court, no matter how conservative he was. In October 1991, Thomas appeared headed for quick Senate confirmation.

Several members of the Senate Judiciary Committee knew that Anita Hill, a former colleague and protégé of Thomas, had accused him—without filing a formal complaint—of sexually harassing her. But they dismissed the issue until journalists broke the story. Following a public outcry, the committee reopened hearings on the nomination. In a highly publicized, televised drama, the two articulate and earnest lawyers exchanged accusations concerning the most intimate aspects of their lives.

If Clarence Thomas had been a woman, one journalist noted, he might have been Anita Hill. The youngest of thirteen children born to a poor, devout Baptist family in rural Oklahoma, Hill excelled in high school and at Oklahoma State University. Like Thomas, she earned a law degree at Yale. Following an introduction by a mutual friend, Thomas hired Hill to assist him in the Department of Education's civil rights office. In 1982 she followed Thomas to the EEOC as a special assistant. A year later she left government to begin teaching law, first at Oral Roberts University and then at the University of Oklahoma.

Reluctant at first to go on record, Hill eventually told the Senate Judiciary Committee that when she worked for Thomas he had harassed her frequently with vivid descriptions of porn flicks, group sex, bestiality, and his own sexual prowess. Many members of the all-male Judiciary Committee condescended to Hill, suggesting her accusations were those of an unstable woman. Why, they asked, had she continued to work for a man who behaved so badly? Why, she and her supporters responded, should she have given up her job because of her boss's misconduct? In a riveting performance, Thomas angrily denied any wrongdoing and characterized the hearing as a "high-tech lynching" by his political opponents. At the time, both a majority of the public and the senators accepted Thomas's version of events. However, the public, and some key senators, were unaware that several other women who had worked with Thomas were prepared—but never called—to testify that he had behaved toward them in ways similar to what Hill described. The committee voted to send Thomas's name to the full Senate, which quickly confirmed him.

Over the next year, perceptions of the Thomas-Hill confrontation changed, with increasing numbers of Americans accepting Hill's veracity. The affair played an important role in galvanizing women against President Bush, and it also brought discussion of sexual harassment into the mainstream. ■

of victory in the Gulf War faded, Americans re-focused their concern on the deteriorating economy. President Bush, who appeared so dynamic and resourceful in managing foreign military ventures, came across as lethargic and disengaged from domestic problems. After first denying that America was experiencing a recession, he insisted that economic problems would solve themselves. But American voters preferred an activist president, certainly on issues that affected their economic livelihood. This set the stage for a political transformation as the 1992 election neared.

CONCLUSION

The Reagan-Bush era represented a major turning point in American politics. The fracturing of the Democratic party was matched by the rise of an assertive, conservative Republican party that directly challenged the New Deal legacy. For the first time since the 1930s, national leaders not only questioned the value of a large, powerful federal government but began to dismantle it. While ordinary Americans did not always agree with the specific programs pushed by the Reagan and Bush administrations, many shared their skepticism toward social programs and appreciated Reagan's efforts to restore the national pride. But the economic and social policies of the Reagan-Bush era failed to reverse many negative trends.

While Reagan's charm and political magic overwhelmed most naysayers, George Bush proved a weak second act to the Reagan revolution. Where Reagan denounced government as the cause of most problems, Bush valued public service and hesitated to crusade against established institutions. Trying to occupy the middle ground between the New Right and the New Deal, he found no place to stand. Officeholders in the 1990s discovered that the American people's tolerance for their elected leaders—like the "sound bites" those leaders used to get elected—had become increasingly brief. ■

FURTHER READING

On America in the 1980s and early 1990s, see: Garry Wills, *Reagan's America* (1988); Lou Cannon, *President Reagan: The Role of a Lifetime* (1991); Michael Rogin, *Ronald Reagan: The Movie* (1987); Haynes Johnson, *Sleepwalking Through History* (1991); Michael Schaller, *Reckoning with Reagan: America and Its President in the 1980s* (1992). On the politics and the economic and social policies of the 1980s, see: Donald T. Regan, *For the Record* (1988); David Stockman, *The Triumph of Politics* (1986); Benjamin Friedman, *Day of Reckoning: The Conse-*

quences of American Economic Policy Under Reagan and After (1988); Herman Schwartz, Packing the Courts (1988); Jane Mayer and Jill Abramson, Strange Justice: The Selling of Clarence Thomas (1994); Kevin Phillips, The Politics of Rich and Poor (1990); Randy Shilts, And the Band Played On: Politics, People, and the AIDS Epidemic (1987); William Julius Wilson, The Truly Disadvantaged: The Inner City, the Underclass and Public Policy (1987); Barbara Ehrenreich, The Worst Years of Our Lives (1990); Nicolaus Mills (ed.), Culture in an Age of Money (1991); Mark Hertsgaard, On Bended Knee (1988); Susan Faludi, Backlash: The Undeclared War Against American Women (1991); Sidney Blumenthal, Pledging Allegiance: The Last Campaign of the Cold War (1990); Jack Germond and Jules Witcover, Whose Broad Stripes and Bright Stars? The Trivial Pursuit of the Presidency, 1988 (1989); James D. Hunter, Culture Wars: The Struggle to Define America (1991); William C. Brennan, America's Right Turn: From Nixon to Bush (1994); E. J. Dionne, Why Americans Hate Politics (1992).

13

From the New Cold War to the New World Order

In August 1984, engaging in some banter before delivering a Saturday morning radio commentary, President Ronald Reagan spoke into a microphone he did not know was on. "My fellow Americans," he declared, "I'm pleased to tell you today that I've signed legislation that will outlaw the Soviet Union forever. We begin bombing in five minutes." The president laughed off criticism of his remark, as if it were something his friend John Wayne might have said while acting in a Hollywood western. But many people thought this incident confirmed that Reagan's presidency had not only restored national pride, but had made America all too ready to end the long-standing stalemate with the Soviets by provoking a showdown. Soviet leaders took Reagan's off-the-cuff joke seriously enough to instruct KGB intelligence officers in Washington to report any indications of war preparations, such as the stockpiling of food or blood in federal buildings.

As a presidential candidate, Ronald Reagan had insisted that "there *are* simple answers" to complex questions. He complained that America suffered from a "Vietnam syndrome," an inability or unwillingness to use force to resist Soviet pressure and defend American friends and interests abroad. Attributing this weakness to guilt over the Vietnam War, Reagan repeatedly praised that struggle as a noble cause. His first secretary of state, General Alexander Haig, echoed this sentiment, declaring that the time had come for Americans to shed their sackcloth and ashes. The new administration pledged to restore America's military superiority, defend its allies, and support anti-Communist movements throughout the world. Unlike Dwight Eisenhower, who had made similar remarks but had restrained military spending, President Reagan pushed through Congress the largest military budgets the United States ever adopted in time of peace. Between 1981 and 1989, total defense spending ballooned from less than $200 billion to over $300 billion per year. At the peak of spending, in 1984, the Pentagon spent over $30 million per hour.

Beneath the rhetoric, however, the president pursued old policies more vigorously than he initiated new ones. His talk of restraining Moscow's "evil empire" harked back to the Truman Doctrine—the policy of containment—and the birth of NATO. His willingness to intervene in Central America and the Caribbean echoed the policies of Dwight Eisenhower, John Kennedy, and Lyndon Johnson. He even forged ties with many conservative Democrats who had chafed under the Carter administration, appointing them to posts as arms negotiators and diplomats.

Midway through his second term, when the Iran-contra scandal erupted, it appeared that Reagan's primary new contribution to foreign policy had been to assemble a team of staffers who engaged in secret, illegal arms deals, flouted congressional authority, contradicted the president's own publicly announced policies, and defied common sense.

Yet, by the end of his administration, Reagan had presided over the most dramatic thawing in relations with the Soviet Union since the collapse of the Grand Alliance in 1945. The American president and Soviet leader Mikhail Gorbachev signed a treaty that eliminated an entire category of nuclear missiles. Like their president did, most Americans discarded Reagan's earlier depiction of the Soviet Union as an "evil empire"; opinion polls showed that Americans felt friendlier toward the Soviets than at any other time since the Second World War.

George Bush, Reagan's successor, continued to reap political benefits from the decline in superpower hostility. As the Soviet Union's domestic problems intensified, Gorbachev withdrew Soviet military support from its satellites in Eastern Europe. Peaceful, popular uprisings quickly toppled Communist governments throughout the region, culminating in the dramatic demolition of the Berlin Wall and the reunification of Germany. By the end of 1991 the Soviet Union had ceased to exist; in its place was a Russian government with a democratically elected president, and a host of ethnic successor states, mostly in central Asia. The "end" of the Cold War, which had dominated and driven international relations since 1945, had a profound effect on the United States and its relations with most of the world.

Meanwhile, as the world's only remaining "superpower," the United States was free to fight a regional war, in the Persian Gulf without fear of Soviet resistance, and it launched a police action to depose a tin horn dictator in Panama. The United States was triumphant in both operations, and President Bush proclaimed the dawn of an American-led "new world order." In fact, the post-Cold War era proved far more chaotic—at home and abroad—than most Americans could have imagined.

REAGAN'S FOREIGN POLICY STYLE

As with many of the Reagan era's domestic programs, a yawning gap existed between the rhetoric and the reality of Reagan's foreign policy. Even the president's admirers admitted that he lived in a world of myths and symbols rather than facts and programs. While Jimmy Carter, with his emphasis on details and process, had failed to articulate any overarching vision, Reagan excelled in evoking sunny images of unity and progress without stipulating the necessary steps to achieve that goal. Reagan let his underlings handle unpleasant (or complicated) announcements. Whatever Americans thought about Reagan's foreign policy, they liked the fact that he made them feel good.

Despite Reagan's reputation as a rigid ideologue, he gave little specific direction to his foreign policy advisers. It is uncertain whether Reagan even thought in terms of a coherent strategy before 1983: until then, stockpiling military hardware and launching covert paramilitary operations passed for a foreign policy in the Reagan administration. Nor did he expend much effort on checking how well his subordinates carried out his orders. During meetings with the National Security Council (NSC), he seldom asked questions and frequently exhibited what aides described as a "glassy look." The president never seemed tempted to use the huge military machine he had created. Convinced that "negotiating from strength" would yield results by itself, Reagan relied on his arms build-up to wring concessions from Moscow and a rollback of Soviet influence. He and his advisers probably hoped that a costly arms race would bankrupt the economically strapped Soviet Union.

Reagan appointed former Kissinger aide General Alexander Haig as secretary of state in 1981, promising him full authority to make and implement foreign policy. But when Haig submitted his agenda (which included a plan to confront Fidel Castro) and asked for a response, presidential counselor Edwin Meese informed him the agenda had been "lost." Appalled by Haig's bellicosity, Reagan and White House aides isolated him soon after his appointment. Haig later described the Reagan policy-making apparatus as a "ghost ship": one heard "the creak of the rigging and the groan of the timbers and sometimes even glimpsed the crew on deck . . . but which of the crew had the helm . . . was impossible to know for sure."

In the absence of central direction, Secretary of State Haig (replaced by George Shultz in 1982), Secretary of Defense Caspar Weinberger, CIA Director William Casey, and six successive national security advisers—Richard Allen, William Clark, Robert McFarlane, John Poindexter, Frank Carlucci, and Colin Powell—each pursued his own tack. For example, Shultz supported arms control negotiations with the Soviets following the U.S. build-up and favored a tough military approach toward minor enemies, such as the Sandinistas in Nicaragua. In contrast, Defense Secretary Caspar Weinberger opposed any deals with Moscow that might limit the immense arms build-up. He appeared to hope that the Soviets would crack in the face of a relentless arms race. At the same time, Weinberger proved reluctant to use force, even against militarily weak guerrillas in Central America. At one cabinet meeting an exasperated Shultz snapped, "If you are not willing to use force, maybe we should cut your budget." Reagan asked his contentious advisers to compromise, a solution NSC head

Robert McFarlane described as "intrinsically unworkable," given the contempt Shultz and Weinberger felt toward each other.

Throughout his first term, Reagan tried to cast the Soviet Union as evil incarnate. The Soviet Union, he remarked, "underlies all the unrest that is going on. If they weren't engaged in this game of dominoes, there wouldn't be any hot spots in the world." This simplistic analysis brushed aside the complex causes of violence in the Middle East, Central America, and Africa. Certainly the Soviets meddled in unstable areas and provided weapons to various groups. But they could not be blamed for creating the violence in Lebanon, El Salvador, and South Africa, for example.

Restoring the CIA's franchise to conduct paramilitary operations in the Third World emerged as a central feature of Reagan's foreign policy. He appointed his friend and campaign manager, William Casey, to head the agency. Casey, who had worked in the Office of Strategic Services during the Second World War, made the CIA an active player in the battle against Soviet influence in the Third World. After convincing Congress to abandon Carter-era restraints on covert operations, the CIA poured money into anti-Communist guerrilla movements in Angola, Mozambique, Afghanistan, and Central America. The administration boasted that "low-intensity warfare," its term for counterinsurgency operations, was a cheap and fairly safe way to battle Moscow for global influence. Covert warfare minimized the risk of a direct confrontation with the Soviets, while giving the administration freedom to act with minimal public knowledge or congressional oversight.

Reagan popularized an idea broached in 1980 by Georgetown University political science professor Jeane Kirkpatrick, whom he later named ambassador to the United Nations. Kirkpatrick drew a distinction between "authoritarian" and "totalitarian" regimes. The former, like the shah's Iran, might eventually evolve toward greater liberty. In contrast, the totalitarian type of government, exemplified by Communist states, was unlikely to become more democratic. Thus, she argued, the United States should support authoritarian rulers against leftist revolutionaries. Reagan employed Kirkpatrick's logic to justify cooperation with the racist, all-white South African regime and to provide military and economic aid to oppressive governments in El Salvador, Guatemala, Chile, Haiti, the Philippines, and Pakistan. Reagan reluctantly agreed to press dictators Ferdinand Marcos of the Philippines and Jean-Claude ("Baby Doc") Duvalier of Haiti into abandoning power only when the alternative to their continued rule seemed to be a left-wing revolution.

Continuing a trend that began in the Nixon years, most foreign aid went to a handful of countries, generally for military purposes. Israel and Egypt each received several billion dollars, and the Philippines,

Turkey, Pakistan, and El Salvador also received large amounts. These six nations absorbed nearly three-fourths of all U.S. foreign assistance. Overall, the United States devoted less than one-third of 1 percent of its gross national product to helping other nations, a lower percentage than that of any other industrialized democracy.

Despite its blanket hostility toward Communist governments, the administration found it possible to act flexibly. For example, Reagan had criticized Carter's extension of full diplomatic recognition to the People's Republic of China in December 1978. He hinted that he might re-establish formal relations with Taiwan, whose government he described as "an American ally." He was determined to sell Taiwan weapons, despite China's opposition. As a result, for two years after Reagan took office, Washington and Beijing criticized each other; China even threatened to downgrade relations with the United States if America sold weapons to Taiwan. But since Reagan valued China's anti-Soviet stance and needed Chinese help in supporting anti-Soviet guerrillas in Afghanistan—and because China needed Western technology and trade—the two nations compromised. In August 1982 they agreed that the United States could continue to sell weapons to Taiwan if Washington promised to reduce its sales over time. President Reagan visited China early in 1984, and he avoided criticizing the Communist government for the rest of his term.

MORE BANG FOR MORE BUCKS: THE NEW ARMS RACE

The pillar of Reagan's foreign policy was his staggering arms build-up. To achieve Reagan's announced goal of "peace through strength," the administration developed an ambitious scheme to boost annual defense spending by more than $100 billion. In 1990 dollars, the military budget soared to above $300 billion a year.

During the build-up, the Department of Defense spent lavishly to procure a variety of advanced weapons, mostly intended for use in a nuclear war with the Soviet Union. These weapons included enhanced-radiation neutron bombs and artillery designed to irradiate Soviet tanks and troops in central Europe; one hundred MX intercontinental missiles, each designed to carry ten nuclear warheads with pinpoint accuracy into Soviet territory; the B-1 intercontinental bomber, intended to replace the fleet of aging B-52s; the "stealth" bomber and fighter, a radar-resistant plane able to penetrate deep inside the Soviet Union; powerful and highly accurate D-5 missiles for mounting on Trident submarines; cruise missiles (slow but accurate pilotless drones); and Pershing II missiles that, when launched from

Europe, could hit targets inside Russia in a few minutes. In addition, the Pentagon planned to float a six-hundred-ship navy, the biggest since World War II.

These weapons systems were immensely powerful, expensive, and controversial. For example, critics charged that the MX missiles were so powerful and accurate that in a crisis the Soviets would be tempted to strike first in order to destroy the missiles before they could be launched. Consequently, American commanders would feel pressured to use the weapons in a pre-emptive strike. Thus, instead of enhancing deterrence by providing a reserve force that could retaliate against a Soviet first strike, the new weapons created a hair-trigger, "use-it-or-lose-it" atmosphere in which nervous strategists on both sides might feel impelled to strike first.

Despite the controversy, Congress appropriated most of the defense funds Reagan asked for. The Democratic party, which controlled the House but not the Senate during Reagan's first six years, mounted little opposition to the administration's arms build-up. The lack of congressional opposition stemmed in part from the fact that two decades of arms limitation talks with the Soviets had borne meager fruit. Moreover, the Democrats were suffering an intense identity crisis because of embarrassment over President Carter's ineffectiveness during the Iranian hostage crisis. And many Democrats appreciated Reagan's tough rhetoric and favored a more assertive foreign policy, even though they feared that the administration might provoke a war.

Although congressional Democrats failed to provide much opposition to the military build-up, at the grassroots level many Americans expressed anxiety over the consequences of the new arms race. In 1982 journalist Jonathan Schell, in *The Fate of the Earth*, described the effects of a single hydrogen bomb dropped on New York City; the book was a best-seller. A year later, over 100 million television viewers watched *The Day After*, a docudrama portraying the devastation of a nuclear war. During this period the grassroots Nuclear Freeze Movement organized large demonstrations calling on both superpowers to cease building new weapons of mass destruction. A 1982 congressional resolution calling for a nuclear freeze was supported by 17 senators and 128 representatives. The next year, the House of Representatives voted in favor of a nuclear weapons freeze.

On the question of arms limitation treaties, the administration adopted a contradictory policy. Reagan denounced Carter's unratified Strategic Arms Limitation Treaty, or SALT-II, claiming it locked in a Soviet advantage; he indicated that he would ignore the treaty's restrictions and build whatever long-range nuclear weapons were needed to close the "window of vulnerability" that exposed the United States to attack. But the Joint Chiefs of Staff pressed Reagan to stay within the SALT-II guidelines because they restrained the Soviets as much as the Americans, if not more. Without admitting it, the Reagan administration honored SALT-II even as it described the treaty as "fatally flawed."

Although Reagan privately chortled that in response to his build-up the Soviets were "squealing like they're sitting on a sharp nail," in public he tried to blunt criticism of his defense policy. In mid-1982 he called for renewed arms control talks with Moscow. But these negotiations—the Strategic Arms Reduction Talks (START) on long-range missiles and the Intermediate Nuclear Forces (INF) talks on medium-range weapons—quickly foundered. In December 1983, the United States began deployment of cruise and Pershing II missiles in Western Europe, in accordance with a decision made at the end of the Carter administration. The Soviet Union denounced the move and canceled further discussions—proving Moscow's bad faith, said Reagan. When Reagan offered a "zero option"—the removal of all Soviet short-range missiles targeted on Europe in exchange for an agreement not to deploy the cruise and Pershing missiles—the Soviets rejected it as an attempt to guarantee an American advantage.

During 1983, the president tried to undermine the nuclear freeze movement and enhance public support for his arms build-up through a bold approach. Beer brewer and Reagan friend Joseph Coors brought physicist Edward Teller to the White House. Teller, a long-standing advocate of nuclear armaments, claimed that a space-based, nuclear-powered "X-ray laser" could produce energy beams capable of shooting down Soviet missiles after they were launched but before they deployed their nuclear warheads. Mounted on orbiting platforms, the lasers could provide a virtual shield over America.

Reagan, who like many people wished for a way to defend civilians against missiles, embraced the idea of a high-technology "fix" that would neutralize Soviet weapons. In a March 1983 speech he presented a startling vision of a peaceful future in which the Strategic Defense Initiative (SDI), as he called it, would render nuclear weapons "impotent and obsolete." Reagan proposed a vast research and development project to perfect a space-based antimissile system along the lines suggested by Teller. Critics promptly dubbed the concept "Star Wars" after the popular fantasy movie of the time.

Soon, defense industry lobbyists launched a campaign to deploy a "space shield." Scientists and arms control advocates retorted that the project violated the existing treaty barring deployment of anti-missile systems and that it would never work as promised. Some critics judged SDI to be little more than a mask for large government subsidies to high-tech industries. Others speculated that SDI proponents hoped to force the Soviets into a costly new defense race that might bankrupt Moscow.

Whatever the motivations may have been, presidents Reagan and Bush spent nearly $20 billion on SDI development over the next nine years. Although the much-touted X-ray laser proved unworkable, the Pentagon agency in charge of the program routinely faked test data to make it appear that a workable system could soon be deployed. Long after the fact, aides to Reagan and Bush justified this deception on the grounds that it intimidated the Soviets into accepting American arms control demands. More likely, the point was to mislead congressional auditors and keep money flowing to defense contractors. By 1993, the Pentagon quietly had shelved most SDI research.

Although the Soviet government denounced Reagan as a warmonger, during the first half of the 1980s it mounted no effective response to American initiatives. The old and ailing Leonid Brezhnev, in power since 1964, presided over a lethargic and corrupt administration during his last years in power. His death in 1982 left his colleagues groping for a successor. The Communist oligarchy selected Yuri Andropov, the government's security chief, as party general secretary. Andropov was considered something of a reformer, but he suffered from kidney disease and spent most of his brief term in office on dialysis. Following his death in 1984, party elders tapped Konstantin Chernenko, a lackluster timeserver, as leader. Chernenko, ill with emphysema, lived only one year thereafter. When asked why he refused to convene a summit with his Soviet counterpart, Reagan quipped, "They keep dying on me." Only in 1985, when the fifty-four-year-old Mikhail Gorbachev emerged as general secretary of the Communist Party, did the Soviet Union have an effective leader.

In the interim, two events gave Reagan opportunities to sharpen his anti-Communist rhetoric. In December 1981, as the Solidarity labor movement threatened to topple Poland's Communist government, Moscow pressured the Polish army to impose martial law. Reagan denounced Moscow for unleashing the "forces of tyranny" against its neighbor. He urged Americans to place "candles of freedom" in their windows in support of the Poles; many Americans did. The president also provided Solidarity with secret financial aid that sustained it in the face of repression. Two years later, in September 1983, a tragic Soviet error outraged Americans even more. A series of navigational mistakes had led Korean Air Lines Flight 007 to stray far off course en route from Alaska to Seoul. After flying for some distance over Soviet territory that included a secret missile test site, the 747 airliner was attacked by a Soviet fighter pilot. All 269 people on board were killed, including a member of Congress.

Although American intelligence intercepts revealed that the Soviets really did think the passenger plane was on a spy mission and had shot at it more out of reflex than premeditation, Reagan immediately branded the event a "crime against humanity" and an "act of barbarism." This version of the incident better justified Reagan's anti-Soviet stance and prompted Congress to spend more money on weapons.

The administration's emotional rhetoric, coupled with the inability of Moscow's doddering leadership to explain its actions, buoyed Reagan's public support and assured continued congressional funding for the administration's defense programs. By this time the Pentagon had so much money to spend that defense contractors could not produce enough ships, tanks, planes, and missiles to fill the orders. Despite a 50 percent increase in procurement spending, factories did not produce 50 percent more tanks, planes, and ships. In many cases, the flood of money caused costs to soar, quality to decline, and corruption to flourish. Many complex weapons, rushed into production with inadequate testing, failed to meet specifications.

The fact that so few people, in or out of government, understood the technical aspects of weapons systems inhibited debate. Often the press and the public focused on marginal details rather than the overall logic of the buying spree. For example, the B-1 and B-2 bombers cost at least $200 million and $1 billion, respectively, per plane; but due to flaws they remained grounded most of the time. Ordinary citizens were not in a position to know if the costs were fair or exorbitant or if lapses in quality were excusable. Consequently, public anger focused on minutiae—on reports that the Pentagon had paid $500 apiece for the toilet seats and hammers carried on these aircraft, for example. Ordinary Americans knew what a toilet seat or hammer cost at their corner hardware store and concluded the taxpayers had been bilked. But who felt knowledgeable enough to assert how much the air force should pay for a stealth bomber?

At the end of the Reagan administration, the Justice Department indicted several Defense Department officials and contractors for illegal actions. The charges included faking quality-control tests and selling competitors' data to certain companies bidding on contracts. Congress passed new procurement regulations in 1988 and stiffened restrictions on Pentagon officials' taking defense-industry jobs immediately after leaving government service. By then, over $2 trillion had been spent on military procurement, much of it for questionable products.

AMERICA AND THE MIDDLE EAST

As it confronted the Soviet Union with a massive arms build-up, the Reagan administration also tried to address some of the thornier problems of the Middle East. Like his predecessors, President Reagan found it difficult to impose American solutions. The Arab-Israeli conflict continued to resist peaceful settlement. Prolonged strife in

Lebanon and Afghanistan remained unresolved, and a bloody war between Iran and Iraq set the stage for further Persian Gulf problems in the 1990s. Making these issues more urgent was the rise in terrorist attacks around the world, many of them against American targets.

By the early 1980s, various armed religious and political factions within Lebanon were embroiled in civil conflict. At the same time, Israel was bombing areas in Lebanon controlled by the Palestine Liberation Organization (PLO), the group responsible for many guerrilla and terrorist attacks on Israeli targets. The PLO was the largest of the political organizations that claimed to represent the Palestinians, who had been displaced from their homeland by the creation of the Israeli state following World War II.

In June 1982, Secretary of State Alexander Haig urged Israel to invade Lebanon in order to destroy the PLO's forces. But when Israel acted on this advice, Haig's colleague, National Security Adviser William P. Clark, contacted PLO representatives in an effort to negotiate a compromise. Haig, already on bad terms with Reagan's inner circle, quit in a huff. The president then appointed George P. Shultz to head the State Department, and Shultz labored mightily to bring some semblance of order to American Middle East policy.

In August, as Israeli forces surrounded Beirut, the United States arranged for the evacuation of the PLO forces it had previously sought to eradicate. Shultz and his aides urged Israel to allow the PLO to establish a new homeland in the West Bank (on the west bank of the Jordan River) in return for guarantees of peace with the Jewish state. To Shultz's dismay, neither Israel nor the Palestinians agreed. Meanwhile, the assassination of Christian Lebanese leader Bashir Gemayel on September 14 sparked Christian massacres of Palestinians living in refugee camps around Beirut.

As the normally chaotic Lebanese political scene approached complete anarchy, the United States, France, and Italy sent peace-keeping forces to Beirut, hoping to shore up Christian Lebanese troops against Muslim forces consisting of Druse and Shiite militias and troops from the Syrian army. The Druse, members of a Syrian and Lebanese Islamic sect that incorporates some aspects of Christianity into their beliefs, had teamed up with members of the Shiite sect, Islam's second-largest denomination (which was frequently in conflict with the Sunni majority) to oppose the Christians in Lebanon and the Jews in Israel. Each of these forces dominated parts of the fragile country. But the peace-keeping mission sparked even greater animosity, as the Lebanese Muslims bitterly resented Western aid to the Christian minority. On April 18, 1983, a suicide squad attacked the American embassy in Beirut, killing 63 people.

Shortly thereafter, American naval ships off Lebanon began shelling Muslim forces. This retaliation, which was interpreted as further

The scene after a terrorist bombing leveled part of the American embassy in Beirut, killing sixty-three people in April 1983. *AP/Wide World Photos.*

pro-Christian intervention, provoked a desperate act of revenge. On October 23 an Islamic terrorist drove a truck filled with explosives into a U.S. Marine barracks near Beirut's airport, killing 241 Marines. French troops were attacked simultaneously.

Although President Reagan offered a moving tribute to the slaughtered young men, he could not explain what they had died for. In his 1984 State of the Union address, he declared that keeping the Marines in Lebanon was "central to our credibility on a global scale." But two weeks later, without explanation, the president ordered American troops out of Beirut, and the warring Lebanese factions resumed their communal slaughter.

Like the conflict in Lebanon, the problem of the Palestinians—who lived either under Israeli occupation or in refugee camps—defied an American solution. Beginning in late 1987, Palestinians living in territory Israel had occupied since 1967 began an *intifadah,* or civilian uprising against Israeli authorities. Israeli troops and police responded harshly, killing some seven hundred Palestinians over the next three years.

In 1988, PLO leader Yasir Arafat declared that his organization would accept Israel's right to exist—an important concession that prompted Washington to begin diplomatic contacts with the PLO. However, not until 1994 did Israeli and Palestinian officials reach even a tentative agreement on terms for partial self-government in areas such as the West Bank and Gaza Strip, which Israel had occupied since 1967. Even then, progress toward settling the Palestinian refugee issue and the Arab-Israeli conflict as a whole proved extremely difficult.

The Iranian hostage crisis during the Carter administration had focused public attention on the vulnerability of Westerners abroad, especially in the Middle East. Throughout the 1980s, incidents of international hostage-taking and terrorism were on the rise, and Americans were among the favorite targets. The risk affected not only diplomats and military personnel, but also businesspeople and other civilians.

Terrorism, some observers noted, was the atomic bomb of the weak; in the 1980s it became the weapon of choice for many frustrated Third World groups, especially those from the Middle East. In reality, the various kidnappings, aircraft and ship hijackings, and bombings were marginal acts in the world arena. On average during the 1980s, more American civilians were killed each year by lightning while playing golf than by terrorist acts. Yet the intense media coverage and the responses of Presidents Carter and Reagan made terrorism a major issue.

The Reagan administration focused much of its antiterrorist sentiment on Libya's demagogic strongman, Muammar Qaddafi. Flush with cash from the sale of oil, Qaddafi bought Soviet military hardware and bankrolled a number of terrorist groups operating in the Middle East and Europe. The American president and State Department, as well as the mass media, blamed him for causing much of the violence in the Middle East and threatening the lives of Americans abroad. The Libyan leader's flamboyant, aggressive style and his fondness for insulting American leaders outraged President Reagan.

Eager—as Secretary of State Shultz phrased it—to put Qaddafi "back in his box," Washington deployed a large naval flotilla in the Gulf of Sidra, on Libya's northern coast. Qaddafi, who claimed the gulf as territorial waters, clashed several times with the Americans as he dared them to cross the "line of death." U.S. and Libyan jets fought air duels over the gulf in 1981 and again in 1988, with the loss of several Libyan planes.

In April 1986, Libyan agents were implicated in the bombing of a Berlin nightclub frequented by American soldiers. Reagan, calling Qaddafi the "mad dog of the Middle East," sent planes to attack Tripoli. One of the targets was Qaddafi's compound. Although the

Libyan leader escaped injury in the raid, one of his infant daughters was killed. Thereafter, Qaddafi remained a bitter critic of the United States but tempered his activities against American allies and interests. The sharp decline of oil prices after 1986 and Qaddafi's continued feuding with his North African neighbors probably had more of a restraining effect on him than the threat of another American air raid.

A bloody nine-year war between Iraq and Iran, fought for regional influence and control of deep-water ports, took the lives of nearly 2 million people between 1980 and 1988. Washington distrusted both the virulent nationalism of Iraqi leader Saddam Hussein and the Islamic fundamentalism of Iran's Ayatollah Khomeini. A victory by either side, American experts feared, would lead one of the two countries to dominate the oil-rich Middle East. To prevent this, Washington played a balancing act, providing secret military aid and intelligence to whichever side appeared to be losing at the time. From 1981 to 1986, this generally meant helping Iran, while after 1986 Washington often assisted Iraq. The United States attempted to coordinate this policy with Israel. But Israel, which feared the nearby threat of Iraq and harbored concern for the safety of several thousand Iranian Jews, more consistently aided Iran.

When Washington began to openly aid the Iraqis in 1987, Iran responded by attacking Western tankers carrying Iraqi oil in the Persian Gulf. Reagan ordered the navy to escort ships carrying petroleum, a policy that resulted in several small clashes with the Iranians. The bloodiest incidents involved cases of mistaken identity. In May 1987 an Iraqi pilot, mistaking the U.S. destroyer *Stark* for an Iranian ship, blasted it with a missile, killing thirty-seven sailors. Washington accepted an apology. A year later, the captain of the USS *Vincennes*, after mistaking a radar blip for an air attack, shot down an Iranian passenger plane, killing 290 civilians. This incident may have prompted Iran to sponsor the December 1988 bombing of a Pan Am flight over Scotland, which killed several hundred people.

Finally exhausted by their vast bloodletting, Iran and Iraq signed a cease-fire in August 1988, but they maintained their territorial claims. During the conflict, Iraq had developed and used poison gas against Iran and had pushed ahead with work on an atomic bomb. Despite these threats, the Reagan and Bush administrations considered Iraq a useful counterforce to Iran and quietly provided financial support to Saddam Hussein. The expansion of Iraqi power had grave consequences, for it led to Iraq's later invasion of Kuwait and the Persian Gulf War of 1991.

When Soviet forces invaded Afghanistan in December 1979, they and their puppet government began a brutal slaughter of Afghanistan's anti-Communist guerrillas, or *mujahidin*. Many of the guerrillas were Islamic fundamentalists who admired the Ayatollah Khomeini's regime in Iran. Despite this fact, the Reagan administration supported their resistance to Soviet domination. The CIA provided military and economic assistance to the *mujahidin,* using neighboring Pakistan (whose own military despots were also developing an atomic bomb) as a base of operations. Millions of Afghans fled the country, most of them resettling in Pakistan.

But the fiercely motivated guerrillas and rugged terrain proved formidable opponents for the Soviet invaders. Once the CIA made shoulder-fired antiaircraft missiles available to them, the *mujahidin* neutralized the Soviet air advantage. American officials described the struggle as the Soviets' Vietnam, a strange analogy for this administration to make in light of Reagan's customary reference to American intervention in Vietnam as a "noble cause."

Nearly a decade after the war began, Moscow's new leader, Mikhail Gorbachev, decided to cut his mounting losses. In 1988 he blamed the costly and unpopular invasion on his dead predecessors and ordered Soviet forces out of Afghanistan. Although the local Communist regime soon collapsed, peace remained elusive. The *mujahidin* quickly divided into rival factions and carved the country into spheres of influence. By 1995, almost two decades of war had left Afghanistan a devastated land.

Ironically, the United States suffered from the "success" of its anti-Soviet strategy. As the 1990s began, some of the Afghan guerrillas took their American-supplied weapons and became soldiers of fortune against "enemies of Islam." Their targets included the Egyptian government, moderate Arab regimes, and New York's World Trade Center, which was bombed in 1993.

ADVENTURES SOUTH OF THE BORDER

Throughout the twentieth century, the United States has intervened frequently in the affairs of its neighbors in Central America and the Caribbean. Derisively called "banana republics," these poor nations were often dominated by a handful of wealthy landowners linked to American corporations—and disciplined by American troops when they strayed from the fold. After the Second World War, the CIA usually handled matters in the region, thereby avoiding the direct use of American troops. The CIA-backed invasions in Guatemala in 1954 and Cuba in 1961, for example. President Johnson did send Marines and army forces to the Dominican Republic in 1965, however, when a leftist politician seemed poised to take power.

The Reagan administration, obsessed by what it perceived as a Communist threat to the Western Hemisphere and hoping to erase the memory of Vietnam with some old-fashioned muscle-flexing, revived the tradition of American military intervention in the region. In the Reagan years the United States invaded one country (Grenada), financed civil wars in two (El Salvador and Nicaragua), and used economic pressure in an effort to topple the government in another (Panama).

The Reagan administration's policy toward Central America often seemed a throwback to the early years of the Cold War. State Department officials warned of a "Moscow-Havana axis," asserting that Cuban agents under the tutelage of the Soviet Union could spread revolution throughout the unstable region. By creating several Cuba-like regimes from Panama to Mexico, officials warned, the Soviet Union would gain control of vital sea lanes and pose a military and economic threat to the United States. Reagan also warned that the consequent invasion of refugees from Central America would destabilize American society.

The administration's critics, such as Connecticut Democratic senator Christopher Dodd, complained that Reagan and his advisers knew "as much about Central America in 1983 as we knew about Indochina in 1963." A former Peace Corps volunteer in Latin America, Dodd believed that "if Central America were not racked with poverty, there would be no revolution." Nevertheless, the administration tried to win public backing by assembling a commission on Central America headed by Henry Kissinger, the former secretary of state. The commission's 1984 report tried, without success, to please all sides. It agreed that many of the region's social and economic problems were rooted in poverty and that Soviet meddling could not be blamed for everything. Although calling for more economic aid, the report stressed the importance of providing much greater military aid to the army in El Salvador and the anti-Communist guerrillas in Nicaragua.

The Reagan administration failed to generate much enthusiasm for its policies in Central America. For a variety of reasons, few members of Congress or ordinary Americans believed that the future of the Free World depended on what regime held power in Managua or Tegucigalpa. Opinion polls taken throughout the 1980s revealed that three-fourths of the public did not know or care what groups the United States favored or opposed in the region. A large majority of respondents opposed sending any troops to Central America, even to stop Communist takeovers.

Unable to build congressional or popular support for direct intervention, the Reagan administration generally relied on a combination of military aid and covert warfare in Central America. For example, between 1981 and 1988, Washington spent $4 billion to $5 billion on military and economic aid to El Salvador. A terribly poor country in which 2 percent of the people controlled nearly all the wealth,

El Salvador had been racked by rural rebellion since the 1920s. Although the country had been nominally ruled since 1979 by a moderate reformer, Christian Democrat José Napoleon Duarte, El Salvador's right-wing military held the real power.

Even with massive American aid, the Salvadoran military could not rout the leftist rebels from their rural and urban bases. The military squandered much of the money and used the arms to wage a fierce campaign of repression against civilians suspected of sympathizing with the rebels or agitating for social change. Army death squads killed as many as seventy thousand peasants, teachers, union organizers, and church workers. Robert D'Aubuisson, a former army officer and the founder of the right-wing ARENA party, was widely judged responsible for this terrorism. Some U.S. politicians, like North Carolina Republican senator Jesse Helms, praised D'Aubuisson, even after his assassins had killed several American church workers and union organizers. Even when the Reagan administration learned that Salvadoran military units trained by Americans had massacred hundreds of unarmed villagers in contested areas, Washington kept the information secret and assailed the integrity of American journalists who reported on the atrocities.

Most Americans ignored developments in Central America, and only a relatively small number voiced disgust at these actions. Congress had only a limited will to defy an otherwise popular president. It placed a cap on the number of American military personnel stationed in El Salvador and required that the president periodically certify that "progress" had occurred in the field of human rights. As long as Reagan did so, Congress approved funds for military and economic aid and asked few questions.

After eight years of bloodshed, Duarte's government had neither defeated the guerrillas nor carried out promised reforms. In 1988 Duarte and his followers lost an election to the ultra-right-wing ARENA party. The war—and the civilian deaths—continued until 1992, when both sides appeared to have worn themselves out. Following a truce, the former guerrillas participated in new elections. International observers questioned the fairness of the vote, which ARENA won, but leftists accepted the outcome. Large-scale killing ceased, although El Salvador remained impoverished and violent.

In contrast to its prolonged and less-than-successful intervention in El Salvador's affairs, the Reagan administration achieved a quick victory with an overt military action in Grenada. A tiny Caribbean island and former British colony, Grenada had been ruled by a Marxist, Maurice Bishop, since 1979. Although the Reagan administration had suspended economic aid to Bishop's government in the early 1980s, Grenada seemed too insignificant to bother with before 1983. Nutmeg, its main commercial export, was important only for a few holiday recipes, such as egg nog. A few U.S. tourists visited the island, but the main American presence consisted of five hundred medical students enrolled in St. George's University School of Medicine. A contingent of armed Cuban construction workers also labored on the island, building an airport that Prime Minister Bishop called a project to boost tourism but Washington labeled a potential Cuban or Soviet air base.

On October 12, 1983, a militant faction of the Marxist New Jewel Movement, led by General Hudson Austin, overthrew Bishop, who had recently softened his anti-Yankee rhetoric. Austin murdered his rival, imposed martial law, and announced a strict curfew. Still, the coup did not seem to affect American interests.

The situation changed abruptly on October 23 with an unrelated incident in another part of the world: the terrorist attack on the Marine barracks in Beirut. Unable to identify the perpetrators or use the vast American military machine to exact revenge, Reagan and his staff felt intense frustration. Seemingly as an afterthought amid the confusion over Beirut, the president's advisers remembered the medical students in Grenada. Although none had been harmed or were known to face danger, administration officials considered their fate sufficiently in doubt to warrant military intervention. Possibly they believed that the rescue of potential American hostages might divert attention from the carnage in Beirut. After consulting with the leaders of a few tiny Caribbean islands that Washington had otherwise ignored, on October 25 Reagan ordered thousands of Marines and army troops to storm ashore and liberate Grenada from what he called a "brutal gang of thugs."

The invasion experienced many logistical problems but resulted in only a handful of American and a few dozen Grenadian casualties. Even though the rescue was more like a comic opera than a war, the Pentagon nevertheless distributed an unprecedented eight thousand medals to the invading force.

Many islanders welcomed the Americans as saviors who might bring peace and prosperity to their tormented island. Free elections soon restored representative government, but Washington rapidly lost interest and failed to fulfill its promises to fund development programs. Grenada returned to its normal poverty and obscurity, searching for a benefactor to complete its airport.

Because of news blackouts, the public learned little about the invasion snafus. Most citizens expressed joy that the United States had "won one for a change." Television pictures of returning medical students falling to their knees and kissing American soil diverted attention from the school director's insistence that the students had never been in danger. In 1984, President Reagan's campaign staff used footage of the grateful medical students to devastating effect in the campaign against Democratic nominee Walter Mondale, who had initially condemned the invasion as a violation of international law.

The celebration of victory in Grenada reflected a wave of jingoism—boisterous nationalism—in the United States that Ronald Reagan both stimulated and exploited. Between 1981 and 1988 a host of immensely popular adventure films and novels portrayed new, all-American heroes who refought and won the war in Vietnam, defeated Soviet troops, and crushed Third World upstarts.

In his seemingly endless series of *Rocky* and *Rambo* films, actor-director Sylvester Stallone beat Russian and North Vietnamese opponents to a bloody pulp. Other films featured similarly simple-minded themes. Martial arts champion Chuck Norris kick-boxed his way through Vietnam, like Stallone, to rescue American prisoners. In the film *Top Gun*, gallant American fliers blasted Libyan and Soviet pilots out of the sky. Tom Clancy's best-selling novel *The Hunt for Red October* portrayed an American victory over Soviet naval forces. In several of these films and novels, the macho hero confronted his superior, demanding to know whether the good guys would be allowed to win this time.

Americans did win big in the 1984 Olympics, held in Los Angeles. In some ways these games exhibited the most overt nationalism since Hitler hosted the 1936 Berlin Olympiad. With the Soviet bloc boycotting the contest, as the United States had done four years earlier, American athletes triumphed in a large number of events. Boisterous crowds waved banners proclaiming "We're Number 1" and chanted "U.S.A., U.S.A." American television networks skipped victory ceremonies in which other countries took the top honors and often declined to broadcast the national anthems of other teams. Riding this wave of patriotism, several television and radio stations changed their call letters to include the sequence USA. The Chrysler Corporation ran ads that paraphrased the president's 1984 re-election slogan, "America Is Back."

Ronald Reagan's landslide victory over Walter Mondale in November 1984 prompted House Speaker Tip O'Neill to tell the president, "In my fifty years in public life, I've never seen a man more popular than you with the American people." During the campaign, polling organizations detected some voter anxiety over Reagan's bellicose rhetoric and his push for ever greater defense spending. To allay these fears, the president's aides had him tone down his hard line toward the Soviet Union and Central America. After his victory, Reagan struck a positive note, declaring that in his second term he would push arms control. "I have no more important goal," he stated, than "reducing and ultimately eliminating nuclear weapons." When National Security Adviser Robert McFarlane asked him to select a couple of foreign policy goals to stress from a long list that included such complicated issues as arms control, the Arab-Israeli conflict, and proxy wars in the Third World, Reagan beamed, "Let's do them all!"

THE IRAN-CONTRA AFFAIR

During Reagan's eight years as president, nothing tarnished his reputation so greatly nor called into question his judgment so seriously as his decision to illegally sell weapons to Iran as part of a scheme to ransom hostages and fund anti-Communist guerrillas in Central America. As the moving force behind a complicated scheme that both violated the law and defied common sense, Reagan came close to destroying his own administration.

In 1980, presidential candidate Reagan denounced Jimmy Carter for abandoning a long-time American client in Central America, Nicaraguan dictator Anastasio Somoza, whose family had ruled Nicaragua as a personal fiefdom since the 1920s. In 1979, Somoza was overthrown by a group of Marxist rebels known as the Sandinistas. Upon taking office, Reagan accused the Sandinista leadership of turning Nicaragua into a "Soviet alley on the American mainland," and a "safe house and command post for . . . international terror." In one especially vivid speech, he evoked an image of Sandinista troops driving a convoy of armed pickup trucks into Harlingen, Texas, a small town on the Mexican border. Cartoonist Garry Trudeau captured the absurdity of this image in a "Doonesebury" strip that pictured a group of "good ol' boys" from Harlingen gazing through the sights of their hunting rifles, prepared to repulse an invasion.

In truth, the Sandinistas hated the United States for its long support of the Somoza dictatorship. They solicited Soviet aid, socialized parts of the economy, and broke their promise to restore full democracy in Nicaragua. But Sandinista human rights abuses paled before the gory record of neighboring El Salvador and Guatemala—regimes Reagan strongly supported. Moreover, since fewer people lived in all of Nicaragua than in some neighborhoods of Mexico City, talk of a grave Sandinista threat to the Western Hemisphere was grossly exaggerated.

In 1981, Reagan ordered CIA director William Casey to offer support to an anti-Sandinista force, the *contra-revolucionarios,* among Nicaraguan exiles. At first the CIA hired Argentine military officers to train the guerrillas. But Argentinean support ended in 1982, when Great Britain and Argentina fought a brief war over control of the Falkland Islands, a bleak British colony in the South Atlantic that was claimed by Argentina. Piqued at Washington's support for Britain, the Argentines quit training the exiles and left it to the CIA to feed and equip them.

The contras, as they were called in the United States—(or "freedom fighters," as Reagan called them)—survived almost entirely on American military and economic aid. By 1985 their ranks had swelled to between ten and twenty thousand men. Some contra political leaders were genuine democrats who had opposed Somoza, but most of the military commanders—who held the real power in the movement—were veterans of Somoza's army.

When members of Congress raised questions about covert operations in Nicaragua, CIA director Casey insisted that the CIA was not utilizing the contras to overthrow the Sandinista regime, but was merely helping them block Sandinista military aid to rebels in El Salvador. Still, Congress grew restive when it became known that the contras had killed thousands of civilians in an effort to seize power within Nicaragua. Representative Edward P. Boland, a Democrat from Massachusetts, sponsored a resolution in 1982 that capped CIA aid to the contras at $24 million and required that none of the funds be used to topple the Nicaraguan government.

To get around this and an even stricter congressional prohibition against aid to the contras, enacted in October 1984, high-level officials in the CIA, the State Department, and the NSC induced several foreign governments to aid the guerrillas in return for American goodwill or repayment through indirect means. To ensure the cooperation of Panama and Honduras in letting arms through to the contras, American officials ignored the fact that men like Panamanian strongman Manuel Noriega were deeply involved in the shipment of cocaine and other drugs to the United States.

Despite the congressional ban on CIA efforts to topple the Sandinistas, CIA director Casey and Lieutenant Colonel Oliver North, an NSC staffer, established a secret fund-raising operation to gather money for the contras. Gradually, this dubious policy in Central America overlapped with even more questionable actions in the Middle East.

In June 1985, Lebanese Shiite terrorists hijacked a TWA flight in Athens, flew it to Lebanon, executed a navy enlisted man on board, and threatened to kill twenty-nine other American passengers unless Israel released seven hundred Lebanese prisoners from its jails. Reagan denounced this extortion but secretly urged the Israelis to comply. They did, winning freedom for the passengers.

Shortly after the TWA incident, Reagan delivered a speech in which he proclaimed that America would never make concessions to terrorists. He called Iran and Libya "outlaw states . . . run by the strangest collection of misfits, Looney Tunes, and squalid criminals since the advent of the Third Reich." Soon, however, the president was approving deals directly with the "Looney Tunes."

Amidst the chaos in Lebanon, Shiite militias linked to Iran had kidnapped several American citizens living in Beirut. Ronald Reagan was deeply moved by the plight of kidnapped Americans. When the grieving families of seven American citizens held hostage in Lebanon pleaded with him to win their loved ones' release, he allowed his natural sympathy for them to supersede the national interest. Unlike the American embassy staff seized in Iran in 1979, these captives were—with the exception of CIA agent William Buckley—private citizens who had continued living in Beirut despite pleas from the State Department to leave. Nevertheless, Reagan wanted everything possible done to win their freedom.

In an attempt to win the hostages' release, the Reagan administration became involved with Iran in July 1985, when an Israeli go-between introduced Iranian businessman Manucher Ghorbanifar to National Security Adviser Robert McFarlane. Ever since the Iranian revolution there had been an American embargo on arms sales to Iran (although Washington had been informally assisting Iran's war against Iraq ever since 1981 by permitting Iran to buy military replacement parts from U.S. allies). Ghorbanifar claimed to represent a "moderate" faction in Iran that wanted to improve relations with Washington, especially after the "imminent" death of the Ayatollah Khomeini. These Iranians asked that Reagan prove his interest in improving relations with Iran by selling them antitank missiles for use against Iraq. In return, they would lobby to free at least four American hostages held in Beirut by pro-Iranian Lebanese.

Ghorbanifar, described in an earlier CIA report as a "con man," won the full trust of Reagan and his NSC staff. During the summer of 1985 the president approved selling Iran one hundred TOW antitank missiles, primarily with the goal of freeing hostages. At the time, U.S. law barred arms sales to Iran because of its support of terrorism. The ban could be overridden only if the president signed a waiver and informed Congress. But Reagan did not want any record of his dealings. To distance himself from the illegal actions, he arranged for Israel to sell American missiles from its stockpile to Iran, which the United States then replaced.

Over the next six months, North and NSC chief McFarlane arranged the sale of several thousand anti-tank and anti-aircraft missiles to Iran. Despite the justification of seeking improved ties with Iranian "moderates," these were primarily arms-for-hostage deals. Yet, the pro-Iranian Lebanese released only one American, Reverend Benjamin Weir, in return. Some of Reagan's advisers, such as Secretary of State Shultz and Defense Secretary Weinberger, opposed the entire scheme. But the president responded by excluding them from the operation and encouraging North and McFarlane to keep trying.

By using profits from weapons sales to Iran, North generated substantial funds for the anti-Communist contras without going to Congress. In his view, the president's aides could legitimately use arms sales profits to aid the contras because the Boland Amendment

Oliver North

Called by one colleague "the world's most powerful lieutenant colonel," Oliver North elicited strong reactions from all who met him. A decorated Vietnam veteran, North joined the staff of the National Security Council early in the Reagan administration on the recommendation of his friend and fellow Marine, National Security Adviser Robert Mc-Farlane. His devotion to anti-terrorist, anti-Communist actions impressed his superiors. Other Reagan aides, including Michael Deaver and Peggy Noonan, saw him differently. Noonan described North as a "true believer" who had the "sunny, undimmed confidence of a man who lacks insight into his own weakness." Deaver placed the colonel's name on a list of persons not allowed to have a private audience with the president, lest they hatch some risky scheme.

North worked closely with the CIA and the State Department during 1985 and 1986 to raise money for the contras. To get around the ban on using public funds to support them, he solicited money from friendly foreign governments and wealthy American conservatives. North perfected a fund-raising pitch that included a slide show with pictures of contras in heroic poses and military hardware with hefty price tags. Especially generous donors, such as Nelson Bunker Hunt and Joseph Coors, received personal thanks from the president. Grateful contras placed a Coors beer logo on one of their military aircraft.

When given responsibility for arranging the ransom of Americans held hostage in Beirut, North conceived what he called "a neat idea." He would overcharge Iran for U.S. missiles drawn from Israeli stockpiles and use the profits to support the rebels in Nicaragua. He jested that the Ayatollah had made a "*contra*bution." Despite several arms sales and a personal trip to Iran in May 1986, North's scheme won the release of only three hostages, who were quickly replaced by new kidnapping victims. Although the "neat idea" generated about $20 million, the contras received only a small portion. North and his colleagues used a substantial amount of this money for pet projects and personal expenses.

In the fall of 1986, North hoped to arrange a mass hostage release to bolster Republican candidates in the November congressional election. Instead, the arms-for-hostages, aid-to-the-contras scheme fell apart. President Reagan fired North, after telling him his life would "make a great movie." As probes into NSC activities began, the colonel led efforts to destroy evidence and pin responsibility on others. When called before a Congressional committee in the summer of 1987 to explain his actions, he pounded the table, thrust out his medal-bedecked chest, and declared that he and the president had had a responsibility to defend the national security against the Communist threat and congressional stupidity. North boasted that he was prepared to "take a spear in the chest" to protect the president—and went on to say that Reagan had

approved everything he did. Impressed by his bravado, a large portion of the TV audience succumbed to what journalists described as "Olliemania."

Although he was convicted of lying to Congress, a federal appeals court overturned North's conviction in 1991. While the facts of his lawbreaking and perjury were not in dispute, the court held that some of the evidence in his trial might have been unfairly influenced by the testimony of witnesses granted immunity from prosecution during the 1987 congressional hearings.

As a private citizen, North became a wealthy man by writing a self-serving memoir, speaking frequently to conservative religious groups, and operating a business selling bullet-proof vests advertised as "God's armor."

In 1994 North captured the Republican nomination for the Senate in Virginia and spent at least $20 million in an unsuccessful bid to unseat incumbent Democrat Charles Robb. Eager to remain a public figure, the next year North followed in the footsteps of his friends and conservative spielmeisters Rush Limbaugh and Watergate burglar G. Gordon Liddy, starting his own radio talk show in Washington, D. C. "You're tuned to true North," he breezily told callers, who chatted with him about the moral squalor of contemporary America. "The colonel," as his call-in audience referred to him, vowed to reenter the political arena. ■

applied only to money appropriated by Congress. This ignored the fact that North's scheme raised funds by selling government property—missiles—at a profit. Federal law required that such profits be returned to the treasury and only be spent on programs approved by Congress. While President Reagan later claimed to know nothing about the diversion of funds, North and his superiors later insisted that the president had approved all their actions.

In February 1986 North arranged the sale of one thousand TOW missiles, netting as much as $10 million for the contra weapons fund. No more hostages were released—in fact, two more Americans were kidnapped in Beirut, and the Iranians demanded more and better weapons as well as intelligence on Iraq. Incredibly, the president approved more arms sales, and again no hostages were received in return. An exasperated North and McFarlane flew to Iran in May 1986. They proposed a trade of all remaining hostages in return for a large weapons shipment, but the Iranians balked. Although the Iranians were eager for more American military equipment, they refused to guarantee the simultaneous freeing of all Americans held in Beirut.

Despite this setback, North continued to wheel-and-deal during the summer and fall of 1986. In July one hostage, Father Lawrence Jenco, was released from captivity in Beirut, but he was promptly replaced by a new victim. An additional arms shipment led to the release of hostage David Jacobsen on November 2. But instead of the hoped-for political boost on the eve of mid-term congressional elections, the White House faced a crisis.

The bizarre scheme began to unravel on October 5, 1986, when Sandinista gunners shot down a plane ferrying weapons to the contras. One crew member, Eugene Hasenfus, survived the crash and confessed to being part of a secret American aid program.

The Iranian connection came to light at the beginning of November—three days before the midterm congressional elections—when *Al Shiraa*, an obscure Lebanese magazine, printed an account of the arms-for-hostages deal. Iranian officials confirmed the story and added that the alleged moderates North had dealt with were actually agents of the Ayatollah Khomeini. Although the revelations had not yet become a major scandal, they perhaps helped the Democrats recapture the Senate in the November 4 election.

President Reagan, North, Poindexter, and Casey rushed to cover up the scandal by lying to Congress and the press about the arms sales and denying any links to operations in Central America. Attorney General Meese mounted a half-hearted investigation, and he virtually encouraged North and his aides to destroy evidence. Nevertheless, in late November Meese announced that he had uncovered documents linking the arms sales to Iran to the diversion of between $10 million and $20 million to the contras. In the hours before Meese went public, Poindexter, North, and NSC secretary Fawn Hall held a "shredding party," destroying some five thousand incriminating documents. When the shredding machine jammed, Hall smuggled sensitive papers out of the building in her boots and underwear. Enough material survived—some of it in back-up files on the main NSC computer—to raise grave concerns about the administration's foreign policy.

As the Iran-contra scandal unfolded, President Reagan insisted he knew nothing about any arms-for-hostages deal or the diversion of profits to the contras. By a wide margin, however, the public no longer believed him. Reagan's overall approval rating plummeted to below 50 percent. Anxious to shift responsibility for the fiasco, he tried to blame the Israelis, who had only acted as middlemen at Reagan's request. When that failed, the president telephoned North, called him a "national hero," and fired him and Poindexter.

Once Attorney General Meese revealed that the NSC staff had sold arms to Iran, diverted millions of dollars to the contras, and lied to Congress, the president was forced to name a special review board to look into the affair. The three-member board was chaired by a former senator from Texas, John Tower. The Tower Commission report in February 1987 began to flesh out the details, showing how the arms deal had devolved into a ransom scheme designed, in part, to raise illegal funds for the contras. The president's action, the group concluded, "ran directly counter" to his public promise to punish terrorism. The report portrayed Reagan as remote, disengaged, uninformed, and easily manipulated.

In a speech delivered on March 4, 1987, the president sidestepped criticism of the affair, humbly accepting the conclusions of the Tower report but denying responsibility. The facts might suggest that he had approved ransom payments, he said, but in his heart he never meant to trade arms for hostages. He also deflected some of the blame by firing Chief of Staff Donald Regan the week the report came out. Although Regan was not a major player in the scandal, firing him gave the appearance of cleaning house.

Following the release of the Tower Commission report, congressional committees began investigating the money trail, trying to discover how the profits were diverted to the contras, who authorized the policy, and who profited from it. Much of the testimony during the summer of 1987 focused on the activities of Oliver North. The telegenic officer dominated the hearings with a vigorous defense of his actions and his president. He chided Congress for ignoring the Sandinista threat and declared that he and Reagan had a moral responsibility to protect national security, even if they had to break the law to do it.

The public inquiry suffered from numerous shortcomings. Congress conducted the hearings at a rapid pace, and administration stonewalling blocked access to crucial documents. North, Poindexter, and other key players lied about their roles, and evidence of their untruthfulness surfaced only later. CIA director Casey died before his involvement could be probed.

In March 1988 a special prosecutor, Lawrence Walsh, indicted North, Poindexter, and eventually numerous other State Department and CIA officials. Most pleaded guilty or were convicted. The Supreme Court later overturned the convictions of North and Poindexter for technical reasons. At his trial in 1990, Poindexter repudiated his testimony before Congress; he declared that the president knew all the details of the Iran-contra operation and had ordered him to break the law and destroy documents. Oliver North made the same claim, writing that "Reagan knew everything."

The trials of several participants in the scandal continued into the early 1990s. President Bush pardoned some senior participants shortly before he left office. The final report on the affair issued by the special prosecutor in January 1994 did little more than chide Reagan for encouraging lawbreaking among his aides.

Although at first it seemed possible that the scandal would topple the Reagan administration, a number of factors mitigated its impact. Members of the House and Senate were reluctant to link President Reagan directly to illegal acts. They feared popular retribution if Congress were blamed for bringing down another chief executive, as they had done to Nixon in 1974. The public grew confused by the complicated story of arms sales and hostage releases and guessed that Reagan, too, might have been more befuddled than cunning.

Ultimately, most Americans cared little about Latin America and did not lose sleep over the diversion of funds to the contras. Although many people resented Reagan's selling arms to the hated ayatollah, the congressional hearings did not concentrate on this part of the drama. Moreover, by the summer of 1987, improved relations with the Soviet Union had distracted attention from the shabby episode. The Democrats, who now controlled both houses of Congress, favored a relaxation of Cold War tensions. With Reagan showing renewed interest in negotiating with the Soviets, they had a strong incentive to mute criticism of his past lapses.

As for Nicaragua, the problem solved itself shortly after Reagan left office. In February 1990 the Sandinistas held free elections. They lost to a moderately conservative coalition and went into political opposition. Significantly, this peaceful transition occurred only after the United States had terminated military aid to the contras.

SUMMIT POLITICS

In the wake of the Iran-contra scandal, a dramatic change inside the Soviet Union helped salvage the Reagan presidency. Unlike all his predecessors since Franklin D. Roosevelt, Ronald Reagan had refused to meet with any Soviet leader during his first term. After his re-election, however, he spent more time with his Kremlin counterpart than any previous president. Reagan met Mikhail Gorbachev on five separate occasions between November 1985 and December 1988.

When Mikhail Gorbachev became general secretary of the Soviet Union's Communist Party in March 1985, he was clearly the best-educated, most worldly, and least dogmatic man to lead his country since Lenin. He blamed his three predecessors for presiding over a twenty-year period of stagnation. Gorbachev recognized that the Soviet Union had fallen far behind most Western and many Asian nations in economic and technological progress. Apart from the defense sector, Soviet industry produced insufficient and shoddy goods. The old methods of central planning and authoritarian control yielded diminishing returns and were ill suited for international competition in the age of high technology. Corruption and despair permeated all aspects of Soviet society. This internal crisis made it nearly impossible for the Soviet Union to continue along the path it had followed for seventy years.

Gorbachev proclaimed new policies of *perestroika* (social and economic restructuring) and *glasnost* (openness and democracy). Incrementally, the Soviet leadership moved toward accepting the principles of representative government and free-market economics. Pulling the Soviet Union out of its torpor, Gorbachev and his colleagues concluded, would require cooperation with the capitalist world as well as domestic liberalization. The Soviet leader traveled around the globe, assuring foreign governments that he represented a new type of communism. Britain's conservative prime minister, Margaret Thatcher, whom Reagan admired, called Gorbachev "charming" and said that he was someone the West could do business with.

Reagan and Gorbachev held a get-acquainted meeting in Geneva in November 1985. Over several dinners they traded insults about human rights and Star Wars and then swapped stories about Hollywood film stars. The leaders met again at Reykjavik, Iceland, in October 1986. Reagan agreed to this summit with almost no advance preparation, fueling speculation that he sought a foreign policy victory on the eve of congressional elections. Gorbachev seized the initiative by proposing a 50-percent cut in long-range missiles and their eventual elimination. In return, the United States would have to abandon plans to deploy the SDI. Although an increasing number of American scientists doubted that the missile shield would ever work as advertised, the Soviets still criticized the program's offensive potential. They may have feared that even a "leaky" anti-missile system would be good enough to stop Soviet ICBMs if both sides cut their missile arsenals down to a small number. In that situation, the SDI system would give the United States an advantage that would allow it to intimidate or attack the Soviet Union with little fear of retaliation.

To the amazement of his advisers, Reagan upped the ante, offering to eliminate all American and possibly all British and French nuclear missiles within ten years. The president even suggested doing away with all types of nuclear weapons. In return, however, the Soviets must accept deployment of the still-unbuilt SDI system. This proposal for a complete elimination of nuclear weapons came out of nowhere, confusing both Gorbachev and Reagan's aides. The Soviets questioned why Reagan proposed to both eliminate nuclear missiles *and* build a vast space-based antimissile system. When Gorbachev balked at accepting SDI, Reagan ended the summit.

Despite this apparent setback, Soviet-American relations improved rapidly. During 1987, in the wake of the Iran-contra scandal, Reagan replaced many of his hard-line, anti-Soviet advisers. Former senator Howard Baker took over as White House chief of staff from Donald Regan. The death of William Casey led to the appointment of FBI director William Webster to head the CIA. Poindexter was replaced by Frank Carlucci as head of the NSC. Caspar Weinberger's resignation a few months later resulted in Carlucci's promotion to defense secretary. Lieutenant General Colin Powell then succeeded Carlucci as NSC chief.

Unlike most of their predecessors, these foreign policy advisers were pragmatic professionals who supported arms control negotiations with the Soviets. Equally important, Nancy Reagan encouraged her husband to pursue an agreement with Gorbachev. A fierce defender of her husband's image, the first lady hoped the president would be remembered for a dramatic lessening of superpower tensions, not the Iran-contra affair.

In the autumn of 1987, Soviet and American negotiators agreed on a treaty to remove all INF missiles (intermediate-range nuclear missiles) from Europe. Although these weapons formed only a small portion of the total nuclear arsenal, the agreement to destroy them represented the first time the two superpowers had agreed to abolish an entire category of weapons. Gorbachev even accepted a long-standing American demand for mutual on-site inspection to ensure compliance.

The Soviets made most of the concessions, dropping their demand that an INF treaty be linked to limits on long-range missiles and SDI. Gorbachev had probably decided that because of technical and economic problems, the Star Wars program would never succeed. Reagan, naturally, claimed that his massive defense build-up had brought the Russians around; he also said that he had known of a Soviet economic crisis since 1986.

In fact, the Soviet economy had been in trouble since long before 1986. Gorbachev, unlike his predecessors, acknowledged the situation publicly and decided to stop bleeding the civilian economy to support the army. He recognized that economic modernization required American, European, and Japanese assistance. They would only provide it if the Soviets improved their domestic and international behavior. Gorbachev also had a far more sophisticated sense of international relations than his predecessors. Since the Bolshevik Revolution, if not before, Russians had measured their national security by the degree to which Moscow dominated or intimidated its neighbors and rivals. As the Soviet Union declined economically, Gorbachev made a virtue of necessity. Reversing the Soviet Union's historical belligerence, he sought to enhance his country's economic and military security through cooperation with neighboring states and other world powers.

Mikhail Gorbachev visited Washington in December 1987 to sign the INF treaty. Undaunted by the Soviet leader's charm, the president quipped, "I don't resent his popularity. Good Lord, I co-starred with Errol Flynn once." This jocularity, apparently so easy and unforced, reaped immense appreciation for Reagan.

Gorbachev revealed a flair for good publicity by hosting a party for American luminaries such as Paul Newman, Yoko Ono, and Henry Kissinger. He charmed members of Congress and the citizens of Washington, D.C., by bounding out of his limousine and grabbing the hands of pedestrians. "I just want to say hello to you," he gushed. One veteran observer of visiting leaders commented, "The man is a PR genius!" Only a tiny number of Reagan's most conservative backers criticized the new friendliness with Moscow.

Apart from the signing of the INF treaty, few substantive Soviet-American agreements were reached during the remainder of Reagan's term. Both leaders, however, enjoyed a boost in their domestic ratings from the improved superpower relations. In a sense, the waning of the Cold War rescued both Reagan and Gorbachev from a host of domestic problems. The two leaders agreed to meet again in Moscow in June 1988. Simply by appearing in the heart of what he had frequently called "the evil empire" and embracing Gorbachev in front of Lenin's tomb, Reagan further blunted the Cold War. Asked if he still considered the Soviets the "focus of evil in the modern world," he answered, "they've changed." Although the United States and Soviet Union still had thirty thousand nuclear weapons aimed at each other, in the new spirit of the time, few people worried.

During 1988, the Soviets withdrew troops from Afghanistan and supported efforts to end civil conflicts in Africa and Southeast Asia. Reagan met Gorbachev again in December in New York, where the Soviet leader announced plans to reduce the Soviet Union's conventional forces. Taking a cue from the president's staff, Gorbachev arranged for Reagan and president-elect George Bush to pose for pictures with him in front of the Statue of Liberty.

THE NEW WORLD ORDER

Reagan's success in burying the Iran-contra scandal and his even more impressive achievement in improving ties with the Soviets dealt Vice President Bush a winning hand in the 1988 election. Clinging to the coattails of the most popular chief executive since Eisenhower, Bush parlayed his own substantial foreign policy expertise (while casting aspersions on Democrat Michael Dukakis's patriotism) into an electoral triumph in November.

The years 1989 through 1991 witnessed some of the most dramatic changes in global politics since 1945. The world order envisioned by Franklin Roosevelt seemed finally to be emerging as the Cold War waned and the United Nations began to function as a forum for global cooperation. As the United States and the Soviet Union ended their rivalry, communism collapsed throughout Eastern Europe. The United States and its allies agreed to provide billions of dollars worth of aid to promote economic reform in the Soviet Union and its former satellites.

Bush assembled an experienced group of policymakers at the beginning of his administration. National Security Adviser Brent Scowcroft, Secretary of Defense Richard Cheney, Secretary of State James Baker III, and General Colin Powell, chairman of the Joint Chiefs of Staff, had all held senior positions in the Ford and Reagan administrations.

Bush's greatest accomplishments in foreign policy were more passive than active. He had the good luck to preside over the peaceful collapse of the Soviet empire and the demise of communism as a global force. Not surprisingly, he claimed credit for the good things that happened on his watch. In some interesting ways, he resembled his Soviet counterpart, Mikhail Gorbachev. Both recognized the need to move their countries beyond the limits of the Cold War. Like Bush, Gorbachev did not push change but rather declined to block internal pressure for reform.

Shortly after Bush took office, Gorbachev permitted free elections to the Soviet parliament. This quickly transformed the nature of Soviet politics. In July 1989, Gorbachev stunned the members of the Warsaw Pact alliance by announcing that Moscow no longer cared how the eastern European states ran their internal affairs. They were free to follow their own road, without Soviet interference. Rather quickly, popular demonstrations challenged the Communist regimes throughout the region. Unlike in the past, the Soviets refused to dispatch troops to prop up unpopular puppets.

From 1961 to 1989 the ugly Berlin Wall stood as a symbol of the repressive Communist regimes of Eastern Europe and the Soviet Union. When the wall was opened in November 1989, jubilant West Berliners climbed on top of it near the Brandenburg Gate to celebrate the apparent end of communism and the imminent reunification of Germany. *UPI/Bettmann Archive.*

In November 1989, after several months of street demonstrations, the East German regime opened the Berlin Wall. Within months, wrecking balls began battering down the wall, the principal symbol of the Cold War. Street vendors began a thriving trade selling chunks of the hated barrier as gifts to tourists. On October 2, 1990, Germany reunited. During the same period, peaceful democratic revolutions brought down the Communist governments in Poland, Hungary, and Czechoslovakia, replacing them with elected parliaments. Only Rumania and Bulgaria experienced bloodshed or major resistance from officials of the old order.

The speed, depth, and relatively peaceful nature of this political revolution caught both American and Soviet leaders by surprise. In removing the Soviet finger from the dike of eastern Europe, Gorbachev unleashed forces Moscow could no longer control. Bush, too, seemed uncertain how to respond to this upheaval in the Communist world. When he visited Eastern Europe during 1989, the most

Democratic Movements in Eastern Europe, 1989–1991

memorable remark he uttered was "there's big stuff, heavy stuff, going on here." He greeted the collapse of communism in Poland by worrying that change might "be more than the market can bear."

Political ferment inevitably spread into the Soviet heartland. Gorbachev, advocating his own version of a "kinder, gentler" communism, hoped that reform would salvage the collapsing economy and convince the nearly twenty ethnic republics that made up the Soviet Union to remain under Moscow's control. But events soon overwhelmed him. The Baltic states of Lithuania, Latvia, and Estonia, annexed by the Soviet Union in 1940, asserted their independence in

"CONGRATULATIONS....YOU WON THE COLD WAR!"

The Cold War had overshadowed United States domestic problems, such as unemployment, economic troubles, and the poor and homeless. *Reprinted with special permission of King Features Syndicate.*

1990. Soon the residents of Armenia, Azerbaijan, Georgia, Moldova, and Ukraine, among others, agitated for independence. Old-line Communists blamed Gorbachev for wrecking the country, while advocates of greater market and political freedoms, such as Boris Yeltsin, criticized him for not moving forward more rapidly. Yeltsin, a former Communist bureaucrat turned reformer, won election as president of the Russian republic in June 1991 and immediately began challenging Gorbachev's authority.

The Bush administration initially seemed unsure of how to deal with Gorbachev. Presidential aides first derided him as a "drugstore cowboy" and a "Stalinist in Gucci shoes." But by the end of 1989 Bush had decided to endorse Gorbachev's gradualist approach, and he held the first of six meetings with the Soviet leader. In November 1990 the two issued a joint message declaring an end to the Cold War. As the president's comfort level with Gorbachev increased, he tried to stem the disintegration of the Soviet Union by criticizing Yeltsin and urging the Soviet republics to remain under Moscow's authority. During a visit to Kiev, the capital of Ukraine, Bush delivered a speech urging its restive population to remain part of the USSR. Critics immediately dubbed the president's policy as "chicken Kiev."

Despite this belated verbal support from Washington, Gorbachev's hold on power grew shakier. The Soviet military and bureaucracy demanded a restoration of order, while dozens of ethnic groups in the

Soviet Union demanded independence. During the summer of 1991 Gorbachev further outraged the old guard by disbanding the Warsaw Pact, signing a wide-ranging missile reduction agreement with the United States, and drafting a treaty to give the Soviet republics greater autonomy under Moscow's umbrella. Hard-liners in the Communist Party apparatus struck back on August 18, arresting Gorbachev at his vacation villa on the Crimean peninsula and proclaiming a new government. The coup failed when Boris Yeltsin and hundreds of thousands of Muscovites took to the streets in defense of Gorbachev. After keeping Gorbachev in captivity for three days, the coup leaders released him and surrendered.

Nevertheless, the botched coup marked a definitive end to the Soviet era. Still clinging to the belief that reformed communism could salvage the Soviet experiment, Gorbachev had lost the power to control events. Meanwhile, Russian president Boris Yeltsin emerged as a symbol of political salvation. During the final months of 1991, some fifteen republics declared their independence from Moscow. On Christmas Day, Gorbachev bowed to reality. He signed a decree dissolving the Soviet Union and resigned, turning power over to Boris Yeltsin, president of the Russian republic. Russia now comprised about 75 percent of the territory of the former Soviet Union.

China, the other Communist giant, followed a very different path from the Soviet Union, stressing free market economic reforms while maintaining authoritarian rule. Dissatisfied with these half steps, in the spring of 1989 Chinese college students in many cities began to demonstrate in favor of democracy. The biggest gathering occurred in Beijing's Tiananmen Square, where tens of thousands of students built a "goddess of democracy" (modeled on the Statue of Liberty) and defied orders to disperse. On June 4, Chinese leader Deng Xiaoping ordered troops and tanks to crush the demonstration. Soldiers took his instructions literally, running down students with tanks and shooting as many as several thousand in the streets. Americans who saw smuggled television pictures of this repression were appalled. But the Bush administration, like its predecessor and successor, concluded that China's influence in Asia and its surging economic power were so important that the United States should not impose stiff sanctions as punishment for mistreating its own citizens. American leaders hoped that the passing of the aging old guard and the development of a vibrant economy linked to foreign markets would encourage greater political pluralism within China.

POST–COLD WAR INTERVENTIONS

The end of the Cold War did not eliminate global instability or challenges to U.S. interests. However, instead of justifying U.S. intervention abroad as a necessary counter to Soviet influence, the Bush administration advanced new rationales for its use of force, including defending human rights, protecting energy supplies, and suppressing the drug trade.

The first foreign military intervention by the Bush administration took place in Panama. Manuel Noriega, a military officer and long-time CIA informant, assumed power in Panama in 1983 following the death of Omar Torrijos, a nationalist who had negotiated Panamanian sovereignty over the Canal Zone. Noriega, most observers agreed, could not be bought, only rented. At various times he cooperated with Colombian drug lords, the contras, Fidel Castro, foreign bankers seeking a safe haven for tainted money, and anyone else willing to pay his price. During most of the 1980s his collaboration with the Colombian drug cartel had been an open secret. However, because he allowed the CIA to use Panama as a conduit to aid the Nicaraguan contras, Washington overlooked his narcotics connection.

As the Nicaraguan conflict wound down in 1988 and 1989, the Reagan administration applied financial pressure on Panama to ease Noriega out of power. But following Bush's election, American priorities changed. The CIA no longer needed Noriega, and with the new administration's high-profile war on drugs, Noriega's open involvement with drug traffickers became an embarrassment to his former patrons in Washington. The general ignored suggestions that he resign and go into genteel exile in France. Instead, in May 1989 he called for snap elections, which he expected to win by rigging the vote. But when opposition candidate Guillermo Endara captured a majority anyway, Noriega voided the election and set his thugs (known as "Dignity Battalions") upon his opponents.

Noriega's affronts, including the beating of a few Americans in Panama, outraged Bush. The president ordered the CIA to organize a revolt among the Panamanian armed forces. When this failed, he dispatched an invasion force of twelve thousand American soldiers on December 20, 1989, assigning them the task of arresting Noriega and installing the winner of the aborted May election as president. During the ensuing three-day conflict, fifty-five members of the Panamanian National Guard and twenty-three Americans lost their lives. Between several hundred to four thousand Panamanian civilians may have died when bombs from U.S. planes accidentally fell on their houses. Nevertheless, the American public strongly backed the invasion, with upwards of 90 percent approving of Bush's action.

Although organized resistance lasted only seventy-two hours, it took two weeks to find Noriega and dislodge him from the Vatican embassy, where he had taken sanctuary. On January 3, 1990, a dazed Noriega surrendered and was taken to Miami to stand trial for drug trafficking. Two years later, after rejecting his claim that he had sold narcotics with Washington's tacit consent, a jury convicted Noriega.

U.S. military power faced a far greater challenge after August 2, 1990, when Iraq seized the tiny, oil rich sheikdom of Kuwait in the Persian Gulf region. Iraqi leader Saddam Hussein had long coveted his southern neighbor, nurturing historic claims that Kuwait was really a "lost" province of Iraq. By annexing Kuwait, he hoped to boost Iraq's ailing economy and play a major role in setting global petroleum prices. The Iraqi leader may well have expected Washington to tolerate his land grab, since both Reagan and Bush had authorized generous loans to his government, provided him with military aid during his war with Iran, and turned a blind eye while Iraq developed chemical and atomic weapons capabilities.

What followed must have stunned Saddam Hussein. Although Kuwait was no democracy, it was a sovereign state and a member of the United Nations. The United States and its allies feared that if the Iraqi seizure of Kuwait went unchallenged, Saddam Hussein would either invade the Saudi oil fields or intimidate the Saudis into following his leadership. This might give Iraq a huge measure of control over Middle East oil reserves and the power to destabilize the economies of the entire industrialized world. To prevent this, President Bush got the United Nations to impose a tight economic embargo on Iraq and sent some 500,000 American troops to Saudi Arabia (including 30,000 women) as part of a twenty-eight-nation coalition force. Even the Soviet Union, Iraq's former patron and arms supplier, supported the sanctions. By January 15, 1991, diplomatic efforts to get Iraq to withdraw from Kuwait had failed. Congress debated the president's request to authorize military retaliation and gave its approval by a narrow margin.

On January 17 Bush ordered American planes to begin bombing Iraqi targets and troops. In launching the so-called Desert Storm attack, the president paraphrased the words of President Woodrow Wilson in declaring that "we have before us the opportunity to forge for ourselves a new world order." For five weeks American and allied planes pounded targets in Iraq and Kuwait. Except for the CNN network, which had a reporter in Baghdad, press coverage was tightly controlled, allowing the Pentagon to release film clips only of bombs that hit their targets rather than those that went astray. Finally, on February 23, U.S. ground forces and those of many coalition members launched a ground offensive that liberated Kuwait and continued on halfway to the Iraqi capital of Baghdad in less than one hundred hours. When President Bush accepted Saddam's plea for a cease-fire on February 27, only 223 allied troops had been killed, compared to tens of thousands of Iraqis. The American commander of Desert Storm, General H. Norman Schwarzkopf, became a media star and then a best-selling author. A Gallup poll reported that 90 percent of Americans—more than ever before—supported the president.

George and Barbara Bush visited American soldiers after the Gulf War. *Diana Walker/Gamma Liaison.*

Although Kuwaiti sovereignty was restored (democracy was never an issue since a ruling family held all power in Kuwait) and Saudi Arabia defended, Saddam Hussein remained in power. Fearing a power vacuum in the region or the triumph of Islamic fundamentalism should the Iraqi regime be completely destroyed, Bush called off the attack before Saddam was crushed. The Iraqi leader turned much of his wrath on dissident groups at home, such as the Kurdish minority, and vowed to someday reclaim Kuwait.

The war had one important unintended consequence. PLO chief Yasir Arafat had professed support for Iraq. This infuriated the Saudis and most other Arab leaders, who then stopped subsidizing the PLO. Suddenly bereft of patrons, Arafat became more conciliatory and soon entered into peace talks with his Israeli enemies.

Triumph in the Cold War, along with easy victories in Panama and Iraq against unsavory enemies, propelled George Bush to unprecedented levels of popularity. Yet, eight months after Desert Storm, polls revealed that only 39 percent of Americans approved of the direction in which he had led the country. The "New World Order," a term first used optimistically after victory in World War I, proved no better a guide for the 1990s than it had in the 1920s and 1930s. The collapse of communism, while it reduced the danger of nuclear war, had allowed simmering ethnic and political conflicts to resurface in the former Soviet Union, Yugoslavia, the Middle East, and Africa. As a real and symbolic enemy, communism and the Soviet Union had unified America's will to intervene in regional conflicts and play the role of world policeman. Absent that unifying symbol, politicians and the public were far less tolerant of calls to send peace-keeping forces into harm's way.

Once the Soviet specter had evaporated and an easy victory been achieved in the Gulf War, Bush's stature quickly diminished. The president's palpable apathy toward domestic issues, his breaking his 1990 "Read my lips, no new taxes" campaign pledge, and the deterioration of the American economy during 1991 and 1992 led over 80 percent of voters in the spring of 1992 to tell a Gallup poll that they were unhappy with the state of the nation. The very phrase "new world order" became an object of popular derision.

Challenged by conservative Patrick Buchanan in the Republican primaries for his "indifference" to domestic concerns, Bush told New Hampshire voters, "Message: I care. . . . Don't cry for me Argentina." Although Bush secured the Republican nomination, he found it difficult to energize his campaign without a foreign enemy. Instead, he unleashed a relentless attack on Democratic candidate Bill Clinton's draft record, opposition to the war in Vietnam, and alleged lack of patriotism. But these accusations, which had served Republicans well since the onset of the Cold War in 1945, fell flat. As memories of the Soviet threat and of Desert Storm faded, millions of Americans worried more about losing their jobs in obsolete factories than about Clinton's draft record. As politicians and pundits remarked in 1992, the Cold War was over. But as they entered an era where economic innovation counted more than the power of nuclear warheads, Americans feared that Japan and Germany had won.

CONCLUSION

In his farewell address delivered in January 1953, President Harry Truman voiced a question that was undoubtedly on the minds of millions of Americans: "Some of you . . . may ask when and how will the Cold War end? I think I can answer that simply. The Communist world has great resources and it looks strong. But there is a fatal flaw in their society. Theirs is a godless system, a system of slavery; there is no freedom in it, no consent." Truman predicted that as "the free world grows stronger, more united, more attractive to men on both sides of the Iron Curtain—and as the Soviet hopes for easy expansion are blocked—then there will have to come a time of change in the Soviet world. Nobody can say for sure when that is going to be, or exactly how it will come about, whether by revolution, or trouble in the satellite states, or by a change inside the Kremlin." But the president whose term of office coincided with the emergence of the global struggle between East and West had no doubt that change would eventually come. "I have a deep and abiding faith in the destiny of free men," Truman concluded. "With patience and courage, we shall some day move on into a new era."

In light of the events of the late 1980s and early 1990s, these words proved prescient. In the long run, the growing economic strength of the United States, Western Europe, and Japan, as well as the allure of democracy, overwhelmed the rigid Soviet police state. For nearly half a century, the U.S. policies of promoting world trade and guaranteeing the security of its major allies created the context for this triumph. Along the way, however, the United States often strayed from the priorities of containment set in the early years of the Cold War. U.S. interventions in the Third World, especially the two-decade-long obsession with Vietnam, now seem to many historians to have been irrelevant and costly diversions from the strategies that secured eventual success.

New economic challenges in Europe and Asia characterized the post–Cold War world. Since the Second World War, steady and usually expanding defense spending had provided an immense government stimulus to the economy. That began to change in 1986, when the Reagan-era military build-up leveled off. Over the next six years, defense spending declined steadily, forcing major job cutbacks in states with large defense industries, like California and Connecticut. While almost certainly a good thing in the long run, this painful economic adjustment to a post–Cold War world contributed to the recession of 1991 and 1992 and the electoral defeat of George Bush.

The demise of the Soviet threat also forced American leaders and citizens alike to ponder what kind of influence they wished the United States to exercise abroad. The world remained full of economic challenges, political trouble spots, and natural disasters. Determining the national interest and deciding on appropriate responses to these hazards fell upon a generation of leaders who had to look beyond the simple truths of the Cold War. ■

F U R T H E R   R E A D I N G

On foreign policy during the 1980s and early 1990s, see: Alexander Haig, *Caveat: Reagan, Realism and Foreign Policy* (1984); Caspar Weinberger, *Fighting for Peace* (1990); George P. Shultz, *Turmoil and Triumph*; Constantine Menges, *Inside the National Security Council* (1988); William Broad, *The Star Warriors* (1985); Strobe Talbott, *Deadly Gambits* (1984); Michael Mandelbaum and Strobe Talbott, *Reagan and Gorbachev* (1987); Kenneth Oye, et al., *Eagle Defiant:*

U.S. Foreign Policy in the 1980s (1983); John Tower, et al., *The Tower Commission Report* (1987); Theodore Draper, *A Very Thin Line: The Iran-Contra Affairs* (1991); Bob Woodward, *Veil* (1987); Jonathan Kwitny, *The Crimes of Patriots: A True Tale of Dope, Dirty Money and the CIA* (1987); Raymond Bonner, *Weakness and Deceit: U.S. Policy and El Salvador* (1984); Mark Danner, *The Massacre at El Mozote: A Parable of the Cold War* (1994); Jane Mayer and Doyle McManus, *Landslide: The Unmaking of the President, 1984–88* (1988); Roy Gutman, *Banana Diplomacy* (1988); Michael Schaller, *Reckoning with Reagan: America and Its President in the 1980s* (1992); Michael R. Beschloss and Strobe Talbott, *At the Highest Levels: The Inside Story of the End of the Cold War* (1993); John L. Gaddis, *The United States and the End of the Cold War* (1992); Alan Friedman, *Spider's Web: The Secret History of How the White House Illegally Armed Iraq* (1993); Rick Atkinson, *Crusade: The Untold Story of the Persian Gulf War* (1993); Stephen R. Graubard, *Mr. Bush's War: Adventures in the Politics of Illusion* (1992); Gale Stokes, *The Walls Came Tumbling Down: The Collapse of Communism in Eastern Europe* (1993).

14

Rumblings of
the Future

As twilight settled over San Francisco on the evening of October 17, 1989, baseball devotees across the country turned on their television sets for the opening pitch of the third game of the World Series. Local fans, 58,000 of whom were in the stands at Candlestick Park, had special reason to tune in, since the Series, nicknamed the "Battle of the Bay Bridge," pitted the National League's San Francisco Giants against the American League's neighboring Oakland Athletics.

Don Robinson, scheduled as the Giants' starting pitcher, was just strapping on his knee brace when the stadium began to rumble and shake. "I thought it was the crowd," Robinson told a reporter. "When the rumbling became more intense, I ran into [Giants manager] Roger Craig's office and lay down under the doorway." Within seconds, water, electricity, communications, and transportation services in the nation's fourth largest metropolitan area had been disrupted by an earthquake along the San Andreas Fault, measuring a devastating 6.9 on the Richter scale.

In fits and starts, reporters, civil defense workers, Red Cross volunteers, and average citizens began to piece together the extent of the damage. A section of Interstate 880 in Oakland had collapsed, crushing dozens of rush hour commuters in their cars. A piece of the upper deck of the Bay Bridge had collapsed. Down on Fisherman's Wharf, a shaken observer commented, "The street had just exploded out of the ground, like someone had hit it with a giant fist from underneath." Fires raged through the city's fashionable Marina District, and burned out of control in Berkeley. The damage was stunning as far south as Santa Cruz, where a pedestrian mall was leveled and scores of houses slid off their foundations. A spokesman for the Nuclear Regulatory Commission announced, much to everyone's relief, that there were no reports of damage at any of the state's six nuclear power plants. For residents of the Bay Area, many of whom prided themselves on their environmental sensitivity, simply living and commuting on the fault line had become riskier than sitting cheek-by-jowl with the Diablo Canyon nuclear reactor.

As the last decade of the twentieth century opened, it seemed to many Americans that the social and physical ground they lived on had become shakier and shakier. For Americans who watched television (which amounted to virtually the whole country) the succession of days sometimes seemed like a series of natural disasters punctuated by social explosions. For middle- and upper-class people, making sense of the world grew more and more difficult, as information flowed in faster and faster. New communications media brought new power, but also sped up the pace of learning and living, making life on earth seem, paradoxically, both more intimate and beyond control. And the middle class worried as economists and demographers solemnly pronounced that their children had become the first American generation that could not expect to live better than their parents, materially or socially.

If those who lived in comfort felt hard-pressed to keep up the pace, poor Americans could view the proliferation of goods and knowledge only from afar, and they fell farther and farther behind. By 1990, one in seven Americans was living below the poverty line. One-quarter of American children between the ages of 3 and 12 received public assistance. Nearly two-thirds of poor families included a head of household who worked full time, yet was unable to adequately support his or her family. Clearly, for people struggling to pull themselves out of poverty, a job was not enough.

A tiny handful of merchant adventurers grew unbelievably rich investing in the communications revolution. Bill Gates, the youthful founder of Microsoft, became America's richest man by cashing in on the boom in personal computers. In the late 1980s, whenever almost anyone switched on his or her desk-top computer, Gates took a piece of the action. Other entrepreneurs found gold in home-shopping cable television channels. Millions of Americans could now watch fashion models and movie stars hawking personalized perfumes and ersatz gemstone jewelry in the privacy of their own homes—but many of those viewers lived amid violence and material desperation. Television glitz, available twenty-four hours a day, cruelly mocked people with no money, no marketable skills, little education, and no hope.

In 1990, the United States was a nation always in motion. City dwellers moved to the suburbs, Texans moved to Florida and California, New Yorkers and Michiganders moved to California and Florida and Texas, too. Chicago, Philadelphia, and Detroit lost hundreds of thousands of people, and Los Angeles gained more than half a million. Nearly three-quarters of Americans over sixteen years of age got up every working morning, got in their cars, and drove—by themselves—to work, averaging 22.4 minutes in transit. As Americans moved, divorced, changed or lost jobs, and loosened ties to family, religion, and government, they became more dependent on the mass media for their information and opinions. In many important ways, the contemporary mass media made people more informed about the wider world than ever before. The speed of satellite communications would have astonished Americans in the World War II era. Yet greater information did not always lead to greater understanding or perspective. Throughout the 1980s and into the 1990s, both television and print journalism concentrated on sensation, scandal, and glamour rather than tackling complex subjects.

Bill Gates

In the mid-1960s, few Americans envisioned the ways in which computers would later revolutionize American life. Even those who were most familiar with the machines could not foresee the time when millions of American families would assume the necessity of owning, and using daily, a personal computer. Being interested in computers then, recalled William H. Gates III, was "not a mainstream thing. I couldn't imagine spending the rest of my life at it." But by the 1990s, Bill Gates would become America's richest man, an inventor and entrepreneurial genius who built his vast fortune on the world's insatiable appetite for computer technology.

The son of a well-to-do Seattle family, Gates first became fascinated with computers as a child of twelve, in 1967, when he and three friends from the exclusive Lakeside School formed the Lakeside Programming Group. One of his first programs was a class schedule for the school, which he engineered so that he would share classes with all the prettiest girls. The school paid him $4,200 for a summer's work. Soon, the Lakeside students were doing consulting work for the Computer Center Corporation, but Gates's penchant for pulling pranks got him into trouble when he hacked into, and crashed, Control Data Corporation's CYBERNET computer system.

By the time Gates was 14, he was president of his own company, Traf-o-Data. The firm earned $20,000 selling traffic-counting systems to municipalities before its customers even found out that the company was run by high school students. He interrupted a thriving career, however, and enrolled at Harvard University in 1973, planning to become a lawyer.

At Harvard, Gates remained fascinated by the possibilities of computer programs, operating systems, and software. In 1975, at the end of his sophomore year, he dropped out, moved to Albuquerque, New Mexico, and with his old Lakeside friend Paul Allen, founded Microsoft. Securing a contract with the Tandy Corporation to develop software for Radio Shack computers, Microsoft grew quickly and moved to Seattle. The company hit the big time when IBM contacted Gates about creating an operating system for a new product, the "personal computer." The result, the MS-DOS operating system, was eventually licensed to more than one hundred companies producing IBM-compatible computers, and by 1981 Microsoft was earning $16 million a year.

Like Thomas Edison, Gates was the rare inventor who mastered the marketplace as well as the laboratory. In the late 1980s, Microsoft introduced its Windows operating system, which allowed users to run IBM-compatible computers with a hand-held "mouse" and on-screen symbols. Windows was as simple to use and "user-friendly" as the operating system pioneered by arch-rival Apple Computer and IBM "clones" were much less expensive than Apple's famous Macintosh model. Soon Windows dominated the market, and Gates, at the age of 32, became a billionaire.

An intensely competitive man, Gates has often been described as aloof, sarcastic, and abrupt, but also as charming, funny, and able to inspire strong loyalty in his employees. The very model of a nineties corporate executive, he puts in long days and works weekends, and he expects employees who aspire to upward mobility to do the same. Microsoft has also earned a reputation as a cutthroat competitor: the Federal Trade Commission has investigated allegations that the company used its dominant position to squelch competition. But however contested his business practices, Gates undeniably had more to do with bringing the computer revolution into American homes and offices than any other individual. ∎

As they approached the uncertainties of the future, Americans perhaps believed too much in the world they saw on television—a world where only celebrities seemed self-assured (and even they, to be sure, had their problems). Since most television stories about ordinary people inevitably involved violence, conflict, or crisis, the world seemed to viewers a threatening place, one that could not be made safe or predictable by rational human action. "We have created rootless, dangling people with little link to the supportive networks—family, friends, school—that sustain some sense of purpose in life," wrote philosopher Cornell West. "The result is lives of what we might call 'random nows,' of fortuitous and fleeting moments preoccupied with 'getting over'—with acquiring pleasure, property, and power by any means necessary."

THE ECONOMY OF THE NINETIES

If the problem of maintaining stability in daily life seemed daunting to some, there were also large, abstract economic troubles looming. Worry about the size of the federal budget deficit overshadowed other public policy considerations in 1989 and 1990. Critics of the borrowing of the 1980s believed that the rising debt would erode capital formation and render American firms unable to compete worldwide. Commentators and politicians unhappy with the federal budget deficit predicted that unless the government made the unpopular decision to raise taxes and cut benefits for the middle class, the American economy would fall behind the economies of Japan and Germany. A recession threatened, but the Federal Reserve refused to lower interest rates unless something was done to reduce the federal budget deficit below the $260 billion expected for 1991.

In the spring of 1990, facing widespread fear of an impending economic calamity, President Bush finally dropped his premier promise of the 1988 campaign—"no new taxes." He entered into negotiations with a small group of congressional leaders to hammer out a budget agreement that would raise taxes, cut middle-class entitlements, and ultimately slice $500 billion from the deficit over five years. In late September, the budget negotiators agreed on a package of income and excise tax increases combined with cuts in such popular programs as Medicare and unemployment insurance. The secretly negotiated agreement nearly came undone, however: its adoption was blocked by an unusual coalition of liberal Democrats angry at the cuts in social programs and conservative Republicans dismayed that Bush had accepted new taxes. Nevertheless, a month later Congress passed a modified version of the budget. The law reduced the burden on elderly recipients of Medicare by increasing payroll taxes on workers. It also raised taxes on the top 2 percent of earners by cutting their deductions, and it boosted taxes on gasoline, alcohol, and big-ticket luxury items. Congress expected these measures to reduce the deficit by $40 billion in the next year and $490 billion over the next five years. From the record of previous plans to lower the deficit, however, observers predicted that such hopes would prove exaggerated. Within a month, officials acknowledged the arrival of the long-anticipated recession, which reduced tax revenues and further strained the government's resources. As a result, the 1991 deficit exceeded $267 billion, the highest in history.

If the government was spending so much money, Americans wondered, what were they getting for their tax dollars? It was evident to anyone who drove, flew, took a train, or got sick that the nation's infrastructure was in disrepair and fundamental social services weren't serving. Estimates for repair of the nation's decaying highways and bridges ranged from $50 billion to $200 billion. Before the long-delayed opening of Denver International Airport in 1995, no new airport had been constructed in the United States since 1974; not surprisingly, the air transportation system suffered bottlenecks, delays, and occasional tragic collisions. The nation's expensive and chaotic health care system also prompted concern. America spent 12 percent of its GNP on health care, 50 to 100 percent more than other industrialized nations. Those who had full medical insurance received the best care in the world, but 37 million people—most of whom worked—had little or no insurance coverage. The uninsured working poor, excluded from the benefits of prohibitively expensive high-tech medicine, lagged far behind more fortunate Americans in their overall health. Moreover, the fact that so many Americans lacked health insurance drove up costs for those who were insured, thereby making health insurance unreachable for even more people. Because the uninsured often waited to go to the doctor until they were really sick or else visited expensive emergency rooms for treatment of relatively minor ailments, health care costs skyrocketed. Drug companies also contributed to the cost of health care, charging arbitrary, inflated prices for high-demand medicines. President Bush seemed unaware that there was any problem with the nation's transportation or health care systems.

The continuing shift of employment from manufacturing to service industries also caused concern. To be sure, some jobs in the service sector paid well. For example, most lawyers and doctors earned handsome livings, and the boom in such upscale professions meant a rising income for certain segments of society. The number of lawyers in the United States increased nearly 50 percent in the 1980s; by 1990 the country had 756,000 lawyers, more than the rest of the world combined. The number of doctors also rose, from 279,000 in 1970 to 554,000 in 1988. An even greater increase occurred among real estate agents, a group that grew from 100,000 members to 800,000 in the twenty years after 1970.

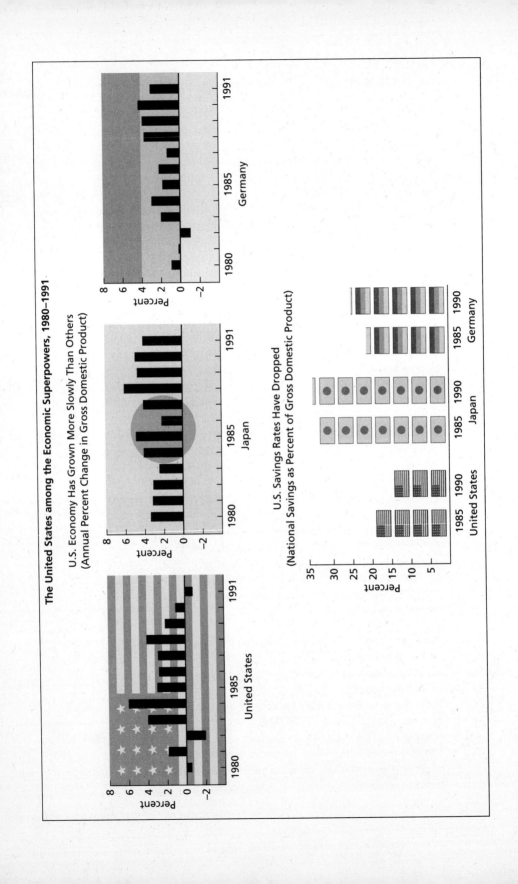

The United States among the Economic Superpowers, 1980–1991

U.S. Economy Has Grown More Slowly Than Others
(Annual Percent Change in Gross Domestic Product)

United States

Japan

Germany

U.S. Savings Rates Have Dropped
(National Savings as Percent of Gross Domestic Product)

Although the increase in upscale service positions was impressive, the vast majority of Americans did not find work as professionals. Those without a college education earned less in the new service jobs than their parents or elder siblings had in manufacturing. Steady work became even more uncertain, because service employers hired during good times and laid employees off during downturns. A so-called K-mart economy developed in many of the booming regions of the Sunbelt, where young, uneducated, unskilled workers found work paying only $4 to $6 per hour in discount stores, supermarkets, fast-food stores, auto repair shops, hair salons, and banks. Towns that had encouraged chain stores to set up branches—and even those where large manufacturing industries had established small local assembly lines—found themselves longing for home-grown businesses and entrepreneurs to create wealth and economic diversity. A city council member in one fast-growing Florida city lamented, "We've had a lot of growth. But it was just quantity, not quality."

During the 1980s, younger workers began finding it harder to make ends meet. The purchasing power of households in which the principal wage earner was less than twenty-five years old fell 19 percent from the beginning of the decade to the end. Households whose major wage earner was twenty-five to thirty-four years old also saw their purchasing power erode in the 1980s. Conditions for most age groups above thirty-five held steady or improved marginally. Only people over sixty-five, whose Social Security and other pension payments were linked to changes in the cost of living, saw their incomes rise significantly. The sense that the younger generation was losing ground helped revive the economic fears of the late 1970s. By 1990, public opinion polls once more reflected a widespread belief that the future would be grimmer than the past and that children would have a harder time achieving economic security than their parents had.

Golden California, the symbol and setting of the American dream, was fast becoming the emblem of all that was tense, puzzling, and frightening about America. As the 1990s wore on, Americans watched one news story after another flash out of the seemingly crazy culture on the fault line; they worried that what L.A. was now, the country would be tomorrow. The West Coast version of the postwar suburban ideal had, by 1990, reshaped a nation now composed primarily of suburbanites, but the view from the picture window was far less tranquil than expected.

And yet, as the 1990s got under way, the California dream persisted and even went global. During the 1980s, as many immigrants came into California as had entered New York in the first decade of the century, mostly from Latin America and Asia. New immigrants

◀ **The United States Among the Economic Superpowers, 1980–1991**

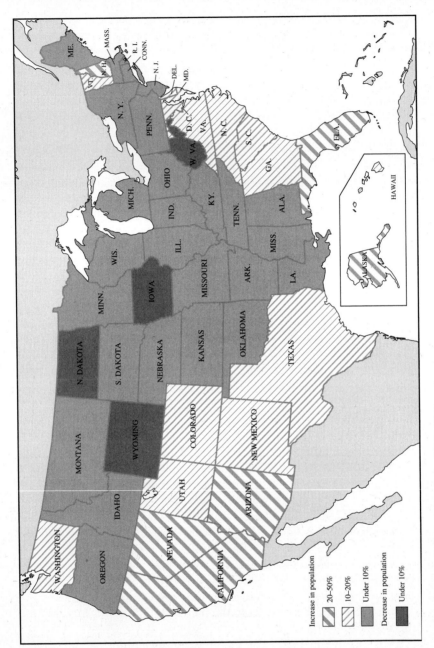

The Continued Shift to the Sunbelt, 1980–1990

Increase in population
- 20–50%
- 10–20%
- Under 10%

Decrease in population
- Under 10%

energized the nation's cities with their ways and their work. The African-American middle class grew, as did black enrollment at colleges and universities. But most African-Americans felt increasingly isolated and abandoned. A new President, the first Democrat in twelve years, spoke glowingly of a promising future, but more and more Americans took the cynical (and understandable) view that their leaders were often short-sighted and unwilling to take actions that might offend important groups or individuals. The millennium neared. Dread mingled with hope.

A NATION OF SUBURBS

In 1990, for the first time, more than half of Americans lived in urban areas with populations of one million or more. Nearly one in four Americans lived in one of five metropolitan areas—New York, Los Angeles, Chicago, San Francisco, and Philadelphia. Suburban expansion powered metropolitan growth. For example, between 1989 and 1990, net migration to the nation's metropolitan areas reached 1.5 million, but its central cities *lost* 2 million residents. The suburbs gained more than 3.5 million. "The suburbs," said geographer Peter Muller, "are no longer sub to the urb."

The most urbanized and fastest-growing region of the nation was the West. Six of the ten largest U.S. cities in 1990 were west of the Mississippi. Cities like Phoenix grew rapidly—24 percent in the 1980s— and their suburbs, like Tempe and Scottsdale, grew even faster, by 40 percent. No American city grew faster in the 1980s than Mesa, Arizona, another Phoenix suburb, with a population that topped 288,000 by the end of the decade, having grown a whopping 89 percent larger than in 1980. Demographers identified a new urban phenomenon, the "edge city," a former suburb or small town—or a massive new development—that had achieved city status on its own, with its own commercial and industrial base. These edge cities formed separate nodes around the old urban cores; clusters of such communities composed the new, multinucleated American metropolis.

Some cities, like Colorado Springs and Albuquerque, tried to maintain a single identity by annexing their borderlands, but they just spawned new suburbs that kept on growing. By 1994, Rio Rancho, New Mexico, a bedroom community just northwest of Albuquerque, had used a combination of low housing prices, corporate tax breaks, and generous water rights to lure high-tech corporations, including Intel, the world's largest manufacturer of computer chips, to build plants. Amid a climate of economic uncertainty, with the memory of the oil bust and the Bush recession fresh in politicians' minds, Western states vied with one another for such economic development.

The urban landscape in 1990 was a product of the almost universal dependence on the private automobile for transportation. Los Angeles, of course, was considered the ultimate car-culture city, but by 1990 its spreading, sprawling suburban form had captured the rest of the country as well, from Boston to Houston. And the more freeways Americans built to carry their cars, the more cars that arrived to add to the congestion. Planners and policymakers did what they could to keep their cities moving. In Houston, corporate employers subsidized van pools, and the city set aside car pool lanes on the main freeways. Portland, Oregon, worked to accommodate "intermodal" transportation, so that commuters could mix public buses, cars, bicycles, and feet as means of getting around. Even Los Angeles sought alternatives to the car; in 1993 it opened the first section of a twenty-three-mile subway running west from downtown.

As Americans moved to the Sunbelt, the regional balance of power in the House of Representatives shifted. After the 1992 election California gained seven seats, for a total of fifty-two. No state had held such a large share of the House since New York had exercised similar power and influence in the 1880s. For its part, New York continued to lose seats, falling from thirty-four to thirty-one. Texas gained three seats, for a total of thirty, only one less than New York; in 1993, Texas overtook New York to become the second largest state. Other Sunbelt states also gained representation, while areas of the traditionally populous industrial East and Midwest saw their leverage in the House decline.

Though the suburban population remained predominately white, an increasing proportion of working- and middle-class blacks, Hispanics, and Asian-Americans also left the cities for the suburbs. Between 1980 and 1990, the black population in the suburbs rose from 5.9 million to 8 million, a 34.4 percent increase. The Hispanic suburban population increased from 5.1 million to 8.7 million during the same period. The Asian-American suburban population also increased dramatically, from 1.5 million to 3.5 million. Some suburban areas, like Prince George's County in Maryland, were predominately nonwhite by 1994. In cities like Washington, D.C., Atlanta, and Dallas, suburbanization among the black middle class was particularly noteworthy.

Western cities like Phoenix, Denver, Portland, Oregon, Salt Lake City, and Albuquerque grew rapidly in the 1990s in part because they offered a combination of low taxes, cheap land, a pleasant climate, and a tractable work force—a formula that previously only southern California had offered. California, by contrast, suffered a deep recession unprecedented in its postwar history. The end of the Cold War spelled trouble for California, a state utterly dependent on billions of dollars in defense contracts. As the federal government cut programs like the B-1 bomber, defense contractors instituted a series of "reorganizations" and "restructurings," which came down to mass layoffs—one thousand at TRW, three thousand at Northrop, another six thousand at Hughes. White-collar employees were no safer than assembly-line workers. McDonnell Douglas asked five thousand managers to resign, then offered them the chance to compete against one another for 2,900 jobs. Plants closed or relocated to Sunbelt cities already lining up the backhoes and the tax breaks. The layoffs and closures had a ripple effect, slowing or stalling business in the state's malls, restaurants, and office complexes. Commercial and residential real estate values spiraled down. California lost 800,000 jobs between 1989 and 1994—more than half of them in Los Angeles County—and economic forecasters gloomily predicted continued job losses in the hundreds of thousands.

In defense-dependent suburbs like Los Angeles County's Lakewood, the recession hit hard. Lakewood, touted as "Tomorrow's City Today," opened for business in the spring of 1950. Meant to be the world's biggest subdivision, larger than Levittown, the original plan called for 17,500 two- and three-bedroom houses to be built on 3,400 acres of former ranchland. The houses (seven floor plans, twenty-one different exteriors) would sell for $8,000 to $10,000. FHA mortgages were available, with no money down for veterans. Lakewood Shopping Center, conceived as the nation's largest retail complex, would anchor the community and provide parking for ten thousand cars. "Everything about this entire project was perfect," recalled developer Mark Taper; 611 houses sold the first week.

Lakewood became home to white migrants from the Midwest and border South, blue-collar and low-level white-collar workers who found jobs at Hughes and McDonnell Douglas and Rockwell, or at the shipyard and naval station in Long Beach. Many of those who grew up in Lakewood stayed, graduating from the high school, only sometimes going on to college, looking for work in the defense and aerospace industries. While Los Angeles County became more multicultural, Lakewood, with a population just under 75,000, remained mostly white.

The Rockwell plant in Lakewood closed in 1992, obliterating a thousand jobs. The closure of the Long Beach naval station in 1996 was expected to take away another nine thousand jobs. Southern California lost more work when McDonnell Douglas moved parts of its production facility to Salt Lake City, and relocated other work to bolster its flagship plant in St. Louis. McDonnell Douglas alone had laid off twenty-one thousand people in Southern California by 1993. The company was said to be talking to Asian investors about moving at least some production to Asia. Half of California aerospace workers laid off in 1989 were still unemployed or had left the state two years later. Only 17 percent went back to work in the aerospace industry, earning close to their original salaries.

The white suburban ideal of the 1950s depended, of course, on plentiful, good-paying jobs for male breadwinners, and on cheerful, domestic women who limited their ambitions to child rearing and contained their sexuality within marriage. Lakewood residents of the 1990s had preserved these ideals to a noteworthy degree, ironically because, like hundreds of thousands of Americans at the mercy of corporations in the midst of "reorganizing", "downsizing," and relocating, maintaining the family income meant clinging to one steady job, usually Dad's, even though the company might fold its tent and move to Utah. But the combination of economic insecurity and social defensiveness produced, in Lakewood, at least one ugly mutation of such traditional "family values."

In the winter of 1993, word began to spread around the community about a group of high school boys, popular athletes, who called themselves the Spur Posse. Small children told of being intimidated, chased by cars, and beaten up by the boys. Rumors of sexual harassment began to circulate. When a pipe bomb blew up on the front porch of a Lakewood house, the high school principal called a meeting of parents suspected of having sons in the Spur Posse, and somebody mentioned the word *"rape."* Several girls came forward to complain that Spur Posse members had forced them into sexual intercourse, sometimes in gang situations, in an effort to compete against each other for sexual "points." A number of boys were taken out of class by sheriff's deputies, arrested, and held for four nights. All were released without being charged, except for one sixteen year-old charged with lewd conduct against a ten-year-old girl. The district attorney concluded that "the arrogance and contempt for young women which have been displayed, while appalling, cannot form the basis for criminal charges."

The Spur Posse boys became instant celebrities, appearing on television talk shows to boast about their conquests, complain about being misunderstood, and blame their behavior on social permissiveness in the United States. "We're a bunch of guys that are—I mean, better than decent-looking. We don't have to go out raping girls," said one. In another instance, a Spur Posse member demonstrated his (and his peers') failure to make the connection between the rising incidences of teenage pregnancy, the threat of AIDS, and the trend toward birth control programs aimed at sexually active high schoolers. "The schools, they're handing out condoms and stuff like that, and like, if

The Boy Scouts of America reflect the growing diversity of the American population. *Lief Skoogfore/Woodfin Camp & Associates.*

they're handing out condoms, why don't they tell us you can be arrested for it?" the young man asked a talk show host.

THE GLOBALIZATION OF AMERICA

As American corporations thought about moving some of their operations out of the United States, eagerly eyeing the cheap labor, minimal environmental regulation, and friendly government officials in Mexico and countries in Asia and the Caribbean, immigrants from those same countries flocked into the United States in search of their own American dreams.

The 1990s shift toward nonwhite minorities was the sharpest of the twentieth century. Whites in general represented about 80 percent of the total population; whites of European background represented about 76 percent. The remainder of the population was primarily African-American, Hispanic, Asian, and Native American. Much of the growth in the nonwhite population came from an additional 7.6 million Hispanics, half of whom were immigrants. Seven million people immigrated legally to the United States during the 1980s, and the vast majority of them were of non-European origin. In California, nonwhites and Latinos contributed a majority of public school students and accounted for 42 percent of the state's population. In New York, 40 percent of public school students were nonwhite. In the telephone book for San Jose, California, there were more people with the surname Nguyen than the surname Jones. Two hundred thousand people of Middle Eastern ancestry lived in the Detroit area. Nearly 1 million Southeast Asians or their children lived in cities across the country. By 1990, four in ten New Yorkers over the age of five spoke a language other than English at home. Around Los Angeles, more people in the suburbs than in the central city did not speak English at home. The immigration trends, combined with the high birth rates among African-Americans, Hispanics, and Asians, led some experts to predict that by the year 2050 a majority of the American population would trace its roots to non-European cultures.

The 1980s had seen one of the largest influxes of immigrants in American history. Even more important, the changing pattern of national origin among immigrants had become pronounced: about 45 percent of the newcomers came from Asia and the Middle East, and another 45 percent came from nations in the Western Hemisphere. No European country was among the top ten places of origin. Countries with extensive cultural, military, or economic ties to the United States—for example, the Philippines, Korea, and Mexico—provided the lion's share of the immigrants.

The diversity of the newcomers made it difficult to generalize about them. Some Asians were highly educated doctors and nurses who joined the staffs of big-city hospitals; some were engineers who pursued careers with high-technology firms. Other Asians from urban backgrounds pooled their resources to establish small retail businesses. Many Vietnamese, Filipinos, and other Asians from rural backgrounds found low-paying employment in service industries or manufacturing. Immigrants from Mexico and the rest of the Western Hemisphere often came from rural areas and had little education or wealth when they arrived. They settled in urban centers of the West, Southwest, and Midwest, where they worked in unskilled service and manufacturing positions.

Newcomers often experienced "exile shock" during their first years in the United States. Even if they had come to America to escape mistreatment or earn a better living, they sometimes felt unhappy with the unfamiliar surroundings and the prevailing materialism of American society. As a Hmong man from the highlands of Cambodia lamented, "Everything is money first." Parents who encouraged their children to adapt to American ways often grew dismayed when those same children rejected their family's traditional customs.

As had been the case during earlier periods of immigration, nativists opposed the admission of strangers on the ground that their presence would undermine American cultural values. Especially during economic downturns, immigrants became the targets of people who felt their own status and well-being threatened. Pete Wilson, the governor of California, was successfully re-elected in 1994 in part due to his support of Proposition 187, a victorious ballot measure based on the idea that the state could solve its economic woes by refusing to educate the children of undocumented immigrants and declining to provide such immigrants with medical care.

Yet most economists and many thoughtful social observers believed that the arrival of the new immigrants enriched the United States. Immigrant workers undeniably provided the labor power needed for the continued expansion of the American economy, and they brought with them cultural variety that injected fresh energy into American cities. The writer David Reiff called Miami "the capital of Latin America." New York mayor David Dinkins called his city a "gorgeous mosaic." New York Telephone announced it would offer customer service in 140 languages, including Fijian, French, Russian, Sioux, Swahili, Twi, and Yiddish, with a California company providing interpreters. In Houston, the immigrant presence enlivened the barren stretches of eight-lane boulevards, supermarkets and strip malls. Along one road on the west side of town, Korean, Thai, Vietnamese, and Chinese businesses and professionals leased mall space and erected bilingual and trilingual roadside signs. Immigrants even managed to create their own public space in Houston, at the Fiesta supermarket, a huge grocery store that stocked seven different kinds of bananas and carried current newspapers from around the globe, including three dailies from different cities in Colombia. In the Fiesta parking lot, vendors set up card tables laden with new and used goods and bargained in five different languages.

The continued movement to the Sunbelt and the allure of the United States for immigrants demonstrated the robustness of American society. But divisions between races and economic classes led to a bleaker picture: a sizable proportion of the American population was trapped in poverty and assailed by racial or ethnic violence. The proportion of Americans living in poverty declined slightly at the end of the eighties to 12.8 percent, yet the poverty rate remained higher than at any time in the 1970s (see figure, page 546). Vast differences existed among ethnic groups. Ten percent of whites were considered poor, versus 26 percent of Hispanics and 30 percent of blacks. Deprivation continued to fall most heavily on single mothers and children. Despite gains made since the 1960s, many elderly were also poor. Half of the people classified as poor were less than eighteen years old or over sixty-five. Half of black children under the age of six were poor.

The plight of the poorest African-Americans also contrasted sharply with the conditions of other people of color. *Time* magazine, which devoted a cover story to the growing ethnic diversity in the

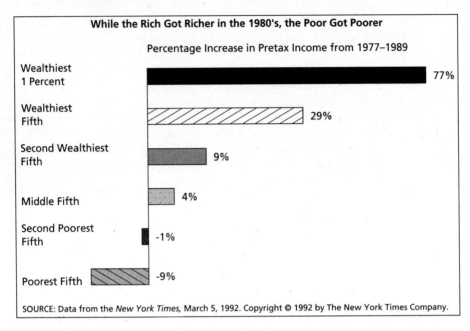

While the Rich Got Richer in the 1980's, the Poor Got Poorer

Percentage Increase in Pretax Income from 1977–1989

Wealthiest 1 Percent	77%
Wealthiest Fifth	29%
Second Wealthiest Fifth	9%
Middle Fifth	4%
Second Poorest Fifth	-1%
Poorest Fifth	-9%

SOURCE: Data from the *New York Times*, March 5, 1992. Copyright © 1992 by The New York Times Company.

Richer and Poorer: Changes in Average Family Income, 1977–1988

United States, reported uneasiness among blacks about the growing size of other nonwhite ethnic groups. Latinos stood to surpass African-Americans as the largest "nonwhite" group early in the twenty-first century. Asians and Latinos fared better than blacks economically, and African-Americans feared that their needs would be increasingly ignored by the larger society.

People of all ethnic backgrounds struggled to balance claims for recognition and respect for one another. Controversies continued over affirmative action programs designed to redress centuries of racial discrimination. The issue erupted into the political arena in October 1990, when President Bush vetoed a civil rights act that would have permitted nonwhites and women greater leeway to sue businesses for discrimination. The president claimed that the act would lead employers to establish rigid hiring and promotion quotas. A small but vocal group of black and Hispanic conservatives agreed. But advocates of affirmative action believed that his veto merely pandered to the resentments of white males, who saw their privileged position being eroded in a more pluralistic society.

The issue of ethnic balance caused special strains in colleges and universities, which faced new difficulties in deciding what should be included in the curriculum and what kinds of people should be hired to teach. Trying to recognize the new cultural diversity of the United States, some universities insisted that students learn something about non-European cultures. Moreover, college administrators—sometimes acting on their own initiative, sometimes in response to pressure—demanded that admission and hiring policies be changed so that a greater proportion of the student body and the faculty would be nonwhite and female. These moves to expand access to professional power and mobility, and to understand the multiple heritage of the United States sometimes produced a backlash. Efforts to broaden the curriculum to include the literature, thought, and art of Asia, Africa, and Latin America provoked complaints from some whites, men, and traditionalists who believed the cultural legacy of the West was being unjustly subordinated. Hiring practices that appeared to favor women or minorities led to bitter arguments about the nature of the university and the importance of traditional academic credentials.

However rancorous the politics of academia had become, the stakes were much higher for those who possessed the least. The term *underclass* was in wide use by the end of the 1980s to describe poor people—mostly urban, disproportionately nonwhite—who had high rates of unemployment and little education, depended on welfare, and often had no legal means of bettering their situation. The idea of an underclass suggested a complete loss of hope for the poorest Americans, especially very poor African-Americans. As Cornell West, professor of Afro-American Studies at Harvard, explained, the nation had not come to terms with "the nihilism that increasingly pervades black communities ... the lived experience of coping with a life of horrifying meaninglessness, hopelessness, and (most important) lovelessness. The frightening result is a numbing detachment from others and a self-destructive disposition toward the world."

Young black men experienced some of the most dire consequences of generations of poverty and deprivation. Nearly one-fourth of black men between the ages of eighteen and thirty had criminal records, were serving jail terms, or were on probation. Although most victims of black criminals were themselves black, the media seized on violent crimes committed by young blacks and Hispanics against middle-class whites. A night of "wilding"—a rampage of rape and mugging—in New York's Central Park, in which a thirty-one-year-old white woman was sexually assaulted and nearly beaten to death, attracted headlines for a year, though the brutal rape of a black woman the same night went unnoticed. At the end of the decade, the murder rate for black men under thirty remained the highest of any group, and a young black man had a greater chance of dying from a gunshot wound than from any other cause.

Reports of the dreadful conditions among the poorest of urban African-Americans might have awakened the revival of a spirit of community that crossed class lines. However, the picture was so bleak that many middle-class and suburban Americans, worried about their own economic status and eager to claim some credit for their ability to hang on, came to hold inner-city residents responsible for their own misery. Consequently, whites paid less attention to information about the racism that was still directed toward African-Americans. Only television, it seemed, had the power to bring racism home to white Americans.

In the early morning hours of a Los Angeles Sunday in March 1991, amateur photographer George Holliday was trying out his new video camera when across the street from his Lake View Terrace apartment a fleet of police cars stopped a white sedan. Holliday began taping the event, and his eighty-one-second video of what ensued would soon become a sight so familiar to American television audiences that still photographs taken from it would be immediately identifiable.

While Holliday's camera rolled unseen, Los Angeles police officers, who had been called in to assist the California highway patrol after a high-speed freeway chase, pulled twenty-five-year-old Rodney G. King from his car, threw him to the ground, tied his hands behind his back, and beat him severely with their batons. Police officers swung fifty-six times, using their batons like baseball bats, and kicked King repeatedly in the head as other officers looked on. King was then booked for evading police officers and violating his parole on a 1989 robbery conviction. No charges were filed.

King went to the hospital with multiple bruises and fractures. Holliday turned the tape over to authorities. By week's end, the video had been played and replayed on local and network television, raising in the starkest terms the often-repeated charges that American law enforcement officers, especially in Los Angeles, did not know the difference between maintaining order and perpetrating violence, particularly where blacks and other people of color were concerned. Civil rights organizations, including the American Civil Liberties Union, the NAACP, and other black and Hispanic advocacy groups, charged that the only difference between the King beating and LAPD business as usual was that *this* incident was caught on video. They pointed to numerous similar incidents, including one involving baseball Hall of Fame member Joe Morgan, who had been awarded $540,000 by a jury after being detained and physically abused by police accusing him of being a drug courier.

Los Angeles police chief Darryl Gates responded to the tape and the accusations by declaring the beating an "aberration." Gates, however, had little credibility with black and Latino Angelenos. He tended to say things the media termed "insensitive." On one occasion he had asserted that blacks died from police officers' choke holds because their bodies were somehow abnormal. On another occasion he suggested to a Senate committee that casual drug users ought to be shot.

Four white officers were ultimately charged with a total of eleven counts of assault on King, who said he was "just glad not to be dead."

When defense attorneys argued that pre-trial publicity had prejudiced potential jurors in Los Angeles, a judge granted a change of venue to Simi Valley, an overwhelmingly white, politically conservative suburban enclave and home of the Ronald Reagan presidential library. The jury, composed of ten non-Hispanic whites, one Asian, and one Hispanic, sat through seven weeks of detailed testimony, and watched the video, in normal time, slow motion, and super slow motion, over and over again.

On April 29, 1992, they acquitted the defendants of all charges. The attorney for one of the police officers said that the defense strategy had been to "put the jurors in the shoes of the police officers. I think we were able to do that . . . to get the jurors to look at the case not through the eyes of the camera." Loyola Law School professor Laurie Levenson observed that "Frankly, the people in Simi Valley worship the police." A juror told television newsman Ted Koppel that "the cops were simply doing what they'd been instructed to do. . . . A lot of those blows, when you watched them in slow motion, were not connecting. . . . When you look at King's body three days after the incident, not that much damage was done."

Los Angeles mayor Tom Bradley (who had been the first African-American to head the LAPD) announced, "Today, the system failed us," but he called for calm and imposed a dusk-to-dawn curfew. Many paid no heed. Reaction to the acquittals was immediate and explosive. Over the next three days, Los Angeles endured widespread arson, looting, shooting, and beatings. An angry crowd set a fire in front of police headquarters at Parker Center, and another in front of City Hall. In south-central Los Angeles, a predominately black and Hispanic area, fires raged, store windows were smashed, looting reigned, and motorists were pulled from their cars and beaten. In an eerie not-quite-replay of the King beating, a news helicopter videotaped the vicious beating of Reginald Denny, a white truck driver, by several young black men at the intersection of Florence and Normandie. The video failed to capture, however, beatings of blacks and Chicanos at the same corner, and it did not include footage of the African-American who rescued Denny from the youths.

The Los Angeles disorder was a lawless riot to some, an uprising against racial tyranny to others. It spawned the battle cry "No Justice, No Peace." Governor Wilson called in the National Guard to reinforce a police department caught off guard. Chief Gates, accused of reacting too slowly, remained uncharacteristically silent throughout the disturbance. The looting spread to affluent, heavily white areas like Beverly Hills, Westwood, and Santa Monica; looters made off with piles of skimpy underclothing from Frederick's of Hollywood. Confrontations broke out between blacks and Koreans in Koreatown, and President Bush added 5,000 federal troops to the 2,400 California National Guardsmen.

The riots following the Rodney King verdict spawned innumerable scenes of violence and disorder. Here, in the aftermath, residents of South Central Los Angeles clean up the neighborhood. © *1992 Jeff Share/Black Star.*

When relative calm returned three days later, more than 3,700 building fires had been set, and some had been allowed to rage out of control because the police lacked the personnel to protect the firefighters. Thirty-eight people, mostly black and Hispanic, had died. Violence had also broken out in San Francisco, Atlanta, New York, and even Madison, Wisconsin. Damage was estimated at $500 million. Most victims were minority business owners and neighborhood bystanders.

Soon, residents of the stricken areas emerged with shovels and brooms to begin cleaning up. Several hundred Koreans gathered along Wilshire Boulevard in an apparently spontaneous demonstration calling for interracial unity and an end to the violence. During the disturbances, Rodney King, stunned, called for calm. Seeming to speak to far larger issues than the immediate emergency, he pleaded, "People, I just want to say, can we all get along? Can we get along? Can we stop making it horrible for the older people and the kids? I mean, we're all stuck here for a while. Let's try to work it out."

The politics of race, class, and gender produced contradictory and troubling circumstances in the 1990s. One bizarre and bloody event involved one of the nation's most recognizable celebrities, football-hero-turned television spokesman O. J. Simpson. Known for his wide smile, eager manner, and jolly television persona, Simpson seemed to personify black success through hard work and a positive attitude. On June 13, 1994, the bodies of Simpson's white ex-wife, Nicole Brown Simpson, and her friend Ronald Goldman were found outside her Brentwood, California townhouse. The two were victims of a knife-wielding assailant who had stabbed and slashed them repeatedly. Simpson appeared grief-stricken at Nicole's funeral, accompanied by the couple's two children, but he was already the only suspect in the case. As police prepared to arrest Simpson, he fled in his white Ford Bronco, driven by his football buddy A.C. Cowling, and television cameras from the national networks soon recorded a bizarre, low-speed chase in which dozens of police vehicles followed Simpson's slow-moving truck along mile after mile of Los Angeles freeway. By the time the chase had neared an end, drivers on the other side of the freeway, tuned in to the story on their car radios, got out of their cars and flocked to the guard rail, cheering "Go O.J.!" much as they would have done if he were still a star running back headed for a touchdown.

As Simpson awaited trial, his public nice-guy image fell to revelations of his history of violence toward his ex-wife. Nicole Simpson, reports revealed, had called police on several occasions, once telling a 911 operator that she feared Simpson would kill her. On one occasion, he had even pleaded no contest to battering her, receiving probation. Advocates for battered women sought to use the case to protest continuing judicial indifference to domestic violence. Some blacks believed that Simpson, although rich and famous, would not receive a fair trail because he was a black man accused of murdering two white people, despite his having hired the highest-priced defense team in history.

The Simpson trial became so grand a public spectacle, crystallizing so many social conflicts, that it sometimes appeared that not only the defendant, but everyone involved, was on trial. A white police detective who worked on the case at the outset was accused of planting evidence in a racist plot to frame the black superstar. A female prosecuting attorney was criticized relentlessly, by some, for her hair style and clothing, and her own bitter divorce and child custody case became front-page news. Though many Americans avowed that they were sick of the media hype and saturation coverage surrounding the case, millions tuned in for daily updates.

ENVIRONMENTAL WORRIES

As Americans began to come to terms with the social tensions that divided them, they also confronted environmental perils. Public fear about the degradation of the environment, muted during the Reagan years by the popular belief that government regulation shackled economic activity, revived during the Bush administration. Bush proclaimed during the 1988 campaign that he wanted to be "the environmental president" as well as "the education president." His media consultants designed a series of television ads showing fouled beaches along the East Coast and raw sewage in Boston Harbor. The latter damaged Dukakis's campaign, despite his accurate riposte that Washington had reneged on a promise to pay for a water treatment plant. Critics disparaged Bush's political opportunism and doubted the depth of his commitment to the environment. Still, Bush achieved better relations with environmentalists than Reagan had, because Bush acknowledged the problem and believed that government had some role in the solution.

After the *Valdez*, a tanker owned by Exxon, ran aground in Alaska's Prince William Sound, causing the largest oil spill in American history, the coast guard demanded that the oil company spend $2 billion to wash the crude oil from the beaches. Environmentalists tried to clean the feathers and fur of thousands of marine animals befouled by the spill. The Justice Department prosecuted the captain of the tanker for operating it while under the influence of alcohol. Having an identifiable villain helped focus public attention on the environment, as did the media-inspired celebration of the twentieth anniversary of the first Earth Day, on April 20, 1990. Across the country people promised to conserve energy, recycle their trash, and patronize businesses that demonstrated concern for the environment.

The record on actual environmental initiatives was mixed. Voters, put off by the price of cleanups, defeated costly environmental initiatives in California and New York in the 1990 election. Five years after the *Valdez* oil spill, the courts settled some $15 billion in damage claims from fishermen and Alaska natives, and scientists were beginning to think that the cleanup had been, on balance, more ecologically disruptive than the original spill. The EPA-administered "Superfund" program to clean up toxic waste sites continued, but some property owners in some places on the agency's list fought designation as Superfund sites, preferring to live with pollution rather than lose all they had invested in their homes and livelihoods if their property was termed contaminated.

Fearful of having to spend money, federal officials responded slowly, even scornfully, to scientific concerns about global warming. Many scientists believed that excessive burning of petroleum had caused a thick layer of carbon dioxide to accumulate in the upper atmosphere, which might turn Earth into a giant greenhouse. Some climatologists and meteorologists feared that the planet's temperature would rise over the next hundred years, melting the polar ice caps, drowning coastal cities, and turning the fertile farmland of the Midwest into desert. Not all scientists agreed, however, and the administration, reluctant to regulate industrial emissions, sided with the skeptics, demanding more studies before taking any action to stem global warming. Though scientists and environmentalists called for conservation measures and new investment on alternative sources of energy, Bush administration officials displayed little inclination to revive the discarded energy policies of the 1970s, which had reduced gasoline use. When reporters criticized Bush for setting a poor example with his gas-guzzling "cigar boat," the former oil man testily replied that he believed Americans should be able to "prudently recreate."

Although the Bush administration, fearful of the costs and the opposition from special interest groups, shied away from a general attack on environmental problems, it did support some environmental laws. Congress approved the first overhaul of the Clean Air Act in thirteen years, setting stricter standards for automobile emissions and requiring municipalities to reduce smog. The measure also addressed for the first time the issue of acid rain: the increasing amount of sulfuric acid in rainfall throughout the Midwest and Northeast, caused by the burning of high-sulfur coal. In addition, Congress increased shipping companies' liability for oil spills and agreed to preserve large coastal areas from Alaska to New England from further development by oil companies. But the Clean Air Act disappointed environmentalists, who pointed out that it included a provision awarding pollution "credits" to companies that complied with emissions standards. Those companies could then sell the credits to corporations that violated the law, bringing polluters into nominal compliance. Conservatives saw the pollution credit as a means of injecting the marketplace into environmental regulation. They reasoned that polluters would soon see the economic advantage of cleaning up. Critics, however, pointed out that pollution credits amounted to a license to continue spewing out toxins, and that the air over credit-purchasing factories, and downwind of them, would remain dirty.

Once the public began to understand that industrial pollution included poisonous substances people could neither see nor smell, environmental concerns spawned grassroots organizing. The movement was particularly strong among poor people and people of color, whose neighborhoods were more likely to play host to polluting industries and toxic waste sites. In East Los Angeles, poor Chicana mothers asserting their right to protect their children from harm organized a group called Mothers of East L.A. to fight a city-sponsored toxic waste incinerator. In Tucson, an investigative reporter named Jane Kay followed up incidents of abnormally high rates of cancer in the overwhelmingly Chicano neighborhood of South Tucson. She also published a series of articles revealing the groundwater pollution that had resulted from the use of tri-chloral ethylene (TCE) as a solvent at the Tucson airport. Kay won a Pulitzer Prize for her stories, but the local branch of the Sierra Club was slow to identify South Tucson's plight as an environmental problem. The Southwest Organizing Project, a group founded in Albuquerque in 1981, argued that predominately nonwhite communities bore a disproportionate burden of toxic industrial sites, and that white-dominated mainstream environmental organizations ignored issues raised by people of color, a combination of circumstances many activists called "environmental racism."

Although the 1990s saw a surge in environmental activism on the part of people of color, some Native American leaders sought to turn environmental problems into community development opportunities. Wendell Chino, tribal chairman of the Mescalero Apaches, declared his intention to seek a permit to open a nuclear waste storage facility on Mescalero land, a project Chino claimed would bring wealth and jobs to the community. When the Mescaleros, to Chino's surprise, rejected the plan in a tribal vote, the chairman insisted on holding another election two weeks later. This time, amid allegations of fraud, the facility was approved. Another tribal chairman, Jacob Viarrial of the Pojoaque Pueblos, decided to put a little pressure on the governor of New Mexico, who opposed a casino gaming license for the tribe. Viarrial went on television to announce that, in light of the state's intransigence about gambling, the Pueblo, whose land was a mere ten miles from Santa Fe, had "no alternative" but to seek licensing as a nuclear waste repository. The governor could have his choice, Villareal implied, between bingo and plutonium on the outskirts of the state's tourist mecca.

Nowhere was the link between government policy and environmental problems clearer than in the case of nuclear waste. The Reagan defense build-up had included a crash program of plutonium processing and nuclear weapons production. Even before the Cold War ended, scientists, policymakers, and activists had begun to worry about mounting evidence of production safety hazards and air, soil, and water contamination around nuclear facilities like the Hanford Reservation in Washington State, the Savannah River facility in South Carolina, and the Rocky Flats installation on a mesa sixteen miles northwest of Denver.

In 1951, the federal government began looking for a place to mass-produce nuclear weapons. Planners settled on the Rocky Flats site because it was close to the bomb laboratory at Los Alamos and near what was then a small city. Additionally, land was cheap, and air conditioning was not needed. Even then, scientists recognized the hazards such a plant might pose to people who lived downwind, but they reasoned that the site was "well-removed from any residential area."

Unfortunately, meteorologists who reported on wind conditions had used bad data. Winds, sometimes clocked at one hundred miles per hour, swept off the mesa constantly, blowing southeast, right over Denver.

Right from the start, Rocky Flats managers put production first, safety second. Leaks of radioactivity occurred regularly. So did fires. A 1969 fire forced a six-month shutdown in weapons production and produced $50 million in damage. Firefighters equipped with radiation detection equipment found plutonium on the ground around the plant, but officials claimed that "There is no evidence that plutonium was carried beyond plant boundaries."

In 1974, the EPA released a study indicating that cattle from a pasture east of Rocky Flats had been more badly contaminated with plutonium than cattle that had been set out to graze on the highly contaminated nuclear test site in Nevada. The government began purchasing thousands of acres of land around the plant. Anti-nuclear activists and concerned physicians began to document increased rates of leukemia and cancers of the lymph nodes, lungs, thyroid, testes, and breast, paralleling patterns seen at Hiroshima and Nagasaki.

By the late 1980s, the Rocky Flats complex was home to a toxic assortment of contaminated holding ponds, waste dumps, and open-air incineration spots. Contaminated materials, often thrown haphazardly into thousands of fifty-five-gallon drums (one scientist called them "barrels of bubbling yuck"), ranged from plutonium-contaminated oil to wipes used to cleanse contaminated instruments. Some of the drums were leaking, threatening the entire Denver water supply. In the fall of 1989, Admiral James Watkins, the Secretary of Energy, declared the plant temporarily closed for "safety improvements." Some scientists suggested that the government simply put a fence around the installation and call it a "National Sacrifice Zone."

Others addressed the problem of long-range storage of nuclear waste. In an effort to store a tiny fraction of the nation's radioactive refuse, the government planned to open a repository, deep underground, outside Carlsbad, New Mexico, in 1988. This facility, called the Waste Isolation Pilot Project (WIPP), was designed only for what was called "low-level" nuclear waste—the miscellany generated as by-products of nuclear manufacturing—rather than "high-level" trash like spent reactor fuel rods. Engineers dug an immense mine, two thousand feet underground, in salt beds. However, the WIPP was perpetually mired in controversy, as scientists and policymakers tried to allay the concerns of New Mexicans determined not to have a nuclear waste dump in their back yard. The site's opening, first slated for 1985, was put off again and again. By the mid-1990s, scientists had identified thousands more contaminated areas at the nation's nuclear sites. Meanwhile, barrels of radioactive garbage continued to pile up around the country, and the United States still had no facility for handling the ever-mounting inventory of nuclear waste.

THE ELECTION OF 1992

On the heels of victory in the Persian Gulf in the spring of 1991, President Bush rode a wave of popularity. At that point, the pundits were calling Bush unbeatable in 1992, a fact not lost on Democratic party heavyweights, who would have had to begin raising money and organizing their campaigns in order to challenge the president in 1992. Mounting such a challenge seemed hopeless to precisely those Democrats that the press had anointed as favorites since 1988: Governor Mario Cuomo of New York, Senator Sam Nunn of Georgia, Senator Bill Bradley of New Jersey, and Senator Al Gore of Tennessee. Each decided not to run.

By the winter of 1991, the field of Democratic candidates looked to many observers like a horse race without a thoroughbred. It included Douglas Wilder, the first black governor of Virginia since Reconstruction, Senators Tom Harkin of Iowa and Bob Kerrey of Nebraska, former senator Paul Tsongas of Massachusetts, former governor Jerry Brown of California, and Governor Bill Clinton of Arkansas. Wilder dropped out early, unable to raise seed money. Harkin, running as an unabashed New Deal Democrat, was next to go. Tsongas stressed the need to make tough choices about the economy—to the delight of "deficit hawks"—and took a pro-business stance that was considered unusual for a Democrat, but many worried that he was too much like Dukakis. Brown staked out the party's left flank, running a shoestring campaign in which he traveled by commercial airliner, stayed in supporters' homes, and relied on small contributions from people who called an 800 number he set up for the campaign. Clinton, previously best known for a soporific keynote speech at the 1988 Democratic convention (the line that got the most applause from the delegates was "In conclusion . . ."), took the tack of concentrating on fund-raising and organization, billing himself as a "New Democrat" who "favored change."

The press set off to cover the New Hampshire primary campaign in a cynical mood, deeming the voters equally turned off to politicians. To the surprise of many reporters, however, New Hampshire voters flocked to candidates' debates and town meetings, asked sophisticated questions, and appeared to be—amazingly—engaged and even optimistic. At first Governor Clinton appeared to be the front-runner. Clinton not only loved to campaign and had the organization to make the long haul, he also gave thoughtful answers to hard questions. He was also thought to have some liabilities, including his wife, Hillary

Rodham Clinton, a nationally prominent attorney and child welfare advocate. Mrs. Clinton had alienated many housewives when she said, in one interview, that she "could have stayed home and baked cookies," but instead she'd made different choices. Nevertheless, polls indicated that Hillary, and consequently her husband, had substantial support among working women, and however strong a presence she projected, Bill was still the candidate. In some polls, Clinton appeared to be ahead by as many as twenty points.

Then, on January 23, the *National Star,* a tabloid newspaper, ran a story featuring a woman named Gennifer Flowers, who claimed that she had had a twelve-year affair with Bill Clinton. Since 1988, when the Miami *Herald* had sent a reporter to Washington, D.C., to try to catch candidate Gary Hart cheating on his wife, the press had deemed candidates' private life fair game. Reporters had created what was commonly referred to as "the character issue," which required their reporting on such things as candidates' sex lives.

When Clinton entered a room packed with more than thirty reporters that morning, he was assailed with questions about Flowers and "the adultery question." An ABC news producer who had watched the press pounce on the candidate declared the spectacle "the worst gang bang I had ever seen." In the ensuing weeks, reporters argued about how much coverage to give the story, but no one seemed to know what to do. Once the line between public and private had been breached, it seemed there were no rules any more. The Gennifer Flowers story was important in the campaign not because it was true, which could not be confirmed, but because it was a political liability for Clinton.

In an effort to confront the charges, Bill and Hillary appeared on a special edition of "60 Minutes," confessing that their marriage had not been perfect, but they loved each other anyway. The Clintons seemed to have defused the Gennifer Flowers story, but another bombshell was soon to come. Allegations began to surface that Clinton had been a Vietnam War draft dodger. Clinton's support in New Hampshire fell from 33 to 17 percent. Tsongas eventually won the battle in New Hampshire, but Clinton, refusing to be beaten, rose again, pronouncing himself "The Comeback Kid." The character issue, it seemed, cut both ways. Many voters sympathized with his marital difficulties or thought such things irrelevant to his qualifications for the presidency. If his opposition to the Vietnam War alienated veterans, it struck a chord with members of his own generation. When he later admitted to having tried marijuana (claiming he "didn't inhale"), few voters under fifty were shocked.

Proving himself a tough and tireless campaigner who knew how to appeal to crowds, Clinton went on to win decisively in the "Super Tuesday" primaries in the South and West as his campaign gathered new steam. Once his grasp on the nomination was assured, he ignored the tradition of choosing a vice presidential candidate who would balance the ticket ideologically and geographically; instead he chose Al Gore. Clinton and Gore were remarkably alike in many ways. Both were southerners, both were moderates in their mid-forties, both were Ivy League-educated intellectuals (Clinton a graduate of Yale Law School, Gore a Harvard B.A.) who loved the details of government and took pride in being called "policy wonks." But Gore brought significant strengths of his own to the ticket. He was a Vietnam veteran, and his homemaker wife, Tipper, had made a name for herself campaigning for warning labels on rock records with graphic lyrics. He was also an avid environmentalist and author of the best-selling, *Earth in the Balance,* which detailed his broad grasp of environmental issues and his passionate commitment to the need for a change in environmental policy. Veterans, housewives, and environmentalists were reassured by Gore. When the Democrats met in New York in July for their convention, New York *Times* political reporter Maureen Dowd sneered that the Democrats had stuffed the big city full of yahoo boosters of the "Double Bubba" ticket. But Clinton and Gore played well in Peoria. Party regulars and Clinton strategists knew an appealing combination when they saw one. The convention, remarkably harmonious, pushed the Clinton ticket nearly twenty points ahead of Bush in the polls.

The Democrats' early troubles should have been George Bush's delights, but he was having problems of his own. His 1988 campaign, in which he had tried to appease "red-meat" Republicans by red-baiting liberals, opposing abortion, and fulminating against Dukakis for coddling criminals, had never really earned him the trust of his party's right wing. Instead, Bush lent the power and credibility of the president's support to rhetoric, policies, and people he couldn't control, from Pat Robertson's Christian Coalition to extreme right-wing ideologues like former Nixon speechwriter and political columnist Pat Buchanan. Buchanan decided to run against Bush, although not many expected him to make much difference. But Bush was hardly an electrifying campaigner, and many voters found him insensitive to the lives of ordinary people. When Buchanan polled 41 percent to Bush's 57 percent in the New Hampshire primary, Bush determined to meet the challenge from the right by co-opting it.

The wild card in the deck was the independent candidacy of Texas billionaire H. Ross Perot. Running as a "populist," the feisty, plain-spoken Perot was willing and able to finance his campaign out of his own pocket. Some people found his description of himself as "the people's candidate," far-fetched, but ironically his immense wealth lent credibility to his claim that he was beholden to no special interests. His candidacy appealed to millions of voters disillusioned with the two main parties. To Democrats concerned about the deficit, Perot proclaimed the need to tighten the nation's belt and launch austerity measures in government. To Republicans worried about the party's turn to the right on social issues, Perot offered a pro-choice position on abortion.

By July, Perot had reached 20 percent in the polls, and strategists in both parties were looking over their shoulders. Perot was a master of the media, using talk shows like "The Larry King Show" to appear sensitive yet strong, a posture the other candidates quickly adopted. By the spring of 1992, Americans were regularly subjected to presidential and vice presidential candidates on "Good Morning America," "Today," "CBS This Morning," and even MTV. Perot, however, lacked the stomach for the grind of traditional campaigning. His public speeches tended to be forced and pugnacious. When he addressed a convention of the NAACP as "you people," he was accused of racial insensitivity, a charge that clearly stung him. He claimed the media had misinterpreted his remarks, and he grew increasingly impatient with his inability to control coverage of his campaign. In the midst of the Democratic convention, Perot dropped out of the race, explaining that he was doing so for personal reasons.

The Republican convention, held in Houston in August, showed television audiences around the country that evangelical Christians and right-wing ideologues had captured the party's rank and file, if not the nomination. Most speakers at the convention emphasized what they called "family values," a theme first voiced by Vice President Dan Quayle. Earlier that summer, Quayle had criticized a television character, Murphy Brown, for having a child out of wedlock, saying the character set a bad example for American women. In a vitriolic tirade, Buchanan bashed gays, accused Hillary Clinton of encouraging children to sue their parents, and, ignoring earlier accusations that he was anti-Semitic, declared that the time had come for "a religious war for the soul of America." Humorists said that they had enjoyed the candidate's references to "Willary Horton" and thought Buchanan's speech probably sounded better in the original German.

The Republicans hoped to capitalize on a backlash against working women by putting their own nurturing, maternal versions of American womanhood on display. Yet, despite the success of a speech by popular first lady Barbara Bush, the strategy failed. Marilyn Quayle, the vice president's wife, sounded a harsh and exclusionary note when she asserted that "not everyone demonstrated, dropped out, took drugs, joined the sexual revolution, or dodged the draft." In an implicit comparison of herself and Hillary Clinton, Quayle (who was also a lawyer) said, "Helping my children as they grow into good and loving teenagers is a daily source of joy for me. There aren't many women who would have it any other way." The press noted that

Christian Coalition leader Pat Robertson had said, in his campaign against a state equal rights amendment in Iowa, that feminism "encourages women to leave their husbands, kill their children, practice witchcraft, destroy capitalism, and become lesbians."

Bush's ratings went up only three points after the convention. Many who watched the convention, including some lifelong Republicans, found the proceedings frighteningly narrow and mean-spirited. Pollsters, moderate party professionals, and many observers, warned that the Republicans were not winning much support by campaigning on moral values in a time of economic uncertainty. President Bush insisted that he would do "whatever it takes" to win and that he was determined to push the character and values questions all the way to election day.

Clinton strategists, having already survived a bruising fight for the nomination, understood that voters in 1992 were far more concerned with the state of the economy than about whether the candidate's wife was too pushy or his libido too strong. They decided to focus their campaign time and money on winnable states, including California and New York, where they were running far ahead, and more hotly contested races in Colorado, Georgia, and Connecticut; they minimized candidate appearances and advertising time in less important and less winnable states like South Carolina. Determined to keep the race focused tightly on the need for change and on economic matters, they daily urged Clinton, Gore, and their various spokespeople to "stay on-message." Lest anyone forget what the message was, Clinton strategist James Carville posted a sign in Clinton headquarters: "It's the economy, stupid."

The Republicans never recovered from the bad press generated by the convention. Bush and Quayle continued to insist that the economy, which a majority of American people saw as "not so good," was just fine and that the real issue was Clinton's "character." But the character issue cut both ways. Voters knew that Bush himself had been on both sides of major issues, from abortion to taxes to balancing the federal budget. Quayle, for his part, had managed to avoid the draft and Vietnam service by using family connections to get into a National Guard unit. Given the extraordinary changes in standards of behavior and belief in the preceding decades, many Americans may have wondered whether their own lives would have stood up to the scrutiny of the press or the rigid codes trumpeted by the Republicans. Unemployment remained above 7 percent, and the deficit continued to balloon, reaching $290 billion in 1992.

Republicans and Democrats both shuddered when Perot re-entered the race little more than a month before election day, claiming that his volunteers had convinced him to come back. But many who had previously considered him an option wondered whether he was really cut out to be president. Showing a goofy paranoid streak that his long-time critics had warned about, he told "60 Minutes" about a Republican conspiracy to disrupt his daughter's wedding, and he claimed he had been the target of assassination attempts, including one in 1970 or 1971, involving a commando unit of Black Panthers hired by the North Vietnamese government. An ABC reporter talked to the man who headed Dallas police operations at the time the Panthers supposedly invaded Perot's Texas compound; the man insisted, "Listen to me—it didn't happen. It did not happen. There were only about eight people here that belonged to the Black Panther party. Two of those people worked for us and they told us every day what was happening." Perot called ABC to complain that the network was out to get him, insisting that "People try to kill me every year." Despite such outbursts, enough American voters were disillusioned with the traditional parties that Perot continued to rise in the polls. He did well in debates with Bush and Clinton, once again using his pugnacious personality to best advantage.

As election day approached, the President's campaign was clearly in trouble. Even nature seemed to be conspiring against Bush, when the most costly natural disaster in the nation's history, Hurricane Andrew, slammed into the Florida coast, leveling huge swaths in the Miami Beach area, and leaving nearly a quarter of a million people homeless. As if that weren't enough, Hurricane Andrew spun out to sea and then returned to hammer away at the Louisiana lowlands, narrowly missing New Orleans. The Federal Emergency Management Agency, the government department charged with handling such matters, responded sluggishly and inefficiently as looters roamed through posh Miami neighborhoods and victims took the law into their own hands, defending their possessions with shotguns. The President went to visit the stricken areas; when reporters asked him why, he replied defensively, "I think it shows that I care."

Trailing in the polls, Bush grew increasingly shrill. He railed at Gore for his environmentalism, telling a crowd that Gore was the "Ozone Man . . . He's crazy, way out, far out, man." Meanwhile Clinton and Gore pounded away at their message of change and economic responsibility to increasingly optimistic crowds who sang along with taped recordings of the campaign's baby boomer theme song, Fleetwood Mac's "Don't Stop (Thinking About Tomorrow)." On election eve, Clinton made a final eleven-state barnstorming tour, playing to huge crowds in the wee hours of the morning. When it was all over, Clinton had rolled up an impressive victory in the electoral college (see map, page 562), vindicating his campaign strategy. However, the results of the popular vote were more mixed, with Clinton winning 43 percent of the vote to Bush's 38 percent and Perot's 15 percent. The president-elect declared that the voters had sent Washington a mes-

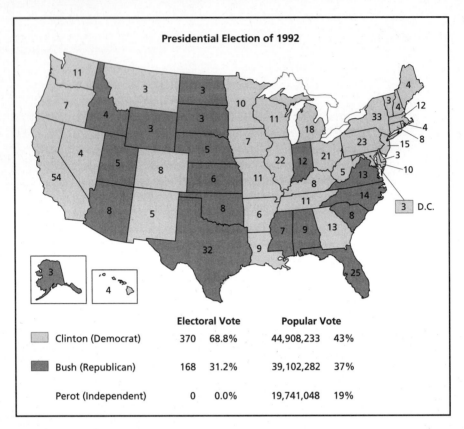

Presidential Election of 1992

	Electoral Vote		Popular Vote	
Clinton (Democrat)	370	68.8%	44,908,233	43%
Bush (Republican)	168	31.2%	39,102,282	37%
Perot (Independent)	0	0.0%	19,741,048	19%

Presidential Election of 1992

sage, and the message was that they wanted change. As if to drive the point home, voters gave the Democrats an increased majority in the Senate. Four women were elected to the Senate as well, including Carol Mosely Braun of Illinois, the first African-American woman to serve there.

The Democrats had polled roughly the same percentage of the popular vote in every presidential election since 1968, when George Wallace split the Democratic coalition, making way for Richard Nixon's election. After 1968, many Wallace voters turned in the direction of the Republican party. In 1992, the Democrats had hoped to turn the tables; after the election, they concentrated on capturing the Perot vote in the years to come.

Senate minority leader Bob Dole saw things differently, however. With Bush's concession speech barely over, Dole was already pointing out that the Democrats would come into the White House having won only a minority of voters; the Republicans, Dole insisted, were determined to represent the majority who did not vote for Clinton.

The Clintons and the Gores celebrate Democratic triumph on election night in Little Rock, Arkansas. © *Ira Wyman/Sygma.*

PRESENT TENSE

When the Democrats took office in January 1993, promising sweeping change and a new spirit of hope, many Americans believed that partisan bickering and gridlock in Washington were at least on the wane, if not yet completely dead. With Democrats in control of both houses of Congress and the presidency, bickering between the executive and legislative branches might subside. Clinton laid out an ambitious agenda that began with economic recovery and went on to include everything from a national service plan to fund college tuition to rebuilding the country's fractured infrastructure, instituting welfare reform, adding 100,000 more police to the nation's streets, and restructuring the country's out-of-control health care system.

To assist him in this task, and to gratify the millions of Hispanics, blacks, and working women who had given him his victory, Clinton pledged to appoint a cabinet that "looked like America." Clinton nominated more African-Americans, Hispanics, and women to cabinet positions than any of his predecessors. Some of Clinton's appointees started out with ambitious plans. Housing and Urban Development secretary Henry Cisneros, formerly mayor of San Antonio, vowed to clean up the mess left behind by his predecessors, a formidable job. Energy Secretary Hazel O'Leary, the first African-American woman to head a cabinet-level department, quietly took the government out of the bomb-making business, and opened millions of classified documents about nuclear experiments and other secret projects to public scrutiny.

But by the 1990s, the novelty of appointing women and minorities to government posts had worn off. Moreover, increasing press scrutiny of their personal lives made it extremely difficult for appointees to be approved by Congress. Clinton's first choice for attorney general, a corporate lawyer named Zoe Baird, was forced to withdraw her name when it was revealed that she had employed an illegal immigrant as a domestic worker and failed to pay Social Security taxes for the woman. The woman who was finally confirmed as attorney general, Miami district attorney Janet Reno, was initially enormously popular. She quickly earned criticism, however, for her handling of a stand-off between followers of religious cult leader David Koresh and agents of the Bureau of Alcohol, Tobacco, and Firearms. The confrontation ended in a fiery conflagration at Koresh's Waco, Texas compound. Many children were killed in the fire. Reno accepted full responsibility for the incident, but this did little to dampen criticism of the ATF's handling of the affair. Two African-American appointees, Commerce Secretary Ron Brown and Agriculture Secretary Mike Espy, were investigated for insider trading and accepting corporate favors. HUD secretary Henry Cisneros was urged to resign amid disclosures that he had made cash payments to a former mistress. Comedians joked that appointees to the Clinton cabinet could expect many fringe benefits, including their own special prosecutors. Clinton's nominee for surgeon general, Dr. Joycelyn Elders, was an African-American woman who, like previous surgeons-general, believed that the office was a bully pulpit. Many senators, however, quailed at the thought of Elders, an outspoken advocate of condom distribution in schools and the legalization of illicit drugs, in charge of the nation's health policy. Even Clinton ultimately found Elders too outspoken, and he fired her. When President Clinton put Mrs. Clinton in charge of the task force that would formulate the administration's health care reform plan, conservatives complained that the first lady had too much influence for someone who had not been elected.

Hillary Clinton aroused strong feelings among both her supporters and her detractors, but her husband was determined to give her a pivotal role in the administration. Many criticized her task force for holding secret meetings and for leaving out key players, including representatives of special interest groups like insurance companies and the American Medical Association. Mrs. Clinton's task force ultimately issued an immensely complicated plan that ran into the thousands of pages. The plan called for a "managed-care" system, which most observers saw as a compromise between a Canadian-style "single-payer," government-run health care program, and the "free-market" approach favored by insurance companies. But delays and equivocations doomed the Clinton plan. Congress whittled away at reform and balked at the idea of "universal coverage"—of enabling the government to guarantee every American health insurance. The insurance industry spent millions airing folksy commercials that featured a middle-class couple worrying that the government would take away their right to choose their own doctors. The Republicans stalled; they knew the public wanted lower costs and better benefits, but they believed that if nothing were done, 1994 voters would blame the Democrats. The failure of Clinton's health care plan did indeed prove disastrous for the president, as well as for his party in the 1994 election.

With the Cold War paradigm no longer dominating American foreign policy, Clinton had to formulate new rules for American engagement abroad. The costs of the Cold War linked the social and the economic—billions that might have gone to alleviate poverty were instead spent on weapons and the appurtenances of the security state. In the Cold War's aftermath, the two superpowers appeared to have become super losers. The American public expressed two deeply held, valid, but often inconsistent principles regarding U.S. involvement in the world's troubles. First, people believed that as the world's only superpower, the United States had a unique responsibility. Instantaneous televised pictures of human suffering in some of the most remote regions of the world tugged at Americans' heartstrings. But, second, Americans wanted U.S. foreign engagements to be brief and inexpensive and result in miniscule American casualties. It proved difficult for the Clinton administration to reconcile these often incompatible aims.

The administration scored its biggest initial success in managing old problems left over from the Cold War. Clinton's secretary of state, Warren Christopher, a veteran of the Johnson and Carter administrations, facilitated agreements between Israel and its many foes. In the summer of 1993, Israel and the Palestine Liberation Organization reached an agreement calling for mutual recognition and the creation of Palestinian self-rule in Gaza and the West Bank. On September 13, 1993, Israeli prime minister Yitzhak Rabin and PLO chairman Yassir Arafat shook hands in a moving ceremony on the south lawn of the White House. Over the next year, Christopher spent a lot of time in the Middle East trying to arrange a comprehensive peace. These efforts bore fruit in the fall of 1994, when Israel and Jordan signed a treaty and pledged cooperation. The Clinton administration also successfully managed the new relationship with Russia, the most powerful of the Soviet Union's successor states. Clinton formed a quick personal bond with Boris Yeltsin, the Russian president, and he helped

Yeltsin survive a coup mounted by ultra-nationalists and Communists in October 1993.

The Clinton administration had less success with other foreign policy problems. Without the Cold War as a framing principle, it was difficult for the administration and the public at large to decide when U.S. interests were sufficiently at stake to warrant engagement. During the campaign of 1992, Clinton faulted the Bush administration for its apparent disregard of the suffering of Bosnian victims of Serb aggression in the civil war in the former Yugoslavia. Clinton suggested that as president he would lift the arms embargo against the mostly Muslim Bosnians and order air strikes against Serb militias. As president, however, he followed a much more cautious approach, authorizing a few intermittent and ineffectual air strikes. When Bosnian Serbs shelled civilians and held hostage hundreds of United Nations peacekeeping forces in June 1995, the Clinton administration could do little except look on in horror.

For the first eight months of his administration, Clinton continued Bush's policy of using tens of thousands of U.S. soldiers to supply food to starving Somalia, a drought-stricken and strife-plagued country in Africa. The famine relief had seemed so successful that the United States and its U.N. allies expanded their mission in Somalia in an effort to create a viable government. But this peace-making enterprise quickly brought U.S. forces into conflict with many armed Somali factions. In the summer of 1993, guerrillas began attacking U.S. soldiers, and in early October twelve American GIs died in a firefight with Somalis. The American public, horrified by pictures of a dead U.S. soldier being dragged through the streets of Mogadishu, demanded that the remaining forces be removed. Clinton ordered them out by March 1994. The loss of life also cost Secretary of Defense Les Aspin his job. He was replaced by William Perry, a strategist, mathematician, and designer of weapons systems.

The bad experience in Somalia made the Clinton administration shy about deploying U.S. forces elsewhere, but television pictures of human suffering made it impossible for the United States to remain disengaged. In the summer of 1994 the administration sent four thousand troops to central Africa to help save nearly 1 million refugees of a hideous civil war in Rwanda from famine and disease. This time, U.S. forces refused to participate in local politics, limiting their mission to humanitarian aid.

In the summer of 1994, Cuba once more became a problem for the United States. The Cuban economy had suffered severely after the collapse of the Soviet Union, because Moscow no longer provided billions in food and fuel. Thousands of desperate Cubans took to boats and rafts to flee the island for Florida. Mindful that a similar 1980 exodus of 120,000 Cubans had embarrassed Jimmy Carter and contributed to his 1980 defeat, Clinton reversed the traditional policy of granting asylum to any Cuban who could reach the United States. Instead of allowing the Cubans entry into Florida, the U.S. coast guard and navy rescued the boat people and deposited them at the U.S. navy base at Guantánamo Bay, Cuba. There they shared a makeshift camp with twenty thousand Haitians also denied entry into the United States. Plans were made to accommodate as many as sixty thousand people at the base, but this arrangement assuredly could not last forever.

Perhaps the Clinton administration's greatest foreign policy success came in Haiti, where the president had pledged to restore a democratically elected government. Haitian army officers had ousted President Jean Bertrand Aristide in September 1991, resuming the brutal repression that had plagued Haiti for generations. In the fall, the United States dispatched a boatload of lightly armed police trainers to the Haitian capital. The military rulers arranged a demonstration by a few dozen thugs near the port, and the Clinton administration ordered the trainers not to disembark. Over the next year, as the military rulers remained in Haiti, the Clinton administration wrestled with the problem of what to do next. Tens of thousands of refugees fled the island, but as Bush had done, Clinton refused to allow them to enter the United States. The U.S. tightened an economic embargo on Haiti and obtained UN authorization for a multilateral invasion to restore Aristide, but neither a majority of the public nor the top military leadership wanted to invade. The Haitian junta remained defiant, so in October 1994 U.S. forces prepared for an invasion that the president clearly hoped to avoid. At the eleventh hour Clinton sent a special delegation to Port-au-Prince, headed by former president Jimmy Carter and including former Joint Chiefs chair Colin Powell and Senator Sam Nunn of Georgia. The Carter delegation managed to reach a settlement with the Haitian military, forestalling the invasion. Soon the military leaders departed the island, and Aristide returned in triumph. American troops were deployed as part of a "transition" effort to ensure that Aristide would be able to take power, but the government had avoided a full-scale invasion while achieving the goal of restoring a democratically-elected leader.

As Majority Leader Dole's early comments suggested, the Republicans in Congress gave Clinton no honeymoon. The president's early successes—passage of a family and medical leave act, a free-trade agreement with Mexico and Canada, and a budget that reduced the deficit for the first time in twelve years—were hard won. Clinton's two moderate appointments to the Supreme Court, Justice Ruth Bader Ginsberg and Justice Stephen Breyer, sailed to confirmation, seemingly his only easy victories. A Clinton-backed ban on assault weapons passed narrowly, but the gun lobby vowed to mount a major campaign against the administration in 1995. Clinton's critics were growing increasingly vocal. His most ambitious proposals—health care reform in particular—faced opposition from such heavily-endowed interests as the insurance industry and the American Medical Association, and it ultimately failed to carry the day. And the character issue continued to plague him. By 1994, a special prosecutor and a congressional committee were investigating the Clintons' investment in a real estate development called Whitewater that had ties to a failed savings and loan in Arkansas. Also, a former employee of the Arkansas state government was suing the president for sexual harassment.

The economy improved immensely under Clinton's stewardship, with growth exceeding 3 percent per year in 1993 and 1994. For the first time in twelve years, the federal government had abandoned the official stance that the market would take care of everything. Government officials grappled with problems ranging from nuclear waste to teenage pregnancy. But Americans continued to feel isolated from the people in power, and many regarded Washington as a foreign country. As president-elect, Bill Clinton had earned the nickname "national empath" for his aching sensitivity to common people's problems. (His campaign lament that "I feel your pain" became a joke even the president laughed at.) The president lamented the capital's insularity and its preoccupation with scandal and gossip. "This is a city," political columnist Molly Ivins said of Washington, "where everybody says what everybody else says." Clinton was heard wondering aloud how he might break through this insularity and keep in touch with the people "beyond the beltway." But nobody seemed to know the answer to this question, least of all members of his party.

The 1994 midterm elections provided plenty of evidence that American voters felt the federal government, particularly the Democrats in charge, had lost touch with their concerns. House minority leader Newt Gingrich crafted the "Contract with America," a position statement, signed by most Republican candidates, that called for scaling back the welfare state, balancing the budget, and reforming government. During the campaign, Republican strategists de-emphasized the social agenda of the Christian Right, focusing instead on the economic issues that had worked so well for the Democrats in 1992. In race after race, voters delivered a stinging rebuke to the Democrats, electing Republicans to governorships and Congress, and defeating such powerful incumbents as Speaker of the House Tom Foley of Washington, Governor Mario Cuomo of New York, and Governor Ann Richards of Texas (who lost to George W. Bush, son of the former president). In Virginia, senatorial candidate Oliver North, the former Marine colonel who had admitted lying to Congress during the Iran-contra scandal, ran with huge financial backing from the Christian

Former House Speaker Richard Gephardt hands the gavel to newly elected Speaker Newt Gingrich. The new Republican majority claimed that it had a mandate to roll back the New Deal and dismantle the Welfare State. *AP/Wide World Photos.*

Right; he only narrowly missed being elected to the same body he had lied to so few years before. Dubbed by some "the revolt of the angry white men," the election swept in a new generation of conservative leaders, some of whom seemed determined to dismantle the federal government. The 39 percent of Americans who went to the polls in 1994 represented a far more affluent and conservative constituency than the American public as a whole. Among the measures passed in the election was Proposition 187, the California initiative to deny most educational and health benefits to illegal immigrants. Although the voters seemed to say they wanted "less government," whether the election was a mandate for a conservative social agenda was less clear: voters elected Republican candidates who vowed to oppose abortion and gay rights, and yet they turned down state ballot initiatives designed to restrict abortion and bar gay rights laws.

When Congress convened in 1995, the Republicans were in control of both houses for the first time since 1946. Bob Dole, the new Senate majority leader, promised change in Washington but expressed less hostility to the Democratic administration than the ultra-conservative congressman, Newt Gingrich, who became Speaker of the House. Gingrich vowed no compromise with the White House and denounced the president and Mrs. Clinton as "Counterculture McGoverniks."

The new Republican leadership announced plans to enact an economic program that included extensive measures, from a constitutional amendment to balance the budget to a "war on welfare." Whether the Republican agenda would succeed in its expressed intention of reversing the New Deal remained to be seen.

CONCLUSION

As they had done since the mid-1960s, American institutions strained to manage continued, rapid change during the 1990s. The strong federal government and assertive presidency characteristic of the postwar epoch remained central features of modern American life. The federal judiciary continued to influence the way people related to one another and their government. But opinions about American government and society were mixed. Some people remained skeptical about the quality of the nation's leadership and the ability of its institutions to meet people's needs.

For forty-five years after the Second World War, the United States was the dominant military and economic power in the world. For nearly all of that time, competition between the Soviet Union and the United States was the primary focus of international relations. The Cold War had helped create the modern American state, in which the president ruled supreme and military spending sped development of the Sunbelt. The post–World War II period also brought extraordinary American prosperity. But the end of the Cold War coincided with the rise of a global free market in which the robust economies of Europe and Japan challenged the pre-eminence of the United States. In some ways this would present a more difficult challenge than the Cold War had been.

By the mid-1990s Americans still had a vast, unfinished agenda for their country. Most thoughtful people believed in the need for concerted action to increase the productivity of American industries; there was also substantial agreement that such tasks as protecting the environment, improving education, reforming the health care system, and restoring the nation's crumbling infrastructure should be given high priority. However, little agreement existed on solutions to any of these important problems, and attempts to achieve consensus were complicated by continuing social conflicts. Lacking a vibrant sense of community, Americans had difficulty coming to terms with the wide differences in wealth and power in their diverse society. Racial animosities, differences between ethnic groups, and the ongoing struggle for equality between women and men left a large gap between the social harmony Americans desired and the reality they saw around them. Politicians, preoccupied with raising money to finance their ever more expensive campaigns, often feared to alienate influential supporters by taking on tough questions. As a result, the American public became increasingly disenchanted with politics.

Before dawn on the morning of January 17, 1994, millions of Los Angeles-area residents were jolted out of bed by a violent earthquake measuring 6.6 on the Richter scale. Power, water, and transportation systems were disrupted for days, buildings were shattered, freeways collapsed. Angelenos, wondering what was next, after the riots of 1992, the fires, floods, and mud slides of 1993, and now this, adjusted. Thousands took the new Metrolink train to work. Roads and bridges were repaired months before expected, and gigantic traffic jams never materialized. Earthquake victims moved in with relatives, stored bottled water, and expressed relief that this quake wasn't "the big one." Yet powerful aftershocks, impossible to anticipate, rattled the city for months to come. And life was like that everywhere in the United States at century's end. No one seemed to know quite what was coming next. ■

FURTHER READING

On American society, see: Sam Roberts, *Who We Are: A Portrait of America Based on the Latest U.S. Census* (1993). On cities and suburbanization, see: Carl Abbott, *The Metropolitan Frontier: Cities in the Modern American West* (1994); Mike Davis, *City of Quartz: Excavating the Future in Los Angeles* (1992). On politics, see: Tom Rosenstiel, *Strange Bedfellows: How Television and the Presidential Candidates Changed Politics, 1992* (1994). On the consequences of atomic energy, see: Tad Bartimus and Scott McCartney, *Trinity's Children: Living Along America's Nuclear Highway* (1993). On economic and social policy, see: David Halberstam, *The Next Century* (1991); Robert Reich, *The Work of Nations: Preparing Ourselves for Twenty-first Century Capitalism* (1991); William Julius Wilson, *The Truly Disadvantaged: The Inner City, the Underclass, and Public Policy* (1987). On the Clinton administration's handling of economic policy, see: Bob Woodward, *The Agenda* (1993). On race relations, see: Cornel West, *Race Matters* (1994). Until books on recent events appear, consult the major journals of public affairs: *The Atlantic Monthly, Dissent, Harper's, The Nation, The New York Review of Books, The New Republic, The National Review,* and *The Public Interest.* These newsweeklies also contain useful information and a variety of interpretations of events: *Business Week, The Economist, Newsweek, Time,* and *U.S. News and World Report.*

INDEX

environment, 551–552; and family, 474–475; health and fitness craze, 469–470; immigration, 476–478; merger mania and junk bonds, 459–460; poverty, 460–463; and Reagan, 444–445; schools, 471–472; underclass, 462–463; yuppies, 460. *See also* Culture of 1980s

Einstein, Albert, 14

Eisenhower, Dwight D., 89, 92, 106–110, 135; Democrats on, 177; and McCarthy, 109, 145, 146, 147; on military-industrial complex, 26; and New Deal, 219; in 1956 election, 134; Reagan contrasted with, 489; and school desegregation, 128; and Warren Court, 128, 133

Eisenhower administration, 108–110, 134–135; foreign policy of, 149–150, 152; and LBJ, 216; and government programs, 93; and Korean War, 88; and National Defense Education Act, 119, 165; and Native Americans, 132–133; and segregation, 127–129, 199

Eisenhower Doctrine, 157

Eisenhower foreign policy, 139–141; and China, 144–145, 153–154; and détente trend, 166–168; and Hungarian uprising, 161–163; and Iranian coup, 154–155; and Korean War, 141–144; and Latin America, 158–161; and Middle East, 156–158; and nuclear weapons testing, 172–173; and Reagan, 489; and space race, 163–166; and Stalin's successors, 144–145; and Third World, 147–150; and Vietnam, 150–153, 252–254

Elders, Jocelyn, 564

Elijah Muhammad, 241, 301

Ellsberg, Daniel, 342–343, 344–345, 386, 426

El Salvador, 492, 502–504; human rights abuses in, 507; and Soviets, 492; U.S. aid to, 492–493, 504

Employment Act (1946), 94, 112

Endara, Guillermo, 523

"Enemies list" of Nixon, 387

Energy problems, and Carter, 429–431

Engel v. *Vitale*, 236

Enola Gay, 50

Entitlement programs, 94–95

Environment: and Bush administration, 552, 553; global warming, 552–553; Great Society programs for, 230; and Love Canal, 430–431; and minorities, 332, 553–554; and Nixon, 370- 371; and nuclear waste, 554, 555–556; and nuclear-weapon production, 169, 554–556; and pesticides, 205; and Reagan years, 551–552; and "Superfund," 431, 552; *Valdez* disaster, 552

Environmental movement, 205–207, 331–332; Earth Day, 331, 370, 552; and People's Park battle, 321

Environmental Protection Agency (EPA), 205, 332, 370–371, 431, 464

Equal Employment Opportunity Commission (EEOC), 324, 325, 484, 485

Equal Pay Act (1963), 324

Equal Pay Act (1973), 377

Equal Rights Amendment (ERA), 327, 373, 408, 420, 475

Ervin, Sam J., Jr., 371, 392, 393, 394–395

Espy, Mike, 564

Estonia, 21, 520

Ethiopia, Italian invasion of, 13

Evans, Rowland, 387

Exchange rates, 380

Exclusionary rule, 236

Executive Order No. 8802, 33

Executive Order No. 9066, 37

Executive Order No. 9835, 74–75

"Executive privilege," 392, 395

Exxon Valdez disaster, 552

Fair Deal, 67

Fair Employment Practices Commission, 122–123, 218

Fair Employment Practices Committee (FEPC), 33

Fair Labor Standards Act, 12

Falkland Islands war, 507

Falwell, Jerry, 416, 472

Family: and hippies, 313; 1970s changes in, 405–409; in 1980s, 474–475; tensions within, 326

Family Assistance Plan (FAP), 369

"Family values": of fifties, 113; and Lakewood, California, 542

Farley, James, 9

Farmer, James, 200–201

Farnham, Marynia, 114

Farouk (king of Egypt), 156

Faubus, Orval, 128–129

Federal Bureau of Investigation (FBI): and anti-Vietnam War groups, 281; and Black Panthers, 302; and Communists, 74; and Watergate, 390, 399; wiretaps by, 339

Federal Communications Commission (FCC), 102, 103, 105

Federal Deposit Insurance Corporation (FDIC), 5, 8

Federal Emergency Relief Administration (FERA), 7

Federal Employee Loyalty Program, 74–75

Federal government: and civil rights, 122–123, 125–130; and education, 119–120; and New Deal, 3–12; science and industry married to, 14, 25; as western land owner ("Sagebrush Rebellion"), 431; and World War II, 22–23, 25–26

Federal Housing Administration, 5, 96, 99

Federal Republic of Germany (West Germany), 55, 63, 191

Hong Kong, 231
Hoover, Herbert C., 3, 4, 5, 31
Hoover, J. Edgar, 75, 76, 182, 183, 186, 339
"Hoovervilles," 3
Hopkins, Harry, 7, 10, 31
Horton, Willie, 480
Hostages, and Iran-contra deals, 508–509
Hot line, between Washington and Moscow, 196
House Committee on Un-American Activities (HUAC), 12, 74, 77–78
Housing: desegregation attempts in north, 242; discrimination in public housing ended, 199–200; fifties boom in, 96–98; and Great Society programs, 226, 243; and minorities, 99
Howard, Roy, 73
Hudson, Rock, 476
Hughes, Charles Evans, 11, 125
Human rights: as Bush intervention rationale, 523; Carter's advocacy of, 432, 433; and Central American policy, 507; and détente with Soviets, 352, 420; presidential certification of progress in, 504
Humphrey, Hubert H., 66, 76; and 1964 Civil Rights Act, 218; and 1964 Democratic convention, 300; and 1968 Chicago police riot, 320; and 1968 election, 290, 291, 292, 320, 383; and 1972 election, 382–383; on Nixon in China, 356; as vice-presidential candidate, 220–221
Hungarian Uprising, 156, 161–163
Hungary, 47, 61, 519
Hunt, E. Howard, 343, 389, 390, 392
Hunt, Nelson Bunker, 510
Hussein (king of Jordan), 247, 359
Hussein, Saddam, 501, 524–525
Huxley, Aldous, 312
Hydrogen bomb, 68, 71, 170. *See also* Nuclear weapons

Ibn Saud (king of Saudi Arabia), 19
Icahn, Carl, 459
Ickes, Harold, 7, 31
Immigration: and Carter years, 433–435; from Cuba, 163, 434, 566; and Displaced Persons Act, 80–81; and Hungarian uprising, 162–163; and Jews from Nazi Germany, 35; and Johnson administration, 230–232; and McCarran-Walter Act, 81; from Mexico, 34, 132, 163, 231, 434, 478; in 1980s, 476–478; in 1990s, 537, 539, 543–545; right-wing vs. left-wing regimes as source of, 434; Truman liberalizes, 65
Immigration and Nationality Act (1952), 81
"Imperial presidency," 362
Impoundment, by Nixon, 371, 372
Income distribution, 112, 459, 536. *See also* Poverty

India, 57, 231, 354
Individualism, and sixties, 333
Indochina War (1946–1954), 72–73, 150–152; and Giap, 279; and Stevenson in 1960 campaign, 134
Indonesia, 160
Inflation: and Arab oil embargo, 380–381; and "bracket creep," 451; Ford's response to, 419; during Kennedy years, 198; during 1950s, 110; of late 1960s, 233–234, 242; in 1970s stagflation, 378–379, 412–413, 428; in 1980s, 458–459; Volcker's policy for, 428, 451; and World War II, 26
Intercontinental ballistic missiles (ICBMs), 141, 183, 350, 493
Interest rates, 233, 428, 451
Intermediate Nuclear Forces (INF) talks and treaty, 495, 516–517
Intermediate-range ballistic missiles (IRBMs), in Cuba, 187, 193
Internal Security Act (1950), 76
International Monetary Fund, 54, 357
Interstate highway system, 101
Intifadah, 499
Iran, 55, 57, 351, 492, 508; U.S. intervention in, 150, 154–155; at war with Iraq, 498, 501, 509
Iran-contra scandal, 456, 489–490, 507–514
Iranian hostage crisis, 432, 437–439, 448, 494, 500
Iraq, 157, 158; and Persian Gulf War, 524–525; at war with Iran, 498, 501, 509
Iron curtain, 52, 54
Islamic fundamentalism, 501
Isolationism, of 1930s, 13
Israel, 144, 155–157, 358–360; and Camp David peace process, 432; foreign aid to, 492; *intifadah* against, 499; and Iran-contra affair, 509, 513; and Iran-Iraq war, 501; Lebanon invaded by, 498; and 1993 agreements, 565; PLO conciliation with, 525; and Six-Day War, 246–247; and Truman, 65; and TWA hijacking, 508; and Yom Kippur War, 358, 359–360
Italy, 4, 13, 166
Ivins, Molly, 568

Jackson, Henry, 164, 351, 352, 422
Jackson, Jesse, 330, 454, 478, 479
Jackson State killings, 323
Jacobsen, David, 512
Jamaica, 231
Japan, 13, 14, 25, 61, 64, 363; as atomic bomb target, 49–52; in World War II, 15–16, 20, 48–52
Japanese-Americans, WWII relocation of, 37–39
Jarvis, Howard, 427
Javits, Jacob, 360, 362
Jaworski, Leon, 397

Jencks v. *United States*, 133
Jenco, Lawrence, 512
Jiang Jieshi (Chiang Kai-shek), 69, 70, 71–72, 73, 153–154
Job Corps, 225, 226
John Birch Society, 219
Johnson, Andrew, 398
Johnson, Lady Bird, 230
Johnson, Lyndon B., 214–216; and consensus, 226; on Diem, 258; and education for science, 119; and Eisenhower, 110; and Kennedy administration, 177; and Kennedy assassination, 207, 208, 209, 210, 217; and 1960 election, 178, 216–217; and 1964 election, 220–222; and 1968 contenders, 289; and Oppenheimer, 71; on presidential opportunities, 450; and space race, 164, 165, 166, 204, 336; as vice-president, 217; withdraws from 1968 election, 237, 287, 288
Johnson administration, 218; foreign policy of, 243–248, 502; Great Society programs, 222–230, 238–243; and immigration, 230–232; and Kennedy administration, 197, 217–218, 244, 258; and Kennedy tax bill, 197; and Kerner Commission, 243, 302; and Reagan, 489; and Vietnam War, 257–265, 277, 280–287, 337–338 (*see also* Vietnam War)
Jones, Jim, and Jonestown, 415
Joplin, Janis, 297, 310–311, 312
Jordan (nation), 157, 246, 247, 358, 359, 565
Judd, Walter, 73
Judicial system: and O. J. Simpson trial, 550–551; and Supreme Court decisions, 236
Junk bonds, 459–460

Kalmbach, Herbert, 388, 390
Kassim, Abdel Karim, 157
Katzenbach, Nicholas deB., 218–219
Kay, Jane, 553
Kearns, Doris, 215
Keating, Charles, 465
Keating, Kenneth, 194
Keats, John (1950s author), 120
Kefauver, Estes, 88–89, 134
Kemp, Jack, 450, 459
Kendall, Donald, 388
Keniston, Kenneth, 297
Kennan, George F., 57–58, 64, 68, 139, 277
Kennedy, Anthony, 468
Kennedy, Edward M., 354, 387, 422, 428, 438, 439
Kennedy, Jacqueline, 176, 190, 208
Kennedy, John F., 92, 176, 181–183; assassination of, 176, 207–210, 241, 401; extramarital liaisons of, 176, 182, 186; and Goldberg, 133; on loss of China, 73; on "missile gap," 166; and 1956 vice-presidential nomination, 134, 178; and 1960 election, 177–181, 216, 388; and 1964 Civil Rights Act, 218; on Nixon's "kitchen debate," 168; and Vietnam, 153, 251–252, 254
Kennedy, Robert: assassination of, 289–290; as attorney general, 182, 183, 218–219; and Cuban missile crisis, 194, 195; and Freedom Riders, 201; and Hoover on JFK liaison, 186; on Khrushchev attitude, 191; in 1960 campaign, 180, 216; and 1968 election, 288, 289
Kennedy administration, 176–177; and Bay of Pigs, 185–186, 188; and Berlin crisis, 190–193; as "Camelot," 210; and civil rights, 177, 198–203; and Commission on the Status of Women, 324; and Cuban missile crisis, 193–196; economic program of, 196–198; foreign policy of, 177, 183–196, 245; and Latin America, 161; Peace Corps, 188–189; and Reagan, 489; and space race, 204–205, 336; and Vietnam, 254–257
Kent State University killings, 323, 329, 340
Kerner, Otto, 243, 302
Kerner Commission, 243, 302
Kerouac, Jack, 120, 308
Kerrey, Bob, 556
Kesey, Ken, 312
Keyes v. *Denver School District No. 1*, 375
Keynes, John Maynard, and Keynesianism 7, 231, 379, 381
Keyserling, Leon, 94
Khomeini, Ayatollah Ruholla, 437, 509, 512
Khrushchev, Nikita, 134, 144, 154, 158, 162, 166–168, 172, 186–187, 190–191, 193, 195, 254
Killian, James, 172
Kim Il Sung, 83
King, Coretta Scott, 131, 180, 318
King, Martin Luther, Jr., 130–131, 202–203, 298–299; assassination of, 289, 318, 330; and Carter, 421; on civil disobedience, 300; and Hoover, 182; and Kennedy, 180, 199; northern desegregation efforts by, 242; and Reagan, 466; and Selma, 227, 301; and Vietnam War, 280–281
King, Martin Luther, Sr., 130, 180, 421, 423
King, Mary, 326, 327
King, Rodney, 548–549, 550
Kinsey, Alfred C., 114
Kirkpatrick, Jeane, 455, 475, 492
Kissinger, Henry, 336–338, 356, 363–364, 387; and Central-America commission, 503; and Chile, 357; and China visit, 353, 355, 356; and détente, 349, 350–352, 356, 420; and economic issues, 363; Gorbachev party for, 517; and Iran, 351; and Middle East, 359–361; and Nixon resignation, 400; and NSC staff wiretaps, 339; Reagan

spending, 457–458; and economic conditions, 451–452, 453, 456–463; and education, 471–472; and hostage release, 439; reality and rhetoric of, 456–457, 490; Supreme Court appointments, 468; WIC program slashed, 461; and women's issues, 475

Reagan foreign policy, 489–493; and arms race, 493–497; in Central America, 456, 489, 491, 502–504, 507–508, 523; and China, 493; Grenada invasion, 504–506; Iran-Contra affair, 456, 489–490, 507–514; and Middle East, 497–502; and North, 510–511; and Soviets, 514–518

Recession: of 1937–1938, 12; of 1954, 197; of 1958, 197; of 1960, 135, 197; of 1979–1980, 429; of 1980s, 451–452; of 1991/1992, 527, 535, 540

Reconstruction Finance Corporation, 5

Redistribution of income, and Great Society programs, 223

Redlining practices, 99

Red Scare (1940s and 1950s), 73–83, 110, 145; and Oppenheimer, 71

Red Scare, first (1919), 73, 75

Reed v. Reed, 377

Reedy, George, 82–83

Refugee Relief Act (1953), 163

Regan, Donald, 455, 513, 516

Rehnquist, William, 371, 374, 468, 482

Religion: and churches in civil-rights movement, 131–132; and conscientious objection, 274; of counterculture, 315; and counterculture drugs, 312; and fifties era, 112–113; increase in "born again" Christians, 472; and 1960 election, 179, 181; and 1970s, 414–416; and Reagan, 472–473, 474; Supreme Court decisions on, 235–236; televangelists, 472–474

Religious Right, 333

Reno, Janet, 564

Republican party: as "big tent," 483; 1960s changes in, 219–220; 1970s changes in, 417

Resolution Trust Corporation, 466

Reston, James, 387

Reuther, Walter, 65, 171

Revenue sharing, under Nixon, 368

Revercomb, William, 163

Rhee, Syngman, 83, 141, 144

Rhodes, James, 323

Rhodes, John, 398

Rice, Donna, 478

Richards, Ann, 568

Richardson, Elliot, 396–397

Ridgeway, Matthew, 87–88

Riesman, David, 120, 121

Robb, Charles, 511

Roberts, Oral, 416, 472, 474

Roberts, Owen, 11

Robertson, Pat, 416, 472, 474, 558, 560

Robeson, Paul, 123

Robinson, Jack Roosevelt (Jackie), 33, 105, 122–123

Robinson, JoAnn Gibson, 130

Robinson, Ruby Doris Smith, 299, 301, 326

Rockefeller, Nelson, 178–179, 220, 417–418, 421, 448

Rock 'n' roll, 115–117, 309–311

Rocky Flats nuclear plant, 103, 554–555

Rodino, Peter, 397

Roe v. Wade, 377–378, 420, 482, 483

Rogers, William P., 337, 351, 354, 356, 359

Rolling Stone magazine, 316–317

Rolling Stones, 309, 315

Rolling Thunder, 262

Roosevelt, Eleanor, 8–9, 10, 32, 44, 65, 324

Roosevelt, Franklin, Jr., 65

Roosevelt, Franklin Delano, 2, 4–5; death of, 40–41; first inaugural address of, 3; on Great Depression danger, 3–4; and Holocaust, 35, 36; and Reagan, 445, 446, 447; and Truman, 64–65, 67; and veterans' benefits, 95

Roosevelt, Kermit, 155

Roosevelt, Theodore, 400

Roosevelt administration, 2; and Eisenhower cabinet, 109; foreign policy of, 12–22; and Great Depression, 2–3; and Holocaust, 35–37; New Deal, 3–12

Roosevelt (New Deal) coalition, 64, 177, 425

Rosenberg, Julius and Ethel, 80, 145

Rosenman, Sam, 10

Rostow, Walt Whitman, 244, 258, 283, 285–286

Roth, William, 450

Roth v. United States, 235

Rubin, Jerry, 306, 317, 321, 333

Ruby, Jack, 209

Ruckelshaus, William, 397

Rumania, 47, 519

Rusk, Dean, 182, 244, 247, 277, 283, 285

Russia (post-Soviet), 522, 565–566

"Rustbelt," 413

Rutledge, Wiley, 32

Rwanda, 566

Sadat, Anwar, 359, 432

"Sagebrush Rebellion," 431

Salinger, J. D., 118, 297

SALT-I, 351, 420

SALT-II, 420, 421, 436, 494–495

Sanctuary movement, 477–478

Sandinistas, 507

SANE, 171, 281

San Francisco earthquake (1989), 530, 571

Sarnoff, David, 101

"Saturday Night Massacre," 396–397

Saudi Arabia, 19, 157, 524, 525

Savings and loan industry, 233–234; scandal in, 464–466
Savio, Mario, 304
Scalia, Antonin, 468
Schell, Jonathan, 494
Schine, David, 145–146
Schlafly, Phyllis, 220, 408
Schlesinger, James, 400
Schneider, Rene, 357
Schwartzkopf, H. Norman, 524
Schwerner, Michael, 299
Scopes, John, 236
Scott, Hugh, 398
Scowcroft, Brent, 518
Scranton, William, 220
SDS (Students for a Democratic Society), 280, 303–307, 321, 322, 326–327
Seale, Bobby, 321
Second Reconstruction, 198
"Secular humanism," 473
Securities Act (1933), 5
Securities and Exchange Commission (SEC), 5, 8, 464
Segregation, racial: school, 125–129, 132; and suburbanization, 97, 99. *See also* Racism
Segretti, Donald, 382
Selma march, 227, 301
"Separate but equal" doctrine, 125, 126
Servicemen's Readjustment Act (1944). *See* GI Bill
Seventies era, 440–441; economic problems of, 412–414, 415, 428–429; family in, 405–409; as "Me Decade," 332, 416; religion and cults, 414–416; and sexual revolution, 409–412
Sex: and AIDS, 475–476; and fifties era, 113, 114–115; Betty Ford on, 420; and Janis Joplin, 311; sixties freedom in, 309–310, 314, 330
Sex discrimination, 95, 218, 377
Sexism, 327
Sexual harassment, and Hill-Thomas hearings, 485
Sheehan, Neil, 342
Shelley v. *Kraemer*, 125
Shepard, Alan, 204
Shilts, Randy, 411
Shriver, Sargent, 225, 226, 384
Shultz, George P., 491–492, 498, 509
Shute, Nevil, 171
"Shuttle diplomacy," 360, 363
Sick, Gary, 439
Sierra Club, 205, 332
Sihanouk, Norodom, 340
"Silent majority," 320
Simpson, Nicole Brown, 551
Simpson, O. J., trial of, 550–551
Simpson-Rodino Act (1986), 478
Sinai Peninsula, 358, 360, 433

Sipuel v. *Board of Regents of the University of Oklahoma*, 125–126
Sirhan, Sirhan, 289, 319
Sirica, John J., 392, 395, 397, 398, 401
Sit-ins, lunch counter, 132, 199
Six-Day War, 246
Sixties era, 296–297; Black Power movement, 302–303; civil rights movement, 297–300; counterculture, 308–317, 321 (*see also* Counterculture); economic growth in, 232–234; and events of 1968/1969, 317–323; legacy of, 329–333; New Left, 303–308, 321; sexual revolution, 309–310, 314, 330, 409; Supreme Court expansion of civil liberties, 234–237; women's liberation, 323–329
Slater, Philip, 297
"Sleaze factor," 455
Smith, Al, 9
Smith, Gerald L. K., 11
Smith, Howard K., 329
Smith, Howard W., 324
Smith, Scott, 410
Smith Act, 76, 133
Smith vs. *Allwright*, 125
SNCC (Student Non-Violent Coordinating Committee), 132, 199, 227, 298, 299–300, 301
Social Security, 109, 461; cost-of-living adjustments to, 370; and Goldwater, 221
Social Security Act (1935), 6, 11
Social Security Administration, 8
Social Security tax, and 1937–1938 recession, 12
Solar Energy Research Institute, 429
Solidarity labor movement, 496
Somalia, 566
Somoza, Anastasio, 507
Sorenson, Theodore, 196, 425–426
Souter, David, 483
South Africa, and Soviets, 492
Southeast Asia Treaty Organization (SEATO), 149, 152, 253, 259
Southern Christian Leadership Conference (SCLC), 298
"Southern strategy," 372–373, 381, 385
Southwest Organizing Project, 332, 554
Soviet-American relations: and atomic bomb, 49, 51; and Cold War, 52–64 (*see also* Cold War); and postwar disputes, 47–48. *See also* Détente
Soviet Union, 47, 55, 525–526; and Afghanistan, 436, 497–498, 501–502, 517; and Castro, 160–161; collapse of, 490, 518–522; COMECON formed by, 64; and Communist China, 70, 71, 144, 154, 353; and Cuban missile crisis, 193–196; deterioration of, 515, 517; and Egypt, 359–360; as "evil empire" (Reagan), 489, 490, 492; as evil empire changed, 517;

Credits (continued from copyright page)

Map and line art credits

Pages 18 and 20: Findley, Carter and John Rothney, *Twentieth Century World*, 2/e. Copyright © 1990 by Houghton Mifflin Company. Used with permission. Pages 24, 28, 462, 536, and 562: From Norton et al., *A People and a Nation*, Fourth Edition. Copyright © 1994 by Houghton Mifflin Company. Used with permission. Page 85: From Paterson et al., *American Foreign Policy: A History*. Copyright © 1988 by D. C. Heath and Company. Reprinted by permission. Pages 63, 98, 111, and 148: Norton, Mary Beth et al., *A People and a Nation*, 3/e. Copyright © 1990 by Houghton Mifflin Company. Used with permission. Page 124: Reprinted from Figure 4.1 in *Dollars and Dreams: The Changing American Income Distribution*, by Frank Levy, © 1987 Russell Sage Foundation. Used with permission of the Russell Sage Foundation. Page 184: Ray, James Lee, *Global Politics*, 4/e. Copyright © 1990 by Houghton Mifflin Company. Used with permission. Page 228: Reprinted by permission of Greenwood Publishing Group, Inc., Westport, CT, from *Voter Mobilization and the Politics of Race: the South and Universal Suffrage, 1952–1984* by Harold W. Stanley. Copyright © 1987 by Harold W. Stanley and published in 1987 by Praeger Publishers. Page 435: Source: *The New York Times*, March 11, 1991. Copyright © 1991 by The New York Times Company. Reprinted by permission. Page 461: From *New York Times*, July 20, 1994. Copyright © 1994 by The New York Times Company. Reprinted by permission. Page 467: From *New York Times*, February 11, 1992. Copyright © 1992 by The New York Times Company. Reprinted by permission. Page 477: Source: *The New York Times*, May 6, 1992. Copyright © 1992 by The New York Times Company. Reprinted by permission. Page 520: McKay, John P., Bennett D. Hill, and John Buckler, *A History of Western Society*, 4/e. Copyright © 1991 by Houghton Mifflin Company. Used with permission. Page 546: Source: Data from the *New York Times*, March 5, 1992. Copyright © 1992 by The New York Times Company.

Text credits

Page 231: Excerpt from *Still the Golden Door* by David Reimers is reprinted by permission of Columbia University Press. Page 296 (song lyrics): Excerpt from "For What It's Worth" by Steven Stills is reprinted courtesy of FM Management. All rights reserved. Page 296 (song lyrics): "For What It's Worth" © 1966 Cotillion Music, Inc., Ten East Music & Springalo Toones. All rights on behalf of Cotillion Music, Inc. administered by Warner-Tamerlane Publishing Corp. All Rights Reserved. Used by permission.